A Christmas Companion

A Christmas Companion

Consultant Editor:
Edel Brosnan

LORENZ BOOKS

First published in 1998 by Lorenz Books

LORENZ BOOKS are available for bulk purchase for sales promotion
and for premium use. For details, write or call the sales director,
Lorenz Books, 27 West 27th Street, New York NY 10011;
(800) 345-9567

Lorenz Books is an imprint of
Anness Publishing Inc.

ISBN 1 85967 775 4

Publisher: Joanna Lorenz
Consultant Editor: Edel Brosnan
Authors: Penny Boylan, Petra Boase, Marion Elliot, Janine Hosegood,
Sue Maggs, Janice Murfitt, Sally Walton, Elizabeth Wolf-Cohen
Photography: Karl Adamson, Edward Allwright, James Duncan,
John Freeman, Michelle Garrett, Mark Wood
Indexer: Vicki Robinson

Previously published in four separate volumes, *Cooking for Christmas, Christmas Treats,
Christmas Crafts* and *Christmas Crafts for Kids*.

Printed and bound in China

1 3 5 7 9 10 8 6 4 2

CONTENTS

Introduction: Christmas Cooking

Christmas is a time for celebrations, for entertaining family and friends and sharing the best of festive food and treats with them. Nonetheless, not even the keenest cook wants to spend the festive season imprisoned in the kitchen! This book features recipes, cook-ahead instructions and freezer tips to help you plan your perfect Christmas. As this is the season for entertaining, all recipes will serve eight people; quantities can be halved or doubled-up, if necessary.

To make your life easier over the holiday period, prepare as much as possible in advance and finish off or reheat on the day. Use the suggested menus or your own variations to draw up shopping lists, and allow yourself plenty of time to shop. On the big day, don't be afraid to draft in the rest of the family to help. All this should give you the freedom to enjoy the company of family and friends.

Christmas is also a wonderful time for giving. There is always so much to organize at this time of year – and organizing and choosing Christmas presents must be near the top of the list. This book is laden with tempting festive treats that you can make yourself, from chocolates, individual puddings and cakes, to flavored oils and spiced vinegars – delightful, delicious presents with a personal touch, for a taste of the true spirit of Christmas.

Sweet Ingredients

Almonds
Almonds may be used blanched or with the skin intact. Blanched almonds, with the skins removed, have a sweet flavor and are ideal for cakes. Almonds with the skin intact are ideal for sweets, and delicious coated in chocolate or caramel.

Angelica
Green angelica stems preserved in sugar are used for cake decorating.

Chocolate
Chocolate in all its many forms is a firm favorite at Christmastime. Milk chocolate has a softer texture and sweeter flavor than plain chocolate. Plain chocolate, with its strong, rich flavor is ideal for melting and cooking. White chocolate is a product made with cocoa butter, which imparts a sweet, delicate flavor without the strong cocoa taste.

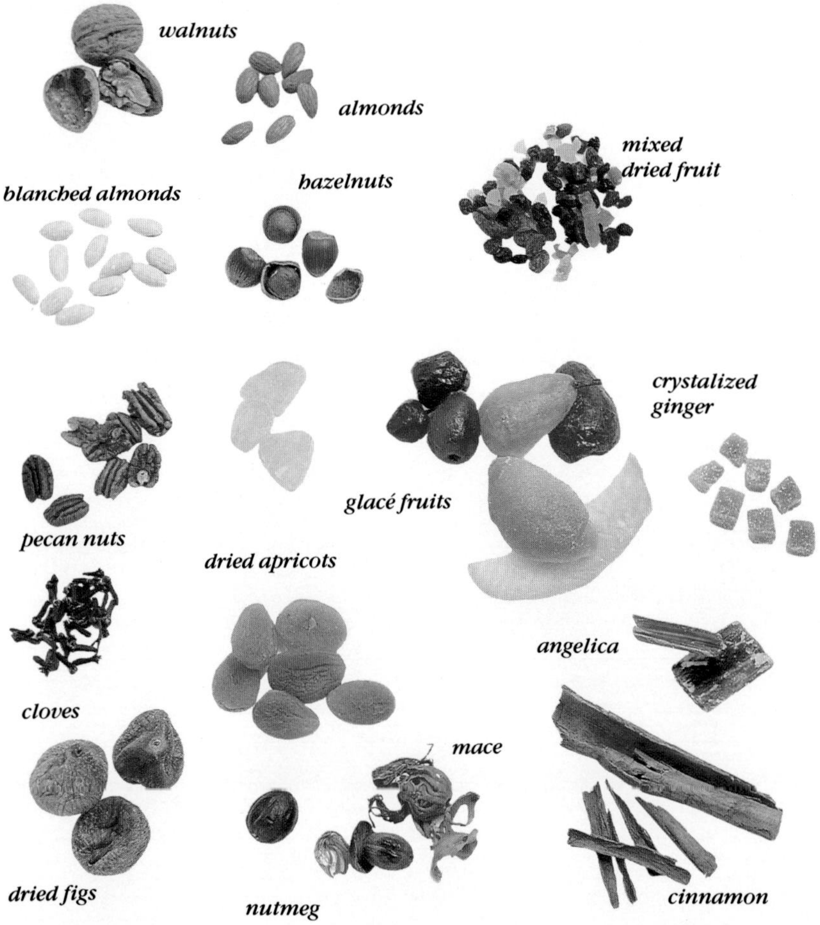

Cinnamon
Cinnamon may be used ground, or as a whole 'stick'. Cinnamon sticks impart a wonderful flavor to oils, vinegars and drinks.

Cloves
Cloves are full of flavor and are a delicious addition to spiced vinegars.

Crystalized ginger
This is preserved ginger root, coated in sugar. Its pungent flavor and crunchy outer layer makes it a good addition to home-made chocolates and candies.

Dates
Fresh or dried, dates are used in cakes, cookies, home-made chocolates and preserves.

Dried fruit
Mixed dried fruit is a blend of raisins, currants, orange and lemon peel and cherries, essential for Christmas cakes and puddings. Dried fruits are very nutritious, and have a very concentrated flavor.

Glacé fruit
Almost any fruit may be preserved in sugar syrup, and the colorful results make beautiful decorations. These can be fairly expensive to buy, but are very simple to make at home.

Hazelnuts
Hazelnuts may be used chopped in praline or cake mixtures, or finely ground.

Mace
Mace is the dried outer skin of the nutmeg, most often used ground. It has a milder flavor than nutmeg.

Nutmeg
Nutmeg can be bought whole, or as a powder. Freshly grated nutmeg has a wonderful flavor and aroma, and will impart a more powerful taste than the powdered form.

Pecan nuts
These nuts are similar to walnuts, but have a milder flavor. They make wonderful eating straight out of the shells, or may be bought as halves, or pieces for decoration and cooking.

Walnuts
Walnuts may be purchased in their shells, as walnut halves (ideal for decoration) or chopped for cake mixtures.

Fresh Fruit

Apples
So many varieties are available at Christmastime, and all have their own characteristics – soft or crisp flesh, red, green or golden skins. Choose firm apples for glacé fruits.

Apricots
Choose firm, ripe apricots for the best color and flavor.

Cherries
Purchase when in season, and use for glacé fruits or fruits in liqueurs. They are available at Christmastime, but are expensive.

Chinese gooseberries
Chinese gooseberries have a paper thin husk which should be peeled back before eating.

Clementines
These are available most of the year and may be used for glacé fruits, preserves or flavoring brandy.

Cranberries
These jewel-bright fruits are a colorful Christmas addition, available fresh at Christmastime, or frozen.

Grapes
A lovely addition to a Christmas fruit bowl. Available red, green or black, with or without seeds.

Kumquats
These tiny orange fruits have a citrus flavor. They may be used for glacé fruits, or making liqueurs, with the skin intact.

Lemons
Buy small lemons with fine skins for the best juice.

Limes
Small limes with smooth, bright green skins have the best flavor.

Lychees
A Christmas treat; choose pink-skinned fruits with sweet white flesh.

Paw paw
An exotic fruit, increasingly available in good supermarkets. Paw paws have a sweet pink flesh. Discard the seeds and skin, and use for glacé fruits or fruits in liqueurs.

Peaches
Peaches are best purchased in the summer, when they are in peak condition. They may sometimes be available at Christmastime – but at a cost. Ensure they are not bruised or damaged when buying. Use for fruits in liqueurs.

Pears
Many varieties of pear are available. Make chutney when they are plentiful.

Plums
These are available all year round, but it is best to make use of indigenous varieties when in season.

Star fruit
These exotic fruits are available all the year round in good supermarkets. They are excellent preserved in liqueurs or used as glacé fruits.

Strawberries
Make the most of strawberries when in season, and bottle or use for preserves.

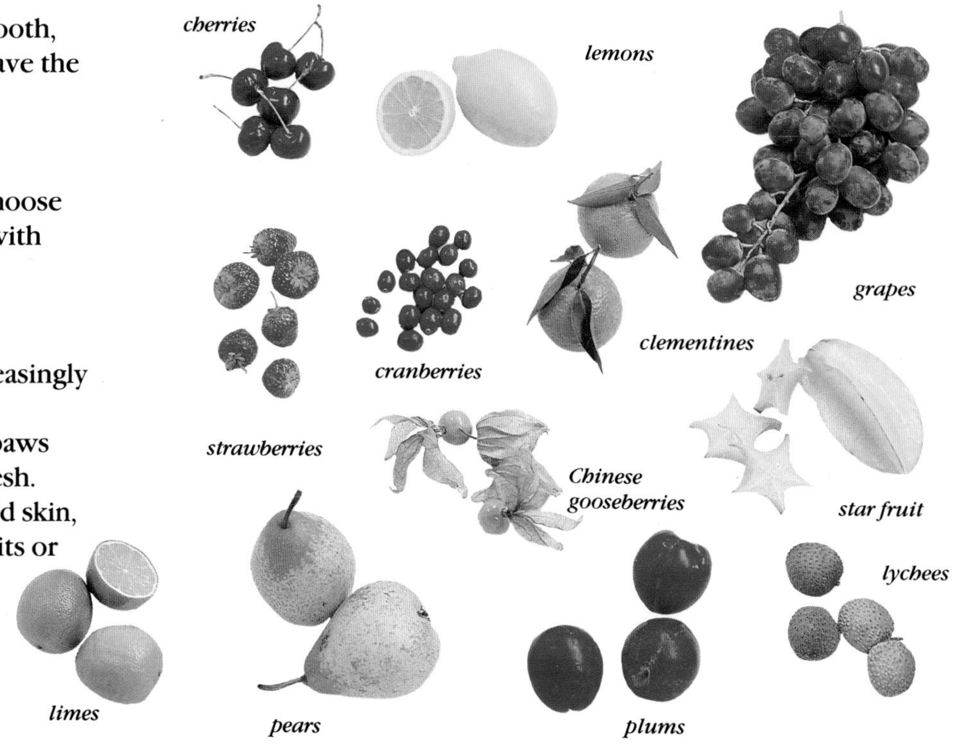

Savory Ingredients

The following are just some of the ingredients used in the savory recipes in this book. Always use the freshest, best quality ingredients available.

Anchovies
These have a very concentrated flavor, and are a great addition to fish pâtés.

Bacon slices
Bacon or fat back keeps home-made pâtés moist and full of flavor.

Bay leaves
Bay leaves are available fresh or dried. They make a flavorful and decorative addition to bottled oils and vinegars.

Basil
A wonderfully aromatic herb used in oils and vinegars.

Celery
Celery imparts a great texture to vegetable chutneys and pickles.

Cheshire cheese
A mild cheese with a crumbly texture, use in potted spreads.

Chilies
Fresh chilies must be handled carefully. Remove the seeds from chilies to lessen their impact.

Dill
Dill is particularly suited to fish dishes. The leaf may be finely chopped and added to pâtés.

Garlic
Fresh heads of garlic divide into single cloves, which may be used crushed or whole.

Ginger root
Use the fresh root grated in sweet or savory dishes.

Jarlsburg cheese
A Norwegian cheese similar to Emmenthal, good for cheese spreads.

Kippers
Kippers are smoked herrings; use in fish pâtés.

Maytag blue cheese
This red, blue-veined cheese is a good addition to cheese spreads.

Olives
Olives, both black and green, impart a strong flavor and color to pâtés and spreads.

Onions
Use large onions for chutneys and small onions pickled whole.

Parmesan cheese
A strongly flavored cheese from Italy. Use freshly grated for the best flavor.

Peppers
Red, yellow and green peppers may be preserved in oil, or used in pepper jelly.

Peppercorns
Green and black peppercorns impart flavor and decoration to oils and vinegars. Pink peppercorns are so-called because of their appearance, but they are not true peppercorns.

Rosemary
Use rosemary sparingly in meat dishes, or add to oils and vinegars.

Sage
Sage is available throughout the year. Use in herbed vinegars and flavored butters.

Salmon
Fresh salmon fillet may be used in pâtés and spreads.

Thyme
Thyme may be added to oils and vinegars, or peppers preserved in oil.

Tomatoes
Cherry tomatoes have the best flavor; larger tomatoes are good for cooking.

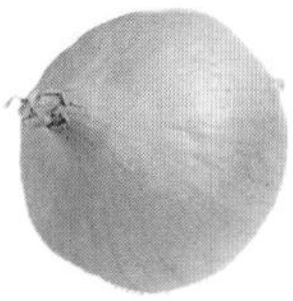

onions

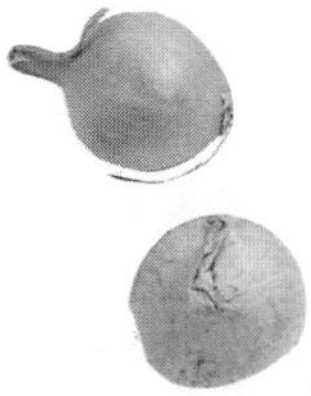

basil

thyme

white peppercorns

pink peppercorns
green peppercorns
bay leaves
ginger
celery
dill
anchovies
olives
kipper
peppers
sage
bacon slices
salmon
chilies
rosemary
Jarlsburg cheese
tomatoes
Parmesan cheese
garlic
Cheshire cheese
Maytag blue cheese

Equipment

Some of the recipes that follow call for specialized items of equipment to obtain the best results. These are readily available from standard kitchenware suppliers. Look after your equipment well and it should never need replacing. Always ensure that metal cutters, pans and utensils are kept in a warm dry place to prevent any discoloration and store piping nozzles in rigid containers to prevent them from being damaged.

Chopping boards
These are for chopping or rolling out pastry or icing, and can be made of wood or acrylic. Acrylic is non-stick and especially good for working with marzipan, icing and sugar.

Cookie sheets
Good quality steel sheets in different sizes and without sides are best as these will not buckle during cooking.

Cooling racks
Wide and narrow mesh racks in a variety of sizes are needed for drying and cooling cakes, icing, chocolate and glacé fruits.

Cutters
A set of round, oval, square, plain or fluted cutters is necessary for cutting out cookies, pastry or icing shapes.

Flour and sugar dredgers
These are used for lightly dusting surfaces with flour before rolling out doughs and for dredging sugar on top of cakes and pastries.

Flower and leaf cutters
Tiny metal cutters are available in almost any shape or size to match any flower bloom or leaf shape.

Flower mat
This mat is invaluable for giving sugar flowers and leaves a natural shape while working the paste; foam sponge may be used as a substitute.

Food mixers and processors
Large food mixers are good for mixing large cake quantities quickly and thoroughly. They are ideal for chopping and crushing or for making pastry or bread doughs and will cut down on preparation time.

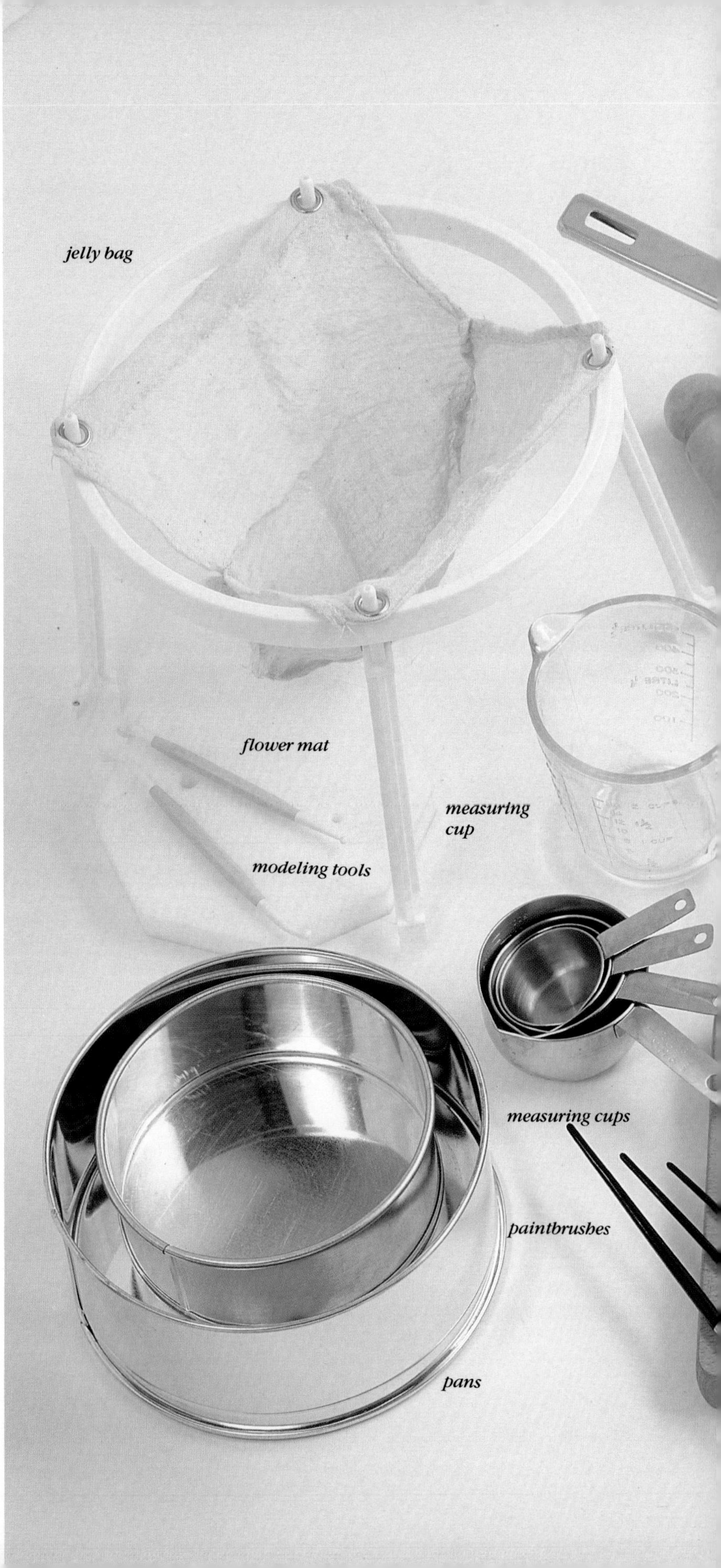

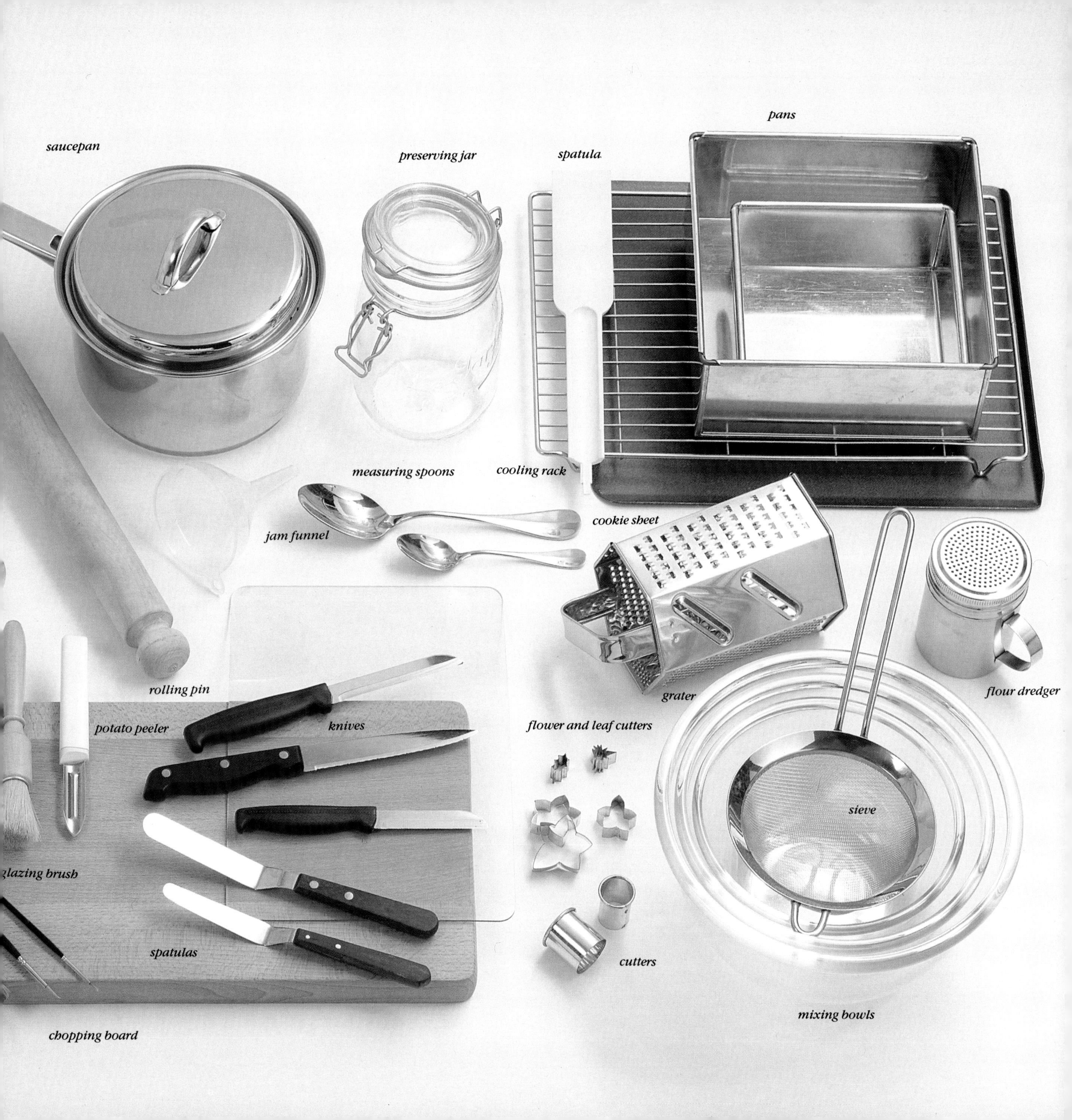
saucepan
preserving jar
spatula
pans
measuring spoons
cooling rack
cookie sheet
jam funnel
rolling pin
grater
flour dredger
potato peeler
knives
flower and leaf cutters
sieve
glazing brush
spatulas
cutters
mixing bowls
chopping board

Glazing brushes
Keep a variety of sizes for glazing cakes, brushing pastry and greasing pans. They are available in small, medium and large sizes.

Graters
A 4- or 6-sided grater with a variety of grating sizes is necessary for many ingredients.

Jam funnels
These are made of stainless steel and are invaluable for filling jars with jam, jelly or chutney without spillage or drips. Use narrow funnels for filling bottles.

Jelly bag
A good quality jelly bag with a very fine weave will ensure that the jelly is crystal clear. A stand is useful but you can improvise with an upturned stool or hook.

Knives
Good quality knives are an investment. Choose a long-bladed knife for slicing, a medium one for chopping and a small knife for paring.

Measuring cups
These are useful for measuring dry ingredients. They can be large or small, heatproof or plastic, for accurate measuring of liquids.

Measuring spoons
These are ideal for the consistent measuring of spoon sizes as general spoons vary widely.

Mixing bowls
Keep several different sizes including heatproof bowls, for whisked mixtures and sugar syrup. The insides should have a smooth rounded finish to ensure thorough mixing.

Modeling tools
These are a good investment if you enjoy cake decoration or modeling. The bone tool is needed for making flowers and the scalpel for cutting out shapes. The scribing tool is invaluable for piercing, marking out and outlining.

Muslin
Very fine cotton muslin is invaluable for straining mixtures in place of a jelly bag, for enclosing pickling spices for flavoring or infusing, and for covering icing to keep it from drying out.

Nozzles
Straight-sided, good quality metal piping nozzles will give a good clean result. They are expensive but should not need replacing if treated with care.

Paintbrushes
A wide selection is available from good cake icing and decorating suppliers. Use paintbrushes for painting on food colorings, sticking sugar pieces together with Gum Glaze and for dusting with food coloring dusts.

Palette
This is useful for keeping small quantities of food coloring dusts separate.

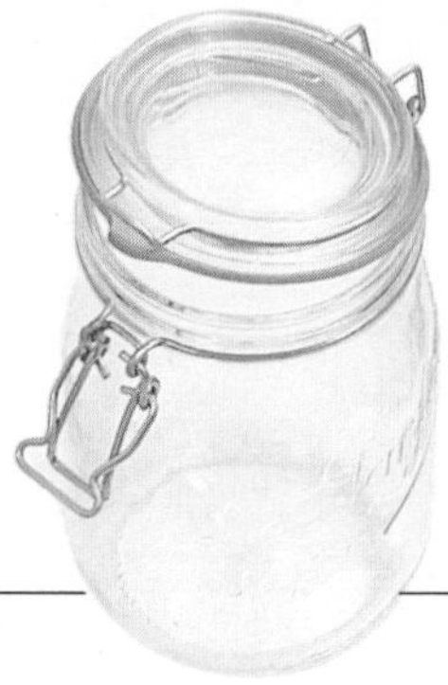

Pans
Round, square or jelly roll cake pans and molds should be of the best quality. Good quality metal pans will not bend or warp during cooking and should never need replacing if they are well looked after.

Pencil, eraser and scissors
These are always necessary for drawing around pan sizes on paper, measuring pan sizes and for cutting out paper templates.

Potato peeler
Use to pare rinds from fruit, or chocolate curls off blocks of chocolate.

Rolling pins
Smooth, straight-ended rolling pins made of wood or acrylic are useful for pastry, dough and icing. Acrylic non-stick rolling pins come in several sizes.

Sieves
Small and fine mesh sieves made of wire or nylon are useful for sieving and straining ingredients and mixtures.

Spatulas
These are essential for all types of cooking especially small, crank-handled spatulas for fine icing and sugar work. They are available with small, medium and large blades.

Useful Techniques

This section contains mini-recipes and lots of tips and useful information on cooking techniques to help you sail through the holiday season. It's worth sitting down a few weeks in advance to make a few plans about what you are going to cook and when is the best time to start.

This section is arranged according to such a plan: it begins with home-made preserves to fill festive jars that will remind you of the treats to come as you make your preparations – you could even give them as presents. Then there are icings you make yourself to decorate a home-made or bought cake. Don't forget the pudding. The recipe in this book can be made up to a month in advance.

Once the festive season gets under way, there are plenty of opportunities for parties and get-togethers of all sorts. The recipes in the Cold Buffets chapter are designed for trouble-free entertaining for large numbers. In this section you will find ideas for cocktail snacks that will supplement the buffet or be perfect for when the neighbours drop by. Ideas for Christmas drinks are also given, including low- and non-alcoholic ideas.

On Christmas Day itself, the information on turkey and its accompaniments will give you all you need for a triumphant celebratory dinner. Follow the turkey with your pudding, accompanied by one of the delicious sweet sauces.

Lastly in this section are some suggested menus for all kinds of occasions over the holiday season. Use them to take the anxiety out of planning, or as a starting point for your own ideas.

Spiced Cranberry and Orange Relish

This is excellent with roast turkey, goose or duck.

Makes about 1 lb

INGREDIENTS
1 1/2 cups fresh cranberries
1 onion, finely chopped
2/3 cup port
1/2 cup superfine sugar
finely grated rind and juice of 1 orange
1/2 tsp English mustard powder
1/4 tsp ground ginger
1/4 tsp ground cinnamon
1 tsp cornstarch
1/3 cup raisins

1 Put the cranberries, onion, port and sugar in a pan. Cook gently for 10 minutes, until tender.

2 Mix the orange juice, mustard powder, spices and cornstarch together. Stir them into the cranberries.

3 Add the raisins and orange rind. Allow to thicken over the heat, stirring with a wooden spoon and then simmer for 2 minutes. Cool, cover and chill ready for serving.

Curried Fruit Chutney

Make this well ahead of Christmas, to serve with cold sliced turkey and ham.

Makes about 2½ lb

INGREDIENTS
- 1⅓ cups dried apricots
- 1⅓ cups dried peaches
- 1⅓ cups dates, pitted
- 1⅓ cups raisins
- 1–2 garlic cloves, crushed
- 1 generous cup light brown sugar
- 1¼ cups white malt vinegar
- 1¼ cups water
- 1 tsp salt
- 2 tsp mild curry powder

1 Put all the ingredients in a large pan, cover and simmer very gently for 10–15 minutes, or until tender.

2 Chop or mince the mixture coarsely in batches in a food processor.

3 Spoon into clean jelly jars. Seal the jars and label them. Store in a cool place for 4 weeks before using.

Ginger, Date, and Apple Chutney

Make this well ahead and store it in airtight jars. Serve with cold sliced meats or pies.

Makes about 3½ lb

INGREDIENTS
- 1 lb cooking apples
- 1 lb dates
- 1⅓ cups dried apricots
- 4 oz crystallized ginger, chopped
- 1–2 garlic cloves, crushed
- 1⅓ cups sultanas
- 1 generous cup light brown sugar
- 1 tsp salt
- 1¼ cups white malt vinegar

1 Peel, core and chop the apples. Pit the dates and chop them roughly. Chop the apricots.

2 Put all the fruit together in a large pan, with the remaining ingredients. Cover and simmer gently for 10–15 minutes, or until tender.

3 Spoon into clean jelly jars. Seal the jars and label them. Store in a cool place for 4 weeks before using.

Preparing Containers for Preserves

It is most important that the containers used to hold preserves have no cracks or chips which could harbour micro-organisms and turn the preserve bad. Ideally, all lids, stoppers and corks should be new, but if you are using old ones ensure they are in good condition without any corrosion, perished rubber seals, or ill-fitting stoppers.

1 To Clean Jars and Bottles: wash them in plenty of hot soapy water using a bottle brush to get into the crevices at the base and around the neck of the container. Rinse well in clean water and dry thoroughly. Do the same for the lids and stoppers. Alternatively use a dishwasher.

2 To Sterilize: a solution of Campden sterilizing tablets and water is best for bottles and corks. Make up and use the solution following the instructions on the packet.

3 Pour the solution into the containers through a funnel, leave for the amount of time specified on the packet, then pour out. Refrigerated syrups, cordials and juices will keep for 4 weeks, but sterilizing with water sterilizing tablets will extend their storage to 1 year.

Melting Chocolate

Working with chocolate can be tricky but these instructions are guaranteed fool-proof.

1 Always use fresh chocolate to ensure a good result. Break the chocolate into small pieces and place in a large, dry, clean bowl over a saucepan of hand-hot water.

2 Ensure that the base of the bowl does not touch the water and there are no spaces between the bowl and the rim of the saucepan which might cause steam and condensation to get into the chocolate, rendering it thick and unusable.

3 Do not beat the chocolate, but stir occasionally while it is melting. Don't try to hurry the process: the chocolate temperature should never exceed 100–110°F, otherwise when it eventually sets, the surface will be dull and covered in streaks.

4 Leave the bowl over hand-hot water during use, unless you want the chocolate to become thicker. Wipe the base of the bowl to remove any condensation.

Fondant Icing

This icing can be used for modeling decorations as well as covering a cake.

Makes enough to cover an 8-inch round cake

INGREDIENTS
4 tablespoons water
1 tablespoons powdered gelatin
2 teaspoons liquid glucose
5 cups confectioner's sugar

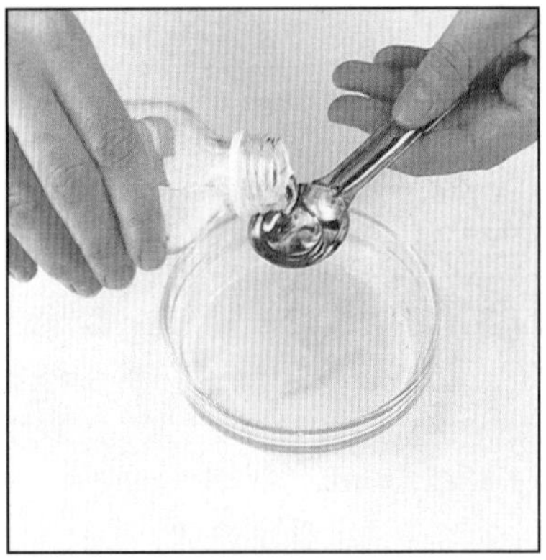

1 Put the water in a small bowl and sprinkle the gelatin over it. Let soak for 2 minutes. Place the bowl in a pan of hot water and let it dissolve over a very gentle heat.

2 Remove the bowl from the hot water and add the liquid glucose to the dissolved gelatin.

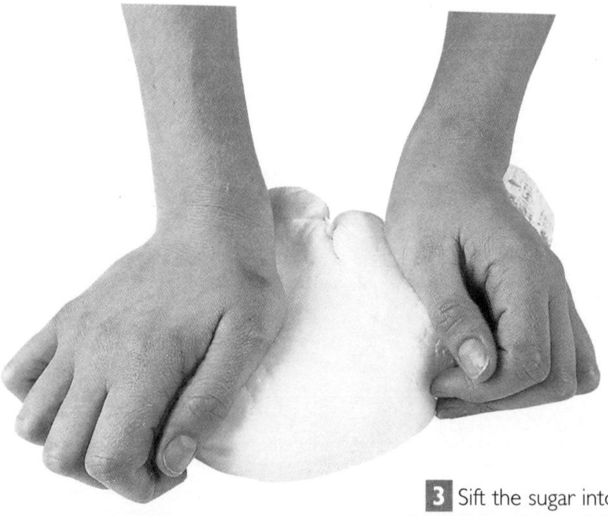

3 Sift the sugar into a bowl and add the gelatin mixture. Mix thoroughly and then knead into a smooth paste. Wrap in plastic wrap until ready to use.

Apricot Glaze

It is always a good idea to make a large quantity of apricot glaze, especially for a celebration cake.

Makes 2 cups

INGREDIENTS
2 cups apricot jam
2 tablespoons water

1 Place the jam and water in a saucepan and heat gently, stirring occasionally until melted.

2 Boil the jam rapidly for 1 minute, then strain through a sieve. Rub through as much fruit as possible, using a spoon, and discard any skins left in the sieve.

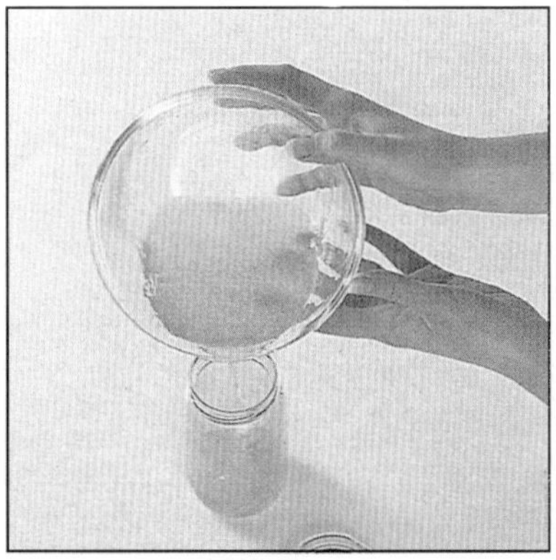

3 Pour the glaze into a sterile jar, seal with a sterile lid and cool. Store in the refrigerator where it will keep well for up to 2 months.

Almond Paste

Use almond paste as a base for royal or fondant icing. It will help to keep the cake moist.

Makes enough to cover an 8 in round cake

INGREDIENTS
4 cups ground almonds
⅞ cup superfine sugar
1½ cups confectioner's sugar
1 tsp lemon juice
¼ tsp almond extract
1 egg

1 Sift the almonds, superfine sugar and confectioner's sugar together into a bowl.

2 With a fork, beat the lemon juice, almond extract and egg together in a small bowl. Stir them into the dry ingredients.

3 Knead together until smooth and wrap in plastic wrap until needed.

Royal Icing

This icing will dry very hard and is a wonderful covering for cakes.

Makes enough to cover an 8 in round cake

INGREDIENTS
2 egg whites
1 tsp lemon juice
1 tsp glycerin (optional)
1 lb confectioner's sugar

1 In a large bowl, beat the egg whites, lemon juice and glycerin (if using) together with a fork.

2 Sift in enough confectioner's sugar to make a thick paste.

3 Using a wooden spoon, beat in the remaining confectioner's sugar until the icing forms stiff peaks. Cover with plastic wrap until ready to use.

Lining a Deep Cake Pan of any Shape

For rich or light fruit cakes, use good quality fixed-base deep cake pans. Ensure that you have the correct size of pan for the quantity of cake mixture.

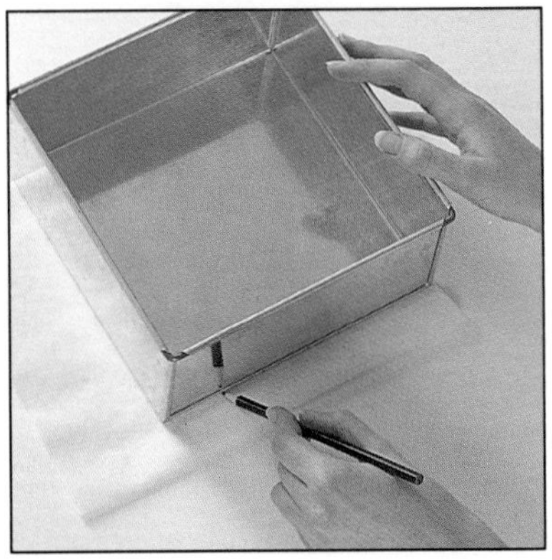

1 Place the pan on a piece of double thickness waxed paper or parchment paper and draw around the base following the pan shape. Cut out the marked shape with a pair of scissors.

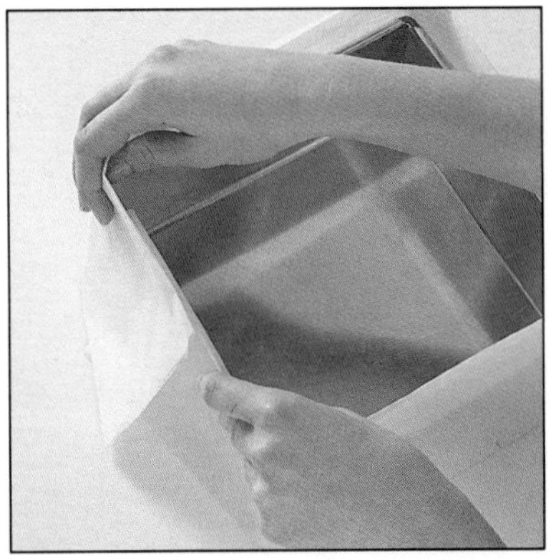

2 Measure and cut a strip of double thickness waxed paper or parchment paper long enough to wrap around the outside of the pan with a small overlap and deep enough to stand 1 in above the top of the pan.

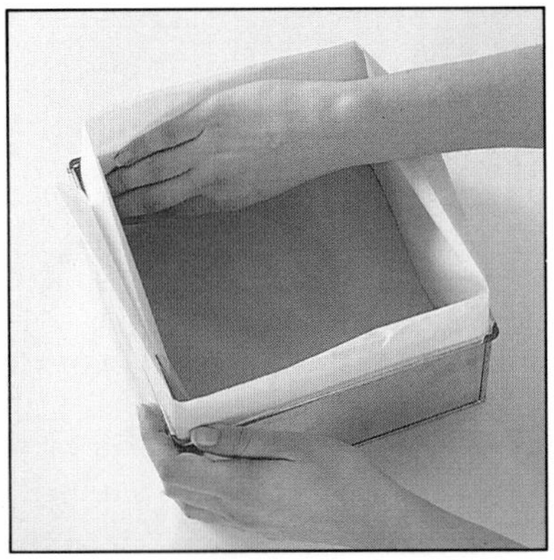

3 Brush the base and sides of the pan with melted fat or oil. Place the cut-out paper shape in the base of the pan and press flat. Fit the double strip of waxed paper or parchment paper inside the pan, pressing well against the sides and making sharp creases where the paper fits into the corners of the pan. Ensure that the paper strip is level and fits neatly without any creases. Brush the base and sides well with melted fat or oil.

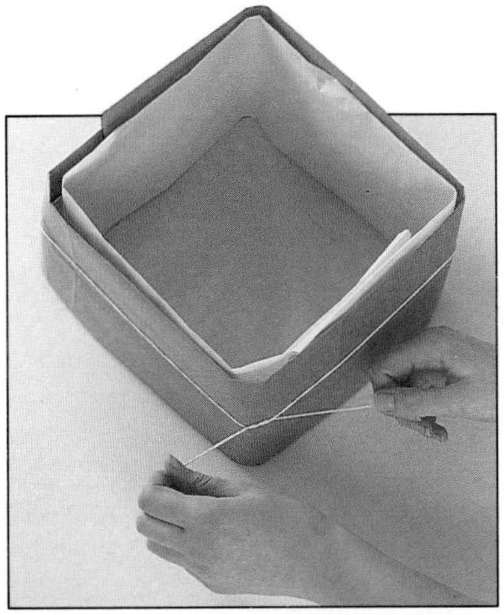

4 Measure and fit a double thickness strip of brown paper around the outside of the pan. Tie securely with string.

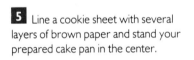

5 Line a cookie sheet with several layers of brown paper and stand your prepared cake pan in the center.

Templates

For gingerbread houses, you may find it easier to use a template for the walls and roof of the house.

1 Draw the dimensions required onto stiff card, and cut out. Position on top of the rolled out dough, and cut around the card shape with a pair of scissors or sharp knife.

Testing Cakes

It is very important to check that cakes are properly baked; otherwise they can be soggy and may sink in the middle.

Testing a Fruit Cake

1 To test if a fruit cake is ready, push a skewer or cake tester into it; if it comes out clean, the cake is done.

2 Fruit cakes are generally left to cool in the pan for 30 minutes. Then turn the cake out carefully, peel away the paper and place on a wire rack.

Testing a Sponge Cake

1 To test if a sponge cake is ready, press down lightly on the center of the cake with your fingertips—if the cake springs back, it is done.

2 To remove the sponge cake from the pan, loosen around the edge by carefully running a small metal spatula around the inside of the pan. Invert the cake onto a wire rack, cover with a second rack, then invert again. Remove the top rack and let cool.

Storing Cakes

Everyday cakes, sponge cakes and meringues can be kept in an airtight container or simply wrapped in plastic wrap or foil: the exclusion of air will ensure that they keep moist and fresh. Store the cakes in a cool, dry place for up to a week; meringues will store for up to one month. Avoid storing cakes in warm, moist conditions as this will encourage mold to grow.

- To store fruit cakes, leave the lining paper on the cakes. Wrap the cakes in a double layer of foil and keep in a cool place. Never seal a fruit cake in an airtight container for long periods of time, as this may encourage mold growth.

- Rich, heavy fruit cakes can be happily stored for up to three months. If you are going to keep a fruit cake for several months before adding a layer of marzipan or icing, pour alcohol, such as brandy, over it a little at a time at monthly intervals, turning the cake each time.

- Light fruit cakes are at their best when first made, or eaten within one month of making.

- For long-term storage, fruit cakes are better frozen in their double wrapping and foil.

- Once fruit cakes have been covered with marzipan or icing, they will keep longer, but iced cakes must be stored in cardboard cake boxes in a warm, dry atmosphere. Damp and cold are the worst conditions, causing the icing to stain and colors to run.

- Freeze a decorated celebration cake in the cake box, making sure the lid is sealed with tape. Take the cake out of its box and thaw it slowly in a cool, dry place. When the cake has thawed, transfer it to a warm, dry place so that the icing dries completely.

PRESENTATION IDEAS

Many of the recipes in this book have been devised to be given as gifts, although they are so delicious you are sure to want to keep a batch yourself. There are many ways of packaging your gifts; the following are just a few ideas.

Marzipan Fruits

Marzipan fruits look so delightful it's a shame to hide them away.

1 Choose a transparent container to show the fruits to best effect. This one is very simple in design, but you may wish to choose a more elaborate, glass container. Carefully position the fruits inside the container.

2 Finish with a co-ordinating ribbon or decoration, secured to the lid with double-sided tape.

Christmas Cakes

These little cakes make ideal gifts. Prettily packaged they are the very essence of Christmas.

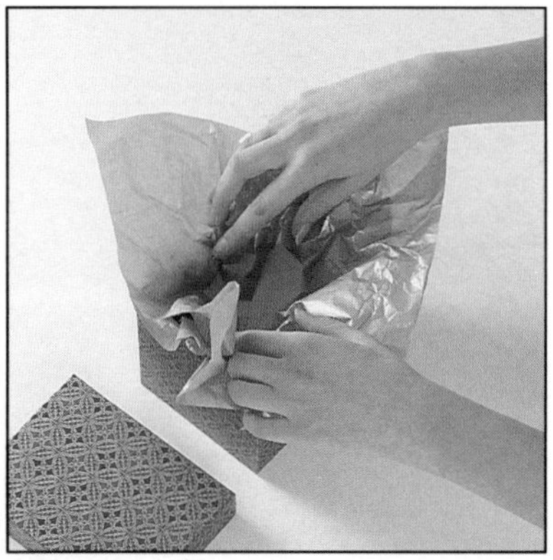

1 For the container, a simple cardboard box covered in decorative paper was used. Line this with tissue paper in a festive color.

2 Carefully place the cake in the box, and cover with the remaining tissue paper. Please note, this packaging is purely decorative, and will not protect the cake if you are planning to send it long distances or in the mail.

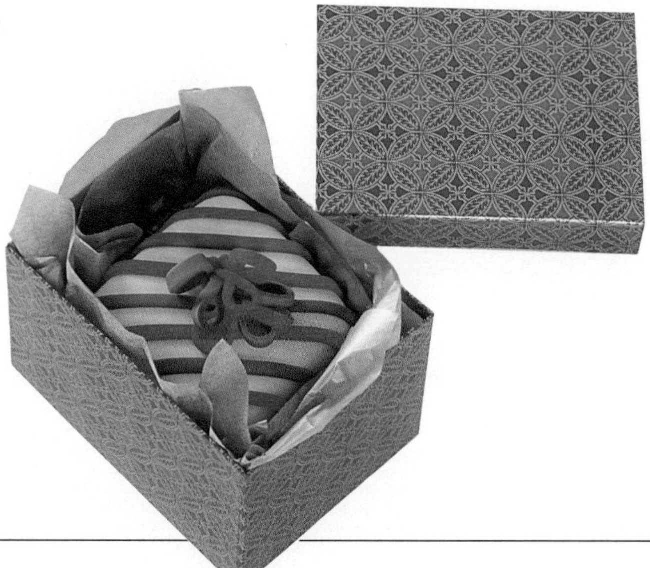

Potted Spreads and Butters

Spreads and flavored butters are enchanting packed in little jars. Sterilize the container as explained earlier, pack with the chosen spread and decorate as follows.

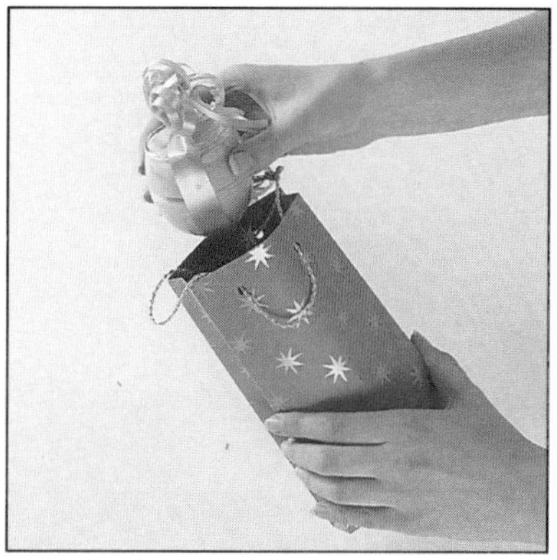

1 Decorate the top with ribbon curls in suitable colors (you may want to reflect the colors of the contents of the jars). Fix the ribbon curls in place with double-sided tape.

2 If you wish to present several assorted jars, pack them in a bag made of decorative wrapping paper.

Cookies and Candies

If your gift will be given, and eaten, relatively quickly, and the contents do not need to be stored in an airtight container, then a pretty box lined with tissue paper may be the answer.

1 Line your chosen container with 3–4 sheets of co-ordinating tissue paper. After positioning the first piece, lay the others on top, alternating the corners to fill the spaces. Crumpled tissue paper has a charm all its own. You may wish to crumple it first, then lightly smooth out.

2 Carefully place the contents inside the box, and fold excess tissue over the top for extra security.

Gift Wrappings

The emphasis on attractive gift wrappings has increased considerably in recent years. It is relatively simple to make small gifts at home and package them beautifully. Personalized gifts are as much a joy to give as receive, and will mean so much more.

There are many stores that specialize in gift wrapping materials. Papers, ribbons, different types of boxes, containers, labels and cards are all available. When making your own Christmas gifts, look out for unusual accessories with which to enhance the packaging of the fruits of your labors.

Boxes
These make wonderful containers for chocolates, candies, cakes or cookies. You will find many different designs, colors and sizes in stationers, paper specialists or large stores.

Fabrics
Choose fabrics printed with Christmas designs to make a simple drawstring bag or stocking shape as a container for a small gift. Cover the tops of preserves with a circle of fabric over the cellophane discs and cover boxes with bright fabrics using a clear fabric adhesive. You can also add ribbons or cut-out shapes.

Gift bags
These are especially useful for packing awkwardly shaped gifts such as pots of preserves or bottles. They come in a variety of sizes and often have a matching gift label attached.

Gift cards and tags
These are often available to co-ordinate with your chosen paper, box or container. You can easily make your own tags by sticking your chosen paper onto a plain piece of card before making a hole in the corner and adding a ribbon.

Glass bottles
There is now an extensive range of recycled glass containers in all sizes, suitable for bottling drinks, flavored oils and herbed vinegars. Many are available complete with their own air-tight stoppers or corks.

Glass jars
Assorted sizes of glass jars with screw-topped lids are invaluable for jams, jellies, savory butters and spreads. Found mostly in kitchen departments or stores, some jars come in wonderful shapes and have corks to seal the tops.

Ribbons
The choice is overwhelming; even the simplest ribbons can transform a gift more than any other packaging.

Small dishes
The choice is quite daunting and is limited only by how much you are willing to pay. Choose from rustic pottery dishes which are fun to receive, or plain white china presented in brightly colored wrapping paper. For a very special gift, choose a fine porcelain dish and place it in a box tied with co-ordinating ribbon.

Tins
These are often sold to store pens and pencils but make excellent air-tight containers for cookies, candies or small cakes, and can be found in many large stores, kitchen stores and stationers.

Right: *Bags and baskets, cards, and tags, ribbons and wrappings of all kinds can be used to enhance your home-made gifts.*

Nutty Cheese Balls

These tasty morsels are perfect for nibbling with drinks.

Makes 32

INGREDIENTS
4 oz cream cheese
4 oz Roquefort cheese
1 cup finely chopped walnuts
chopped fresh parsley, to coat
paprika, to coat
salt and freshly ground black pepper

1 Beat the two cheeses together until smooth using an electric beater.

2 Stir in the chopped walnuts and season with salt and pepper.

3 Shape into small balls (about a rounded teaspoonful each). Chill on a baking sheet until firm.

4 Roll half the balls in the chopped parsley and half in the paprika. Serve on toothpicks.

Salami and Olive Cheese Wedges

Genoa salami is delicious with the olives.

Makes 24

INGREDIENTS
8 oz cream cheese
1 tsp paprika
½ tsp English mustard powder
2 tbsp stuffed green olives, chopped
8 oz sliced salami
sliced olives, to garnish

1 Beat the cream cheese with the paprika and mustard and mix well. Stir in the chopped olives.

2 Spread the salami slices with the olive mixture and stack five slices on top of each other. Wrap in plastic wrap and chill until firm. With a sharp knife, cut each stack into four wedges. Garnish with additional sliced olives and serve with a toothpick through each wedge, to hold the slices together.

Spiced Mixed Nuts

Spices are a delicious addition to mixed roasted nuts.

Makes 2 cups

INGREDIENTS
2/3 cup brazil nuts
2/3 cup cashew nuts
2/3 cup almonds
1 tsp garam masala
1/2 tsp ground coriander
1/2 tsp salt
2 tbsp butter, melted

1 Preheat the oven to 350°F. Put all the nuts and spices and the salt on to a baking tray and mix well.

2 Pour the melted butter over and bake for 10–15 minutes, stirring until golden brown.

3 Drain on paper towels and allow to cool before serving.

Herby Cheese Crackers

Use a selection of festive shapes for cutting out these crackers.

Makes 32

INGREDIENTS
3 cups all-purpose flour
1/2 tsp cayenne pepper
1 tsp English mustard powder
3/4 cup butter
6 oz sharp Cheddar cheese, grated finely
1 tbsp mixed dried herbs
1 egg, beaten
salt and freshly ground black pepper

1 Preheat the oven to 400°F. Sift the flour, cayenne pepper and mustard powder together into a bowl or food processor.

2 Rub the butter into the flour and add the cheese, herbs and seasoning. Stir in the beaten egg to bind, and knead to a smooth dough.

3 On a lightly floured work surface, roll the dough out thinly. Stamp it into small biscuits with cutters. Bake for 10–15 minutes, or until golden. Cool on a wire rack. Store in an airtight container.

Mulled Red Wine

Excellent to serve on a cold winter's evening; it will really get the party started.

Makes 2½ cups

INGREDIENTS
1 bottle red wine
⅓ cup light brown sugar
2 cinnamon sticks
1 lemon, sliced
4 whole cloves
⅔ cup brandy or port
lemon slices, to serve

1 Put all the ingredients, except the brandy or port, into a large pan. Bring the wine to a boil to dissolve the sugar. Remove from the heat, cover the pan and leave it to stand for 5 minutes, to allow the flavors to infuse.

2 Strain to remove the spices and lemon slices.

3 Add the brandy and serve warm, with a fresh slice of lemon.

Sparkling Cider Punch

This is a very refreshing, sparkling drink, best served as cold as possible.

Makes 10½ cups

INGREDIENTS
1 orange
1 lemon
1 apple
4 cups sparkling cider, chilled
4 cups lemonade, chilled
2½ cups apple juice, chilled
fresh mint sprigs, to serve

1 Slice all the fruit into a large bowl.

2 Add the cider, lemonade and apple juice. Serve cold with sprigs of fresh mint.

Spiced Fruit Cocktail

This non-alcoholic fruit drink is a real treat.

Makes 8¾ cups

INGREDIENTS
2½ cups orange juice, chilled
1¼ cups pineapple juice, chilled
pared rind and juice of 1 lemon
4 whole cloves
1 cinnamon stick, broken into pieces
4 tbsp superfine sugar
orange slices
ice cubes
2½ cups sparkling mineral water, chilled
2½ cups ginger ale, chilled

1 Mix the orange and pineapple juices together in a large bowl. Add the lemon rind and juice, spices and sugar. Chill.

2 Put the orange slices and ice cubes in a serving bowl. Strain the fruit juice mixture into the bowl. Add the mineral water and ginger ale.

Fruit Punch

This is a quick punch to assemble. Make sure that all the ingredients are well chilled.

Makes 10¼ cups

INGREDIENTS
1 bottle white wine, chilled
1 bottle red wine, chilled
3 tbsp orange-flavored liqueur
1 orange, cut in quarters and sliced
seedless grapes
ice cubes
4 cups sparkling lemonade

1 Empty the wines and liqueur into a large bowl.

2 Add the orange pieces, grapes and ice and finally the sparkling lemonade.

Prune, Orange and Nut Stuffing

You could also finely chop the reserved turkey liver and mix it into this stuffing.

Serves 8 (enough to stuff a 10 lb turkey)

INGREDIENTS
1 cup pitted prunes
4 tbsp red wine or sherry
1 onion, finely chopped
2 tbsp butter
4 cups fresh white bread crumbs
finely grated rind of 1 orange
2 eggs, beaten
2 tbsp chopped fresh parsley
1 tbsp mixed dried herbs
large pinch of ground allspice
large pinch of grated nutmeg
1 cup chopped walnuts or pecans
2 celery stalks, finely chopped
salt and freshly ground black pepper

1 Put the prunes and red wine or sherry in a small pan, cover and simmer gently until tender. Set aside to cool.

2 Cook the onion gently in the butter until tender, about 10 minutes.

3 Cut each prune into four pieces. Mix all the ingredients in a large bowl and season well with salt and pepper.

Rice, Mushroom and Leek Stuffing

The rice gives this stuffing a crumbly, light texture.

Serves 8 (enough to stuff a 10 lb turkey)

INGREDIENTS
½ cup rice
2 tbsp butter
3 cups leeks, washed and sliced
2½ cups mushrooms, chopped
2 celery stalks, finely chopped
½ cup chopped walnuts
1 egg, beaten
4 tbsp chopped fresh parsley
2 tsp dried thyme
finely grated rind of 1 lemon
2 cooking apples, peeled, cored and diced
salt and freshly ground black pepper

1 Cook the rice in plenty of boiling, salted water for 12 minutes until tender. Drain the rice thoroughly and let it cool. Melt the butter in a frying-pan and cook the leeks and mushrooms until tender. Increase the heat and cook to evaporate any remaining moisture in the pan. Set aside to cool.

2 Mix all the remaining ingredients thoroughly together in a large bowl and season with salt and pepper.

3 Add the rice, and the leek and mushroom mixture to the bowl and mix together thoroughly.

Making Bacon Rolls

If you want to wrap pitted prunes or chicken livers inside each strip cut the bacon strips in half after stretching them.

1 Remove the rind from the rashers of bacon and stretch them with the back of a large knife.

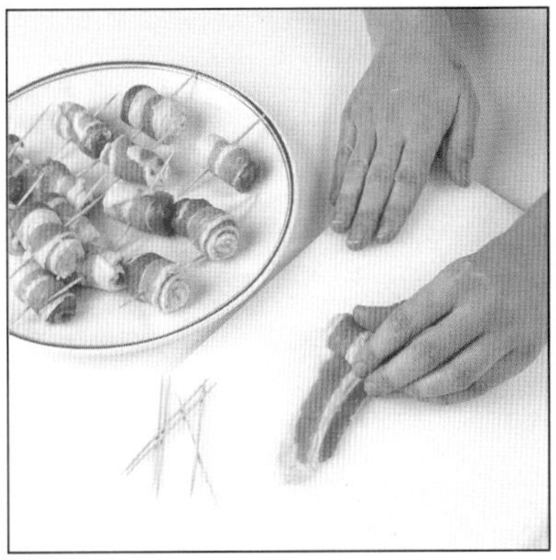

2 Roll the strips up neatly.

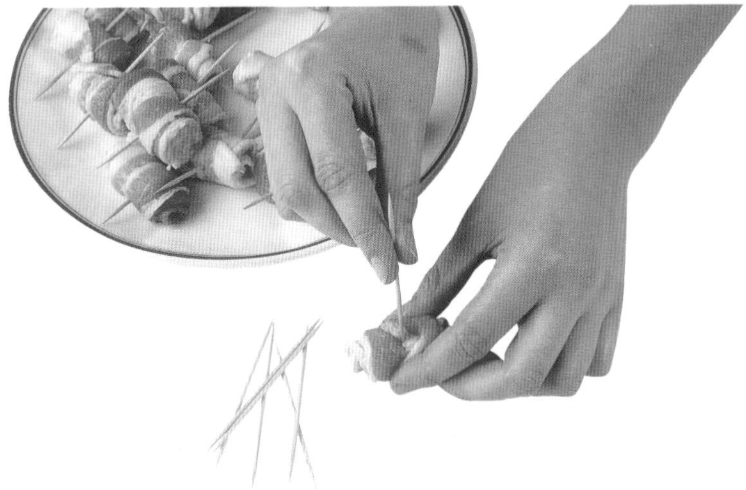

3 Skewer the bacon rolls with toothpicks. Broil the rolls until crisp, turning them halfway through cooking.

Roasting Potatoes

Floury potatoes make the best crisp roast potatoes. Garlic or rosemary can be added to the oil, to flavor the potatoes during cooking.

1 Preheat the oven to 400°F. Peel the potatoes and cut large potatoes in half. Parboil them for 10 minutes. Drain. Score the surface of each potato with a fork. Roll them in flour and tap them to remove any excess. Heat 1 in olive oil in a shallow roasting pan until smoking hot.

2 Put the potatoes in the hot oil and baste them to coat them in oil. Roast for about an hour.

3 Baste and turn the potatoes twice during cooking. Drain them on paper towels and sprinkle them with salt.

Carving a Turkey

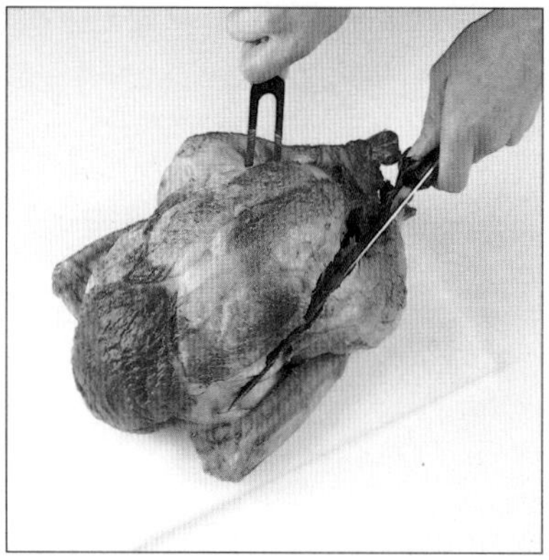

1 First remove the leg, by cutting the skin between the breast and leg. Press the leg flat, to expose the joint. Cut between the bones through the joint.

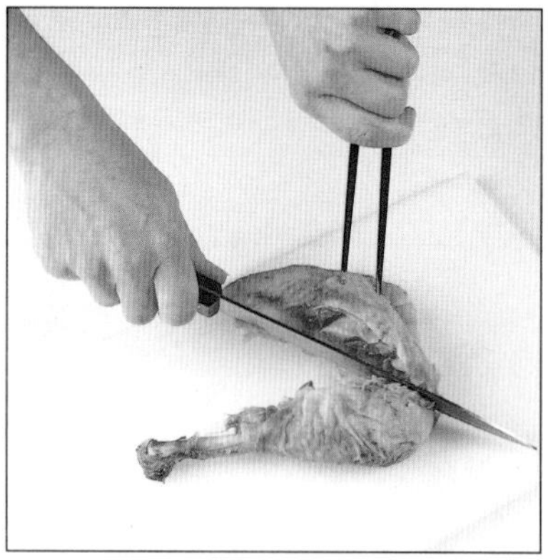

2 Cut the leg in two, through the joint.

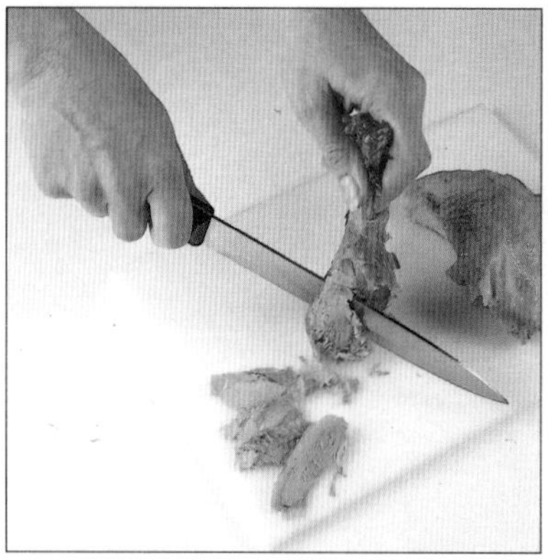

3 Carve the leg into slices.

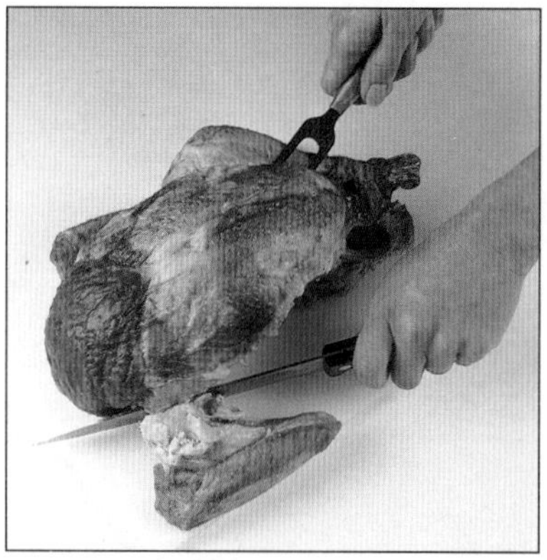

4 Remove the wing, cutting through the joint in the same way as for the leg.

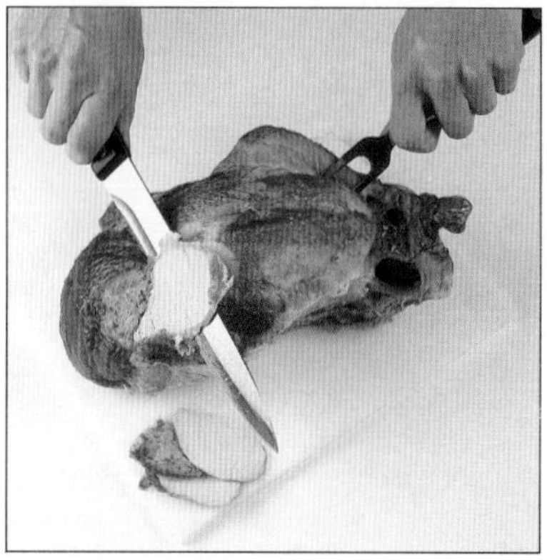

5 Carve the breast in thin slices, starting at the front of the breast. Then carve slices from the back of the breast, alternating the slices between front and back, until all the breast has been carved.

Times for Roasting Turkey

When choosing a turkey for Christmas, you should allow about 1 lb of dressed (plucked and oven-ready) bird per person. A good sized turkey to buy for Christmas is 10 lb. This will serve about 12 people, with leftovers for the following day.

Thaw a frozen turkey, still in its bag, on a plate at room temperature (65–70°F) until the legs are flexible and there are no ice crystals in the cavity of the bird. Remove the giblets from the cavity as soon as the bird has thawed enough.

Oven-ready weight	Thawing time	Number of servings	Cooking time
8 lb	18 hours	8–10 people	2½–3½ hours
10 lb	19 hours	12–14 people	3½–4 hours
12 lb	20 hours	16–18 people	3¾–4½ hours
14 lb	24 hours	18–20 people	4–5 hours

These times apply to a turkey weighed after stuffing and at room temperature. Cook in a moderate oven, 350°F, covered with butter and bacon strips and loosely covered with foil.

To test whether the turkey is fully cooked, push a skewer into the thickest part of the leg and press the flesh; the juices should run clear and free from any blood. The legs take longer than the breast to cook; keep the breast covered with foil until the legs are cooked. The foil can be removed for the final hour of cooking, to brown and crisp the skin. The turkey should be basted with the juices from the roasting pan, every hour of cooking.

Plan for the turkey to be ready 15–20 minutes before you want to serve dinner. Remove it from the oven and allow the flesh to relax before carving it.

Brandy or Rum Butter

Serve with Christmas pudding or mince pies.

Makes about 3/4 cup

INGREDIENTS
6 tbsp unsalted butter
6 tbsp superfine sugar
finely grated rind of 1 small orange
3 tbsp brandy or rum

1 Whisk the butter, sugar and orange rind together until soft and fluffy.

2 Gradually whisk in the brandy or rum. Chill until ready to serve.

Whisky Sauce

This is another delicious accompaniment to Christmas pudding or mince pies.

Makes about 2 1/2 cups

INGREDIENTS
2 tbsp cornstarch
2 1/2 cups milk
2 tbsp superfine sugar
4 tbsp whisky
grated nutmeg

1 In a small bowl, mix the cornstarch with 1 tbsp of the milk to make a smooth paste.

2 Bring the remaining milk to a boil, remove from the heat and pour a little on to the cornstarch mixture and mix the cornstarch into the pan.

3 Return to the heat, stirring constantly until thickened. Simmer for 2 minutes. Turn off the heat and add the sugar and whisky. Pour into a serving pitcher and sprinkle with the grated nutmeg.

SUGGESTED MENUS

Christmas Dinner for 8 People

Cheese and Pesto Pastries

Roast Turkey, stuffing balls, sausages, Bacon Rolls and gravy

Roast Potatoes and Brussels Sprouts with Chestnuts and Carrots

Steamed Christmas Pudding with Whisky Sauce

Vegetarian Christmas Dinner for 8 People

Christmas Salad with mini bread rolls

Cheese and Spinach Quiche or Vegetarian Christmas Pie

Vegetable Crumble or Brussels Sprouts with Chestnuts and Carrots

Crunchy Apple and Almond Flan

New Year's Eve Party for 8 People

Smoked Salmon Salad

Roast Goose with Caramelized Apples, with Port and Orange Gravy

Gratin Dauphinois and Sweet and Sour Red Cabbage

Chocolate and Chestnut Yule Log

Hot Supper for 12 People

Roquefort Tartlets and Stilton with Herbs Spread and Melba toast

Spiced Lamb with Fruit Pilaf

Sweet and Sour Red Cabbage

Iced Praline Torte and Ruby Fruit Salad

New Year's Day Lunch for 12 People

Warm Shrimp Salad with herb and garlic bread

Baked Country Ham with Cumberland Sauce

Vegetable Gnocchi

Deluxe Mincemeat Tart

Cold Buffet Lunch for 12 People

Layered Salmon Terrine

Fillet of Beef with Ratatouille

Turkey Rice Salad

Ginger Trifle and Almond Mincemeat Tartlets

Countdown to Christmas

This at-a-glance timetable will help you plan and organize your Christmas cooking. If you have chosen your menu from one of those suggested previously, the table below suggests when the components may be prepared.

Late Autumn
Make preserves and relishes such as Cranberry and Orange Relish or Curried Fruit Chutney to serve with cold meats.

November
Second week
Make Moist and Rich Christmas Cake.

Third week
Feed Moist and Rich Christmas Cake (optional).

Fourth week
Make Christmas Pudding.
Decide on Christmas dinner menu.
Order turkey, goose, beef or ham.
Continue to feed Moist and Rich Christmas Cake (optional).

December
First week
Make Light Jeweled Fruit Cake.
Make mincemeat for Deluxe Mincemeat Tart.
Continue to feed Moist and Rich Christmas Cake (optional).
Compile complete shopping list for main Christmas meals under headings for different stores, or for the various counters at the supermarket.
Continue to add to list throughout the week.

Second week
Make Almond Paste to cover Moist and Rich Christmas Cake.
Shop for dry goods such as rice, dried fruits and flour.
Order special bread requirements.
Order milk, cream and other dairy produce.
Make Brandy or Rum Butter.

Third week
Make Cheese and Pesto Pastries and other pastry-type cocktail savories and freeze.
Cover Moist and Rich Christmas Cake with royal icing, leave one day, then cover and store.

Fourth week
Shop for chilled ingredients.
Buy wines and other drinks.

21 December
Check thawing time for frozen turkey, duck, beef or other meat. Large turkeys (25 lb) need 86 hours (3½ days) to thaw in the refrigerator, or 40 hours at room temperature.
Make a note to take the meat from the freezer at the appropriate time.

23 December
Shop for fresh vegetables, if not possible to do so on 24 December.
Make Cheese and Spinach Quiche and freeze, if not making on Christmas Day.
Make Crunchy Apple and Almond Flan.

24 December
Shop for fresh vegetables, if possible.
Assemble Christmas Salad and refrigerate dressing separately.
Make stuffing for poultry.
Cook poultry giblets to make gravy.
Defrost Cheese and Pesto Pastries.
Prepare Bacon Rolls by threading them on to toothpicks.
Make Whisky Sauce to serve with Christmas Pudding.

Christmas Day
This timetable is planned for Christmas Dinner to be served at 2.00pm. If you wish to serve it at a different time, please adjust the times accordingly.

Stuff poultry. Make forcemeat balls with any leftover stuffing, or spoon it into greased ovenproof dishes.
Set table, if not already done.

Put steamer or large saucepan on cooker and bring water to a boil.
Put Christmas Pudding on to steam.

To cook a 10 lb turkey
9.05am Set oven to 425°F.
9.25am Put turkey in oven.
9.45am Reduce heat to 350°F. Baste turkey now and at frequent intervals.
12.15pm Put potatoes around meat. Remove foil from turkey and baste again.
12.45pm Turn the potatoes. Increase heat to 400°F. Put any dishes of stuffing in oven.
1.45pm Remove turkey and potatoes from oven, put on heated dish, cover with foil and keep warm. Make gravy and broil bacon rolls.

To cook vegetarian menu
11.15am Make pastry for Cheese and Spinach Quiche, if not cooking from frozen. (If you are making Christmas Pie, begin 20 minutes earlier to allow time to chill the assembled pie.)
11.45am Put pastry in the fridge and chill. Prepare sprouts for Brussels Sprouts with Chestnuts and Carrots.
12.15pm Preheat oven for Cheese and Spinach Quiche. Remove pastry from fridge and assemble. (For Christmas Pie, chill assembled dish for 20 minutes before baking. Preheat oven 10 minutes before removing pie from fridge.)
1.00pm Put quiche or pie in oven.
1.20pm Simmer chestnuts for 10 minutes.
1.30pm Simmer sprouts for 5 minutes.
1.35pm Simmer carrots for 5 minutes.
1.40pm Gently reheat all vegetables together.
1.45pm Remove quiche or pie from oven.
2.00pm Serve first course.

Cheese and Pesto Pastries

These pastries can be made ahead and frozen uncooked. Freeze them in a single layer and then transfer them to a freezer-proof container. To serve, arrange the pastries on baking trays, brush them with oil and bake from frozen for 5–10 minutes longer than the recommended time.

Serves 8

INGREDIENTS
8 oz frozen chopped spinach
2 tbsp pine nuts
4 tbsp pesto sauce
4 oz Gruyère cheese
½ cup grated Parmesan cheese
2 × 10 oz packet of frozen filo pastry, thawed
2 tbsp olive oil
salt and freshly ground black pepper, to taste

Parmesan

olive oil

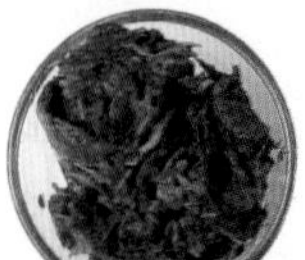

spinach

filo pastry

pesto sauce

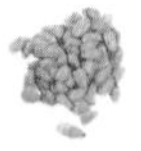

pine nuts

1 Preheat the oven to 375°F. Prepare the filling; put the frozen spinach into a pan, and heat gently, breaking it up as it defrosts. Increase the heat to evaporate any excess moisture. Transfer to a bowl and cool slightly.

2 Put the pine nuts into a frying pan and stir over a very low heat until they are lightly toasted. Chop them and add them to the spinach, with the pesto and Gruyère and Parmesan cheeses. Season to taste.

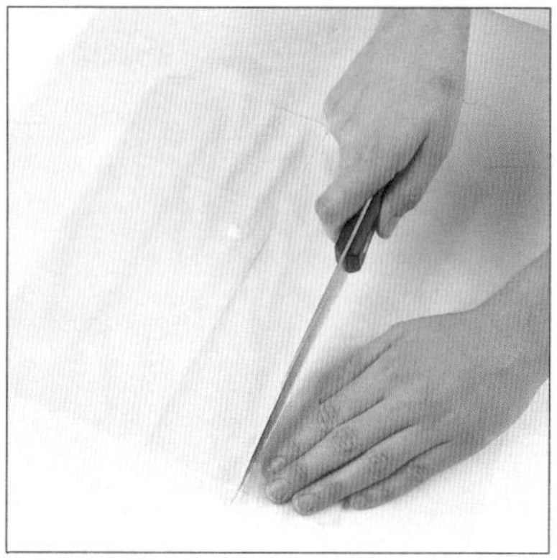

3 Unwrap the filo pastry and cover it with plastic wrap and a damp dish towel (to prevent it from drying out). Take one sheet at a time and cut it into 2 in wide strips. Brush each strip with oil.

4 Put a teaspoon of filling on one end of each strip of pastry. Fold the end over in a triangle, enclosing the filling.

5 Continue to fold the triangle over and over again until the end of the strip is reached. Repeat with the other strips, until all the filling has been used up.

6 Place the pastries on baking trays, brush them with oil and bake for 20–25 minutes, or until golden brown. Cool on a wire rack. Serve warm.

Christmas Salad

A light first course that can be prepared ahead and assembled just before serving.

Serves 8

Ingredients
mixed red and green lettuce leaves
2 sweet pink grapefruit
1 large or 2 small avocados, peeled and cubed

For the dressing
6 tbsp light olive oil
2 tbsp red wine vinegar
1 garlic clove, crushed
1 tsp Dijon mustard
salt and freshly ground black pepper

For the caramelized orange peel
4 oranges
4 tbsp superfine sugar
4 tbsp cold water

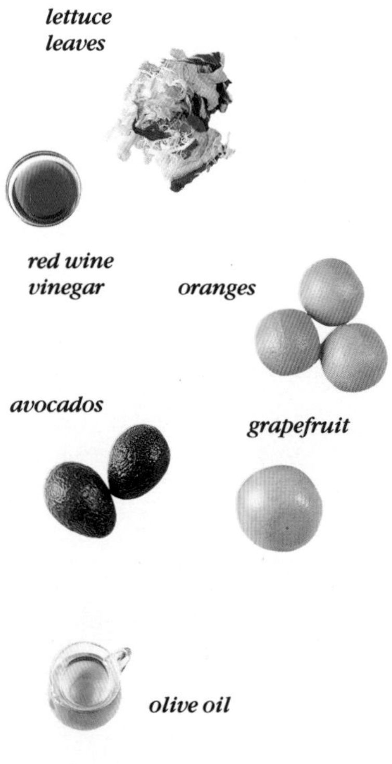

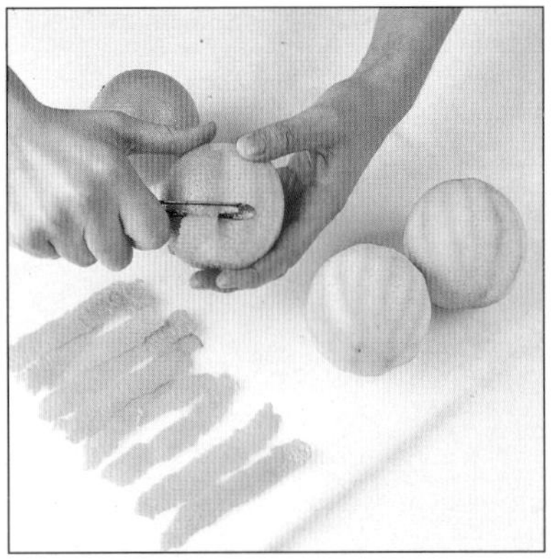

1 To make the caramelized peel, using a vegetable peeler, remove the rind from the oranges in thin strips and reserve the fruit. Scrape away the white pith from the underside of the rind with a sharp knife, and cut the rind in fine shreds.

2 Put the sugar and water in a small pan and heat gently until the sugar has dissolved. Then add the shreds of orange rind, increase the heat and boil steadily for 5 minutes, until the rind is tender. Using two forks, remove the orange rind from the syrup and spread it out on a wire rack to dry. (This can be done the day before). Reserve the syrup to add to the dressing.

3 Wash and dry the lettuce and tear the leaves into bite-sized pieces. Wrap them in a clean, damp dish towel and keep them in the fridge. Cut the pith off the oranges and grapefruit. Holding the fruit over a bowl to catch any juice, cut them into segments, removing all the pith.

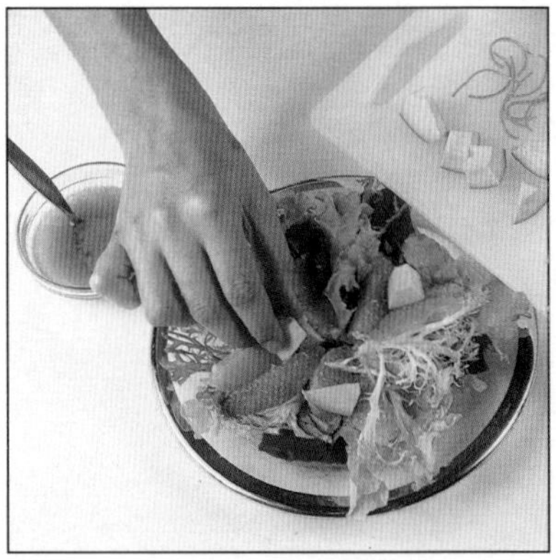

4 Put all the dressing ingredients into a screw-top jar and shake the jar vigorously to emulsify the dressing. Add the reserved orange-flavored syrup and adjust the seasoning to taste. Arrange the salad ingredients on individual plates with the avocados, spoon over the dressing and scatter on the caramelized peel.

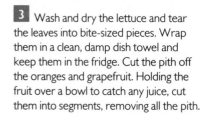

Warm Shrimp Salad with Spicy Marinade

The ingredients can be prepared in advance; if you do this, cook the shrimp and bacon just before serving, spoon over the salad and serve with hot herb and garlic bread.

Serves 8

INGREDIENTS
8 oz large, cooked, shelled shrimp
8 oz smoked lean bacon, chopped
mixed lettuce leaves
2 tbsp chopped fresh chives

FOR THE LEMON AND CHILI MARINADE
1 garlic clove, crushed
finely grated rind of 1 lemon
1 tbsp lemon juice
4 tbsp olive oil
1/4 tsp chili paste, or a large pinch dried ground chili
1 tbsp light soy sauce
salt and freshly ground black pepper

1 In a glass bowl, mix the shrimp with the garlic, lemon rind and juice, 3 tbsp of oil, the chili paste and soy sauce. Season with salt and pepper. Cover with plastic wrap and let marinate for at least one hour.

2 Gently cook the bacon in the remaining oil until crisp. Drain on a paper towel.

3 Wash and dry the lettuce, tear the leaves into bite-sized pieces and arrange them in individual bowls or on plates.

4 Just before serving, put the shrimp with their marinade into a large frying-pan, bring to a boil, add the bacon and cook for one minute. Spoon over the salad and sprinkle with chopped chives. Serve immediately.

Smoked Salmon Salad

To save time, prepare all the ingredients in advance and assemble them on the plates just before serving. The dressing can be made the day before and kept in the fridge.

Serves 8

INGREDIENTS
4 thin slices white bread
oil, for frying
paprika, for dusting
mixed lettuce leaves
1 oz Parmesan cheese
8 oz smoked salmon or trout, thinly sliced
1 lemon

FOR THE VINAIGRETTE DRESSING
6 tbsp olive oil
2 tbsp red wine vinegar
1 garlic clove, crushed
1 tsp Dijon mustard
1 tsp honey
1 tbsp chopped fresh parsley
½ tsp fresh thyme
2 tsp capers, chopped
salt and freshly ground black pepper

lettuce leaves

lemon

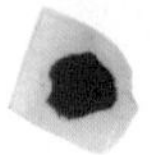
paprika

bread

smoked salmon

1 First make the dressing. Put all the ingredients into a screw-top jar and shake the jar well to emulsify the dressing. Season to taste.

2 With a small star-shaped cutter, stamp out as many shapes from the slices of bread as possible. Heat 1 in oil in a shallow frying-pan until the oil is almost smoking (test it with a cube of bread, it should sizzle on the surface and brown within 30 seconds). Fry the croûtons, in small batches, until golden brown all over. Remove the croûtons with a slotted spoon and let them drain on paper towels. Dust with paprika and let cool.

3 Wash the lettuce, dry the leaves and tear them into small bite-sized pieces. Wrap in a clean, damp dish towel and keep the lettuce in the fridge until ready to serve.

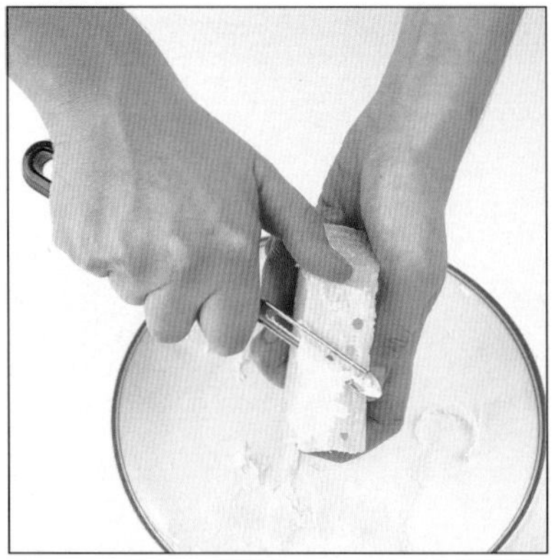

4 Cut the Parmesan cheese into shavings with a vegetable peeler. Put into a dish and cover with plastic wrap.

5 Cut the salmon or trout into ½ in strips no more than 2 in long. Cut the lemon into eight thin wedges.

6 To assemble the salad, arrange the lettuce on individual plates, scatter over the Parmesan flakes and arrange the salmon strips on top. Shake the dressing vigorously to emulsify it again and spoon a little over each salad. Scatter over the croûtons, place a lemon wedge on the side of each plate and serve immediately.

Roquefort Tartlets

These can be made in shallow tartlet pans to serve hot as a first course. You could also make them in mini pie pans, to serve warm as bite-sized snacks with a drink before a meal.

Makes 12

INGREDIENTS
1½ cups all-purpose flour
large pinch of salt
½ cup butter
1 egg yolk
2 tbsp cold water

FOR THE FILLING
1 tbsp butter
1 tbsp all-purpose flour
⅔ cup milk
4 oz Roquefort cheese, crumbled
⅔ cup heavy cream
½ tsp dried mixed herbs
3 egg yolks
salt and freshly ground black pepper

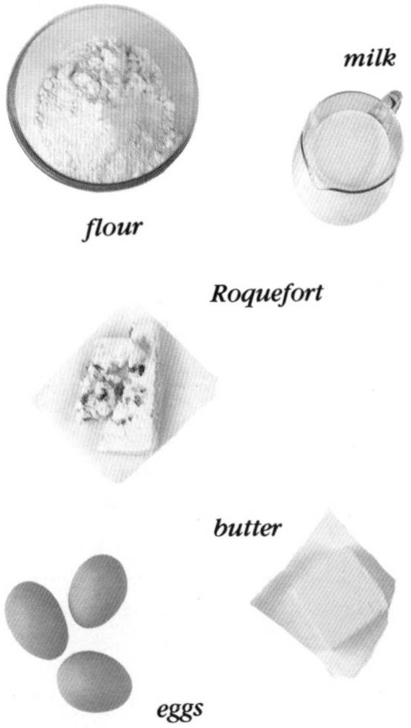

1 To make the pastry, sift the flour and salt into a bowl and rub the butter into the flour until it resembles bread crumbs. Mix the egg yolk with the water and stir into the flour to make a soft dough. Knead until smooth, wrap in plastic wrap and chill for 30 minutes. (You can also make the dough in a food processor.)

2 Melt the butter, stir in the flour and then the milk. Boil to thicken, stirring continuously. Off the heat beat in the cheese and season. Cool. Bring the cream and herbs to a boil. Reduce to 2 tbsp. Beat into the sauce with the eggs.

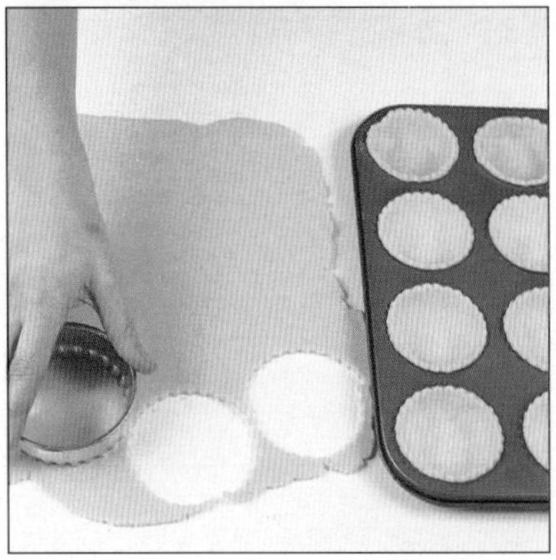

3 Preheat the oven to 375°F. On a lightly floured work surface, roll out the pastry ⅛ in thick. Stamp out rounds with a fluted cutter and use to line your chosen tartlet pans.

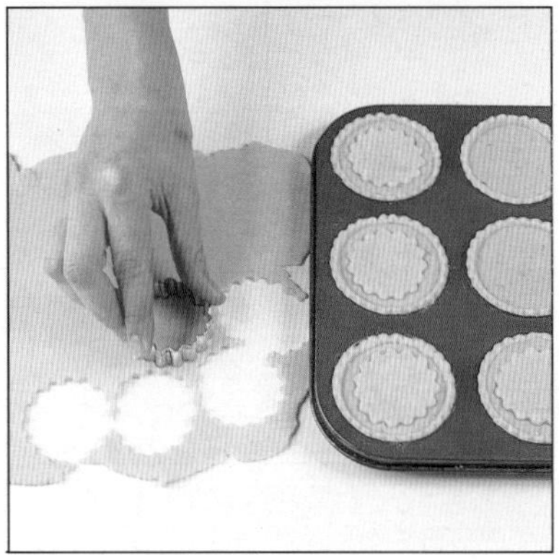

4 Divide the filling between the tartlets; they should be filled only two-thirds full. Stamp out smaller fluted rounds or star shapes for the tops and lay on top of each tartlet. Bake for 20–25 minutes, or until puffed and golden brown.

Stilton with Herbs Spread and Melba Toast

Make this the day before and serve it in small ramekins with the crisp Melba toast, as an hors d'oeuvre or first course. The Melba toast will keep in an airtight container for a day or two.

Serves 8

INGREDIENTS
8 oz blue Stilton or other blue cheese
4 oz cream cheese
1 tbsp port
1 tbsp chopped fresh parsley
1 tbsp chopped fresh chives, plus extra to garnish
½ cup finely chopped walnuts
salt and freshly ground black pepper

FOR THE MELBA TOAST
12 thin slices white bread

1 Put the Stilton, cream cheese and port into a bowl or food processor and beat until smooth.

2 Stir in the remaining ingredients and season with salt and pepper to taste.

3 Spoon into individual ramekins and level the tops. Cover with plastic wrap and chill until firm. Sprinkle with chopped chives before serving. To make the melba toast, preheat the oven to 350°F. Toast the bread lightly on both sides.

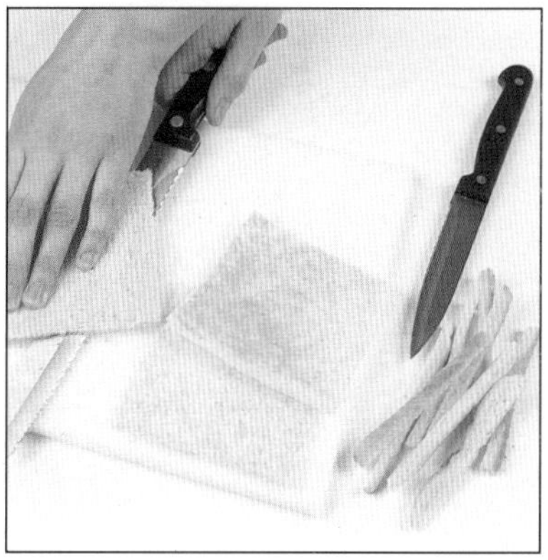

4 While the toast is still hot, cut off the crusts, and cut each slice horizontally in two. While the bread is still warm, place it in a single layer on baking trays and bake for 10–15 minutes, until golden brown and crisp. Continue with the remaining slices in the same way. Serve warm with the Stilton spread.

Baked Country Ham with Cumberland Sauce

Serve this delicious cooked meat and sauce either hot or cold. The country ham must be soaked overnight before cooking to remove any strong salty flavor resulting from the curing process.

Serves 8–10

INGREDIENTS
5 lb smoked or unsmoked country ham
1 onion
1 carrot
1 celery stalk
bouquet garni sachet
6 peppercorns

FOR THE GLAZE
whole cloves
4 tbsp light brown or demerara sugar
2 tbsp corn syrup
1 tsp English mustard powder

FOR THE CUMBERLAND SAUCE
juice and shredded rind of 1 orange
2 tbsp lemon juice
½ cup port or red wine
4 tbsp red currant jelly

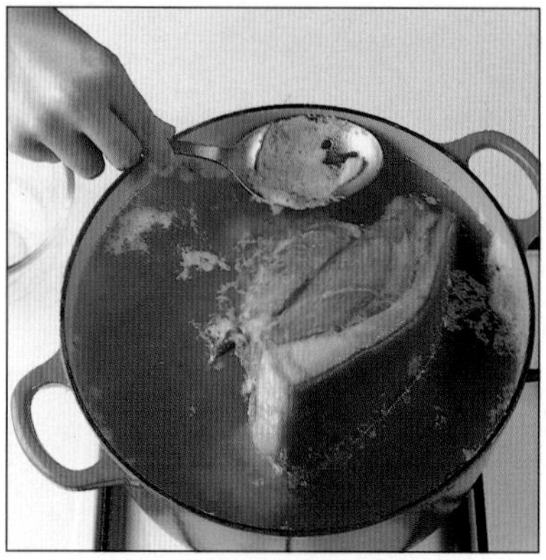

1 Soak the ham overnight in a cool place in plenty of cold water to cover. Discard this water. Put the ham into a large pan and cover it again with more cold water. Bring the water to a boil slowly and skim any scum from the surface with a slotted spoon.

2 Add the vegetables and seasonings, cover, and simmer very gently for 2 hours. (The meat can also be cooked in the oven at 350°F. Allow 30 minutes per lb.)

3 Leave the meat to cool in the liquid for 30 minutes. Then remove it from the liquid and strip off the skin neatly with the help of a knife (use rubber gloves if the ham is too hot to handle).

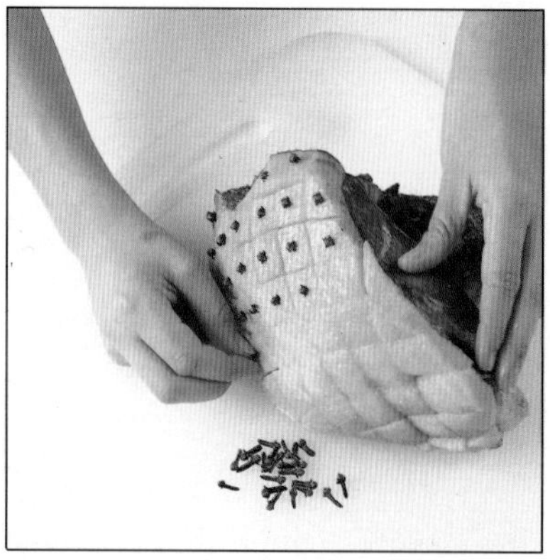

4 Score the fat in diamonds with a sharp knife and stick a clove in the center of each diamond.

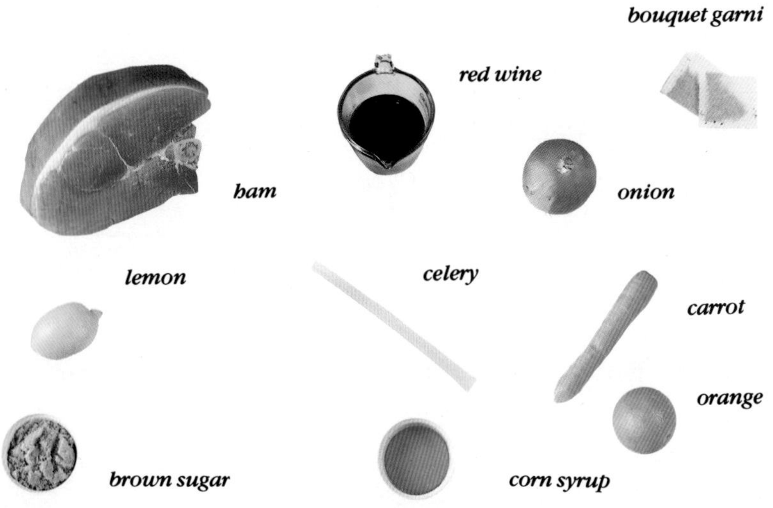

5 Preheat the oven to 350°F. Put the sugar, corn syrup and mustard powder in a small pan and heat gently to melt them. Place the ham in a roasting pan and spoon over the glaze. Bake it until golden brown, about 20 minutes. Put it under a hot broiler, if necessary, to get a good color. Allow to stand in a warm place for about 15 minutes before carving (this allows the flesh to relax and makes carving much easier).

6 For the sauce, put the orange and lemon juice into a pan with the port and red currant jelly, and heat gently to melt the jelly. Pour boiling water over the orange rind, drain, and add to the sauce. Cook gently for 2 minutes. Serve the sauce hot, in a sauce boat.

Roast Turkey

Serve with stuffing balls, bacon rolls, roast potatoes, Brussels sprouts and gravy.

Serves 8

INGREDIENTS
10 lb oven-ready turkey, with giblets (thawed overnight if frozen)
1 large onion, peeled and stuck with 6 whole cloves
4 tbsp butter, softened
10 sausages
salt and freshly ground black pepper

FOR THE STUFFING
8 oz lean bacon, chopped
1 large onion, finely chopped
1 lb bulk pork sausage
⅓ cup rolled oats
2 tbsp chopped fresh parsley
2 tsp dried mixed herbs
1 large egg, beaten
⅔ cup dried apricots, finely chopped

FOR THE GRAVY
2 tbsp all-purpose flour
1⅞ cups giblet stock

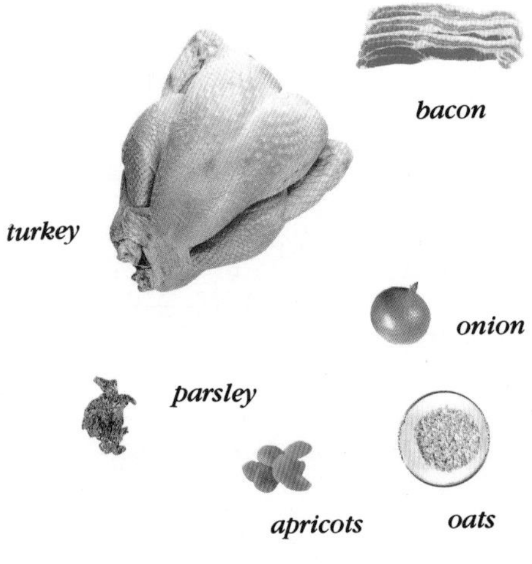

1 Preheat the oven to 400°F. Adjust the oven shelves to allow for the size of the turkey. For the stuffing, cook the bacon and onion gently in a pan until the bacon is crisp and the onion tender. Transfer to a large bowl and mix in all the remaining stuffing ingredients. Season well with salt and pepper.

2 Stuff the neck-end of the turkey only, tuck the flap of skin under and secure it with a small skewer or stitch it with thread (do not over-stuff the turkey or the skin will burst during cooking). Reserve any remaining stuffing.

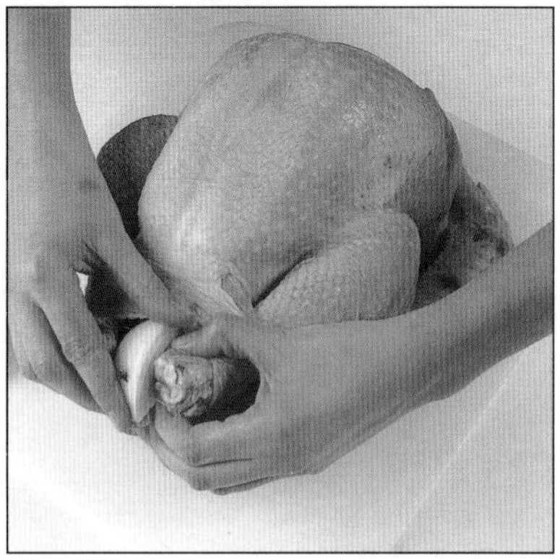

3 Put the whole onion studded with cloves in the body cavity of the turkey and tie the legs together. Weigh the stuffed bird and calculate the cooking time; allow 15 minutes per 1 lb plus 15 minutes over. Place the turkey in a large roasting pan.

4 Spread the turkey with the butter and season it with salt and pepper. Cover it loosely with foil and cook it for 30 minutes. Baste the turkey with the pan juices. Then lower the oven temperature to 350°F and cook for the remainder of the calculated time (about 3½ hours for a 10 lb bird). Baste it every 30 minutes or so.

5 With wet hands, shape the remaining stuffing into small balls or pack it into a greased ovenproof dish. Cook in the oven for 20 minutes, or until golden brown and crisp. About 20 minutes before the end of cooking put the sausages into an ovenproof dish and put them in the oven. Remove the foil from the turkey for the last hour of cooking and baste it. The turkey is cooked if the juices run clear when the thickest part of the thigh has been pierced with a skewer.

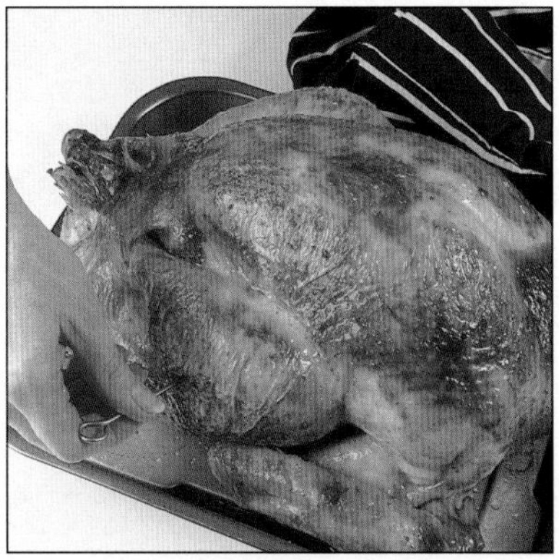

6 Transfer the turkey to a serving plate, cover it with foil and let it stand for 15 minutes before carving. To make the gravy, spoon off the fat from the roasting pan, leaving the meat juices. Blend in the flour and cook for 2 minutes. Gradually stir in the stock and bring to a boil. Check the seasoning and pour into a sauce boat. Remove the skewer or string and pour any juices into the gravy. To serve, surround the turkey with sausages, bacon rolls and stuffing balls.

Roast Duck with Orange

Most of the meat on a duck is on the breast. It is easier to cut the whole breast off each side of the carcass and slice it thinly on a board. The ducks can be cooked the day before, sliced and reheated in some of the gravy. The remaining gravy, with the orange segments, can be reheated gently just before serving.

Serves 8

Ingredients
4 oranges, segmented, with rind and juice reserved
2 × 5 lb oven-ready ducks, with giblets
salt and freshly ground black pepper

For the sauce
2 tbsp flour
1¼ cups giblet stock
⅔ cup port or red wine
1 tbsp red currant jelly

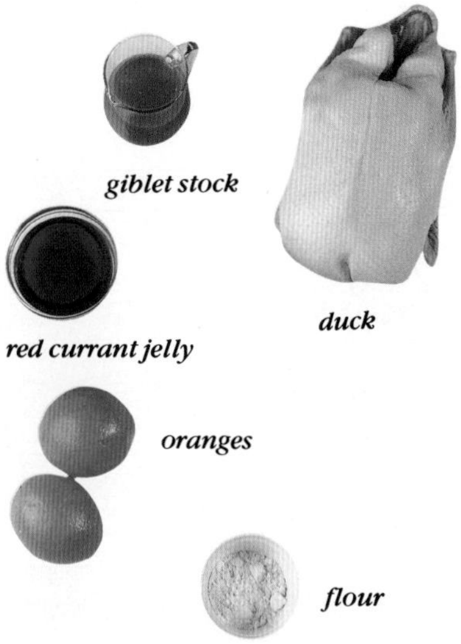

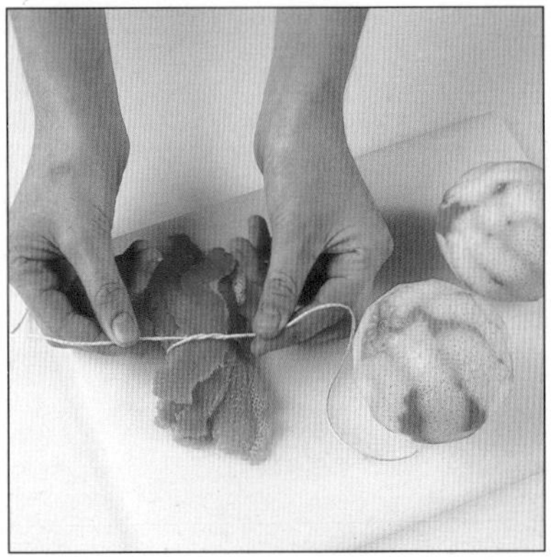

1 Preheat the oven to 350°F. Tie the orange rind with string and place it inside the cavities of the ducks.

2 Place the ducks on a rack in a roasting pan, season and cook for 30 minutes per 1 lb (about 2½ hours), until the flesh is tender and the juices run clear. Pour off the fat into a bowl halfway through the cooking time.

3 Transfer the ducks to a carving board and remove the orange rind from the cavities. To make the sauce, remove any fat from the roasting pan, leaving the sediment and juices behind. Sprinkle in the flour and cook gently for 2 minutes. Blend in the rest of the ingredients and reserved orange rind, coarsely chopped. Bring to a boil and simmer for 10 minutes; then strain into a pan, and add the orange segments, with their juice.

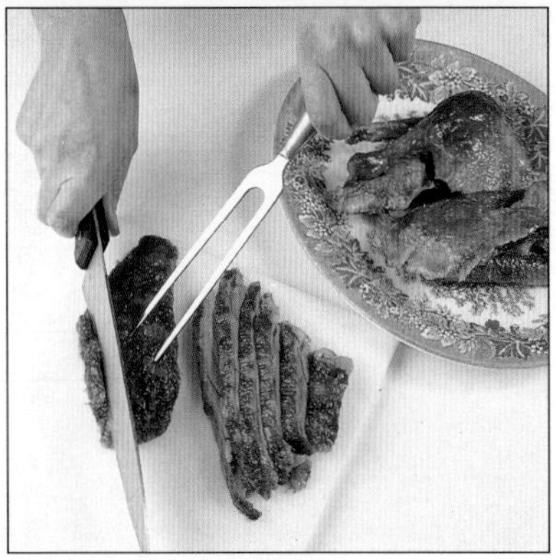

4 To carve the ducks, remove the legs and wings, cutting through the joints. Cut the two end joints off the wings and discard them. Cut the breast meat off the carcass in one piece and slice it thinly. Arrange the slices on a warm serving plate with the legs and the wing joints. Spoon some of the hot sauce over and serve the rest separately in a sauce boat.

Spiced Lamb with Fruit Pilaf

This wonderfully rich and spicy dish is excellent for a New Year's Eve party. It can be made the day before and reheated gently in the oven before serving. It freezes well too.

Serves 8

Ingredients
- 3 tbsp olive oil
- $2\frac{1}{2}$ lb boneless leg of lamb, cut into $1\frac{1}{2}$ in cubes
- 2 large onions, chopped
- 2–3 garlic cloves, crushed
- 2 tbsp flour
- 1 tsp ground cumin
- 1 tsp ground coriander
- $\frac{1}{2}$ tsp ground allspice
- 3 tbsp tomato paste
- $1\frac{1}{4}$ cups lamb stock
- $\frac{2}{3}$ cup red wine
- salt and freshly ground black pepper

For the fruit pilaf
- 3 tbsp butter
- 1 onion, chopped
- 1 tsp ground turmeric
- $1\frac{3}{4}$ cups long grain rice
- $3\frac{2}{3}$ cups stock
- $\frac{2}{3}$ cup dried apricots, chopped
- $\frac{2}{3}$ cup pistachio nuts

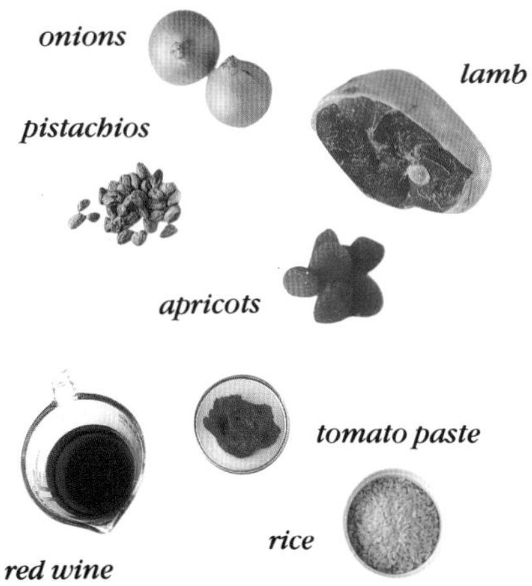

1 Preheat the oven to 350°F. Heat the oil in a casserole and brown the meat a few pieces at a time. Remove the lamb after it has browned and keep it warm.

2 Lower the heat, add the onions and garlic to the casserole and cook gently until tender, about 5 minutes, stirring occasionally. Stir in the flour and spices and cook slowly for 3–4 minutes.

3 Stir in the tomato paste, stock and wine, blending them in gradually until the sauce is smooth. Bring to a boil to thicken, and season. Replace the meat, cover the casserole and cook it in the preheated oven for 45–55 minutes, or until the lamb is tender. (Cook for half the time if you are cooking ahead and planning to reheat the next day.)

4 To make the pilaf, melt the butter and cook the onion until tender. Stir in the turmeric and rice and cook for 2 minutes. Then add the stock and season. Bring to a boil, cover and cook in the oven for 20–30 minutes, or until the rice is tender and all the liquid has been absorbed. Stir in the apricots and pistachio nuts, cover and let stand for 10–15 minutes.

Roast Goose with Caramelized Apples and Port and Orange Gravy

Choose a young goose with a pliable breast bone.

Serves 8

INGREDIENTS
10–12 lb goose, with giblets
salt and freshly ground black pepper

FOR THE APPLE AND NUT STUFFING
2 cups prunes
⅔ cup port or red wine
1½ lb cooking apples, peeled, cored and cubed
1 large onion, chopped
4 celery stalks, sliced
1 tbsp mixed dried herbs
finely grated rind of 1 orange
goose liver, chopped
1 lb bulk pork sausage
1 cup chopped pecans or walnuts
2 eggs

FOR THE CARAMELIZED APPLES
4 tbsp butter
4 tbsp red currant jelly
2 tbsp red wine vinegar
8 small apples, peeled and cored

FOR THE GRAVY
2 tbsp all-purpose flour
2½ cups giblet stock
juice of 1 orange

1 The day before you want to cook the goose, soak the prunes in the port or red wine. Then pit each one and cut it into four pieces, reserving the port.

2 Mix with all the remaining stuffing ingredients and season well. Moisten with half the reserved port.

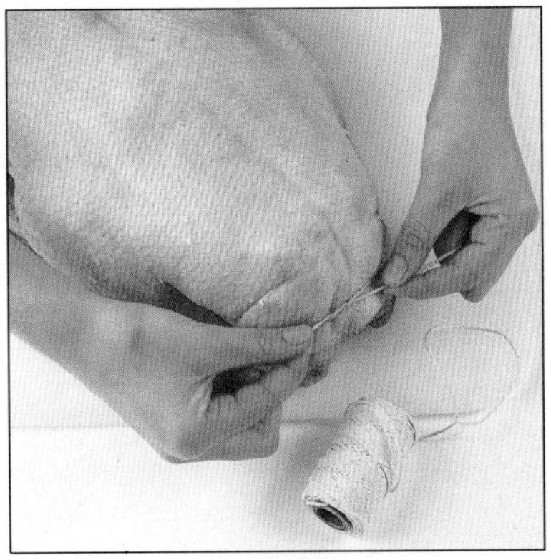

3 Preheat the oven to 400°F. Stuff the neck-end of the goose, tucking the flap of skin under and securing it with a small skewer. Remove the excess fat from the cavity and pack it with the stuffing. Tie the legs together to hold them in place.

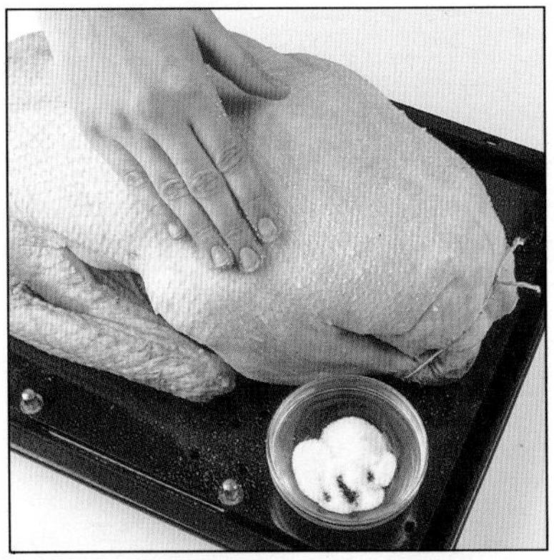

4 Weigh the stuffed goose and calculate the cooking time: allow 15 minutes per 1 lb. Put the bird on a rack in a roasting pan and rub the skin with salt. You may prick the skin all over to help the fat run out. Roast it for 30 minutes, then reduce the heat to 350°F and roast for the remaining cooking time. Pour off any fat produced during cooking into a bowl. The goose is cooked if the juices run clear when the thickest part of the thigh has been pierced with a skewer. Pour a little cold water over the breast to crisp the skin.

5 Meanwhile, prepare the apples. Melt the butter, red currant jelly and vinegar in a small roasting pan or a shallow ovenproof dish. Put in the apples, baste them well and cook in the oven for 15–20 minutes. Baste the apples halfway through the cooking time. Do not overcook them or they will collapse.

6 Place the goose on a serving dish and let it stand for 15 minutes before carving to make the gravy. Pour off the excess fat from the roasting pan, leaving any sediment in the bottom. Stir in the flour, cook gently until golden brown, and then blend in the stock. Bring to a boil, add the remaining reserved port, orange juice and seasoning. Simmer for 2–3 minutes. Strain into a gravy boat. Surround the goose with the caramelized apples and spoon the red currant glaze over.

Tenderloin of Pork Wrapped in Bacon

This easy-to-carve roast is served with an onion and prune gravy.

Serves 8

INGREDIENTS
3 large pork fillets, weighing about 2½ lb in total
8 oz lean bacon
2 tbsp butter
⅔ cup red wine

FOR THE PRUNE STUFFING
2 tbsp butter
1 onion, very finely chopped
1⅓ cups mushrooms, very finely chopped
4 ready-to-eat prunes, pitted and chopped
2 tsp dried mixed herbs
2 cups fresh white bread crumbs
1 egg
salt and freshly ground black pepper

TO FINISH
16 ready-to-eat prunes
⅔ cup red wine
16 pickling onions
2 tbsp all-purpose flour
1¼ cups fresh or canned chicken stock

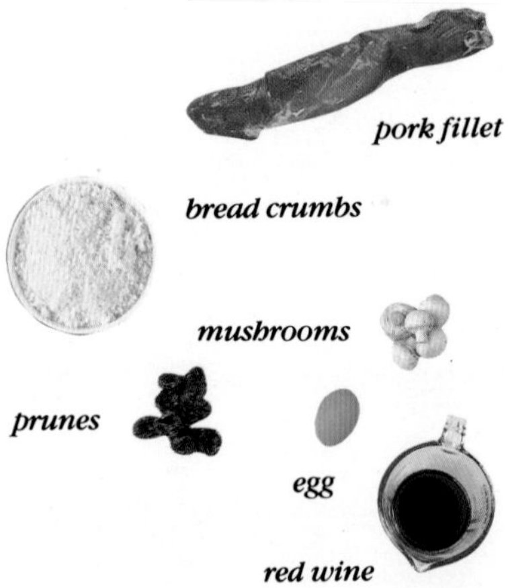

1 Preheat the oven to 350°F. Trim the fillets, removing any sinew and fat. Cut each fillet lengthways, three-quarters of the way through, open them out and flatten.

2 For the stuffing, melt the butter and cook the onion until tender, add the mushrooms and cook for 5 minutes. Transfer to a bowl and mix in the remaining stuffing ingredients. Spread the stuffing over two of the fillets and sandwich together with the third fillet.

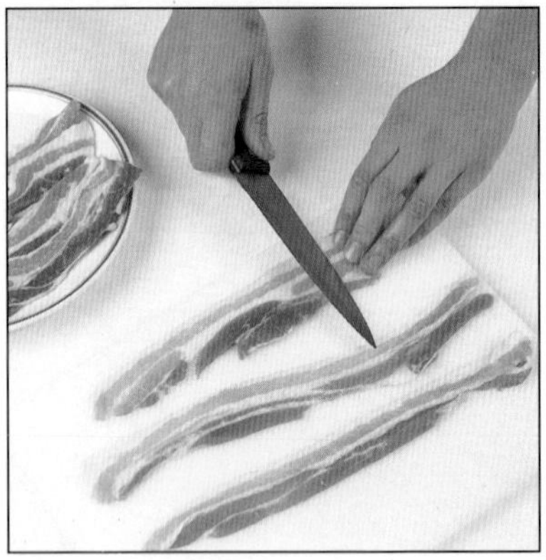

3 Stretch each strip of bacon with the back of a large knife.

4 Lay the strips overlapping across the meat. Cut lengths of string and lay them at ¾ in intervals over the bacon. Cover with a piece of foil to hold in place, and roll the tied fillets over. Fold the bacon strips over the meat and tie the string to secure them in place. Roll the fillets back on to the bacon joins and remove the foil.

5 Place in a roasting pan and spread the butter over the pork. Pour around the wine and cook for 1¼ hours, basting occasionally with the liquid in the roasting pan, until evenly browned. Simmer the remaining prunes in the red wine until tender. Boil the onions in salted water for 10 minutes, or until just tender. Drain and add to the prunes.

6 Transfer the pork to a serving plate, remove the string, cover loosely with foil and leave to stand for 10–15 minutes, before slicing. Remove any fat from the roasting pan, add the flour to the sediment and juices and cook gently for 2–3 minutes. Then blend in the stock, bring to a boil and simmer for 5 minutes. Adjust the seasoning to taste. Strain the gravy on to the prunes and onions, reheat and serve in a sauce boat with a ladle.

Individual Beef Wellingtons

The sauce can be made the day before and reheated just before serving. The Wellingtons can be made several hours before cooking, as long as the meat is quite cold before you wrap it in pastry. Keep them in the refrigerator before cooking.

Serves 8

INGREDIENTS
2 tbsp olive oil
8 beef fillet steaks, cut 1 in thick, weighing about 4 oz each
2 lb puff pastry, thawed if frozen
8 oz smooth liverwurst or pâté
2 tbsp chopped fresh parsley
2 tbsp chopped fresh chives
1 egg, beaten with 1 tbsp water

FOR THE SAUCE
2 tbsp butter
1 onion, finely chopped
1⅓ cups mushrooms, finely chopped
2 tbsp all-purpose flour
½ tsp tomato paste
½ tsp superfine sugar
⅔ cup red wine
1¼ cups beef stock
salt and freshly ground black pepper

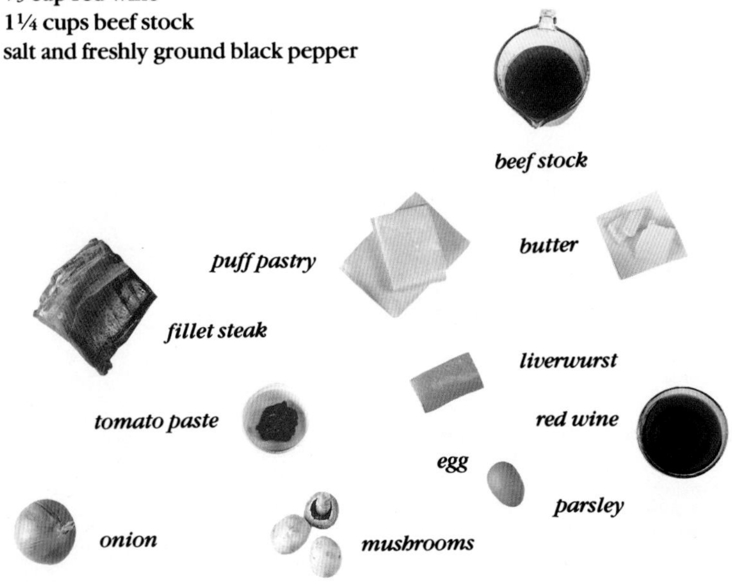

1 Heat the oil in a large frying pan and quickly brown the steaks on both sides. Transfer to a plate and leave to cool. Preheat the oven to 400°F.

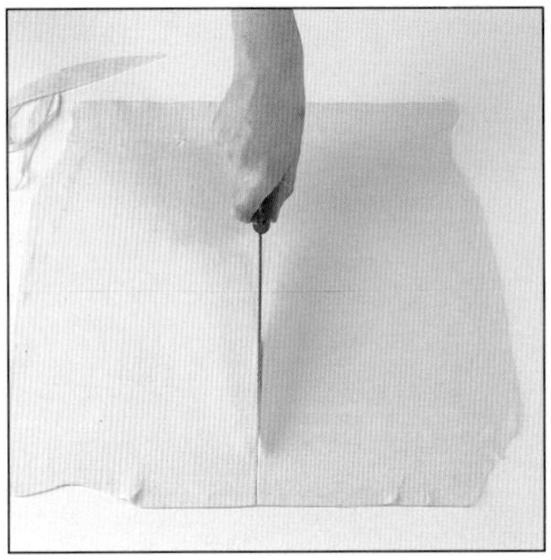

2 Divide the pastry in two equal halves. On a lightly floured work surface, roll each piece out thinly and trim to a 16 in square. Cut into four 8 in squares. (Save the trimmings for the decoration.)

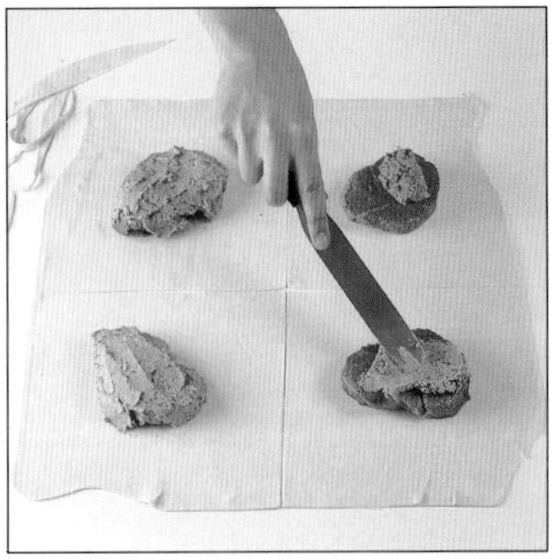

3 Mix the liverwurst or pâté with the herbs. Place a cold filet steak on each piece of pastry and divide the wurst or pâté between each. Spread evenly over the top and sides.

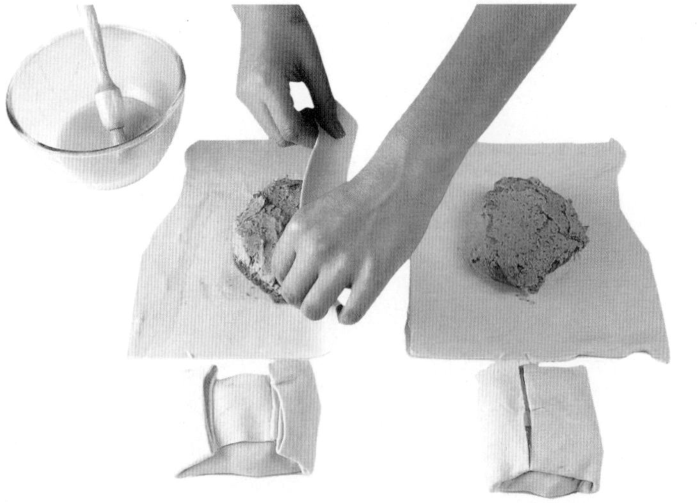

4 Brush the pastry with beaten egg and fold the sides over like a package. Pinch the edges to seal.

5 Place on baking trays, seam-side down and decorate the tops with a lattice cut from the trimmings. When ready to cook them, brush the pastry all over with beaten egg and bake for 25 minutes, or until golden brown. (Do not brush the Wellingtons with egg until just before baking, as the egg dries in the fridge.)

6 To make the sauce, heat the butter and cook the onion until tender. Add the mushrooms and cook for 5 minutes, stirring occasionally. Stir in the flour, tomato paste and sugar and blend in the red wine and stock. Bring to a boil and simmer for 10 minutes. Season to taste, then strain into a gravy boat and serve separately.

Filo Vegetable Pie

This marvelous pie makes a delicious main course for vegetarians or is an excellent accompaniment to cold sliced turkey or other meat dishes.

Serves 6–8

INGREDIENTS
8 oz leeks
11 tbsp butter
8 oz carrots, cubed
8 oz mushrooms, sliced
8 oz Brussels sprouts, quartered
2 garlic cloves, crushed
4 oz cream cheese
4 oz Roquefort or Stilton cheese
⅔ cup heavy cream
2 eggs, beaten
8 oz apples
8 oz/1 cup cashew nuts or pine nuts, toasted
12 oz frozen filo pastry, defrosted
salt and freshly ground black pepper

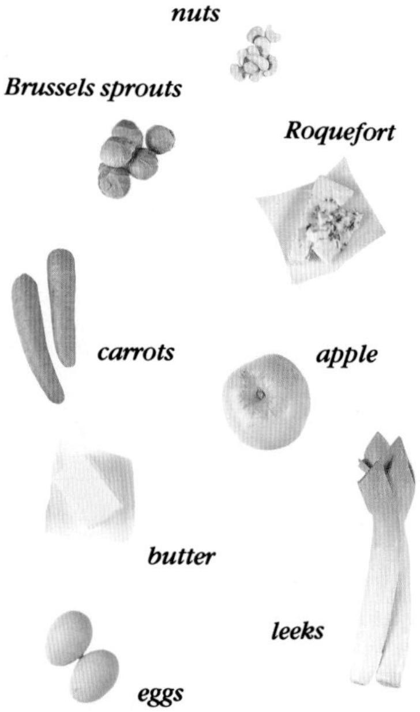

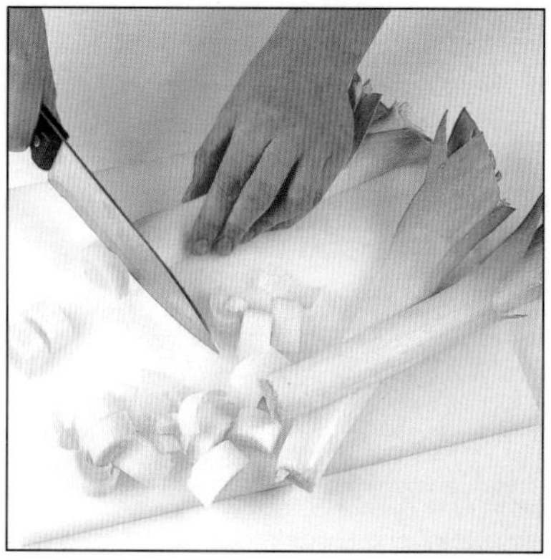

1 Preheat the oven to 350°F. Cut the leeks in half through the root and wash them to remove any sand, separating the layers slightly to check they are clean. Slice into ½ in pieces, drain and dry on paper towels.

2 Heat 3 tbsp of the butter in a large pan and cook the leeks and carrots, covered, over a medium heat for 5 minutes. Add the mushrooms, sprouts and garlic and cook for another 2 minutes, stirring to coat them with the butter. Turn the vegetables into a bowl and let them cool.

3 Whisk the cream cheese and blue cheese, cream, eggs and seasoning together in a bowl. Pour them over the vegetables. Peel and core the apples and cut into ½ in cubes. Add them to the vegetables, with the toasted nuts.

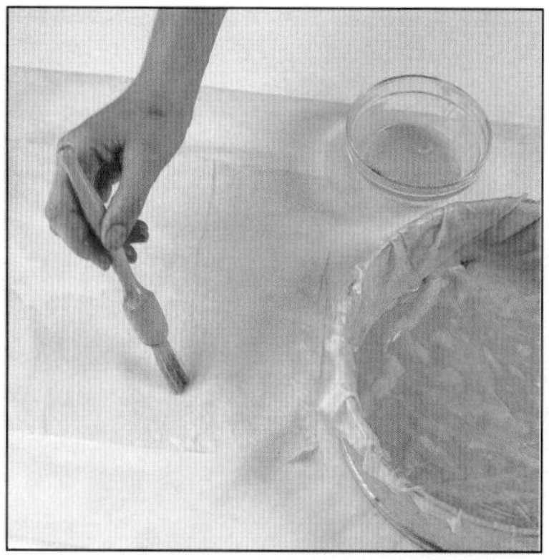

4 Melt the remaining butter. Brush the inside of a 9 in loose-based springform cake pan with melted butter. Brush two-thirds of the filo pastry sheets with butter one at a time, and use them to line the base and sides of the pan, overlapping the layers so that there are no gaps.

5 Spoon in the vegetable mixture and fold over the excess filo pastry to cover the filling.

6 Brush the remaining filo sheets with butter and cut them into 1 in strips. Cover the top of the pie with these strips, arranging them in a rough mound. Bake for 35–45 minutes until golden brown all over. Allow to stand for 5 minutes, and then remove the cake pan and transfer to a serving plate.

BROS & HOWSON
TO HIS MAJESTY

Cheese and Spinach Quiche

This quiche freezes well and can be reheated. It's an excellent addition to a festive buffet party and is popular with vegetarians too. If you don't have a lattice cutter, cut the pastry into strips and make a lattice following the instructions given for the Deluxe Mincemeat Tart.

Serves 8

INGREDIENTS
½ cup butter
2 cups all-purpose flour
½ tsp English mustard powder
½ tsp paprika
large pinch of salt
4 oz Cheddar cheese, finely grated
3–4 tbsp cold water
1 egg, beaten, to glaze

FOR THE FILLING
1 lb frozen spinach
1 onion, chopped
pinch of grated nutmeg
8 oz cottage cheese
2 large eggs
2 oz Parmesan cheese, grated
⅔ cup light cream
salt and freshly ground black pepper

1 Rub the butter into the flour until it resembles fine bread crumbs. Rub in the next four ingredients. Bind to a dough with the cold water. Knead until smooth, wrap and chill for 30 minutes.

2 Put the spinach and onion in a pan, cover, and cook slowly. Increase the heat to evaporate any water. Season with salt, pepper and nutmeg. Turn the spinach into a bowl, cool slightly. Add the remaining filling ingredients.

3 Preheat the oven to 400°F. Put a baking tray in the oven to preheat. Cut one-third off the pastry for the lid. On a lightly floured surface, roll out the remaining pastry and use it to line a 9 in loose-based cake pan. Press the pastry well into the edges and make a narrow lip around the top edge. Remove the excess pastry with a rolling pin. Pour the filling into the pie crust.

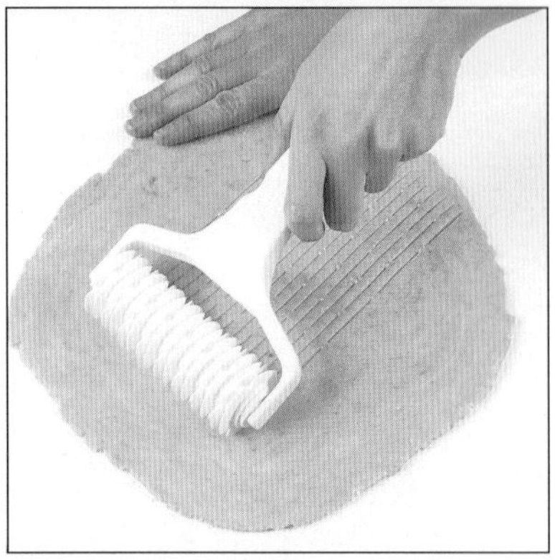

4 Roll out the remaining pastry and cut it with a lattice pastry cutter. Carefully open the lattice. With the help of a rolling pin, lay it over the quiche. Brush the joins with egg glaze. Press the edges together and trim off the excess pastry. Brush the pastry lattice with egg glaze and bake on the hot baking tray for 35–40 minutes, or until golden brown. Serve hot or cold.

Gratin Dauphinois

This dish can be made and baked in advance; reheat it in the oven for 20–30 minutes. This is a good alternative to roast potatoes and it needs no last-minute attention.

Serves 8

INGREDIENTS
butter, for greasing
3½ lb potatoes
2–3 garlic cloves, crushed
½ tsp grated nutmeg
4 oz Cheddar cheese, grated
2½ cups milk
1¼ cups light cream
2 large eggs, beaten
salt and freshly ground black pepper

1 Preheat the oven to 350°F. Butter a 10 cup shallow ovenproof dish. Scrub and peel the potatoes and slice them thinly.

2 Layer the potatoes in the dish, with the garlic, nutmeg and two-thirds of the grated cheese and season well.

3 Whisk the milk, cream and eggs together and pour them over the potatoes, making sure the liquid goes all the way to the bottom of the dish.

4 Scatter the remaining cheese on top and bake for 45–50 minutes, or until golden brown. Test the potatoes with a sharp knife; they should be very tender.

Cheese, Rice and Vegetable Strudel

Based on a traditional Russian dish called 'Koulibiac', this makes a perfect vegetarian main course or an unusual accompaniment to cold leftover turkey or sliced ham.

Serves 8

INGREDIENTS
- 7⁄8 cup long grain rice
- 2 tbsp butter
- 1–2 leeks, thinly sliced
- 12 oz mushrooms, sliced
- 8 oz Gruyère or Cheddar cheese, grated
- 8 oz feta cheese, cubed
- 2 tbsp raisins
- ½ cup chopped almonds or hazelnuts, toasted
- 2 tbsp chopped fresh parsley
- 10 oz package frozen filo pastry, thawed
- 2 tbsp olive oil
- salt and freshly ground black pepper

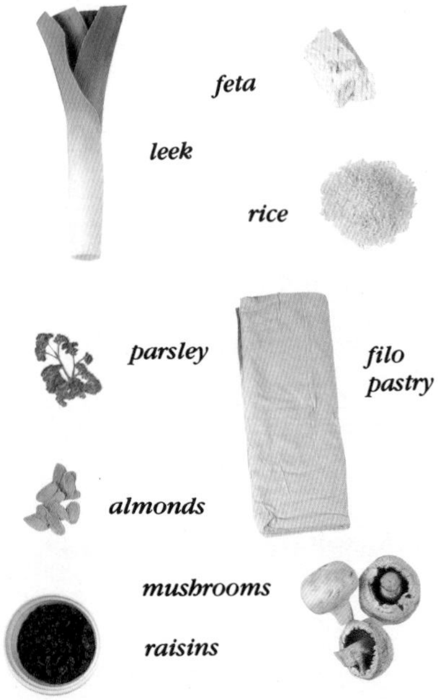

1 Cook the rice in boiling, salted water for 10–12 minutes, until tender. Drain, rinse under cold running water and set aside. Melt the butter and cook the leeks and mushrooms for 5 minutes. Transfer to a bowl to cool.

2 Add the well-drained rice, the cheeses, raisins, toasted nuts, parsley and season to taste (be careful with the salt as the feta cheese is very salty).

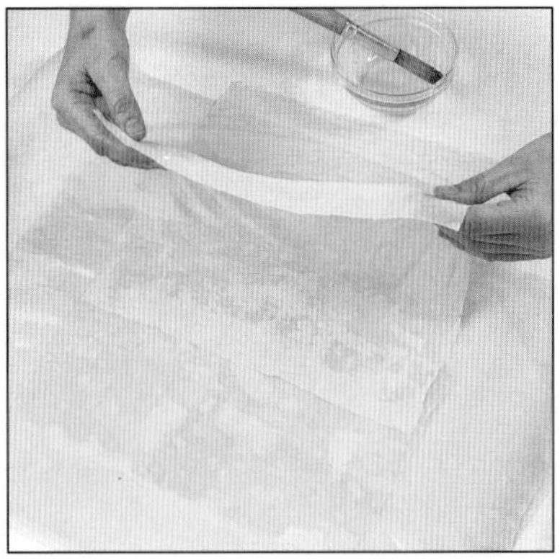

3 Preheat the oven to 375°F. Unwrap the filo pastry. Cover it with a piece of plastic wrap and a damp cloth while you work. Lay a sheet of filo pastry on a large piece of wax paper and brush it with oil. Lay a second sheet, overlapping the first by 1 in. Put another sheet with its long side running at right angles to the long sides of the first two. Lay a fourth sheet in the same way, overlapping by 1 in. Continue in this way, alternating the layers of two sheets so that the join between the two sheets runs in the opposite direction for each layer.

4 Place the filling along the center of the pastry and shape it neatly with your hands into a rectangle approximately 4 × 12 in.

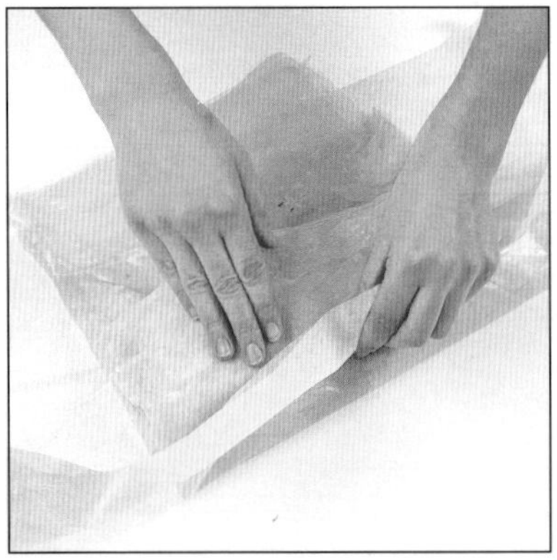

5 Fold the pastry over the filling and roll it over, with the help of the wax paper, so that the join is hidden underneath.

6 Lift the strudel on to a greased baking tray and tuck the edges under, so that the filling does not escape during cooking. Brush with oil and bake for 30–40 minutes, until golden and crisp. Let the strudel stand for 5 minutes before cutting.

Vegetable Cheese Puff

This makes a light vegetarian supper, or a main meal served with a salad and baked potatoes.

Serves 4

INGREDIENTS
4 tbsp butter
⅔ cup water
⅔ cup all-purpose flour
2 eggs, beaten
¼ tsp English mustard
2 oz Cheddar or Gruyère cheese, cubed
salt and freshly ground black pepper
2 tsp chopped fresh parsley, to garnish

FOR THE FILLING
2 tbsp butter
1 onion, sliced
1 garlic clove, crushed
2⅔ cups mushrooms, sliced
1 tbsp all-purpose flour
1 × 14 oz can tomatoes
1 tsp superfine sugar
8 oz zucchini, sliced thickly

FOR THE TOPPING
1 tbsp grated Parmesan cheese
1 tbsp bread crumbs, toasted

1 Preheat the oven to 400°F. To make the choux pastry, melt the butter in a pan, add the water and bring to a boil. As soon as the liquid is boiling, draw the pan off the heat and beat in the flour all at once, until a smooth paste is formed. Turn into a large bowl and allow to cool slightly.

2 With an electric whisk, beat the eggs gradually into the paste until the mixture is glossy but firm. Season with salt, pepper and mustard powder. Fold in the cheese. Set aside.

3 To make the filling, melt the butter in a pan and cook the onion gently until tender. Add the garlic and mushrooms and cook for 2–3 minutes. Stir in the flour and the tomatoes and their juice. Bring to the boil, stirring, to thicken. Season with salt, pepper and sugar to taste. Lastly add the sliced zucchini.

4 Butter a 5 cup ovenproof dish. Spoon the choux pastry in rough mounds around the sides of the dish and turn the filling into the center. Sprinkle the Parmesan cheese and bread crumbs on top of the filling. Bake for 35–40 minutes, until the pastry is well risen and golden brown. Sprinkle with chopped parsley and serve hot.

Vegetable Crumble with Anchovies

The anchovies may be left out of this dish in order that vegetarians can enjoy it, but they give the vegetables a delicious flavor. Serve as an accompaniment to sliced turkey or ham.

Serves 8

INGREDIENTS
1 lb potatoes
8 oz leeks
2 tbsp butter
1 lb carrots, chopped
2 garlic cloves, crushed
2⅓ cups mushrooms, sliced
1 lb Brussels sprouts, sliced
1 × 1½ oz can anchovies, drained
salt and freshly ground black pepper

FOR THE CHEESE CRUMBLE
4 tbsp all-purpose flour
4 tbsp butter
1 cup fresh bread crumbs
2 oz Cheddar cheese, grated
2 tbsp chopped fresh parsley
1 tsp English mustard powder

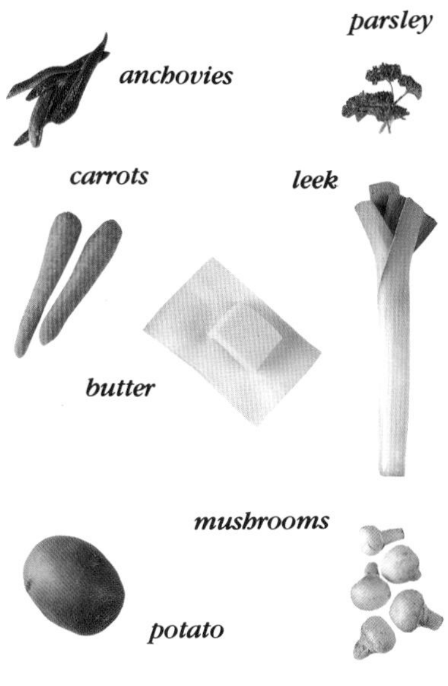

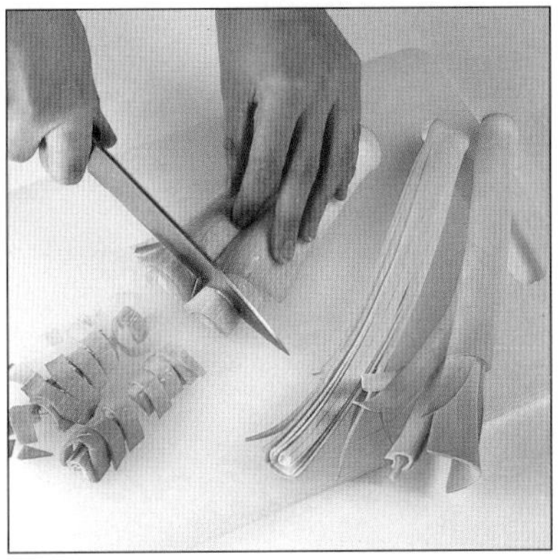

1 Peel and halve the potatoes and parboil them in salted water until just tender. Drain and cool. Cut the leeks in half lengthwise and wash them thoroughly to remove any sand. Drain and slice in ½ in pieces.

2 Melt the butter and cook the leeks and carrots for 2–3 minutes. Add the garlic and mushrooms and cook for a further 3 minutes. Add the sprouts. Season with pepper. Transfer to a 10 cup ovenproof dish.

3 Preheat the oven to 400°F. Chop the anchovies and scatter them over the vegetables. Slice the potatoes and arrange them on top.

4 To make the crumble, sift the flour into a bowl and rub in the butter or process in a food processor. Add the bread crumbs and mix in the remaining ingredients. Spoon over the vegetables and bake for 20–30 minutes.

Vegetable Gnocchi

This delicious vegetarian main course can be assembled well ahead of time and cooked in the oven without any last-minute preparation.

Serves 8

INGREDIENTS
1 lb frozen spinach
1 tbsp butter
¼ tsp grated nutmeg
8 oz ricotta or farmer's cheese
4 oz Parmesan cheese, grated
2 eggs, beaten
1 cup all-purpose flour
2 oz Cheddar cheese, grated
salt and freshly ground black pepper

FOR THE SAUCE
4 tbsp butter
4 tbsp all-purpose flour
2½ cups milk

FOR THE VEGETABLE LAYER
2 tbsp butter
2 leeks or onions, sliced
4 carrots, sliced
4 celery stalks, sliced
4 zucchini, sliced

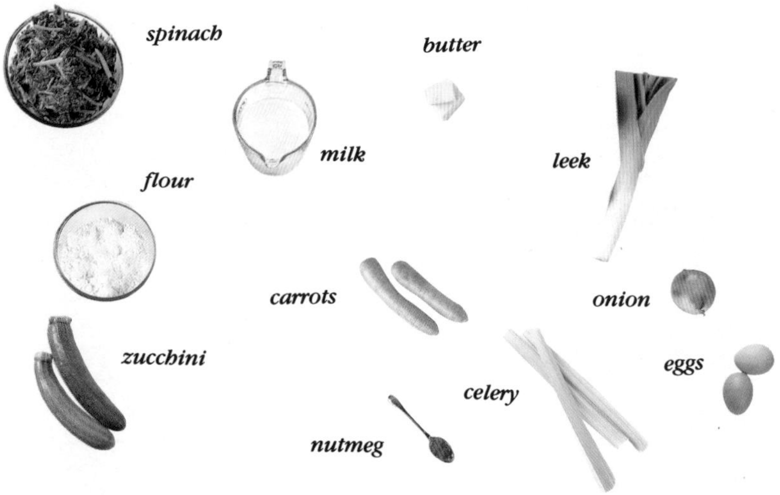

1 Put the spinach in a large pan with the butter and heat gently to defrost it. Then increase the heat to drive off any moisture. Season with salt, pepper and nutmeg. Turn into a bowl and mix in the ricotta or farmer's cheese, Parmesan cheese, eggs and flour. Beat until smooth.

2 Shape the mixture into ovals with two dessertspoons and place them on a lightly floured tray. Place in the refrigerator for 30 minutes.

3 Have a large shallow pan of boiling, salted water ready. Cook the gnocchi in two batches, for about 5 minutes (the water should simmer gently and not boil). As soon as the gnocchi rise to the surface, remove them with a slotted spoon and let them drain on a clean dish towel.

4 Preheat the oven to 350°F. For the sauce, melt the butter in a pan, add the flour and blend in the milk. Bring to a boil to thicken and season to taste.

5 For the vegetable layer, melt the butter and cook the leeks, carrots and celery until tender, about 5 minutes. Add the zucchini, season with salt and pepper and stir to mix. Turn into a 10 cup ovenproof dish.

6 Place the drained gnocchi on top, spoon over the sauce and sprinkle with grated cheese. Bake for 30 minutes, until golden brown. Broil if necessary.

Brussels Sprouts with Chestnut and Carrots

Be sure to allow plenty of time to peel the chestnuts; it is fussy work but well worth the effort.

Serves 8

INGREDIENTS
1 lb fresh chestnuts
1⅞ cups vegetable stock
1 lb Brussels sprouts
1 lb carrots
2 tbsp butter
salt and freshly ground black pepper

carrots

butter

chestnuts

Brussels sprouts

1 Using a sharp knife, peel the raw chestnuts, leaving the brown papery skins intact. Bring a small pan of water to a boil, drop a handful of chestnuts into the water for a few minutes, and remove with a slotted spoon. The brown papery skins will slip off easily.

2 Put the peeled chestnuts in a pan with the stock. Cover the pan and bring to a boil. Simmer for 5–10 minutes, until tender. Drain.

3 Remove the outer leaves from the sprouts, if necessary, and trim the stalks level. Cook in a pan of boiling, salted water for about 5 minutes, or until just tender. Drain and rinse under cold running water to stop the cooking.

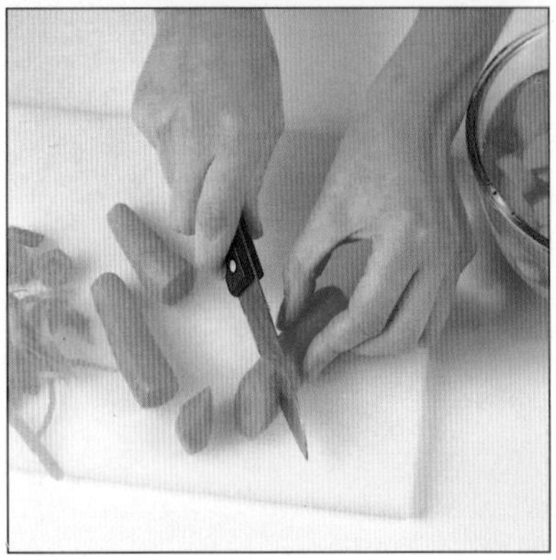

4 Peel the carrots and cut them in ½ in diagonal slices. Put them in a pan with cold water to cover, bring to a boil and simmer until just tender, 5–6 minutes. Drain and rinse under cold running water. Melt the butter in a heavy-based pan, add the chestnuts, sprouts and carrots and season with salt and pepper. Cover with a lid and reheat, occasionally stirring the vegetables in the pan.

Sweet and Sour Red Cabbage

The cabbage can be cooked the day before and reheated for serving. It is a good accompaniment to goose, pork or strong-flavored game dishes. The crispy bacon added at the end of cooking is optional and can be omitted.

Serves 8

INGREDIENTS
2 lb red cabbage
2 tbsp olive oil
2 large onions, sliced
2 large apples, peeled, cored and sliced
2 tbsp cider vinegar
2 tbsp brown sugar
8 oz lean bacon (optional)
salt and freshly ground black pepper

1 Preheat the oven to 350°F. Cut the cabbage into quarters through the stalk and shred it finely with a sharp knife or in a food processor, discarding the hard core.

2 Heat the oil in a large ovenproof casserole. Cook the onion over a gentle heat for 2 minutes.

3 Stir the cabbage, apples, vinegar, sugar and seasoning into the casserole. Cover with a tight-fitting lid and cook for about 1 hour, or until very tender. Stir halfway through cooking.

4 Chop the bacon, if using, and fry it gently in a pan until crisp. Stir it into the cabbage just before serving.

Vegetarian Christmas Torte

A sophisticated mushroom torte with a cheese-soufflé topping. Serve hot with cranberry relish and Brussels Sprouts with Chestnuts and Carrots.

Serves 8

INGREDIENTS
2 cups all-purpose flour
¾ cup butter
2 tsp paprika
4 oz Parmesan cheese, grated
1 egg, beaten with 1 tbsp cold water
1 tbsp Dijon mustard

FOR THE FILLING
2 tbsp butter
1 onion, finely chopped
1–2 garlic cloves, crushed
12 oz mushrooms, chopped
2 tsp dried mixed herbs
1 tbsp chopped fresh parsley
1 cup fresh white bread crumbs
salt and freshly ground black pepper

FOR THE CHEESE TOPPING
2 tbsp butter
2 tbsp all-purpose flour
1¼ cups milk
1 oz Parmesan cheese, grated
3 oz Cheddar cheese, grated
¼ tsp English mustard powder
1 egg, separated

1 To make the pastry, sift the flour into a bowl and rub in the butter until the mixture resembles fine bread crumbs. Stir in the paprika and Parmesan cheese. Bind to a soft pliable dough with the egg and water. Knead until smooth, wrap in plastic wrap and chill for 30 minutes.

2 For the filling, melt the butter and cook the onion until tender. Add the garlic and mushrooms and cook, uncovered, for 5 minutes, stirring occasionally. Increase the heat and drive off any liquid in the pan. Remove the pan from the heat and stir in the dried herbs, parsley, bread crumbs and seasoning. Allow to cool.

3 Preheat the oven to 375°F. Put a baking sheet in the oven. On a lightly floured surface, roll out the pastry and use it to line a 9 in loose-based cake pan, pressing the pastry well into the edges and making a narrow rim around the top edge. Chill for 20 minutes.

4 For the cheese topping, melt the butter in a pan, stir in the flour and cook for 2 minutes. Gradually blend in the milk. Bring to a boil to thicken and simmer for 2–3 minutes. Remove the pan from the heat and stir in the cheeses, mustard powder and egg yolk, and season well. Beat until smooth. Whisk the egg white until it holds soft peaks; fold the egg white into the topping.

5 To assemble the torte, spread the Dijon mustard evenly over the base of the crust. Spoon in the mushroom filling and level the surface.

6 Pour over the cheese topping and bake the torte on the hot baking tray for 35–45 minutes until set and golden.

Game Terrine

Any game can be used to make this country terrine. The ovenproof dish that it is cooked in must have a lid, to seal in all the flavors during the long cooking time.

Serves 8

INGREDIENTS
8 oz lean bacon
8 oz lamb or pork liver, ground
1 lb ground pork
1 small onion, finely chopped
2 garlic cloves, crushed
2 tsp dried mixed herbs
8 oz game (e.g., hare, rabbit, or pheasant)
4 tbsp port or sherry
1 bay leaf
½ cup all-purpose flour
1¼ cups jelly stock, made with beef stock and gelatin
salt and freshly ground black pepper

1 Remove the rind from the bacon and stretch each strip with the back of a heavy knife. Use the rindless bacon strips to line a 4 cup terrine.

2 In a bowl, mix together the ground pork and liver with the onion, garlic and dried herbs. Season with salt and pepper.

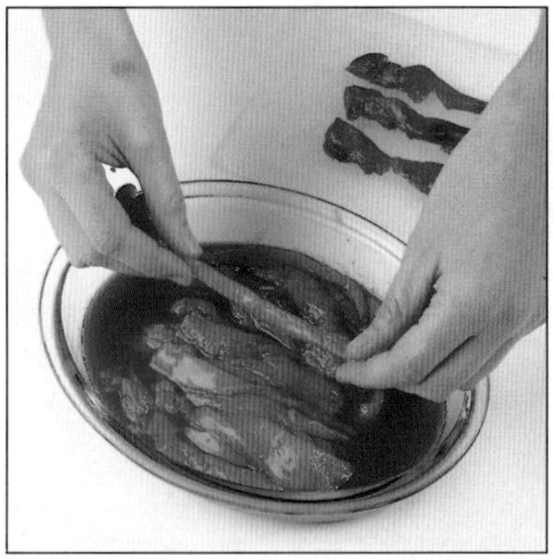

3 Cut the game into thin strips and put it into a bowl with the port or sherry. Season with salt and pepper and leave to marinate for 1 hour.

4 Put one-third of the ground mixture into the terrine, pressing it well into the corners. Cover with half the strips of game and repeat these layers, ending with a ground layer. Level the surface and lay the bay leaf on top.

5 Preheat the oven to 325°F. Put the flour into a small bowl and mix it to a firm dough with 2–3 tbsp cold water. Cover the terrine with a lid and seal it with the flour paste. Place the terrine in a roasting pan and pour enough hot water around to come halfway up the sides of the dish. Cook in the oven for 2 hours.

6 Remove the lid and weight the terrine down with a 4 lb weight. Leave to cool. Remove any fat from the surface and cover with warmed jelly stock. Let set overnight before turning out.

Turkey and Cranberry Pie

The cranberries add a tart layer to this turkey pie. Cranberry sauce can be used if fresh cranberries are not available. The pie freezes well.

Serves 8

INGREDIENTS
1 lb bulk pork sausage
1 lb lean ground pork
1 tbsp ground coriander
1 tbsp dried mixed herbs
finely grated rind of 2 large oranges
2 tsp grated fresh ginger root or ½ tsp ground ginger
2 tsp salt
1 lb turkey breast fillets, thinly sliced
4 oz fresh cranberries
freshly ground black pepper

FOR THE PASTRY
4 cups all-purpose flour
1 tsp salt
⅔ cup shortening
⅔ cup mixed milk and water

TO FINISH
1 egg, beaten
1¼ cups jelly stock, made with chicken stock and gelatin

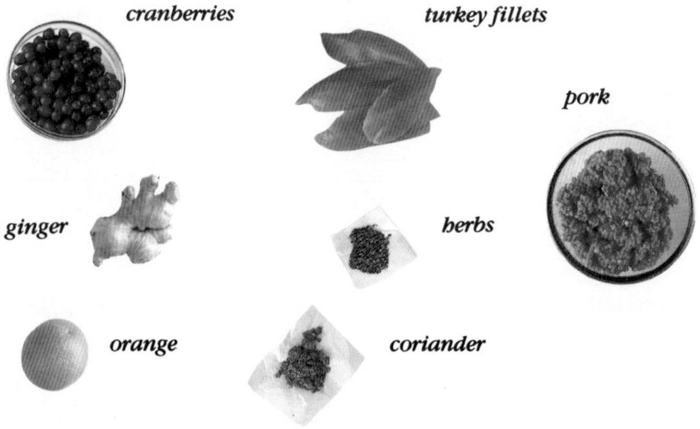

1 Preheat the oven to 350°F. Place a baking sheet in the oven to preheat. In a bowl, mix together the sausage, pork, coriander, herbs, orange rind, ginger and salt and pepper.

2 To make the pastry, put the flour into a large bowl with the salt. Heat the shortening in a small pan with the milk and water until just beginning to boil. Take the pan off the heat and let cool slightly.

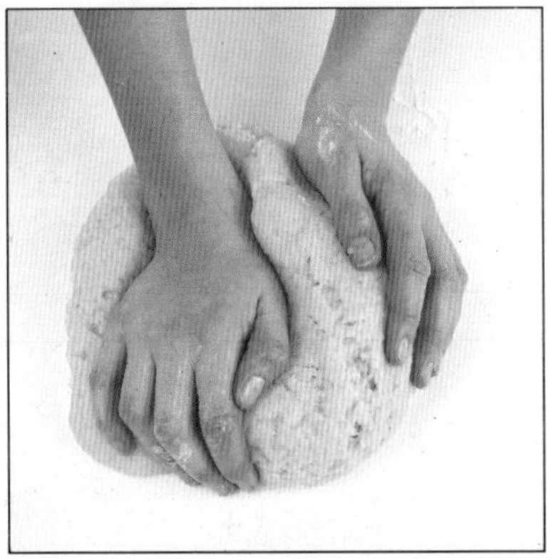

3 Using a wooden spoon, quickly stir the liquid into the flour until a very stiff dough is formed. Turn on to a work surface and knead until smooth. Cut one-third off the dough for the lid, wrap it in plastic wrap and keep it in a warm place.

4 Roll out the large piece of dough on a floured surface and line the base and sides of a well-greased 8 in loose-based, springform cake pan. Work with the dough while it is still warm, as it will crack and break if it is left to get cold.

5 Put the turkey pieces between two pieces of plastic wrap and flatten with a rolling pin to a thickness of ⅛ in. Spoon half the pork mixture into the base of the pan, pressing it well into the edges. Cover with half of the turkey slices and then the cranberries, followed by the remaining turkey and finally the rest of the pork mixture.

6 Roll out the rest of the dough and cover the filling, trimming any excess and sealing the edges with a little beaten egg. Make a steam hole in the center of the lid and decorate the top by cutting pastry trimmings into leaf shapes. Brush with beaten egg. Bake for 2 hours. Cover the pie with foil if the top gets too brown. Place the pie on a wire rack to cool. When cold, use a funnel to fill the pie with liquid jelly stock. Let set for a few hours or overnight, before unmolding the pie to serve it.

Turkey Rice Salad

A delicious, crunchy salad to use up leftover turkey during the holiday festivities.

Serves 8

INGREDIENTS
1¼ cups brown rice
⅔ cup wild rice
2 red apples, quartered, cored and chopped
2 celery stalks, coarsely sliced
4 oz seedless grapes
3 tbsp lemon or orange juice
⅔ cup thick mayonnaise, homemade or store bought
12 oz cooked turkey, chopped
salt and freshly ground black pepper
frilly lettuce leaves, to serve

1 Cook the brown and wild rice together in plenty of boiling salted water for 25 minutes, or until tender. Rinse under cold running water and drain thoroughly.

2 Turn into a large bowl and add the apples, celery and grapes. Beat the lemon or orange juice into the mayonnaise, season with salt and pepper and pour over the rice.

3 Add the turkey and mix well to coat with the lemon or orange mayonnaise.

4 Arrange the frilly lettuce over the base and around the sides of a serving dish and spoon the rice on top.

Ham and Bulgur Wheat Salad

This unusual, nutty salad uses up leftover cooked ham for a quick meal on New Year's Day.

Serves 8

INGREDIENTS
8 oz bulgur wheat
3 tbsp olive oil
2 tbsp lemon juice
1 red bell pepper
8 oz cooked ham, diced
2 tbsp chopped fresh mint
2 tbsp raisins
salt and freshly ground black pepper
sprigs of fresh mint and lemon slices, to garnish

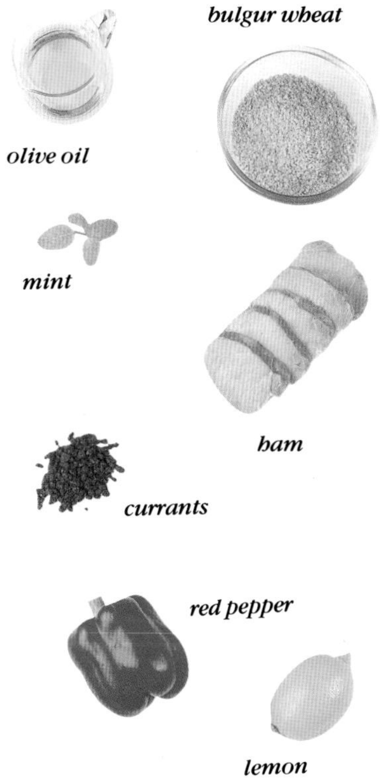

1 Put the bulgur wheat into a bowl, pour over enough boiling water to cover and leave to stand until all the water has been absorbed.

2 Add the oil, lemon juice, and seasoning to taste. Toss to separate the grains using two forks.

3 Quarter the pepper, removing the stalk and seeds. Cut it into wide strips and then into diamonds. Add the pepper, ham, mint and currants. Transfer to a serving dish and garnish with sprigs of fresh mint and lemon slices.

COOK'S TIP

This salad can also be made with 8 oz couscous instead of the bulgur wheat. Cover the couscous with boiling water as in step 1.

Layered Salmon Terrine

This elegant fish mousse is perfect for a buffet table or first course. Slice with a sharp knife.

Serves 8

INGREDIENTS

- ⅞ cup milk
- 4 tbsp butter
- ⅔ cup all-purpose flour
- 1 lb fresh haddock fillet, boned and skinned
- 12 oz fresh salmon fillet, boned and skinned
- 2 eggs, beaten
- 4 tbsp heavy cream
- 4 oz smoked salmon or trout, cut in strips
- salt and freshly ground black pepper

1 Heat the milk and butter in a saucepan until the milk is boiling, take the pan off the heat and beat in the flour until a thick smooth paste forms. Season with salt and pepper, turn out on to a plate and let cool.

2 Put the haddock into a food processor and process it until smooth. Put it into a bowl. Process the salmon fillet in the same way and put it into a separate bowl. Add an egg and half the cream to each of the fish mixtures. Beat in half the milk and flour paste to each mixture.

3 Preheat the oven to 350°F. Butter a 2 lb loaf pan and line it with a piece of wax paper. Lay strips of smoked salmon or trout diagonally over the base and up the sides of the lined pan.

4 Carefully spoon the haddock mixture into the pan and level the surface. Cover with the salmon mixture and fold any overlapping smoked salmon strips over the filling.

5 Cover the loaf pan with a piece of buttered wax paper and then a layer of foil. Place it in a roasting pan and pour enough hot water around to come halfway up the sides of the pan. Cook for 40 minutes, or until firm to the touch.

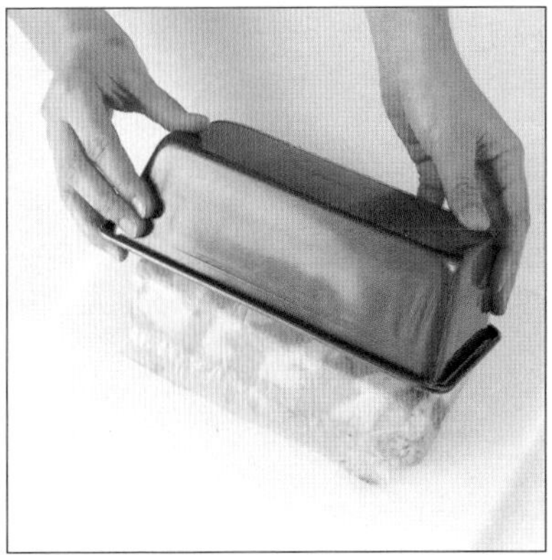

6 Remove from the oven and stand for 10 minutes. Turn the terrine out on to a serving plate and serve it warm or let cool.

Fillet of Beef with Ratatouille

This succulent rare beef is served cold with a colorful garlicky ratatouille.

Serves 8

INGREDIENTS
1½–2 lb fillet of beef
3 tbsp olive oil
1¼ cups jelly stock, made with beef stock and gelatin

FOR THE MARINADE
2 tbsp sherry
2 tbsp olive oil
2 tbsp soy sauce
2 tsp grated fresh ginger root or 1 tsp ground ginger
2 garlic cloves, crushed

FOR THE RATATOUILLE
4 tbsp olive oil
1 onion, sliced
2–3 garlic cloves, crushed
1 large eggplant, cubed
1 small red bell pepper, seeded and sliced
1 small green bell pepper, seeded and sliced
1 small yellow bell pepper, seeded and sliced
8 oz zucchini, sliced
1 lb tomatoes, skinned and quartered
1 tbsp chopped fresh mixed herbs
2 tbsp French dressing
salt and freshly ground black pepper

1 Mix all the marinade ingredients together in a shallow dish, put the beef in and turn it over to coat it. Cover with plastic wrap and leave for 30 minutes, to allow the flavors to penetrate the meat.

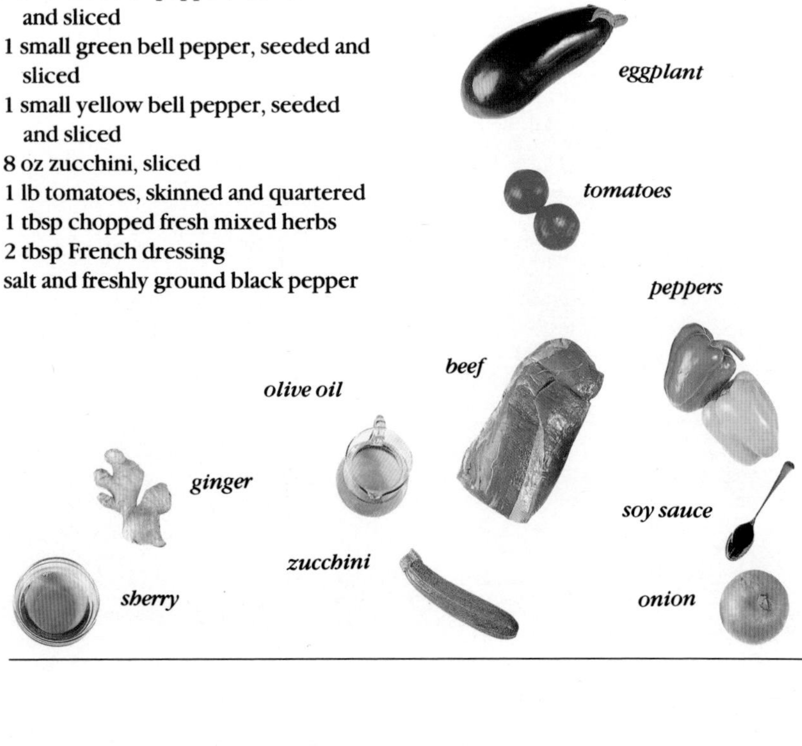

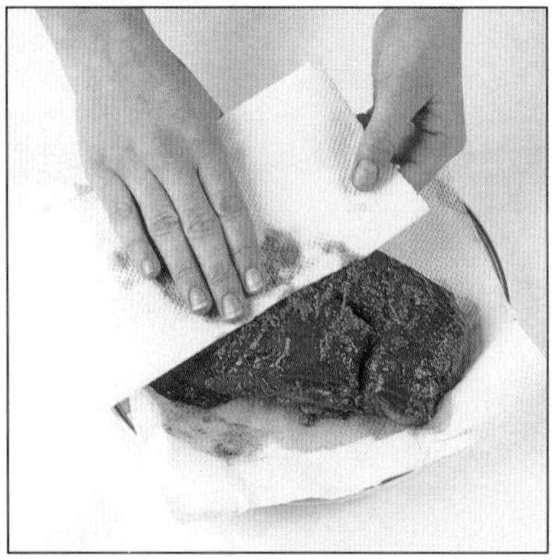

2 Preheat the oven to 425°F. Lift the fillet out of the marinade and pat it dry with paper towels. Heat the oil in a frying-pan until smoking hot and then brown the beef all over to seal it. Transfer to a roasting pan and roast for 10–15 minutes, basting it with the marinade. Lift the beef on to a plate and let it cool.

3 Meanwhile, for the ratatouille, heat the oil in a large casserole and cook the onion and garlic over a low heat until tender. Add the eggplant and cook for a further 5 minutes, until soft. Add the sliced peppers and zucchini and cook for 2 minutes. Then add the tomatoes, herbs and seasoning and cook for a few minutes longer.

4 Turn the ratatouille into a dish and cool. Drizzle with a little French dressing. Slice the beef and arrange overlapping slices on a serving platter. Brush the slices with cold jelly stock which is on the point of setting.

5 Leave the jelly to set completely, then brush with a second coat. Spoon the ratatouille on to the dish and serve.

Salmon and Pea Ring

A stunning pea and fish mousse with salmon chunks set in it. Serve it hot or cold as a starter, with a delicious herb and lemon sauce.

Serves 8

INGREDIENTS
1 lb fresh haddock, filleted, skinned and cubed
4 oz frozen peas, cooked and cooled
2 eggs
4 tbsp heavy cream
1 lb fresh salmon, filleted, skinned and cubed
salt and freshly ground black pepper
small bunch watercress, to garnish

FOR THE HERB AND LEMON SAUCE
⅔ cup fish stock
8 oz low-fat cream cheese
1 tbsp lemon juice
1 tbsp chopped fresh parsley
1 tbsp chopped fresh chives

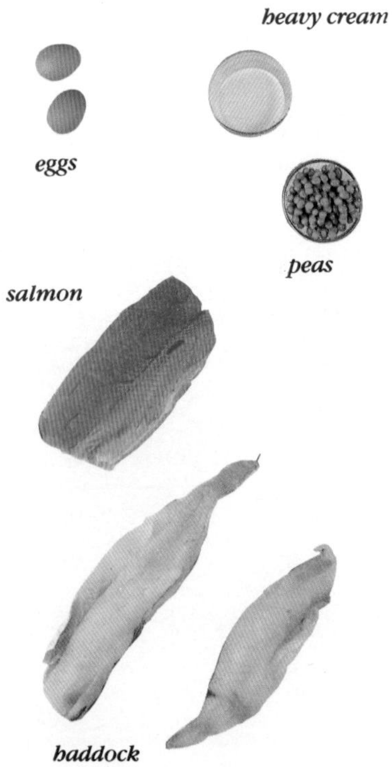

1 Check the fish for any stray bones. Preheat the oven to 350°F. Put the haddock and cooked peas into a food processor and process them until smooth.

2 Add the eggs, cream and seasoning to the food processor and mix together thoroughly.

3 Transfer to a bowl and fold in the cubed salmon pieces. Butter a 1¾ pint/ 4 cup ring mold and spoon in the fish mixture. Level the top and cover it with buttered paper and foil. Put the ring mold into a roasting pan and pour hot water around to come halfway up the sides of the pan. Poach in the oven for 40 minutes, or until the ring is firm to the touch.

4 Meanwhile, make the sauce. Put the fish stock and cream cheese in a pan and heat gently to melt. Whisk until smooth. Add the lemon juice and herbs and season to taste. Turn the fish mould out on to a serving plate and garnish it with a bunch of watercress in the center. Serve it warm or cold, with the sauce.

Chocolate and Chestnut Yule Log

This is based on the French Bûche de Noël, traditionally served at Christmas. Make it some time in advance and freeze it. It's an excellent dessert for a party.

Serves 8

INGREDIENTS
¼ cup all-purpose flour
2 tbsp cocoa powder
pinch of salt
3 large eggs, separated
large pinch of cream of tartar
8 tbsp superfine sugar
2–3 drops almond extract
sifted cocoa powder and holly sprigs, to decorate

FOR THE FILLING
1 tbsp rum or brandy
1 tsp powdered gelatin
4 oz dark chocolate, broken into squares
4 tbsp superfine sugar
8 oz canned chestnut purée
1¼ cups heavy cream

1 Preheat the oven to 350°F. Grease and line a 9 × 13 in jelly roll pan and line the base with non-stick baking paper. Sift the flour, cocoa and salt together on to a piece of wax paper.

2 Put the egg whites into a large clean bowl and whisk them until frothy. Add the cream of tartar and whisk until stiff. Gradually whisk in half the sugar, until the mixture will stand in stiff peaks.

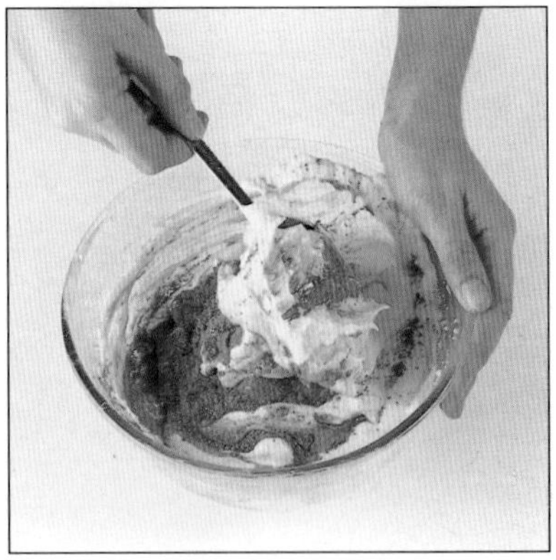

3 Put the egg yolks and the remaining sugar into another bowl and whisk until thick and pale. Add the almond extract. Stir in the sifted flour and cocoa mixture. Lastly, fold in the egg whites, using a metal spoon, until everything is evenly blended. Be careful not to overmix.

4 Turn the batter into the prepared jelly roll pan and level the top. Bake for 15–20 minutes, or until springy to the touch. Have ready a large piece of wax paper dusted liberally with superfine sugar. Turn the jelly roll on to the paper, remove the lining paper, and roll it up with the wax paper still inside. Let cool completely on a wire rack.

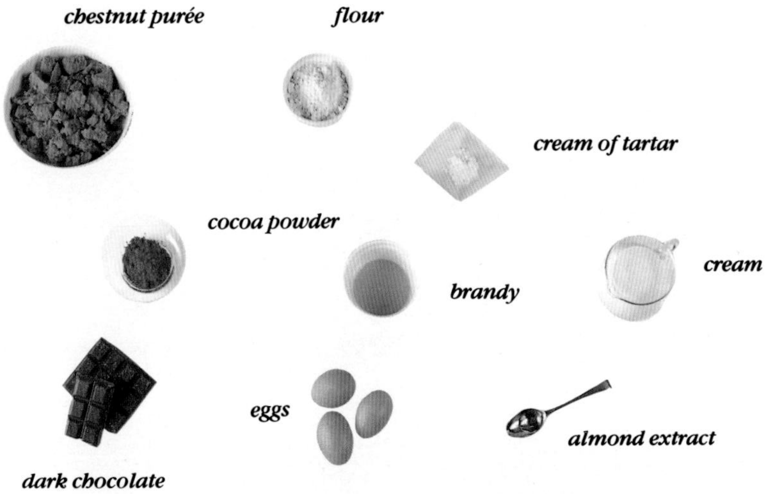

5 Put the brandy in a cup and sprinkle the gelatin over; leave to become spongy. Melt the chocolate in a 2½ cup bowl over a pan of hot water. Melt the gelatin over hot water and add to the chocolate. With an electric beater, whisk in the sugar and chestnut purée. Remove from the heat and let cool. Whisk the cream until it holds soft peaks. Fold the two mixtures together evenly.

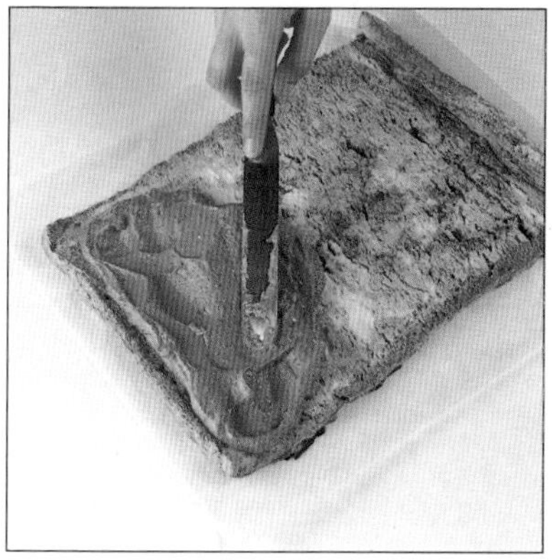

6 Unroll the cake carefully, spread it with half the filling and roll it up again. Place it on a serving dish and spread over the rest of the chocolate cream to cover it. Mark it with a fork to resemble a log. Chill until firm. Dust the cake with sifted cocoa powder and decorate the plate with sprigs of holly.

Ginger Trifle

This is a good way to use up leftover cake, whether plain, chocolate or gingerbread. You can substitute honey for the ginger and syrup, if you prefer. This pudding can be made the day before.

Serves 8

INGREDIENTS
8 oz gingerbread or other cake
4 tbsp Grand Marnier or sweet sherry
2 ripe pears, peeled, cored and cubed
2 bananas, thickly sliced
2 oranges, segmented
1–2 pieces preserved ginger, finely chopped, plus 2 tbsp syrup

FOR THE CUSTARD
2 eggs
4 tbsp superfine sugar
1 tbsp cornstarch
1⅞ cups milk
few drops vanilla extract

TO DECORATE
⅔ cup heavy cream, lightly whipped
¼ cup chopped almonds, toasted
4 candied cherries
8 small pieces angelica

1 Cut the gingerbread into 1½ in cubes. Put them in the bottom of a 3 pint/7½ cup glass bowl. Sprinkle the Grand Marnier or sherry over and let soak in.

2 To make the custard, whisk the eggs, sugar and cornstarch together in a bowl with a little of the milk. Heat the remaining milk until it is almost boiling. Pour it on to the egg mixture, whisking all the time. Return to the pan and stir over the heat until thickened. Simmer for 2 minutes, to cook the cornstarch. Add the vanilla extract and let cool.

3 Mix all the prepared fruit with the finely chopped preserved ginger and syrup. Spoon into the bowl on top of the gingerbread. Spoon over the custard to cover and chill until set.

4 Cover the top with whipped cream and sprinkle on the toasted almonds. Arrange the candied cherries and angelica around the edge.

Ruby Fruit Salad

After a rich main course, this port-flavored fruit salad is light and refreshing. Use any fruit that is available.

Serves 8

INGREDIENTS
1¼ cups water
8 tbsp superfine sugar
1 cinnamon stick
4 cloves
pared rind of 1 orange
1¼ cups port
2 oranges
1 small ripe cantaloupe or honeydew melon
4 small bananas
2 apples
8 oz seedless grapes

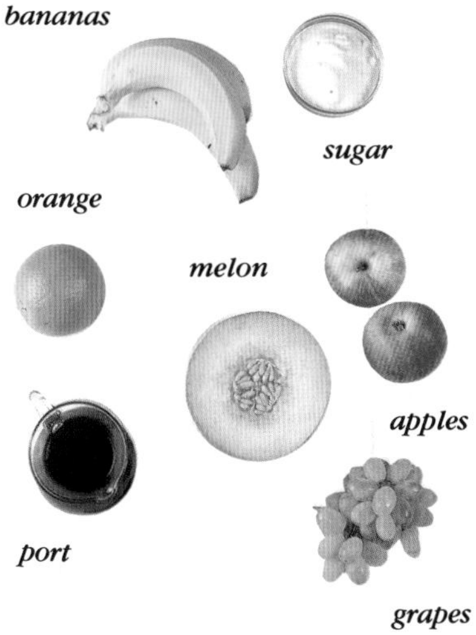

1 Put the water, sugar, spices and pared orange rind into a pan and stir over a gentle heat to dissolve the sugar. Then bring to a boil, cover with a lid and simmer for 10 minutes. Let cool, then add the port.

2 Strain the liquid (to remove the spices and orange rind) into a bowl. With a sharp knife, cut off all the skin and pith from the oranges. Then, holding each orange over the bowl to catch the juice, cut away the segments, by slicing between the membrane that divides each segment and allowing the segments to drop into the syrup. Squeeze the remaining pith to release any juice.

3 Cut the melon in half, remove the seeds and scoop out the flesh with a melon baller, or cut it in small cubes. Add it to the syrup.

4 Peel the bananas and cut them diagonally in ½ in slices. Quarter and core the apples and cut them in small cubes. Leave the skin on, or peel them if it is tough. Halve the grapes if large or leave them whole. Stir all the fruit into the syrup, cover with plastic wrap and chill for an hour before serving.

Christmas Pudding

This recipe makes enough to fill one 5 cup mold or two 2½ cup molds. It can be made up to a month before Christmas and stored in a cool, dry place. Steam the pudding for 2 hours before serving. Serve with brandy or rum butter, whisky sauce, custard or whipped cream, topped with a decorative sprig of holly.

Serves 8

INGREDIENTS
- ½ cup butter
- 1 heaped cup soft dark brown sugar
- ½ cup self-rising flour
- 1 tsp ground allspice
- ¼ tsp grated nutmeg
- ½ tsp ground cinnamon
- 2 eggs
- 2 cups fresh white bread crumbs
- 1 cup sultanas
- 1 cup raisins
- ½ cup currants
- 3 tbsp mixed candied citrus peel, chopped finely
- ¼ cup chopped almonds
- 1 small apple, peeled, cored and coarsely grated
- finely grated rind of 1 orange or lemon
- juice of 1 orange or lemon, made up to ⅔ cup with brandy, rum or sherry

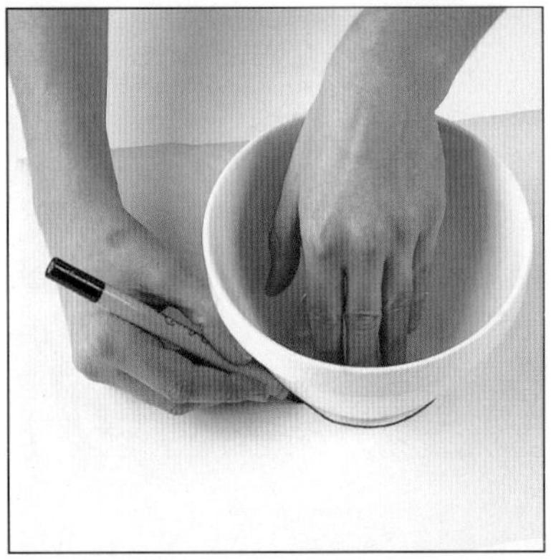

1 Cut a disc of wax paper to fit the base of the mold(s) and butter the disc and mold(s).

2 Whisk the butter and sugar together until soft. Beat in the flour, spices and eggs. Stir in the remaining ingredients thoroughly. The mixture should have a soft dropping consistency.

3 Turn the mixture into the greased mold(s) and level the top.

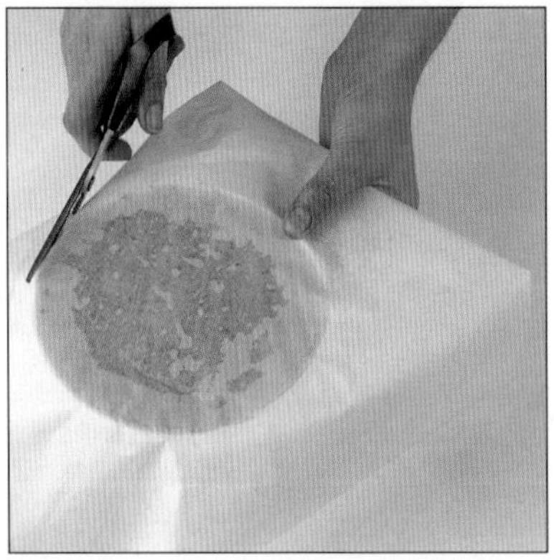

4 Cover with another disc of buttered wax paper.

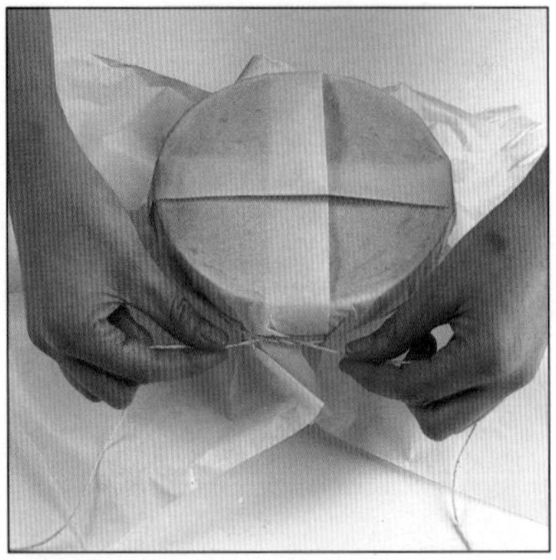

5 Make a pleat across the center of a large piece of wax paper and cover the mold(s) with it, tying it in place with string under the rim. Cut off the excess paper. Pleat a piece of foil in the same way and cover the mold(s) with it, tucking it around the bowl neatly, under the wax frill. Tie another piece of string around the mold(s) and across the top, as a handle.

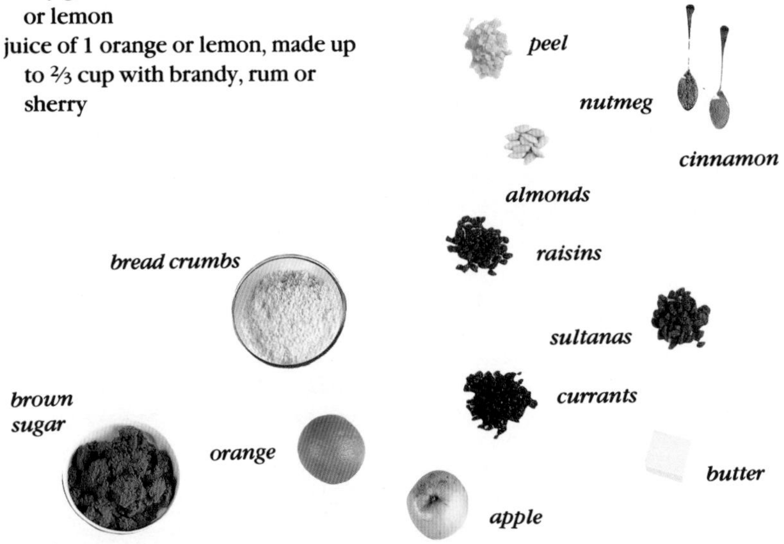

6 Place the mold(s) in a steamer over a pan of simmering water and steam for 6 hours. Alternatively, put the mold(s) into a large pan and pour enough boiling water around to come halfway up the mold(s) and cover the pan with a tight-fitting lid. Check the water is simmering and top it up with boiling water as it evaporates. When the pudding(s) have cooked, let cool completely. Then remove the foil and wax paper. Wipe the mold(s) clean and replace the wax paper and foil with clean pieces, ready for reheating.

TO SERVE

Steam for 2 hours. Turn on to a plate and let stand for 5 minutes, before removing the pudding mold (the steam will rise to the top of the mold and help to loosen the pudding).

De Luxe Mincemeat Tart

The mincemeat can be made up and kept in the fridge for up to two weeks. It can also be used to make individual mince pies.

Serves 8

INGREDIENTS
- 2 cups all-purpose flour
- 2 tsp ground cinnamon
- ⅔ cup walnuts, finely ground
- ½ cup butter
- 4 tbsp superfine sugar, plus extra for dusting
- 1 egg
- 2 drops vanilla extract
- 1 tbsp cold water

FOR THE MINCEMEAT
- 2 apples, peeled, cored and coarsely grated
- 1⅓ cups raisins
- ⅔ cup ready-to-eat dried apricots, chopped
- ⅔ cup ready-to-eat dried figs or prunes, chopped
- 8 oz green grapes, halved and seeded
- ½ cup chopped almonds
- finely grated rind of 1 lemon
- 2 tbsp lemon juice
- 2 tbsp brandy or port
- ¼ tsp ground allspice
- generous ½ cup light brown sugar
- 2 tbsp butter, melted

1 To make the pastry, put the flour, cinnamon and walnuts in a food processor. Add the butter and process until the mixture resembles fine bread crumbs. Turn into a bowl and stir in the sugar. Using a fork, beat the egg with the vanilla extract and water. Gradually stir the egg mixture into the dry ingredients. Gather together with your fingertips to form a soft, pliable dough. Knead briefly on a lightly floured surface until smooth; then wrap the dough in plastic wrap and chill it for 30 minutes.

2 Mix all the mincemeat ingredients together thoroughly in a bowl.

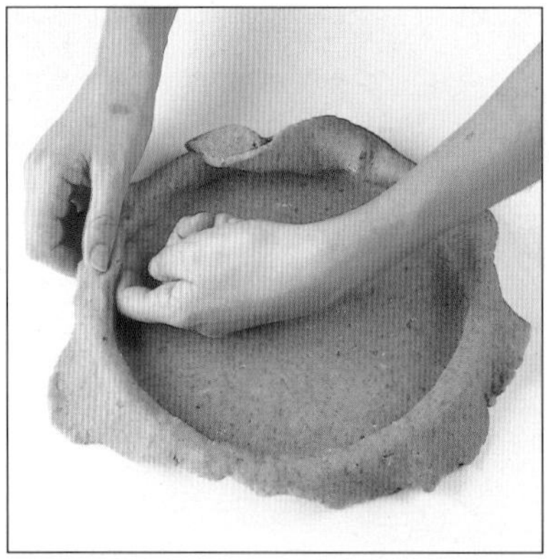

3 Cut one-third off the pastry and reserve it for the lattice. Roll out the remainder and use it to line a 9 in, loose-based cake pan. Take care to push the pastry well into the edges and make a ¼ in rim around the top edge.

4 With a rolling pin, roll off the excess pastry to neaten the edge. Fill the pastry crust with the mincemeat.

5 Roll out the remaining pastry and cut it into ½ in strips. Arrange the strips in a lattice over the top of the pastry, wet the joins and press them together well. Chill for 30 minutes.

6 Preheat the oven to 375°F. Place a baking sheet in the oven to preheat. Brush the pastry with water and dust it with superfine sugar. Bake it on the baking sheet for 30–40 minutes. Transfer to a wire rack and let cool for 15 minutes. Then carefully remove the cake pan. Serve warm or cold, with sweetened, whipped cream.

Iced Praline Torte

Make this elaborate torte several days ahead, decorate it and return it to the freezer until you are nearly ready to serve it. Allow the torte to stand at room temperature for an hour before serving, or leave it in the refrigerator overnight to soften.

Serves 8

INGREDIENTS
1 cup almonds or hazelnuts
8 tbsp superfine sugar
⅔ cup raisins
6 tbsp rum or brandy
4 oz dark chocolate, broken into squares
2 tbsp milk
1⅞ cups heavy cream
2 tbsp strong black coffee
16 ladyfinger cookies

TO FINISH
⅔ cup heavy cream
½ cup slivered almonds, toasted
½ oz dark chocolate, melted

1 To make the praline, have ready an oiled cake pan or baking sheet. Put the nuts into a heavy-based pan with the sugar and heat gently until the sugar melts. Swirl the pan to coat the nuts in the hot sugar. Cook slowly until the nuts brown and the sugar caramelizes. Watch all the time, as this will only take a few minutes. Turn the nuts quickly into the pan or on to the tray and let them cool completely. Break them up and grind them to a fine powder in a food processor.

2 Soak the raisins in 3 tbsp of the rum or brandy for an hour (or better still overnight), so they soften and absorb the rum. Melt the chocolate with the milk in a bowl over a pan of hot, but not boiling water. Remove and let cool. Lightly grease a 5 cup loaf pan and line it with wax paper.

3 Whisk the cream in a bowl until it holds soft peaks. Whisk in the cold chocolate. Then fold in the praline and the soaked raisins, with any liquid.

4 Mix the coffee and remaining rum or brandy in a shallow dish. Dip in the ladyfingers and arrange half in a layer over the base of the prepared loaf pan.

5 Cover with the chocolate mixture and add another layer of soaked lady-fingers. Freeze overnight.

6 Dip the pan briefly into warm water to loosen the torte and turn it out on to a serving plate. Cover with whipped cream. Sprinkle the top with toasted slivered almonds and drizzle the melted chocolate over the top. Return the torte to the freezer until it's needed.

Spiced Pears in Red Wine

Serve these pears hot or cold, with lightly whipped cream. The flavors improve with keeping, so you can make this several days before you want it.

Serves 8

INGREDIENTS
2½ cups red wine
1⅛ cups superfine sugar
2½ in cinnamon stick
6 cloves
finely grated rind of 1 orange
2 tsp grated ginger root
8 even-sized firm pears, with stems
1 tbsp brandy
2 tbsp almonds or hazelnuts, toasted, to decorate

1 Choose a pan large enough to hold all the pears upright in one layer. Put all the ingredients except the pears, brandy and almonds into the pan and heat slowly until the sugar has dissolved. Simmer for 5 minutes.

2 Peel the pears, leaving the stems on, and cut away the flower end. Arrange them upright in the pan. Cover with a lid and simmer *very* gently until they are tender. The cooking time will vary depending on their size and how ripe they are, but will be about 45–50 minutes.

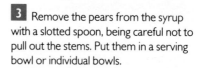

3 Remove the pears from the syrup with a slotted spoon, being careful not to pull out the stems. Put them in a serving bowl or individual bowls.

4 Bring the syrup to a boil and boil it rapidly until it thickens and reduces. Let cool slightly, add the brandy and strain over the pears. Sprinkle on the toasted nuts to decorate.

Frozen Grand Marnier Soufflés

These sophisticated little desserts are always appreciated and make a wonderful end to a special meal.

Serves 8

INGREDIENTS
1 cup superfine sugar
6 large eggs, separated
1 cup milk
½ oz powdered gelatin, soaked in
 3 tbsp cold water
1⅞ cups heavy cream
4 tbsp Grand Marnier

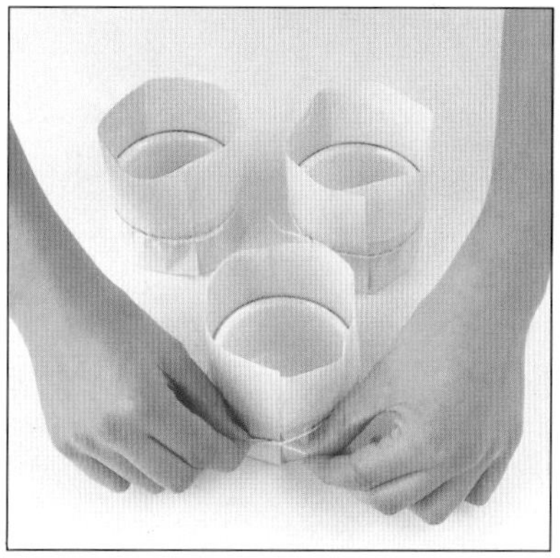

1 Tie a double-collar of wax paper around eight ramekins. Put 6 tbsp of the sugar in a bowl with the egg yolks and whisk until pale.

2 Heat the milk until almost boiling and pour it on to the yolks, whisking all the time. Return to the pan and stir it over a gentle heat until it is thick enough to coat the spoon. Remove the pan from the heat. Stir the soaked gelatin into the custard. Pour into a bowl and leave to cool. Whisk occasionally, until the custard is on the point of setting.

3 Put the remaining sugar in a pan with the water and dissolve it over a low heat. Bring to a boil and boil rapidly until it reaches the soft ball stage or 240°F on a sugar thermometer. Remove from the heat. In a clean bowl, whisk the egg whites until they are stiff. Pour the hot syrup on to the whites, whisking all the time. Let cool.

4 Whisk the cream until it holds soft peaks. Add the Grand Marnier to the cold custard and fold the custard into the cold meringue, with the cream. Quickly pour into the prepared ramekins. Freeze overnight. Remove the paper collars. Leave the soufflés at room temperature for 30 minutes before serving.

White Amaretto Mousses with Chocolate Sauce

These little desserts are extremely rich, and derive their flavor from Amaretto, an almond-flavored liqueur, and amaretti, little almond-flavored cookies.

Serves 8

INGREDIENTS
- 4 oz amaretti or macaroon cookies
- 4 tbsp Amaretto liqueur
- 12 oz white chocolate, broken into squares
- ½ oz powdered gelatin, soaked in 3 tbsp cold water
- 1⅞ cups heavy cream

FOR THE CHOCOLATE SAUCE
- 8 oz dark chocolate, broken into squares
- 1¼ cups light cream
- 4 tbsp superfine sugar

1 Lightly oil eight individual 4 fl oz molds and line the base of each mold with a small disc of oiled wax paper. Put the cookies into a large bowl and crush them finely with a rolling pin.

2 Melt the Amaretto and white chocolate together gently in a bowl over a pan of hot but not boiling water (be very careful not to overheat the chocolate). Stir well until smooth; remove from the pan and let cool.

3 Melt the gelatin over hot water and blend it into the chocolate mixture. Whisk the cream until it holds soft peaks. Fold in the chocolate mixture, with 4 tbsp of the crushed cookies.

4 Put a teaspoonful of the crushed cookies into the bottom of each mold and spoon in the chocolate mixture. Tap each mold to disperse any air bubbles. Level the tops and sprinkle the remaining crushed cookies on top. Press down gently and chill for 4 hours.

5 To make the chocolate sauce, put all the ingredients in a small pan and heat gently to melt the chocolate and dissolve the sugar. Simmer for 2–3 minutes. Let cool completely.

6 Slip a knife around the sides of each mold, and turn out on to individual plates. Remove the wax paper and pour round a little dark chocolate sauce.

Crunchy Apple and Almond Flan

Do not be tempted to put any sugar with the apples, as this makes them produce too much liquid. All the sweetness is in the pastry and topping.

Serves 8

INGREDIENTS
75 g/3 oz/6 tbsp butter
175 g/6 oz/1½ cups plain flour
25 g/1 oz/scant ⅓ cup ground almonds
25 g/1 oz/2 tbsp caster sugar
1 egg yolk
15 ml/1 tbsp cold water
¼ tsp almond essence
sifted icing sugar, to decorate

FOR THE CRUNCHY TOPPING
115 g/4 oz/1 cup plain flour
¼ tsp ground mixed spice
50 g/2 oz/4 tbsp butter, cut in small cubes
50 g/2 oz/4 tbsp demerara sugar
50 g/2 oz/½ cup flaked almonds

FOR THE FILLING
675 g/1½ lb cooking apples
25 g/1 oz/2 tbsp raisins or sultanas

1 To make the pastry, rub the butter, by hand or in a processor, into the flour until it resembles fine breadcrumbs. Stir in the ground almonds and sugar. Whisk the egg yolk, water and almond essence together and mix them into the dry ingredients to form a soft, pliable dough. Knead the dough lightly until smooth, wrap in clear film and leave in a cool place to rest for 20 minutes.

2 Meanwhile, make the crunchy topping. Sift the flour and mixed spice into a bowl and rub in the butter. Stir in the sugar and almonds.

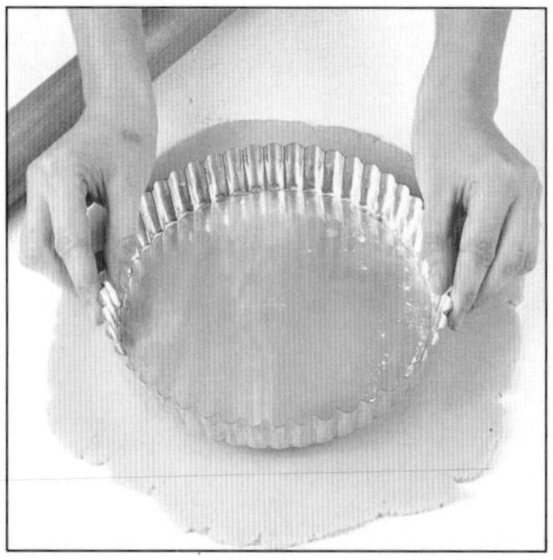

3 Roll out the pastry on a lightly floured surface and use it to line a 23 cm/9 in loose-based flan tin, taking care to press it neatly into the edges and to make a lip around the top edge.

4 Roll off the excess pastry to neaten the edge. Chill for 15 minutes.

5 Preheat the oven to 190°C/375°F/Gas 5. Place a baking sheet in the oven to preheat. Peel, core and slice the apples thinly. Arrange the slices in the flan in overlapping, concentric circles, doming the centre. Scatter over the raisins or sultanas. The flan will seem too full at this stage, but as the apples cook the filling will drop slightly.

6 Cover the apples with the crunchy topping mixture, pressing it on lightly. Bake on the hot baking sheet for 25–30 minutes, or until the top is golden brown and the apples are tender (test them with a fine skewer). Leave the flan to cool in the tin for 10 minutes. Serve warm or cold, dusted with sifted icing sugar.

Double Chocolate Snowball

This is an ideal party dessert as it can be prepared at least one day ahead and decorated on the day.

Serves 12–14

INGREDIENTS

12 oz bittersweet or semi-sweet chocolate, chopped
1½ cups superfine sugar
1¼ cups unsalted butter, cut into small pieces
8 eggs
¼ cup orange-flavored liqueur or brandy (optional)
cocoa for dusting

WHITE CHOCOLATE CREAM

7 oz fine quality white chocolate, broken into pieces
2 cups heavy or whipping cream
1 tbsp orange-flavor liqueur (optional)

1 Preheat the oven to 350°F. Line a 1½ quart round ovenproof bowl with aluminum foil, smoothing the sides. In a bowl over a pan of simmering water, melt the bittersweet or semi-sweet chocolate. Add sugar and stir until chocolate is melted and sugar dissolves. Strain into a medium bowl. With an electric mixer at low speed, beat in the butter, then the eggs, one at a time, beating well after each addition. Stir in the liqueur or brandy and pour into the prepared bowl. Tap gently to release any large air bubbles.

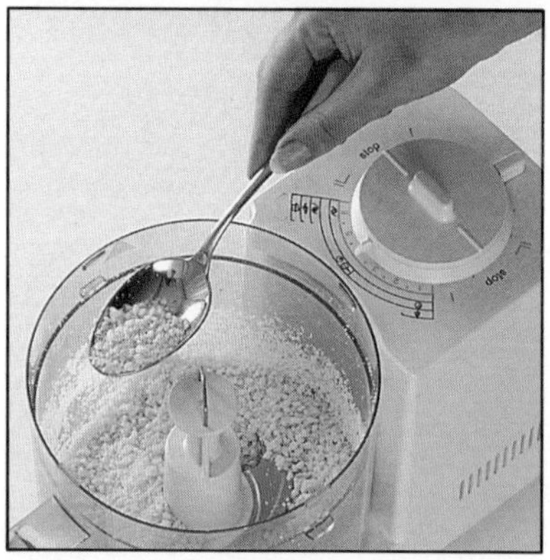

2 Bake for 1¼–1½ hours until the surface is firm and slightly risen, but cracked. The center will still be wobbly: this will set on cooling. Remove to rack to cool to room temperature; the top will sink. Cover with a dinner plate (to make an even surface for unmolding); then cover completely with clear film or foil and refrigerate overnight. To unmold, remove plate and film or foil and place a serving plate over the top of the mold. Invert mold on to plate and shake firmly to release the dessert. Carefully peel off foil. Cover until ready to decorate.

3 In a food processor fitted with a metal blade, process the white chocolate until fine crumbs form. In a small saucepan, heat ½ cup cream until just beginning to simmer. With the food processor running, pour cream through the feed tube and process until the chocolate is completely melted. Strain into a medium bowl and cool to room temperature, stirring occasionally.

4 In another bowl, with the electric mixer, beat the cream and chocolate mixture until soft peaks form, add liqueur and beat for 30 seconds or until cream holds its shape, but not until stiff. Fold a spoonful of cream into the chocolate mixture to lighten it, then fold in remaining cream. Spoon into a piping bag fitted with a star tip and pipe rosettes over the surface. If you wish, dust with cocoa.

Poached Figs with Mascarpone Quenelles

Quenelles are an edible garnish – here they are made of mascarpone, but they can be formed in the same way with other creamy-textured foods such as meringue, ice cream or sorbet.

Serves 6

INGREDIENTS
18 fresh figs
1½ cups red wine
½ cup granulated sugar
3 strips of orange zest

FOR THE QUENELLES
1¼ cups mascarpone cheese
scant ½ cup fromage frais
2–3 tablespoons confectioners' sugar, sifted
2 tablespoons Madeira

1 Place the figs in a saucepan with the red wine, granulated sugar and orange zest. Bring to a boil, then simmer for 5–10 minutes, until tender. Using a slotted spoon, transfer the figs to a bowl. Bring the red wine syrup back to a boil and cook until reduced by half. Cool slightly.

2 Make the quenelles. Beat together the mascarpone cheese and fromage frais. Sift over the confectioners' sugar, add the Madeira and stir to combine.

3 Take two large metal spoons. Scoop up a spoonful of the mascarpone mixture and invert the second spoon on top of it. Push down and scoop the mixture onto the second spoon.

4 Invert the first spoon a third of the way over the mixture, push down and scoop as before. This will create an oval wedge. Repeat this action to create an oval with three sides. Ease gently off the spoon and place on individual plates next to the warm figs, with a little syrup spooned around them.

Chocolate Box with Caramel Mousse and Berries

Do not add caramel shards too long before serving the Chocolate Box as moisture may cause them to melt.

Serves 8–10

INGREDIENTS
10 oz semi-sweet chocolate, broken into pieces

CARAMEL MOUSSE
4 × 2 oz Heath bars, coarsely chopped
1½ tbsp milk or water
1½ cups heavy cream
1 egg white

CARAMEL SHARDS
½ cup granulated sugar
¼ cup water

TOPPING
4 oz fine quality white chocolate, chopped
1½ cups heavy cream
1 lb mixed berries or cut up fruits such as raspberries, strawberries, blackberries or sliced nectarine and orange segments

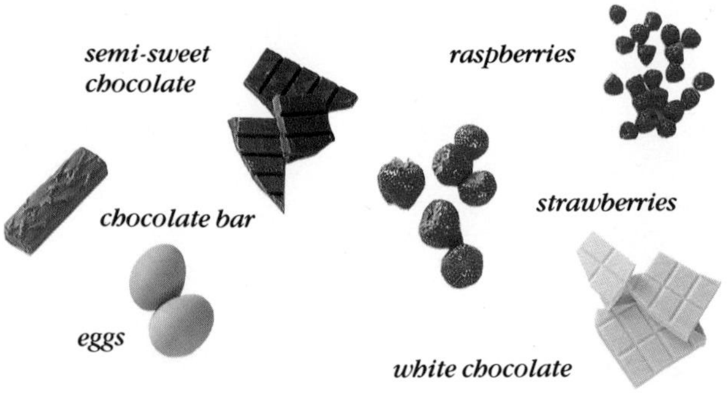

1 Prepare the chocolate box. Turn a 9 in square baking pan bottom-side up. Mold a piece of foil around the pan, then turn it right side up and line it with the foil, pressing against the edges to make the foil as smooth as possible.

2 Place the semi-sweet chocolate in a bowl over a saucepan of hot water. Place saucepan over low heat and stir until chocolate is melted and smooth. Immediately pour melted chocolate into the lined pan and tilt to coat bottom and sides evenly, keeping top edges of sides as straight as possible. As chocolate coats sides, tilt pan again to coat the corners and sides again. Refrigerate until firm, 45 minutes.

3 In a medium bowl, place the Heath bars and milk or water. Place over a pan of hot water over medium heat and stir until melted. Remove from heat and cool for 10 minutes, stirring occasionally. In a bowl with electric mixer, whip cream until soft peaks form. Stir a spoonful of cream into caramel mixture, then fold in remaining cream. In another bowl with electric mixer and cleaned beaters, beat egg white until just stiff; fold into mousse mixture. Pour into the box. Refrigerate for several hours or overnight.

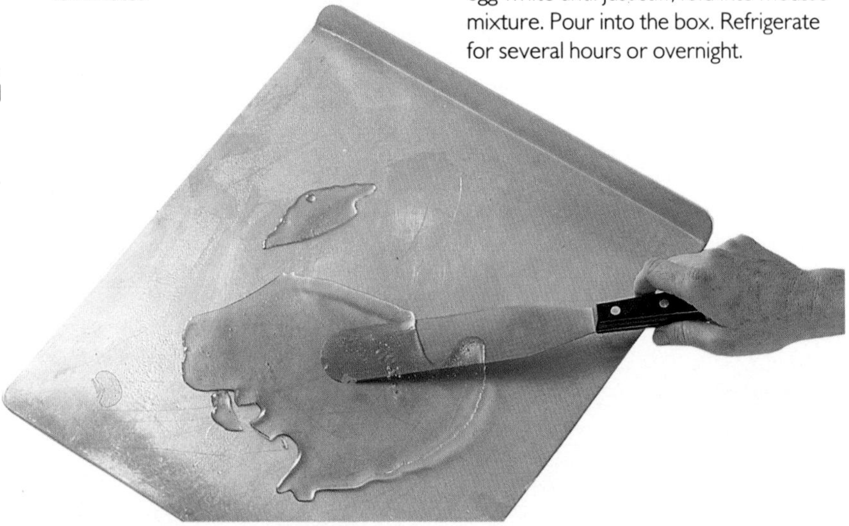

4 Meanwhile prepare the caramel shards. Lightly oil a cookie sheet. In a small saucepan over low heat, dissolve the sugar in the water, swirling pan gently. Increase the heat and boil mixture until sugar begins to turn a pale golden color, 4–5 minutes. When mixture is a golden caramel color, immediately pour on to the oiled sheet, tilt sheet to distribute caramel in an even layer; *do not touch – caramel is dangerously hot*. Cool completely, then using a metal spatula lift off cookie sheet and break into pieces. Set aside to decorate.

5 In a small saucepan over low heat, melt the white chocolate and ½ cup cream until smooth, stirring frequently. Strain into a medium bowl and cool to room temperature, stirring occasionally. In another bowl with electric mixer, beat the remaining cream until firm peaks form. Stir a spoonful of cream into the white chocolate mixture, then fold in remaining whipped cream. Using foil as a guide, remove mousse-filled box from the foil by peeling foil carefully from sides, then bottom. Slide on to serving plate.

6 Spoon chocolate-cream mixture into a medium piping bag fitted with a star tip and pipe a decorative design of rosettes or shells over the surface of the set mousse. Decorate the cream-covered box with the fruits and Caramel Shards.

Moist and Rich Christmas Cake

The cake can be made 4–6 weeks before Christmas. During this time, pierce the cake with a fine needle and spoon over 2–3 tbsp brandy.

Makes 1 × 8 in cake

INGREDIENTS
1⅓ cups sultanas
1 cup currants
1⅓ cups raisins
4 oz prunes, pitted and chopped
¼ cup candied cherries, halved
⅓ cup mixed candied citrus peel, chopped
3 tbsp brandy or sherry
2 cups all-purpose flour
pinch of salt
½ tsp ground cinnamon
½ tsp grated nutmeg
1 tbsp cocoa powder
1 cup butter
1 generous cup dark brown sugar
4 large eggs
finely grated rind of 1 orange or lemon
⅔ cup ground almonds
½ cup chopped almonds

TO DECORATE
4 tbsp apricot jam
10 in round cake board
1 lb almond paste
1 lb white fondant icing
8 oz royal icing
1½ yd ribbon

1 The day before you want to bake the cake, put all the dried fruit to soak in the brandy or sherry, cover it with plastic wrap and leave overnight. Grease a 8 in round cake pan and line it with a double thickness of wax paper.

2 The next day, preheat the oven to 325°F. Sift together the flour, salt, spices and cocoa powder. Whisk the butter and sugar together until light and fluffy and beat in the eggs gradually. Finally mix in the orange or lemon rind, the ground and chopped almonds and the dried fruits (with any liquid). Fold the flour mixture into the dried fruit mixture.

3 Spoon into the prepared cake pan, level the top and give the cake pan a gentle tap on the work surface to settle the mixture and disperse any air bubbles. Bake for 3 hours, or until a fine skewer inserted into the middle comes out clean. Transfer the cake pan to a wire rack and let the cake cool in the pan for an hour. Then carefully turn the cake out on to the wire rack, but leave the paper on, as it will help to keep the cake moist during storage. When the cake is cold, wrap it tightly in foil and store it in a cool place.

4 Warm then sieve the apricot jam to make a glaze. Remove the paper from the cake and place it in the center of the cake board and brush it with hot apricot glaze. Cover the cake with a layer of almond paste and then a layer of fondant icing. Pipe a border around the base of the cake with royal icing. Tie a ribbon around the sides.

5 Roll out any trimmings from the fondant icing and stamp out 12 small holly leaves with a cutter. Make one bell motif with a cookie mold, dusted first with sifted confectioner's sugar. Roll 36 small balls for the holly berries. Leave on wax paper to dry for 24 hours. Decorate the cake with the leaves, berries and bell, attaching them with a little royal icing.

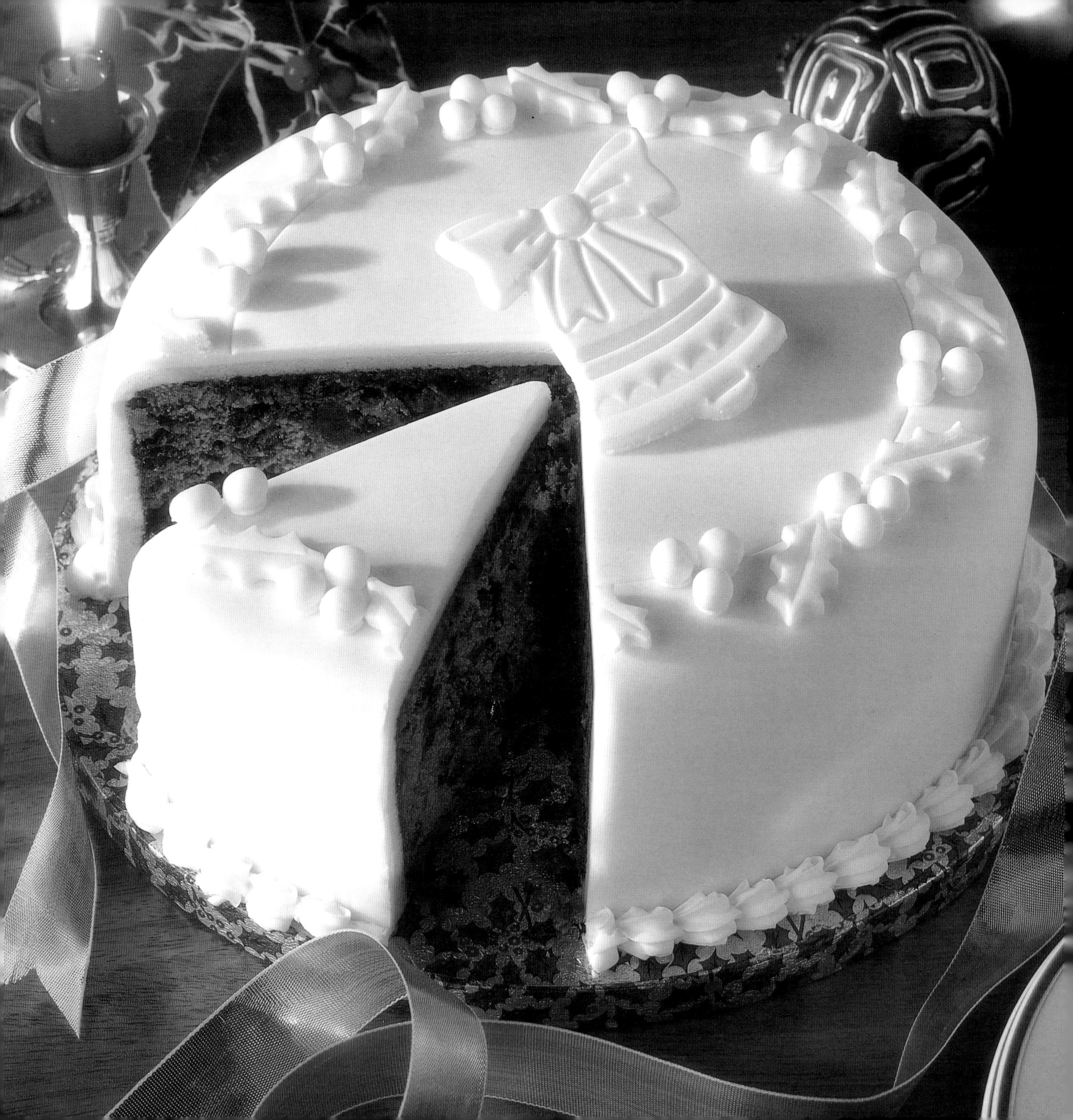

Glazed Christmas Ring

A good, rich fruit cake is a must at Christmas. This one is particularly festive, with its vibrant, glazed fruit-and-nut topping.

Serves 16–20

INGREDIENTS
1⅓ cups golden raisins
1 cup raisins
1 cup currants
1 cup dried figs, chopped
6 tablespoons whiskey
3 tablespoons orange juice
½ pound (2 sticks) butter
1 cup dark brown sugar
5 eggs
2¼ cups all-purpose flour
1 tablespoon baking powder
1 tablespoon pumpkin pie spice
⅔ cup candied cherries, chopped
1 cup Brazil nuts, chopped
⅓ cup chopped mixed candied peel
⅓ cup ground almonds
grated rind and juice of 1 orange
2 tablespoons thick-cut orange marmalade

TO DECORATE
1 cup thick-cut orange marmalade
1 tablespoon orange juice
¾ cup mixed-color candied cherries
1½ cups whole Brazil nuts
⅔ cup dried figs, halved

1 Place the golden raisins, raisins, currants and figs in a large bowl. Pour in 4 tablespoons of the whiskey and the orange juice and let soak overnight.

2 Preheat the oven to 325°F. Grease and double line a 10-inch ring or tube pan with baking parchment.

3 Cream the butter and sugar together until pale and light. Beat in the eggs one at a time, beating well after each addition, until incorporated. Add a little flour if the mixture starts to curdle.

4 Sift the flour, baking powder and pumpkin pie spice together. Fold into the creamed mixture. Add the remaining ingredients, reserving the whiskey, then stir in the soaked fruit. Transfer the mixture to the prepared pan, smooth the surface and make a small dip around the center. Bake for 1 hour, reduce the oven temperature to 300°F and bake for another 1¾–2 hours.

5 Test the cake with a skewer to make sure it is done, then remove it from the oven. Prick the cake all over with a skewer and spoon the reserved whiskey over. Allow to cool in the pan for 30 minutes, then transfer to a wire rack, remove the paper and cool completely.

6 To decorate, heat the marmalade and orange juice together in a pan and boil gently for 3 minutes. Stir in the cherries, nuts and figs. Remove from the heat and let cool slightly.

7 Spoon the candied fruits and nuts over the cake in an attractive pattern and let stand until set.

Light Jeweled Fruit Cake

If you want to cover the cake with marzipan and icing omit the whole-almond decoration. The cake can be made up to two weeks before eating it. For serving, brush the top with hot apricot jam and tie a pretty ribbon around the sides.

Makes 1 × 8 in cake

INGREDIENTS
½ cup currants
⅔ cup sultanas
1 cup candied cherries (mixed red, green and yellow), quartered
⅓ cup mixed candied citrus peel, finely chopped
2 tbsp rum, brandy or sherry
1 cup butter
1⅛ cups superfine sugar
finely grated rind of 1 orange
finely grated rind of 1 lemon
4 eggs
½ cup chopped almonds
⅔ cup ground almonds
2 cups all-purpose flour

TO FINISH
2 oz whole blanched almonds (optional)
1 tbsp apricot jam

1 The day before you want to bake the cake, soak the currants, sultanas, candied cherries and the mixed peel in the rum, brandy or sherry. Cover with plastic wrap and leave overnight. The next day, grease and line an 8 in round cake pan or a 7 in square cake pan with a double thickness of wax paper.

2 Preheat the oven to 325°F. In a large bowl, whisk the butter, sugar and orange and lemon rinds together until they are light and fluffy. Beat in the eggs, one at a time.

3 Mix in the chopped almonds, ground almonds, soaked fruits (with their liquid) and the flour, to make a soft dropping consistency. Spoon into the cake pan and level the top. Bake for 30 minutes.

4 Arrange the whole almonds in a pattern on top of the cake. Do not press them into the cake or they will sink during cooking. Return the cake to the oven and cook for a further 1½–2 hours, or until the center is firm to the touch. Let the cake cool in the pan for 30 minutes. Then remove it and let it cool completely on a wire rack, but leave the paper on, as it helps to keep the cake moist while it is stored. When cold, wrap the cake in foil and store it in a cool place. Remove the paper before serving, and heat then strain the apricot jam. Brush the glaze over the cake. Let cool.

Panettone

This famous fruit cake comes from Italy, where it is often served with a glass of red wine.

Makes 1 cake

INGREDIENTS
- ⅔ cup lukewarm milk
- 1 envelope (2¼ teaspoons) active dry yeast
- 3 cups all-purpose flour
- 6 tablespoons sugar
- 2 teaspoons salt
- 2 eggs, plus 5 egg yolks
- 12 tablespoons (1½ sticks) butter
- ⅔ cup raisins
- grated rind of 1 lemon
- ½ cup chopped candied peel

1 Mix the milk and yeast in a large warmed bowl and let sit for 10 minutes, until frothy. Stir in 1 cup of the flour, cover loosely and leave in a warm place for 30 minutes. Sift in the remaining flour. Make a well in the center and add the sugar, salt, eggs and egg yolks.

2 Stir with a spoon, then with your hands to obtain a soft, sticky dough.

3 Soften the butter, then smear it on top of the dough and work it in. Cover and let rise in a warm place for 3 4 hours, until the dough has doubled in bulk.

4 Line the bottom of an 8¾-cup charlotte mold with baking parchment, then grease well. Punch down the dough and transfer to a floured surface. Knead in the raisins, lemon rind and candied peel. Shape the dough and fit it into the prepared mold.

5 Cover the mold with a plastic bag and let the dough rise for about 2 hours, until it is well above the top of the mold.

6 Preheat the oven to 400°F. Bake for 15 minutes, cover the top with foil and lower the heat to 350°F. Bake for 30 minutes more. Allow to cool in the mold for about 5 minutes, then transfer to a wire rack, remove the paper and cool completely.

COOK'S TIP

If you do not have a charlotte mold, you can use a perfectly clean 2-pound coffee or fruit can.

Death by Chocolate

There are many versions of this cake; this is a very rich one which is ideal for a large party, as it can serve up to twenty chocolate lovers.

Serves 18–20

INGREDIENTS
8 oz fine quality bittersweet chocolate, chopped
½ cup unsalted butter, cut into pieces
⅔ cup water
1¼ cups granulated sugar
2 tsp vanilla extract
2 eggs, separated
⅔ cup buttermilk or sour cream
2 cups flour
2 tsp baking powder
1 tsp baking soda
pinch of cream of tartar
chocolate curls
raspberries and confectioners' sugar to decorate (optional)

CHOCOLATE FUDGE FILLING
1 lb fine quality couverture chocolate or bittersweet chocolate, chopped
1 cup unsalted butter
⅓ cup brandy or rum
¾ cup seedless raspberry preserve

CHOCOLATE GANACHE GLAZE
1 cup heavy cream
8 oz couverture chocolate or bittersweet chocolate, chopped
2 tbsp brandy

1 Preheat oven to 350°F. Grease a 10 in springform pan and line base with parchment paper or waxed paper. In a saucepan over medium-low heat, heat chocolate, butter and water until melted, stirring frequently. Remove from heat, beat in sugar and vanilla and cool.

In a bowl, beat yolks lightly, then beat into cooled chocolate mixture; gently fold in buttermilk or sour cream. Into a bowl, sift flour, baking powder and baking soda, then fold into chocolate mixture. In a bowl with an electric mixer, beat egg whites and cream of tartar until stiff peaks form; fold in chocolate mixture.

2 Pour mixture into prepared pans and bake for 45–50 minutes until cake begins to shrink away from side of pan. Remove to a wire rack to cool for 10 minutes (cake may sink in center, this is normal). Run a sharp knife around the edge of pan, then unclip pan and carefully remove side. Invert cake on to wire rack, remove bottom of pan and cool completely. Wash and dry pan.

3 Prepare filling. In a saucepan over medium heat, heat chocolate, butter and 4 tbsp brandy until melted, stirring frequently. Remove from heat and set aside to cool and thicken. Cut cake crosswise into three even layers. Heat the raspberry preserve and remaining brandy until melted and smooth, stirring frequently. Spread a thin layer over each of the cake layers and allow to set.

4 When the filling is spreadable, place the bottom cake layer back in the pan. Spread with half the filling, top with the second layer of cake, then spread with the remaining filling and top with the top cake layer, preserve side down. Gently press layers together, cover and refrigerate for 4–6 hours or overnight.

bittersweet chocolate

eggs

chocolate curls

raspberries

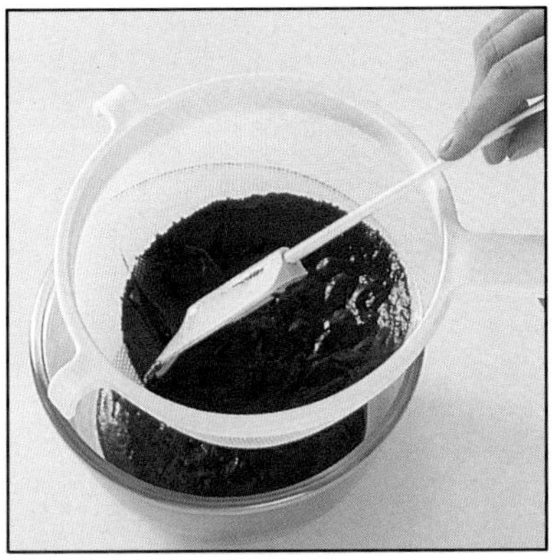

5 Carefully run a sharp knife around edge of cake to loosen, then unclip and remove side of pan. Set cake on wire rack over a cookie sheet to catch any drips. In a medium saucepan, bring the cream to a boil. Remove from heat and add chocolate all at once, stirring until melted and smooth. Stir in the brandy and strain into a bowl. Allow to stand for 4–5 minutes to thicken slightly.

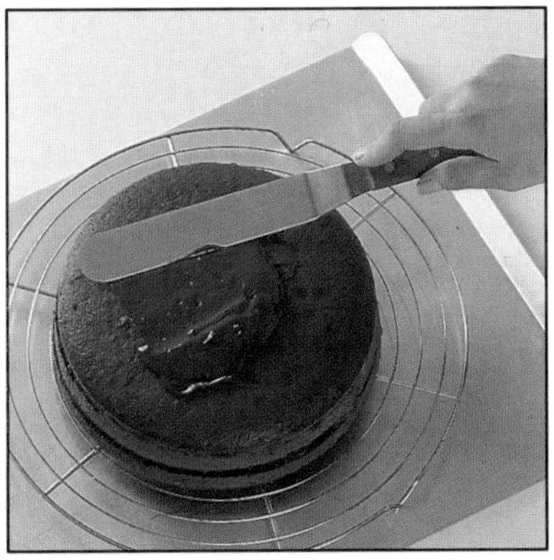

6 Beginning from the center of the bowl and working out towards the edge, whisk the glaze until smooth and shiny. Pour over the cake using a metal spatula to help smooth top and sides; allow glaze to set. Slide cake on to serving plate and decorate with chocolate curls and raspberries. Dust with confectioners' sugar. Do not refrigerate glaze or it will become dull.

Passion Cake

A complete change from the traditional rich Christmas cake. The icing thickens quickly as it cools and will become difficult to spread, so have the cake on a serving plate and a spatula ready to spread the icing once it is ready. The cake will stay moist for days.

Serves 8

INGREDIENTS
10 tbsp butter
scant 1 cup light brown sugar
2 eggs, beaten
6 oz carrots, finely grated
finely grated rind of 1 orange
large pinch of salt
1 tsp ground cinnamon
½ tsp grated nutmeg
1¾ cups self-rising flour
1 tsp baking powder
⅔ cup raisins
½ cup chopped walnuts
2 tbsp milk

FOR THE ICING
2¼ cups granulated sugar
⅔ cup water
pinch of cream of tartar
2 egg whites

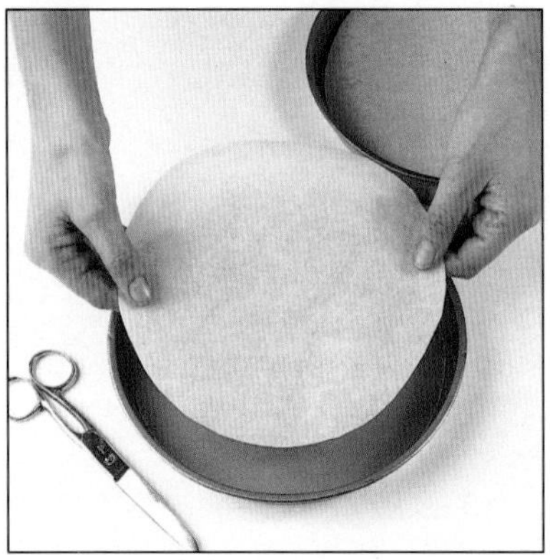

1 Preheat the oven to 375°F. Grease and line the bases of two 8 in square cake pans.

2 In a bowl, whisk together the butter and sugar until pale and fluffy. Beat in the eggs gradually, and then stir in the remaining ingredients to make a soft dropping consistency.

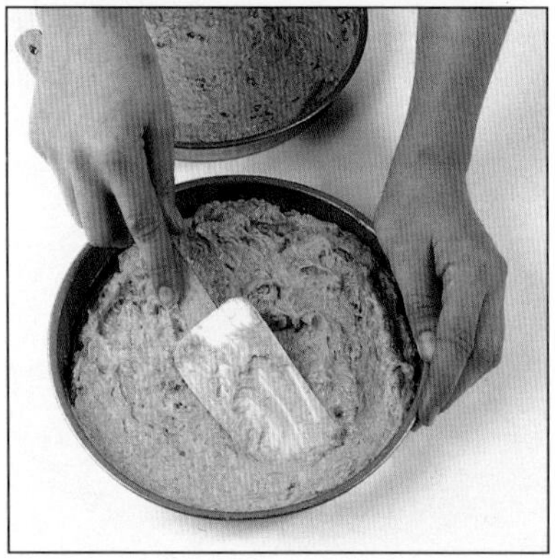

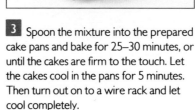

3 Spoon the mixture into the prepared cake pans and bake for 25–30 minutes, or until the cakes are firm to the touch. Let the cakes cool in the pans for 5 minutes. Then turn out on to a wire rack and let cool completely.

4 For the icing, put the sugar and water in a pan and heat them very gently to dissolve the sugar. (Swirl the pan to mix the sugar, do not stir it with a spoon.) Add the cream of tartar and bring to a boil. Boil to 240°F or to the soft ball stage. Quickly dip the base of the pan in cold water. Whisk the egg whites until they are stiff and pour the syrup over them, whisking all the time. Continue whisking until the icing loses its satiny appearance and will hold its shape. Quickly sandwich the cakes with the icing and spread the rest over the cake.

Almond Mincemeat Tartlets

These little tartlets are a welcome change from traditional mince pies. Serve them warm with brandy- or rum-flavored custard. They freeze well and can be reheated for serving.

Makes 36

INGREDIENTS
2½ cups all-purpose flour
generous ¾ cup confectioner's sugar
1 tsp ground cinnamon
¾ cup butter
⅔ cup ground almonds
1 egg yolk
3 tbsp milk
1 lb jar mincemeat
1 tbsp brandy or rum

FOR THE LEMON SPONGE FILLING
½ cup butter or margarine
8 tbsp superfine sugar
1½ cups self-rising flour
2 large eggs
finely grated rind of 1 large lemon

FOR THE LEMON ICING
1 generous cup confectioner's sugar
1 tbsp lemon juice

1 For the pastry, sift the flour, icing sugar and cinnamon into a bowl or a food processor and rub in the butter until it resembles fine bread crumbs. Add the ground almonds and bind with the egg yolk and milk to a soft, pliable dough. Knead the dough until smooth, wrap it in plastic wrap and chill it for 30 minutes.

2 Preheat the oven to 375°F. On a lightly floured surface, roll out the pastry and cut out 36 fluted rounds, to line the patty pans, with a pastry cutter. Mix the mincemeat with the brandy or rum and put a small teaspoonful in the bottom of each crust. Chill for 10 minutes.

3 For the lemon sponge filling, whisk the butter or margarine, sugar, flour, eggs and lemon rind together until smooth. Spoon on top of the mincemeat, dividing it evenly, and level the tops. Bake for 20–30 minutes, or until golden brown and springy to the touch. Remove and let cool on a wire rack.

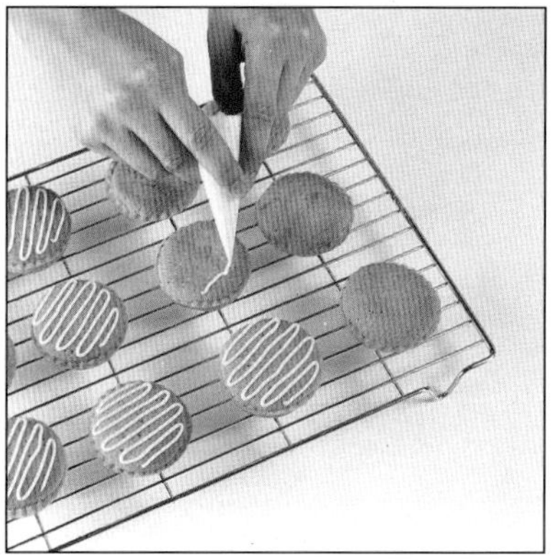

4 For the lemon icing, sift the confectioner's sugar and mix with the lemon juice to a smooth, thick, coating consistency. Spoon into a piping bag and drizzle a zigzag pattern over each tart. If you're short of time, simply dust the tartlets with sifted confectioner's sugar.

Christmas Cookies

These are great fun for children to make as presents. Any shape of cookie cutter can be used. Store them in an airtight tin. For a change, omit the lemon rind and add 1/3 cup of ground almonds and a few drops of almond extract.

Makes about 12

INGREDIENTS
6 tbsp butter
generous 1/2 cup confectioner's sugar
finely grated rind of 1 small lemon
1 egg yolk
1 1/2 cups all-purpose flour
pinch of salt

TO DECORATE
2 egg yolks
red and green edible food coloring

1 In a large bowl, beat the butter, sugar and lemon rind together until pale and fluffy. Beat in the egg yolk, and then sift in the flour and the salt. Knead together to form a smooth dough. Wrap in plastic wrap and chill for 30 minutes.

2 Preheat the oven to 375°F. On a lightly floured surface, roll out the dough to 1/8 in thick. Using a 2 1/2 in fluted cutter, stamp out as many cookies as you can, with the cutter dipped in flour to prevent it from sticking to the dough.

3 Transfer the cookies on to lightly greased baking trays. Mark the tops lightly with a 1 in holly leaf cutter and use a 1/4 in plain piping nozzle for the berries. Chill for 10 minutes, until firm.

4 Meanwhile, put each egg yolk into a small cup. Mix red food coloring into one and green food coloring into the other. Using a small, clean paintbrush, carefully paint the colors on to the cookies. Bake the cookies for 10–12 minutes, or until they begin to color around the edges. Let them cool slightly on the baking trays, and then transfer them to a wire rack to cool completely.

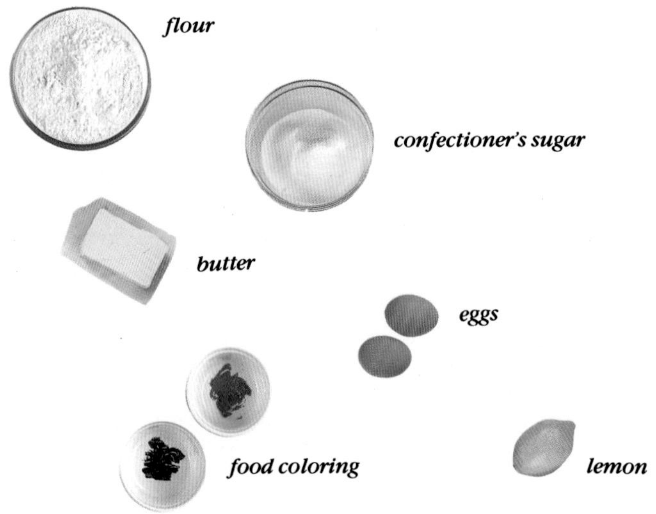

Chocolate Kisses

These rich little cookies look pretty mixed together on a plate and dusted with confectioner's sugar. Serve them with ice cream or simply with coffee.

Makes 24

INGREDIENTS
- 3 oz dark chocolate, broken into squares
- 3 oz white chocolate, broken into squares
- ½ cup butter
- 8 tbsp superfine sugar
- 2 eggs
- 2 cups all-purpose flour
- confectioner's sugar, to decorate

1 Put each chocolate into a small bowl and melt it over a pan of hot, but not boiling, water. Set aside to cool.

2 Whisk together the butter and confectioner's sugar until they are pale and fluffy. Beat in the eggs, one at a time. Then sift in the flour and mix well.

3 Halve the mixture and divide it between the two bowls of chocolate. Mix each chocolate in thoroughly. Knead the doughs until smooth, wrap them in plastic wrap and chill them for 1 hour. Preheat the oven to 375°F.

4 Shape slightly rounded teaspoonfuls of both doughs roughly into balls. Roll the balls in the palms of your hands to make neater ball shapes. Arrange the balls on greased baking sheets and bake them for 10–12 minutes. Dust with sifted confectioner's sugar and then transfer them to a wire rack to cool.

Ginger Florentines

These colorful, chewy cookies are delicious served with ice cream and are certain to disappear as soon as they are served. Store them in an airtight container.

Makes 30

INGREDIENTS
4 tbsp butter
8 tbsp superfine sugar
3 rounded tbsp mixed candied cherries, chopped
2 rounded tbsp candied orange peel, chopped
½ cup slivered almonds
½ cup chopped walnuts
1 tbsp crystallized ginger, chopped
2 tbsp all-purpose flour
½ tsp ground ginger

TO FINISH
2 oz dark chocolate, or chocolate chips, melted
2 oz white chocolate, or chocolate chips, melted

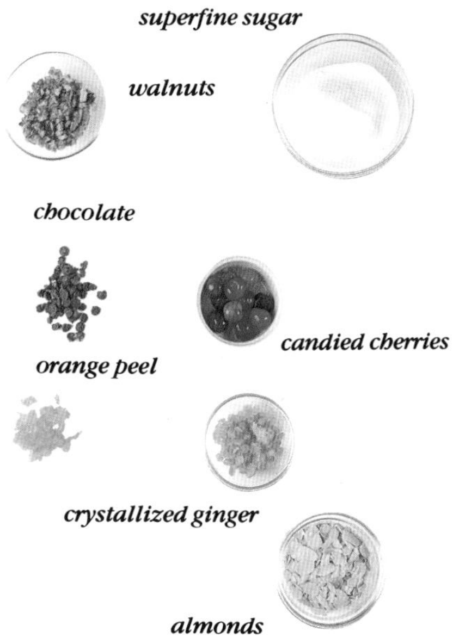

1 Preheat the oven to 350°F. Whisk the butter and sugar together until they are light and fluffy. Thoroughly mix in all the remaining ingredients, except the melted chocolate.

2 Cut a piece of non-stick baking parchment to fit your baking trays. Put 4 small spoonfuls of the mixture on to each tray, spacing them well apart to allow for spreading. Flatten the cookies and bake them for 5 minutes.

3 Remove the cookies from the oven and flatten them with a wet fork, shaping them into neat rounds. Return to the oven for 3–4 minutes, until they are golden brown.

4 Let them cool on the baking trays for 2 minutes, to firm up, and then carefully transfer them to a wire rack. When they are cold and firm, spread the melted dark chocolate on the undersides of half the biscuits and spread the melted white chocolate on the undersides of the rest.

Rosehip Cordial

If you get the chance to collect rosehips from the hedges, this cordial makes a wonderfully Christmassy drink. If you can't find rosehips, replace them with black currants.

Makes 7½ cups

INGREDIENTS
11¼ cups water
6 cups rosehips
4 cups granulated sugar

rosehips

COOK'S TIP

To sterilize, dissolve one crushed water sterilizing tablet in 1 tbsp of boiled water and add to each 2½ cups of cordial. Pour the cordial into the sterilized bottles and seal with a cork or stopper. Store the cordial in the fridge.

1 Sterilize 4 small bottles. Place 7½ cups of water in a large heavy-based saucepan and bring to a boil. Put the rosehips in a food processor and process until finely chopped. Add to the boiling water, bring back to a boil, cover with a lid and turn off the heat. Leave to infuse for 15 minutes.

2 Suspend a jelly bag and place a bowl underneath. Sterilize the jelly bag by pouring boiling water through the bag, then discard the water and replace the bowl. Strain the rosehips through the jelly bag and leave until the pulp is almost dry.

3 Return the pulp to the saucepan with another 3¾ cups of water, bring to a boil, cover and infuse for 10 minutes as above and strain, mixing the 2 juices together. Pour the juices back into a clean saucepan and boil to reduce the mixture by half, to about 4 cups. Stir in the sugar, heat gently until dissolved, then boil for 5 minutes. Sterilize the cordial if it is going to be kept for longer than 4 weeks.

Christmas Spirit

This colorful drink has a sharp but sweet taste. It is excellent served as a winter warmer or after a meal, but it is also good as a summer drink with crushed ice.

Makes 3 cups

INGREDIENTS
2 cups cranberries
2 clementines
2 cups granulated sugar
1 cinnamon stick
2 cups vodka

cranberries

clementines

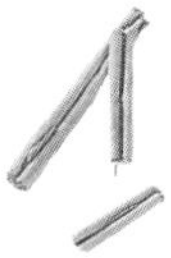
cinnamon sticks

1 Sterilize a large jar and lid. Place the cranberries in a food processor or use a pestle and mortar to crush them evenly. Spoon the cranberries into the jar. Pare the rind thinly from the clementines taking care not to include the white pith. Squeeze the juice and add with the rind to the jar.

2 Add the sugar, cinnamon stick and vodka to the jar and seal with the lid or a double thickness of plastic, and tie down securely. Shake the jar well to combine all the ingredients.

3 Store in a cool place for 1 month, shaking the jar daily for 2 weeks, then occasionally. When the drink has matured, sterilize some small pretty bottles and using a funnel with a filter paper inside, strain the liquid into the bottles and cork immediately. Label clearly and tie a gift tag around the neck.

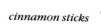

Brandy Alexander

A warming digestif, made from a blend of crème de cacao, brandy and double cream, that can be served at the end of the meal with coffee.

Serves 1

INGREDIENTS
1 measure/$1^1/_2$ tablespoons brandy
1 measure/$1^1/_2$ tablespoons crème de cacao
1 measure/$1^1/_2$ tablespoons heavy cream
whole nutmeg, to decorate

crème de cacao

nutmeg

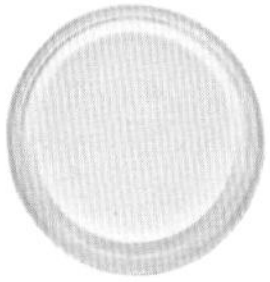
heavy cream

brandy

VARIATION
Warm the brandy and the heavy cream gently and add to a blender with the crème de cacao. Blend until frothy. Serve with a cinnamon stick.

1 Half fill the cocktail shaker with ice and pour in the brandy, crème de cacao and the cream.

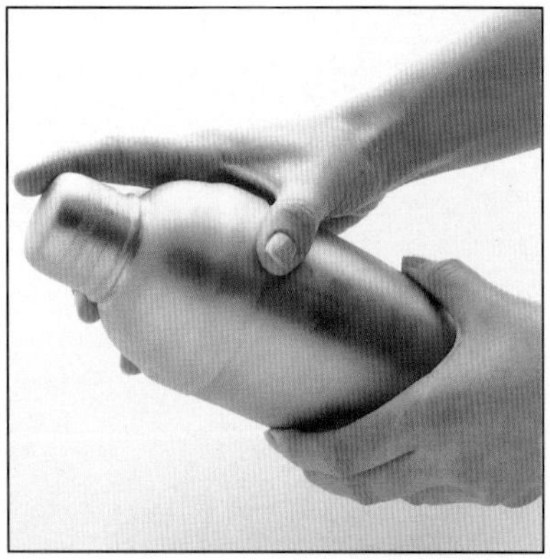

2 Shake for about 20 seconds to mix thoroughly.

3 Strain the chilled cocktail into a small wine glass.

4 Finely grate a little nutmeg over the top of the cocktail.

Brandy Blazer

A warming after-dinner tipple, ideally served with fresh vanilla ice cream or caramelized oranges.

Serves 1

INGREDIENTS

$^1/_2$ orange
1 lemon
2 measures/3 tablespoons Cognac
1 sugar cube
$^1/_2$ measure/2 teaspoons Kahlúa
orange rind, threaded
 on to a cocktail stick, to decorate

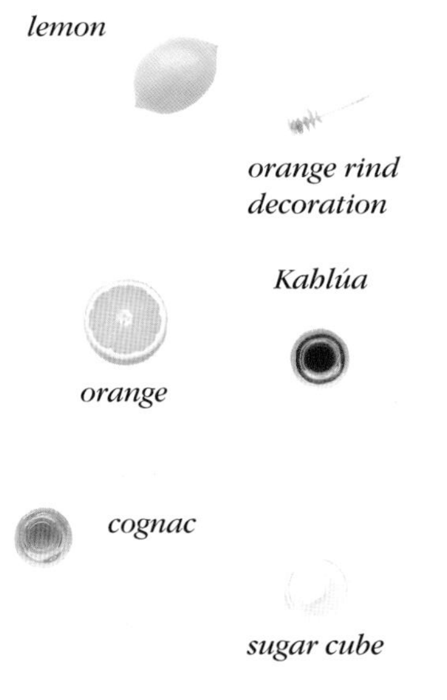

VARIATION

Pour the hot Cognac and Kahlúa mix into freshly brewed coffee and serve the drink black.

1 Pare the rind from the orange and lemon, removing and discarding as much of the white pith as possible.

2 Put the Cognac, sugar cube, lemon and orange rind in a small pan.

3 Heat gently, then remove from the heat, light a match and pass the flame close to the surface of the liquid. The alcohol will burn with a low, blue flame for about a minute. Blow out the flame.

4 Add the Kahlúa to the pan and strain into a heat-resistant liqueur glass. Decorate with a toothpick threaded with orange rind, then serve warm.

Apricot Bellini

This is a version of the famous apéritif served at Harry's Bar in Venice. Instead of the usual peaches and peach brandy, apricot nectar and apricot brandy make this a tempting variation.

VARIATION

Instead of apricots and apricot brandy, use fresh raspberries and raspberry-infused gin or syrup.

Serves 6–8

INGREDIENTS

3 apricots
2 teaspoons lemon juice
2 teaspoons sugar syrup
2 measures/3 tablespoons apricot brandy or peach schnapps
1 bottle *brut* champagne or dry sparkling wine, chilled

lemon juice

apricots

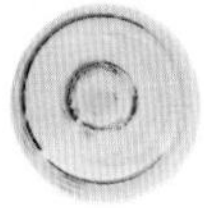

sparkling wine

apricot brandy

sugar syrup

1 Plunge the apricots into boiling water for 2 minutes to loosen the skins.

2 Peel and pit the apricots. Discard the pits and skin.

3 Process the apricot flesh with the lemon juice until you have a smooth purée. Sweeten to taste with sugar syrup, then strain.

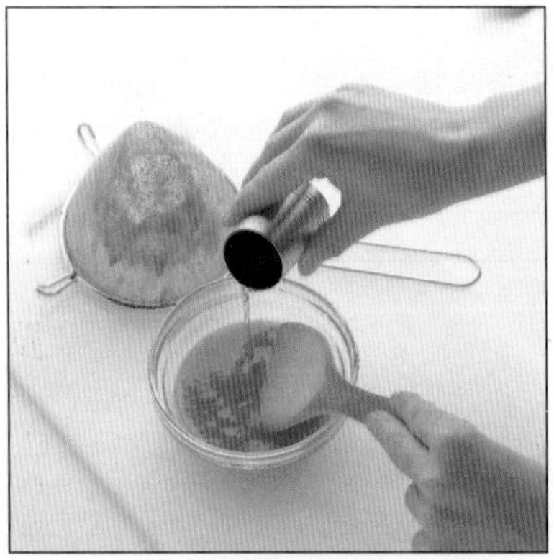

4 Add the brandy or peach schnapps to the apricot nectar and stir together.

5 Divide the apricot nectar among chilled champagne flutes.

6 Finish the drinks with chilled champagne or sparkling wine.

Festive Liqueurs

These are easier to make than wines and may be made with a variety of flavors and spirits. All these liqueurs should be allowed to mature for 3 months before drinking.

Makes 3¾ cups of each liqueur

PLUM BRANDY
1 lb plums
1 cup raw sugar
2½ cups brandy

FRUIT GIN
3 cups raspberries, black currants or purple plums
1½ cups granulated sugar
3 cups gin

CITRUS WHISKY
1 large orange
1 small lemon
1 lime
1 cup granulated sugar
2½ cups whisky

1 Sterilize 3 jars and lids. Wash and halve the plums, remove the pits and finely slice. Place the plums in the sterilized jar with the sugar and brandy. Crack 3 pits, remove the kernels and chop. Add to the jar and stir until well blended.

2 Place the raspberries, blackcurrants or plums into the prepared jar. If using plums, prick the surface of the fruit using a stainless steel pin to extract its juice. Add the sugar and gin and stir until well blended.

3 To make the Citrus Whisky, first scrub the fruit. Using a sharp knife or potato peeler pare the rind from the fruit, taking care not to include the white pith. Squeeze out all the juice and place in the jar with the fruit rinds. Add the sugar and whisky, stir until well blended.

4 Cover the jars with lids or double thickness plastic tied well down. Store the jars in a cool place for 3 months.

5 Shake the Fruit Gin every day for 1 month, and then occasionally. Shake the Plum Brandy and Citrus Whisky every day for 2 weeks, then occasionally. Sterilize the chosen bottles and corks or stoppers for each liqueur.

6 When each liqueur is ready to be bottled, strain, then pour into the bottles through a funnel fitted with a filter paper. Fit the corks or stoppers and label with a festive label.

Virgin Prairie Oyster

A superior pick-me-up and a variation on the Bloody Mary. The tomato base can be drunk without the raw egg yolk if it does not appeal to you. Use only fresh free-range eggs.

Serves 1

INGREDIENTS
¾ cup tomato juice
2 teaspoons Worcestershire sauce
1–2 teaspoons balsamic vinegar
1 egg yolk
cayenne pepper, to taste

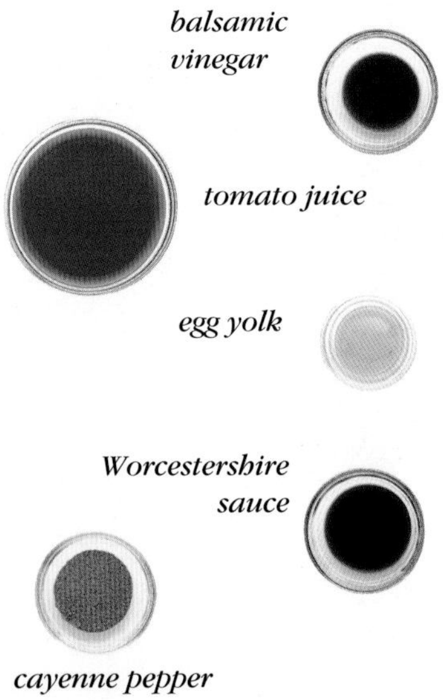

1 Measure the tomato juice into a large bar glass and stir over plenty of ice until well chilled.

2 Strain into a tall tumbler half filled with ice cubes.

3 Add the Worcestershire sauce and balsamic vinegar to taste and mix with a swizzle stick.

4 Float the egg yolk on top and lightly dust with cayenne pepper.

VARIATION

Shake together equal quantities of fresh grapefruit juice and tomato juice with a dash of Worcestershire sauce. Strain into a tall and narrow highball glass.

Volunteer

This drink is ideal for a lazy summer afternoon. It's also a fine cocktail to serve the designated driver at a party. It was devised and drunk during a very rough channel crossing in too small a boat!

Serves 1

INGREDIENTS

2 measures/3 tablespoons lime cordial
2–3 dashes angostura bitters
7 measures/⅔ cup chilled tonic water
decorative ice cubes, to serve
frozen slices of lime, to decorate

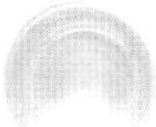

tonic water

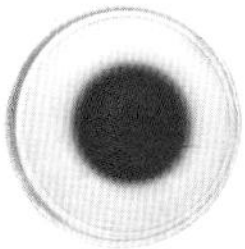

angostura bitters

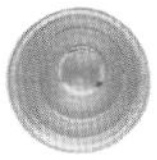

lime cordial

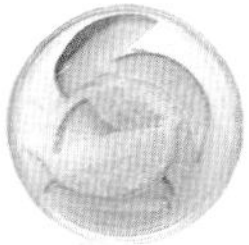

frozen lime slice

1 Place the lime cordial at the bottom of the glass and shake in the angostura bitters to taste.

2 Add a few decorative ice cubes to the glass, if liked.

3 Finish with tonic water and add the frozen lime slices.

VARIATION

Use fresh lime or grapefruit juice and a splash of sugar syrup instead of the lime cordial, and finish with ginger ale.

Chocolate Boxes

These tiny chocolate boxes make the perfect containers for handmade chocolates or candies. Use white or milk chocolate with dark trimmings to vary the theme.

Makes 4

INGREDIENTS
8 squares plain, or milk chocolate, melted
2 squares white chocolate

DECORATION
handmade chocolates or candies, to fill
2 yd ribbon, ½ in wide

milk chocolate

plain chocolate

white chocolate

1 Line a large cookie sheet with parchment paper. Remove the bowl of melted chocolate from the heat and wipe the condensation off the base of the bowl.

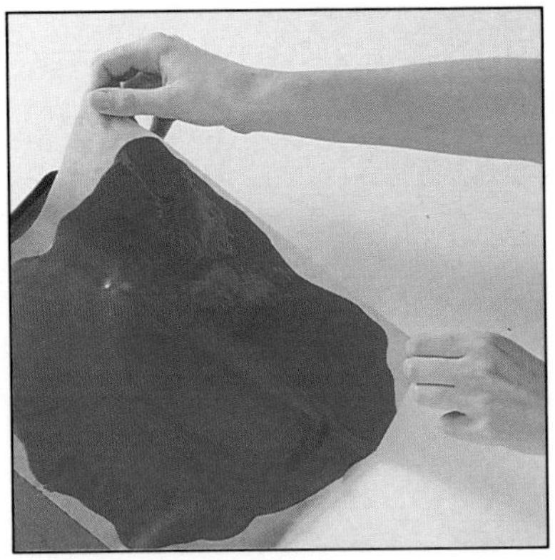

2 Pour all but 1 tbsp of the chocolate over the parchment paper and quickly spread to the edges using a metal spatula. Pick up 2 corners of the paper and drop; do this several times on each side to level the surface of the chocolate.

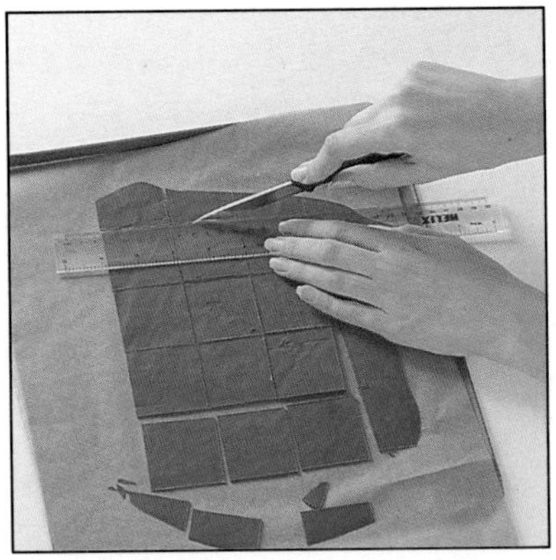

3 Leave the chocolate until almost set but still pliable. Place a clean piece of parchment paper on the surface, invert the chocolate sheet and peel the paper away from the back of the chocolate. Using a ruler and a scalpel or sharp knife, measure and cut the chocolate sheet into 2 in squares to form the sides of the boxes. Measure and cut out 2¼ in squares for the lids and bases of each of the boxes.

4 To assemble the boxes, paint a little of the remaining melted chocolate along the top edges of a chocolate square using a fine brush. Place the side pieces in position one at a time, brushing the side edges to join the 4 squares together to form a box. Leave to set. Repeat to make the remaining 3 boxes.

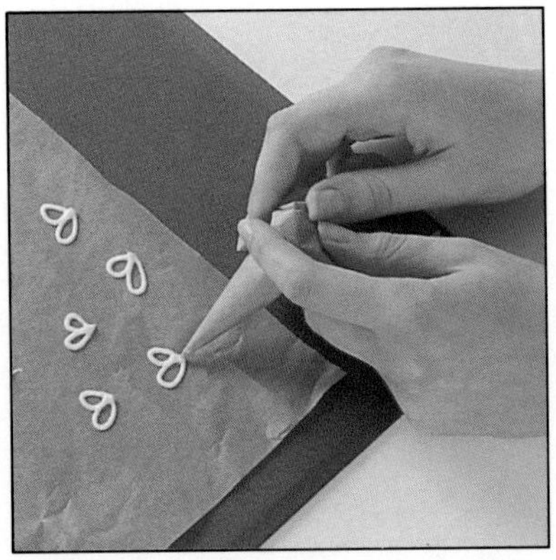

5 Melt the white chocolate and spoon into a waxed paper piping bag. Fold down the top and snip off the point. Pipe 20 chocolate loops onto a sheet of parchment paper and leave them to set.

6 Decorate the sides of the boxes with chocolate loops, each secured with a bead of white chocolate. Alternatively, wrap a ribbon carefully around each box and tie a bow, having filled the boxes with chocolates or candies. Pack into gift boxes.

Fruit Fondant Chocolates

These chocolates are simple to make using pre-formed plastic molds, yet look very professional. Fruit fondant is available from sugarcraft stores and comes in a variety of flavors including coffee and nut. Try a mixture of flavors using a small quantity of each, or use just a single flavor.

Makes 24

Ingredients
8 squares plain, milk or white chocolate
1 cup real fruit liquid fondant
3–4 tsp cooled boiled water

Decoration
1 tbsp melted plain, milk or white chocolate

milk chocolate

plain chocolate

white chocolate

1 Melt the chocolate. Use a piece of cotton wool to polish the insides of the chocolate molds, ensuring that they are spotlessly clean. Fill up the shapes in one plastic tray to the top, leave for a few seconds, then invert the tray over the bowl of melted chocolate allowing the excess chocolate to fall back into the bowl. Sit the tray on the work surface and draw a metal spatula across the top to remove the excess chocolate and to neaten the edges. Chill until set. Repeat to fill the remaining trays.

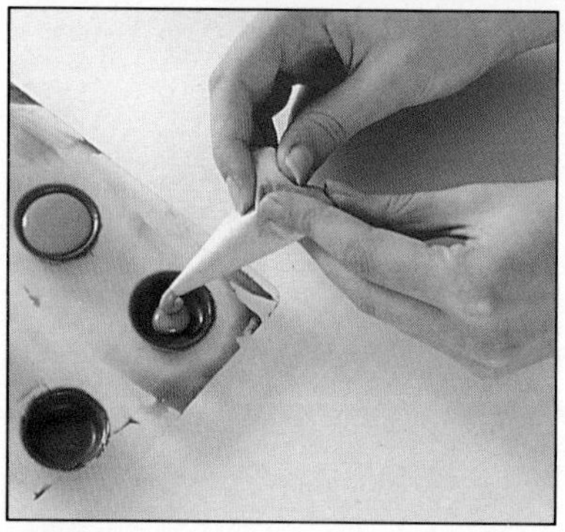

2 Sift the fruit fondant mixture into a bowl. Gradually stir in enough water to give it the consistency of thick cream. Place the fondant in a waxed paper piping bag, fold down the top and snip off the end. Fill each chocolate case almost to the top by piping in the fondant. Leave for 30 minutes or until a skin has formed on the surface of the fondant.

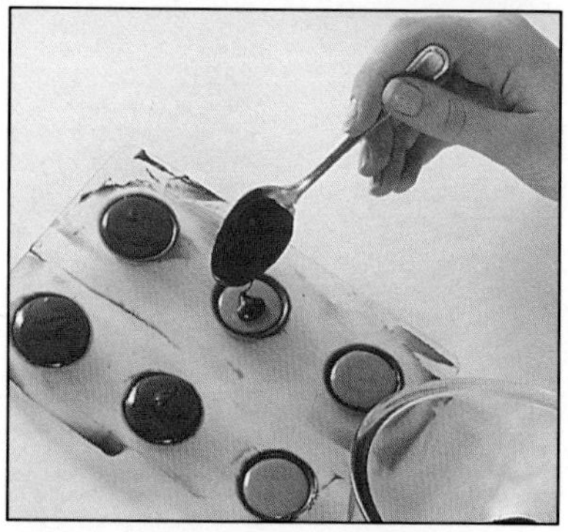

3 Spoon the remaining melted chocolate over the fondant to fill each mold level with the top. Chill until the chocolate has set hard. Invert the tray and press out the chocolates one by one. Place the melted chocolate of a contrasting color into a waxed paper piping bag, fold down the top, snip off the point and pipe lines across the top of each chocolate. Allow to set, then pack into pretty boxes and tie with ribbon.

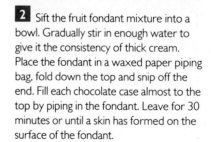

Chocolate Truffles

These are popular with almost everybody; simply use different combinations of chocolate and flavorings to make your favorites.

Makes 60

INGREDIENTS
4 squares plain chocolate
4 squares milk chocolate
6 squares white chocolate
¾ cup heavy cream

FLAVORINGS
2 tbsp dark rum
2 tbsp Tia Maria
2 tbsp apricot brandy

COATINGS
3 tbsp coarsely grated plain chocolate
3 tbsp coarsely grated milk chocolate
3 tbsp coarsely grated white chocolate

milk chocolate

plain chocolate

white chocolate

1 Melt each type of chocolate in a separate bowl. Place the cream in a small saucepan and heat gently until hot but not boiling. Allow to cool. Stir ⅓ of the cream into each of the bowls and blend evenly. Add the rum to the plain chocolate and whisk until the mixture becomes lighter in color. Whisk the Tia Maria into the milk chocolate and lastly whisk the apricot brandy into the white chocolate.

2 Allow the 3 mixtures to thicken, giving them an occasional stir, until they are thick enough to divide into equal spoonfuls. Line 3 cookie sheets with parchment paper. Place about 20 teaspoons of each flavored chocolate mixture, well spaced apart, onto the 3 cookie sheets and chill until firm enough to roll into small balls.

3 Place each of the grated chocolates into separate dishes. Shape the plain chocolate truffles into neat balls and roll in grated plain chocolate to coat evenly. Repeat with the milk chocolate truffles and grated milk chocolate and the white chocolate truffles and grated white chocolate. Chill the truffles until firm, then arrange neatly in boxes, bags or tins and tie with festive ribbon.

Chocolate Nut Clusters

If you do not possess a sugar thermometer, you can test cooked sugar for 'soft ball stage' by spooning a small amount into a bowl of cold water: it should form a soft ball when rolled between finger and thumb.

Makes about 30

INGREDIENTS

2¼ cups heavy cream
2 tbsp unsalted butter, cut into small pieces
1½ cups corn syrup
1 cup granulated sugar
½ cup (packed) brown sugar
pinch of salt
1 tbsp vanilla extract
3 cups hazelnuts, pecans, walnuts, brazil nuts or unsalted peanuts, or a combination
14 oz semi-sweet chocolate, chopped
2 tbsp white vegetable fat

semi-sweet chocolate

brazil nuts

walnuts

hazelnuts
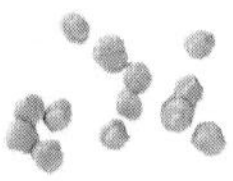

peanuts

pecans

1 Lightly oil 2 cookie sheets with vegetable oil. In a large heavy-based saucepan over medium heat, cook the cream, butter, corn syrup, sugars and salt, stirring occasionally, until sugars dissolve and butter melts, about 3 minutes. Bring to a boil and continue cooking, stirring frequently, until caramel reaches 240°F (soft ball stage) on a sugar thermometer, about 1 hour.

2 Place bottom of saucepan into a pan of cold water to stop cooking or transfei caramel to a smaller saucepan. Cool slightly, then stir in vanilla.

3 Stir nuts into caramel until well-coated. Using an oiled tablespoon, drop tablespoonfuls of nut mixture on to prepared sheets, about 1 in apart. If mixture hardens, return to heat to soften. Refrigerate clusters for 30 minutes until firm and cold, or leave in a cool place until hardened.

4 Using a metal spatula, transfer clusters to a wire rack placed over a cookie sheet to catch drips. In a medium saucepan, over low heat, melt chocolate and white vegetable fat, stirring until smooth. Cool slightly.

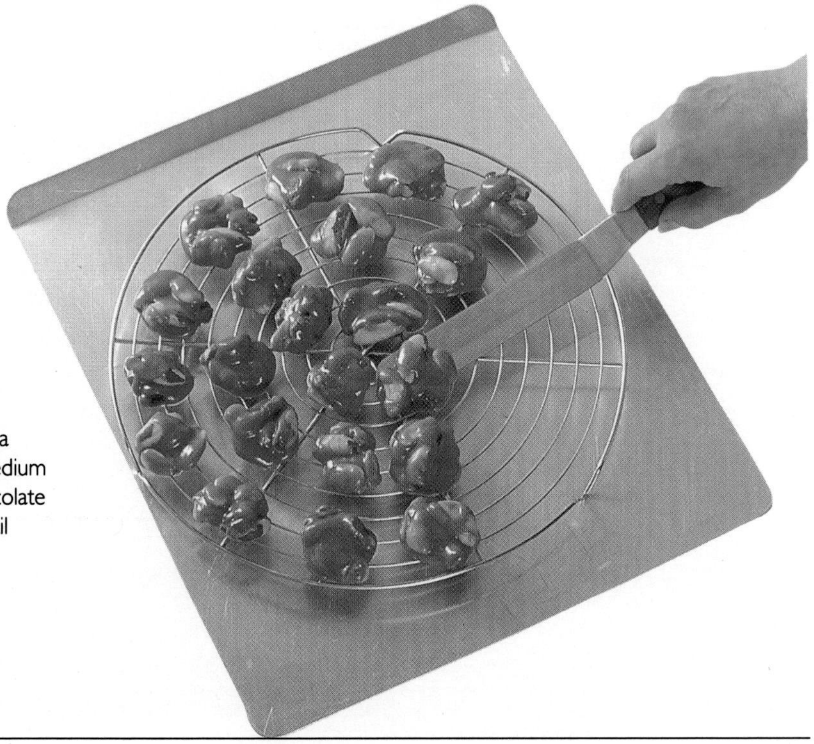

5 Spoon chocolate over each cluster, being sure to cover completely. Alternatively, using a fork, dip each cluster into chocolate and lift out, tapping on edge of saucepan to shake off excess.

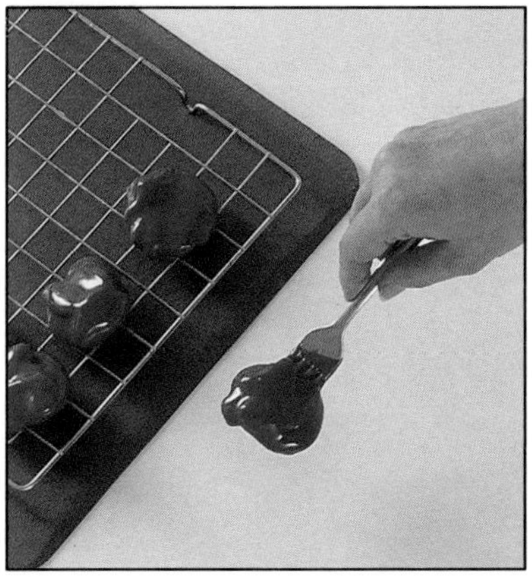

6 Place on a wire rack over a cookie sheet. Allow to set for 2 hours until hardened. Store in an airtight container.

Chocolate Christmas Cups

To crystalize cranberries for decoration, beat an egg white until frothy. Dip each berry first in the egg white then in superfine sugar. Place on sheets of waxed paper to dry.

Makes about 35 cups

INGREDIENTS
70–80 foil or paper candy cases
10 oz semi-sweet chocolate, broken into pieces
6 oz cooked, cold Christmas pudding
⅓ cup brandy or whisky
chocolate leaves and crystallized cranberries to decorate

semi-sweet chocolate

brandy

1 Place the chocolate in a medium bowl over a saucepan of hot water. Place saucepan over low heat until chocolate is melted, stirring frequently until chocolate is smooth. Using a pastry brush, brush or coat the bottom and side of about 35 candy cases. Allow to set, then repeat, reheating melted chocolate if necessary, applying a second coat. Leave to cool and set completely, 4–5 hours or overnight. Reserve remaining chocolate.

2 Crumble the Christmas pudding in a small bowl; sprinkle with brandy or whisky and allow to stand for 30–40 minutes, until brandy is absorbed.

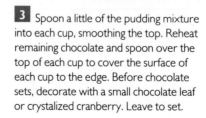

3 Spoon a little of the pudding mixture into each cup, smoothing the top. Reheat remaining chocolate and spoon over the top of each cup to cover the surface of each cup to the edge. Before chocolate sets, decorate with a small chocolate leaf or crystalized cranberry. Leave to set.

4 When completely set, carefully peel off the cases and place in clean foil cases. Decorate with chocolate leaves and crystalized berries.

Chocolate Peppermint Crisps

If you do not have a sugar thermometer, test cooked sugar for 'hard ball stage' by spooning a few drops into a bowl of cold water; it should form a hard ball when rolled between fingers.

Makes 30 crisps

INGREDIENTS
¼ cup granulated sugar
¼ cup water
1 tsp peppermint extract
8 oz bittersweet or semi-sweet chocolate, chopped

bittersweet chocolate

peppermint extract

1 Lightly brush a large cookie sheet with flavorless oil. In a saucepan over medium heat, heat the sugar and water, swirling pan gently until sugar dissolves. Boil rapidly until sugar reaches 280°F on a sugar thermometer (see introduction). Remove pan from heat and add peppermint extract; swirl to blend. Pour on to the cookie sheet and allow to set and cool completely.

2 When cold, break into small pieces. Place in a food processor fitted with the metal blade and process until fine crumbs form; do not over-process.

3 Line 2 cookie sheets with parchment paper or waxed paper. Place chocolate in a small bowl over a small saucepan of hot water. Place over very low heat until chocolate has melted, stirring frequently until smooth. Remove from heat and stir in peppermint mixture.

4 Using a teaspoon, drop small mounds on to prepared sheets. Using the back of the spoon, spread to 1½ in rounds. Cool, then refrigerate to set for about 1 hour. Peel off the paper and store in airtight containers with waxed paper between the layers.

Chocolate Christmas Cakes

This recipe may also be made as one 8 in square cake but 4 individual cakes look even more tempting and may be packed into pretty boxes.

Makes 4

INGREDIENTS
$2\frac{1}{2}$ cups self-rising flour
1 tbsp baking powder
$\frac{1}{4}$ cup cocoa powder
1 cup 2 tbsp superfine sugar
$\frac{2}{3}$ cup sunflower oil
$1\frac{1}{2}$ cups water

ICING AND DECORATION
6 in square silver cake boards
6 tbsp Apricot Glaze (see Introduction)
$2\frac{1}{4}$ lb marzipan
2 lb chocolate fondant
red, yellow and green food colorings
2 yd red ribbon
2 yd green ribbon

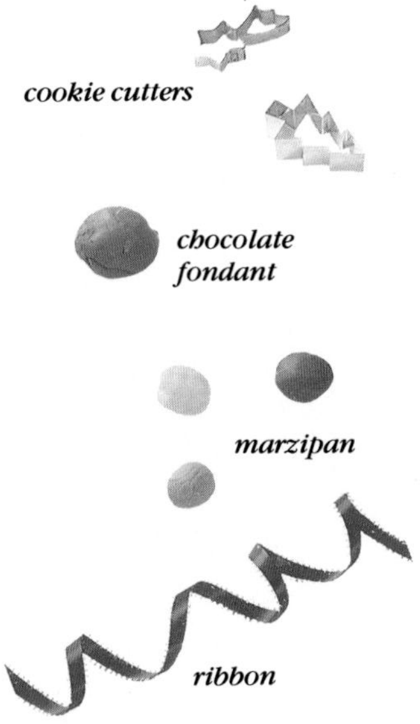

1 Preheat the oven to 325°F. Grease an 8 in square cake pan and line with waxed paper. Sift the flour, baking powder, cocoa powder and sugar into a mixing bowl.

2 Add the oil and water and mix together with a wooden spoon, beating until smooth and glossy. Pour into the prepared pan and bake in the oven for about 1 hour or until the cake springs back when pressed in the center.

3 Cool the cake in the pan for 15 minutes, then turn out, remove the paper and invert onto a wire rack. When completely cold, cut into 4 equal pieces, place each on a separate cake board and brush with Apricot Glaze.

4 Divide the marzipan into 4 equal pieces and roll out a piece large enough to cover one cake. Place over the cake, press neatly into shape and trim off the excess marzipan at the base of the board. Knead the trimmings together and repeat to cover the remaining 3 cakes.

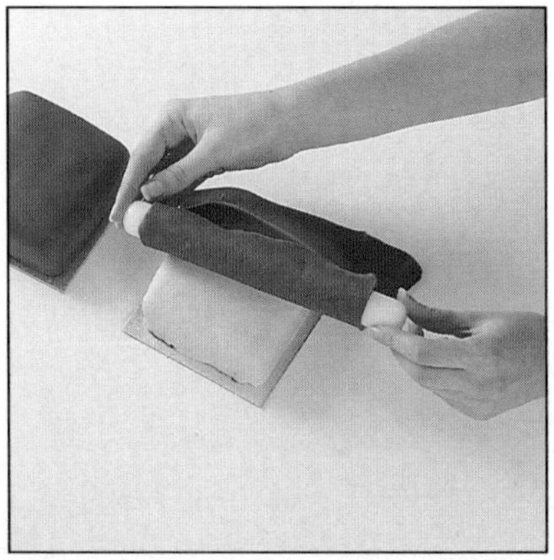

5 Divide the chocolate fondant into 4 pieces and repeat the process, rolling out each piece thinly to cover each cake. Color the remaining marzipan $\frac{1}{3}$ red, $\frac{1}{3}$ yellow and $\frac{1}{3}$ green with the food colorings. Thinly roll out each piece and cut into $\frac{1}{2}$ in strips.

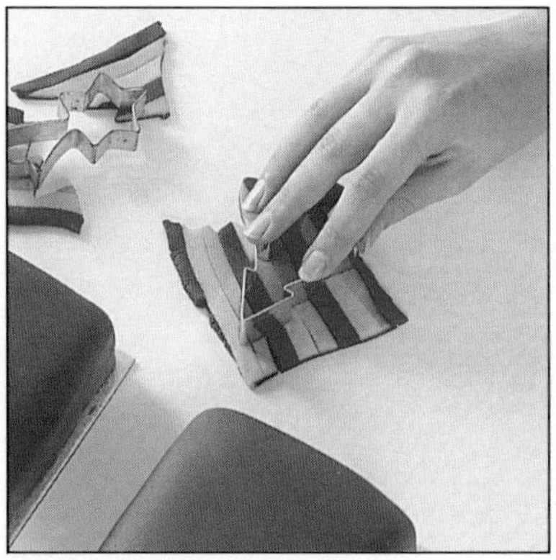

6 Lay alternate strips together and cut out 4 shapes using cookie cutters. Arrange the shapes on top of each cake. Measure and fit the red and green ribbons around each cake and tie a bow. Pack into pretty boxes, tie with ribbons and label.

Festive Gingerbread

These brightly decorated gingerbread cookies are fun to make and may be used as edible Christmas tree decorations.

Makes 20

INGREDIENTS
2 tbsp corn syrup
1 tbsp black molasses
¼ cup light brown sugar
2 tbsp butter
1½ cups flour
¾ tsp baking soda
½ tsp ground cinnamon
1½ tsp ground ginger
1 egg yolk

ICING AND DECORATION
½ quantity Royal Icing (see Introduction)
red, yellow and green food colorings
brightly colored ribbons

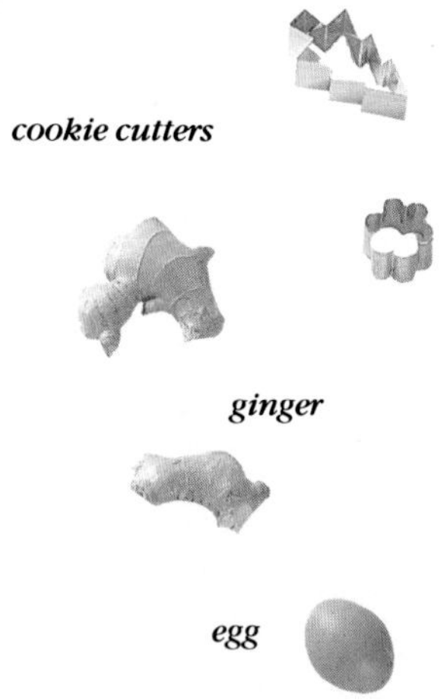

1 Preheat the oven to 375°F. Line several cookie sheets with parchment paper. Place the syrup, molasses, sugar and butter into a saucepan. Heat gently, stirring occasionally, until the butter has melted.

2 Sift the flour, baking soda, cinnamon and ginger into a bowl. Using a wooden spoon stir in the molasses mixture and the egg yolk and mix to a soft dough. Knead on a lightly floured surface until smooth.

3 Roll out the dough thinly and using a selection of festive cutters, stamp out as many shapes as possible, kneading and re-rolling the dough as necessary. Arrange the shapes well spaced apart on the cookie sheets. Make a hole in the top of each shape using a drinking straw if you wish to use the cookies as hanging decorations.

4 Bake in the oven for 15–20 minutes or until risen and golden and leave to cool on the cookie sheets before transferring to a wire rack using a metal spatula.

5 Divide the Royal Icing into 4 and color ¼ red, ¼ yellow and ¼ green using the food colorings. Make 4 waxed paper piping bags and fill each one with the different colored icings. Fold down the tops and snip off the points.

6 Pipe lines, dots, and zigzags on the gingerbread cookies using the colored icings. Leave to dry. Thread ribbons through the holes in the cookies.

Festive Shortbread

Light, crisp shortbread looks so professional when shaped in a mold, although you could also shape it by hand.

Makes 2 large or 8 individual shortbreads

INGREDIENTS
¾ cup plain flour
¼ cup cornstarch
¼ cup superfine sugar
½ cup unsalted butter

flour

sugar

butter

1 Preheat the oven to 325°F. Lightly flour the mold and line a cookie sheet with parchment paper. Sift the flour, cornstarch and sugar into a mixing bowl. Cut the butter into pieces and rub into the flour mixture until it binds together and you can knead it into a soft dough.

2 Place the dough into the mold and press to fit neatly. Invert the mold onto the cookie sheet and tap firmly to release the dough shape. Bake in the oven for 35–40 minutes or until pale golden.

3 Sprinkle the top of the shortbread with a little sugar and cool on the cookie sheet. Wrap in cellophane paper or place in a box tied with ribbon.

Christmas Tree Cookies

These cookies make an appealing gift. They look wonderful hung on a Christmas tree or in front of a window to catch the light.

Makes 12

INGREDIENTS
1½ cups plain flour
5 tbsp butter
3 tbsp superfine sugar
1 egg white
2 tbsp orange juice
8 oz colored fruit candies

DECORATION
colored ribbons

1 Preheat the oven to 350°F. Line 2 cookie sheets with parchment paper. Sift the flour into a mixing bowl. Cut the butter into pieces and rub into the flour until the mixture resembles fine breadcrumbs. Stir in the sugar, egg white and enough orange juice to form a soft dough. Knead on a lightly floured surface until smooth.

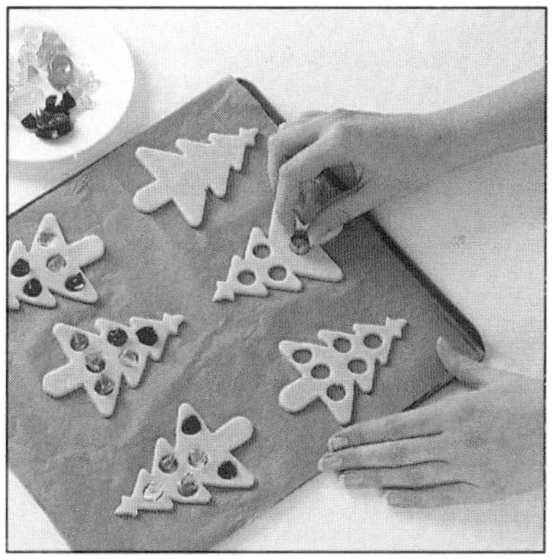

2 Roll out thinly and stamp out as many shapes as possible using a Christmas tree cutter. Transfer the shapes to the lined cookie sheets well spaced apart. Knead the trimmings together. Using a ½ in round cutter or the end of a plain meringue piping nozzle, stamp out and remove 6 rounds from each tree shape. Cut each candy into 3 and place a piece in each hole. Make a small hole at the top of each tree to thread through the ribbon.

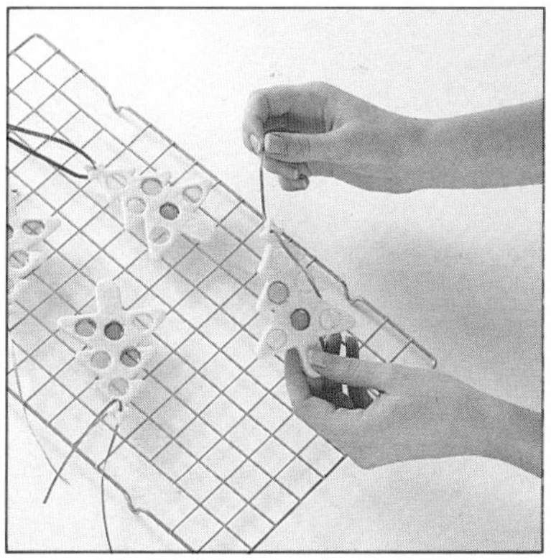

3 Bake in the oven for 15–20 minutes, until the cookies are slightly gold in color and the candies have melted and filled the holes. Cool on the cookie sheets. Repeat until you have used up the remaining cookie dough and candies. Thread short lengths of ribbon through the holes so that you can hang up the cookies.

Gingerbread House

This gingerbread house makes a memorable family gift, especially if filled with lots of little gifts and surprises.

Makes 1

INGREDIENTS
6 tbsp corn syrup
2 tbsp black molasses
⅓ cup light brown sugar
5 tbsp butter
4 cups flour
1 tbsp ground ginger
1 tbsp baking soda
2 egg yolks
8 oz barley sugar candies

ICING AND DECORATION
1 quantity Royal Icing (see Introduction)
10 in square silver cake board

black molasses

cookie cutters

barley sugar candies

eggs

corn syrup

1 Preheat the oven to 375°F. Line several cookie sheets with parchment paper. Cut out the templates. Place the syrup, molasses, sugar and butter in a saucepan and heat gently, stirring occasionally until melted.

2 Sift the flour, ginger and baking soda into a bowl. Add the egg yolks and pour in the molasses mixture, stirring with a wooden spoon to form a soft dough. Knead on a lightly floured surface until smooth and place in a polythene bag. Cut off ⅓ of the dough and roll out thinly.

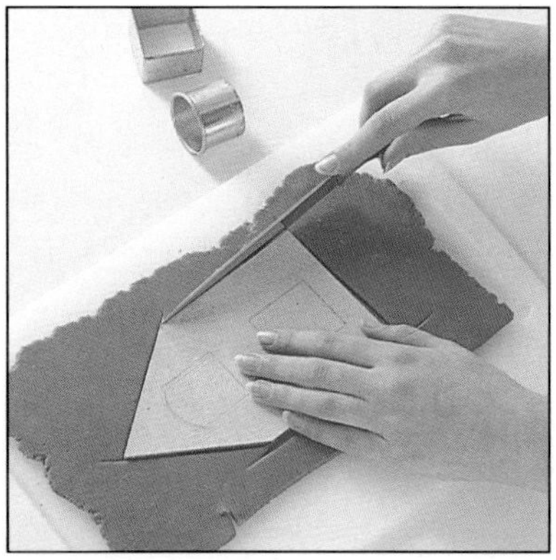

3 Place the template for the end walls at one end and cut neatly round the shape using a sharp knife. Repeat to cut another end wall. Place on the cookie sheet. Using a 1 in round cutter, stamp out 1 round window for each piece. Cut a door shape on each end wall, using the square cutter, then rounding off the tops. Place a candy in each of the windows and bake in the oven for 8–10 minutes until the candy has filled the frame and the gingerbread is golden brown. Cool on the cookie sheet.

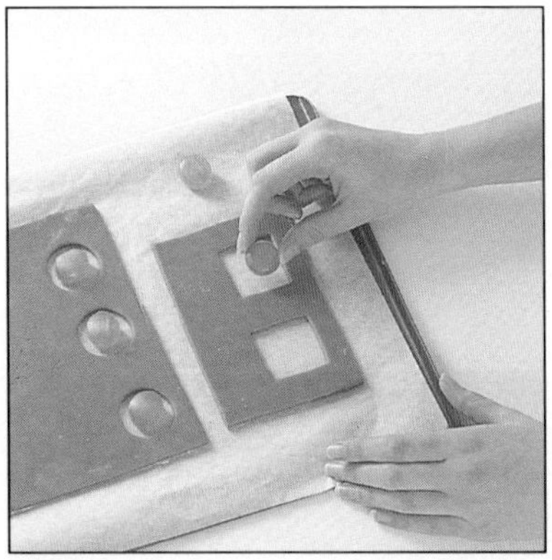

4 Repeat the above instructions using the remaining dough for the 2 side walls and the 2 roof pieces. Using a 1 in square cutter, stamp out 2 window shapes for each wall piece. Using a 1 in round cutter, stamp out 3 round windows for each roof piece. Place candies in the openings and bake as before.

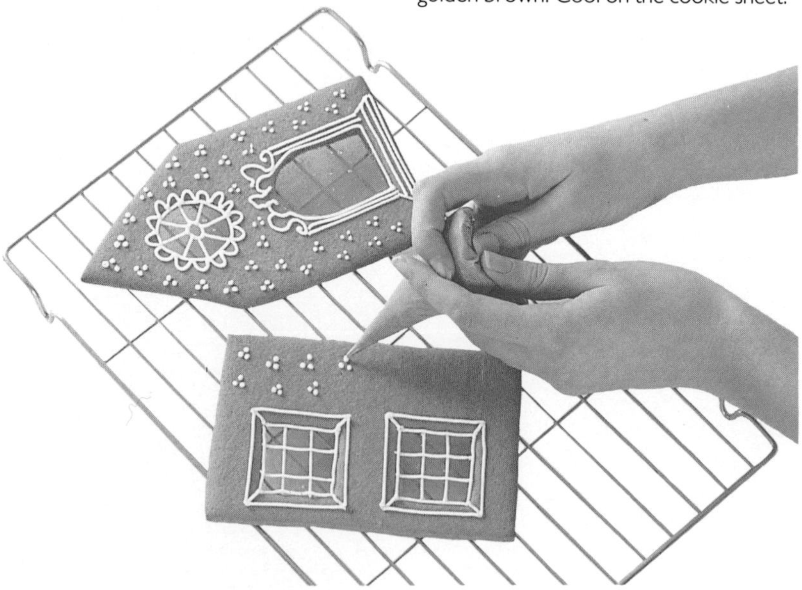

5 Make the Royal Icing. Place some of the icing in a waxed paper piping bag fitted with a No. 2 plain writing nozzle. Pipe lines, loops and circles around the windows, doors and on the walls and roof to decorate. Pipe beads of icing in groups of 3 all over the remaining spaces and leave flat to dry.

Templates for the Gingerbread House

1 For the side wall, measure and cut out a rectangle 6 in × 4 in from stiff cardboard.

2 For the pitch of the roof, measure and cut out a rectangle 7 in × 4 in. Measure 4 in up each long side and mark these points. Mark a center point at the top of the short edge. Draw a line from each of the side points to the top point. Cut out.

3 For the roof, measure and cut out a rectangle 8 in × 6 in from stiff cardboard.

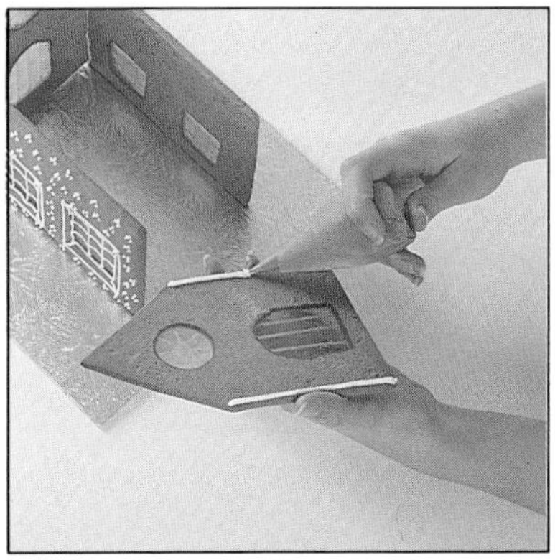

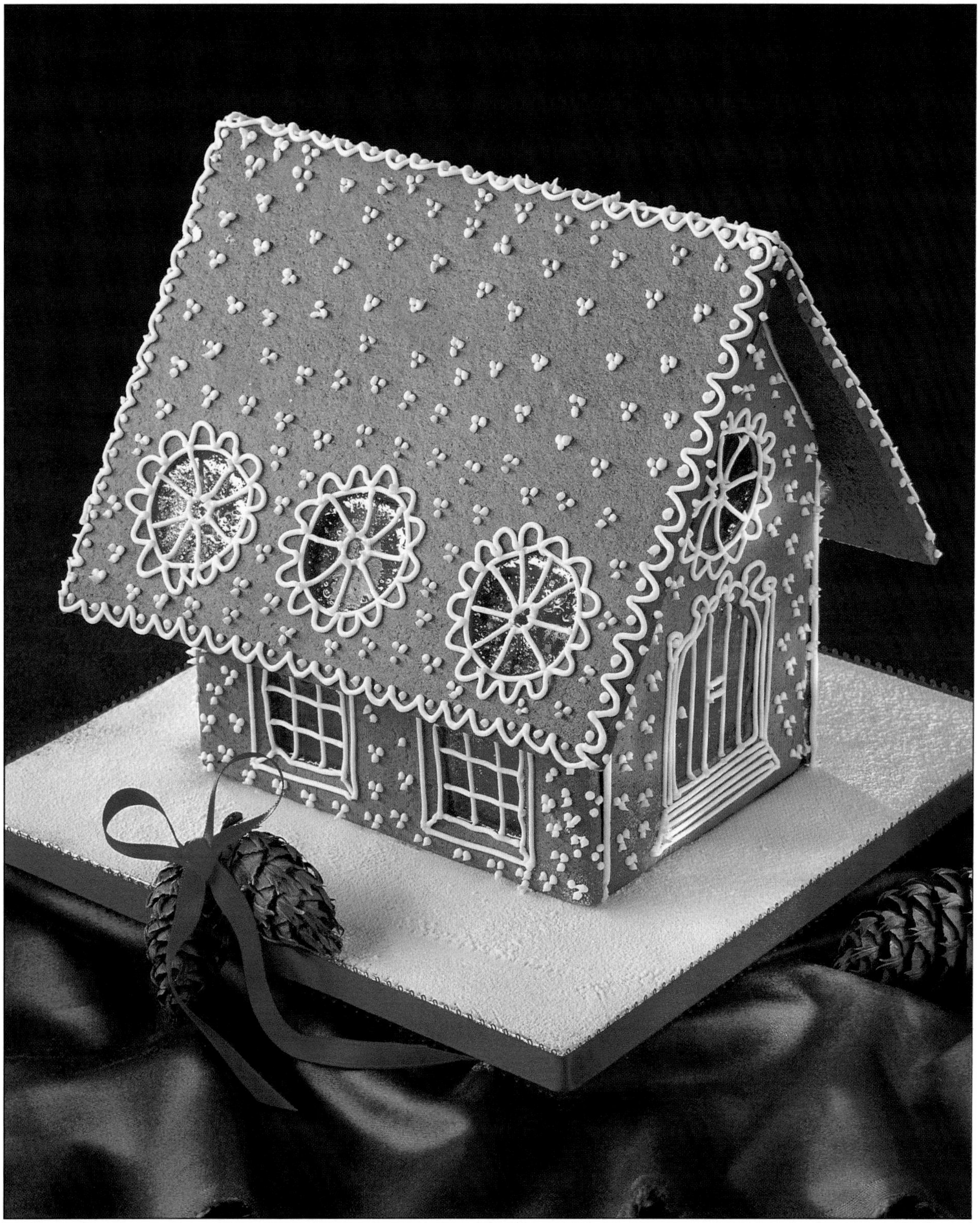

6 To assemble the house, pipe a line of icing on the side edges of the walls and side pieces. Stick them together to form a box shape on the cake board. Pipe a line of icing following the pitch of the roof on both end pieces and along the top of the 2 roof pieces. Press gently in position and support the underneath of each roof while the icing sets. Pipe the finishing touches to the roof and base of the house. Dust the cake board with confectioners' sugar to look like snow. Wrap ribbon around the edges of the board.

Cheese Biscuits

These crispy cheese biscuits are irresistible, and will disappear in moments. Try using different cheeses sprinkled with a variety of seeds to give alternative flavors.

Makes about 80

INGREDIENTS
1 cup flour
½ tsp salt
½ tsp cayenne pepper
½ tsp powdered mustard
½ cup butter
½ cup grated Cheddar
½ cup grated Gruyère
1 egg white, beaten
1 tbsp sesame seeds

sesame seeds

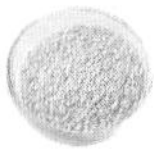

cayenne pepper

egg

Cheddar

Gruyère

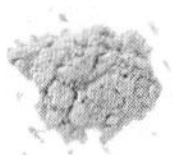

powdered mustard

1 Preheat the oven to 425°F. Line several cookie sheets with parchment paper. Sift the flour, salt, cayenne pepper and mustard into a mixing bowl. Cut the butter into pieces and rub into the flour mixture until it begins to cling together.

2 Divide the mixture in half, add the Cheddar to 1 half and the Gruyère to the other. Using a fork, work each mixture into a soft dough and knead on a floured surface until smooth.

3 Roll out both pieces of dough very thinly and cut into 1 in squares. Transfer to the lined cookie sheets. Brush the squares with beaten egg white, sprinkle with sesame seeds and bake in the oven for 5–6 minutes or until slightly puffed up and pale gold in color. Cool on the cookie sheets, then carefully remove with a metal spatula. Repeat the process until you have used up all the biscuit dough. Pack into tins or boxes and tie with ribbon.

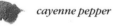

Cocktail Biscuits

Tiny savory biscuits are always a welcome treat. Try using different flavors and shapes and pack the biscuits into brightly colored tins.

Makes about 80

INGREDIENTS
3 cups flour
½ tsp salt
½ tsp black pepper
1 tsp whole grain mustard
¾ cup butter
½ cup grated Cheddar
1 egg, beaten

FLAVORINGS
1 tsp chopped nuts
2 tsp dill seeds
2 tsp curry paste
2 tsp chili sauce

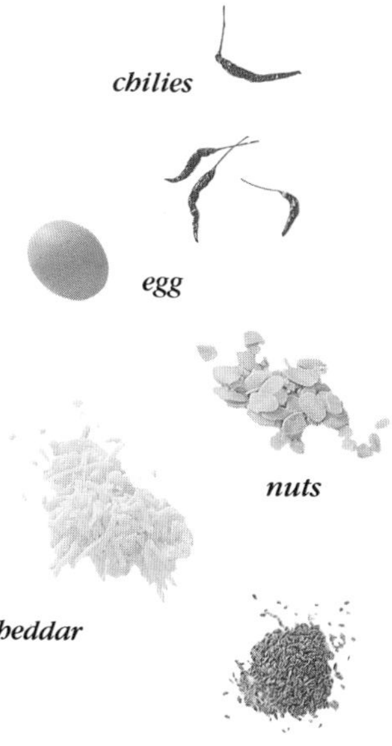

1 Preheat the oven to 400°F. Line several cookie sheets with parchment paper. Sift the flour into a mixing bowl and add the salt, pepper and mustard. Cut the butter into pieces and rub into the flour mixture until it resembles fine breadcrumbs. Use a fork to stir in the cheese and egg, and mix together to form a soft dough. Knead lightly on a floured surface and cut into 4 equal pieces.

2 Knead chopped nuts into one piece, dill seeds into another piece and curry paste and chili sauce into each of the remaining pieces. Wrap each piece of flavored dough in plastic wrap and leave to chill in the fridge for at least an hour. Remove from the plastic wrap and roll out one piece at a time.

3 Using a heart-shaped cutter, stamp out about 20 shapes from the curry-flavored dough and use a club-shaped cutter to cut out the chili-flavored dough. Arrange the shapes well spaced apart on the cookie sheets and bake in the oven for 6–8 minutes or until slightly puffed up and pale gold in color. Cool on wire racks. Repeat with remaining flavored dough using spade- and diamond-shaped cutters. Knead any trimmings together, re-roll and stamp out and bake as above.

Tiny Cheese Puffs

These bite-sized portions of choux pastry are the ideal accompaniment to a glass of wine.

Makes about 45

INGREDIENTS
1 cup all-purpose flour
½ teaspoon salt
1 teaspoon dry mustard powder
pinch cayenne pepper
1 cup water
½ cup butter, cut into pieces
4 eggs
¾ cup finely diced Gruyère cheese
1 tablespoon chives, finely chopped

1 Preheat the oven to 400°F. Lightly grease 2 large baking trays. Sift together the flour, salt, dry mustard, and cayenne pepper.

2 In a medium-size saucepan, bring the water and butter to a boil over medium-high heat. Remove the pan from the heat and add the flour mixture all at once, beating with a wooden spoon until the dough forms a ball. Return to the heat and beat constantly for 1 to 2 minutes to dry out. Remove from the heat and cool for 3 to 5 minutes.

3 Beat 3 of the eggs in to the dough, one at a time, beating well after each addition. Beat the fourth egg in a small bowl and add a teaspoon at a time beating until the dough is smooth and shiny and falls slowly when dropped from a spoon. (You may not need all the fourth egg; reserve any remaining egg for glazing.) Stir in the diced cheese and chives.

4 Using 2 teaspoons, drop small mounds of dough 2 inches apart on to the baking trays. Beat the reserved egg with 1 tablespoon water and brush the tops with the glaze. Bake for 8 minutes, then reduce the oven temperature to 350°F and bake for 7 to 8 minutes longer until puffed and golden. Remove to a wire rack to cool. Serve warm.

VARIATION

For Ham and Cheese Puffs, add ½ cup finely diced cooked ham with the cheese. For Cheesy Herb Puffs, stir in 2 tablespoons chopped fresh herbs or green onions with the cheese.

COOK'S TIP

The puffs can be prepared ahead and frozen. Reheat in a hot oven for 5 minutes, until crisp, before serving.

Striped Cookies

These cookies may be made in different flavors and colors and look wonderful tied in bundles or packed into boxes. Eat them with ice cream or light desserts.

Makes 25

INGREDIENTS
1 square white chocolate, melted
red and green food coloring dusts
2 egg whites
⅓ cup superfine sugar
½ cup flour
4 tbsp unsalted butter, melted

egg

icing bag

white chocolate

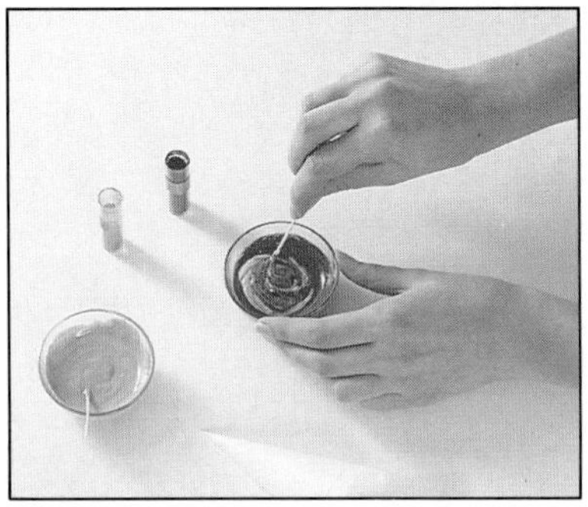

1 Preheat the oven to 375°F. Line 2 cookie sheets with parchment paper. Divide the melted chocolate in 2 and add a little food coloring dust to each half to color the chocolate red and green. Using 2 waxed paper piping bags, fill with each color chocolate and fold down the tops. Snip off the points.

2 Place the egg whites in a bowl and whisk until stiff. Add the sugar gradually, whisking well after each addition, to make a thick meringue. Add the flour and melted butter and whisk until smooth.

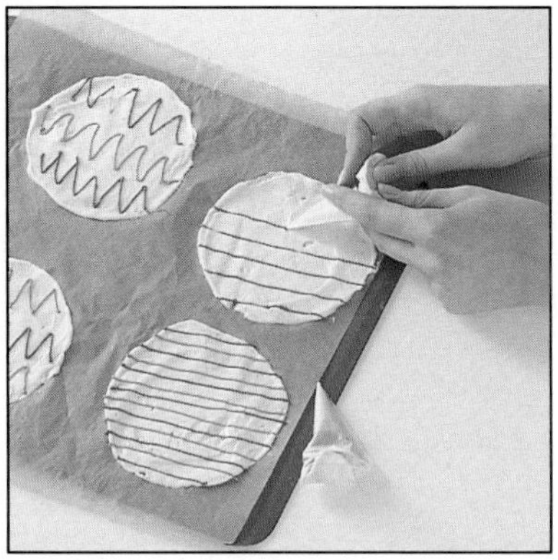

3 Drop 4 separate teaspoonfuls of mixture onto the cookie sheets and spread into thin rounds. Pipe lines or zigzags of green and red chocolate over each round. Bake in the oven for 3–4 minutes or until pale golden in color. Loosen the rounds with a metal spatula and return to the oven for a few seconds to soften. Have 2 or 3 lightly oiled wooden spoon handles at hand.

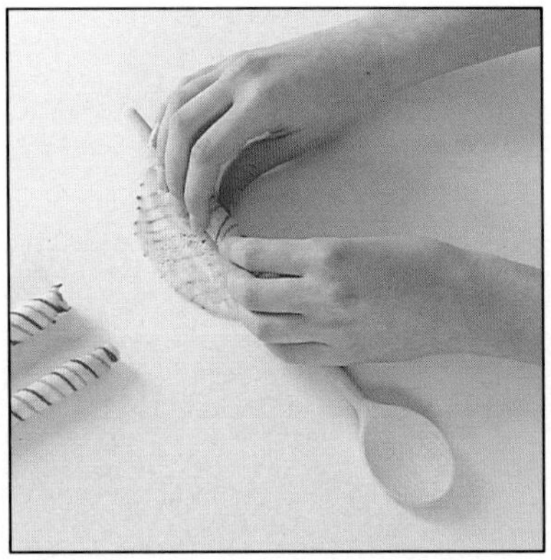

4 Taking one round cookie out of the oven at a time, roll it around a spoon handle and leave for a few seconds to set. Repeat to shape the remaining cookies.

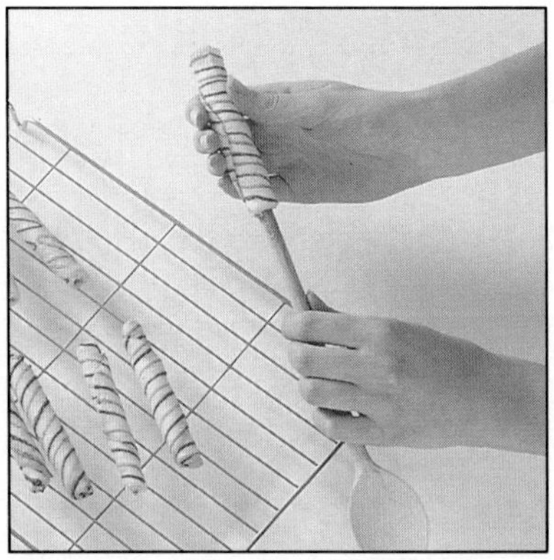

5 When the cookies are set, slip them off the spoon handles onto a wire rack. Repeat with the remaining mixture and the red and green chocolate until all the mixture has been used, baking only one sheet of cookies at a time. If the cookies are too hard to shape, simply return them to the oven for a few seconds to soften.

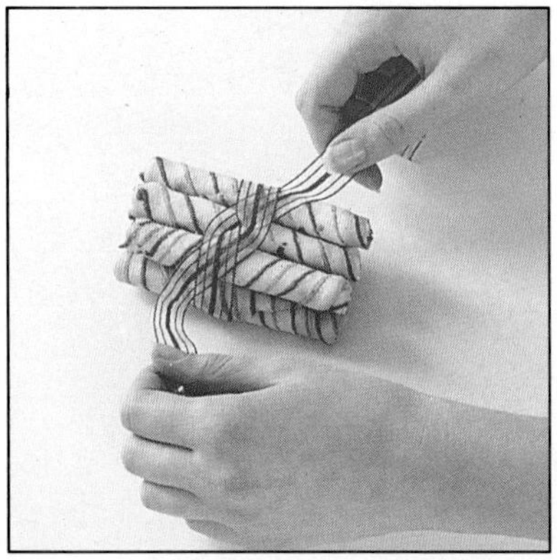

6 When the cookies are cold, tie them together with colored ribbon and pack into boxes, tins or glass jars.

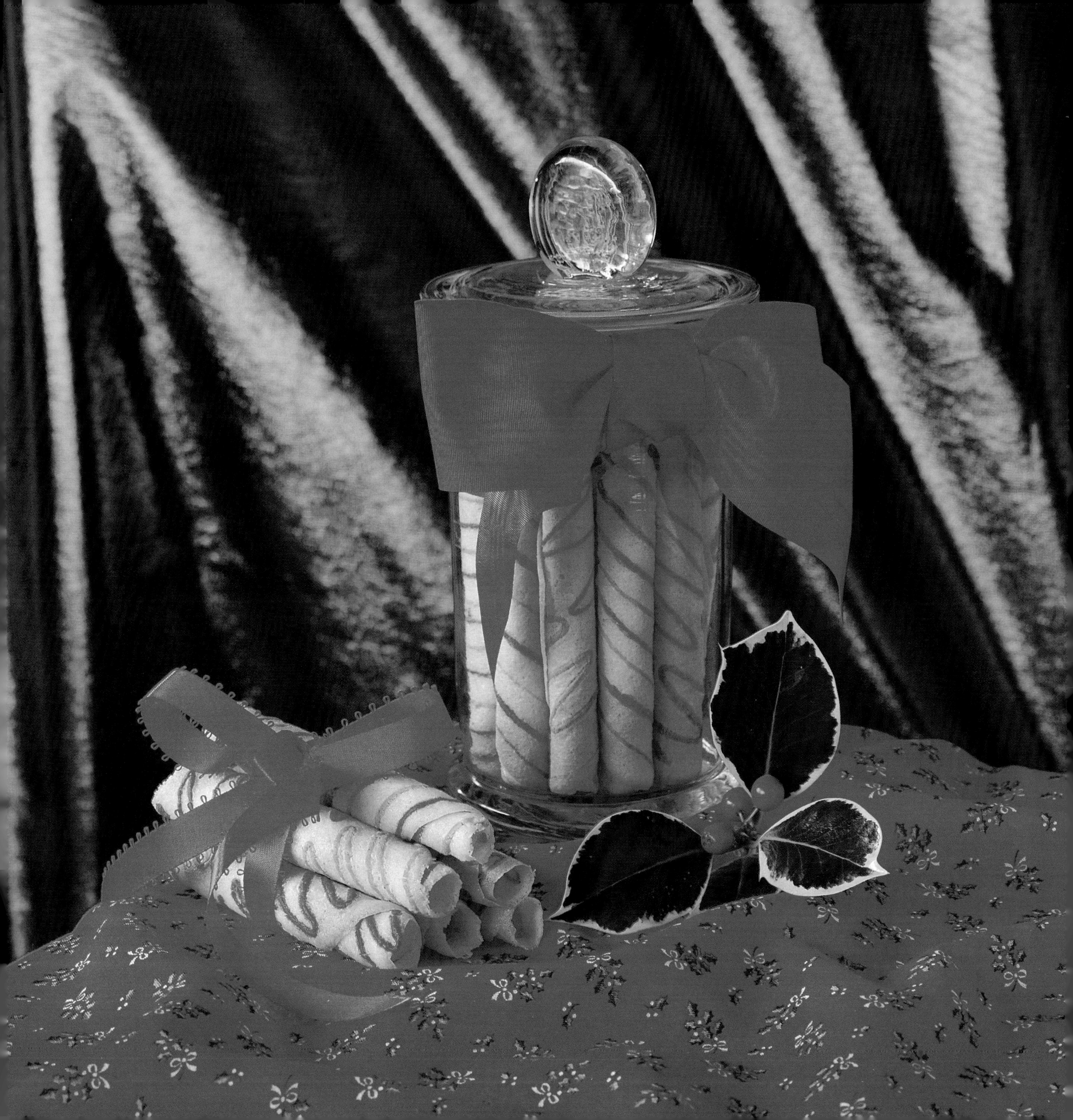

Mini Iced Christmas Cakes

A personal Christmas cake makes an extra special gift. Try improvising with your own designs, decorations and color schemes

Makes 1 large or 4 individual cakes

INGREDIENTS
1½ cups mixed dried fruit
¼ cup glacé cherries, sliced
½ cup slivered almonds
grated rind of ½ lemon
1 tbsp brandy
1 cup flour
½ tsp ground cinnamon
⅓ cup ground almonds
½ cup unsalted butter, softened
½ cup dark brown sugar
½ tbsp black molasses
2 eggs

ICING AND DECORATION
4 in square cake boards
4 tbsp Apricot Glaze (see Introduction)
1½ lb white marzipan
2 lb ready-to-roll icing
red and green food colorings

1 Prepare a 6 in square cake pan. Place the mixed dried fruit, cherries, almonds, lemon rind and brandy into a large mixing bowl. Stir until thoroughly blended, cover with plastic wrap and leave for 1 hour or overnight.

2 Preheat the oven to 300°F. Sift the flour and mixed spice into another bowl, add the ground almonds, butter, sugar, molasses and eggs. Mix together with a wooden spoon and beat for 2–3 minutes until smooth and glossy. Alternatively use a food mixer or processor for 1 minute. Fold the fruit into the cake mixture until evenly blended. Place the mixture in the prepared pan, level the top and make a slight dent in the center.

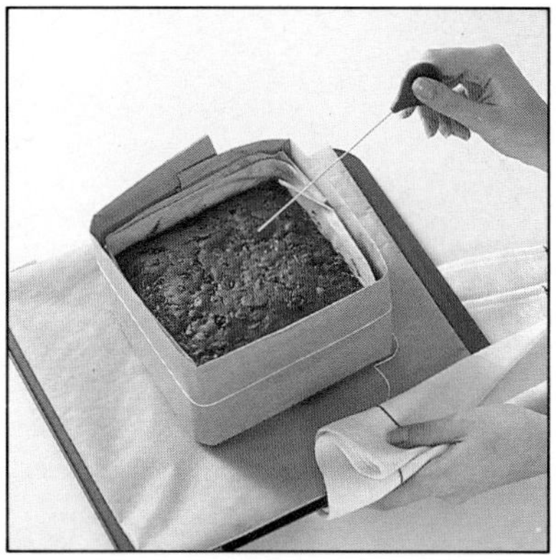

3 Bake the cake in the center of the oven for 2¼–2½ hours or until a skewer inserted into the center of the cake comes out clean. Leave the cake to cool in the pan. Spoon over a little extra brandy if desired. Remove the cake from the pan and wrap in foil until required.

lemon

glacé cherries

almonds

marzipan

4 Remove the lining paper and cut the cake into 4 square pieces. Place each cake on a small cake board and brush evenly with Apricot Glaze. Cut the marzipan into 4 pieces and roll out a piece large enough to cover one cake. Place over the cake, smooth over the top and sides and trim off the excess marzipan at the base. Repeat to cover the remaining 3 cakes.

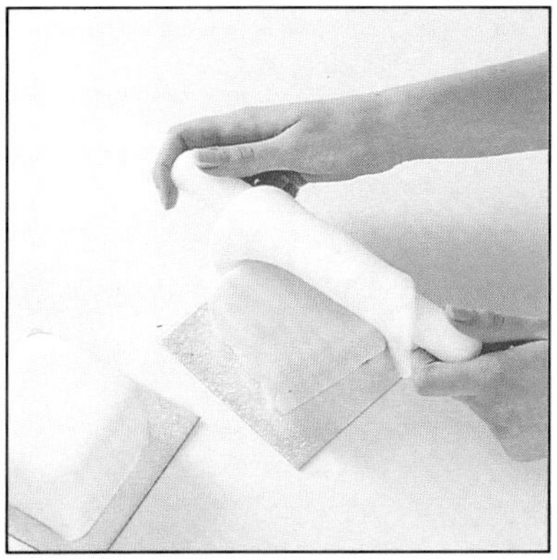

5 Cut the ready-to-roll icing into 5 pieces, roll 4 pieces out thinly to cover each cake, smoothing the tops and sides and trimming off the excess icing at the bases. Knead the trimmings together with the remaining piece of icing and cut into 2 pieces. Color one piece red and the other piece green using the food colorings. Roll out ½ of the red icing into a 10 × 6 in oblong.

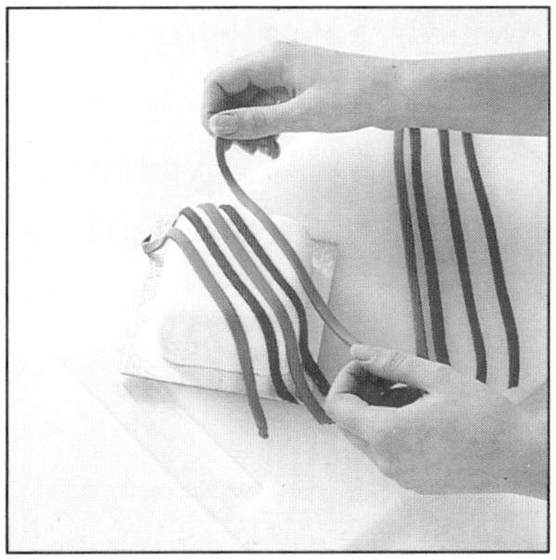

6 Cut the icing into ¼ in strips and place diagonally across the cake working from corner to corner. Trim the strips at the base of the cake. Brush the ends of the strips with a little water and press onto the cake. Make a few loops of icing and place on top of the cake. Repeat to decorate the remaining cakes with green and finally red and green strips of icing. Pack into boxes when dry.

Mini Black Buns

Black bun is a traditional Scottish recipe with a very rich fruit cake mixture cooked inside a bun dough. This variation uses marzipan in place of the dough.

Makes 4

INGREDIENTS
- 4 tbsp butter, melted, plus extra for brushing
- 1 cup mixed dried fruit
- ¼ cup glacé cherries, chopped
- ½ cup chopped almonds
- 2 tsp grated lemon rind
- 2 tbsp superfine sugar
- 1 tbsp whisky
- ½ cup flour
- 1 tsp ground cinnamon
- 1 egg, beaten

DECORATION
- 2 tbsp Apricot Glaze (see Introduction)
- 1 lb white marzipan
- purple and green food colorings

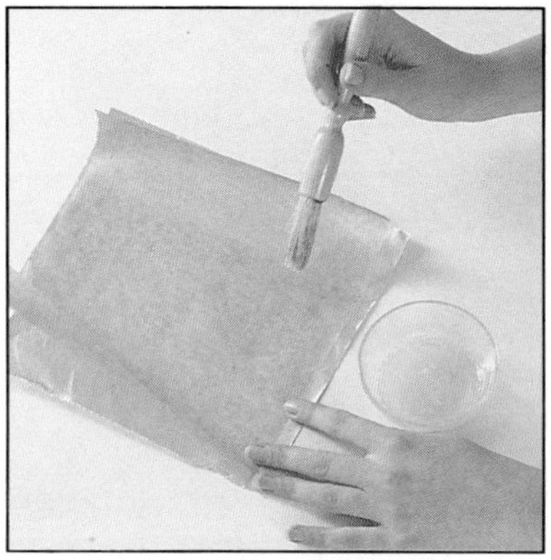

1 Preheat the oven to 300°F. Cut out 6 in squares of waxed paper and 4 squares of foil. Place the waxed paper squares on top of the foil squares and brush with a little melted butter.

2 Place the dried fruit, cherries, almonds, lemon rind, sugar, whisky, sifted flour and cinnamon into a large mixing bowl. Using a wooden spoon, stir until well mixed. Add the melted butter and egg and beat together until well blended.

3 Divide the mixture between the 4 paper and foil squares, draw up the edges to the center and twist to mold the mixture into rounds. Place on a cookie sheet and bake in the oven for 45 minutes or until the mixture feels firm when touched. Remove the foil and bake for a further 15 minutes. Open the paper and cool on a wire rack.

4 Remove the paper and brush each cake with Apricot Glaze. Cut off ¼ of the marzipan for decoration and put to one side. Cut the remainder into 4 pieces.

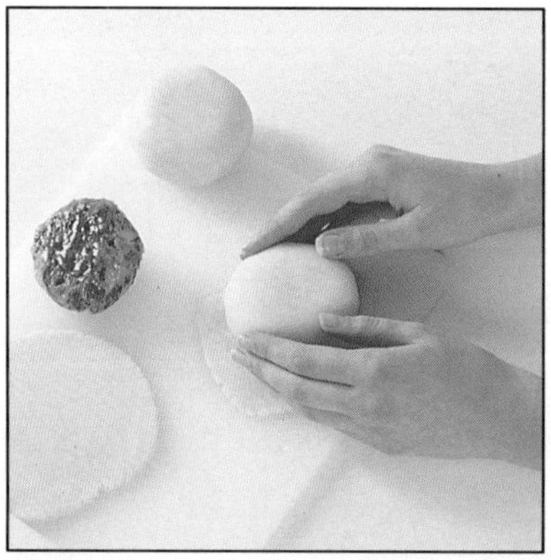

5 Roll out each piece thinly and cover the cakes, tucking the joins underneath. Roll each cake in the palms of your hands to make them into round shapes. Prepare a hot broiler and place the cakes onto a cookie sheet lined with foil.

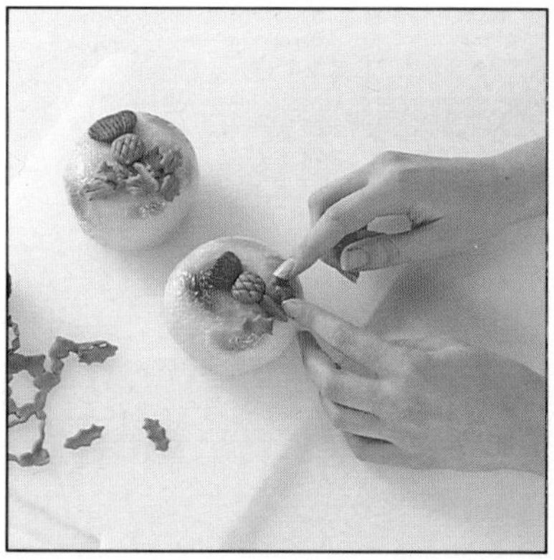

6 Broil the cakes until the marzipan is evenly browned. Leave until cold. Color ½ of the remaining marzipan purple and ½ green with food colorings. Cut out 4 purple thistle shapes, green leaves and stems and arrange them on top of each cake, moistening with a little water to stick. Wrap in cellophane and place into small cake boxes.

Individual Fruit Cakes

These delicious little fruit cakes may be topped with almonds or covered with glacé fruits.

Makes 3

INGREDIENTS
1 cup raisins
1 cup currants
1 cup golden raisins
¼ cup glacé cherries, sliced
¾ cup orange and lemon peel
grated rind of 1 orange
2¾ cups flour
½ tsp baking powder
1 tsp ground cinnamon
1 cup unsalted butter, softened
1 cup superfine sugar
5 eggs

TOPPING
½ cup whole blanched almonds
¼ cup glacé cherries, halved
½ cup glacé fruits, sliced
3 tbsp Apricot Glaze (see Introduction)

1 Preheat the oven to 300°F. Prepare 5 in round cake pans. Place all the fruit and the orange rind into a large mixing bowl. Mix together until evenly blended. In another bowl sift the flour, baking powder and cinnamon. Add the butter, sugar and eggs. Mix together with a wooden spoon and beat for 2–3 minutes until smooth and glossy. Alternatively use a food mixer or processor for 1 minute.

2 Add the mixed fruit to the cake mixture and fold in using a plastic scraper until well blended. Divide the cake mixture between the 3 pans and level the tops. Arrange the almonds in circles over the top of one cake, the glacé cherries over the second cake and the mixed glacé fruits over the last one. Bake in the oven for approximately 2–2½ hours or until a skewer inserted into the center of the cakes comes out clean.

3 Leave the cakes in their pans until completely cold. Turn out, remove the paper and brush the tops with Apricot Glaze. Leave to set, then wrap in cellophane paper or plastic wrap and place in pretty boxes.

Spiced Christmas Cake

This light cake mixture is flavored with spices and fruit. It can be served with a dusting of confectioners' sugar and decorated with holly leaves.

Makes 1

INGREDIENTS
1 cup butter, plus extra for greasing mold
1 tbsp fresh white breadcrumbs
1 cup superfine sugar
¼ cup water
3 eggs, separated
2 cups self-rising flour
1½ tsp ground cinnamon
2 tbsp chopped angelica
2 tbsp orange and lemon peel
¼ cup glacé cherries, chopped
½ cup walnuts, chopped
confectioners' sugar, to dust

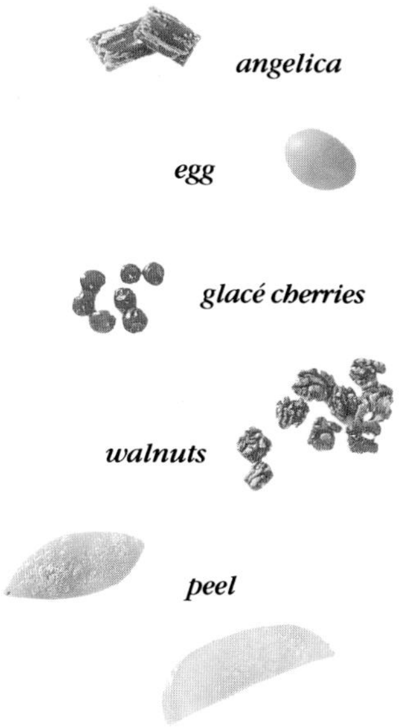

1 Preheat the oven to 350°F. Brush an 8 in, 2½ pint fluted ring mold with melted butter and coat with breadcrumbs, shaking out any excess.

2 Place the butter, sugar and water into a saucepan. Heat gently, stirring occasionally, until melted. Boil for 3 minutes until syrupy, then allow to cool. Place the egg whites in a clean bowl, whisk until stiff. Sift the flour and cinnamon into a bowl, add the angelica, orange and lemon peel, cherries and walnuts and stir well to mix. Add the egg yolks.

3 Pour the cooled mixture into the bowl and beat together with a wooden spoon to form a soft batter. Gradually fold in the egg whites using a plastic spatula until the mixture is evenly blended. Pour into the prepared mold and bake for 50–60 minutes or until the cake springs back when pressed in the center. Turn out and cool on a wire rack. Dust thickly with sugar and decorate with a sprig of holly.

Novelty Christmas Cakes

These individual cakes can be packed in their own little boxes to make unusual gifts for children.

Makes 2

INGREDIENTS
1 cup self-rising flour
1 tsp baking powder
1 tbsp cocoa powder
½ cup superfine sugar
½ cup soft margarine
2 eggs

DECORATION
3 tbsp Apricot Glaze (see Introduction)
2 × 6 in thin round cake boards
12 oz ready-to-roll icing
350 g/12 oz white marzipan
red, black, green, yellow and brown food colorings
white and red glitter flakes

1 Preheat the oven to 325°F. Grease and line the bases of 2 × 6 in round sandwich pans. Place all the cake ingredients into a large mixing bowl. Mix together with a wooden spoon and beat for 2–3 minutes until smooth and glossy.

2 Divide the mixture between the 2 pans, smooth the tops and bake in the oven for 20–25 minutes or until the cakes spring back when pressed in the center. Loosen the edges of the cakes and invert onto a wire rack. Remove the paper.

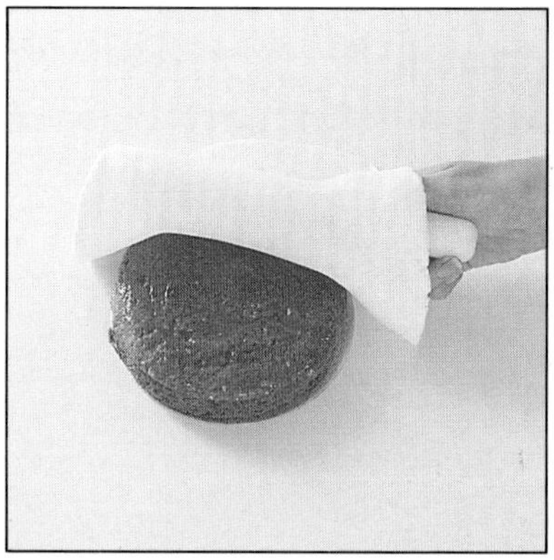

3 Brush both the cakes with Apricot Glaze and place on their cake boards. To make the clown cake, roll out ⅓ of the icing to a round large enough to cover one cake. Place the icing over the cake, smooth the surface and trim off the excess at the base. Mold 2 ears from the trimmings and press into position.

4 Color ⅓ of the marzipan red and shape a mouth and nose; reserve the remainder. Color a small piece of marzipan black and roll out thin lengths to outline the mouth and make the eyebrows and 2 crosses for the eyes. Color another small piece green for the ruffle. Color another small piece yellow and grate coarsely to make the hair. Stick in position with Apricot Glaze and sprinkle with the white glitter flakes.

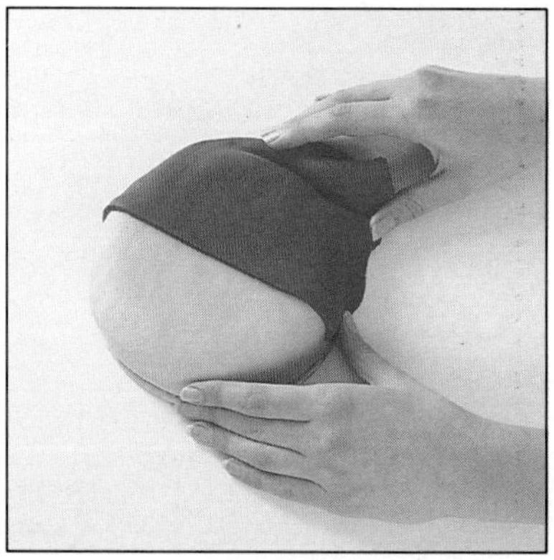

5 To make the Santa Claus cake, color the remaining marzipan skin tone using a tiny amount of brown coloring and roll out thinly to cover ⅔ of the second cake. Trim to fit. Roll out ¾ of the red marzipan thinly and cover the remaining ⅓ of the cake to make the hat. Gather the excess together at one side for the hat. Mold a nose and mouth from the remaining red marzipan.

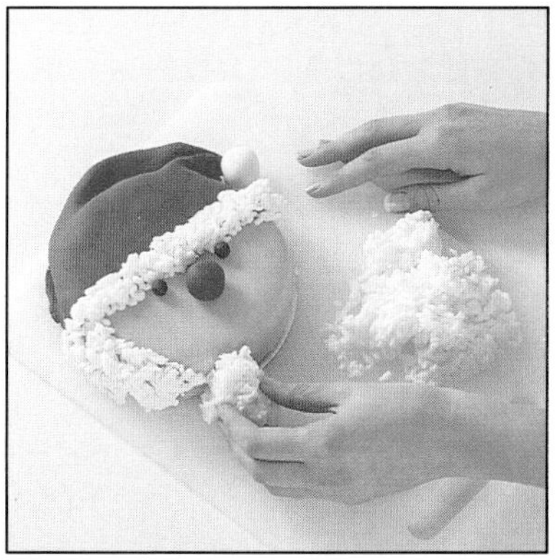

6 Coarsely grate the remaining white icing and use to trim the hat and to shape the beard, moustache and eyebrows. Gently press a small ball of grated icing together to make a bobble for the hat. Shape 2 black eyes and press in position. Sprinkle red glitter flakes onto the hat to give a sparkle. Pack each cake into a small box with a lid and write a name tag.

Flavored Vinegars

Flavored vinegars look extra special if you pour them into beautifully shaped bottles. Use fresh herbs and flowers, spices and soft fruits.

Makes 2½ cups of each flavor

INGREDIENTS
good quality red and white wine vinegar or cider vinegar

HERB VINEGAR
1 tbsp mixed peppercorns
2 lemon slices
4 garlic cloves
rosemary, thyme and tarragon sprigs

SPICE VINEGAR
1 tbsp allspice berries
2 mace blades
2 tsp star anise
2 cinnamon sticks
1 orange

FRUIT VINEGAR
3 cups raspberries
3 cups gooseberries
3 cups blackberries or elderberries

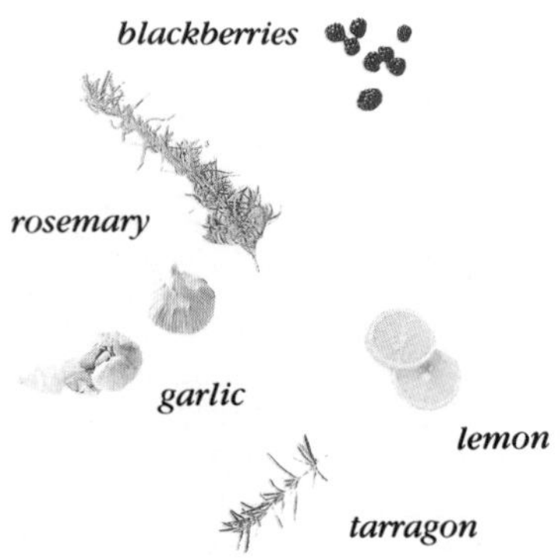

1 Sterilize 2 bottles with corks or caps. To the first bottle add the peppercorns, lemon slices and garlic cloves. Place the herb sprigs together and trim the stems so they vary in length. Insert them into the bottle, placing the short ones in first.

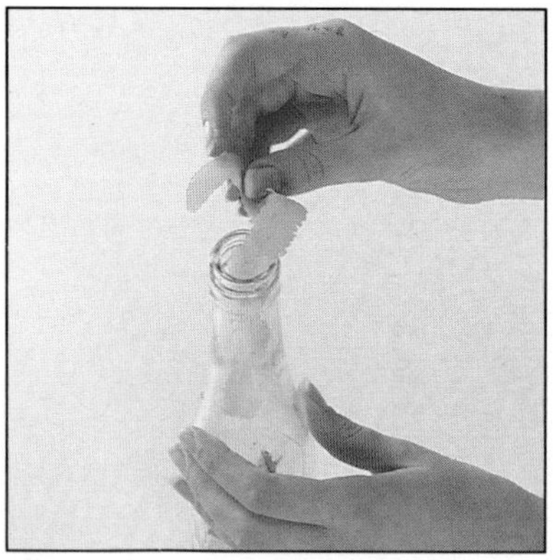

2 Into the second bottle add the allspice berries, mace, star anise and cinnamon sticks. Cut 2 slices from the orange and insert into the bottle. Pare the rind from the remaining orange, taking care not to include any pith. Insert into the bottle.

3 Using white wine vinegar, fill the bottle containing the herbs up to the neck. Repeat to fill the bottle containing the spices with red wine vinegar. Cork or cap the bottles and store in a cool place.

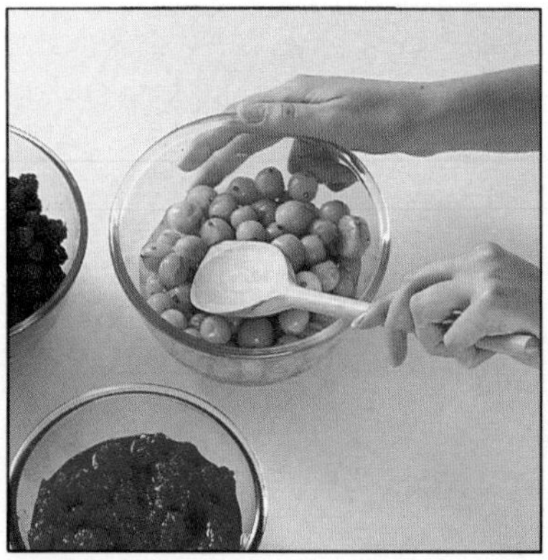

4 Wash the raspberries, gooseberries and blackberries or elderberries separately and place into separate bowls. Crush with a wooden spoon.

5 Pour each fruit into a separate clean wide-necked jar and add 2½ cups of white wine vinegar. Cover and leave for 3–4 days in a cool place. Shake the jars occasionally to mix well.

6 Strain each fruit separately through a jelly bag or a muslin-lined sieve into a stainless steel saucepan and boil for 10 minutes. Pour into sterilized bottles or jars and seal with lids or tops with plastic coated linings. Use all vinegars within 6 months.

Fresh Fruit Preserve

The wonderfully fresh flavor of this fruit spread makes it a welcome gift. To vary the recipe, use a mixture of soft fruits, or other individual fruits such as strawberries or blackberries.

Makes 2 lb

INGREDIENTS
3½ cups raspberries
4 cups superfine sugar
2 tbsp lemon juice
½ cup liquid pectin

raspberries

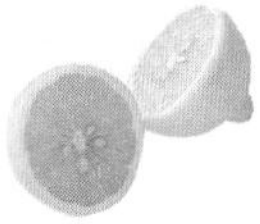

lemon

1 Place the raspberries in a large bowl and lightly crush with a wooden spoon. Stir in the sugar. Leave for 1 hour at room temperature, giving the mixture an occasional stir to dissolve the sugar.

2 Sterilize several small jars or containers, and their lids if being used. Add the lemon juice and liquid pectin to the raspberries and stir until thoroughly blended.

3 Spoon the raspberry mixture into the jars, leaving a ½ in space at the top if the preserve is to be frozen. Cover the surface of each preserve with a waxed paper disc and cover with a lid or cellophane paper and an elastic band. Don't use a screw-topped lid if the preserve is to be frozen. Allow to cool, then label and freeze for up to 6 months, or refrigerate for up to 4 weeks.

Flavored Oils

Any good quality oils may be flavored with herbs, spices, peppers, olives or anchovies. They look attractive in the kitchen, as well as being ready flavored for use in cooking or salad dressings.

Makes 1¼ cups of each flavor

INGREDIENTS
olive, grapeseed or almond oil

HERB OIL
sage, thyme, oregano, tarragon and rosemary sprigs
1 bay leaf sprig

SPICED OIL
2 tbsp whole cloves
3 mace blades
1 tbsp cardamom pods
1 tbsp coriander seeds
3 dried chilies
1 bay leaf sprig
2 lime slices
2 cinnamon sticks

MEDITERRANEAN OIL
2 mini red peppers
3 black olives
3 green olives
3 anchovy fillets
1 bay leaf sprig
strip of lemon rind

1 Have ready 3 bottles and corks which have been sterilized and are completely dry inside. Place all the fresh herb sprigs together and trim to fit inside the first bottle. Insert the short lengths first and arrange them using a long skewer, adding them stem by stem.

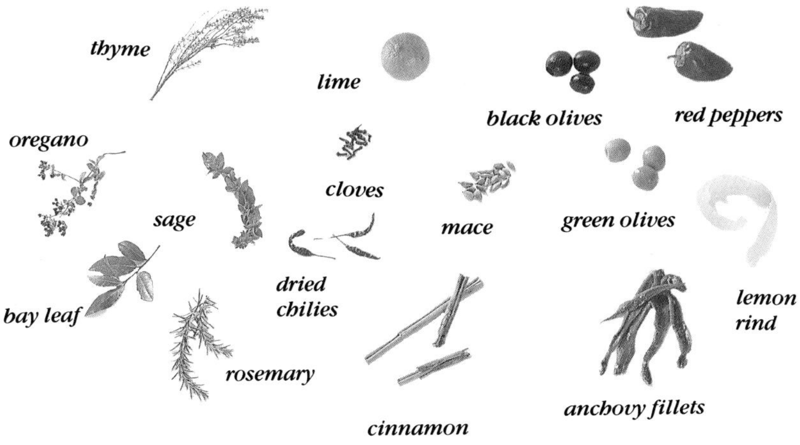

2 Add the cloves, mace, cardamom pods, coriander seeds and chilies to the second bottle. Insert the bay leaf, lime slices and cinnamon sticks.

3 Grill the mini red peppers until they are tender, turning once. Add the olives, anchovies and peppers to the last bottle. Insert the bay leaf sprig and strip of lemon rind. Fill each bottle with the chosen oil and cork or cap. Label clearly and keep cool until required.

Red Pepper and Rosemary Jelly

This wonderful amber-colored jelly may be made with either red or yellow peppers and flavored with any full-flavored herbs. It is delicious with cold meat, poultry, fish or cheeses.

Makes 4 lb

INGREDIENTS
8 tomatoes, chopped
4 red peppers, seeded and chopped
2 red chilies, seeded and chopped
rosemary sprigs
1¼ cups water
1¼ cups red wine vinegar
½ tsp salt
5 cups granulated sugar with added pectin
1 cup liquid pectin

1 Place the tomatoes, peppers, chilies, a few rosemary sprigs and the water into a stainless steel saucepan and bring to a boil. Cover and simmer for 1 hour or until the peppers are tender and pulpy.

2 Suspend a jelly bag and place a bowl underneath. Sterilize the jelly bag by pouring through boiling water. Discard the water and replace the bowl.

3 Pour the contents of the saucepan slowly into the jelly bag. Allow the juices to drip through slowly for several hours but do not squeeze the bag or the jelly will become cloudy. Sterilize the jars and lids required.

4 Place the juice into a clean saucepan with the vinegar, salt and sugar. Discard the pulp in the jelly bag. Heat gently, stirring occasionally, until the sugar has dissolved. Boil rapidly for 3 minutes.

5 Remove the saucepan from the heat and stir in the liquid pectin. Skim the surface with a piece of paper towelling to remove any foam.

6 Pour the liquid into the sterilized jars and add a sprig of rosemary to each jar. Place a waxed disc onto the surface of each and seal with a lid or cellophane paper and a rubber band. Allow to cool, then label and decorate with ribbons.

Crab Apple and Lavender Jelly

This fragrant, clear jelly looks even prettier with a sprig of fresh lavender suspended in the jar. Try using other fruits such as apples, quince or rosehips.

Makes about 2 lb

INGREDIENTS
5 cups crab apples
7½ cups water
lavender stems
4 cups granulated sugar

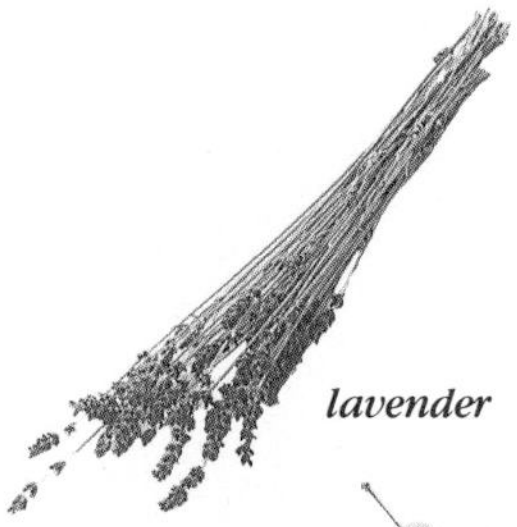

lavender

crab apples

1 Cut the crab apples into chunks and place in a preserving pan with water and 2 stems of lavender. Bring to a boil and cover the pan with a piece of foil or a lid and simmer very gently for 1 hour, giving the mixture an occasional stir, until the fruit is pulpy.

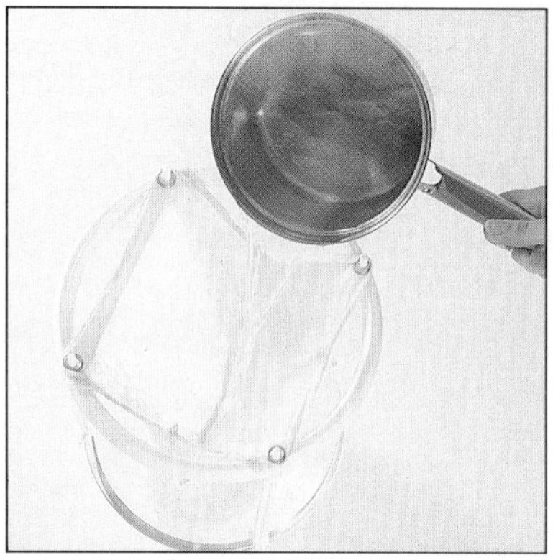

2 Suspend a jelly bag and place a bowl underneath. Sterilize the jelly bag by pouring through some boiling water. Discard the water and replace the bowl.

3 Pour the contents of the saucepan slowly into the jelly bag. Allow the juice to drip slowly through for several hours but do not squeeze the bag or the jelly will become cloudy.

4 Discard the pulp and measure the quantity of juice in the bowl. To each 2½ cups of juice add 2 cups of sugar and pour into a clean pan. Sterilize the jars and lids required.

5 Heat the juice gently, stirring occasionally, until the sugar has dissolved. Bring to a boil and boil rapidly for about 8–10 minutes until setting point has been reached. When tested, the temperature should be 221°F. If you don't have a sugar thermometer, put a small amount of jelly on a cold plate and allow to cool. The surface should wrinkle when you push your finger through the jelly. If not yet set, continue to boil and then re-test.

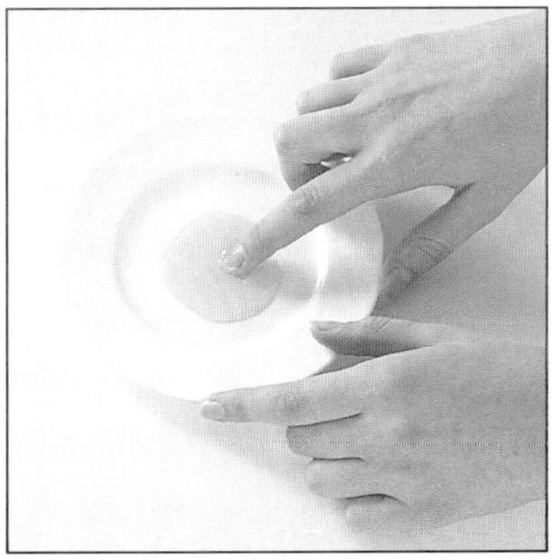

6 Remove the pan from the heat and use a slotted spoon to remove any froth from the surface. Carefully pour the jelly into a pitcher, then fill the warm sterilized jars. Dip the lavender quickly into boiling water and insert a stem into each jar. Cover with a disc of waxed paper and with cellophane paper and a rubber band. Label when cold.

Peppers in Olive Oil

The wonderful flavor and color of these peppers will add a Mediterranean theme to festive foods. Bottle the peppers separately or mix the colors together for a gift that tastes as good as it looks.

Makes enough to fill 3 × 1 lb jars

INGREDIENTS
3 red peppers
3 yellow peppers
3 green peppers
1¼ cups olive oil
½ tsp salt
½ tsp freshly ground black pepper
3 thyme sprigs

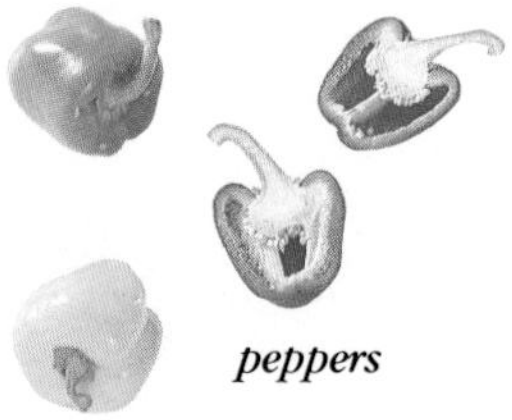

peppers

thyme

1 Prepare a hot broiler or preheat the oven to 400°F. Put the whole peppers on a broiling pan or onto a cookie sheet. Place under the broiler or in the oven and cook for about 10 minutes until the skins are charred and blistered all over. Turn frequently during cooking.

2 Allow the peppers to cool for at least 5 minutes, then peel off the skins. Remove the cores, seeds and stalks. Slice each of the peppers thinly, keeping each color separate, and place each into a separate dish.

3 Pour ⅓ of the olive oil over each of the peppers. Sprinkle with salt and pepper and add a sprig of thyme to each dish. Stir to blend well. Sterilize 3 jars and lids and fill each with a mixture of peppers, or keep them separate. Top up each jar with the oil. Screw firmly down and label.

Christmas Chutney

This chutney makes the perfect accompaniment to cold meats, pâtés and cheese. It has a sweet but spicy flavor and the fruits may be changed for quince, greengage or rhubarb.

Makes 4 lb

INGREDIENTS
9 plums, pitted
16 pears, peeled and cored
2 apples, peeled and cored
4 stalks celery
1 lb onions, sliced
1 lb tomatoes, skinned
½ cup raisins
1 tbsp grated fresh ginger root
2 tbsp pickling spice
3¾ cups cider vinegar
2 cups granulated sugar

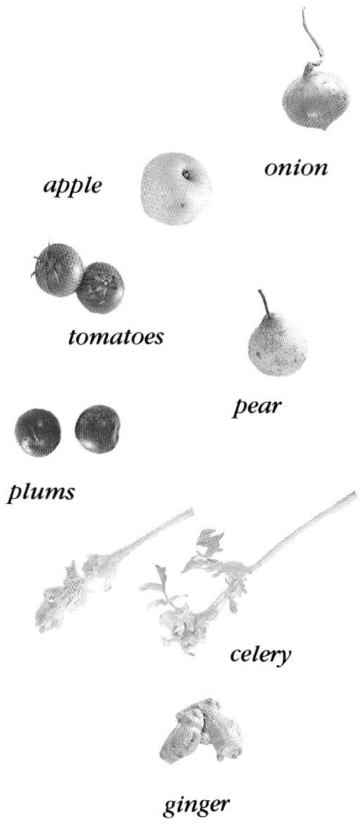

1 Chop the plums, pears, apples, celery and onions and cut the tomatoes into quarters. Place all these ingredients with the raisins and ginger into a very large saucepan.

2 Place the pickling spice into a piece of muslin and tie with string to secure. Add to the saucepan with half the vinegar and bring to the boil, giving the mixture an occasional stir. Cook for about 2 hours.

3 Meanwhile sterilize the jars and lids. When all the ingredients are tender, stir in the remaining vinegar and the sugar. Boil until thick, remove the bag of spices and fill each jar with chutney. Cover with a wax paper disc and plastic lid and label when cold.

Fruits in Liqueurs

These eye-catching fruits in liqueurs are best made when the fruits are plentiful, cheap and in season. Choose from apricots, clementines, kumquats, cherries, raspberries, peaches, plums or seedless grapes and team them with rum, brandy, kirsch or Cointreau just to name a few.

Makes 1 lb

INGREDIENTS
3 cups fresh fruit
1 cup granulated sugar
⅔ cup liqueur or spirits

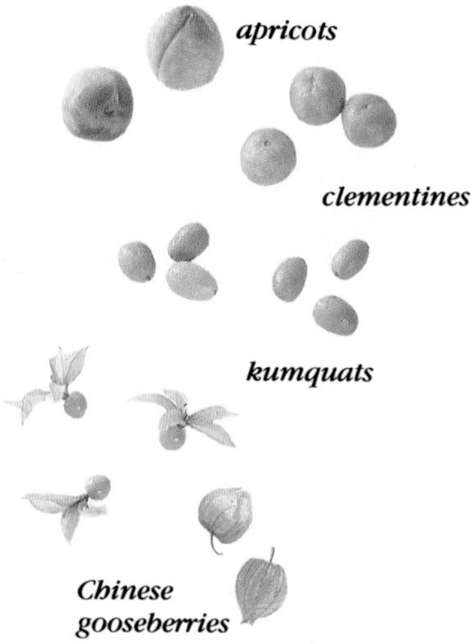

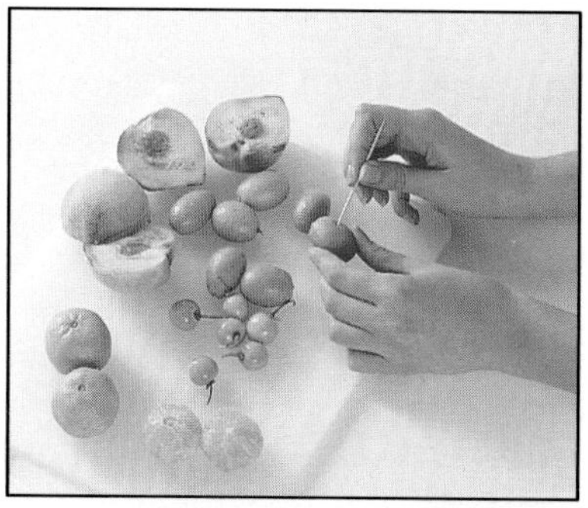

1 Wash the fruit, halve and pit apricots, plums or peaches. Peel back and remove the husk from Chinese gooseberries, hull strawberries or raspberries, and prick kumquats, cherries or grapes all over with a toothpick. Pare the rind from clementines using a sharp knife, taking care not to include any white pith.

2 Place ½ cup of the sugar and 1 ¼ cups of water into a saucepan. Heat gently, stirring occasionally, until the sugar has dissolved. Bring to a boil.

3 Add the fruit to the syrup and simmer gently for 1–2 minutes until the fruit is just tender, but the skins are intact and the fruits are whole.

4 Carefully remove the fruit using a slotted spoon and arrange neatly into the warmed sterilized jars. Add the remaining sugar to the syrup in the pan and stir until dissolved.

5 Boil the syrup rapidly until it reaches 230°F or the thread stage. Test by pressing a small amount of syrup between 2 teaspoons; when they are pulled apart, a thread should form. Allow to cool.

6 Measure the cooled syrup, then add an equal quantity of liqueur or spirit. Mix until blended. Pour over the fruit in the jars until covered. Seal each jar with a screw or clip top, label and keep for up to 4 months.

Anchovy Spread

This delicious spread has a concentrated flavor and is best served with plain toast.

Makes $2\frac{1}{2}$ cups

INGREDIENTS
2 × 2 oz cans anchovy fillets in olive oil
4 garlic cloves, crushed
2 egg yolks
2 tbsp red wine vinegar
1¼ cups olive oil
¼ tsp freshly ground black pepper
2 tbsp chopped fresh basil or thyme

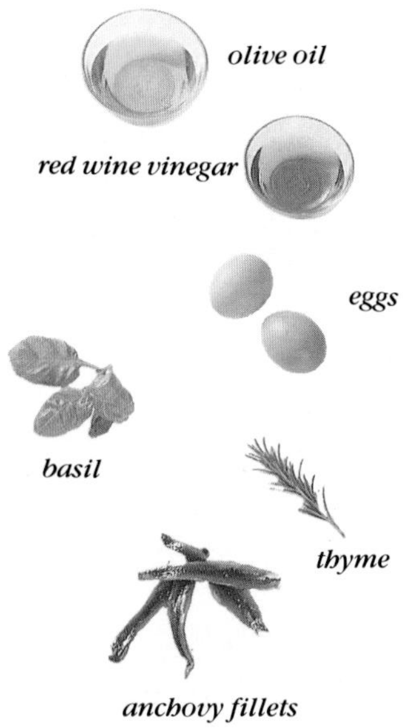

1 Drain the oil from the anchovies and reserve. Place the anchovies and garlic in a food processor. Process until smooth. Add the egg yolks and vinegar, and process until the egg and vinegar have been absorbed by the anchovies.

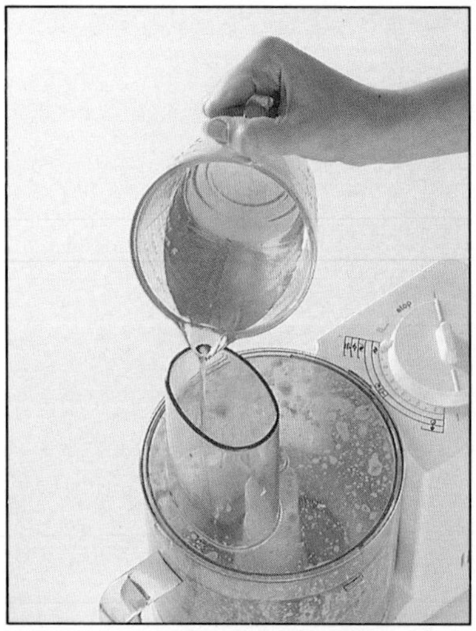

2 Measure out the oil into a measuring cup and add the reserved anchovy oil. Set the food processor to a low speed and add the oil drop by drop to the anchovy mixture until it is thick and smooth.

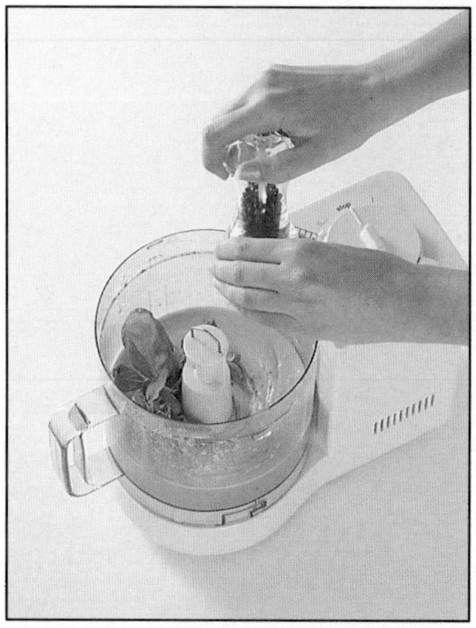

3 Add some freshly ground black pepper and fresh herbs, and blend until smooth. Spoon the mixture into small sterilized jars, cover and label. Store in the fridge.

Smoked Salmon Pâté

This luxury pâté makes a fine gift for a special person. Pack the pâté in a pretty dish to give as part of the gift. Store in the fridge.

Makes enough to fill 4 small ramekin dishes

INGREDIENTS
12 oz fresh salmon fillet
¼ tsp salt
½ tsp freshly ground black pepper
1 tbsp chopped fresh dill, plus sprigs to garnish
4 slices smoked salmon
½ cup cottage or cream cheese
5 tbsp unsalted butter
1 cup fresh white breadcrumbs
1 tsp lemon juice
2 tbsp Madeira

lemon

dill

salmon fillet

smoked salmon

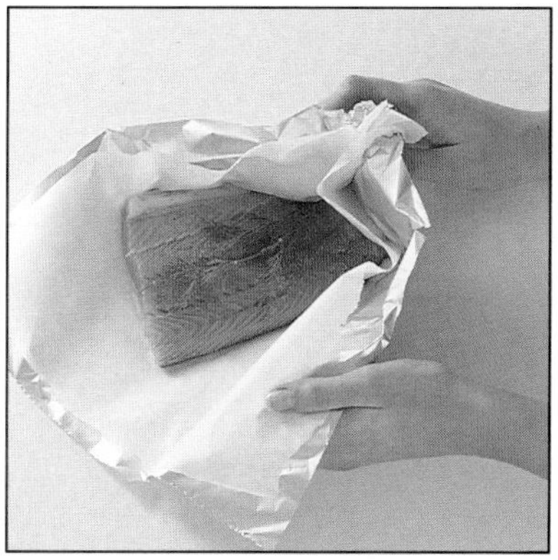

1 Preheat the oven to 375°F. Put the salmon fillet on a large piece of waxed paper placed on top of a sheet of foil. Sprinkle with salt, pepper and dill. Seal the foil and place on a cookie sheet. Cook in the oven for 10 minutes or until just tender. Leave until cold and remove the skin, saving any of the juices.

2 Cut out 4 pieces of smoked salmon to fit the bases of the 4 individual dishes. Cut out 4 strips to fit around the inside edges of each dish. Cover and chill.

3 Place the cooked salmon, its juices, the cheese, butter, breadcrumbs, lemon juice and Madeira into a food processor. Process until smooth. Divide the mixture between the dishes and press it down to fill each dish evenly. Cover the top with another piece of smoked salmon and decorate with a sprig of dill. Cover with plastic wrap and chill.

Savory Butters

This selection of 8 tiny pots of unusual flavored butters can be used as garnishes for meat, fish and vegetables, as a topping for canapés or as a tasty addition to sauces.

Makes about 1/4 cup of each flavor

INGREDIENTS
2 cups unsalted butter
2 tbsp Stilton
3 anchovy fillets
1 tsp curry paste
1 garlic clove, crushed
2 tsp finely chopped fresh tarragon
1 tbsp prepared horseradish
1 tbsp chopped fresh parsley
1 tsp grated lime rind
1/4 tsp chili sauce

Stilton

lime

tarragon

garlic

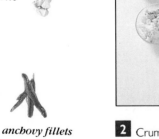

parsley

anchovy fillets

1 Place the butter in a food processor. Process until light and fluffy. Divide the butter into 8 portions.

2 Crumble the Stilton and mix together with a portion of butter. Pound the anchovies to a paste in a pestle and mortar and mix with the second portion of butter. Stir the curry paste into the third, and the crushed garlic into the fourth portion.

3 Stir the tarragon into the fifth portion and the horseradish into the sixth portion. Into the seventh portion add the parsley and the lime rind, and to the last portion add the chili sauce. Pack each flavored butter into a tiny sterilized jar and label clearly. Store in the fridge.

Potted Cheese Rarebit

An instant 'cheese on toast' in a pot. Try using Gruyère cheese instead of the Cheddar as a variation. You may wish to serve it with a sprinkling of Worcestershire sauce or a bit of chopped anchovy.

Makes 1½ lb

INGREDIENTS
4 tbsp butter
1 tbsp herbed French mustard
½ tsp freshly ground black pepper
½ cup ale or cider
1 lb mature Cheddar, grated

Cheddar

black pepper

French mustard

1 Place the butter, mustard, pepper and ale or cider into a saucepan. Heat gently, stirring occasionally, until boiling.

2 Add the cheese, take off the heat and stir until the cheese has melted and the mixture is creamy.

3 Pour the mixture into sterilized pots, cover and leave until cold. Chill to set, then label.

Farmhouse Pâté

This pâté is full of flavor and can be cut into slices for easy serving. You can make the pâté in 4 individual dishes, or make 1 pâté in a 1 lb container.

Makes 1 lb

INGREDIENTS
8 slices bacon
2 chicken breasts
8 oz chicken livers
1 onion, chopped
1 garlic clove, crushed
½ tsp salt
½ tsp freshly ground black pepper
1 tsp chopped anchovy fillet
1 tsp ground mace
1 tbsp chopped fresh oregano
1 cup fresh white breadcrumbs
1 egg
2 tbsp brandy
⅔ cup chicken stock
2 tsp gelatin

TO GARNISH
strips of pimento and black olives

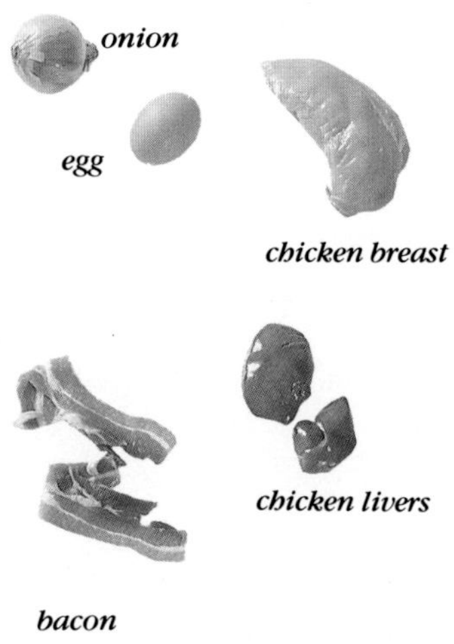

1 Preheat the oven to 325°F. Press the bacon slices flat with a knife to stretch them. Line the base and sides of each dish with bacon and neatly trim the edges.

2 Place the chicken breasts and livers, onion and garlic into a food processor. Process until smooth. Add the salt, pepper, chopped anchovy, mace, oregano, breadcrumbs, egg and brandy. Process until smooth.

3 Divide the mixture between the dishes and fill to the top. Cover each with double thickness foil and stand the dishes in a roasting pan. Add enough hot water to come halfway up the side of the dishes.

4 Bake in the center of the oven for 1 hour or until firm to touch. Release the foil to allow the steam to escape. Place a weight on the top of each dish to flatten the surface until cool.

5 Pour the juices from each dish into a measuring cup and make up to ⅔ cup with chicken stock. Heat in a small saucepan until boiling. Blend the gelatin with 2 tbsp water and pour into the hot stock, stir until dissolved. Allow to cool thoroughly.

6 When the pâté is cold, arrange strips of pimento and black olives on the top of each. Spoon the cold gelatin mixture over the top of each and chill until set. Cover each with plastic wrap. Store in the fridge until required.

Christmas Cards

These decorative sugar greeting cards make ideal gifts. The Modeling Paste may be cut to any size and a variety of cutters or piping nozzles used to create the design. Double the quantity of Modeling Paste to make more cards.

Makes 4

INGREDIENTS
½ quantity Modeling Paste
gold, green, red and purple food colorings
brown, red, green and purple food coloring pens
½ yd each of ⅛ in wide brown, red, green and purple ribbon

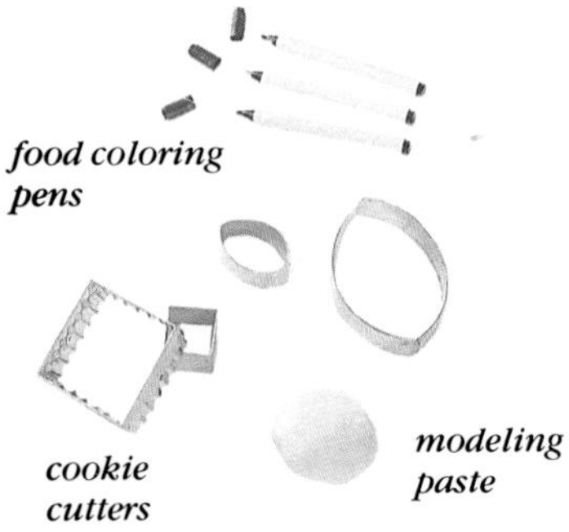

1 Make the Modeling Paste. Color the paste a pale cream color using a few drops of gold food coloring and cut into 4 pieces. Taking a piece at a time, roll out until the paste is ⅛ in thick. Using a 3½ in fluted oval cutter, stamp out 2 oval shapes. Stamp out a small oval from the center of one shape using a 2 in plain oval cutter.

2 Using a No. 1 plain writing nozzle, carefully stamp out tiny holes in each fluted shape around the edge of each oval. Make 2 holes ½ in apart in the center of the left-hand side on both shapes so they match together when the ribbon is threaded through. Place the oval shape with the cut-out center on a board. Using a small heart-shaped cutter, stamp out a series of hearts around the cut-out section. Use the plain nozzle to cut holes between the heart shapes.

MODELING PASTE

INGREDIENTS
1½ cups confectioners' sugar
1 tbsp gum tragacanth
1 tsp liquid glucose
1–2 tbsp water

1 Sift the icing sugar and gum tragacanth into a bowl. Make a well in the center and add the liquid glucose and water. Mix together with your fingers to form a soft paste. Dust a surface with confectioners' sugar and knead the sugarpaste until smooth, and free from cracks.

2 Place in a plastic bag or wrap in plastic wrap and seal well to exclude all the air. Leave for 2 hours before use, then re-knead and use small pieces at a time, leaving the remaining Modeling Paste well sealed. Use a little margarine instead of sugar when kneading, rolling out or molding the paste, to prevent it from becoming dry and brittle.

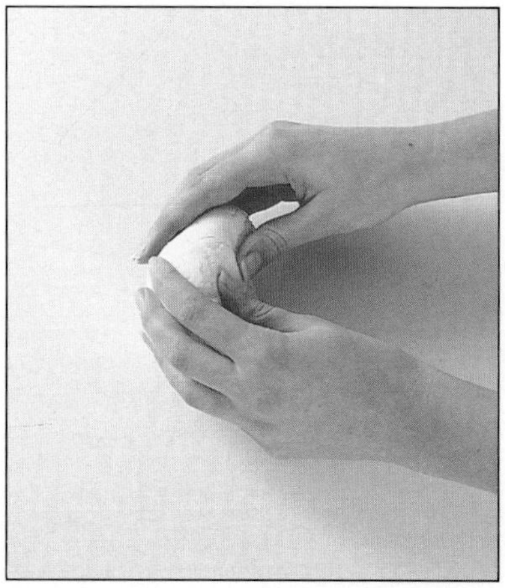

3 Leave the pieces to dry on a piece of foam sponge. Repeat to make 3 more cards in different shapes and sizes. When the cards are dry, arrange the 2 pieces of each card with the cut centers on top. Mark a series of dots within the cut-out center, matching each food coloring pen to the ribbon color, and write the name or greeting inside. Alternatively, cut out tiny holly leaves and berries and apply to the front of the card. Thread the ribbon through the holes to secure the cards together. They will keep indefinitely if stored in a cool, dry place.

Sugar Boxes

These delightful boxes may be made in any size or shape you choose. Decorate them with a freehand design or apply cut out decorations if you prefer.

Makes 4

INGREDIENTS
1 quantity Modeling Paste
1 quantity Gum Glaze
green and red food coloring dusts or ready-blended food colorings

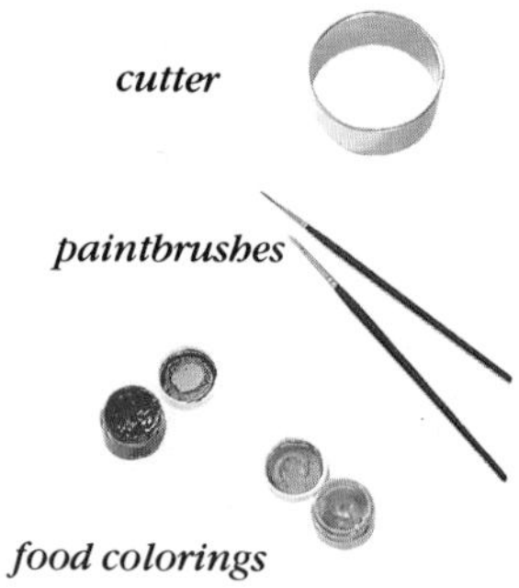

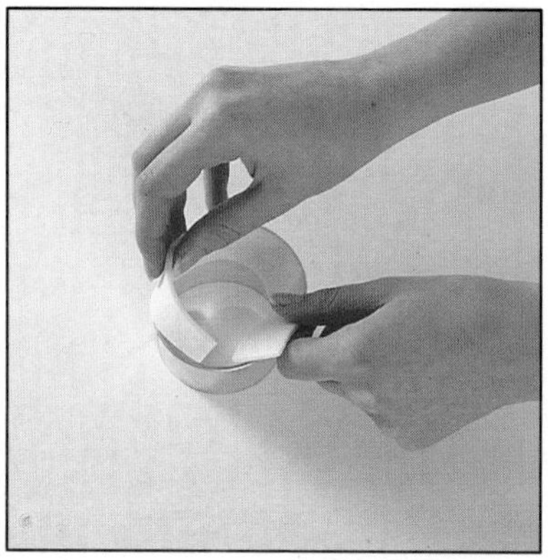

1 Measure around the outside of a plain round 3 in cutter with a length of string and cut it to size. Dust the outside of the cutter with cornstarch. Roll out a small piece of Modeling Paste thinly and cut to the length of the string and to the depth of the cutter. Gently ease the strip to fit inside the cutter so that the edges overlap, cutting away any excess paste. Brush the cut ends of the joins with a little Gum Glaze and press together to join neatly. Run a knife between the paste and the cutter to ensure the ring moves freely. Remove the cutter when the paste is firm.

2 Roll out another piece of paste thinly. Stamp out 2 rounds using the same cutter and place on a foam sponge. Mold a small knob for the lid, brush the underneath with Gum Glaze and press in position on the lid.

3 Brush the base edge of the box with Gum Glaze and place it in position on the round base. Repeat to make another 3 boxes. Leave all the pieces in a warm place to dry overnight. Using a fine pencil, draw a freehand design of holly leaves and berries, hearts, or your chosen design onto the side and lid of the box. Using food coloring dust mixed with a little Gum Glaze or ready-blended food colorings, and a fine paintbrush, paint one color at a time, cleaning the brush well before using each new color, until all the design has been painted. When dry, fill with a small gift or candies.

GUM GLAZE

INGREDIENTS
1 tbsp gum arabic
1 tbsp water

1 Gum Glaze is much more effective than egg white for sticking together sugar paste items. It dries very quickly and sets the sugar paste. Blend the gum arabic with the water using a small whisk and beat until smooth and free from lumps. Place in a tiny screw-topped jar or container.

Napkin Rings

These pretty rings may be used as a table decoration and taken home afterwards as a keepsake.

Makes 4

INGREDIENTS
1 quantity Modeling Paste
red, green, gold and silver glitter food coloring dusts
2 tbsp Royal Icing (see Introduction)

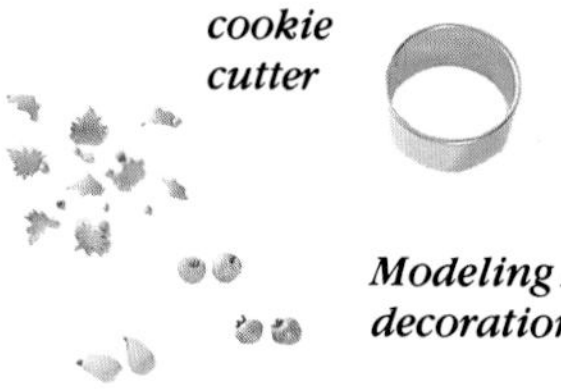

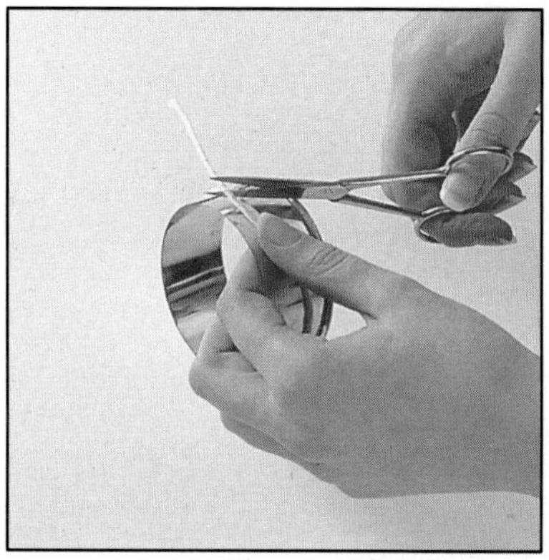

1 Make the Modeling Paste. Measure a piece of string to fit around the outside of a 3 in plain cutter and cut to size.

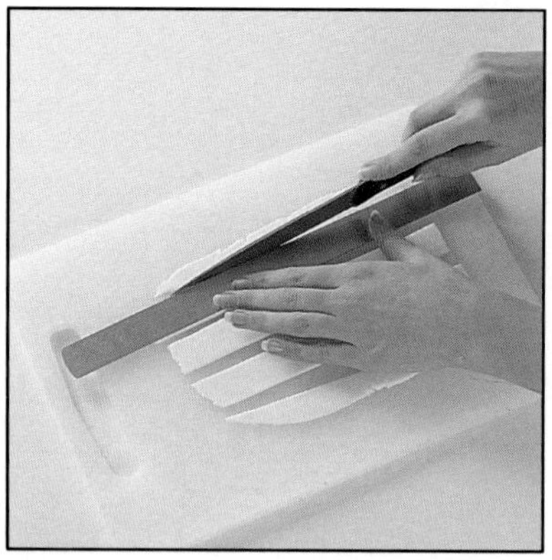

2 Roll out a small piece of Modeling Paste to the length of the string and measuring 1 in wide, and ⅛ in thickness. Using a knife, cut out the measured shape and round off both ends.

3 Brush the surface of the Modeling Paste with red glitter dust to color evenly. Place the strip of paste inside the cutter so the ends just meet. When the paste has set remove the cutter.

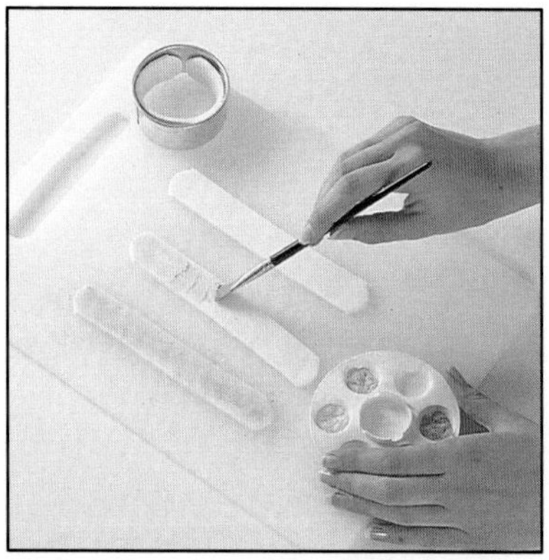

4 Color the remaining strips green, silver and gold, and make another 3 napkin ring shapes. Place all 4 rings on a foam sponge and leave in a warm dry place for 48 hours until completely dry and hard.

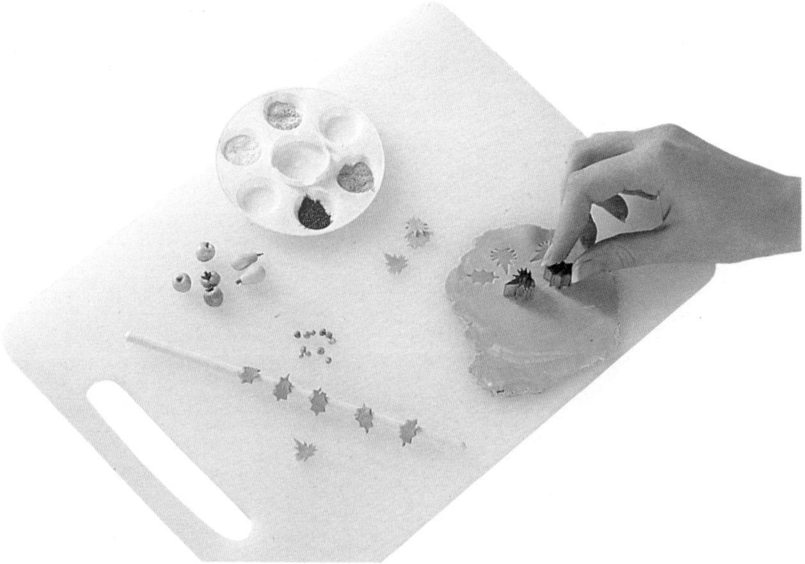

5 To make the decorations, use some Modeling Paste to form a selection of tiny fruits and vine leaves following the instructions for Marzipan Fruits. Color each fruit and leaf using the glitter dust and allow to dry. Using holly and ivy leaf cutters, make a selection of leaves and berries, rolling out the paste thinly and coloring with green and red glitter dusts. Mark the veins on the leaves with a knife and bend each leaf to dry over a wooden dowel or acrylic skewer.

6 Apply the holly, ivy leaves and berries to the red and green napkin rings, securing each piece with a little Royal Icing. Arrange the fruit and vine leaves on the gold and silver napkin rings, securing them with Royal Icing. Leave overnight to dry and pack into individual boxes.

Hanging Christmas Decorations

Decorations made from sugar Modeling Paste dry as hard as ceramic tiles. Many shapes and designs may be accomplished by imagination and flair. Ready-to-roll icing may be used instead of Modeling Paste but allow much longer for drying.

Makes 6

INGREDIENTS
1 quantity Modeling Paste or
8 oz ready-to-roll icing or fondant
1 quantity Gum Glaze
red and green food colorings
1½ yd red ribbon, ½ in wide
3 yd green ribbon, ½ in wide

1 Make the Modeling Paste and Gum Glaze or use ready-to-roll icing or fondant instead. Color ⅓ of the paste a bright red and ⅔ a rich green using the red and green food colorings, and knead until evenly colored and smooth. Keep in a plastic bag.

2 Using ½ of the green paste, roll out to a thickness of about ¼ in. Using a 3 in plain round pastry cutter, stamp out 3 rounds. Using a 2 in plain cutter, stamp out the center of each round to leave 3 rings. Take a small cocktail heart cutter and stamp out 3 heart shapes. Place all these cut-outs on a piece of foam sponge.

3 Brush the surface of one ring with Gum Glaze. Press some of the green paste through a garlic press, allowing the strands to fall evenly over the ring. Repeat to cover the remaining 2 rings. Roll out the red paste and using a 3 in heart-shaped cutter, stamp out 3 hearts and secure the small hearts in the center of each large heart using a little Gum Glaze. Make a hole in the top of each wreath and heart. Form lots of tiny berries and arrange at intervals on the wreath. Leave all pieces to dry hard, then thread ribbon through each.

Gold and Silver Christmas Bell Decorations

These are simply made by pressing sugar or Modeling Paste into a set of different sized bell-shaped molds. They can be colored, decorated or left plain.

Makes 6

INGREDIENTS

1 quantity Modeling Paste or 8 oz ready-to-roll icing or fondant
1 quantity Gum Glaze
cornstarch, to dust
1 tsp gin or vodka
gold and silver food coloring dusts
1½ yd gold ribbon, ⅛ in wide
1½ yd silver ribbon, ⅛ in wide

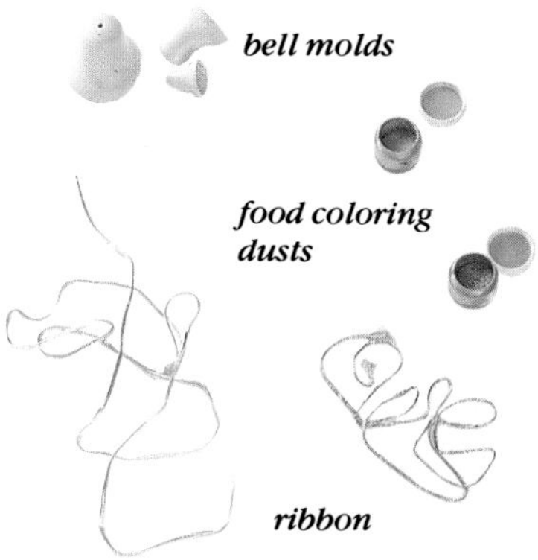

1 Make the Modeling Paste and Gum Glaze. Cut the paste into 6 even-sized pieces, returning 5 to the plastic bag. Lightly dust a work surface with cornstarch and shake a little into the inside of the largest bell mold.

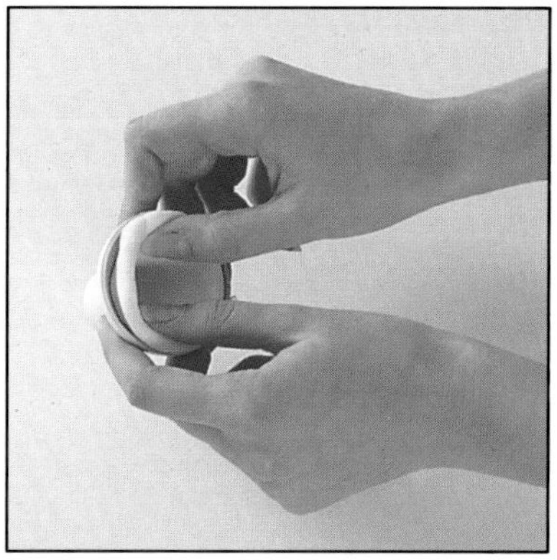

2 Gently ease the paste around the inside of a bell mold keeping the paste smooth. When the top end of the bell is smooth and a good shape, work down to the rim of the bell and trim off the excess with a knife. Pierce a hole in the top of the bell using a stainless steel needle. Repeat to make the medium- and small-sized bells, leave to dry. When the bells are hard, ease them out of the molds and repeat to make another set.

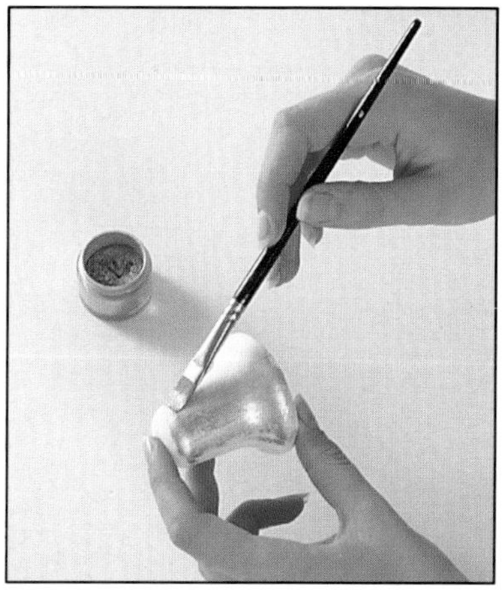

3 Using a fine paintbrush brush the outside of one bell with alcohol. Dust with gold food coloring dust to coat evenly. Repeat to color one set gold and one set silver. Cut each ribbon into 3 pieces. Mold 6 pea-shapes of paste for the 'clappers' and color 3 gold and 3 silver. Make a hole in the center of each, brush with Gum Glaze and insert the gold and silver ribbons. Thread the ribbon through each bell until the clapper is just above the rim. Press a small piece of paste, brushed with Gum Glaze, to the top of the bell to hold the ribbon in position, and tie the ribbon in a loop.

Candle Centerpiece

This arrangement of festive foliage and Christmas roses can be made in advance. Choose a brightly colored candle for the center.

Makes 1

INGREDIENTS
1 quantity Modeling Paste
1 quantity Gum Glaze
dark and light green and red food colorings
yellow and green food coloring dusts
2 tbsp Royal Icing (see Introduction)

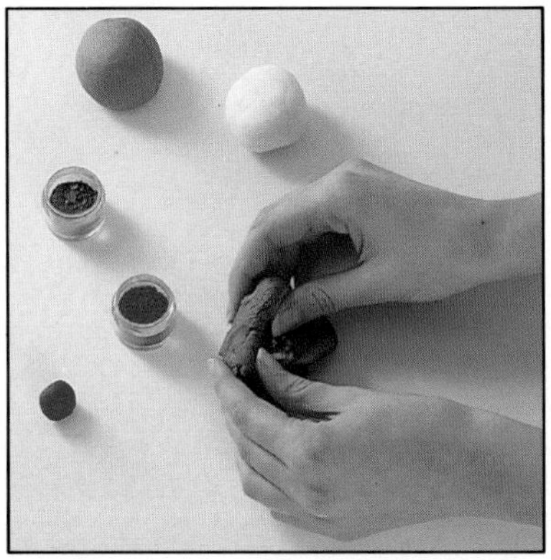

1 Make the Modeling Paste and Gum Glaze. Keep well sealed in a plastic bag during use. Divide the modeling paste into 3 pieces. Color 1 piece dark green and 1 piece light green using the food colorings. Place in the plastic bag. Take a pea-sized piece from the remaining white paste and color it bright red for the holly berries. Seal well.

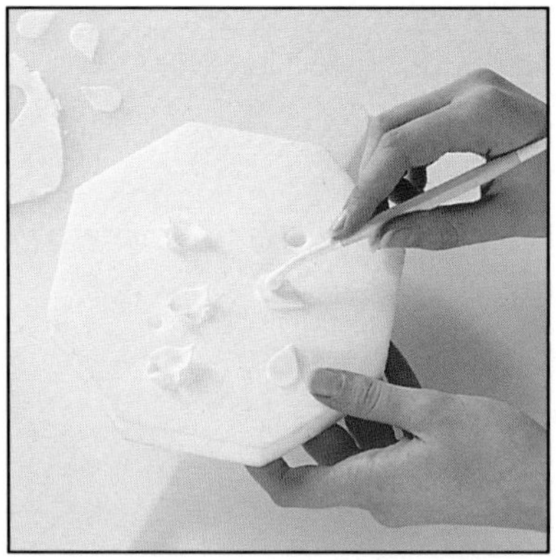

2 To make the rose: roll out a small piece of white paste on an acrylic board so thinly that you can almost see through it. Using a Christmas rose cutter, cut out 5 petal shapes. Soften the edges by using a bone tool on a flower mat or piece of foam sponge and make them slightly cup-shaped. Roll out a tiny piece of dark green paste and cut out a calyx and place on the flower mat or foam.

3 Brush the calyx with a little Gum Glaze and arrange the petals on it one at a time so that they overlap slightly, and stick them together with Gum Glaze. Position the flower over the hole in the flower mat or pierced hole if you are using foam sponge. Mold a tiny piece of white paste into a bead shape, brush with Gum Glaze and dip into yellow food coloring dust.

4 Place the yellow bead in the center of the rose and place the rose over a round cutter to support the petals while drying. Leave to dry in a warm place and repeat to make another 4 roses.

5 Roll out the light green paste. Using large and small-sized holly cutters, stamp out 8 large and 8 small holly leaves. Mark in the veins with a knife and bend over an acrylic skewer or wooden dowel to give each leaf a realistic shape. Roll out the dark green paste and cut out 8 medium-sized ivy leaves. Leave to dry. Mold lots of tiny red berries. Brush the surface of each leaf with Gum Glaze and green food coloring dust to give them a gloss.

6 Knead the remaining green colored pastes together and roll into 2 × 10 in pencil thin lengths. Twist together to form a rope and join the ends together to make a circle. Place on a board. Arrange the Christmas roses, holly and ivy leaves around the ring and add a few berries. Secure each element with a little Royal Icing. Leave to set hard in a warm place.

Marzipan Fruits

These eye-catching and realistic fruits will make a perfect gift for lovers of marzipan.

Makes 1 lb

INGREDIENTS
1 lb white marzipan
yellow, green, red, orange and burgundy food coloring dusts
2 tbsp whole cloves

marzipan

cloves

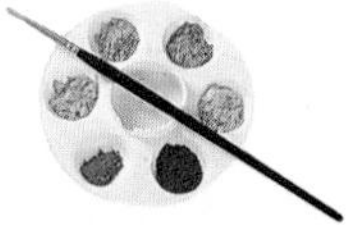

food coloring dusts

1 Cover a cookie sheet with parchment paper. Cut the marzipan into quarters. Take 1 piece and cut it into 10 even-sized pieces. Place a little of each of the food coloring dusts into a palette, or place small amounts spaced apart on a plate. Cut ⅔ of the cloves into 2 pieces, making a stem and core end.

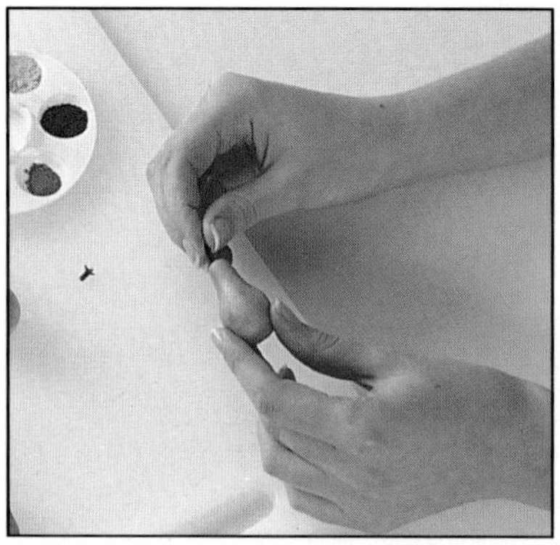

2 Taking the 10 pieces, shape each one into a neat ball. Dip 1 ball into the yellow food coloring dust and roll between the palms of the hands to color. Re-dip into the green coloring and re-roll to tint a greeny-yellow color. Using your forefinger, roll one end of the ball to make a pear shape. Press a clove stem into the top and a core end into the base. Repeat with the remaining 9 balls of marzipan. Place on the cookie sheet.

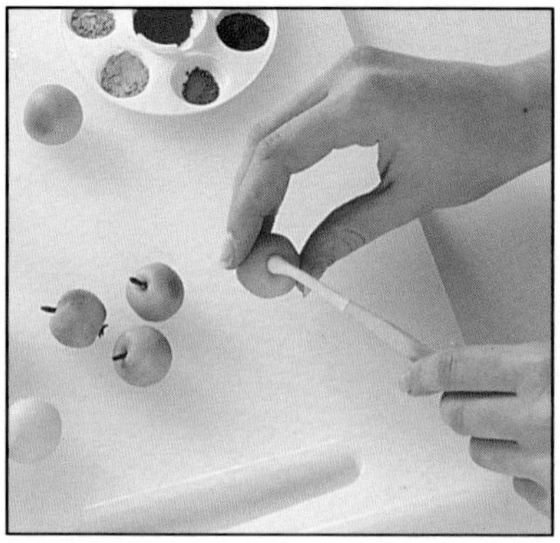

3 Cut another piece of the marzipan into 10 pieces and shape into balls. Dip each piece into green food coloring dust and roll in the palms to color evenly. Add a spot of red coloring dust and roll to blend the color. Using a ball tool or the end of a paintbrush, indent the top and base to make an apple shape. Insert a stem and core.

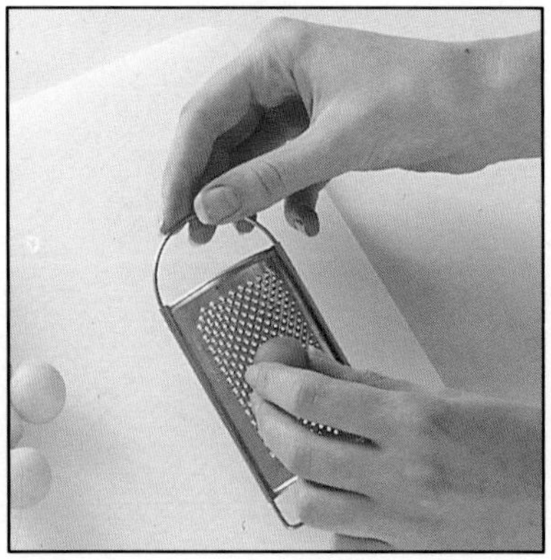

4 Repeat as above using another piece of the marzipan to make 10 orange colored balls. Roll each over the surface of a fine grater to give the texture of an orange skin. Press a clove core into the base of each.

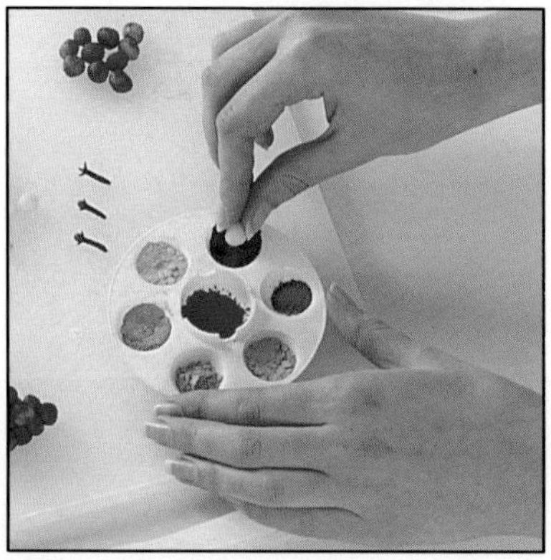

5 Take the remaining piece of marzipan, reserve a small piece, and mold the rest into lots of tiny marzipan beads. Color them burgundy with the food coloring dust. Place a whole clove on the cookie sheet. Arrange a cluster of burgundy beads in the shape of a bunch of grapes. Repeat with the remaining burgundy beads of marzipan to make another 3 bunches of grapes.

6 Roll out the remaining tiny piece of marzipan thinly and brush with green food coloring dust. Using a small vine leaf cutter, cut out 8 leaves, mark the veins with a knife and place 2 on each bunch of grapes, bending to give a realistic appearance. When all the marzipan fruits are dry, pack into gift boxes.

Turkish Delight

Turkish Delight is always a favorite at Christmas, and this versatile recipe can be made in minutes. Try different flavors such as lemon, crème de menthe and orange and vary the colors accordingly.

Makes 1 lb

INGREDIENTS
2 cups granulated sugar
1¼ cups water
1 oz powdered gelatin
½ tsp cream of tartar
2 tbsp rose-water
pink food coloring
3 tbsp confectioners' sugar, sifted
1 tbsp cornstarch

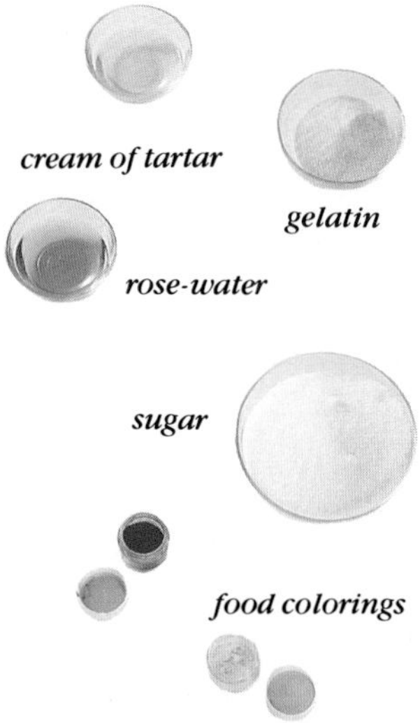

1 Wet the insides of 2 × 7 in shallow square pans with water. Place the sugar and all but 4 tbsp of water into a heavy-based saucepan. Heat gently, stirring occasionally, until the sugar has dissolved.

2 Blend the gelatin and remaining water in a small bowl and place over a saucepan of hot water. Stir occasionally until dissolved. Bring the sugar syrup to a boil and boil steadily for about 8 minutes or until the syrup registers 260°F on a sugar thermometer. Stir the cream of tartar into the gelatin, then pour into the boiling syrup and stir until well blended. Remove from the heat.

3 Add the rose-water and a few drops of pink food coloring to tint the mixture pale pink. Pour the mixture into the pans and allow to set for several hours or overnight. Dust a sheet of waxed paper with some of the sugar and cornstarch. Dip the base of the pan in hot water. Invert onto the paper. Cut into 1 in squares using an oiled knife. Toss in confectioners' sugar to coat evenly.

Orange, Mint and Coffee Meringues

These tiny, crisp meringues are flavored with orange, coffee and mint chocolate sticks and liqueurs. Pile into dry, air-tight glass jars or decorative tins.

Makes 90

Ingredients.
8 chocolate mint sticks
8 chocolate orange sticks
8 chocolate coffee sticks
½ tsp crème de menthe
½ tsp orange curaçao or Cointreau
½ tsp Tia Maria
3 egg whites
¾ cup superfine sugar
1 tsp cocoa powder

Tia Maria
eggs
crème de menthe
chocolate mint sticks

1 Preheat the oven to 225°F. Line 2–3 cookie sheets with parchment paper. Chop each flavor of chocolate stick separately and place each into separate bowls, retaining a teaspoonful of each flavor stick. Stir in the liquid flavorings to match the chocolate sticks.

2 Place the egg whites in a clean bowl and whisk until stiff. Gradually add the sugar, whisking well after each addition until thick. Add ⅓ of the meringue to each bowl and fold in gently using a clean plastic scraper until evenly blended.

3 Place about 30 teaspoons of each mixture onto the cookie sheets, well spaced apart. Sprinkle the top of each meringue with the reserved chopped chocolate sticks, matching the flavors. Bake in the oven for 1 hour or until crisp. Allow to cool and dust lightly with cocoa.

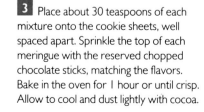

Creamy Fudge

A good selection of fudge always makes a welcome change from chocolates. Mix and match the flavors to make a gift-wrapped assortment.

Makes 2 lb

INGREDIENTS
- 4 tbsp unsalted butter, plus extra for greasing
- 2 cups granulated sugar
- 1¼ cups heavy cream
- ⅔ cup milk
- 3 tbsp water (this can be replaced with orange, apricot or cherry brandy, or strong coffee)

FLAVORINGS
- 1 cup plain or milk chocolate chips
- 1 cup chopped almonds, hazelnuts, walnuts or brazil nuts
- ½ cup chopped glacé cherries, dates or dried apricots

walnuts

almonds

glacé cherries

hazelnuts

plain chocolate chips

1 Butter a 8 in shallow square pan. Place the sugar, cream, butter, milk and water or other flavoring into a large heavy-based saucepan. Heat very gently, stirring occasionally using a long-handled wooden spoon, until all the sugar has completely dissolved.

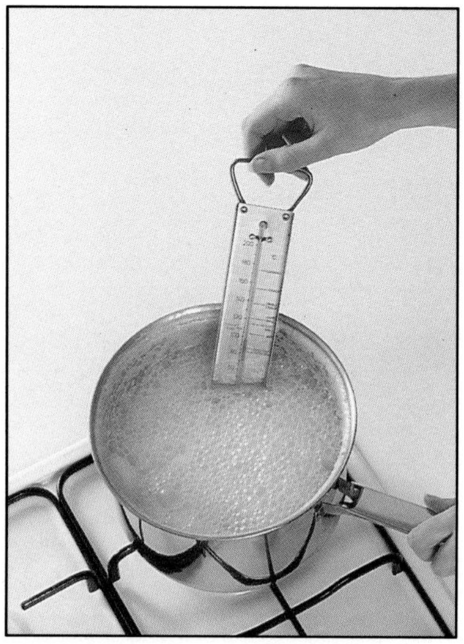

2 Bring the mixture to a boil and boil steadily, stirring only occasionally to prevent the mixture from burning over the base of the saucepan. Boil until the fudge reaches just under soft ball stage, 230°F for a soft fudge.

3 If you are making chocolate flavored fudge, add the chocolate at this stage. Remove the saucepan from the heat and beat thoroughly until the mixture starts to thicken and become opaque.

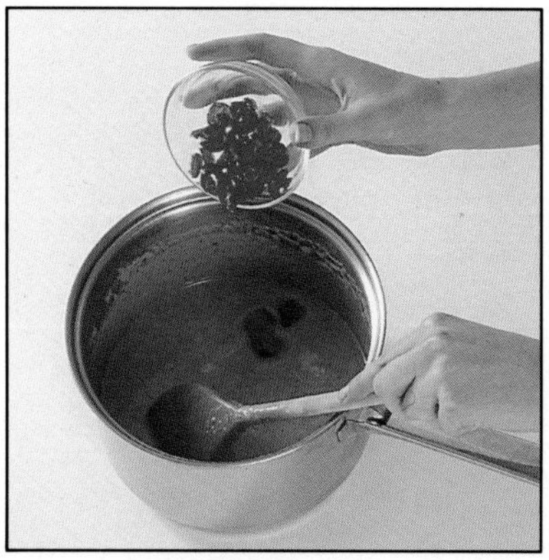

4 Just before this consistency has been reached, add chopped nuts for a nutty fudge, or glacé cherries or dried fruit for a fruit-flavored fudge. Beat well until evenly blended.

5 Pour the fudge into the prepared pan, taking care as the mixture is exceedingly hot. Leave the mixture until cool and almost set. Using a sharp knife, mark the fudge into small squares and leave in the pan until quite firm.

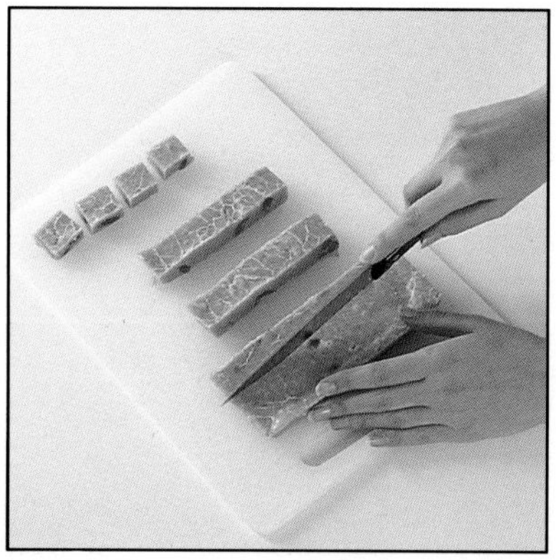

6 Turn the fudge out onto a board and invert. Using a long-bladed knife, cut into neat squares. You can dust some with confectioners' sugar and drizzle others with melted chocolate if desired.

Macaroons

These little macaroons can be served as petit-fours or with coffee. To make chocolate macaroons, replace the cornstarch with cocoa powder.

Makes 30

INGREDIENTS
½ cup ground almonds
¼ cup superfine sugar
1 tbsp cornstarch
¼–½ tsp almond extract
1 egg white, whisked
15 slivered almonds
4 glacé cherries, quartered
confectioners' sugar or cocoa, to dust

egg

glacé cherries

almonds

1 Preheat the oven to 325°F. Line 2 cookie sheets with parchment paper. Place the ground almonds, sugar, cornstarch and almond extract into a bowl and mix together well using a wooden spoon.

2 Stir in enough egg white to form a soft piping consistency. Place the mixture into a nylon piping bag fitted with a ½ in plain piping nozzle.

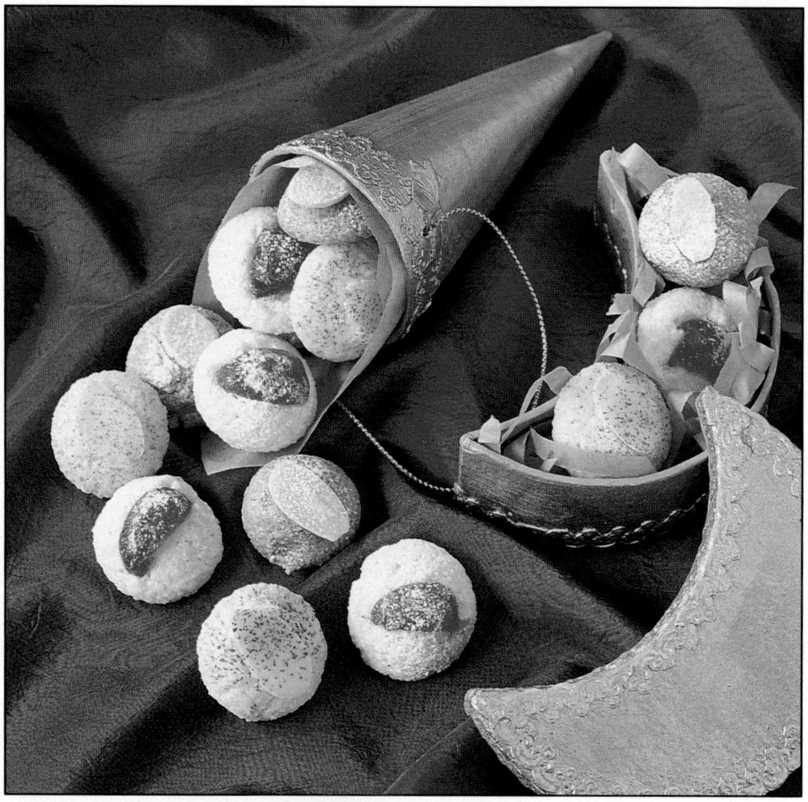

3 Pipe about 15 rounds of mixture onto each cookie sheet well spaced apart. Press a slivered almond onto half the macaroons and quartered glacé cherries onto the remainder. Bake in the oven for 10–15 minutes until firm to touch. Cool on the paper and dust with sugar or cocoa before removing from the paper.

Truffle Christmas Puddings

Truffles disguised as Christmas puddings are great fun to make and receive. Make any flavored truffle, and decorate them as you like.

Makes 20

INGREDIENTS
20 plain chocolate truffles
1 tbsp cocoa powder
1 tbsp confectioners' sugar
1 cup white chocolate chips, melted
2 oz white marzipan
green and red food colorings
yellow food coloring dust

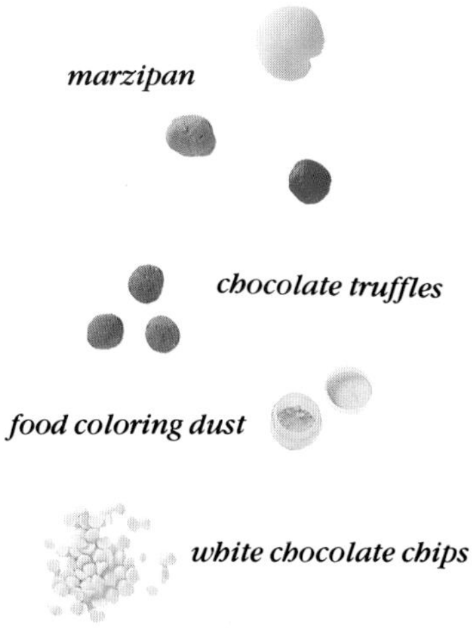

1 Make the truffles following the recipe in this book. Sift the cocoa and sugar together and coat the truffles.

2 Spread ⅔ of the melted white chocolate over a piece of parchment paper. Pick up the corners and shake to level the surface. Using a 1 in daisy cutter, stamp out 20 rounds when the chocolate has just set. Place a truffle on the center of each daisy shape, secured with a little of the reserved melted chocolate. Leave to set.

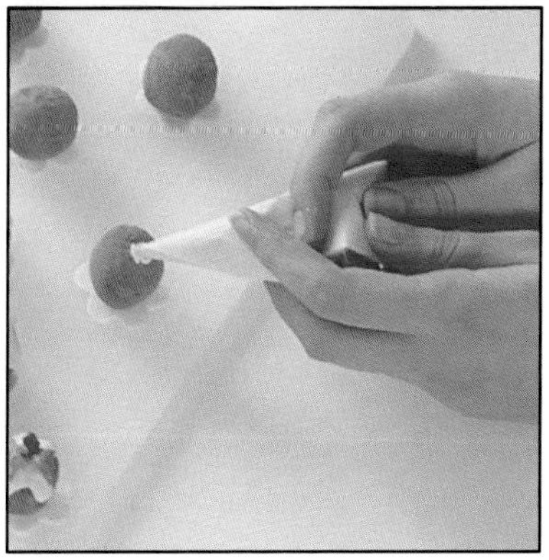

3 Color ⅔ of the marzipan green and ⅓ red using the food colorings. Roll out the green thinly and stamp out 40 leaves using a tiny holly leaf cutter. Mark the veins with a knife. Mold lots of tiny red beads. Color the remaining white chocolate with yellow food coloring dust and place in a waxed paper piping bag. Fold down the top, cut off the point and pipe over the top of each truffle to resemble custard. Arrange the holly leaves and berries on the top. When set, arrange in gift boxes and tie with ribbon.

Marshmallows

These light and fragrant mouthfuls of pale pink mousse are flavored with rose-water. Try using orange-flower water as a contrast, and color the sweets with a hint of orange food coloring.

Makes 1¼ lb

INGREDIENTS
oil, for greasing
3 tbsp confectioners' sugar
3 tbsp cornstarch
¼ cup cold water
3 tbsp rose-water
1 oz powdered gelatin
pink food coloring
2 cups granulated sugar
2 level tbsp liquid glucose
1 cup boiling water
2 egg whites

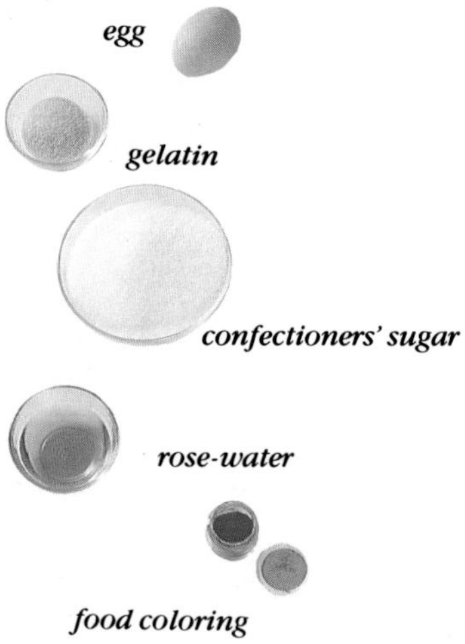

1 Lightly oil an 11 × 7 in jelly roll pan. Sift together the confectioners' sugar and cornstarch and use some of this mixture to coat the inside of the pan evenly. Shake out the excess.

2 Mix together the cold water, rose-water, gelatin and a drop of pink food coloring in a small bowl. Place over a saucepan of hot water and stir occasionally until the gelatin has dissolved.

3 Place the sugar, liquid glucose and boiling water in a heavy-based saucepan. Stir over a low heat to dissolve the sugar completely. Ensure that there are no sugar crystals around the water line; if so, wash these down with a brush dipped in cold water.

4 Bring the syrup to a boil and boil steadily without stirring until the temperature reaches 260°F on a sugar thermometer. Remove from the heat and stir in the gelatin mixture.

5 While the syrup is boiling, whisk the egg whites stiffly in a large bowl using an electric hand whisk. Pour a steady stream of syrup onto the egg whites while whisking continuously for about 3 minutes or until the mixture is thick and foamy. At this stage add more food coloring if the mixture looks too pale.

6 Pour the mixture into the prepared pan and allow to set for about 4 hours or overnight. Sift some of the remaining confectioners' sugar mixture over the surface of the marshmallow and the rest over a board or cookie sheet. Ease the mixture away from the pan using an oiled metal spatula and invert onto the board. Cut into 1 in squares, coating the cut sides with the sugar mixture. Pack into glass containers or tins and seal well.

Glacé Fruits

These luxury sweetmeats are very popular at Christmas and they cost a fraction of the store price if made at home. The whole process takes about 4 weeks, but the result is well worth the effort. Choose one type of fruit, or select a variety of fruits such as cherries, plums, peaches, apricots, star fruit, pineapple, apples, oranges, lemons, limes and clementines.

Makes 24 pieces

INGREDIENTS
1 lb fruit
4½ cups granulated sugar
1 cup powdered glucose

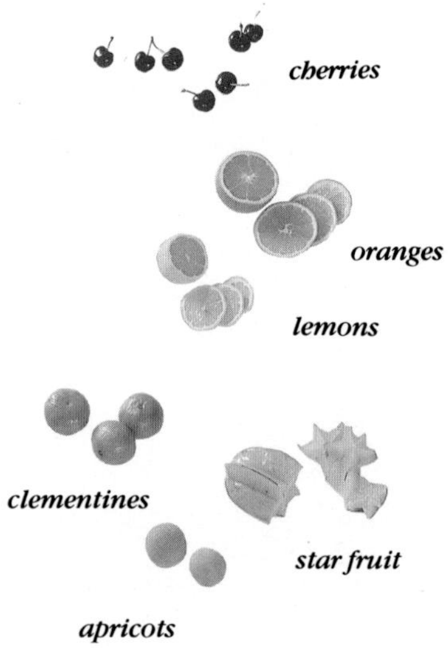

1 Remove the pits from cherries, plums, peaches and apricots. Peel and core pineapple and cut into cubes or rings. Peel, core and quarter apples and thinly slice citrus fruits. Prick the skins of cherries with a stainless steel needle so the syrup can penetrate the skin.

2 Place enough of the prepared fruit in a saucepan to cover the base, keeping individual fruit types together. Add enough water to cover the fruit and simmer very gently, to avoid breaking it, until almost tender. Use a slotted spoon to lift the fruit and place in a shallow dish, removing any skins if necessary. Repeat as above until all the fruit has been cooked.

3 Measure 1¼ cups of the liquid, or make up this quantity with water if necessary. Pour into the saucepan and add 4 tbsp sugar and the glucose. Heat gently, stirring occasionally, until dissolved. Bring to a boil and pour over the fruit in the dish, completely immersing it, and leave overnight.

4 DAY 2. Drain the syrup from the fruit into the saucepan and add 4 tbsp sugar. Heat gently to dissolve the syrup and bring to a boil. Pour over the fruit and leave overnight. Repeat this process each day, draining off the syrup, dissolving 4 tbsp sugar, boiling the syrup and immersing the fruit and leaving overnight on Days 3, 4, 5, 6 and 7.

5 DAY 8. Drain the fruit, dissolve ½ cup sugar in the syrup and bring to a boil. Add the fruit and cook gently for 3 minutes. Return to the dish and leave for 2 days. DAY 10. Repeat as above for Day 8; at this stage the syrup should look like clear honey. Leave in the dish for at least a further 10 days, or up to 3 weeks.

6 Place a wire rack over a tray and remove each piece of fruit with a slotted spoon. Arrange on the rack. Dry the fruit in a warm dry place or in the oven at the lowest setting until the surface no longer feels sticky. To coat in sugar, spear each piece of fruit and plunge into boiling water, then roll in granulated sugar. To dip into syrup, place the remaining sugar and ¾ cup of water in a saucepan. Heat gently until the sugar has dissolved, then boil for 1 minute. Dip each piece of fruit into boiling water, then quickly into the syrup. Place on the wire rack and leave in a warm place until dry. Place the fruits in paper candy cases and pack into boxes.

INTRODUCTION: CHRISTMAS CRAFTS

There's no time like Christmas. Sooner or later we all get swept up in its huge, warm embrace. It's an unrivalled opportunity to exercise your creativity as you decorate your home and plan your Christmas table. Lighten up the dark days of winter with the glint of gold, the enchanting glow of candlelight and the scent of freshly gathered evergreens. The craft ideas in this book will spark your creative energy and help you make the best of the festive season.

You'll find suggestions for traditional, colorful tree ornaments, or you might prefer the elegant monochromatic arrangements of gold or silver. If you'd rather avoid Christmas glitz, you may find inspiration in a rustic scheme, using materials such as homespun fabrics, garden raffia, and twigs and greenery you could collect on a winter walk.

Don't stop at decorations: make your own gift-wrap and tags – and gifts too. Find out how to make your own party crackers and you'll be able to fill them with personalized treats for your guests. All the projects are simple to make following the detailed step-by-step instructions.

There are craft projects especially for children, so they can share in the fun and sense of satisfaction of creating personalized cards, gift-wrap, decorations and presents. There is no better way to enter into the true spirit of the season.

Once you've discovered the satisfaction that comes from creating your own Christmas you'll no longer be content with ready-made decorations. Assemble a collection of rich fabrics, gold paper, ribbons, glitter and paint and use them to turn your home into a welcoming haven every Christmas.

Papers, Paints and Decorating Materials

Build up a store of interesting materials for your decorating projects: save pretty boxes, foil wrappings and packaging material. Specialist crafts suppliers offer a huge range of paints and papers. Remember that gold papers, markers and paints tend to be in short supply near Christmas so it's best to stock up beforehand. Below are some key materials for Christmas crafts.

Crayons and Pens
Stencil crayons come in a range of plain and metallic colours. They are oil-based and dry out to form a skin which must be scraped away each time they are used. Allow the work to dry thoroughly for a permanent finish. Gold (magic) marker pens are an alternative to paint when you need a fine line.

Decorative Papers
The choice is endless here. Look for double-sided and metallic crepe paper, especially in unusual colours such as bronze. Gold papers and foils come in various textures, matt and shiny, and add a touch of luxury to your work. Don't forget the basics: add your own decorations to brown parcel wrap (packaging paper), white paper and card (cardboard).

Glitter and Glitter Paints
There is an amazing selection of different types of glitter to choose from now. As well as the old-fashioned tubes of coloured glitter to sprinkle on, you can buy coloured glitter suspended in clear paint and tubes of glittery fabric paints.

Lino-Cutting Tool
I used this to cut decorative grooves in citrus fruit. A traditional implement, used by chefs, is known as a canelle knife.

Metal Foils
Copper and aluminium foils are available from crafts suppliers in a heavier gauge than ordinary kitchen foil.

Paints
Gold spray paint is useful for covering large areas, but look out for different shades of gold in water-based and oil-based paints. Watercolour inks have a wonderful translucent vibrancy that is quite different to the matt effect of gouache paint. Try to use special stencil paint for stencilling on fabric and paper as it has a creamy texture and will not bleed easily.

Papers
There is a tremendous range of decorative papers available from stationers, crafts suppliers and art shops. It is always worth stocking up at Christmas time as the shops tend to have an even larger selection than usual.

Polystyrene Shapes (Forms)
These are available from crafts suppliers and come in a large range of different shapes.

Oil-based Paints
These paints are used for decorating surfaces that will need washing, such as glass and ceramics. Read the manufacturer's instructions before you use them. Clean brushes with (distilled) turpentine or white spirit (paint thinner). Glass (relief) outliner paint comes in a tube and is squeezed directly on to the surface. It needs a long drying time but sets rock hard.

White Emulsion (Latex) Paint
This is a cheaper alternative to white gouache paint for covering the surface of papier mâché. For added strength, mix in some PVA (white) glue.

Willow Twigs
Perfect for rustic decorations or for hanging on the tree, willow twigs grow straight and regular, and are an excellent material for weaving wreaths. Leave them in their natural state, or paint or spray them.

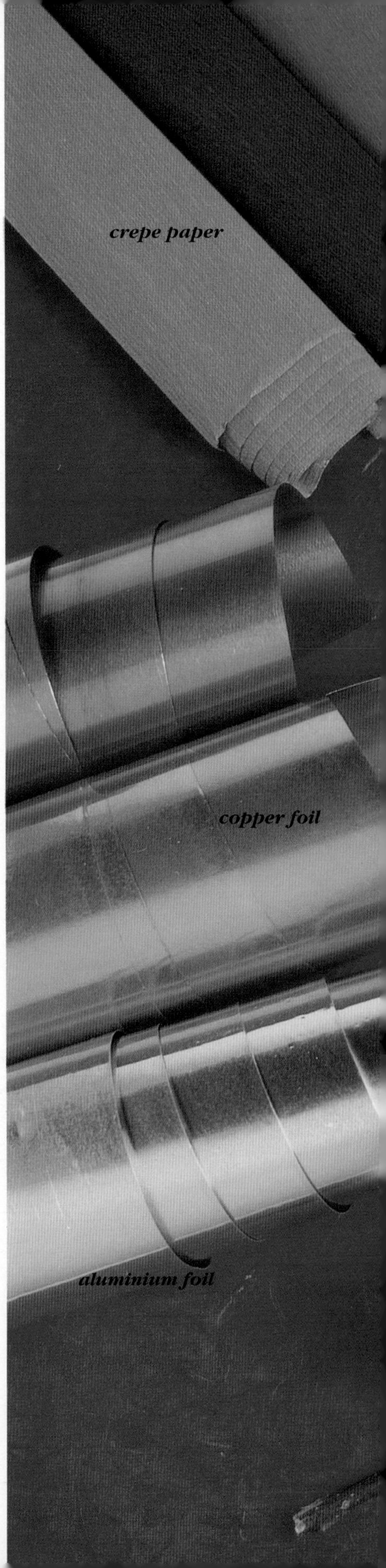

metallic
crepe paper
gold spray paint
e 170g 3
card
(cardboard)
stencil crayons
gold relief
outliner
GUITAR OIL PASTEL
GUITAR OIL-PASTEL
ARTISTS
IRISÉ
white
paper
white emulsion
(latex) paint
1.25 US fl.oz
e 37ml
PERMANENT WHITE
jaune orangé
Couleurs
vitrail
cerne relief
oil-based
glass paint
gouache
foam board
lino-cutting tool
ENGLAND
decorative
papers
watercolour
inks
gold water-
based paint
glitter paint
polystyrene
shapes (forms)
glitter
gold oil-based
paint
CONTAIN NO XYLENE
gold (magic)
marker pen
willow twigs
foil wrappers

Fabrics, Ribbons, Trims and Threads

One of the joys of making your own original decorations lies in using high-quality, sumptuous materials: you can create an impression of great luxury with very small amounts of beautiful fabrics, so hunt around for pretty colours and interesting textures as well as unusual ribbons and braids.

Buttons
Many people collect buttons for pleasure. For decorations, keep a supply of gold buttons and always save real mother-of-pearl buttons from shirts that are no longer used. Be on the look out for odd luxury buttons on old jackets which you can use in decorations.

Checked Cotton, Ticking, Wool, Calico, Hessian (Burlap) and Linen
As an antidote to all the richness of traditional Christmas fabrics, simple country-style homespun materials are perfect for naïve decorations. Age fabrics by washing well, then dipping in strong tea. Hessian (burlap) is normally used for upholstery, but its rustic texture and honey colour work very well with bright colours and gold.

Cords and Braids
Gold is the most festive colour for cords and braid, although rich dark colours make an interesting alternative for trimming items you may wish to leave out for the rest of the year. Use fine gold cord to make loops for hanging decorations for the tree.

Polyester Wadding (Batting)
This is invaluable for stuffing since it is lightweight and very soft. It can also be purchased in lengths, for quilting, which can be cut to shape when a light padding is needed.

Ribbons
Wide satin ribbon is the kind most often used for the projects in this book. It is readily available in a versatile range of sizes and colours, sometimes with printed designs. Collect special ribbons when you see them for making tree ornaments and decorating floral displays. Wire-edged ribbon is particularly good for making bows since it holds its shape.

Sequins and Beads
Sequins, seed pearls (heads) and glass beads add instant opulence to any decorative piece. They are available from crafts suppliers in a multitude of shapes and colours. You can also buy plastic "gemstones" to make jewelled ornaments for the tree.

Silks, Taffeta, Organza (Organdy) and Lamé
Use these luxurious fabrics for both decorations and gifts. You'll find plenty of gold shades to choose from in the run-up to Christmas, but wonderful striped and checked silk can be found all year round.

String and Raffia
I have used thin garden twine for several of the projects in this book: its soft brown colour and rustic appearance suit the naïve decorations. Sisal parcel string and natural (garden) raffia are also used.

Tapestry Canvas
You will need white canvas with 24 holes to 5 cm (12 holes to 1 in) for the needlepoint projects in this book.

Threads
A well-stocked sewing box filled with every shade of sewing thread one could ever need is every dressmaker's dream. Start with essential black and white threads and build up your collection as you sew. Stranded embroidery thread (floss) has six strands: for all but the boldest stitches you'll probably want to use two or three. Cut a length, then pull the strands gently apart. Tapestry wool (yarn) is made for canvas work and is very hard-wearing. Don't be tempted to substitute knitting wool (yarn) or you will be frustrated by constant breaks as you stitch.

Velvet
In rich, dark colours, velvet is especially Christmassy. It is available in light weights for dressmaking and heavier weights for furnishing (upholstering). Look for textured and two-toned velvets.

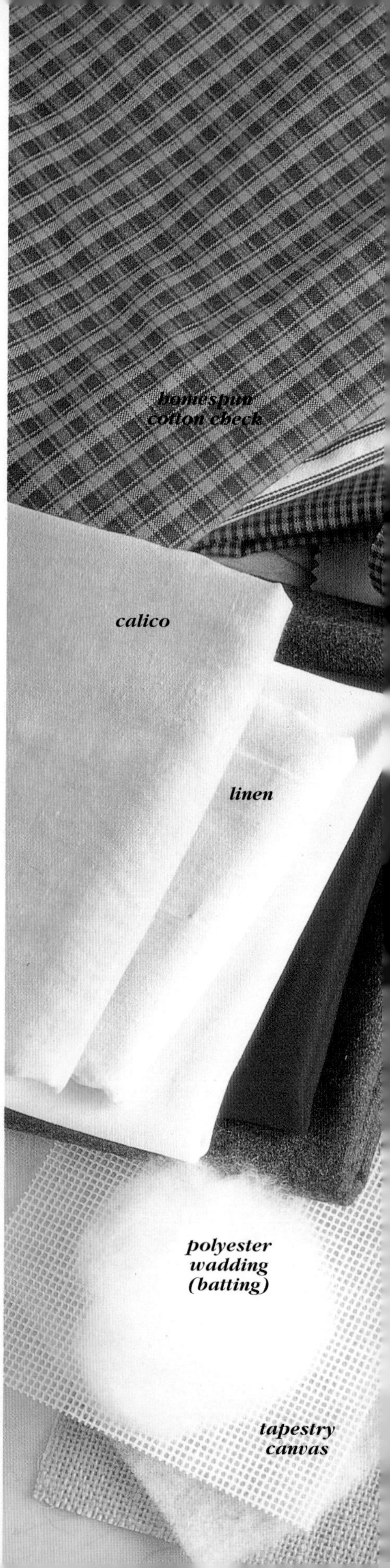

pleated organza
lamé
cotton ticking
velvet
gold netting
fine gold cord
decorative braid
sequin ribbon
gold braid
plastic gemstones
silk
mother-of-pearl buttons
glass beads
sequins
wool
satin ribbons
sewing thread
garden twine
stranded embroidery thread (floss)
sisal (parcel string)
quilting wadding (batting)
bessian (burlap)
natural (garden) raffia
tapestry wool (yarn)

Equipment

It's sensible to make sure you have everything you need for your project before you begin. The following list of invaluable equipment includes artists' materials, office supplies and some general bits and pieces you probably already have around the home.

Adhesive Tape
Double-sided adhesive (cellophane) tape allows you to join paper invisibly. It is also a good substitute for glue when you don't wish to dampen a surface, when using crepe paper, for example. Masking tape is indispensable for securing stencils and patterns in position.

Craft Knife
Craft knives have extremely sharp blades. Use them (on a cutting mat) for cutting out stencils and for accurate cutting of paper against a metal ruler. Change the blade frequently and keep out of the reach of children.

Foam Rollers
These come in assorted sizes and are easily washable. Use them with stencil paint and for sponging water-based paints on to paper or fabrics.

Glue
PVA (white) glue is a thick liquid that dries to a transparent sheen. It will stick most surfaces together. It can also be diluted with water when making papier mâché or as a protective coating. After use, wash brushes out in water straight away. Glue-sticks are excellent for sticking paper neatly and are safe for children to use.

Hole Punch
Useful for making neat holes for the handles of gift bags and for punching a single hole in home-made gift tags.

Hot Glue Gun
The best thing to use when you need a glue that dries almost instantly and is very strong and clean. The nozzle delivers a small dot of hot, melted glue at the squeeze of the trigger.

Metal Ruler
This provides a safe edge to work against when cutting paper with a craft knife; you can also use it for measuring and marking out. Use a dressmaker's tape for longer measurements.

Paintbrushes
Old brushes are useful for applying glue and emulsion (latex) paint mixed with PVA (white) glue. Stencil brushes are wide and stiff. You will also need a fine-tipped brush for more delicate work and a medium bristle brush for applying metallic craft paint, which should be cleaned with white spirit (paint thinner) or a commercial brush cleaner.

Pencils and Pens
A soft pencil that can easily be erased is useful for tracing and transferring motifs. Keep an old ballpoint pen that has run out of ink for making embossed foil decorations. For marking light fabrics you can use a vanishing fabric marker: the best fade naturally and don't need to be washed out.

Pins and Needles
Use dressmaker's pins to hold fabrics in place. You'll need an ordinary sewing needle for seams and an embroidery needle with a large eye to thread stranded embroidery thread (floss). A tapestry needle is fairly broad, with a large eye and a blunt point.

Plastic Adhesive
This malleable substance is used for attaching objects and paper to surfaces from which it can later be removed cleanly. It is useful when working with candles to keep them upright in their holders.

Saucers and Jars
Keep old saucers and jars for mixing paint and glue. Keep the lids of the jars, too, so that the contents don't dry out.

Scissors
You will need one pair for cutting paper and another for fabrics: never use the latter on paper as it will blunt them very quickly. A small pair of needlework scissors with pointed ends is useful for embroidery.

Secateurs (Pruning Shears)
For heavy-duty foliage trimming and for the twig decorations.

Stapler
A staple gun is indispensable for attaching fabrics to wood or board. An ordinary office stapler will secure paper, fabric and thin card (cardboard).

Stencil Card (Cardboard)
Specially made for stencilling, this card (cardboard) is coated in a water-resistant oil so that you can wipe it clean between stencils and when changing colours. Transfer your image to the card (cardboard) using a soft pencil and cut it out with a craft knife.

Tracing Paper
Another essential. When you've traced a motif you can cut it out to use as a pattern, or transfer it by rubbing the back side of the paper with a soft pencil, positioning the template, and then tracing over the outline again from the front of the paper.

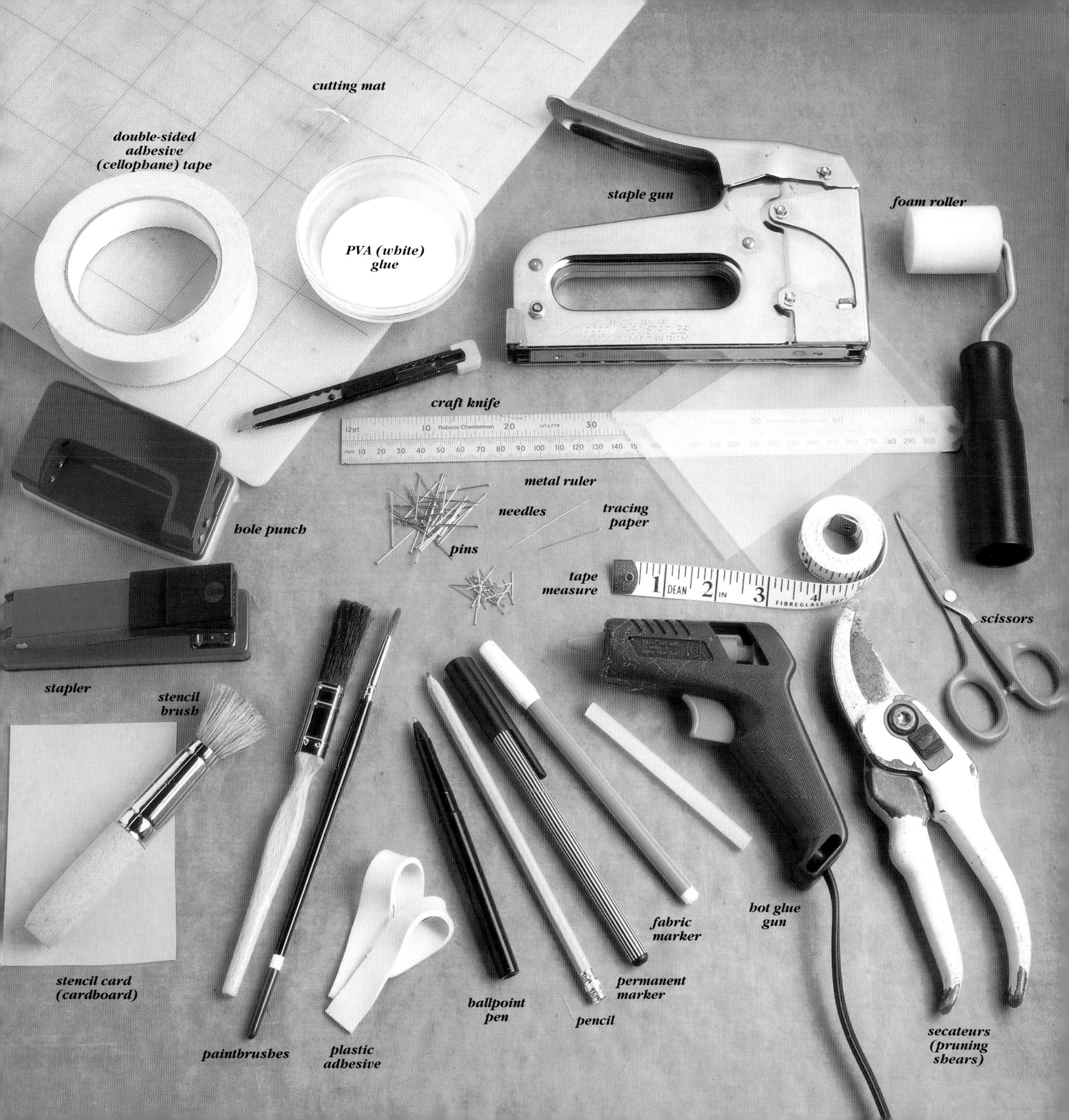
cutting mat
double-sided adhesive (cellophane) tape
PVA (white) glue
staple gun
foam roller
craft knife
metal ruler
hole punch
needles
tracing paper
pins
tape measure
scissors
stapler
stencil brush
hot glue gun
fabric marker
permanent marker
ballpoint pen
pencil
stencil card (cardboard)
paintbrushes
plastic adhesive
secateurs (pruning shears)

Techniques

The projects in this book use straightforward techniques that are easy and satisfying to master. If you're doing something you haven't tried before, practise on a spare piece of fabric or paper until you're confident.

Stem Stitch

This embroidery stitch is perfect for working the outline of a design, is very simple and quick to do and creates a neat edge.

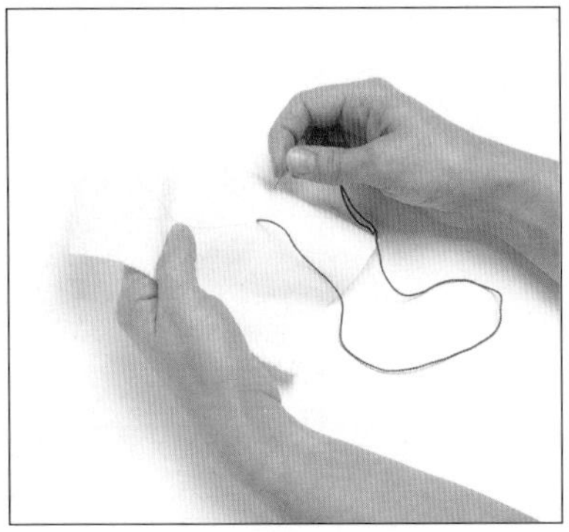

1 Cut a length of embroidery thread (floss) about 30cm (12in), thread the needle and knot the end. Bring the threaded needle up through the fabric directly through the line you have traced for the design.

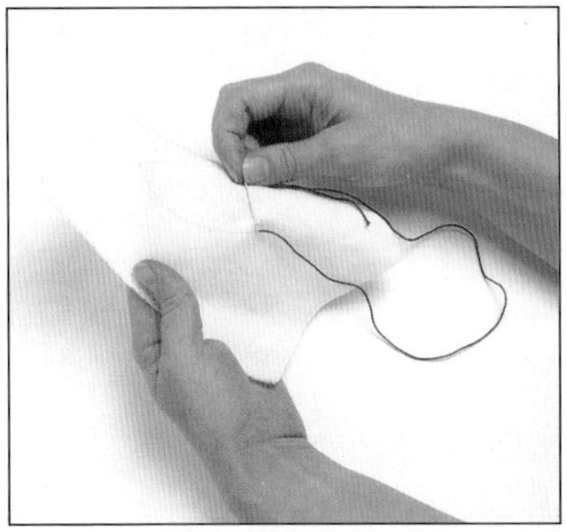

2 Put the needle back into the fabric a short way along the traced line and in the same movement bring the needle up again about halfway back towards the place where your first stitch emerged. Always keep to the traced outline.

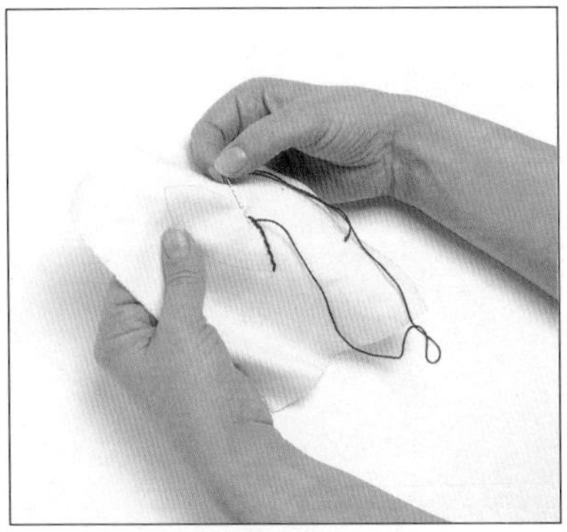

3 Put the needle into the fabric a little further along the line, making a stitch equal in length to the first. Work the whole of the outline in evenly spaced stitches, repeating step two throughout and always bringing the needle out on the same side of the previous stitch.

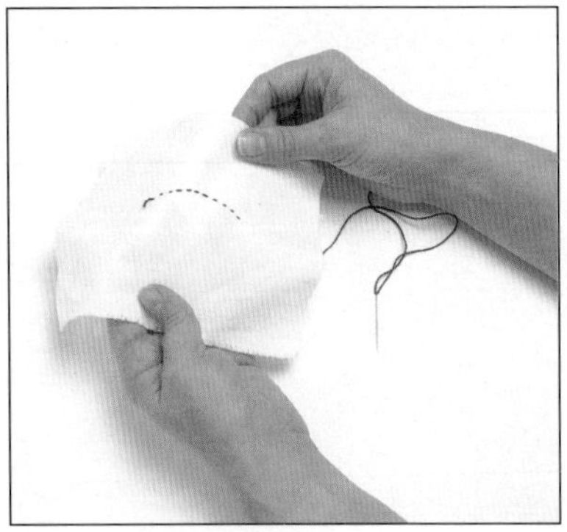

4 The back of the work will look like short running stitches.

Needlepoint Tent Stitch

This is the stitch used on canvas for needlepoint designs. When working from a chart, one square on the chart represents one intersection of the canvas. Tent stitch is usually worked horizontally.

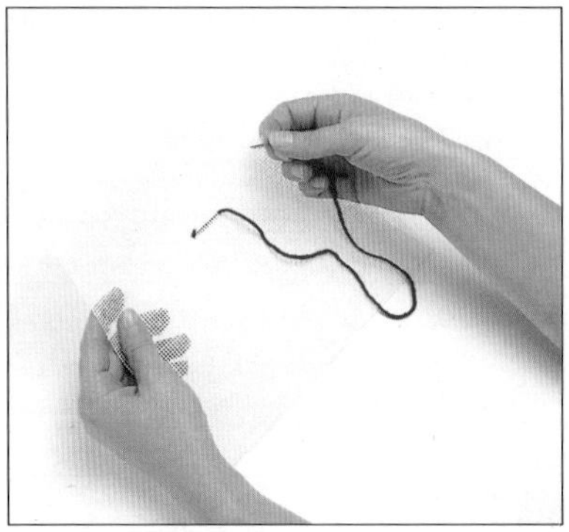

1 Cut a 45 cm (18 in) length of tapestry wool (yarn), thread the needle and knot the end. Begin with the knot on the right side of the canvas. Bring the needle up 2.5 cm (1 in) away. The first few stitches are worked over this thread to secure it. Then cut the knot off neatly.

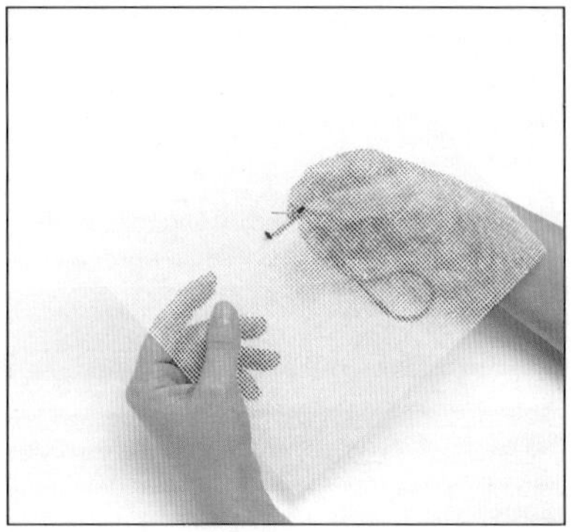

2 To work from right to left, bring your needle up through the canvas at the top left of a stitch and put it back in the square diagonally down to the right, working across one intersection of tapestry canvas.

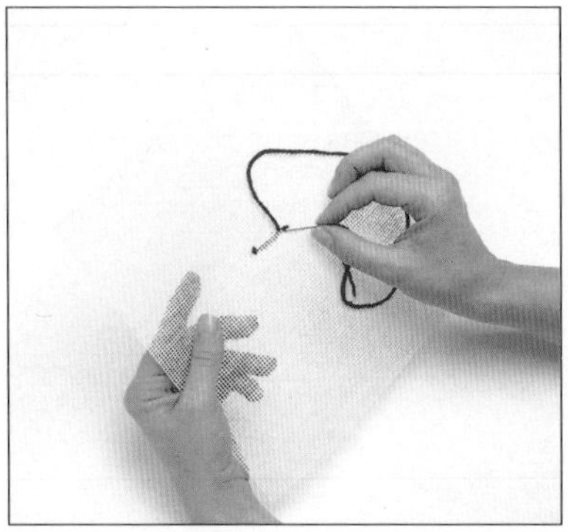

3 Bring the needle up again through the hole directly to the left of the top of the stitch you made in step two. Repeat to make a row of stitches. The stitches on the back are always longer.

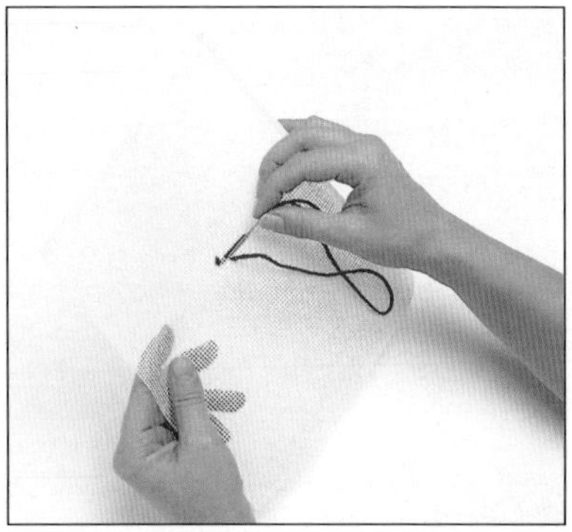

4 To work from left to right, bring the needle out at the bottom of a stitch and put it back diagonally up to the left, across one intersection of canvas. All the stitches must slant in the same direction.

French Knots

French knots are used in embroidery to give a lovely raised effect. They are perfect for adding decorative detail to embroidery. To make a large French knot, use the full six strands of embroidery thread (floss).

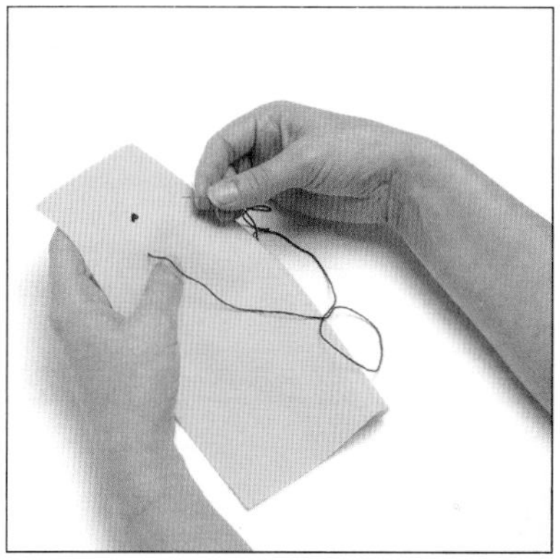

1 Thread the needle with embroidery thread (floss). Bring the needle up through the fabric at the point where you want the knot to be.

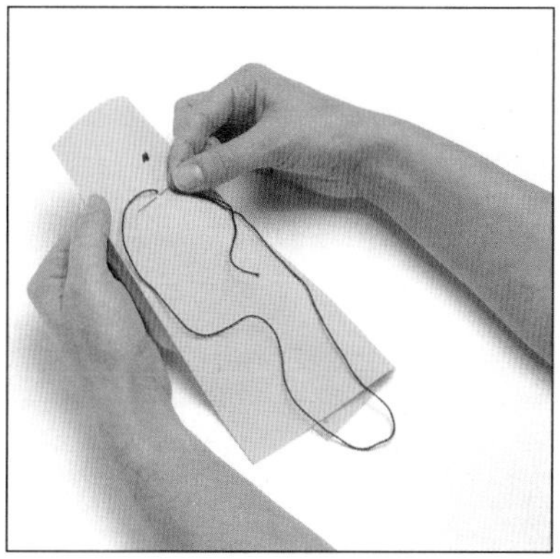

2 Make a small stitch at the same point and with the needle still in the fabric, pick up the end of the thread as it emerges from the fabric.

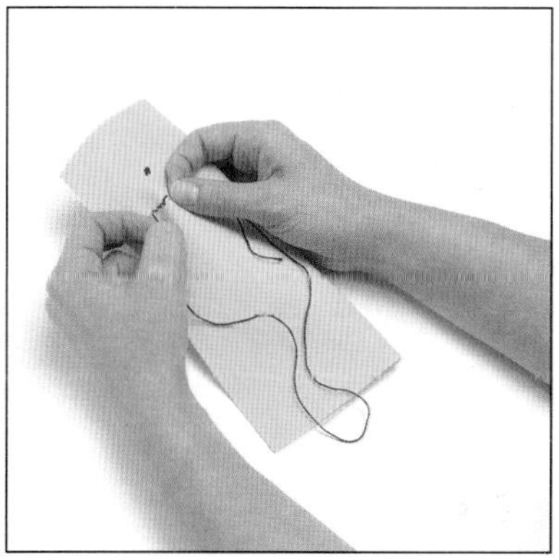

3 Wrap the thread two or three times around the needle, then pull the needle out through these threads.

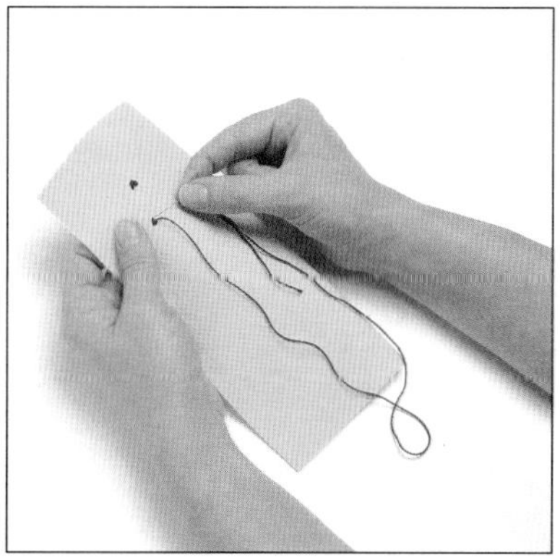

4 Secure the stitch by pulling the needle back through the fabric at the point where you began the stitch.

Blanket Stitch

This stitch is traditionally used to finish the raw edges of non-fraying fabrics, such as wool and felt. It is very decorative when it is worked in a colour that contrasts with the fabric.

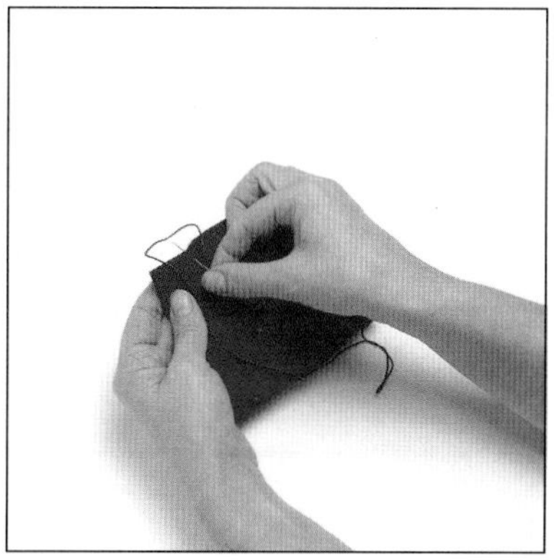

1 Bring the needle out from the back of the fabric a little way in from the raw edge. Insert the needle from the front to one side of the first stitch and the same distance from the edge.

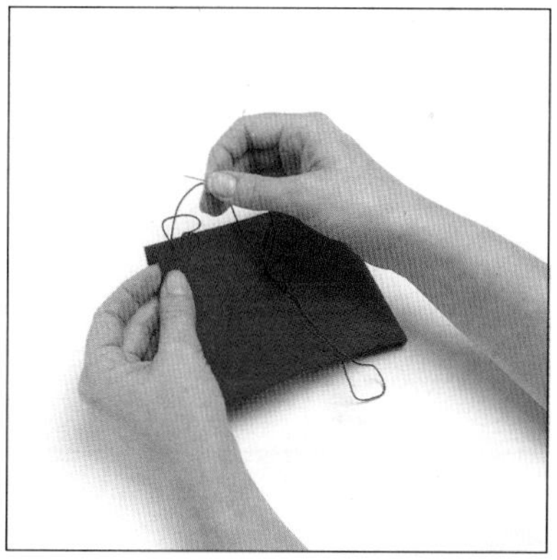

2 As you pull the needle through, take it through the loop between the two stitches and gently pull up the slack. Repeat, inserting the needle from the front and pulling it through the loop.

3 To turn a corner, work three stitches into the same hole, changing the angle.

Making Templates

You may need to enlarge the templates in this book to the size you require before you use them. If you do not have access to a photocopier, follow the instructions for the grid system of enlarging templates at the back of this book

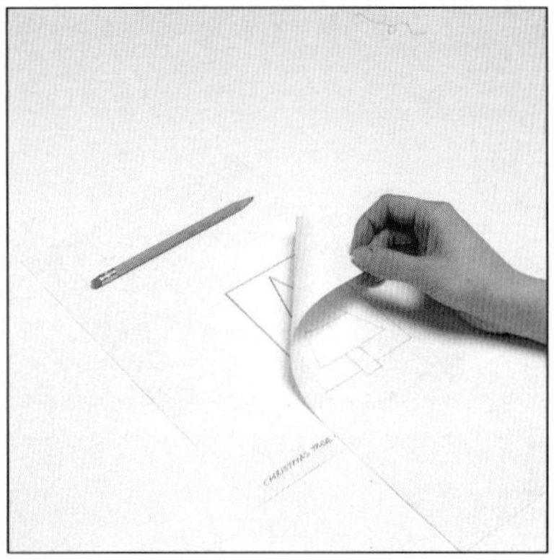

1 Photocopy the template you are going to use, enlarging it as many times as is necessary to achieve the required correct size.

2 If you wish to use the photocopy again, or you need to trace the design on to another sheet of paper or other material, make a tracing with a soft pencil on thin plain paper or tracing paper.

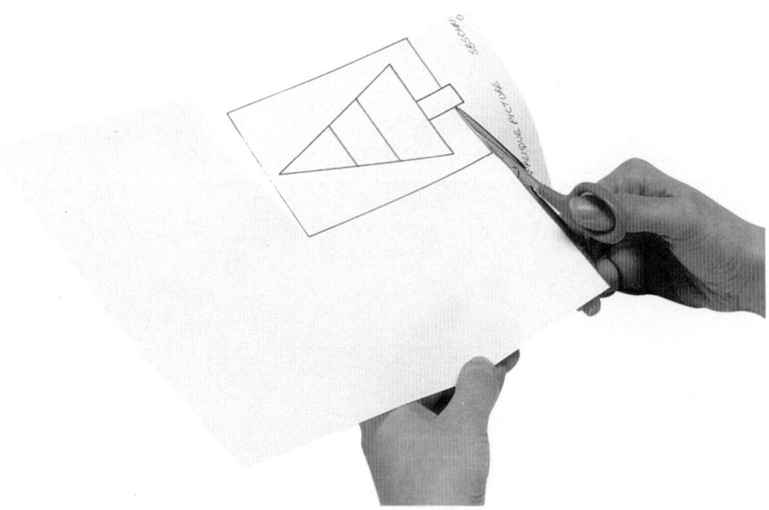

3 If you are going to use the photocopy as your template, cut it out ready to draw around. If you are working with fabric, pin the template to the fabric and draw around it lightly with tailor's chalk or a fabric marker pen.

Stencilling

Stencilling is a satisfying and easy way to produce repeated designs on paper, wood or fabric. You can cut your motif out of stencil card (cardboard) or clear acetate sheet.

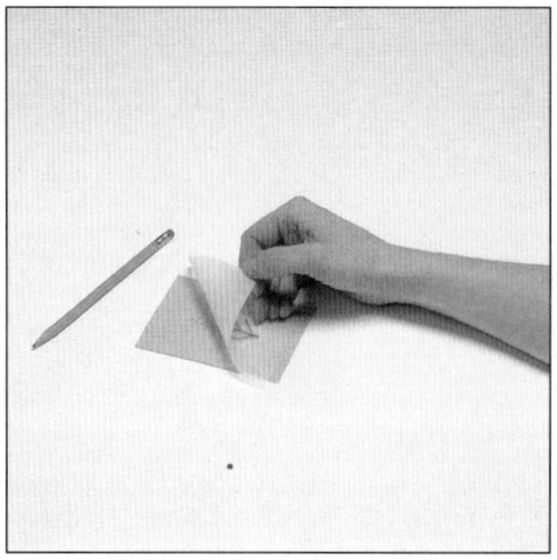

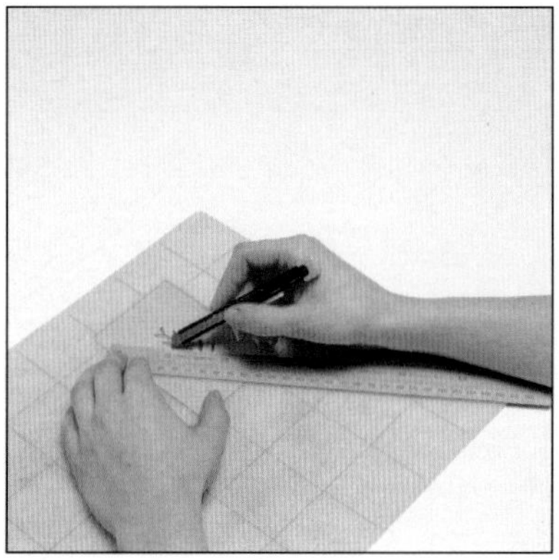

1 Trace the motif on to tracing paper. Turn over and rub the back side with a soft pencil. Position the tracing face up over the stencil card (cardboard) and draw around the outline of the design.

2 Using a craft knife and cutting mat, cut the motif carefully from the card.

3 Place the stencil on the surface you wish to decorate, securing it with masking tape if necessary. Brush the paint through the stencil. Do not overload the brush: it is better to repeat the process until you achieve the desired effect, otherwise paint may bleed under the edges of the stencil. Lift off the stencil carefully.

Stamping

Stamping is great fun and so easy to do. The stamps used in this book were very simply made from thin cellulose kitchen sponge cloths, which are easy to cut into simple shapes using scissors.

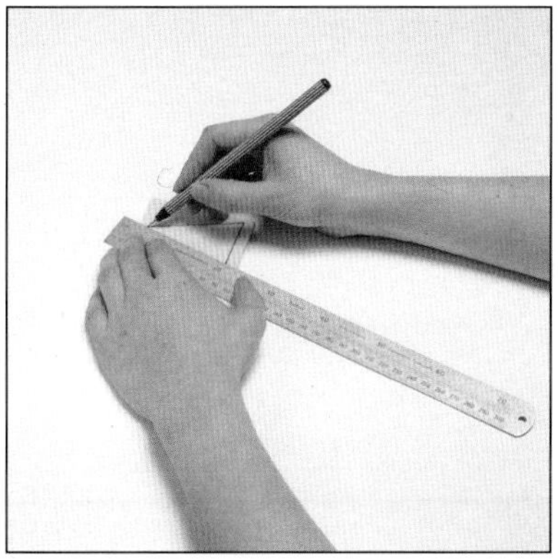

1 Draw your motif directly on to the sponge with a fine (magic) marker pen, following a paper template if necessary.

2 Cut out the motif with scissors and use a glue stick to attach it securely to a piece of corrugated cardboard.

3 Brush stencil paint directly on to the sponge, coating it well.

4 Press the stamp on to the surface to be decorated, using even pressure. Re-apply paint between each stamping to get consistent prints.

Working with Metal Foil

The aluminium and copper foil used in this book are thicker than kitchen foil, and are available from crafts suppliers. However, they are still thin enough to cut with ordinary scissors. Take great care as the edges are sharp. Use a dried-out ballpoint pen to emboss designs: this will keep the work and your hands much cleaner.

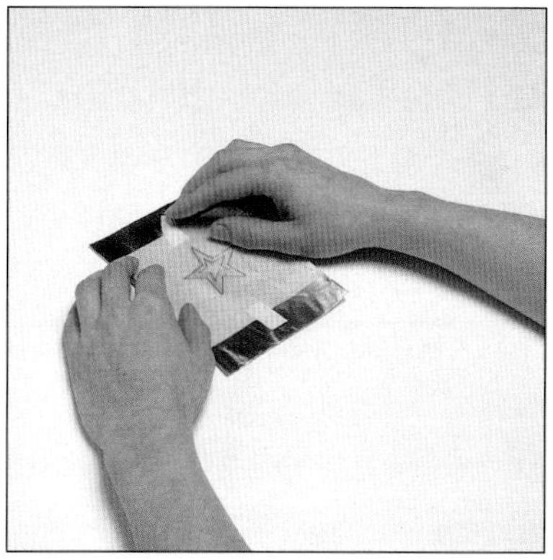

1 Position a tracing of your motif over a piece of foil and secure it with masking tape.

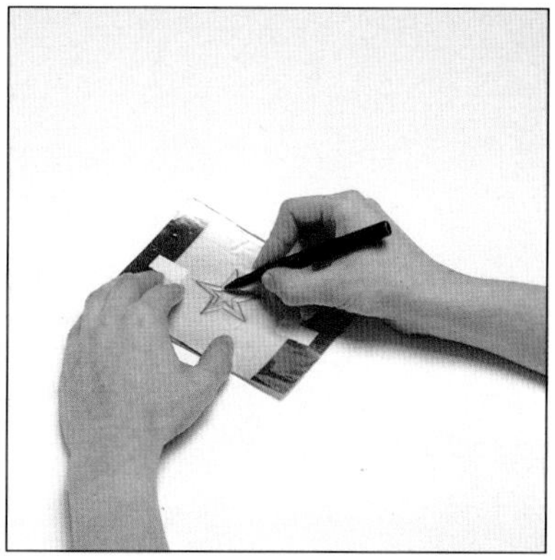

2 Draw the outline of the motif over the tracing paper with a ballpoint pen, pressing into the foil as you work. You can add more detail at this stage.

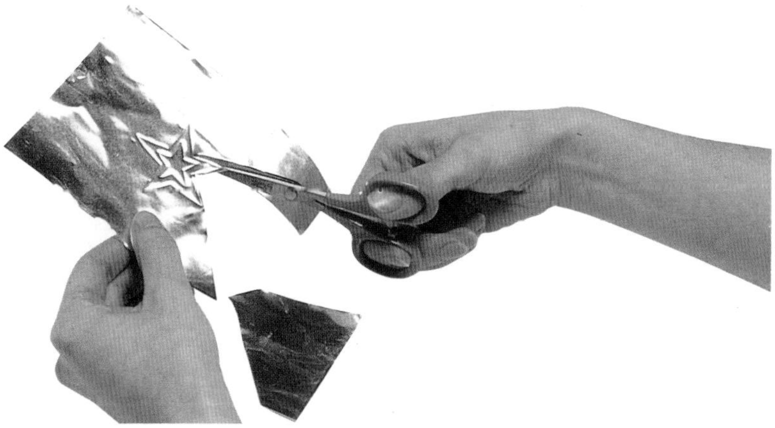

3 Remove the tracing paper and check the embossing, going over it again if necessary. Cut out the motif, leaving a narrow border of about 2 mm ($^1/_{16}$ in) all around the edge. Don't cut into the embossed outline.

HINTS AND TIPS FOR KIDS

If you always worry about what presents to give your friends and family at Christmas, this book is the perfect solution to all your problems. There are lots of exciting gift-wraps, cards, decorations and gifts to make, so leave your piggybank alone and get creative!

To avoid running out of time, it's always a good idea to plan ahead and start making your presents early. When you have read through the projects and decided what presents and decorations you want to make, study the equipment and materials lists carefully to check what basic items you need. Don't worry if you can't find exactly the same materials as appear in each project; the best part about making your own presents is that there is so much to choose from that you can pick the shapes and colors that you like the best!

Once your family has caught the craft bug, a handy tip is to start a recycling box or bag and fill it with useful odds and ends that can be used in the projects, for example, jam jars, cereal boxes, old wrapping paper, paper towel tubes, corks and candy wrappers.

Children will be able to make a lot of the projects by themselves, but they may need adult help for some of them, so be sure to help when the project says to do so.

When you have finished making all your presents and decorations, help the kids store them in a safe place away from prying eyes, until it is Christmas Day.

Materials for Kids

It helps to explain each material to the children before starting the project.

Artificial gemstones
These look like jewels and can be glued on to projects for an added touch of sparkle.

Beads
Beads can be made from wood, plastic, metal or glass. They can be glued or sewn on.

Bells
These can be bought from craft shops or large department stores and make a festive jingling sound.

Braids
Braid comes in many widths and can be glued or sewn on.

Buttons
These can be used for decoration and can be glued or sewn on.

Cardboard tubes
These can be found in the middle of rolls of tin foil and toilet paper.

Christmas cards
These can be cut up and glued on to a whole range of projects.

Coloured paper
This paper is very useful! It comes in different thicknesses and colours, and is available from most stationers and art shops.

Corrugated cardboard
Corrugated cardboard has ridges and comes in many thicknesses.

Cotton sewing thread
Thread is used for sewing fabric together. Always try to match the colours of your sewing thread and your fabric.

Cotton wool (balls)
This can be used to add texture. It is available from supermarkets and chemists (drugstores).

Doily
This is a lace-like paper, sometimes with a top layer of gold or silver foil. It is useful for making a snowflake effect.

Elastic
Elastic comes in many different widths and strengths.

Embroidery thread (floss)
This is a thick, strong thread which comes in a wide variety of colours.

Enamel paint
This type of paint gives good coverage and can be used to paint both plastic and metal.

Felt
Felt is easy to cut and will not fray. It is available from art and craft shops in a variety of colours.

Foil sweet (candy) wrappers
These give a shiny decorative effect to gifts and ornaments. Remember to save the wrappers whenever you have some sweets (candies).

Glitter
Glitter always adds a Christmassy touch to projects. Take care not to spill your glitter on the floor!

Glitter glue
This is a ready-made mix of glitter and clear glue. It makes decorating projects very easy.

Jam jars
These are useful containers for storing sequins and gemstones.

Letter and number transfers
Transfers can be bought from art shops. They are an easy way of making sure you have neatly written words and numbers.

Metallic foil
This can be bought from art and craft shops. It is thicker than tin foil but can be cut with scissors.

Mini pom-poms
These can be bought from art and craft shops, or you can easily make your own at home.

Modelling clay
This is great for making moulded shapes. It comes in lots of colours.

Neoprene
This is a special fabric that is like a soft rubber. It is easy to cut and glue on to projects for decoration.

Paints
There are many different types of paint, such as fabric, acrylic, poster and watercolour. Always paint in a well-ventilated area.

Paper baubles (styrofoam balls)
These are very light and can be painted and decorated to make fun decorations. Buy them from art and craft shops.

Pine cones
Look out for these the next time you go for a walk near woodland, or buy them from a florist's shop.

Ribbon
This comes in a variety of colours, textures and widths. It can be tied in pretty bows and wrapped around presents, or use it for hanging decorations.

Rope
This is thicker and stronger than string. Glue rope on to a block of wood and use as a printing block.

Sequins
These shiny decorations can be glued or sewn on to paper, cardboard or fabric.

Squeezy paint
This is great for decorating projects and you may find it easier to use than an ordinary paintbrush for painting small details and patterns.

Sticky-backed plastic (contact paper)
This has a paper backing, so that after you have cut out your shape, you can peel the backing off and stick the shape in place.

Tinsel
A Christmas favourite which can be cut up and used to decorate many projects.

Tissue paper
This is a delicate, transparent paper. It is available in many colours and can be used in lots of ways for decoration.

Wool (yarn)
This comes in many different colours and is available from department stores or craft shops.

tinsel
pine cones
cardboard tubes
jar
enamel paint
squeezy paint
mini pom-poms
rope
braids
bells
poster paints
glitter glue
wool (yarn)
beads
corrugated cardboard
metallic foil
glitter
embroidery thread (floss)
elastic
tissue paper
cotton sewing thread
ribbon
modelling clay
coloured paper
neoprene
artificial gemstones
metallic foil
felt
sequins
aaaaaaa
ccccddd
eeeeeef
hhhhhiii
Christmas cards
buttons
scourer pad (sponge)
paper bauble (styrofoam ball)
transfers
doily
cotton wool
corks
sweet (candy) wrappers
sticky-backed plastic (contact paper)

Equipment for Kids

This is a range of the equipment used in projects for kids in this book. You will probably have many items, but it may be worth buying one or two new tools.

Badge findings
These are glued or sewn on to the back of badges. They can be bought from specialist shops.

Compass
A very useful tool for drawing different sized circles with.

Corks
Corks are useful to dab into paint and then print with.

Double-sided sticky tape
A type of tape that is sticky on both sides.

Earring findings
These are glued on to the back of earrings so that they can then be clipped on to your ears.

Eraser
An eraser is useful for rubbing out any pencilled markings you may have made.

Fabric scissors
These sharp scissors are used to cut fabric. They should always be handled with care.

Felt-tip pens
Felt-tip pens are useful for drawing around templates.

Foam roller
These are taken from ordinary hair rollers. They are very good for printing dots. Wash the roller each time you use a new colour.

Glue stick
A glue stick is less messy than most other types of glue. This type shows up as a purple colour until it dries so that you can see where you are gluing. It is used for sticking paper to paper.

Gold pen
A special effect pen that can be used for writing messages in cards and for decorating paper.

Hair clip (barrette)
Hair clips (barrettes) can be bought from specialist craft shops. They can be decorated with fabric or neoprene. You will need to use a strong glue to stick the materials on to the clip.

Hole punch
This is used for punching holes in paper or cardboard.

Knife
Use this sharp tool for cutting. Always cut onto a firm surface and ask an adult to help you.

Needles
These have a very sharp point and are used in sewing projects. Ask an adult to help you if you need to use a needle.

Paintbrushes
These come in a variety of thicknesses. Store your brushes with the bristles facing upwards.

Palette
A palette is useful for mixing paint. If you don't have one, an old saucer is just as good.

Paper fasteners
These are used for holding two pieces of paper together so the top piece can spin around.

Paper scissors
These are used for cutting paper, cardboard or metallic foil. They should be of the type that are made specially for children and have rounded blades.

Pencil
A soft pencil is useful for making tracings and transferring them to cardboard and paper.

Pencil sharpener
This is useful for sharpening lead and coloured pencils.

Pinking shears
When you cut fabric or paper with these scissors you get an attractive crinkly edge.

Pins
These are sharp and are used for pinning pieces of fabric together.

PVA (white) glue
Always use a non-toxic glue and work in a well-ventilated area. PVA (white) glue is good for gluing cardboard and fabric.

Ring finding
This can be glued to the back of a small project to turn it into a ring. Use a strong glue to stick the materials on to the ring back.

Safety pins
These are useful for holding pieces of material together, or for taping to the back of badges.

Sandpaper
Rub wood and glazed ceramics with sandpaper, to make the surface smooth for painting.

Scourer pad (sponge)
This is ideal for cutting into shapes to make printing blocks.

Single hole punch
This can be used for punching single holes in paper, cardboard, neoprene or felt.

Sponge
Lightly dip a sponge into paint and sponge over a stencil, or use it to make prints.

Sticky tape
This can be used for sticking paper, cardboard and foil.

Strong glue (epoxy)
Always use a non-toxic and solvent-free glue. Strong glue is useful for sticking heavier cardboard together.

Tracing paper
This is a lightweight transparent paper. It is used to trace and transfer templates and designs.

Varnish
Always use a non-toxic, water-based varnish and work in a well-ventilated area. Varnish is used to protect a wooden surface that has been decorated with paint or pieces of paper or cardboard.

Water container
This is a special container with a safety lid. If you don't have one, a clean jam jar is just as good.

Wood
Glue a length of string in a coil on a block of wood, to make a printing block.

PVA (white) glue
strong glue
hole punch
wood
sandpaper
glue stick
single hole punch
compass
paintbrushes
foam roller
tracing paper
palette
scourer pad (sponge)
water container
badge finding
hair clip (barrette)
ring finding
safety pin
earring findings
sponge
pencil
felt-tip pen
gold pen
ballpoint pen
badge findings
needles
pins
pencil sharpener
paper fasteners
fabric scissors
knife
eraser
varnish
paper scissors
ruler
pinking shears
double-sided sticky tape

Tracing

Some of the projects in this section have patterns that you can transfer directly to paper or use to make templates. Tracing is the quickest way to make copies of a pattern so that you can easily transfer it to another piece of paper or cardboard.

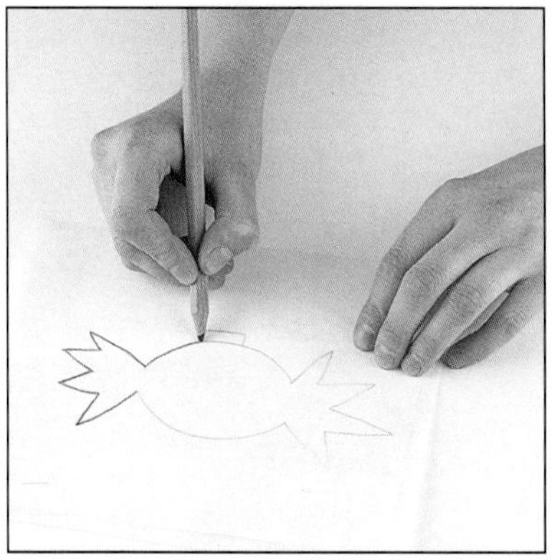

1 Lay your piece of tracing paper on the pattern and use a soft pencil to draw over the image, making a dark line.

2 Turn the sheet of tracing paper over and place it on a scrap of paper. Scribble over the lines with your pencil.

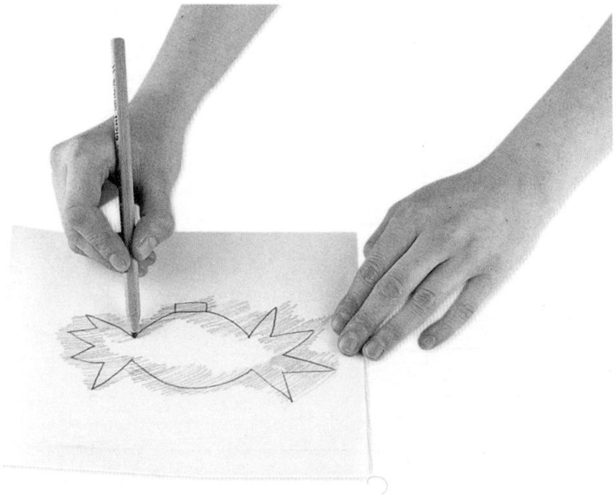

3 Turn the tracing right-side up again and place it on an appropriate piece of paper or cardboard. Carefully draw over the lines to transfer the tracing to the paper or cardboard. Lift up the tracing paper and you will see that your outline is now on the paper or cardboard.

Scaling-up

Sometimes you will want to make a project bigger than the template given and will need to scale-up the size of the template. It is very easy to make a template bigger – all you need is a piece of plain paper, a pencil and a ruler. You could use a photocopier instead, if you prefer.

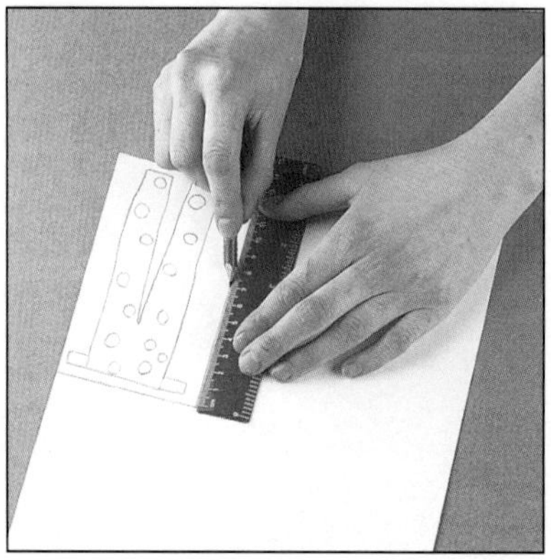

1 Trace the template and transfer it to a sheet of paper. Draw a box around the template. Draw two diagonal lines through the box, from each of the bottom corners.

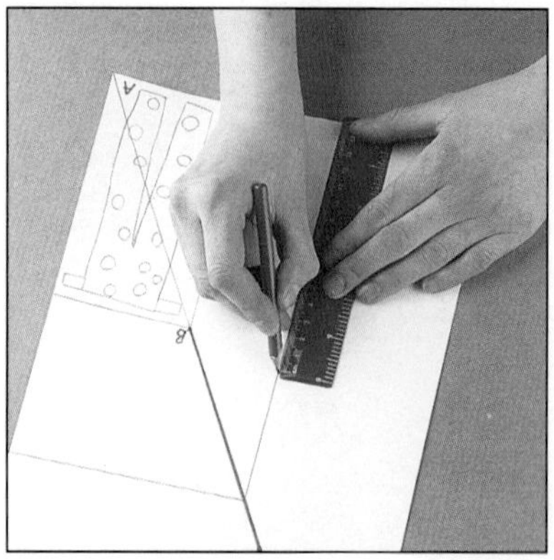

2 Draw a box for the new image on the same piece of paper. Make the box as large as you want your scaled-up image to be. Draw two diagonal lines through the new box, as before.

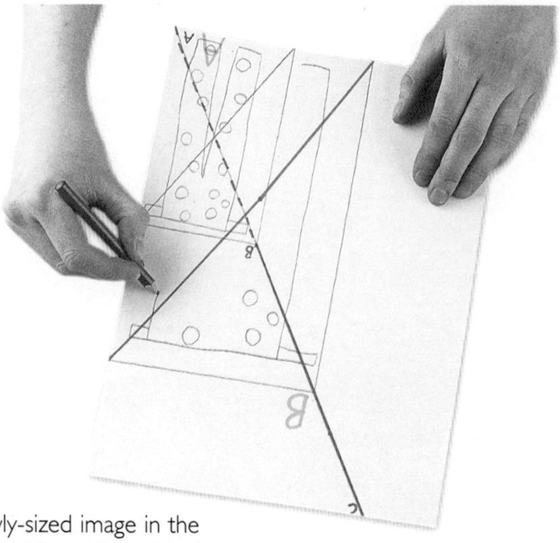

3 Draw the newly-sized image in the box, looking very carefully at the original.

Folding Paper

Paper can be folded in a variety of ways. One of the simplest methods is to fold a sheet of paper into sections like a concertina (accordion). You can hang the finished design as a decoration.

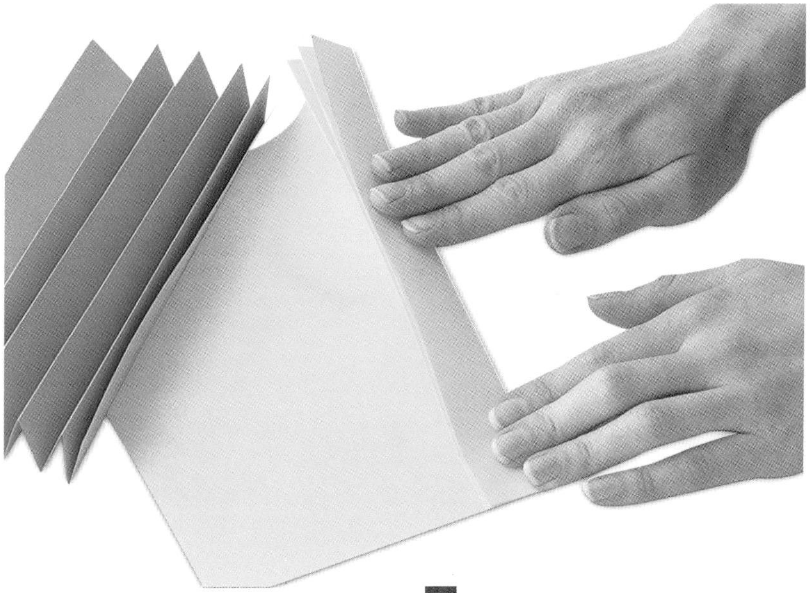

1 Fold two sheets of paper in contrasting colours into sections about 2.5 cm (1 in) wide.

2 Fold each piece of paper in the middle to make a semi-circle. Join the two ends together with a staple.

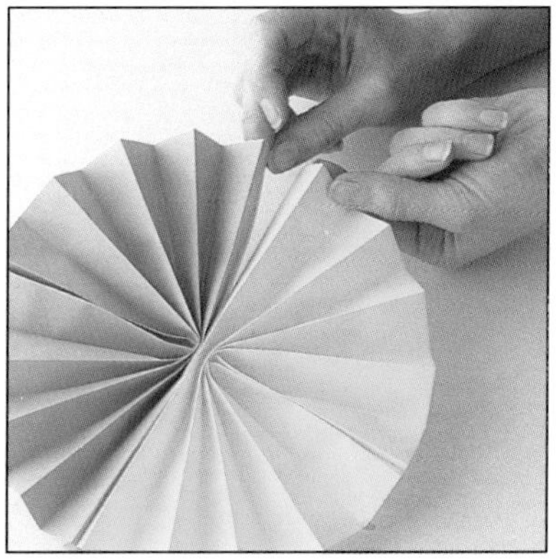

3 With the help of an adult, join the two semi-circles together at the outside edges to form a circle.

Flattening and Cutting up a Box

Cardboard is used for many of the projects in this book. Old boxes are the best source of cardboard, and you can flatten them out easily.

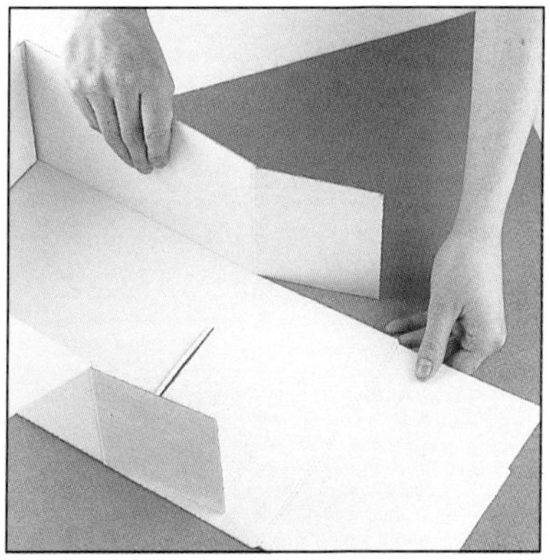

1 Remove any tape that is holding the box together and press the box flat.

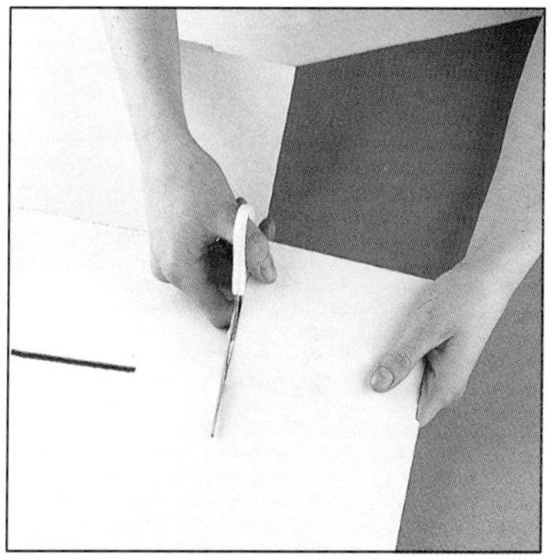

2 Cut the box into pieces, ready for use in your various projects.

Re-using Foil Wrappers

Coloured foil is great for decorations, and you don't have to buy it specially. Save old sweet (candy) wrappers made of pretty colours, and cut them into different shapes.

1 Flatten the sweet (candy) wrappers and chocolate cases and smooth them out with your hands. Cut up the wrappers and use as decorations for your projects. Sweet wrappers and chocolate cases are always cheerful and will make your projects look really festive!

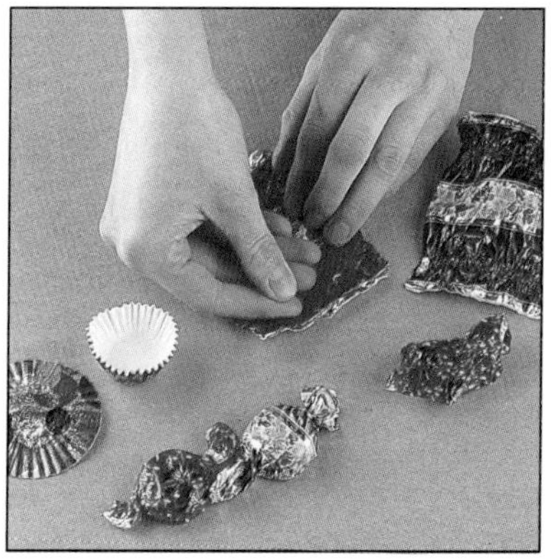

Using a Compass

This is an old-fashioned instrument that is still one of the best tools you can use to draw neat circles. You will also need a freshly sharpened pencil.

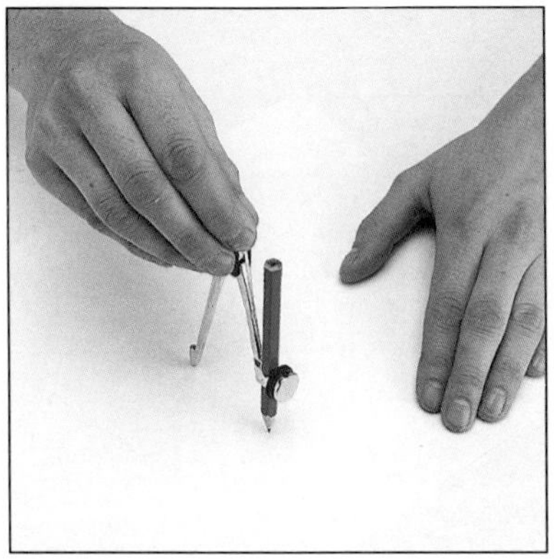

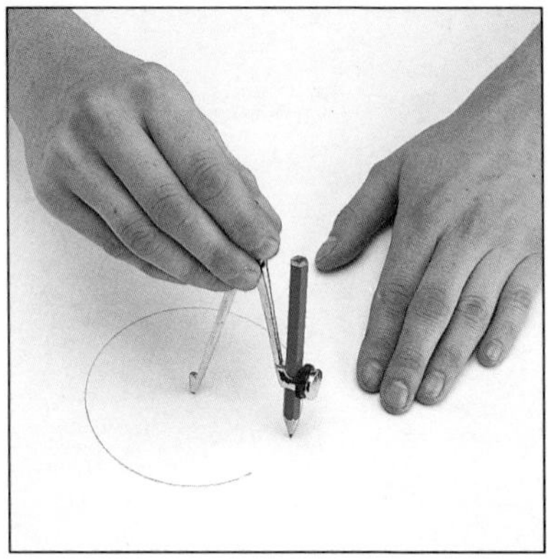

1 Place the point of the compass on the piece of paper or cardboard that you want to draw the circle on. The point of the compass is sharp so be careful when you use it.

2 Decide on how large you need your circle to be and pull out the arm of the compass. Place the pencil on the surface and, holding the top of the compass, draw the circle.

Saving Glitter

This handy tip shows you how to save glitter and avoid making a mess.

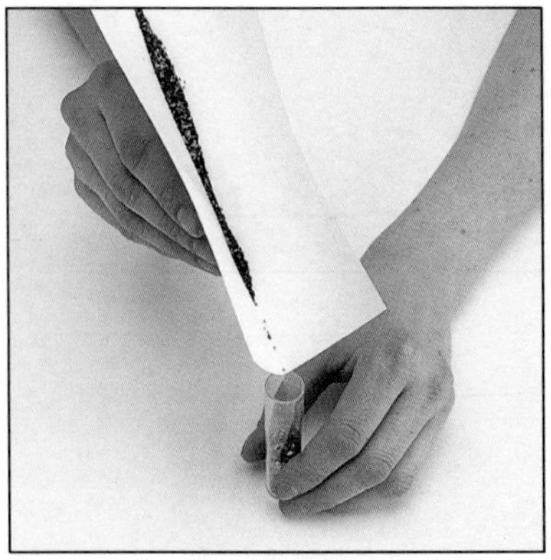

1 Fold a scrap of paper in half and then open it out and lay it under the project you are working on. When you have sprinkled the glitter over the project, fold the paper in half again and place the end of the paper by the crease over the glitter tube and carefully pour it back into the tube.

Mixing Paints

If you only have the basic primary colours (red, yellow and blue) of paint, try mixing them together to make new colours.

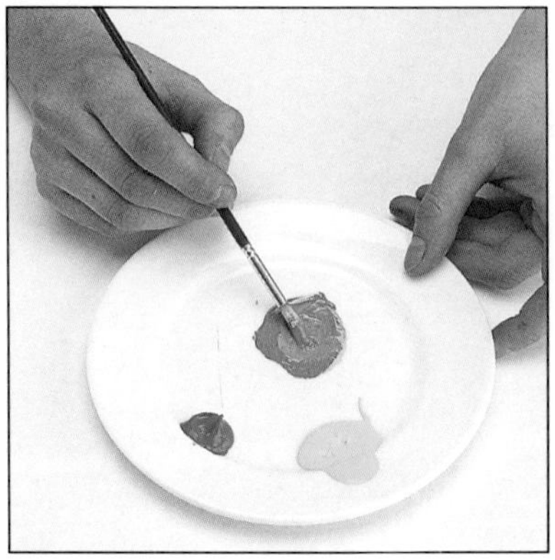

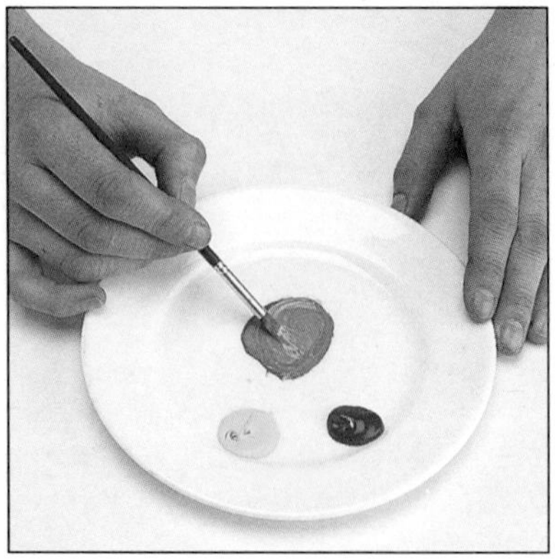

1 Mix yellow and blue paints together to make green. For a bright green use mainly yellow paint.

2 Mix yellow and red paints together to make orange. For a dark orange use mainly red paint.

3 Mix blue and red paints together to make purple. For a deep royal purple use mainly blue paint.

Fixing Jewelry Findings

These are small metal attachments that are glued on to the back of your projects to turn them into pieces of jewelry. The findings should be glued on with strong glue.

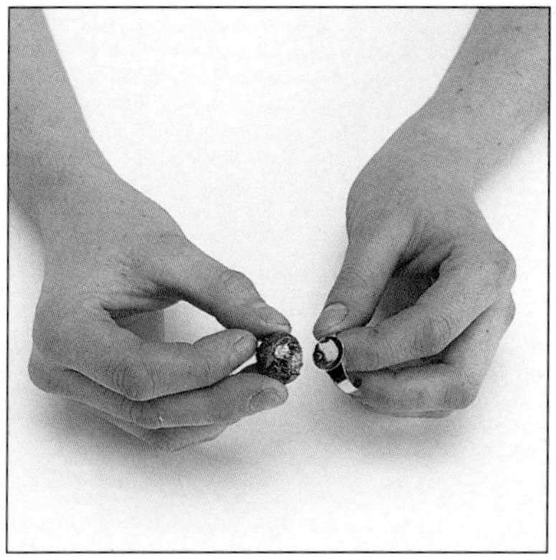

1 This is a brooch or badge finding. Let the glue harden completely before pinning the badge on to your clothes. For clip-on earring findings, when you glue them on to your project, open them out and keep them open until the glue has hardened. With an adjustable ring finding, simply squeeze the two metal sides together to make it smaller or pull them out gently to make it larger.

Curling

Thin strips of paper can be pulled with a pencil to create gentle curls. The curls are especially good for adding extra decoration to your wrapped Christmas presents.

1 Cut thin strips of paper about 1 cm (½ in) wide. Holding a strip of paper in one hand, pull a pencil down its length several times. Don't pull too hard or you'll tear the paper. The paper will form gentle curls. To make tighter curls, roll the strips around a pencil.

Using a Hole Punch

This is a single hole punch which can be bought from specialist craft shops or large department stores. It is useful for making holes and polka-dots.

1 Punch through felt to make holes or neat mini dots which can then be glued on to other surfaces.

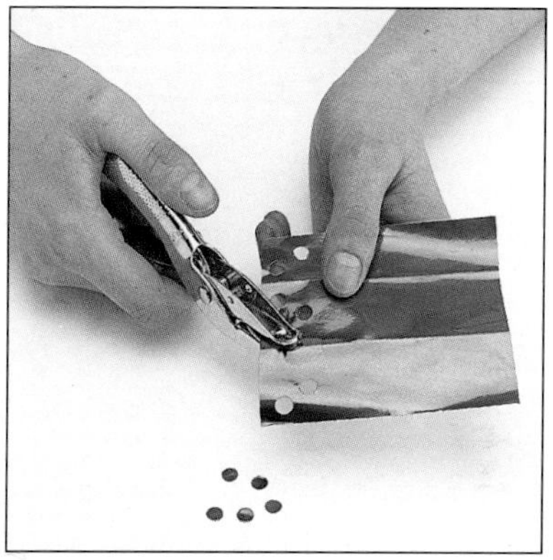

2 If you want to make a lot of paper dots at one time, fold a piece of paper in half and then in half again and punch through it.

3 When you have made a gift tag, punch a hole at one end of it so that you can thread a piece of ribbon or string through it.

Gilded Glass Spheres

With a gold glass (relief) outliner, you can turn plain glass tree decorations into unique gilded ornaments. Don't be too ambitious with your designs: you'll find that simple repeating motifs such as circles, triangles and stars are best to begin with and can be the most effective.

YOU WILL NEED
plain glass tree ornaments
white spirit (paint thinner)
gold glass (relief) outliner
paper tissues
jam jar
wire-edged ribbon
scissors

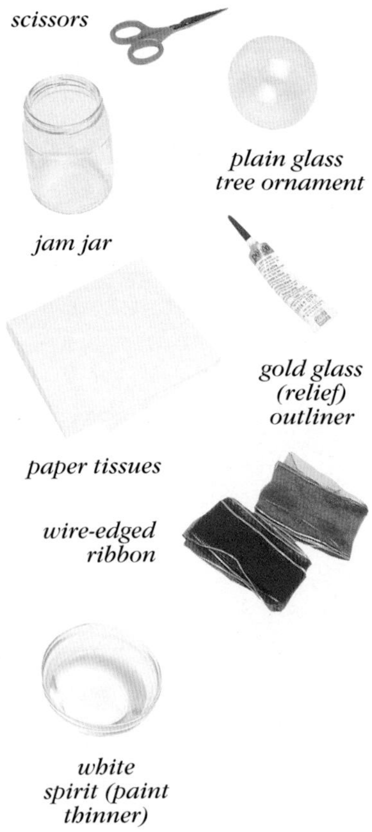

1 Clean the glass with detergent and wipe it with white spirit (paint thinner) to remove all traces of grease.

2 Working on one side only, gently squeeze the gold glass (relief) outliner on to the glass in your chosen design. If you make a mistake, wipe the outliner off quickly with a paper tissue while it is still wet.

3 Rest the sphere in an empty jam jar and leave for about 24 hours to dry thoroughly. Decorate the other side and leave to dry again.

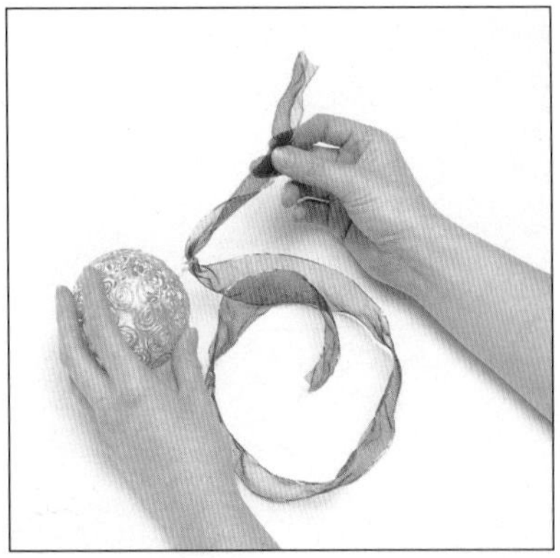

4 Thread a length of wire-edged ribbon through the top of the ornament and tie it in a bow.

Festive Wine Glasses

With the same gold glass (relief) outliner used to decorate the glass ornaments, you can also transform plain, everyday wine glasses. Add clear, stained-glass colours for a jewelled effect, to give your Christmas dinner the air of a medieval feast.

YOU WILL NEED
plain wine glasses
white spirit (paint thinner)
gold glass (relief) outliner
oil-based glass paints
fine paintbrush
old glass or jar
paper towel

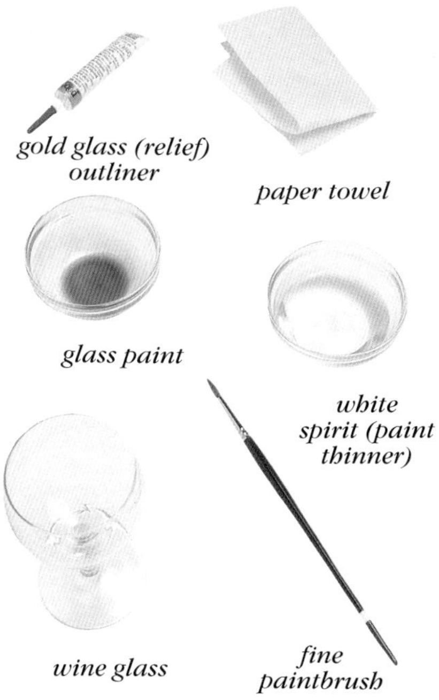

1 Wash the glasses with detergent and wipe over with white spirit (paint thinner) to remove all traces of grease.

2 Pipe your design directly on to the glass with the gold outliner. Leave to dry thoroughly for at least 24 hours.

3 Check the colour and get the feel of the rather viscous glass paint by practising on an old glass or jar first. Use a fine paintbrush to colour in your design, and be careful not to get paint on the gold relief. Try to finish with each colour before changing to the next one. Clean the brush with white spirit (paint thinner) between each colour.

CRAFT TIP

When planning your design, it's best to avoid the rim of the glass as the relief outliner will feel bumpy against the drinker's lips. The paint colours can be mixed if you wish.

Gilded Christmas Plate

Seek out reasonably priced plain white plates and turn them into glowing works of art with ceramic paint. There's no need to reserve them for Christmas: this crown and star design will look lovely at any time.

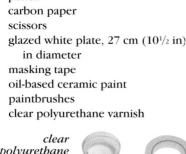

YOU WILL NEED
tracing paper
pencil
carbon paper
scissors
glazed white plate, 27 cm ($10^1/_2$ in) in diameter
masking tape
oil-based ceramic paint
paintbrushes
clear polyurethane varnish

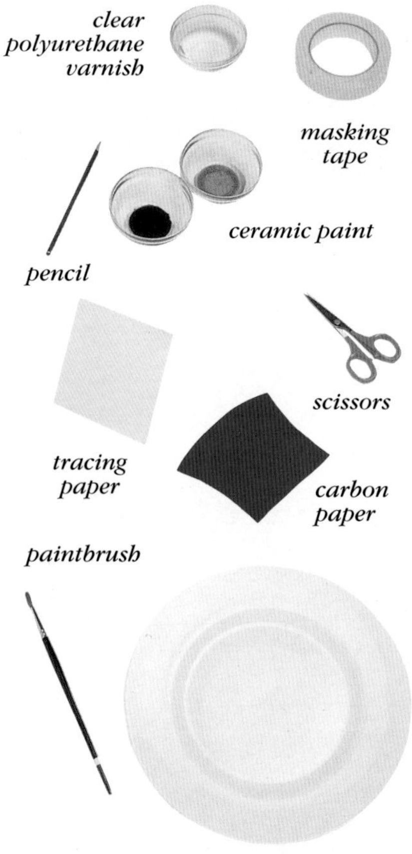

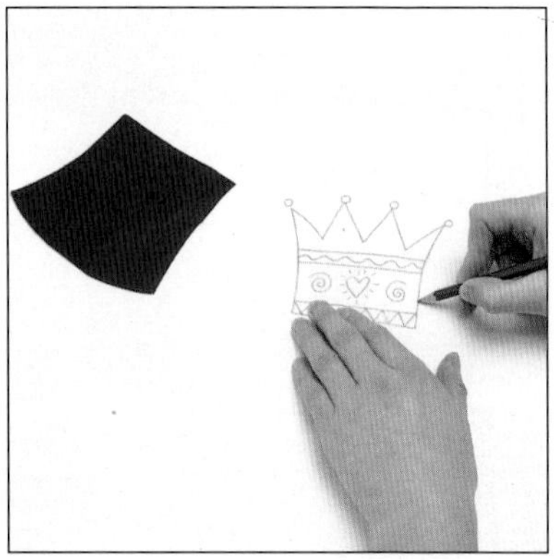

1 Trace the crown, star and swirl from the back of the book. Cut pieces of carbon paper to the size of the tracings.

2 Starting with the crown, secure the carbon paper and the tracing to the plate with masking tape. Draw over the motif to transfer it to the plate. Plan the positions of the stars and swirls, spacing them evenly around the rim, and transfer them in the same way.

3 Paint in the coloured areas of the crown and the centres of the stars and swirls with ceramic paint, following the manufacturer's instructions. Start at the centre and work outwards so that your hand does not smudge the paint. Fill in the background with a medium brush.

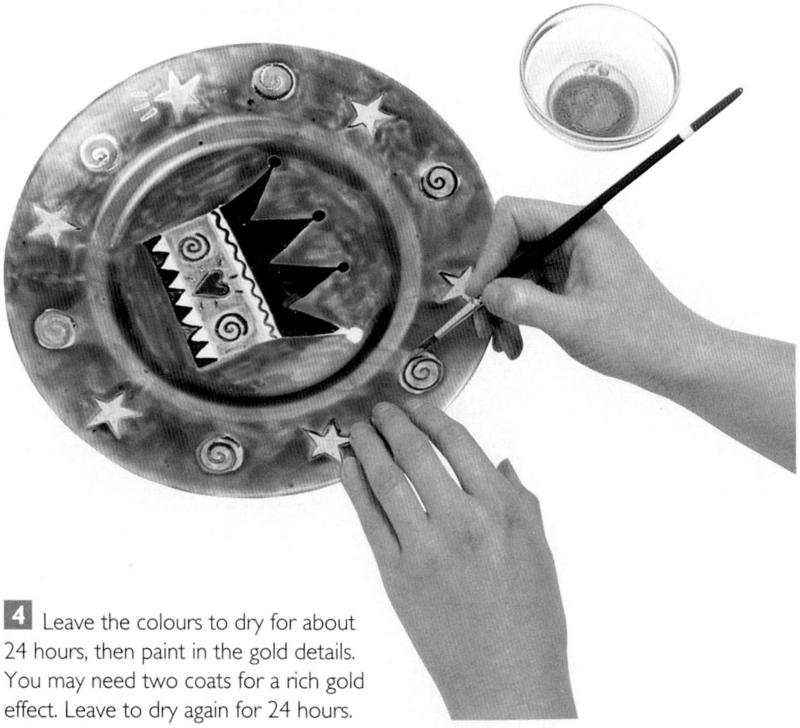

4 Leave the colours to dry for about 24 hours, then paint in the gold details. You may need two coats for a rich gold effect. Leave to dry again for 24 hours.

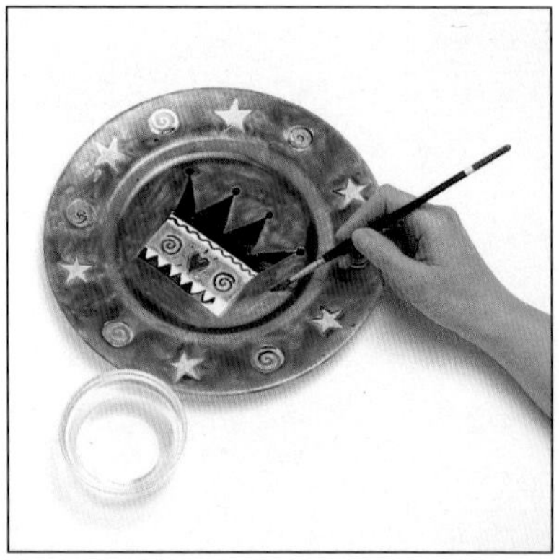

5 Cover the plate with clear varnish to protect the surface. The decorated plate is not suitable for food use.

Star Candle-holder

Pretty boxes, especially if they have an unusual shape, are always worth hoarding for future craft projects. This star-shaped chocolate box makes a perfect Christmas candle-holder.

YOU WILL NEED
small, rigid chocolate box with a lid
metal screw-cap from a bottle
pen
craft knife
newspaper
PVA (white) glue
paintbrush
white emulsion (latex) paint
gold (magic) marker pen
watercolour inks

1 Place the bottle cap exactly in the centre of the box lid and draw around it.

2 Divide the circle into narrow pie sections and cut them with a craft knife. Fold them down into the box. Push the bottle cap into the hole so that its rim is just below the surface of the box (this will hold the candle).

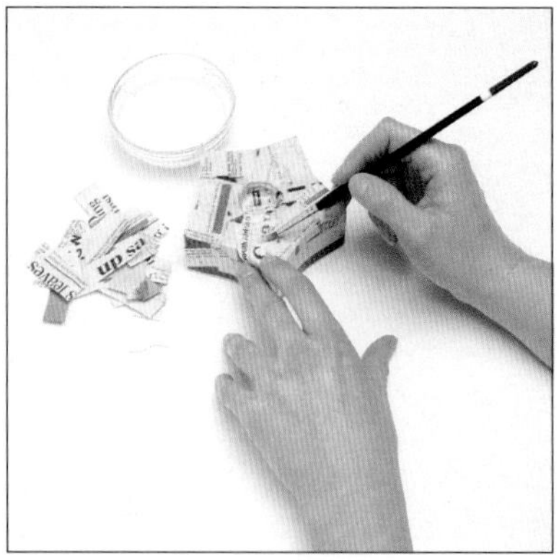

3 Tear the newspaper into strips about 1 x 5 cm (½ x 2 in). Dilute the PVA (white) glue slightly with water. Paint a strip liberally with glue on both sides and stick it on to the box, flattening it with the paintbrush loaded with more glue. Apply a layer of newspaper all over the box in this way, beginning around the bottle cap to cover the join. Press the paper neatly over awkward corners. When the first layer is dry, apply a second and let that dry thoroughly.

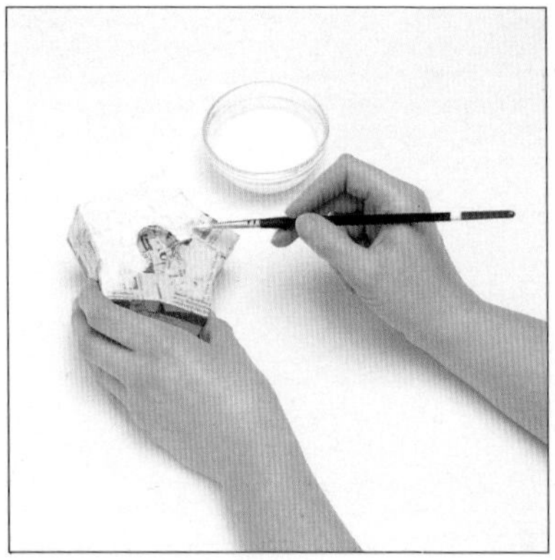

4 Mix a little white emulsion (latex) paint with the glue and paint the whole box white.

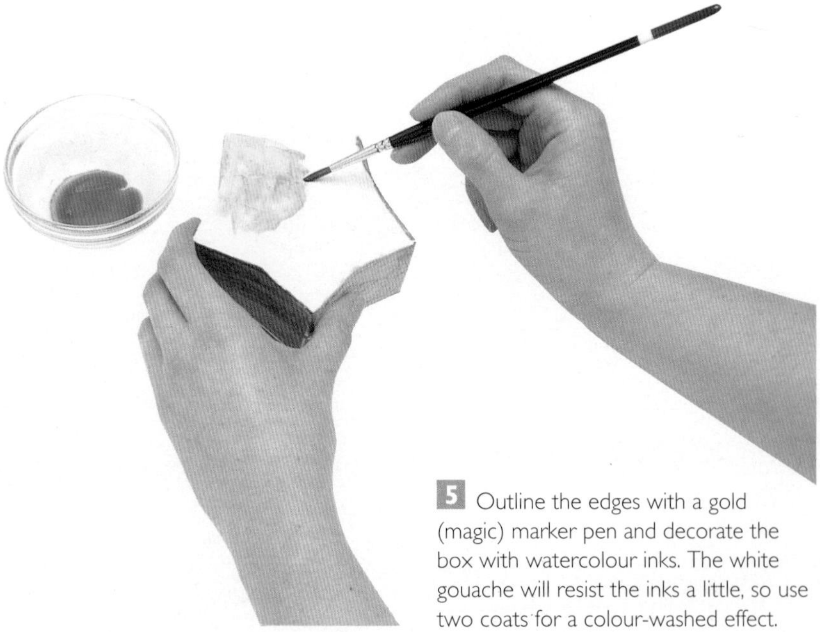

5 Outline the edges with a gold (magic) marker pen and decorate the box with watercolour inks. The white gouache will resist the inks a little, so use two coats for a colour-washed effect.

Gold Crown Tablecloth

Set the festive tone with this lovely white and gold tablecloth. The stencilling is easy and enjoyable to do, but it's important to plan your design carefully before you start work with the paint so that the motifs are evenly spaced.

YOU WILL NEED
white cotton fabric 135 cm (54 in) square
iron
pins
stencil card (cardboard)
craft knife
masking tape
gold stencil paint
stencil brush
fine paintbrush
sewing machine
white thread

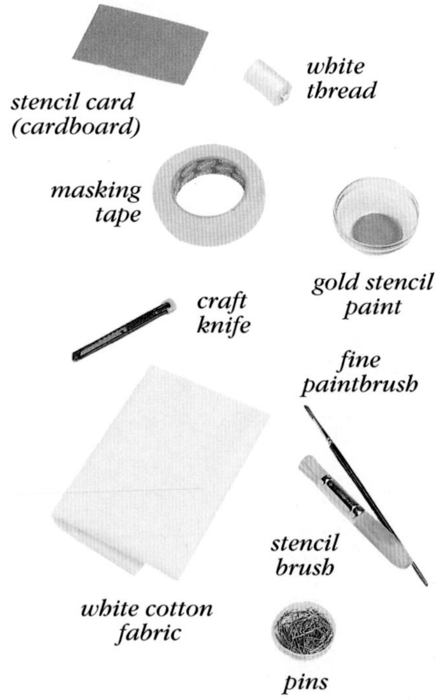

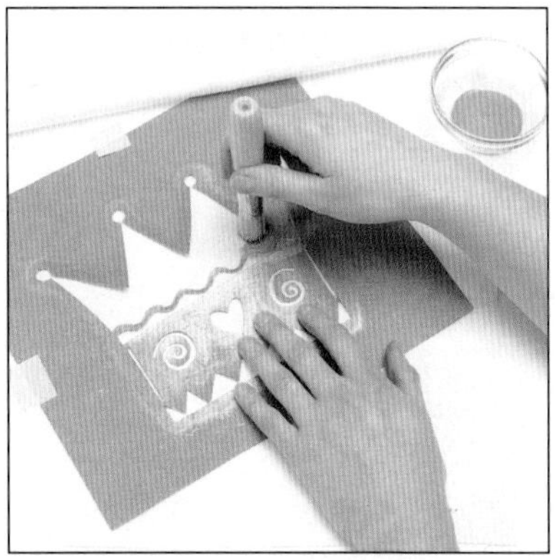

1 Iron the fabric to remove creases, then fold in quarters and press the folds. Fold each quarter to find the centre point, press and mark with pins. Copy the crown and shooting star templates from the back of the book, transfer on to stencil card (cardboard) and cut out with a craft knife. Stencil the crowns in the corners, then the edges and centre.

2 Stencil the shooting stars between the crowns, all pointing in the same direction around the edge of the cloth.

3 Complete the stars by touching up the gaps left by the stencil with a fine brush and gold stencil paint.

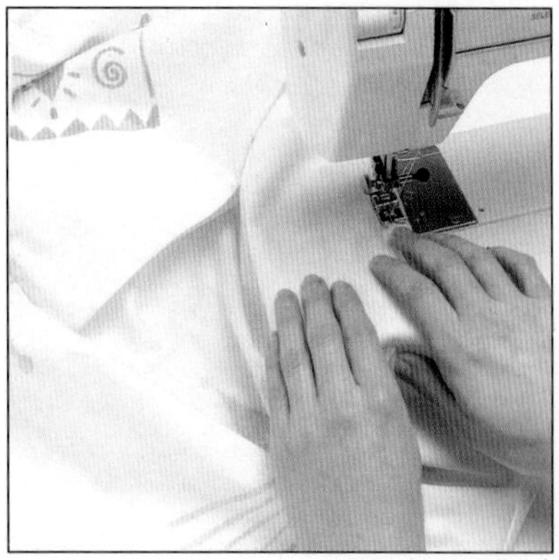

4 Press on the wrong side of the fabric to fix the paint. Hem the fabric all around the edge on a sewing machine.

CRAFT TIP

Don't overload your brush as too much paint may bleed underneath the edges of the stencil.

Holly Leaf Napkin

The Christmas table deserves something more distinctive than paper napkins, and your guests will love these specially embroidered cotton ones in festive but definitely non-traditional colours. The holly leaf motif is quick and easy to work in stem stitch.

YOU WILL NEED
paper for template
scissors
50 cm (20 in) square of washable cotton fabric in hot pink for each napkin
pins
tailor's chalk
stranded embroidery thread (floss) in acid green, acid yellow and bright orange
needle

1 Trace the holly leaf motif from the back of the book and use it to make a paper template. Pin it to one corner of the fabric, allowing room for a hem, and draw round it with tailor's chalk.

2 Using three strands of embroidery thread (floss) and working in stem stitch, embroider the outline of the holly leaf in acid green and the veins in acid yellow.

3 Fold under and pin a 5 mm ($\frac{1}{4}$ in) double hem all around the napkin.

4 Using three strands of bright orange embroidery thread (floss), work a neat running stitch evenly around the hem.

Sparkling Flowerpot

This flowerpot is covered with the foil wrapped around chocolates and candies. You'll need to prepare in advance by eating plenty of foil-wrapped candies. Choose the colours carefully, and don't forget to save the wrappers! Fill the pot with baubles (balls) for a table decoration.

YOU WILL NEED
coloured foil candy wrappers
terracotta flowerpot
PVA (white) glue
paintbrush

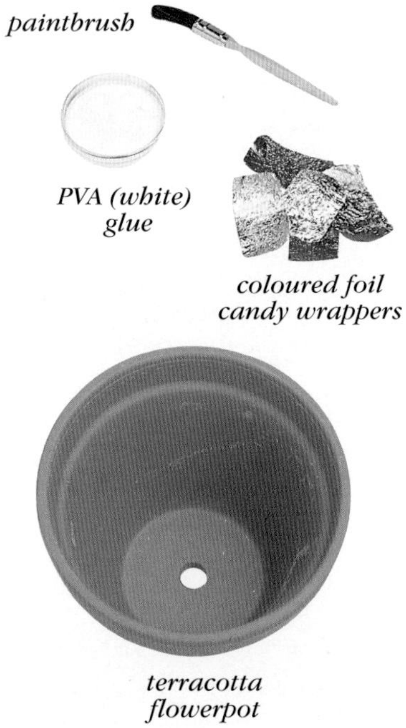

1 Smooth out the coloured foils and select as many rectangular shapes as possible. If any wrappers have tears, you may be able to hide these by overlapping them with perfect pieces.

2 Paint the flowerpot all over with PVA (white) glue to seal the surface.

3 Paint the back of a piece of foil with glue and apply it to the pot, smoothing it with the paintbrush and brushing on more glue to secure it. Continue adding the foils in an attractive pattern. When the pot is completely covered, seal it inside and out with another coat of glue.

CRAFT TIP

Although you can arrange the foils in a haphazard manner for a crazy patchwork effect, this project looks best if you keep to a more regular design by placing the foil pieces horizontally and vertically.

Silver Crown Candle-holder

Masses of night-lights (tea-lights) make a lovely glowing addition to your decorative scheme: dress them up for Christmas with these easy foil crowns. Make sure the candles you buy come in their own foil pots to contain the hot wax.

YOU WILL NEED
night-light (tea-light)
heavy-gauge aluminium foil
ruler
scissors
masking tape
dried-out ballpoint pen
glue-stick

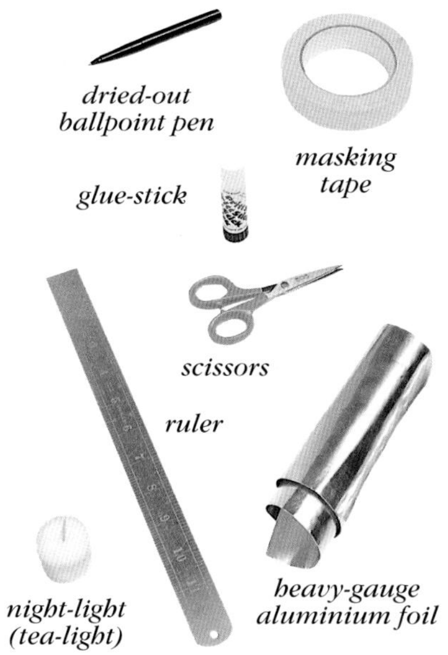

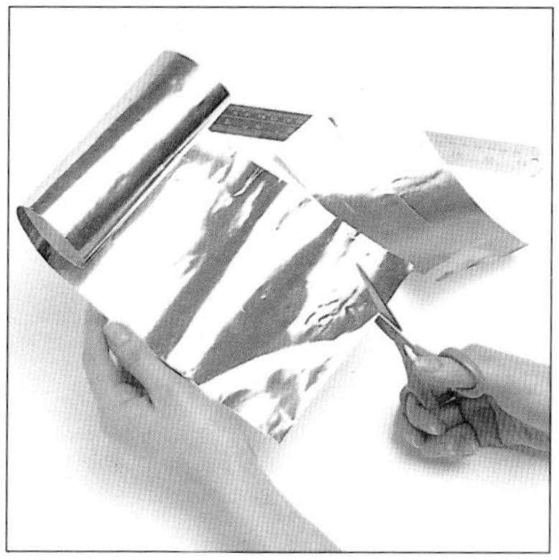

1 Cut a rectangle of foil to fit around the night-light (tea-light) and overlap by about 4 cm (1 1/2 in). The foil should stand at least 3 cm (1 1/4 in) higher than the night-light (tea-light).

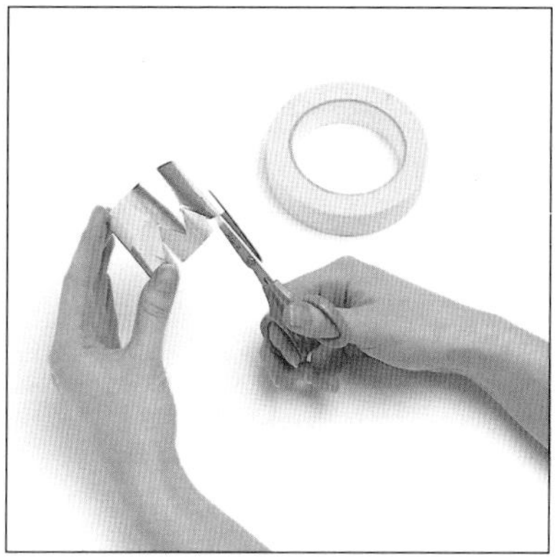

2 Wrap the foil in a circle around the candle and secure with a piece of masking tape. Cut the points of the crown freehand with scissors.

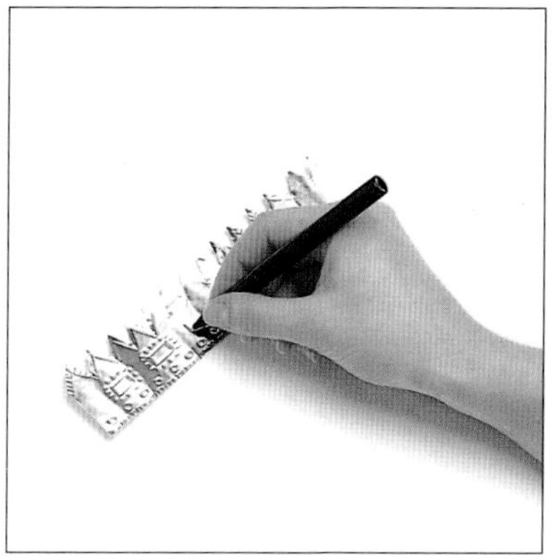

3 Remove the tape and lay the foil flat on a protected surface. Emboss a design on the foil with a dried-out ballpoint pen, making sure that it will meet neatly when the crown is joined up.

4 Roll the finished design tightly around the night-light (tea-light) to get a good candle shape and stick it together finally with a glue-stick.

SAFETY TIP

Never leave burning candles unattended and do not let the candle burn down to within 10 cm (2 in) of any flammable material.

Velvet Fruits

A lavish bowl full of sumptuous apples and pears in rich, fruity-coloured velvets will look like a still-life painting. You may not be able to eat them, but these fruits feel delicious!

YOU WILL NEED
paper for templates
small amounts of dress-weight velvet in red, plum and green
pins
scissors
sewing machine
matching thread
polyester wadding (batting)
needle

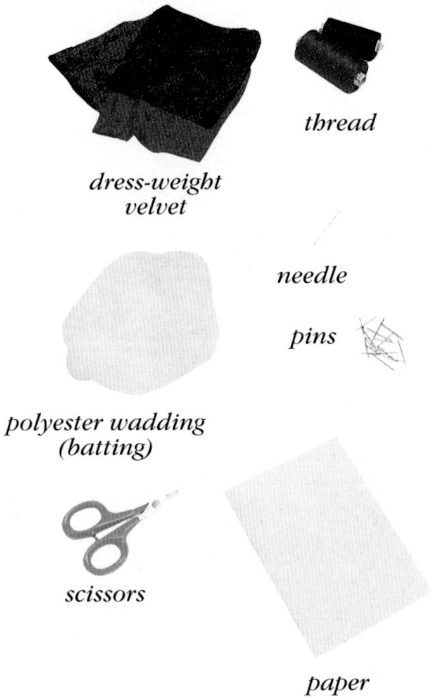

1 Trace the pear, apple and leaf shapes at the back of the book and enlarge as required. Transfer to paper and cut out the templates. Pin to the velvet and cut out, adding a 5 mm (1/4 in) seam allowance all round. You will need four sections for the pear and three for the apple.

CRAFT TIP

You could also use this idea to create other velvet objects on a festive theme. Why not try making some stars or holly leaves following the other templates at the back of the book?

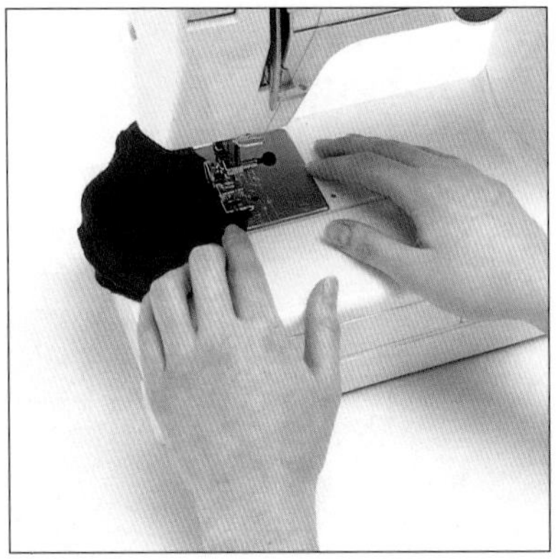

2 With wrong sides together, pin together the side seams and machine stitch, leaving the top of the fruits open. Turn to the right side.

3 Cut two pieces of green velvet for each leaf. Machine stitch together, leaving the end open, and turn to the right side. Gather the end with a needle and thread to give a realistic leaf shape.

4 Stuff each fruit with polyester wadding (batting). Sew up the opening at the top with a needle and thread, catching in the leaf as you sew.

White Christmas Tree

Stand this abstract, modern interpretation of the traditional star-topped Christmas tree on a side-table or the mantelpiece. It looks best as part of a cool, monochrome arrangement in white or gold.

YOU WILL NEED
hot glue gun
coarse sisal (parcel) string
large polystyrene cone
scissors
small polystyrene star
white emulsion (latex) paint
paintbrush
gold paint

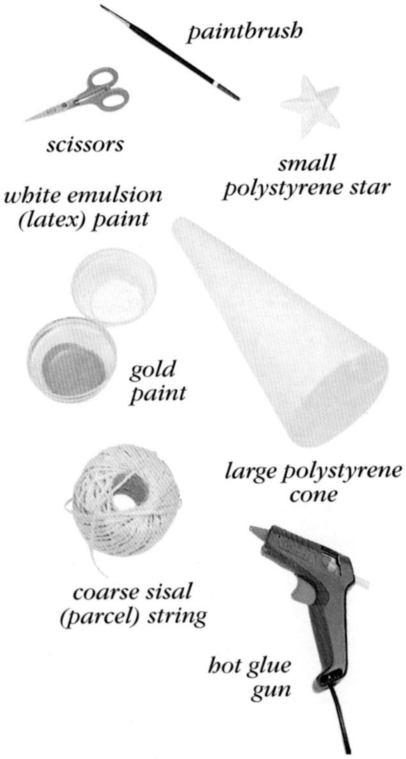

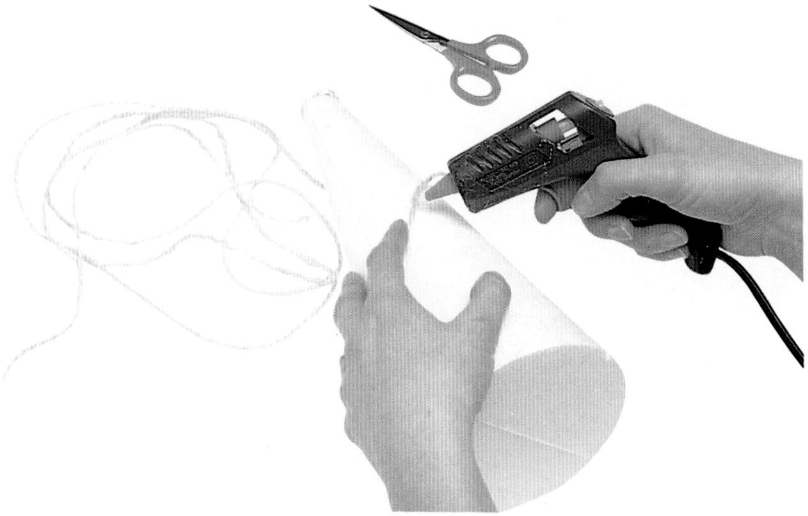

1 With a hot glue gun, attach the end of the string to the base of the cone. Wind the string up the cone towards the point, then down to the base again, gluing it as you work and securing it when it crosses. Each time you reach the base, cut the string and start again from another point so that the cone is evenly covered.

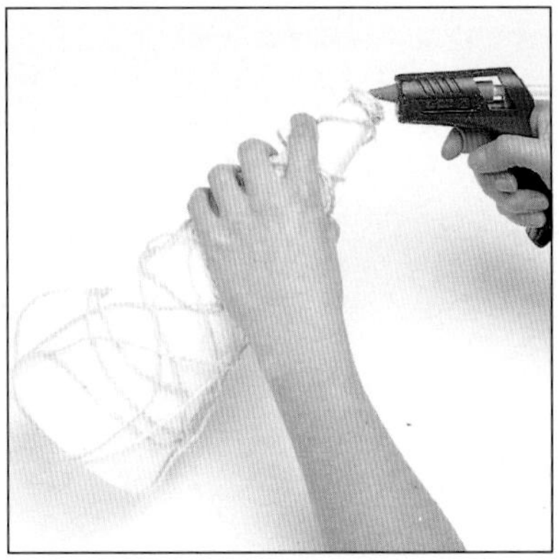

2 Wind a short length of string in a coil and glue it to the top of the cone for the star to sit on.

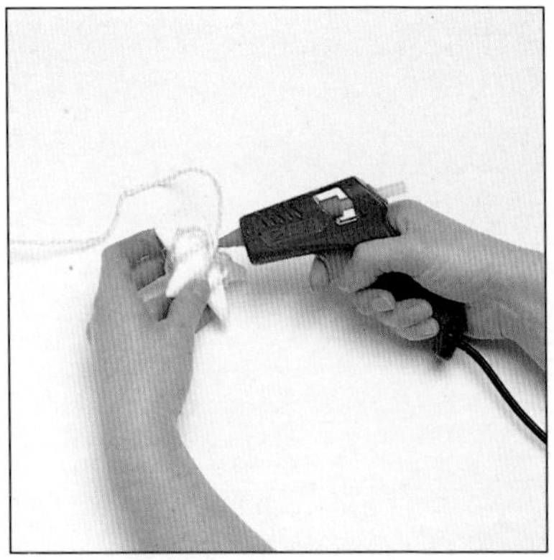

3 Wind and glue string around the star in the same way. Hide the raw ends under the string. Glue the star to the top of the cone.

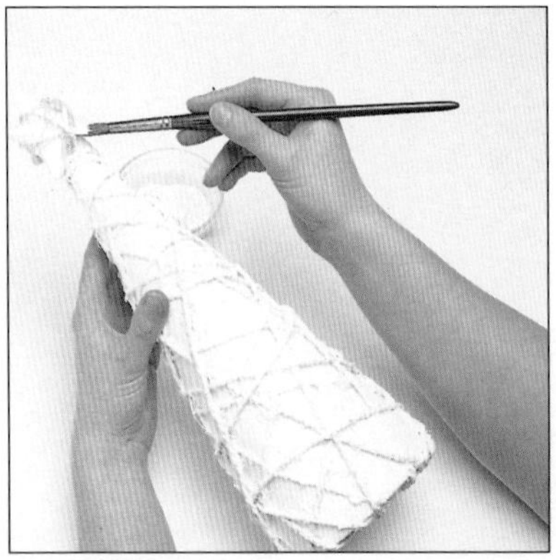

4 Paint the cone and star with several coats of white emulsion (latex) paint, covering the string and filling in any unsightly dents in the polystyrene.

5 Finish by brushing roughly over the string with gold paint.

CRAFT TIP

Make sure the ends of the string are evenly spaced around the base of the cone so that it stands upright.

Silk-wrapped Candle Pot

Here's a simple way to incorporate a beautiful piece of silk in to your decorative scheme. Match all the rich colours of the fabric when you are choosing the candles. Play safe with candles and never leave them burning unattended.

YOU WILL NEED
terracotta flowerpot
corrugated cardboard
gold paper
marker pen
scissors
double-sided adhesive (cellophane) tape
square of silk fabric to fit comfortably around the pot
newspaper or tissue paper
selection of coloured candles in various sizes
plastic adhesive

1 Try out the candles in the flowerpot to find a suitable height at which they should stand. Cut out a circle of cardboard to fit in the pot at this level as a base for the candles.

2 Cut a larger circle of gold paper and use it to cover the cardboard. Fold the edges under neatly and secure with double-sided adhesive (cellophane) tape.

3 Neaten the edges of the silk and stand the flowerpot in the centre of the square. Take two opposite corners and bring them up over the sides of the pot, tucking them inside. Tie the other two corners together at the front and arrange the folds of the silk in a pleasing manner.

4 Pad the base of the pot firmly with newspaper or tissue paper then place the gold disc inside. Arrange the candles on the disc, then secure them with small pieces of plastic adhesive.

Willow Twig Napkin Rings

You can decorate with natural, homespun materials but still achieve a sparkling effect if you choose bright, glowing colours. Using glue to assemble these rings reinforces the fabric and is a welcome short-cut if making a large quantity.

YOU WILL NEED
willow twigs
secateurs (pruning shears)
11 x 22 cm (4¼ x 8½ in) coarsely woven cotton fabric per ring
fabric glue
paintbrush
stranded embroidery thread (floss)
needle
scissors
pins
matching thread

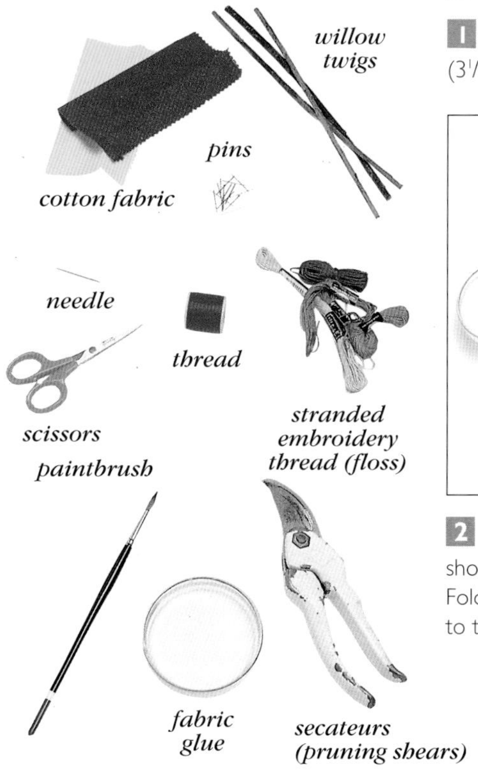

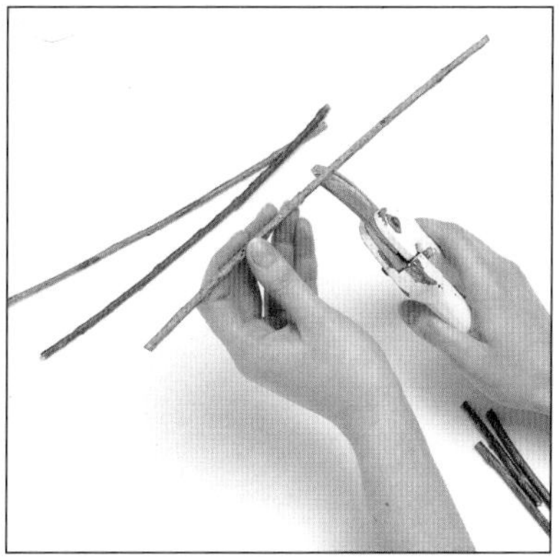

1 Cut four pieces of twig, each 9 cm (3½ in) long.

2 Make a 1 cm (½ in) hem along one short end of the fabric and glue it down. Fold the long sides of the fabric rectangle to the centre and glue.

3 Position the twigs evenly across the centre of the right side of the fabric. Using three strands of embroidery thread (floss) oversew the twigs on to the napkin ring.

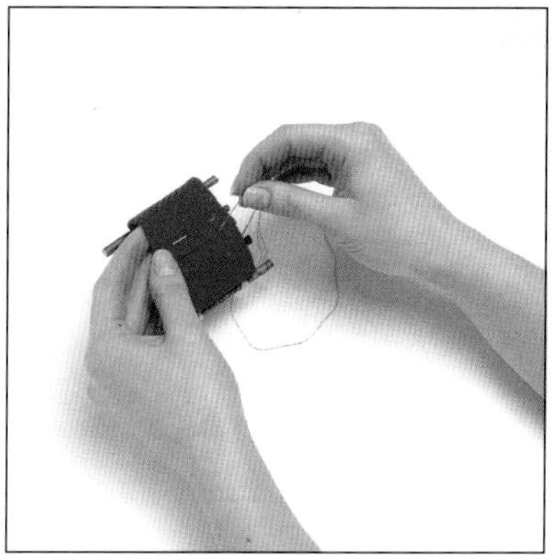

4 Pin the ends of the ring together, tucking the raw edge into the folded edge. Slip-stitch together.

The Christmas Mantelpiece

In restrained tones of cream and green, this elegant arrangement concentrates on contrasting shapes and textures. Placing it in front of a mirror makes it doubly effective. The key to success is scale: use the largest-leaved ivy and the thickest candles you can find to make a really stylish design statement.

YOU WILL NEED
- polystyrene balls
- double-sided adhesive (cellophane) tape
- scissors
- reindeer moss
- ivory candles of various heights and widths
- foil dishes (for baking or take-out food)
- plastic adhesive
- stems of ivy
- florist's wire

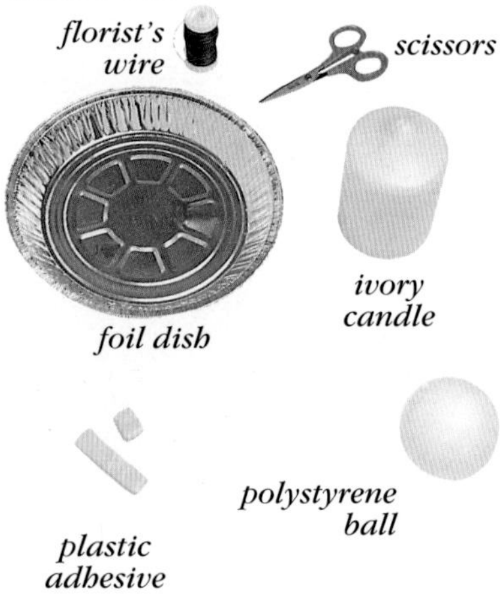

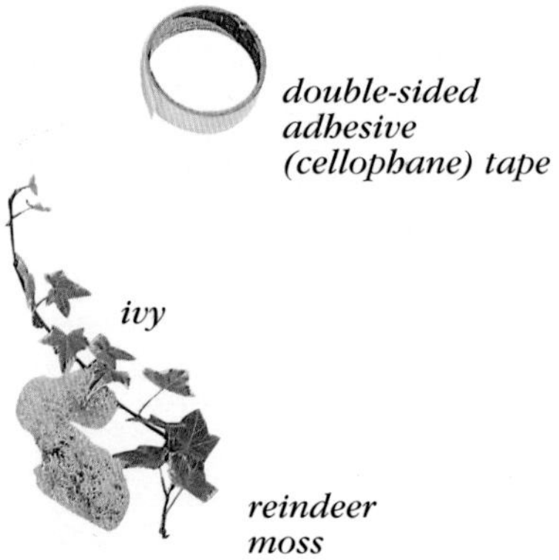

1 To make the moss balls, cover the polystyrene shapes all over with double-sided adhesive (cellophane) tape.

2 Press the moss gently on to the balls, covering well so that none of the polystyrene can be seen.

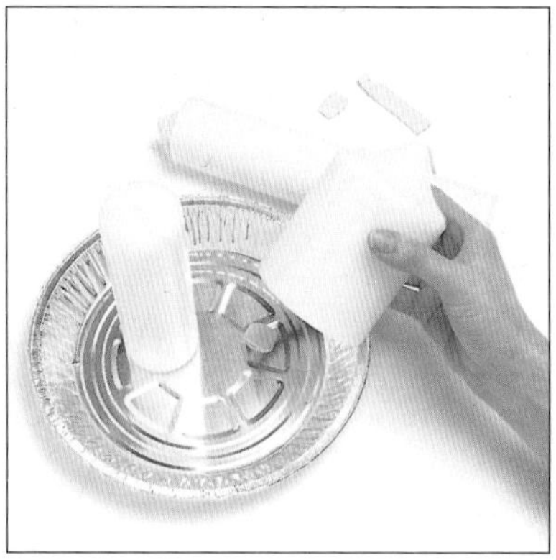

3 Arrange the candles on foil dishes, to protect the mantelpiece from hot, dripping wax. Secure the candles in the dishes with pieces of plastic adhesive.

4 Wire together small bunches of ivy and attach them to a longer main stem to make a lush garland. Arrange the candles on the mantelpiece and drape the garlands in front of them. Position the moss balls around the candles.

SAFETY TIP

Never leave burning candles unattended and do not allow the candle to burn down to within 5cm (2in) of the foliage or other decoration materials.

Christmas Crackers

Making your own Christmas crackers is really rewarding and it's great fun watching friends and family pull them open to discover the treats inside. Make exactly the number you need for your party and collect small gifts to put in them.

YOU WILL NEED
- double-sided crepe paper in bright colours
- craft knife
- metal ruler
- cutting mat
- thin card (cardboard) in black and white
- double-sided adhesive (cellophane) tape
- cracker snaps
- paper hats, jokes and gifts to go in the crackers
- narrow black ribbon
- gold paper-backed foil
- corrugated cardboard
- gold crepe paper
- fine gold cord

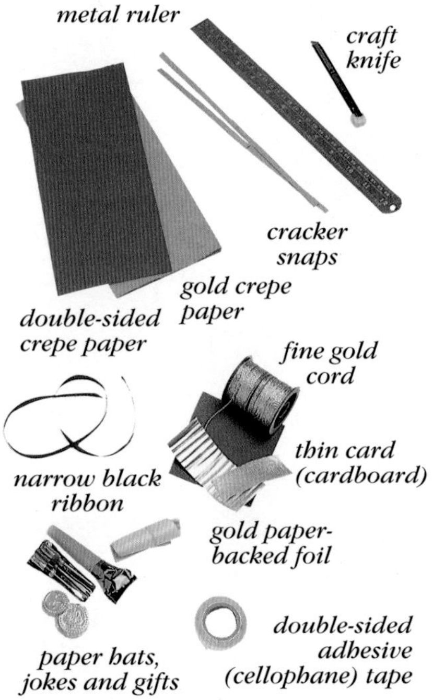

1 For each cracker, cut two rectangles of crepe paper measuring 25 x 20 cm (10 x 8 in). Join, overlapping the ends, to make a rectangle 45 x 20 cm (18 x 8 in).

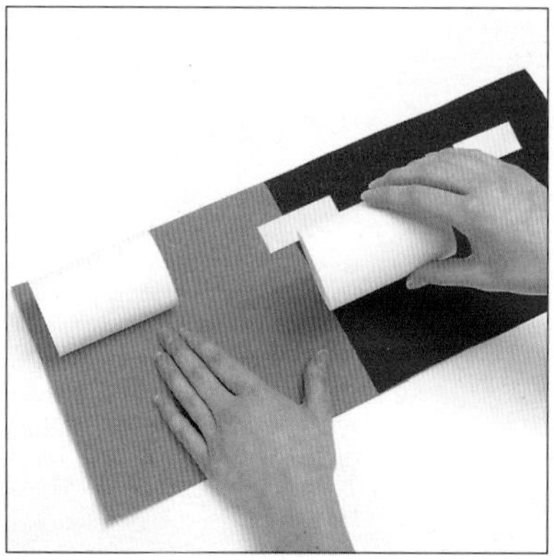

2 Cut three pieces of thin white card (cardboard) 22 x 10 cm (9 x 4 in). Roll each into a cylinder, overlapping the short ends by 3.5 cm (1 1/4 in). Lay strips of double-sided adhesive (cellophane) tape across the crepe paper with which to attach the card cylinders: one in the centre and the other two about 4 cm (1 1/2 in) in from each end of the rectangle. Roll up and secure the edge with double-sided tape.

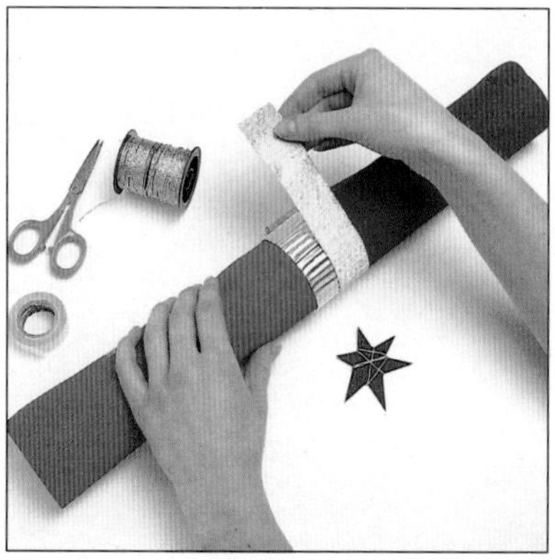

3 Decorate the cracker with strips of the gold papers. To make the corrugated paper, lay a strip of paper-backed foil over a piece of corrugated cardboard and ease the foil into the ridges with your thumb. Cut a simple star shape out of thin black card (cardboard), wrap some fine gold cord around it and stick it on top of the gold decorations (use one of the star templates at the back of the book or draw your own).

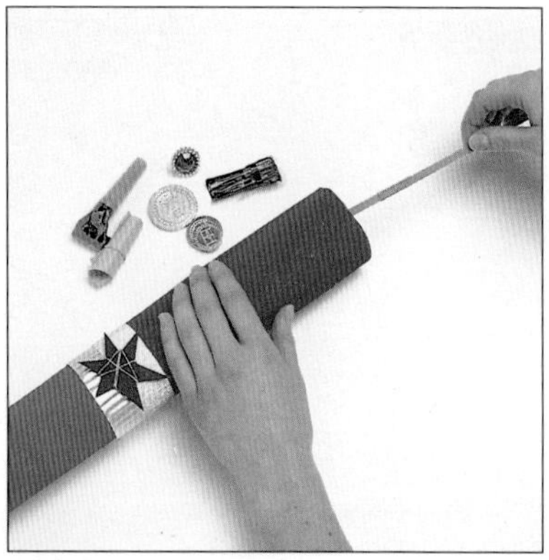

4 Insert the snap and place the novelties and a paper hat in the central section of the cracker.

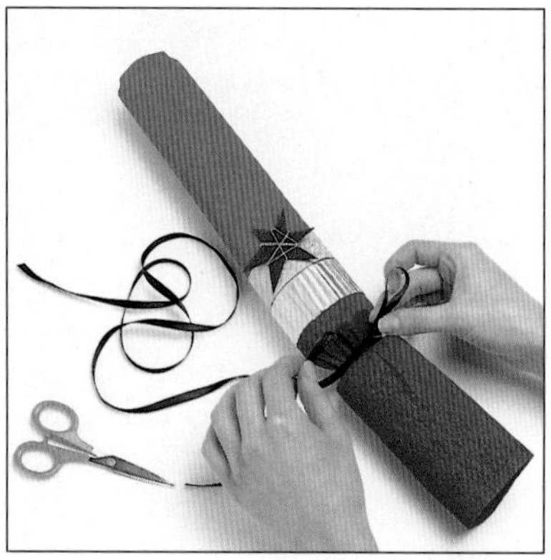

5 Tie up the ends with narrow black ribbon, easing the crepe paper gently so that you can tie the knots very tightly.

6 Complete the cracker by folding the edges of the crepe paper over the ends of the cardboard cylinders.

Citrus Centrepiece

Perhaps because they're at their best at this time of year, oranges feature in many traditional Christmas recipes and their warm spicy smell readily evokes the festive season. A sparkling glass bowl of citrus fruits brings a flash of sunshine into the house in the depths of winter and makes a glowing, fragrant centrepiece.

CRAFT TIP

If you are using a lino-cutting tool for this project, paint the blade with a coat of clear nail varnish to prevent it discolouring the fruit.

YOU WILL NEED
oranges, lemons and limes
V-shaped lino-cutting tool or canelle knife
sharp knife
wire-edged ribbon
scissors
florist's stub (floral) wire
glass dish or bowl
sprigs of fresh bay leaves
secateurs (pruning shears)

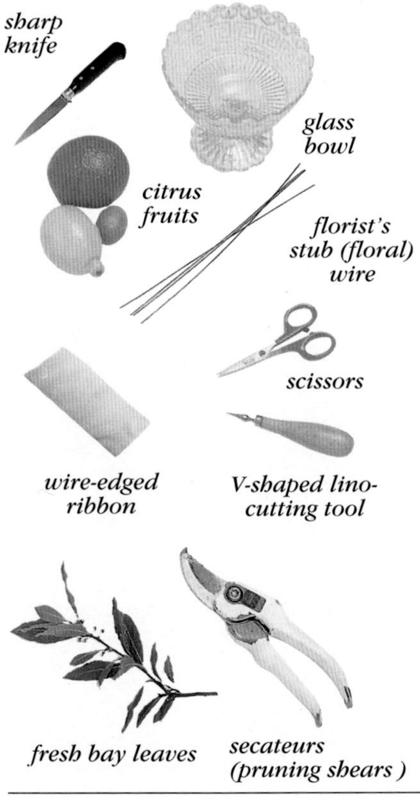

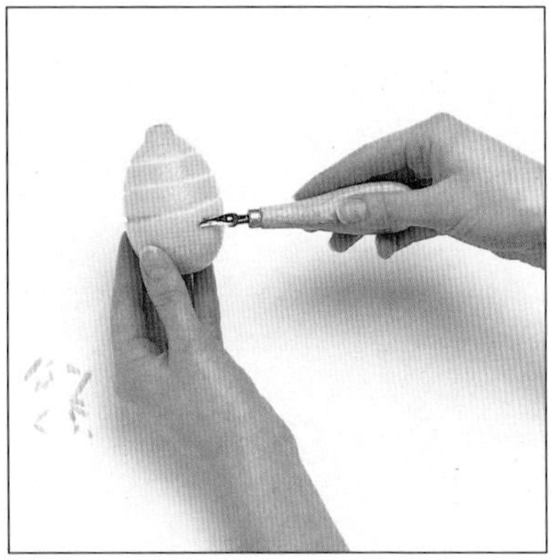

1 Use the lino-cutting tool or canelle knife to cut grooves in the peel of the fruits and reveal the white pith beneath. Follow the contours of the fruit in a spiral or make straight cuts.

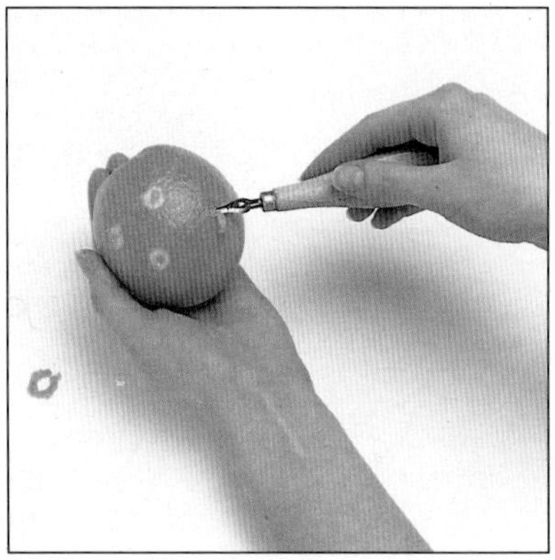

2 On other fruits, try making an overall pattern of small circles. Practise the patterns on spare fruits you intend to cook with or eat.

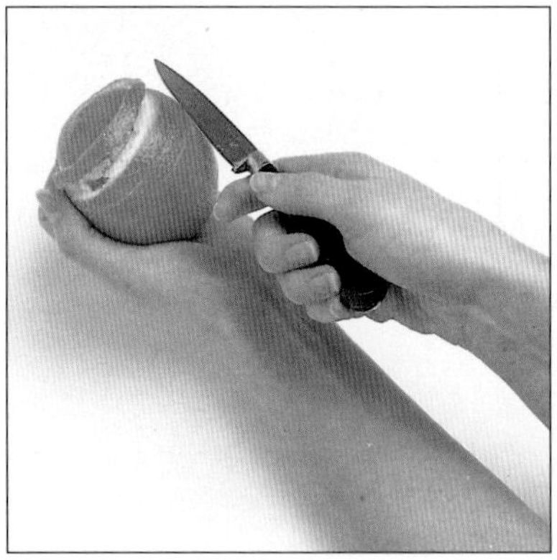

3 With a very sharp knife, cut thin spirals of orange peel as long as possible to drape over the arrangement.

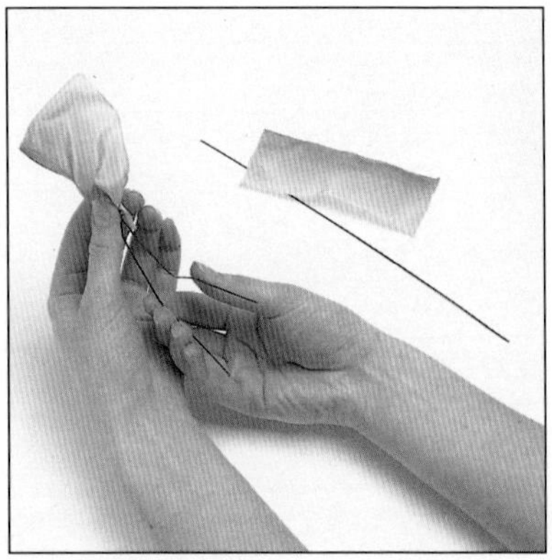

4 Cut short lengths of wire-edged ribbon, fold into loops and secure the ends with florist's stub (floral) wire.

5 Arrange the fruits in your chosen container, tucking in the ribbon loops and adding a few sprigs of fresh green bay leaves.

Silk Purses

Ribbons are available in a great range of widths and colours and you need only a small amount of each to make these delicate little purses to hang on your tree. Use luxurious satins or sheer organza (organdy), with contrasting colours for generous bows around the top.

YOU WILL NEED
an assortment of ribbons
scissors
pins
matching thread
needle
fine gold cord
polyester wadding (batting)

1 Cut enough ribbon to make a pleasing purse shape when folded in two, short sides together, allowing for the raw edges to be folded down at the top. To make a striped purse, pin and stitch three narrower lengths together using running stitch.

2 With the wrong sides together, sew up the sides of the purse by hand, or using a sewing machine if you prefer.

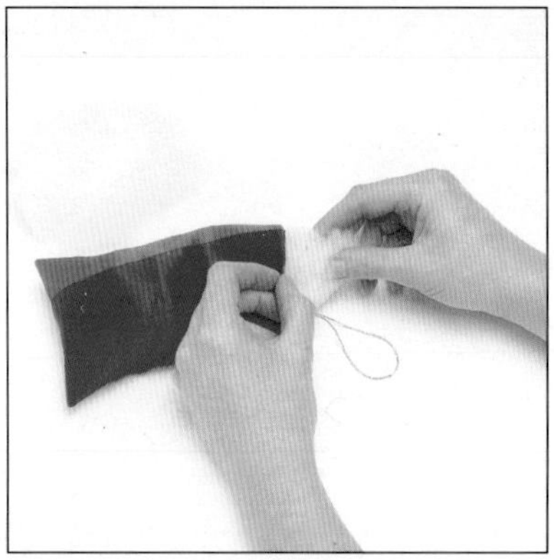

3 Turn the purse right side out and tuck the raw edges inside. Stitch on a loop of fine gold cord for hanging. Stuff lightly with polyester wadding (batting).

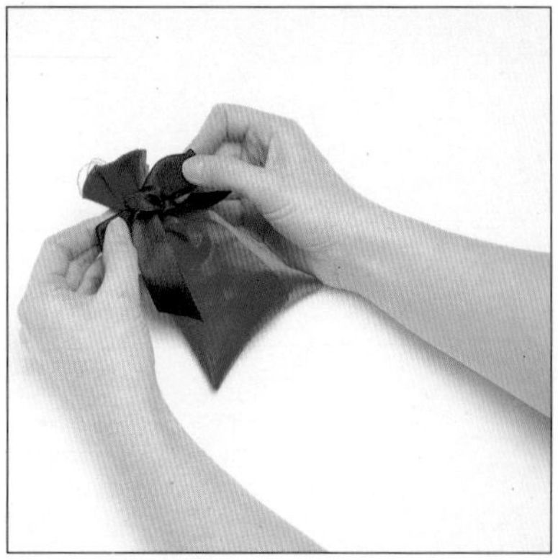

4 Gather the top of the purse together and tie with another piece of ribbon, finishing with a pretty bow.

Victorian Boots

Use the richest fabrics you can find to make these delicate boots: fine raw silks and taffetas in glowing colours are perfect. The two sides of the decoration should harmonize well.

YOU WILL NEED
thin white card (cardboard)
pencil
stapler
scissors
scraps of fabric
fabric glue
paintbrush
fine gold cord

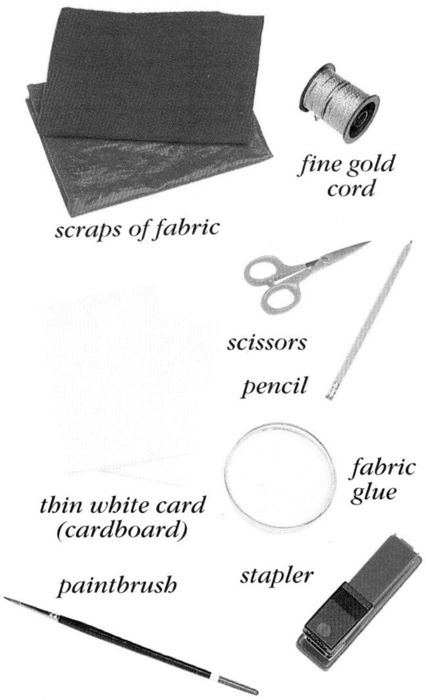

1 Trace the boot motif from the back of the book and transfer it on to thin card (cardboard). Fold the card in two and staple the layers together at the edges so that you can cut out two exactly matching templates. Cut the boots out with scissors.

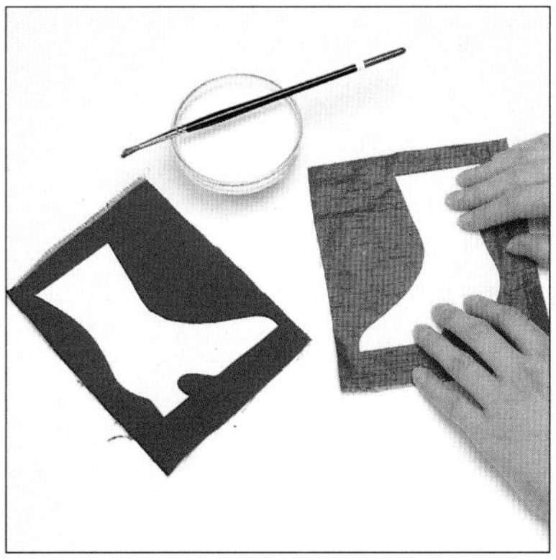

2 Separate the templates. Turn one over and glue each on to a piece of coordinating fabric.

3 Cut around each boot leaving an allowance of barely 1 cm (1/2 in). Snip the excess fabric around all the curves and stick down firmly to the back of the card.

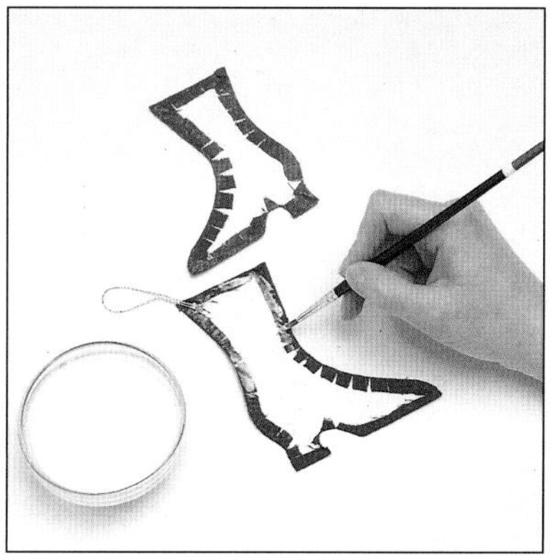

4 Glue a loop of cord to the back of one card for hanging, then glue the two sides of the boot together and leave to dry thoroughly.

Glitter Keys

A simple idea for transforming everyday objects into fantasy tree decorations. Once you've picked up the glitter habit, you may find you want to cover all kinds of other things – and why not?

YOU WILL NEED
old keys in various shapes and sizes
PVA (white) glue
old paintbrush
sheets of scrap paper
coloured glitter
fine gold cord

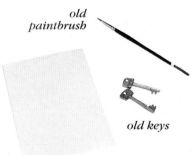

old paintbrush

old keys

scrap paper

PVA (white) glue

coloured glitter

fine gold cord

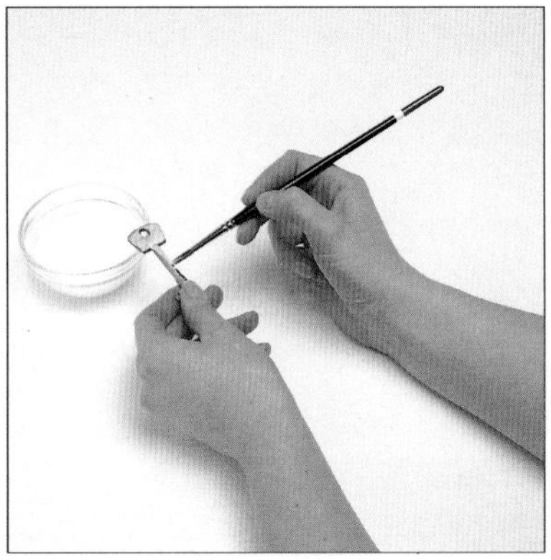

1 Using an old paintbrush, cover one side of the key with a coat of undiluted PVA (white) glue.

2 Lay the key on a sheet of scrap paper and sprinkle generously with glitter. Repeat with the other keys, using a separate sheet of paper for each one. Allow to dry completely.

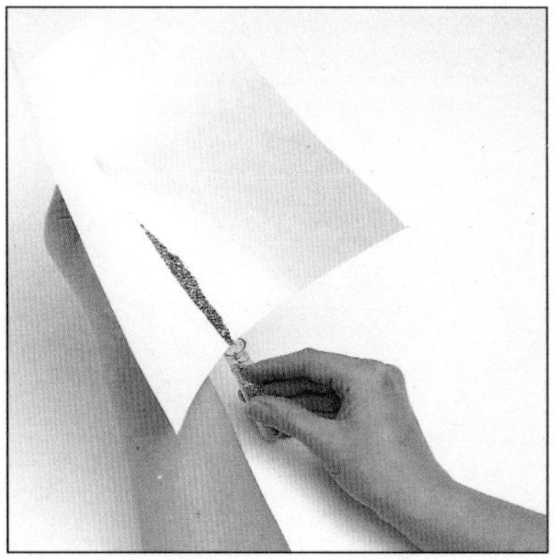

3 Remove the key. Pinch the paper to make a groove for the spare glitter to run into. Pour it back into the container. Glue the remaining areas of the keys and repeat the process. Add further layers to build up quite a thick coating. Tie a loop of gold cord to each key for hanging.

CRAFT TIP

PVA (white) glue dries to a transparent glaze, so you can brush it on over glitter you have already applied when building up the layers on the keys.

Ornamental Keys

Gold paint and fake gems can turn a bunch of old keys into something truly wonderful – fit to unlock a fairy-tale castle or treasure chest.

YOU WILL NEED
- old keys in assorted shapes and sizes
- gold spray paint
- gold braid
- hot glue gun
- flat-backed fake gems in assorted colours

gold spray paint

scissors

gold braid

old keys

flat-backed fake gems

hot glue gun

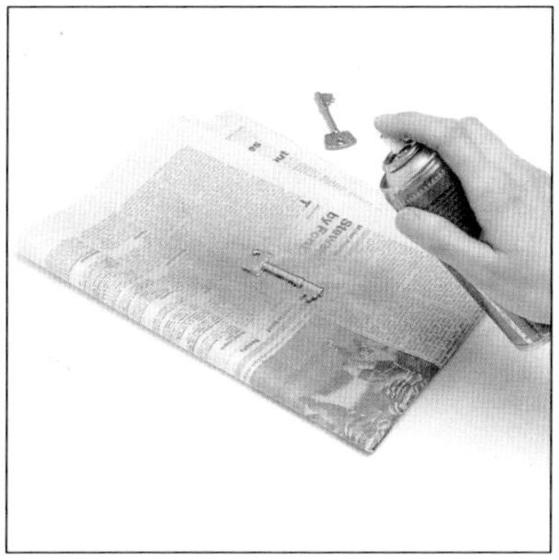

1 Make sure the keys are free of rust. Working with one side at a time, spray with gold paint and allow to dry.

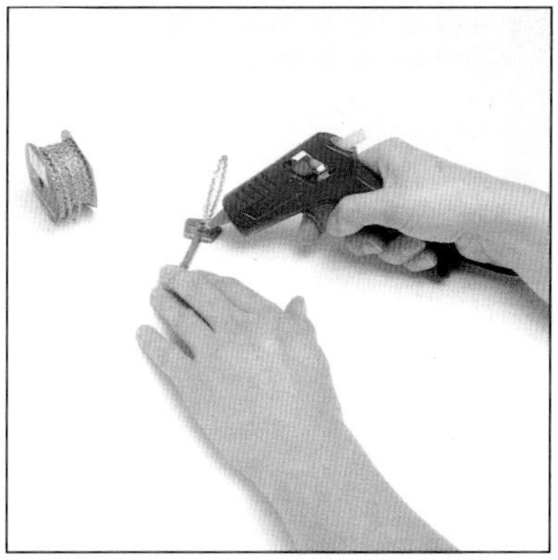

2 Cut the gold braid to a suitable length for hanging the key. Fold in half and attach the ends to the key with the hot glue gun

3 Cover the ends of the braid by gluing a jewel over them. Arrange two or three more jewels on the key and glue them on. Allow to dry thoroughly.

Carnival Mask

A stunning decoration inspired by the traditional costume of the masked Harlequin. Use the fragile foil from candy wrappers for part of the design to mimic the expensive look of fine gold leaf.

YOU WILL NEED
tracing paper
thin white card (cardboard)
scissors
craft knife
pencil
ruler
metallic crayons in gold and lilac
glitter paint
PVA (white) glue
glitter
foil candy wrappers
sequins
gold doily
matt gold paper
glue-stick
fine gold cord
gold button

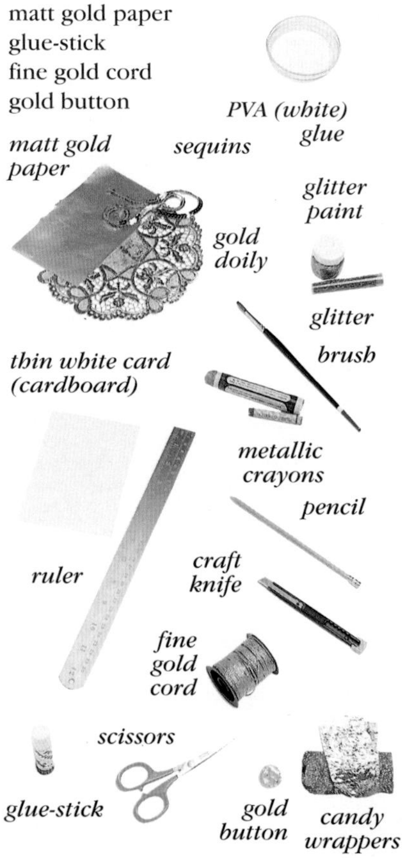

1 Trace the template from the back of the book and transfer it to thin white card (cardboard). Cut out the mask shape and eye holes. Use a soft pencil to draw in the diagonals for the diamonds.

2 Decorate the diamond shapes in different colours and textures. Use metallic crayons, adding glitter paint on some for texture. Paint PVA (white) glue on to others and sprinkle with glitter. When dry, coat thinly with more glue to fix the glitter. Cut diamonds from the candy wrappers and glue these on last to cover any rough edges.

3 Trim the eye holes with rows of gold sequins and the edging cut from a gold doily.

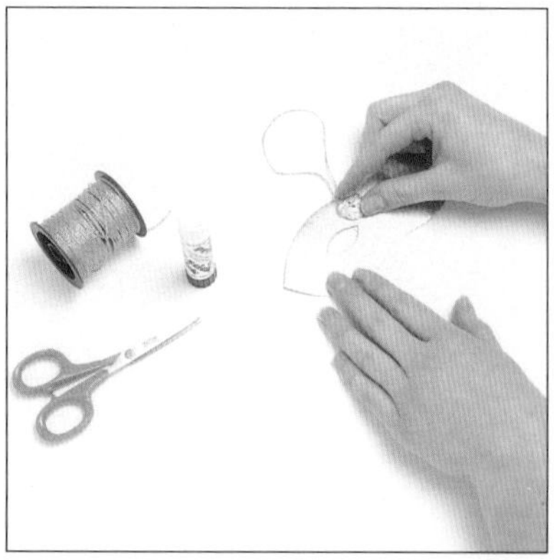

4 Use the template to cut a second mask shape from matt gold paper. Glue this to the back of your mask. Attach a loop of fine gold cord for hanging, covering the ends with a gold button.

Lacy Silver Gloves

Dainty Victorian ladies' gloves make a pretty motif for a traditional glittering tree ornament. Use translucent glass paints, which adhere well and let the foil shine through the colour.

YOU WILL NEED
tracing paper
heavy-gauge aluminium foil
masking tape
dried-out ballpoint pen
scissors
oil-based glass paints
paintbrush
fine gold cord

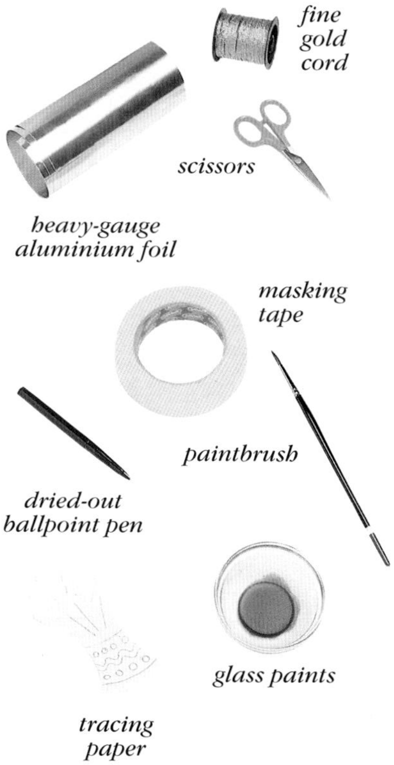

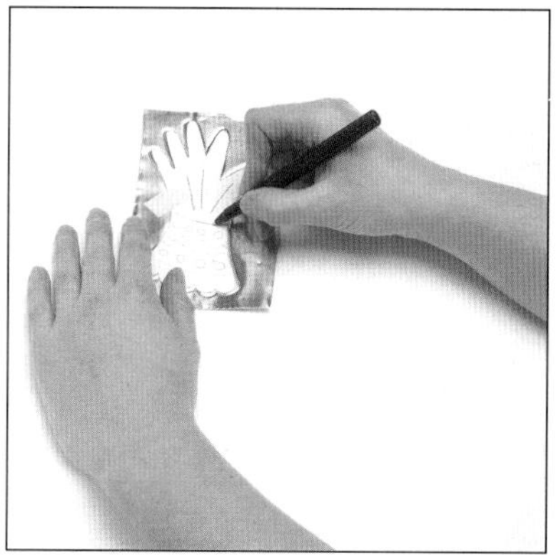

1 Trace the template from the back of the book and attach the tracing to a piece of foil with masking tape. Draw over the design to transfer it to the foil. Remove the tracing and complete the embossing with an old ballpoint pen.

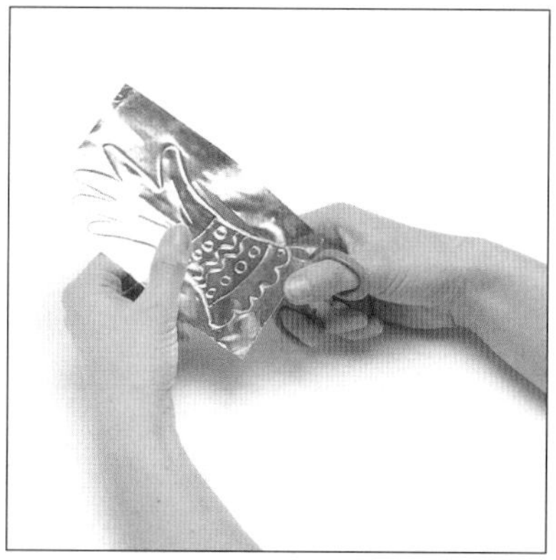

2 Cut out the glove, leaving a narrow border of about 2 mm (1/16 in) all around the edge: don't cut into the embossed outline. Make a hole in one corner of the glove with the point of the scissors.

3 Paint the design with glass paints, keeping the colours within the embossed outlines. Allow to dry completely for at least 24 hours.

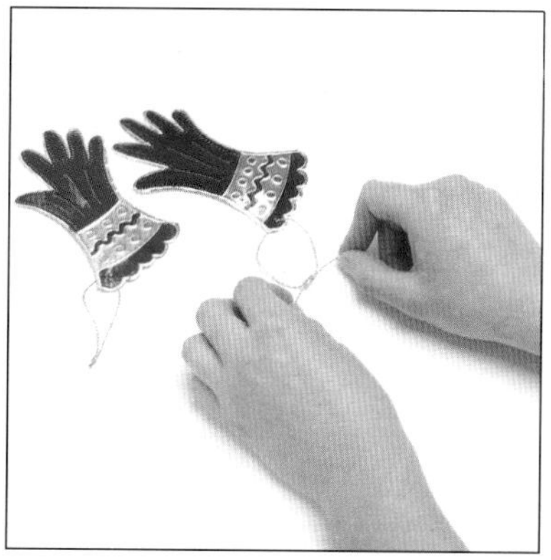

4 Thread a loop of fine gold cord through the hole for hanging.

Gilded Rosettes

These flower-like ornaments can be hung on the tree or used to decorate a sumptuously wrapped gift for someone special. Gold lamé makes an opulent setting for an ornate gilt button, but ring the changes with luxurious velvets too.

YOU WILL NEED
paper for template
pencil
small pieces of silk, lamé or dress-weight velvet
pins
scissors
matching thread
needle
fine gold cord
ornate buttons
hot glue gun

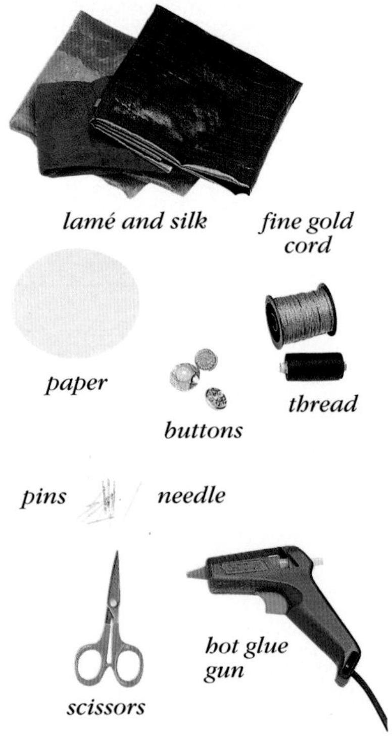

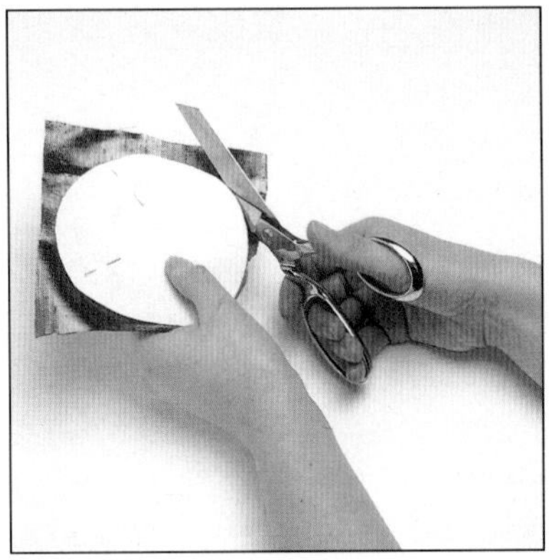

1 Draw and cut out a circular template about 12 cm (5 in) in diameter, pin to a single layer of fabric and cut out (there is no need for a seam allowance).

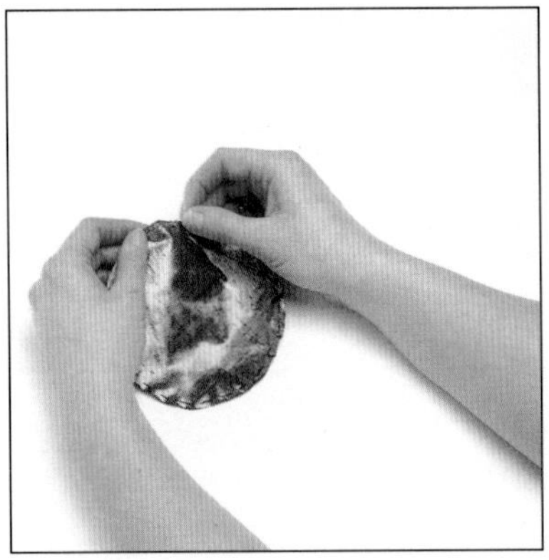

2 Using double thread, sew in running stitch all round the circle 5 mm ($^1/_4$ in) from the edge. Pull the thread taut to form the rosette and secure the ends.

3 Thread a loop of fine gold cord through the top of the rosette for hanging the decoration.

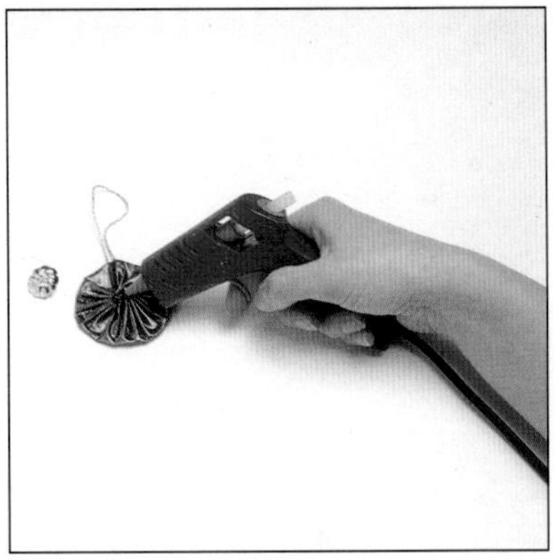

4 Using a hot glue gun, attach a button in the centre to cover the raw edges.

Exotic Ornaments

These sequinned and beaded balls look like a collection of priceless Fabergé treasures, yet they're simple and fun to make. Hang them on the tree or pile them in a dish for a show-stopping decoration.

YOU WILL NEED
- silky covered polystyrene balls
- paper for template
- pins
- gold netting
- scissors
- double-sided adhesive (cellophane) tape
- gold braid
- sequins in a variety of shapes and colours
- small glass and pearl beads
- brass-headed pins, 1 cm (½ in) long

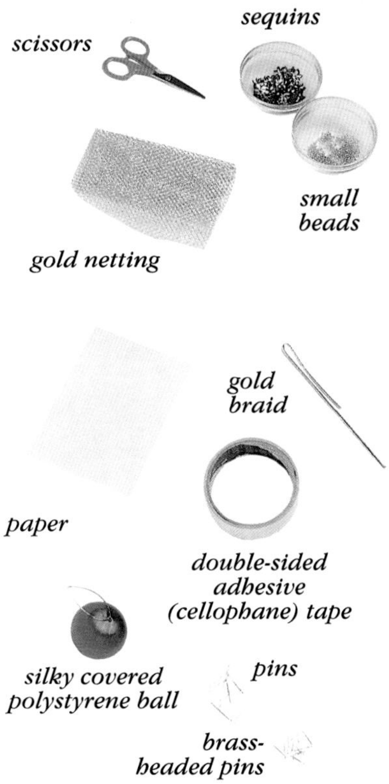

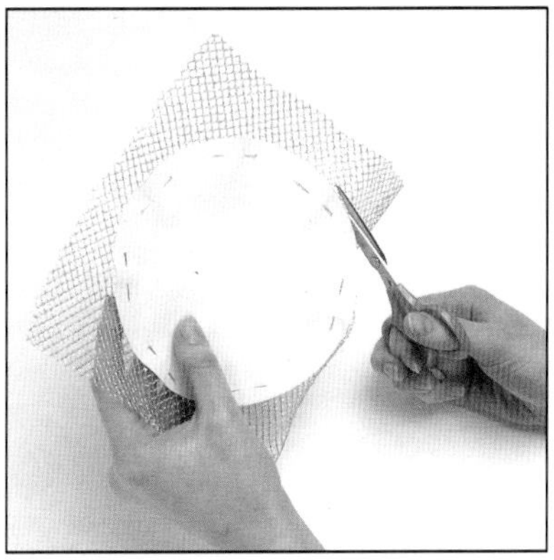

1 Cut a circle to completely cover the ball and make a paper template. Pin to the gold netting and cut out.

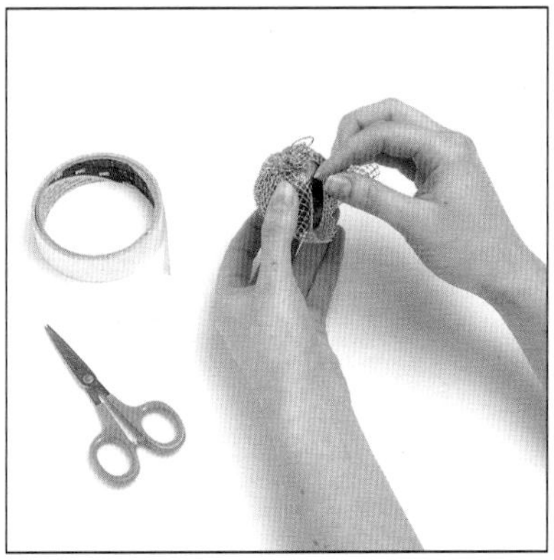

2 Secure the netting to the ball using tiny pieces of double-sided adhesive (cellophane) tape. The tape and raw edges will be hidden later with sequins.

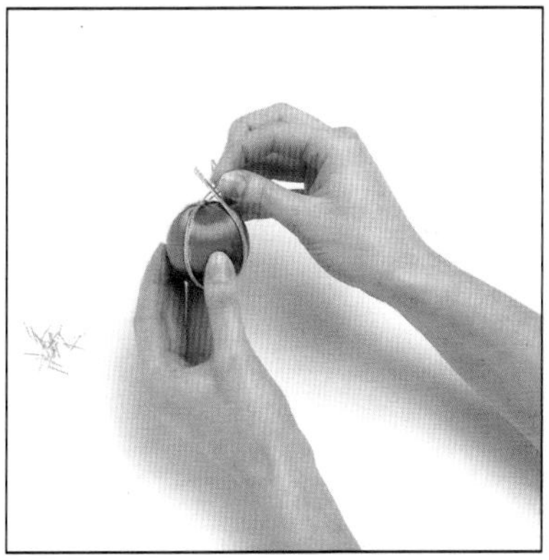

3 For an alternative design cut lengths of gold braid and pin around the ball to make a framework for your sequins.

4 Attach a loop of gold thread to the ball with a brass-headed pin. Thread a bead and sequin on to a brass-headed pin and gently press into the ball. Repeat until each design is complete.

CRAFT TIP

Silk-covered balls are available as ready-made tree ornaments. When you are working out your designs, use simple repeating patterns and avoid using too many colours on each one, since this can look too busy.

Christmas Balls

Plain Christmas tree balls can be transformed into totally unique decorations. Customize the balls by adding surface decorations with a hot glue gun – ribbons, sequins, fake gemstones, eyelets, glitter glue and fabric paints, for example.

YOU WILL NEED
red and gold balls
hot glue gun
decorations – sequins, gem stones, glitter glue, metallic stars
tweezers
fancy gold cord
scissors

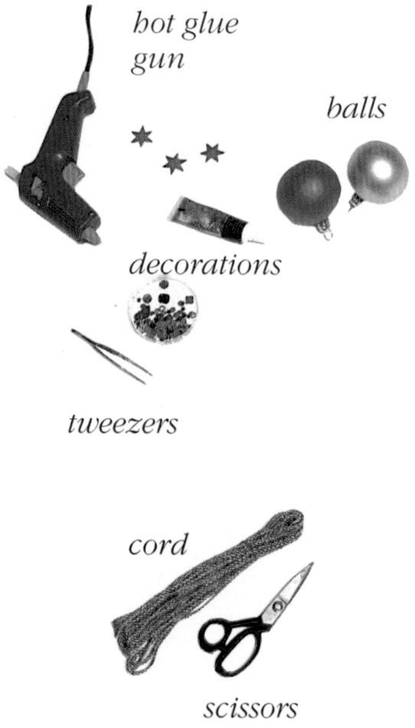

1 Draw stripes of glue down the red ball with the glue gun to divide it into quarters. Sprinkle it immediately with sequins.

2 Place a dot of glue in the middle of each panel and stick on a metallic star.

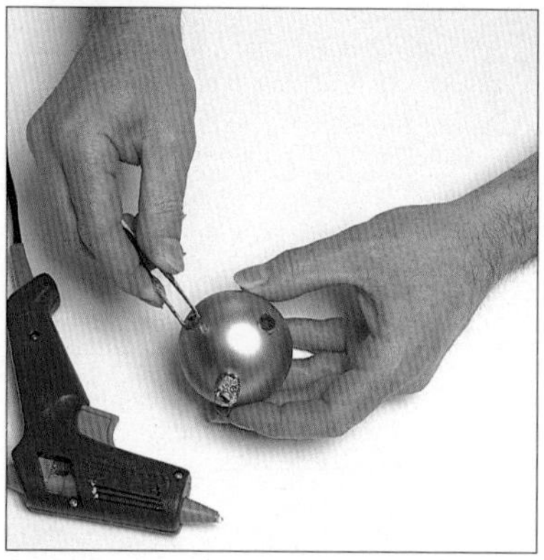

3 Stick the gemstones around the gold ball with the glue gun. Position them with the tweezers.

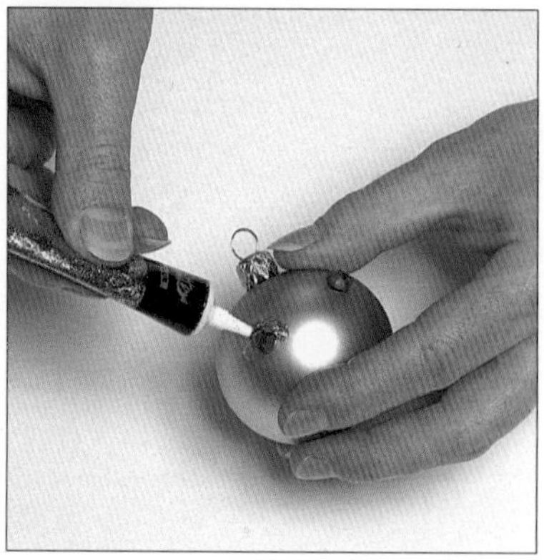

4 Surround each gemstone with a setting of glitter glue. Finally, thread all the balls with gold cord, and tie them on to gifts or a Christmas tree.

Button Garland

An assortment of old buttons can be given new life as an original garland for the Christmas tree. Use fairly large ones for this project: save your little shirt buttons for other decorative ornament

YOU WILL NEED
an assortment of buttons
garden twine
scissors
hot glue gun

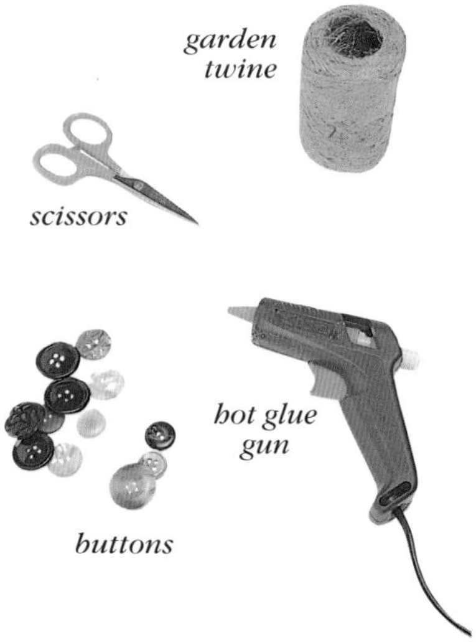

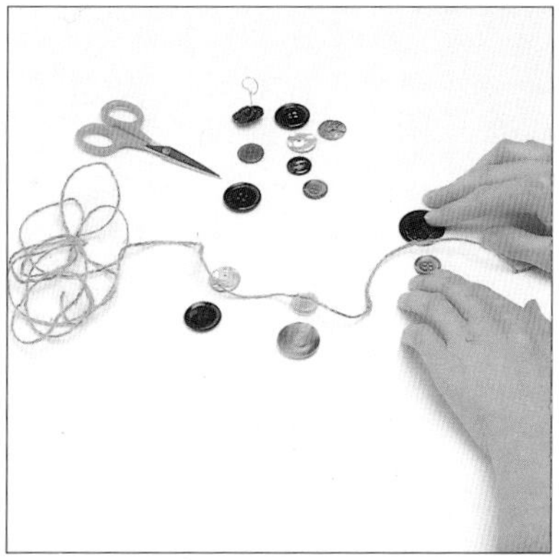

1 Spread all your buttons out so that you can choose a variety of colours and sizes. Balance the weight of the buttons by using small ones with larger ones, and choose a pleasing combination of colours to go along the garland.

2 Heat the hot glue gun and put a dot of glue on the back of a button. Lay the twine on top and wait a few seconds for the glue to harden.

SAFETY TIP

Take care with your fingers when using the hot glue gun as hot glue may squeeze through the holes in the buttons and cause a burn.

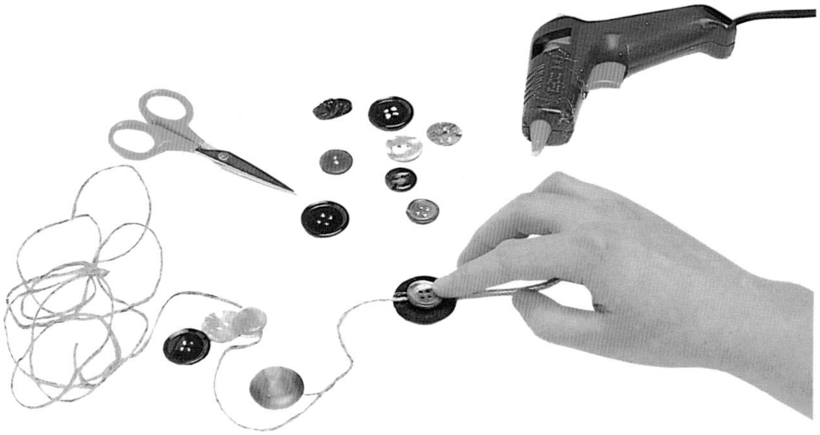

3 Glue a second button on the other side of the twine. Glue buttons all along the string in the same way, spacing them evenly. The length of your garland will depend on the size of your tree and the number of buttons you have.

A Country Angel

This endearing character, with her homespun clothes and tightly knotted hair, is bound to be a friend for many Christmases to come.

YOU WILL NEED
- 40 x 24 cm- (16 x 10 in-) piece natural calico
- 40 x 26 cm- (16 x 10 $^1/_4$ in-) piece check cotton homespun or small-scale gingham
- 30 x 22 cm (12 x 9 in)-piece blue and white ticking
- tea
- paper for templates
- scissors
- fabric marker pen
- sewing machine
- matching thread
- polyester wadding (batting)
- twigs
- secateurs (pruning shears)
- fine permanent (magic) marker
- stranded embroidery thread (floss) in brown
- needle
- garden twine
- scrap of red woollen fabric
- fabric stiffener (starch)
- copper wire
- all-purpose glue

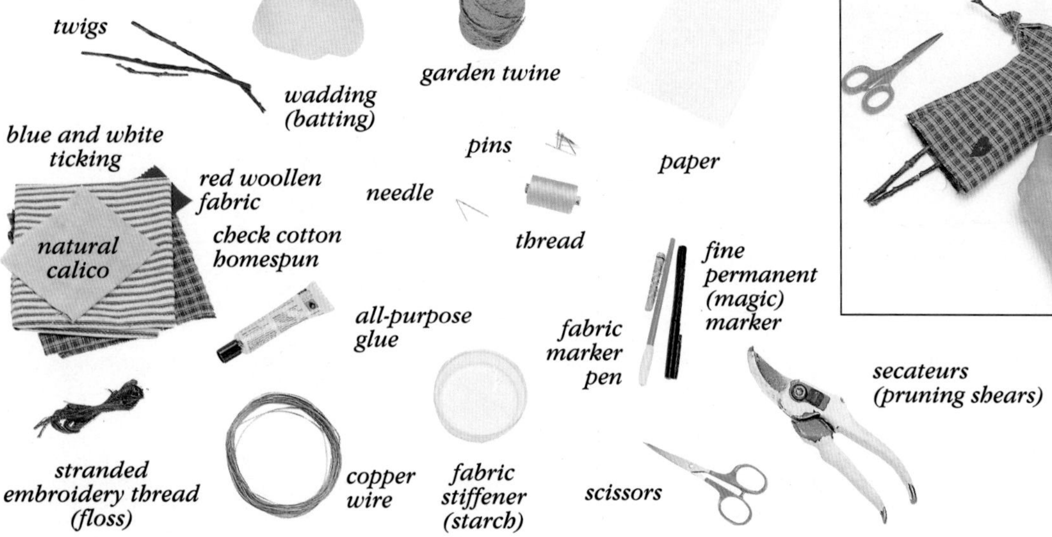

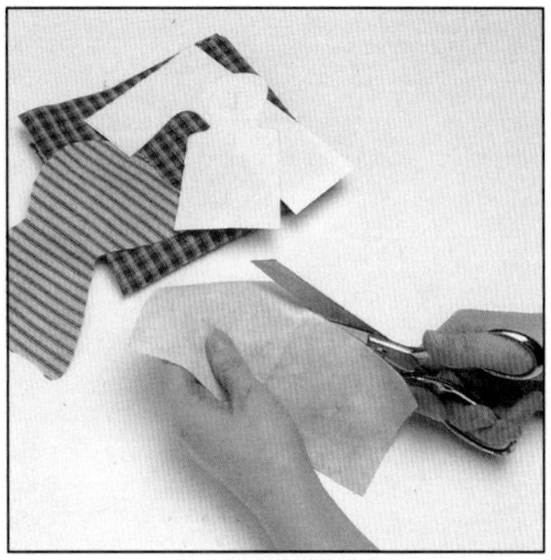

1 Begin by washing all the fabrics to remove any chemicals. While they are still damp, soak them in tea. Don't worry if the colouring is uneven as this adds to their rustic, aged appearance. Trace the patterns for the head, dress and wings from the back of the book. Cut the head and torso out of doubled calico, leaving a 1 cm ($^1/_2$ in) seam allowance.

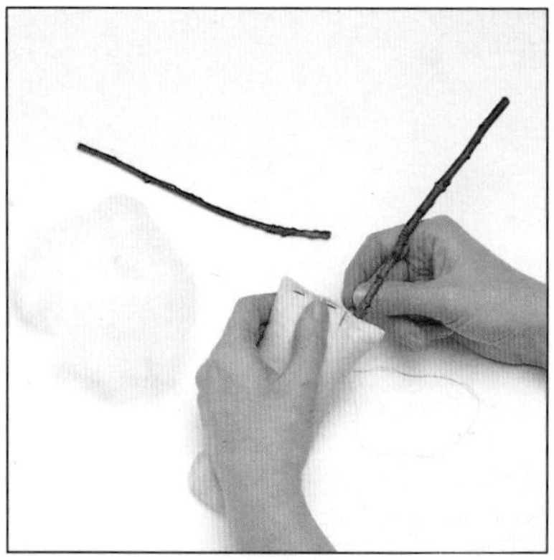

2 Machine stitch the two body pieces right sides together leaving the lower edge open. Clip the curves and turn to the right side. Stuff softly with polyester wadding (batting). Cut two twigs about 20 cm (8 in) long and stick them into the body to make the legs. Sew up the opening, securing the legs as you go.

3 With a very fine permanent (magic) marker, draw the eyes, nose and mouth on to the face. Make heavy French knots with embroidery thread around the top of the face for the hair.

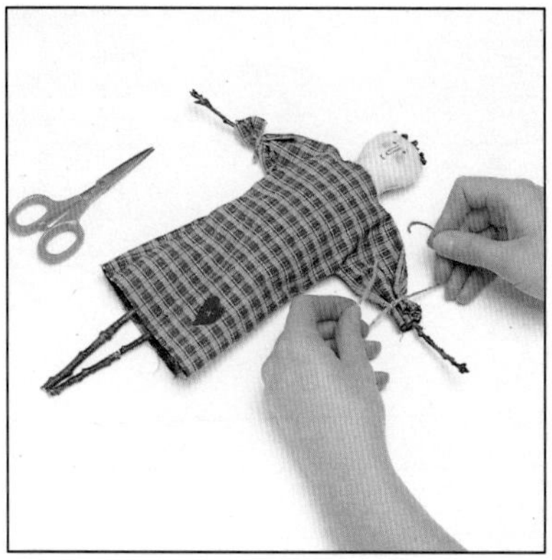

4 Use the paper pattern to cut out the dress from the check fabric. Sew up the sides, leaving the sleeves and hem with raw edges. Cut a slit in the top for the neck and turn the dress to the right side. Cut a small heart from the red woollen fabric and attach to the dress with a single cross stitch in brown embroidery thread (floss). Put the dress on the angel, then place short twigs inside the sleeves, securing them tightly at the wrists with garden twine. The twigs should be short enough to let the arms bend forwards.

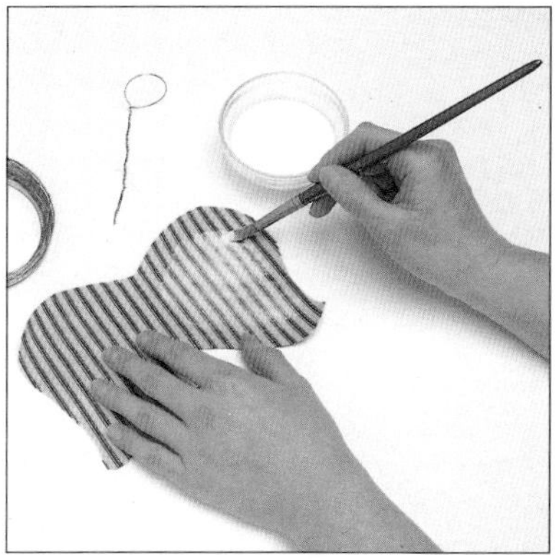

5 Cut the wings out of the ticking and fray the raw edges slightly. Apply fabric stiffener (starch) liberally to the wings to soak them thoroughly. Lay them completely flat to dry.

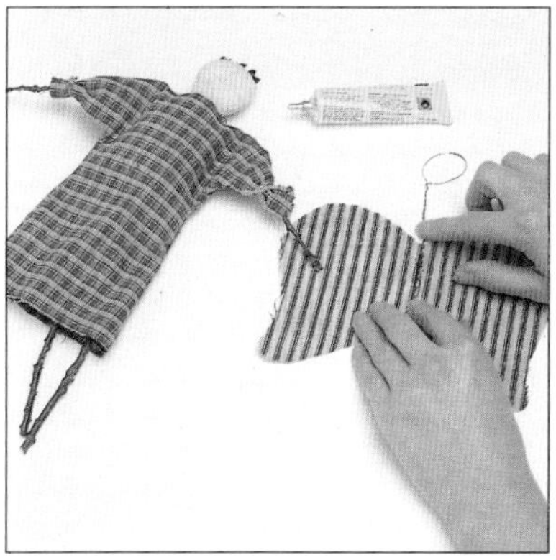

6 Make a halo from copper wire, leaving a long end to glue to the wings. Stitch the wings securely to the back of the body through the dress.

Raffia Balls

Here's another idea to decorate the natural Christmas tree. Instead of glitzy glass ornaments, hang up these little balls covered in creamy, undyed raffia. Their subtle shade and interesting texture go really beautifully with the tree's soft green branches.

YOU WILL NEED
fine copper wire
scissors
small polystyrene balls
double-sided adhesive (cellophane) tape
natural (garden) raffia

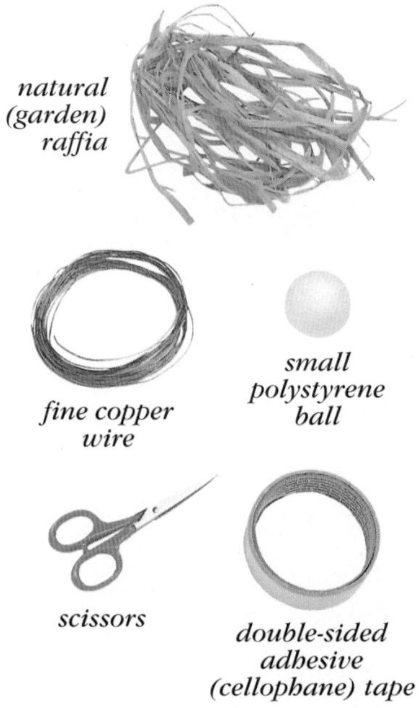

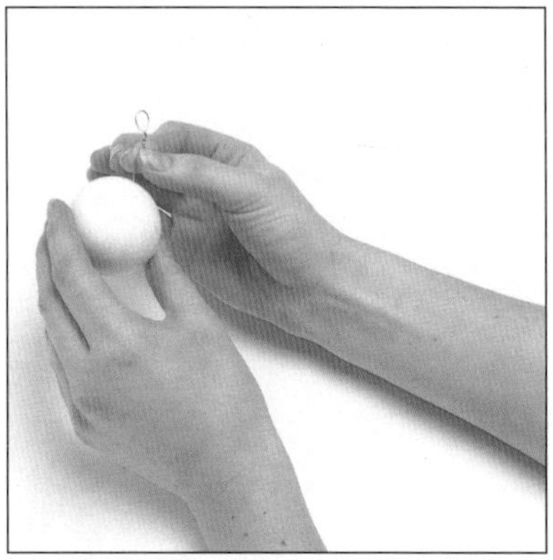

1 Cut a short piece of wire and make it into a loop. Stick the ends into a polystyrene ball.

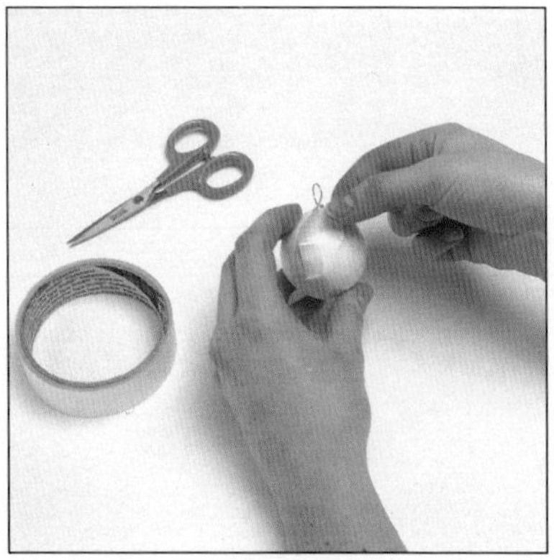

2 Cover the ball completely in double-sided adhesive (cellophane) tape.

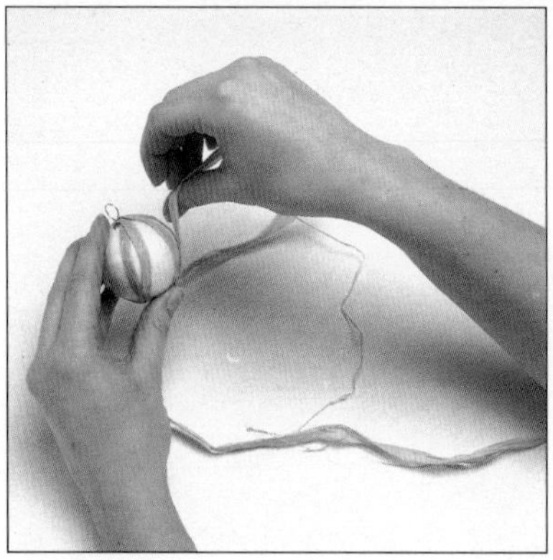

3 Arrange the hank of raffia so that you can remove lengths without tangling them. Holding the first 10 cm (4 in) of the strand at the top of the ball, wind the raffia around the ball working from top to bottom and covering it as evenly as possible.

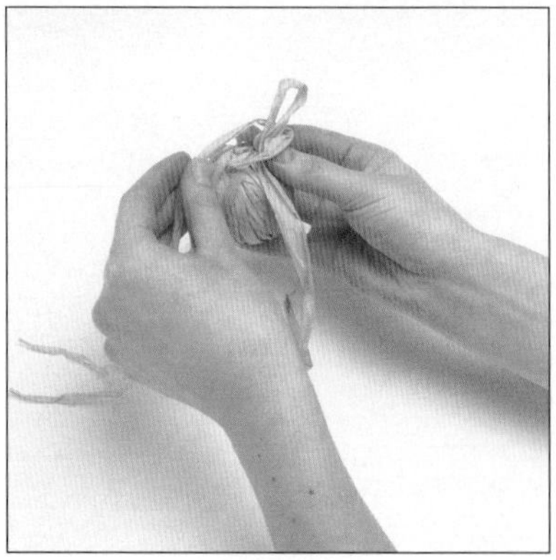

4 When you have finished covering the ball, tie the end of the raffia to the length you left free at the beginning. Using a few lengths of raffia together, form a loop with which to hang the decoration and finish with a bow.

CRAFT TIP

As an alternative, try using coloured raffia for a more varied effect.

Twiggy Stars

Buy a bundle of willow twigs or, better still, hunt for them in winter woods and gardens. These pretty stars would look equally effective hanging on the tree or in a window.

YOU WILL NEED
willow twigs
secateurs (pruning shears)
stranded embroidery thread (floss)
checked cotton fabric
scissors
natural (garden) raffia

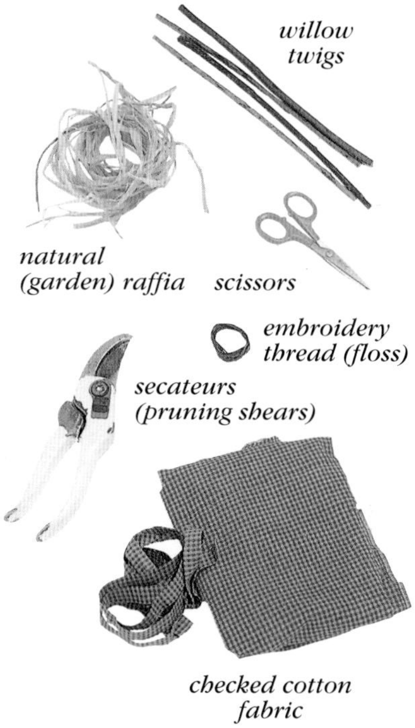

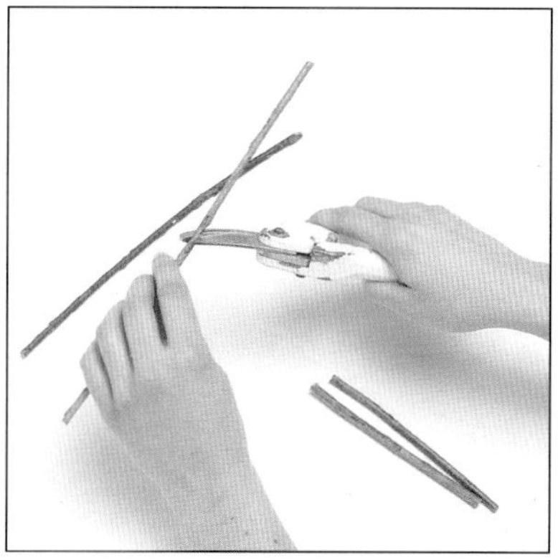

1 Cut the twigs into lengths of 15 cm (6 in) using the secateurs (pruning shears. You will need five for each star.

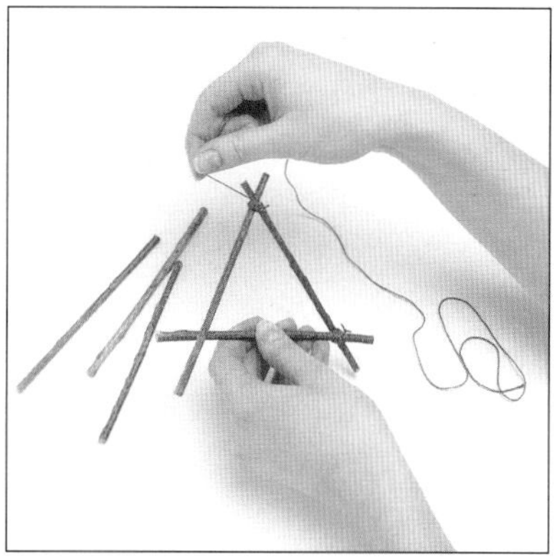

2 Tie the first pair of twigs together near the ends with a length of embroidery thread (floss), winding it around and between to form a "V" shape. Repeat with the remaining twigs, arranging them under and over each other as shown in the photograph to form a five-pointed star.

3 Cut the fabric into strips approximately 15 x 2 cm (6 x 3/4 in).

4 Tie a length of fabric in a double knot over the thread securing each point of the star. Attach a loop of raffia to hang the decoration.

Tiny Knitted Socks

Miniature socks would be a charming addition to the tree, especially appropriate for a baby's first Christmas. They're lightly stuffed with wadding (batting), but if you prefer you could wrap up a tiny present to peep out of the top.

ABBREVIATIONS
K: knit; P: purl; st: stitch; Sl: slip st from one needle to the other; psso: pass the slipped stitch over the one just worked; K2 tog: pick up two stitches and knit them together.

YOU WILL NEED
4-ply knitting yarn in off-white
set of four double-ended knitting needles in a size suitable for your yarn
polyester wadding (batting)
needle

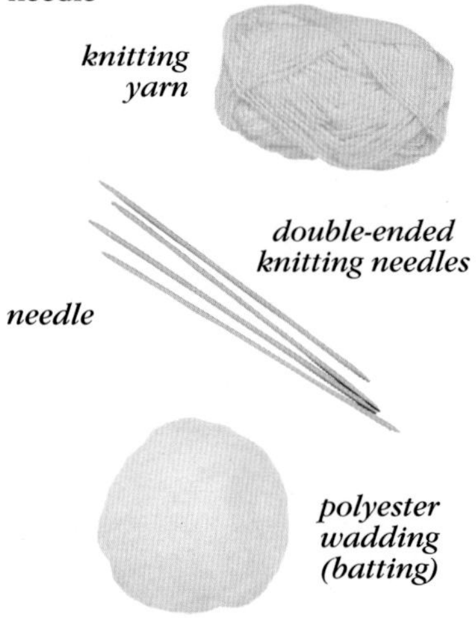

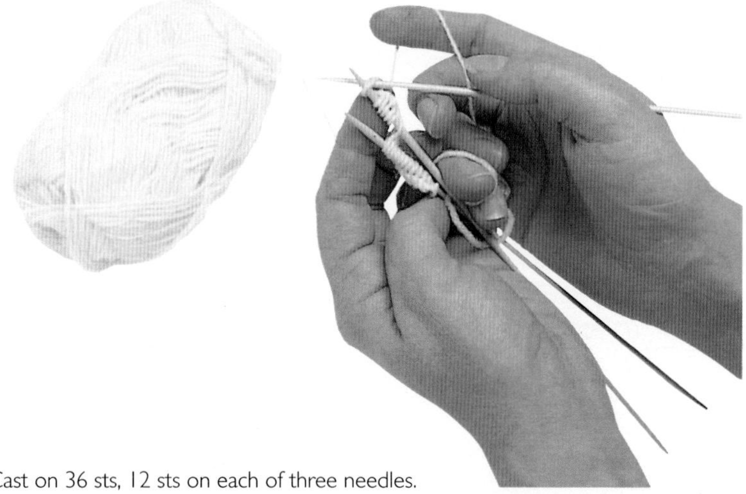

1 Cast on 36 sts, 12 sts on each of three needles.

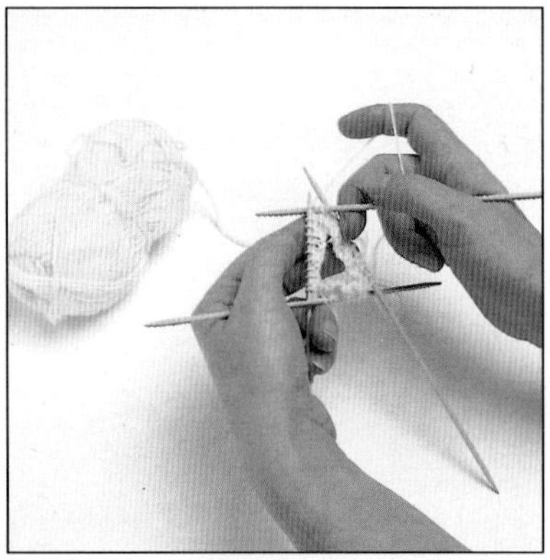

2 Work rib of K2, P2 for 2.5 cm (1 in).

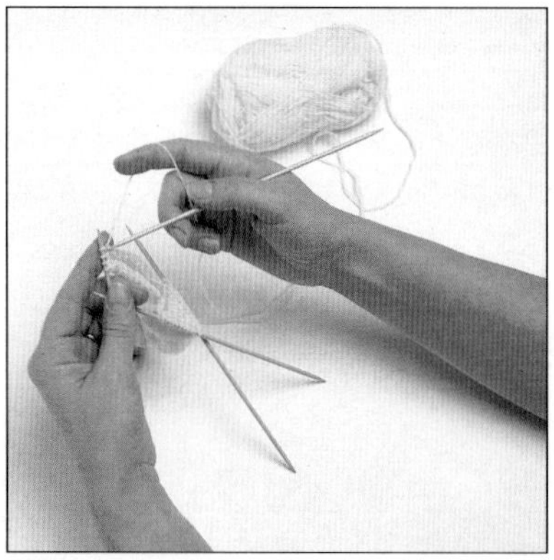

3 Work a further 5.5 cm (2¼ in) in stocking stitch. Shape the heel: knit 10 rows in stocking stitch on one set of 12 sts only. Continuing on these 12 sts only, K3, Sl1, K1, psso, K2, K2 tog, K3, turn and P back. Next row: K2, Sl1, K1, psso, K2, K2 tog, K2, turn and P back. Next row: K1, Sl1, K1, psso, K2, K2 tog, K1. Turn and P back. Next row: K1, Sl1, K1, psso, K2 tog, K1. This leaves 4 sts on the needle.

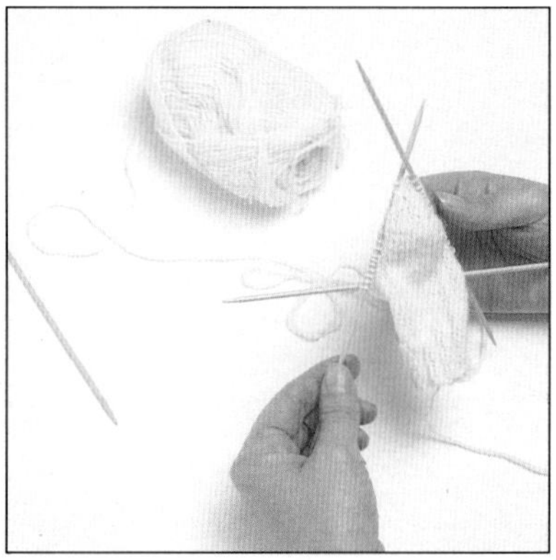

4 Turn the heel: pick up 10 sts along each side of the heel and arrange 16 sts on each needle with one division at the centre of the heel just worked: this will be the beginning of the round. Now work around the whole sock in continuous rows. 1st round: K13, K2 tog, K1; K1, Sl1, K1, psso, K10, K2 tog, K1; K1, Sl1, K1, psso, K13. 2nd round: K12, K2 tog,K1; K1, Sl1, K1, psso, K8, K2 tog, K1; K1, Sl1, K1, psso, K12. 3rd round: K11, K2 tog, K1; K1, Sl1, K1, psso, K6, K2 tog, K1; K1, Sl1, K1, psso, K11. 4th round: K10, K2 tog, K1; K10; K1, Sl1, K1, psso, K10.

Work 22 plain rounds in K for foot.

Shape the toe: 1st round: K1, Sl1, K1 psso, K6, K2 tog, K1 (12 sts); K1, Sl1, K1, psso, K4, K2 tog, K1 (10 sts); K1, Sl1, K1, psso, K6, K2 tog, K1 (12 sts). 2nd round: K1, Sl1, K1, psso, K4, K2 tog, K1 (10 sts); K1, Sl1, K1, psso, K2, K2 tog, K1 (8 sts); K1, Sl1, K1, psso, K4, K2 tog, K1 (10 sts). 3rd round: K1, Sl1, K1, psso, K2, K2 tog, K1 (8 sts); K1, Sl1, K1, psso, K2, K2 tog, K1 (8 sts); K1, Sl1, K1, psso, K2, K2 tog, K1 (8 sts). 4th round: K1, Sl1, K1, psso, K1, K2 tog, K1 (7 sts); K1, Sl1, K1, psso, K1, K2 tog, K1 (7 sts); K1, Sl1, K1, psso, K1, K2 tog, K1 (7 sts).

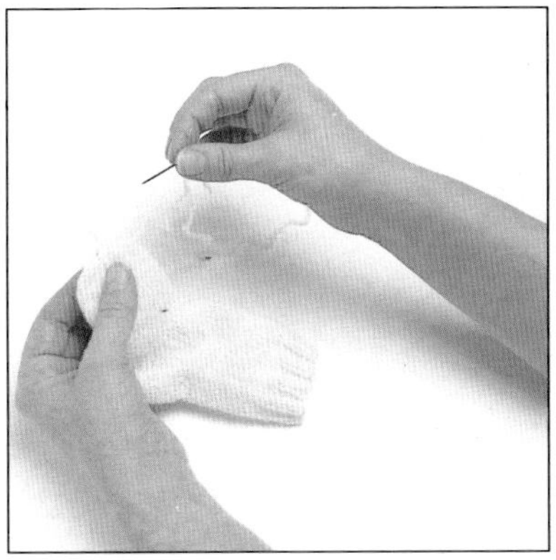

5 Break off the wool, thread all the remaining stitches on it, draw up and fasten securely. Press gently using steam and pad lightly with polyester wadding (batting). Make a loop at the top for hanging, using the cast-on end.

CRAFT TIP

Try to keep an even tension when knitting. Don't pull the yarn too tightly around the needles or the work will start to pucker.

Pearl Houses and Hearts

Almost everyone has a collection of little creamy-white buttons that can be turned into these lovely pearly tree decorations. Try to include some real mother-of-pearl buttons, which have a beautiful sheen and interesting tonal variations.

YOU WILL NEED
paper for template
scissors
plain corrugated cardboard
pencil
masking tape
craft knife
garden twine
hot glue gun
selection of mother-of-pearl and plastic buttons in various sizes

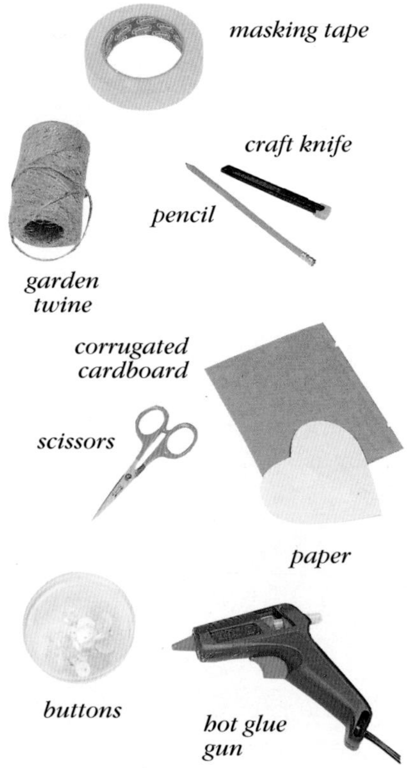

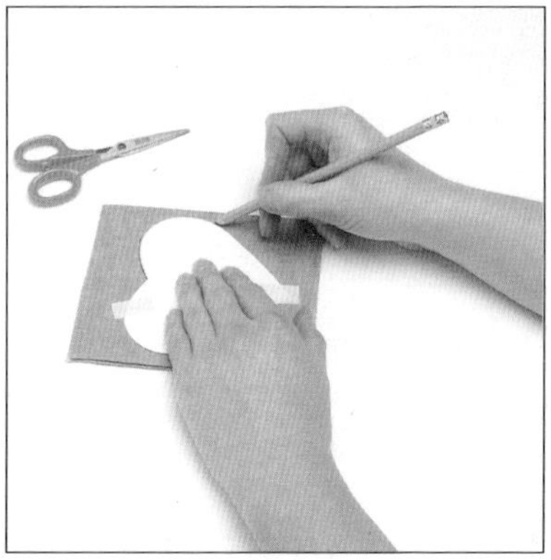

1 Make paper templates for the house and heart and secure them to the corrugated cardboard with masking tape. Draw around the templates.

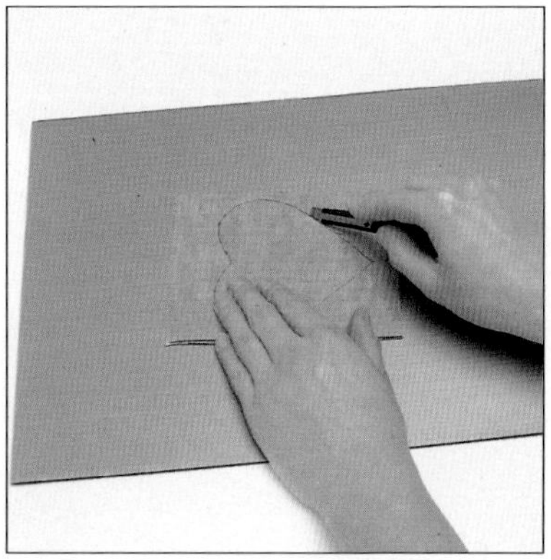

2 Cut out the shapes using a craft knife. Cut a short length of garden twine and glue it in a loop at the top of the ornament with the glue gun.

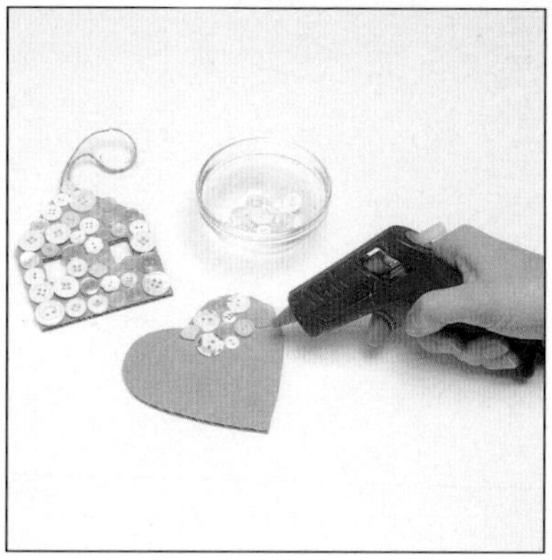

3 Arrange the buttons all over the shapes, covering them completely. Choose different sizes to fit neatly together. When you are happy with your arrangement, attach the buttons individually with the hot glue gun.

4 On the back of each decoration, conceal the ends of the twine by gluing a button over them.

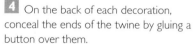

Warm Woolly Heart

A plump, soft heart edged in bold blanket-stitch will make an original addition to your rustic tree. Subtly coordinated fabrics give prominence to its unusual textures – everyone will want to touch it.

YOU WILL NEED
- paper for template
- scraps of two coordinating woollen fabrics
- scissors
- polyester wadding (batting)
- pins
- contrasting stranded embroidery thread (floss)
- needle
- garden twine

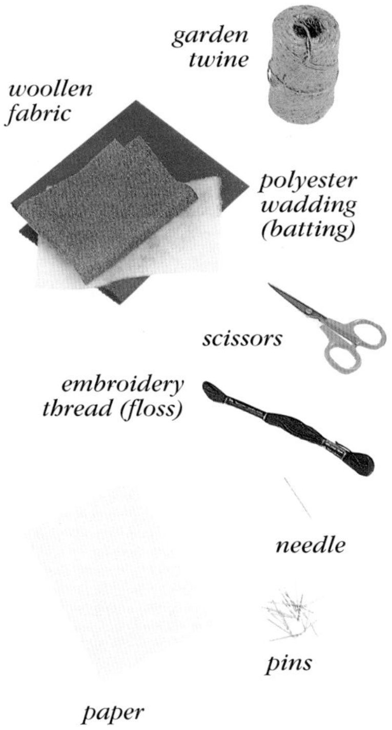

1 Trace the template from the back of the book and use it to cut out two hearts, one from each fabric. Cut two small strips for the appliqué cross. Use the template again to cut out a piece of wadding (batting), then trim off about 1 cm (½ in) all round the edge.

2 Pin the cross pieces on the contrasting fabric and attach with large oversewing stitches, using three strands of embroidery thread (floss).

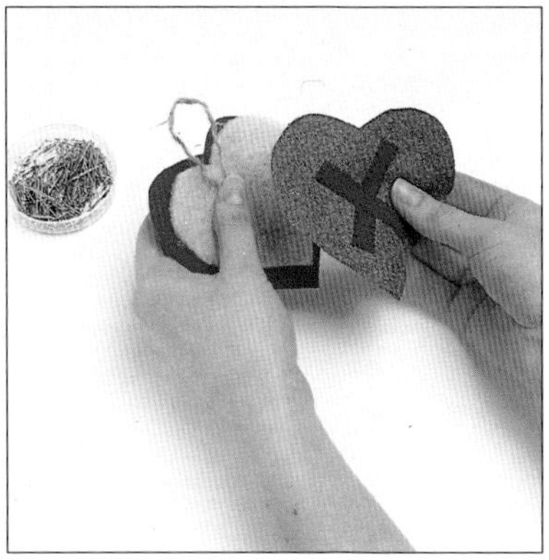

3 Pin all the layers together, sandwiching the wadding between the fabric hearts. Make a loop of twine for hanging the ornament and insert the ends in the top.

4 Stitch all around the edges in blanket stitch with three strands of embroidery thread (floss). Make sure the twine is secured as you go.

CRAFT TIP

Cut out the appliqué cross freehand. It doesn't matter if the strips are not exactly true: this will add to the heart's rustic appearance.

Paper Sculpture Birds

These birds have a bright, crisp, contemporary feel, with a touch of folk art in the painting. Imagine a Christmas tree covered with these bright, colourful little birds – a project for all the family. They also look great on gifts, and several of them strung on nylon would make a fabulous mobile.

YOU WILL NEED
- pencil
- stiff (heavy) coloured paper
- scissors
- ruler
- stapler
- hole punch
- paints
- saucers
- paintbrush
- fine cord

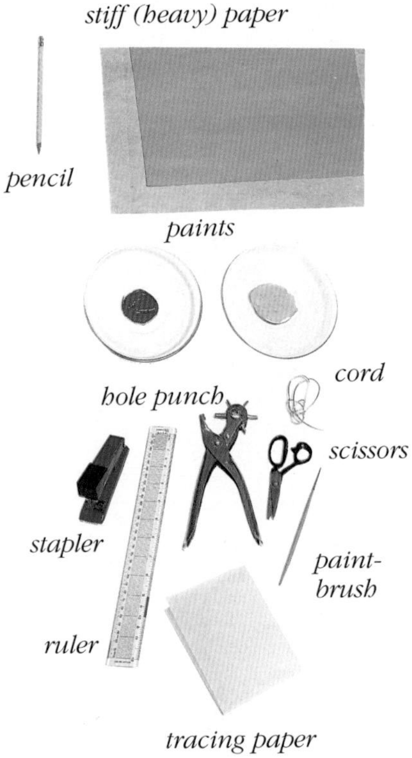

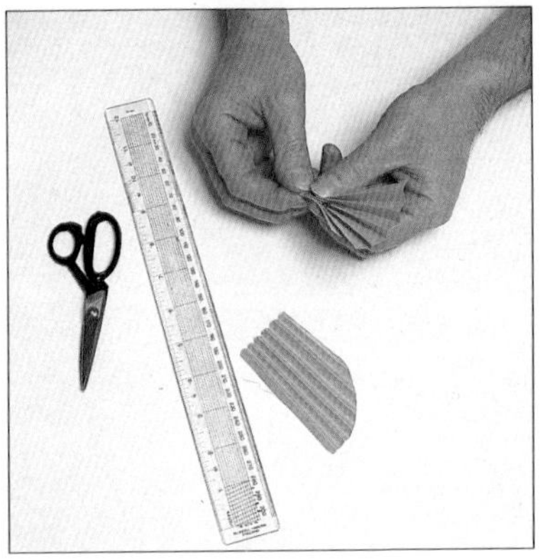

3 Use the blunt edge of the scissors to score fold lines at 0.5 cm (¼ in) intervals across the wings, then pleat them.

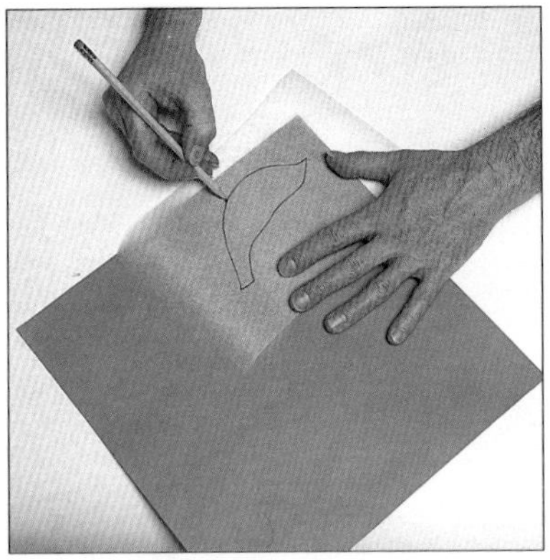

1 Trace the pattern on page 18 then transfer it to the coloured papers.

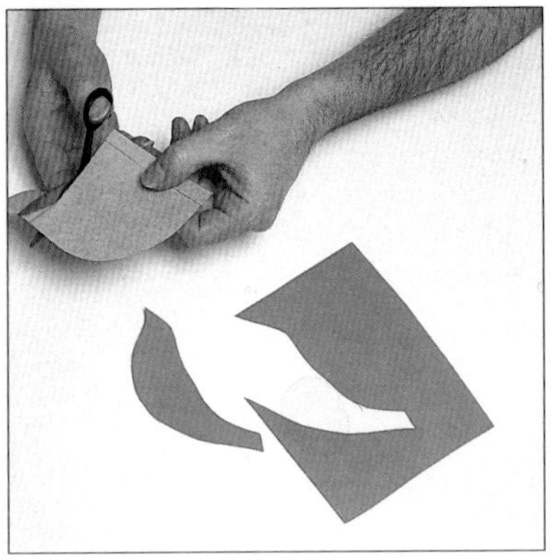

2 Cut out the bird body and wing shapes.

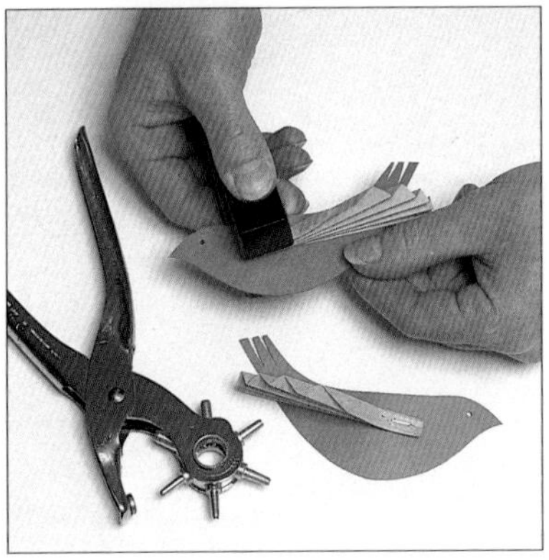

4 Staple a wing to each half of the bird and fan the wings out. Punch a small hole through both sides for the bird's eyes.

5 Paint spots on the underside of the bird bodies and when dry add a small contrasting spot in the middle of each.

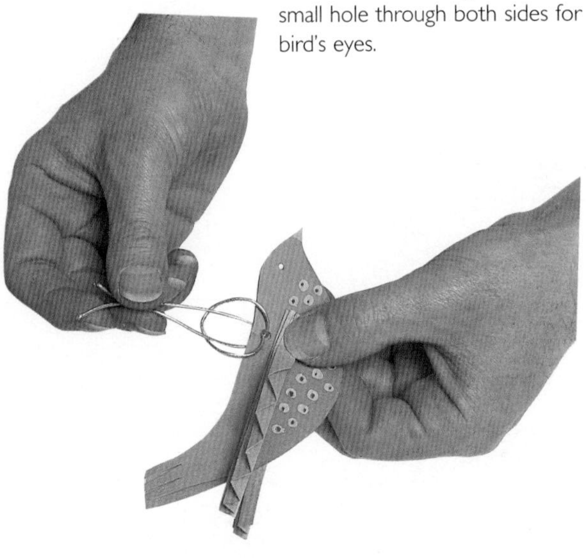

6 Punch a hole through the top of the bird, about halfway along, and thread it through with fine cord.

Santa's Toy Sack

Leave this gorgeous sack by the fireplace on Christmas Eve and Santa's guaranteed to fill it. Alternatively, it would be a wonderful way to deliver all your gifts if you're visiting friends. The contrast in texture between the luxurious satin ribbons and the coarse weave of the sack is novel and effective.

YOU WILL NEED
1.6 x 1.1 m (63 x 43 in) hessian (burlap), washed
tape measure
scissors
pins
sewing machine
selection of contrasting satin ribbons, 3.5 – 4.5 cm (1¼ – 1¾ in) wide
bodkin or safety pin
matching thread
needle

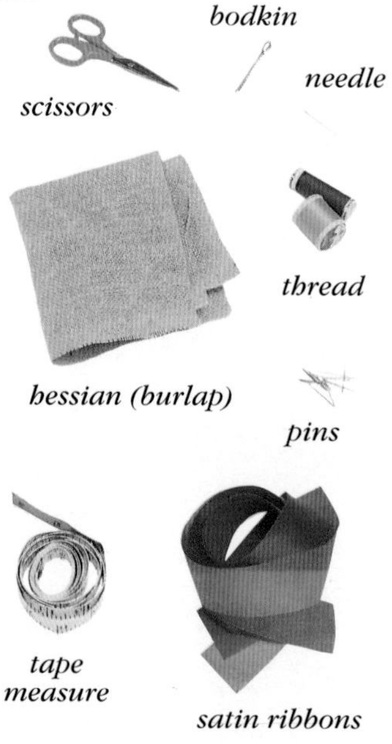

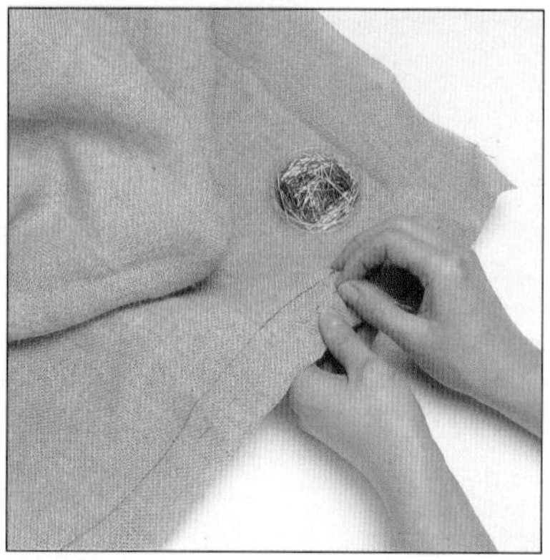

1 Trim the washed hessian (burlap) so that it measures 1 x 1.5 m (39 x 59 in). Fold it in half, right sides together, bringing the shorter sides together, and pin across the bottom and up the side, making a seam allowance of approximately 4 cm (1½ in).

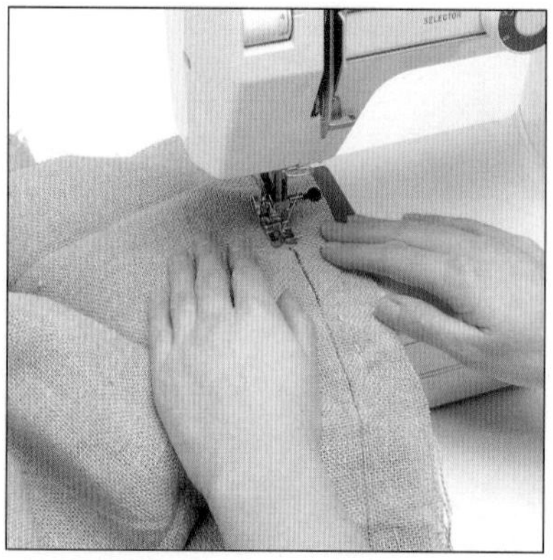

2 Machine stitch the bottom and one side of the sack.

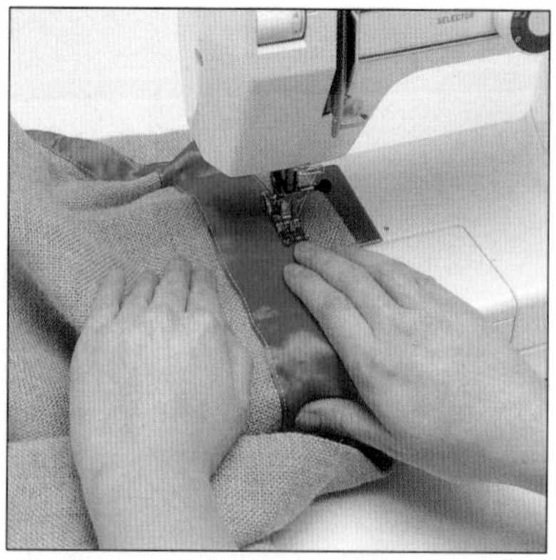

3 Still working on the wrong side, turn down the top edge by approximately 7 cm (3 in). Pin, then cover the raw edge with a length of satin ribbon. Fold under the raw ends of the ribbon to leave an opening. Machine stitch close to the top and bottom edges of the ribbon.

4 With a bodkin, or safety pin, thread a length of contrasting ribbon through the channel you have created. Make sure it is long enough to make a generous bow when the top of the sack is gathered up. Turn the sack right side out.

5 Using a double thread, stitch along one edge of a length of ribbon in running stitch. Draw the ribbon up into gathers. Cut to length allowing for joining the ends, flatten out and measure how much you need to make a rosette. Then cut all the ribbons to this length. Gather again and secure tightly, joining the raw edges invisibly from the wrong side.

6 Make enough rosettes in assorted colours to make a pleasing arrangement on the front of the sack. Stitch on the rosettes by hand.

CRAFT TIP

Hessian (burlap) is not pre-shrunk, so wash the fabric before you begin to make the sack. Use your machine's hottest setting, then press with a steam iron or damp cloth to remove all the creases.

Appliqué Christmas Tree

A charmingly simple little picture which you can frame or mount on card (cardboard) as a seasonal greeting for a special person. Contrasting textures in the homespun fabrics and simple, childlike stitches give it a naïve appeal.

YOU WILL NEED
scraps of homespun fabrics in greens, red and orange
scissors
matching thread
needle
coarse off-white cotton
pins
stranded embroidery thread (floss)
gold embroidery thread (floss)
iron
picture frame

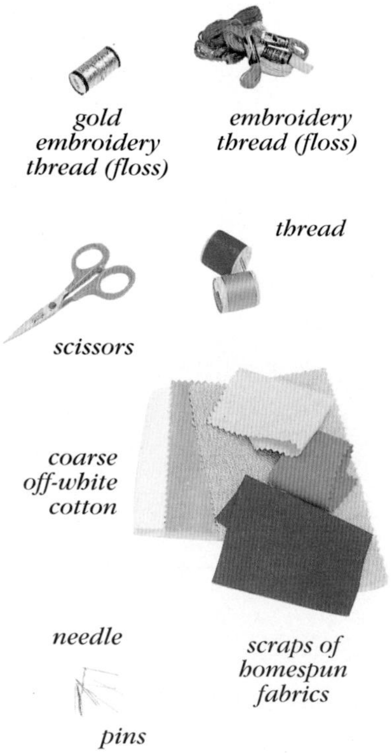

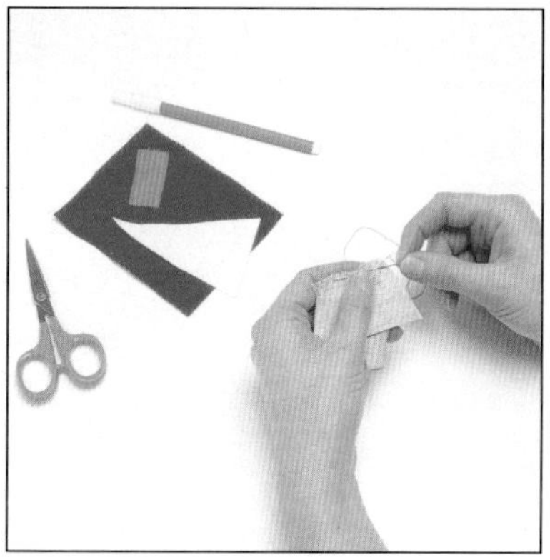

1 Following the template at the back of the book, cut out the pieces for the Christmas tree from three different shades and textures of green fabric. Cut out a red rectangle for the background and an orange stem. Join the three sections of the tree with running stitches.

2 Pin all the pieces to a backing of off-white cotton large enough to fill your picture frame.

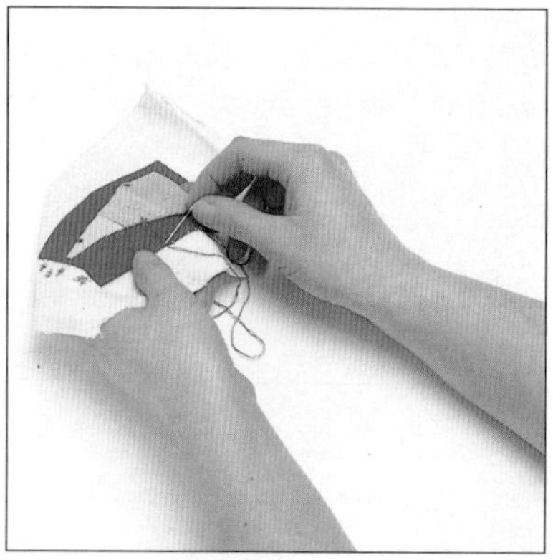

3 Sew the pieces together invisibly in slip-stitch, tucking the edges under with your needle as you sew. Aim for a slightly uneven, naïve appearance. Add gold stars and coloured stitch details using three strands of embroidery thread (floss). Press gently before framing.

Heavenly Gold Star

Collect as many different kinds of gold paper as you can find to cover this sparkling star with its subtle variations of texture. It makes a lovely wall or mantelpiece decoration, and would look equally splendid at the top of the tree.

YOU WILL NEED
- assorted gold paper: candy wrappers, metallic crepe paper, gift-wrap etc
- polystyrene star
- fine wire
- scissors
- masking tape
- PVA (white) glue
- paintbrush
- gold glitter paint

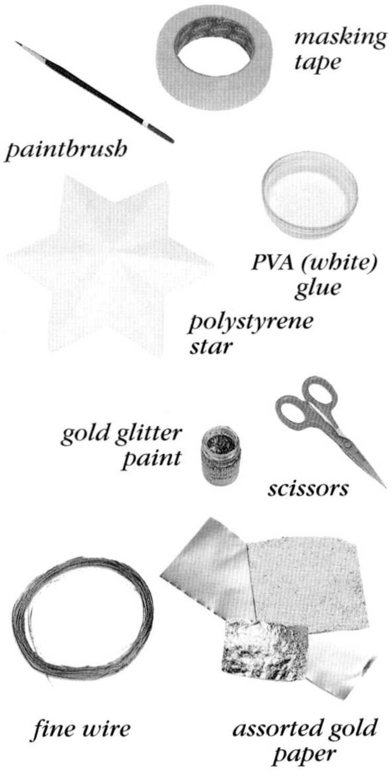

1 Tear the various gold papers into odd shapes of slightly different sizes.

2 Dilute the PVA (white) glue with a little water. Paint it on to the back of a piece of gold paper and stick on to the polystyrene star. Paint more glue over the piece to secure it. Work all over the front of the star, using different papers to vary the texture and colour.

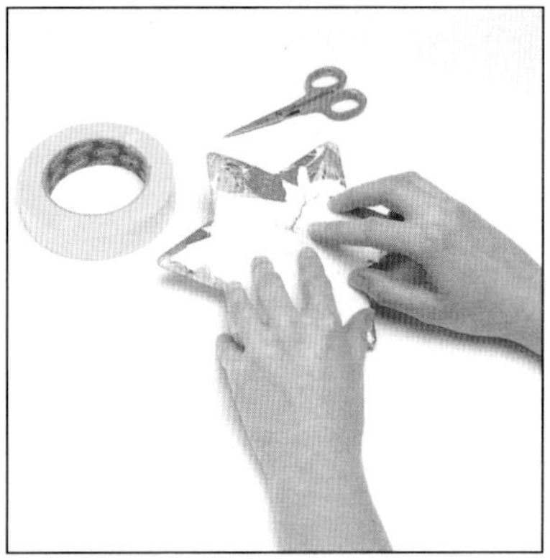

3 Make a loop of wire and stick the ends into the back of the star for hanging. Secure with masking tape. Cover the back with gold paper in the same way as the front.

4 Leave to dry, then cover with a coat of gold glitter paint.

Velvet Stocking

This rather grown-up stocking is so grand that it's just asking to be filled with exquisite treats and presents. Make it in rich, dark colours for a really Christmassy look.

YOU WILL NEED
paper for templates
dress-weight velvet in three toning colours
scissors
pins
tailor's chalk
sewing machine
matching thread
decorative braid
sequin ribbon
gold satin fabric
sewing needle
gold buttons

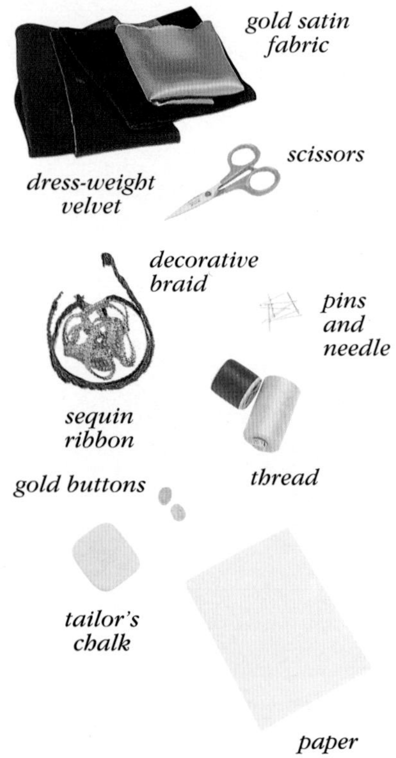

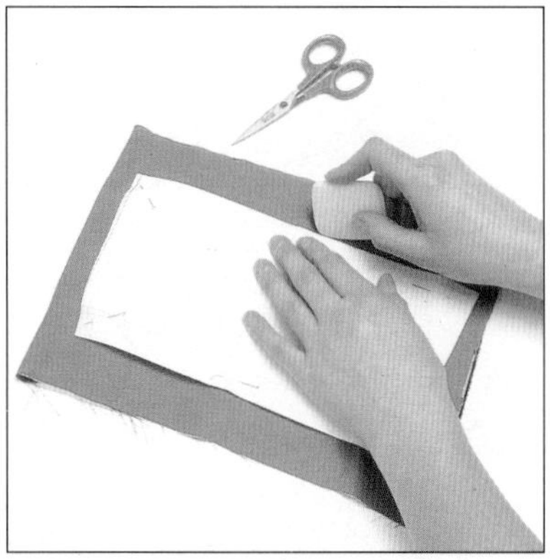

1 Copy the template for the cuff from the back of the book and increase to the size required. Place the template against a folded edge of the gold satin fabric. Pin and draw around the pattern piece with tailor's chalk. Cut out two cuffs, leaving a narrow seam allowance.

2 As for step 1, make a template for the stocking and divide into three sections. Place the template for each section on a double thickness of each colour velvet. Pin and draw around each piece with tailor's chalk. Cut out, leaving a narrow seam and pin together.

3 Once the three sections of velvet and the gold cuff for each side have been pinned together, machine stitch each seam and tidy any loose ends of thread.

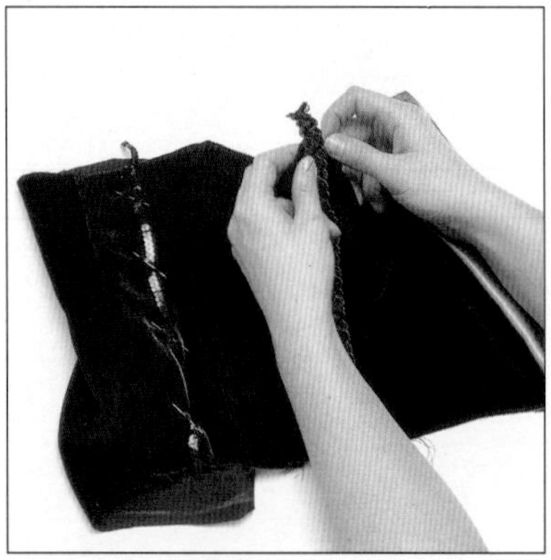

4 On the right side of each piece, pin a strip of decorative braid and a row of sequins. Sew these on invisibly by hand.

5 With right sides together, machine stitch the two sides of the stocking and the cuff together. Turn through, then fold down the gold satin inside to form a deep cuff. Turn in the raw edge of the cuff and stitch down to neaten, catching it to the seams of the velvet stocking.

6 Trim the satin cuff with a few gold buttons and attach a loop of decorative braid for hanging.

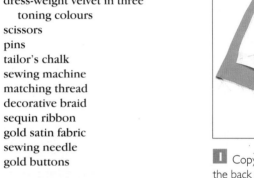

Christmas Countdown

Christmas is coming! Excitement builds as the windows of an Advent calendar are opened day by day. Paint the façade of this three-dimensional house in hot, bright colours with lots of gilding.

YOU WILL NEED
tracing paper
pencil
thin white card (cardboard)
craft knife
metal ruler
cutting mat
gouache paints
paintbrush
white cartridge (heavy) paper
watercolour inks
gold (magic) marker pen
glue-stick
white polystyrene-filled mounting board
cup sequins

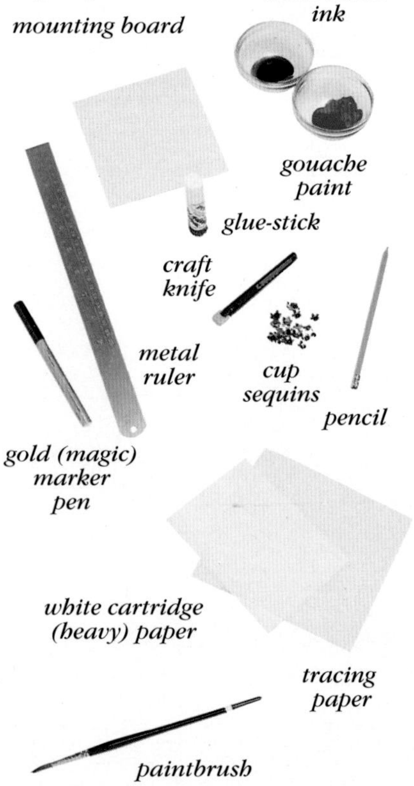

1 Enlarge and trace the template for the front of the Advent calendar and transfer it on to a sheet of white card (cardboard). Cut around three sides of each window with a craft knife.

2 Turn over the sheet and paint the backs of the windows and a little of the area around them with gouache paint, so that they will look neat when the windows are opened.

3 Using the front tracing again, mark the window frames on cartridge (heavy) paper and draw on the inside motifs. Paint with watercolour inks and draw in details with a gold (magic) marker pen. Cut out and attach with a glue-stick.

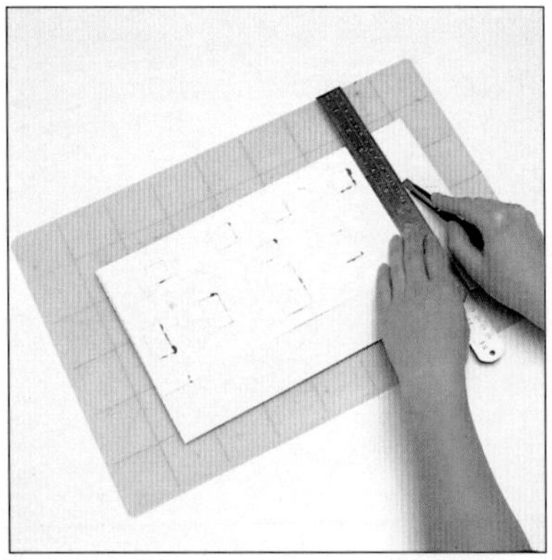

4 Cut the work into three sections; the first being the main doorway and windows, the second the three middle windows and two towers and the third the top central panel. Cut three pieces of mounting board, making the largest the size of the whole calendar with two more graded steps to go in front.

5 Mount the sections on the boards, gluing the edges, and glue the sections together. Paint the front of the calendar, carefully avoiding getting any paint inside the windows. Add details and number the windows with a gold (magic) marker pen. Don't forget to paint the edges of the mounting boards.

6 Finish the calendar with shiny multi-cup sequins. Using a glue-stick, attach them all around the edges of the Advent calendar.

Needlepoint Pincushion

This pincushion won't take long to stitch and makes a lovely gift for a needlework enthusiast. The starry theme and trimming of glossy cord give it a Christmassy feel, but its subtle shading will make it a joy to use all year round.

YOU WILL NEED
23 cm (9 in) square of white needlepoint canvas with 24 holes per 5 cm (12 holes per in)
ruler
waterproof (magic) marker pen
masking tape
small lengths of tapestry wool (yarn) in 12 shades
scissors
tapestry needle
coordinating furnishing fabric for backing
matching thread
needle
polyester wadding (batting)
70 cm (3/4 yd) decorative cord

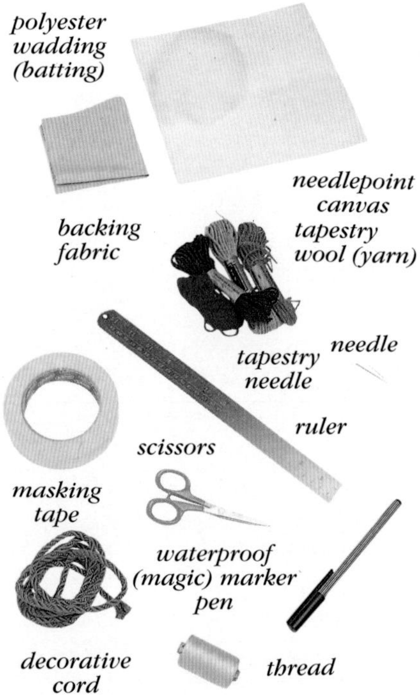

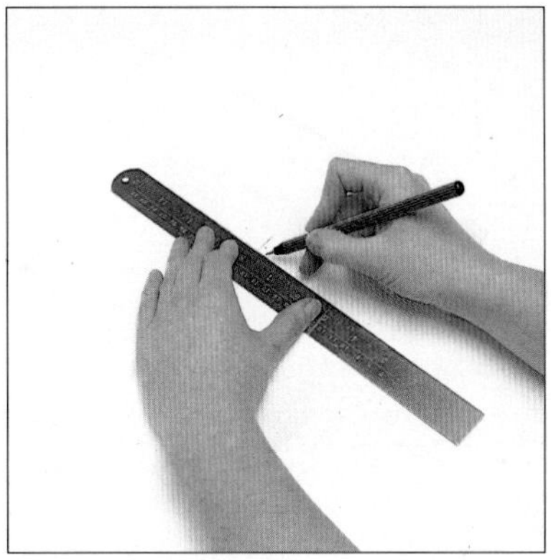

1 To prepare the canvas, draw a vertical line down the centre and a horizontal line across the centre with a waterproof (magic) marker pen.

2 Bind the edges of the canvas with masking tape to prevent the yarn from catching as you work. Select three colours for each corner star.

3 Work the design from the chart at the back of the book in tent stitch, beginning in the centre and counting each square as one intersection of canvas threads. Complete all four squares. Remove the masking tape. Press with a steam iron, pulling the canvas gently back into a square. Dry quickly so that the canvas does not distort.

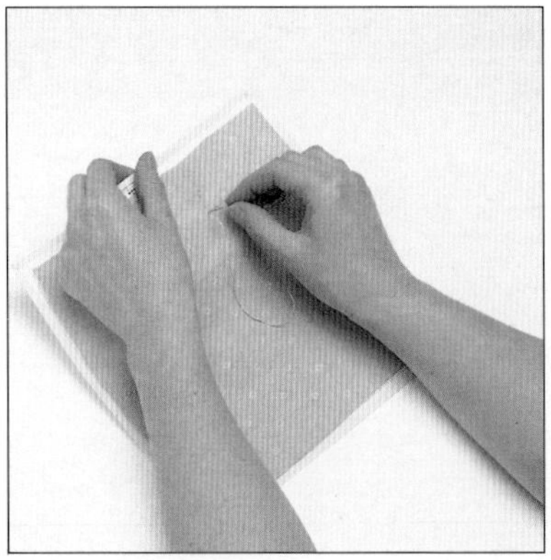

4 Cut a square of backing fabric and pin it to the canvas right sides together. Machine or hand stitch around the edges, leaving a gap on one side. Trim the seams and corners and turn to the right side. Stuff with polyester wadding (batting) to make a nice plump shape.

5 Beginning near the opening, hand stitch the cord around the edges of the cushion. Make a knot in the cord as you reach each corner. Push both ends of the cord into the opening and sew it up neatly, securing the cord as you stitch.

CRAFT TIP

This pincushion is ideal for using up small quantities of tapestry wool (yarn) left over from other projects, but if you do use scraps make sure you will have enough to complete the design.

Yuletide Pot-pourri

Scour ethnic food shops for large bags of bay leaves, cardamom and other exotic ingredients for pot-pourri. Try to include dried flowers (I used hibiscus flowers) for colour and texture.

YOU WILL NEED
oranges
paring knife
large bowl
selection of dried herbs, flowers
and barks
orris root powder
essential oils
decorative box
cellophane (plastic wrap)
ribbon

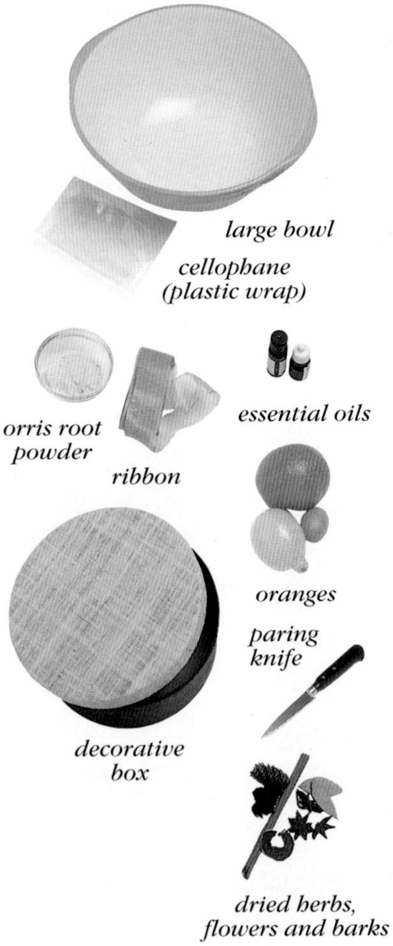

1 Pare the rind from several oranges, keeping the strips as long as possible. Dry them in the lowest shelf of a very low oven and store in a dry place until you are ready to use them. Slices of orange can be dried in the same way and are very decorative in pot-pourri.

2 Mix all the ingredients for the pot-pourri in a large bowl. Do not be tempted to use too many different ingredients or the result will be an untidy-looking mixture.

3 Add the orris root powder, which is used as a fixative for the fragrance, sparingly at first: you do not want to see any residue in the finished mixture. Toss the mixture. Sprinkle with your chosen essential oils.

4 Line a decorative box with a large piece of cellophane (plastic wrap) and fill generously with the pot-pourri. Gather up the edges and secure with a ribbon.

Fun Wreath

Although every house deserves an elegant fresh Christmas wreath on the front door, all the family can have plenty of fun making this rather alternative wreath. Think of it as a seasonal joke and load it with all the ephemera of Christmas past and present.

YOU WILL NEED
newspaper
adhesive tape
string
scissors
gold spray paint
hot glue gun
assortment of novelties, candies and decorations

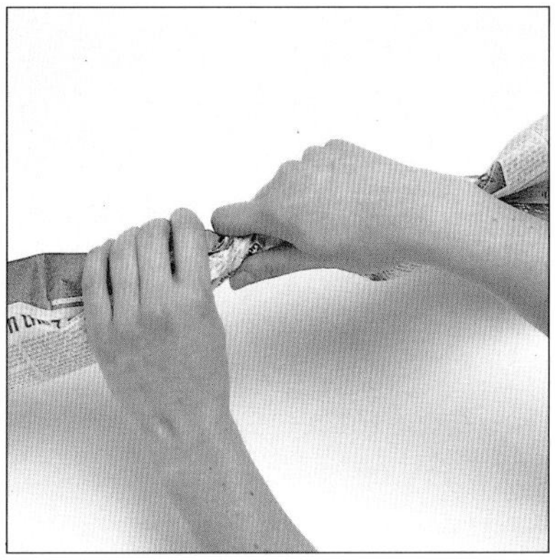

1 Join two sheets of newspaper together down their short sides with adhesive tape. Scrunch up the paper along its length, squeezing it together while gently twisting it to make a paper rope. When it is quite tightly twisted join the ends with tape to make a ring.

2 Make a second ring in the same way, cutting it a little shorter so that it will fit inside the first ring. Bind the two rings together with string.

3 Spray the ring on both sides with gold paint and leave to dry.

4 Using a hot glue gun, cover the ring completely with an assortment of Christmas ephemera, such as old decorations, cracker novelties, candies, decorated pine cones, and bows from gift wrappings.

Fragrant Herb Pillow

This lovely scented sachet looks as if it has been thickly encrusted with gold. It's made using a cutwork technique in which the different fabrics are revealed as if by magic. It's enjoyable to make and a wonderful gift to receive. Choose fabrics of similar weights but different textures and shades of gold, such as taffeta and lamé.

YOU WILL NEED
four 17 cm (6½ in) squares of different gold fabrics
pins
matching thread
sewing machine
sharp-pointed scissors
two 25 cm (10 in) squares of gold fabric chosen from the selection above
gold braid
needle
fragrant herbs or pot-pourri to fill

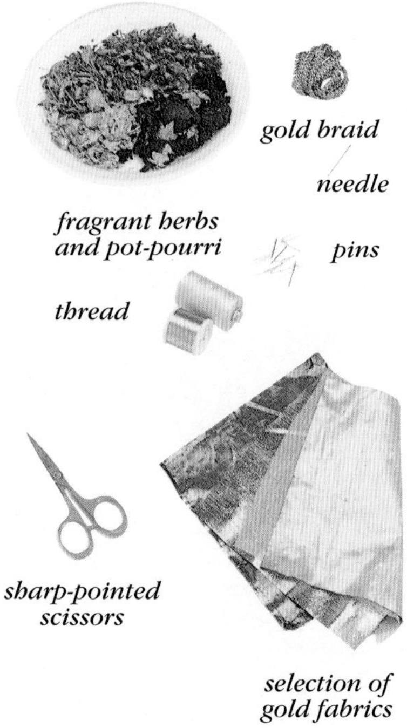

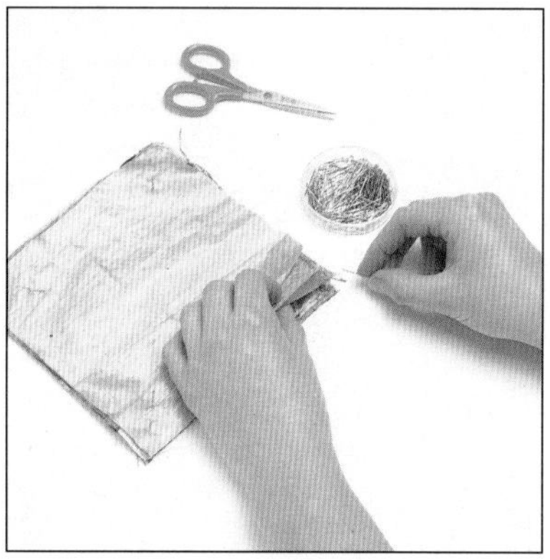

1 Pin the four 17 cm (6½ in) squares of different gold fabric together, all with right sides facing up.

2 Sewing through all four layers, machine stitch across the middle of the square in both directions, then stitch a simple star motif in each quarter. Don't worry if the four stars don't match each other exactly: you are aiming for a freehand effect.

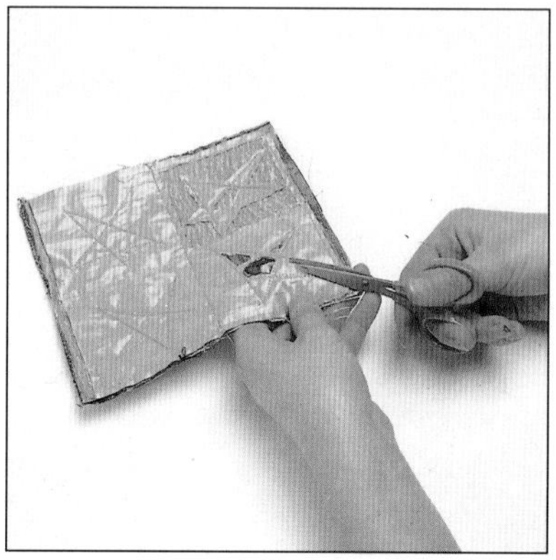

3 With the point of the scissors, pierce the top layer of fabric, then cut out a section of a star. Work around each star, cutting through different areas and layers to reveal the one below until you are pleased with the effect.

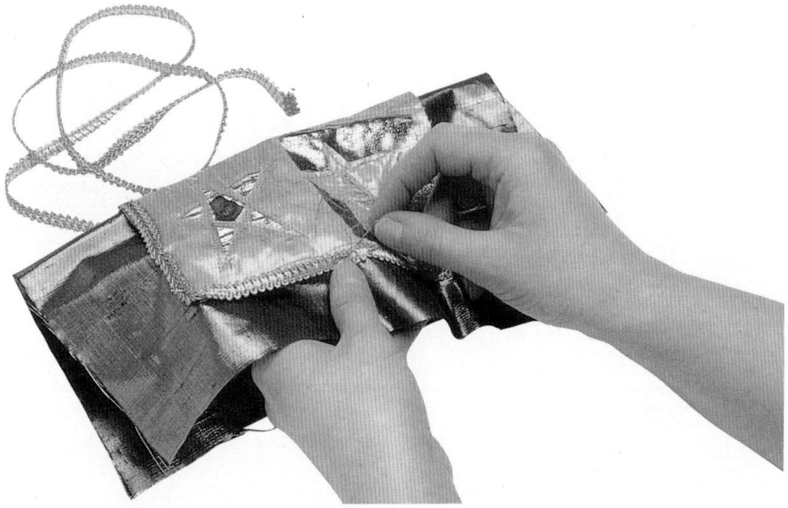

4 Pin the appliqué square in the centre of the right side of one of the large squares and machine stitch all around the edge. Hand-stitch a length of gold braid over the seam to hide the raw edges.

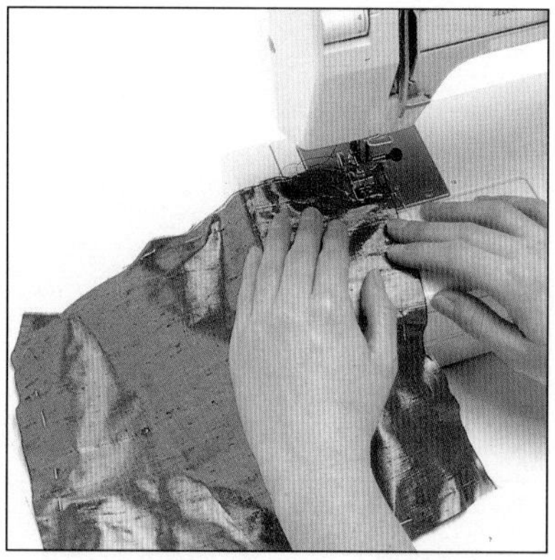

5 Pin the other gold square to the front of the cushion, right sides together, and machine around the edge with a 1 cm (½ in) seam allowance, leaving an opening down one side.

CRAFT TIP

It is essential to use really sharp, pointed small scissors for this type of appliqué as you will be cutting away through small areas, some of which may be quite delicate and difficult to manoeuvre around.

6 Turn the work right side out, fill loosely with fragrant herbs or pot-pourri and slip-stitch the opening.

Painted Candles

Plain coloured candles can easily be dressed up for Christmas with gold paint. Use them yourself, but don't forget that they make excellent gifts too. Present them as a set with a coordinating, handmade wrapper.

YOU WILL NEED
coloured candles
gold paint
paintbrush
ribbon
tube of fabric glitter paint
gold gift-wrap
pencil
scissors
cartridge (heavy) paper
watercolour inks

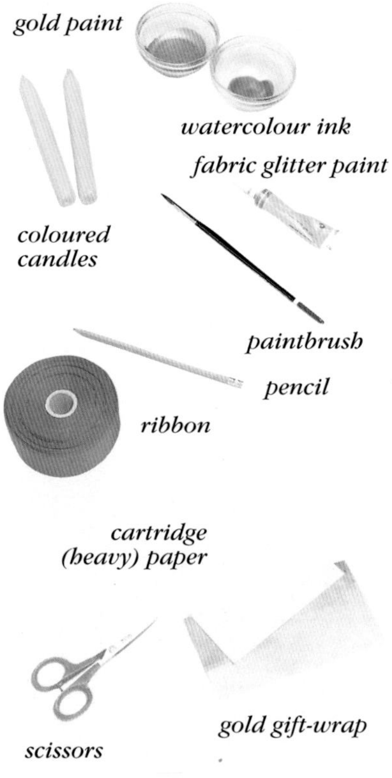

1 Paint the candles with spots or stripes, building up the colour in several layers if the candles resist the paint. Allow to dry between coats.

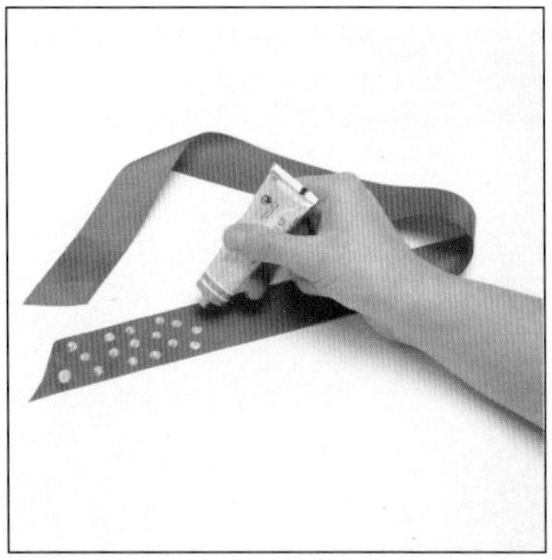

2 Apply gold dots on the ribbon with fabric glitter paint. The glitter effect will begin to show only as the paint dries.

3 Fold a strip of gold gift-wrap over several times. Mark a semi-circle at the top and bottom and cut it out. Unfold the paper to reveal a scalloped edge.

4 Paint a sheet of cartridge (heavy) paper in watercolour ink to coordinate with the candles. Allow to dry then tear into strips. Wrap a set of candles in the scalloped gold paper, then a strip of the painted paper, finishing off with a bow of glitter ribbon.

Painted Card Holders

With your mantelpieces and shelves filled with beautiful decorations, you need to find an attractive and original way to display your Christmas cards. With our painted clothes pegs (pins) and colourful "clothesline", you can hang them all the way up the stairs.

YOU WILL NEED
wooden clothes pegs (pins)
gouache paints
jam jar
paintbrush
thick cotton twine
scissors

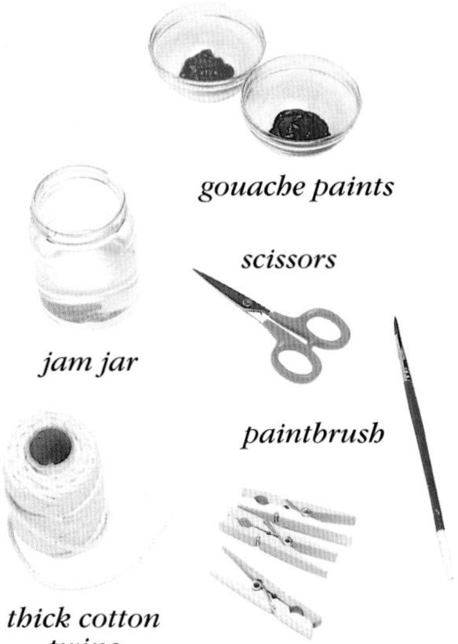

1 Separate the halves of each clothes peg (pin) by removing the spring.

2 Paint the pegs (pins) with gouache paint in an assortment of bright colours. Allow to dry then reassemble.

CRAFT TIP

Attach the pegs (pins) to the twine at regular intervals or according to the sizes of cards you are hanging. Leave a good length at each end of the twine for tying.

3 Paint the cotton twine in a bright colour. Allow to dry.

Front Door Wreath

Take a break from traditional red berries and ribbons with this fresh-looking arrangement. The vibrant orange kumquats are perfectly set off by the cool blue spruce.

YOU WILL NEED
- fresh greenery: sprays of bay leaves and blue spruce
- secateurs (pruning shears)
- florist's wire
- kumquats
- green chillies
- pine cones
- ready-made willow wreath
- wire-edged ribbon
- pins
- scissors

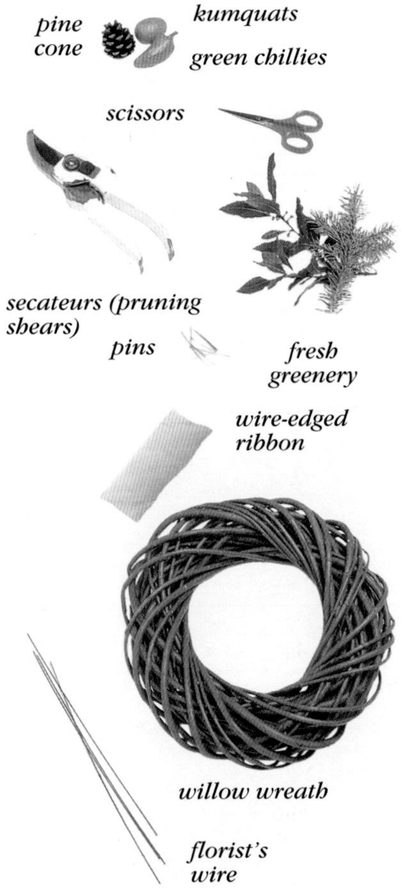

1 Trim the greenery into sprigs suitable for the size of the wreath, wiring pieces together here and there to fill them out.

2 Twist a piece of wire around each stem, leaving a length to insert into the willow wreath.

3 Wire the kumquats and chillies by sticking a piece of wire through the base then bending the ends down and twisting them together. Wind a piece of wire around the base of each pine cone.

4 Attach the greenery, fruits and cones to the wreath, twisting the ends of the wires to secure them.

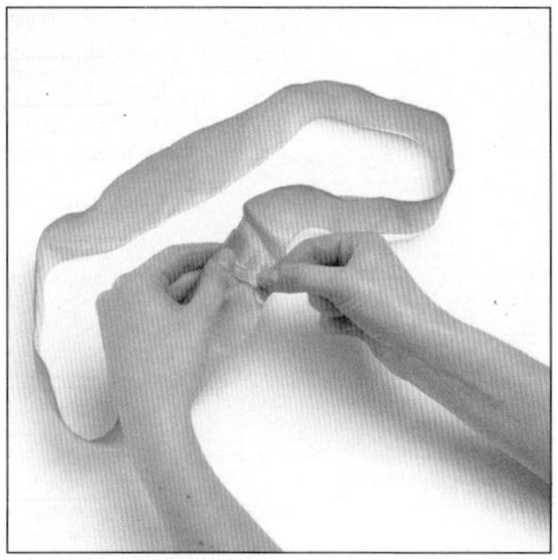

5 Reserving a short length of ribbon for the centre of the bow, join the ends together with a pin.

6 Fold the ribbon over on itself to make four loops.

7 Pinch the centre of the loops together and secure with a wire. Cover this with the remaining piece of ribbon and wire the bow to the wreath.

Picture Bulletin board

Show off your prettiest Christmas cards on this bright and cheerful bulletin board. After the cards have come down it will be equally useful for the rest of the year.

YOU WILL NEED
large picture frame
gold spray paint
piece of soft board to fit snugly inside the frame
hessian (burlap) to cover the soft board with a 2.5 cm (1in) overhang
staple gun
ribbons in various widths and colours
drawing pins (thumb tacks)

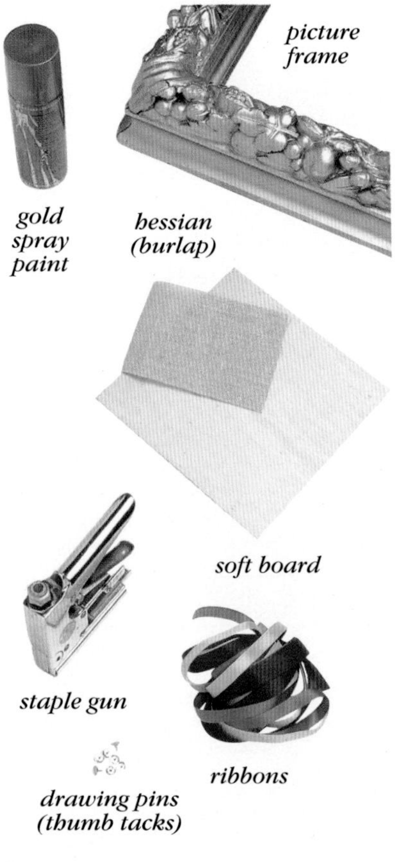

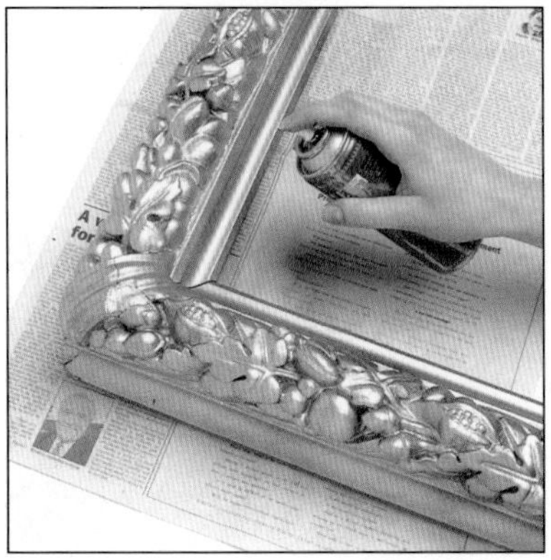

1 Clean and repair your frame if it is an old one. Spray with gold paint and allow it to dry.

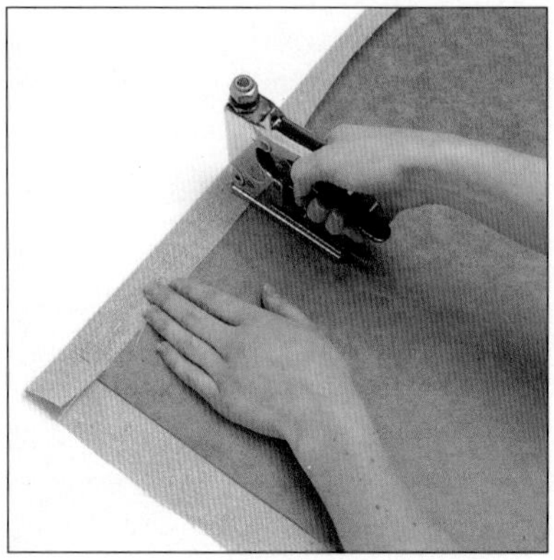

2 Cover the soft board with the hessian (burlap), securing the edges at the back with a staple gun. Make sure the fabric is evenly stretched, securing it at points opposite one another.

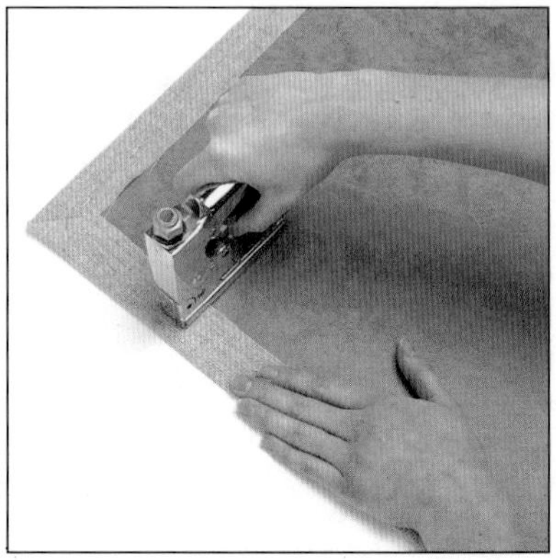

3 Fold the corners neatly and secure the fabric all around the edge of the board.

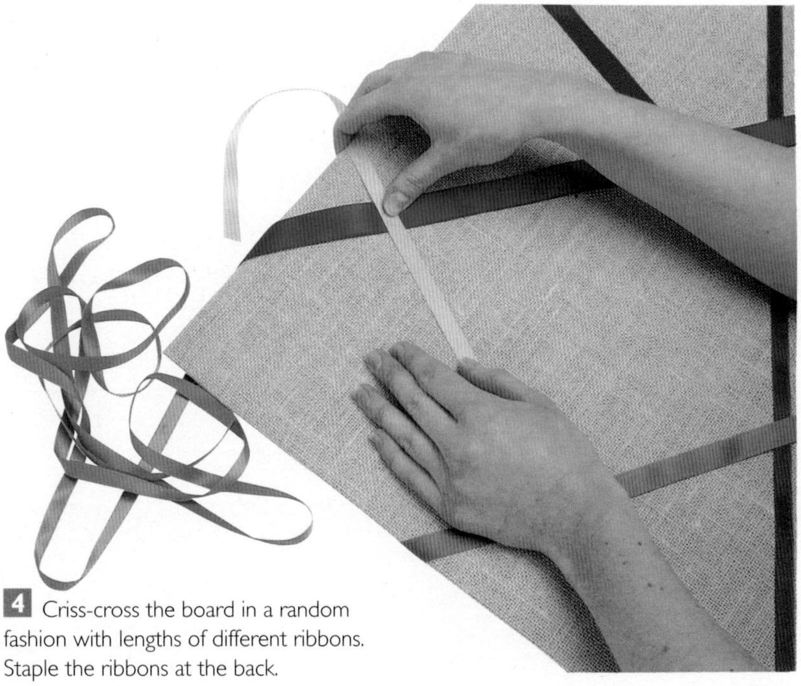

4 Criss-cross the board in a random fashion with lengths of different ribbons. Staple the ribbons at the back.

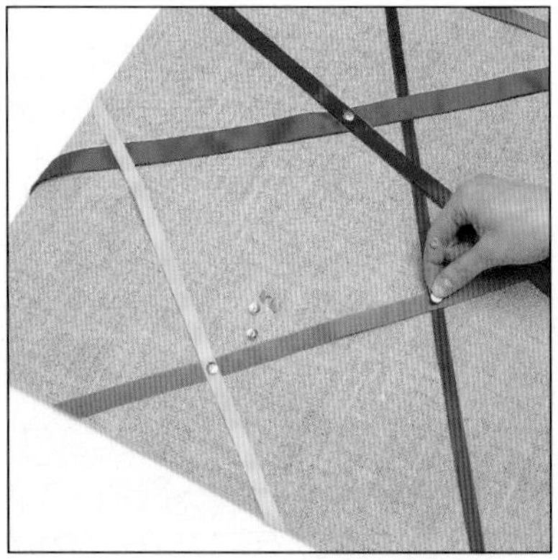

5 Secure the ribbons with drawing pins (thumb tacks) at each point where they cross. Place the board inside the frame.

Collage Gift-wrap

Look along the racks on the newspaper stand for interesting foreign scripts to incorporate in this fascinating gift-wrap. The newspaper is painted with translucent watercolour inks so that the print shows through.

YOU WILL NEED
foreign language newspaper
watercolour inks
paintbrush
white cartridge (heavy) paper
coloured card (cardboard)
stencil card (cardboard)
craft knife
gold and black stencil paint
cellulose kitchen sponge
scissors
corrugated cardboard
plain gold gift-wrap
glue-stick

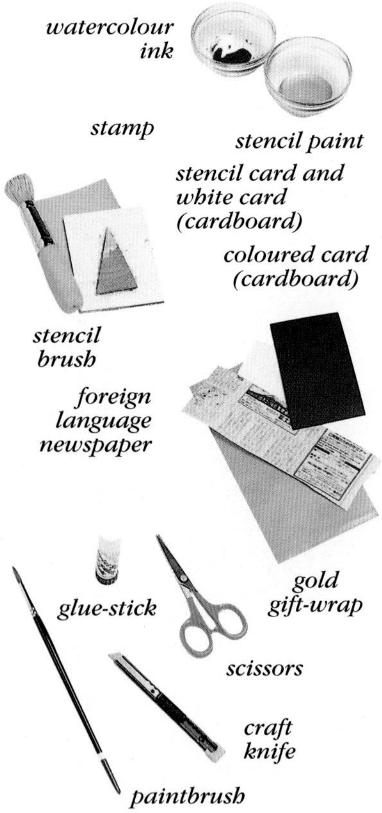

1 Paint sections of the newspaper in bright watercolour inks.

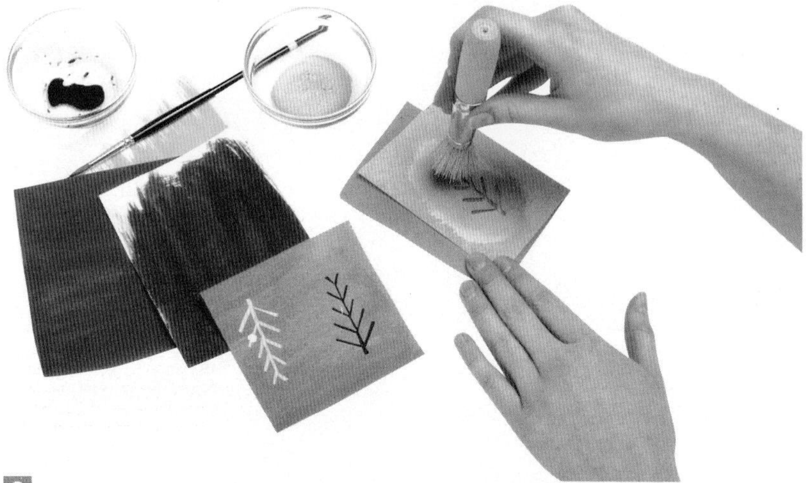

2 Transfer the Christmas tree template at the back of the book to a piece of stencil card (cardboard) and cut out. Paint plain white cartridge (heavy) paper in different coloured inks or use coloured card (cardboard). Stencil the paper in black and gold.

3 Cut a triangular Christmas tree shape out of kitchen sponge and stick it to a piece of corrugated cardboard. Stamp some of the coloured newsprint with gold trees.

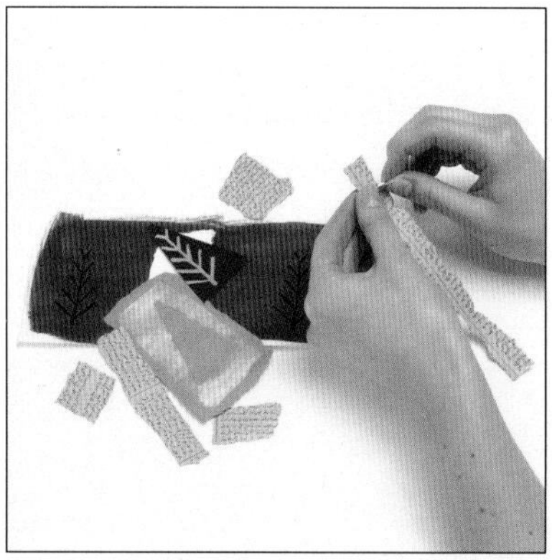

4 Tear strips, rectangles and simple tree shapes from the coloured newsprint. Tear around the stamped and stencilled motifs, and cut some out with scissors to give a different texture.

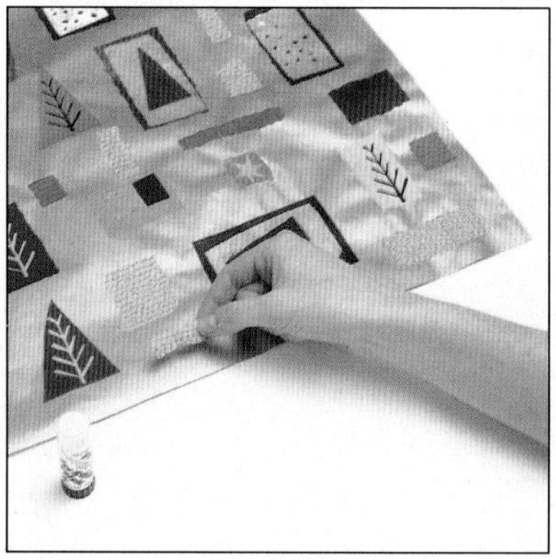

5 Arrange the motifs on the gold gift-wrap and attach them down using a glue-stick.

Christmas Tree Gift Tags

As with the gift-wrap on the previous pages, spend some time making yourself a selection of stamped, stencilled and painted motifs before you begin to assemble the gift tags.

YOU WILL NEED
craft knife
metal ruler
cutting mat
thin card (cardboard) in various colours
tracing paper
pencil
paper for templates
cellulose kitchen sponge
scissors
corrugated cardboard
glue-stick
stencil paint in gold and black
stencil card (cardboard)
white cartridge (heavy) paper
paintbrush
watercolour inks
white oil crayon
brown parcel wrap (packaging paper)
hole punch
fine gold cord

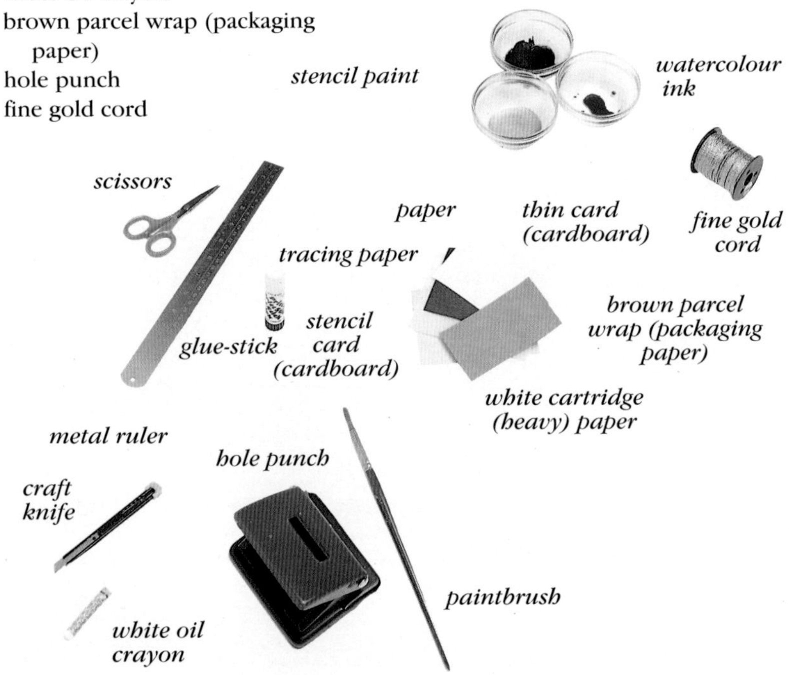

1 Using a craft knife and a metal ruler, cut out tags from thin card (cardboard) in various colours.

2 Trace the Christmas tree motif from the back of the book and make a paper template. Draw around this on a rectangle of kitchen sponge and cut out carefully with scissors, so that you have a positive and negative image to use as stamps. Mount each stamp on a piece of cardboard with a glue-stick. Stamp both motifs in gold on to a selection of papers in different textures and colours (use tracing paper as well).

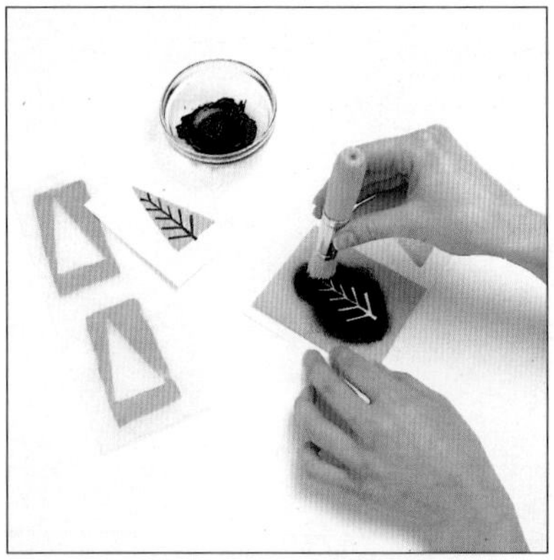

3 Trace the Christmas tree branch pattern and transfer it to a piece of stencil card. Cut out using a craft knife and stencil in black and gold on to a selection of papers and on some of the stamped motifs.

4 Paint plain white cartridge (heavy) paper with watercolour ink in bright colours and cut out a simple star motif.

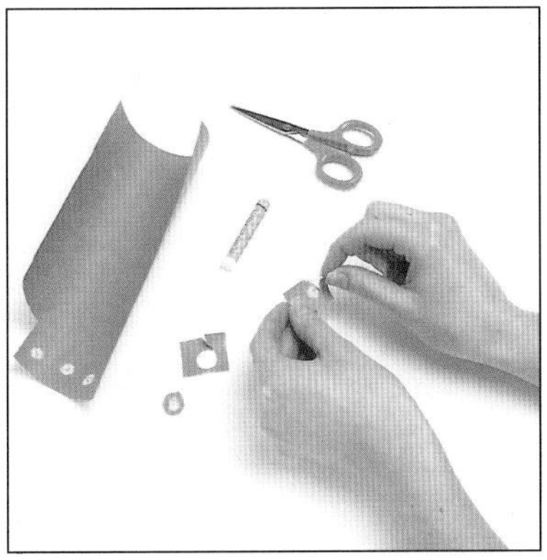

5 Use a white oil crayon to scribble spots on brown parcel wrap (packaging paper) for snowflakes. Tear them out individually leaving a border of brown paper around each one.

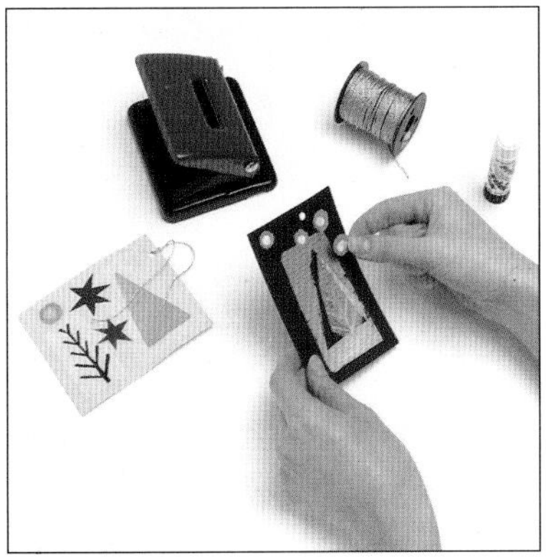

6 Assemble the tags. Cut or tear out a selection of motifs and arrange them on the cards. Attach with the glue-stick. Punch a hole in the top and thread each with a loop of fine gold cord.

Crayon Gift-wrap

See how easy it can be to transform humble brown parcel wrap (packaging paper) into stylish and original gift-wraps. Both suggestions are quick to do but allow at least 24 hours for the oil pastels to dry before using the paper.

YOU WILL NEED
- brown parcel wrap (packaging paper)
- masking tape
- gold paint
- old plate
- sponge roller
- gold oil crayon
- oil pastel crayons in black, white and colours

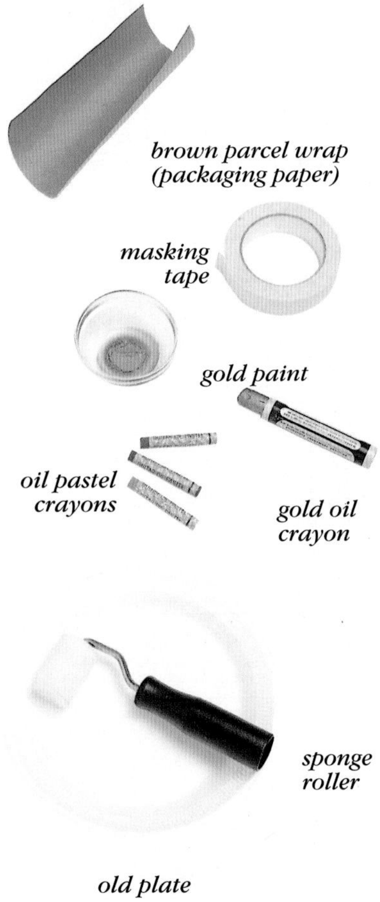

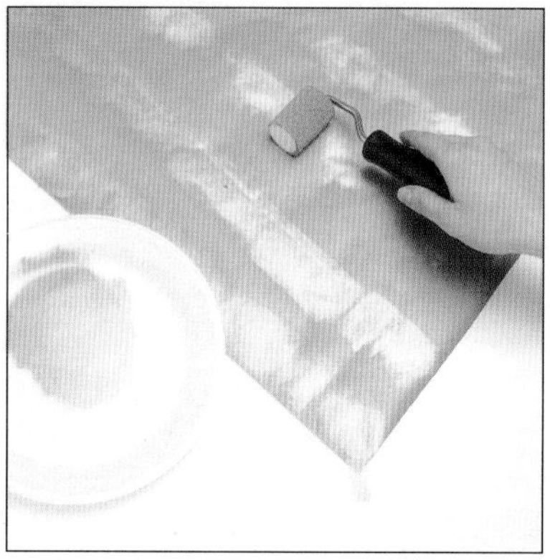

1 Secure the brown parcel wrap (packaging paper) with masking tape. Spread gold paint on an old plate. Using a sponge roller, apply the paint in wide gold lines up the sheet. Leave to dry.

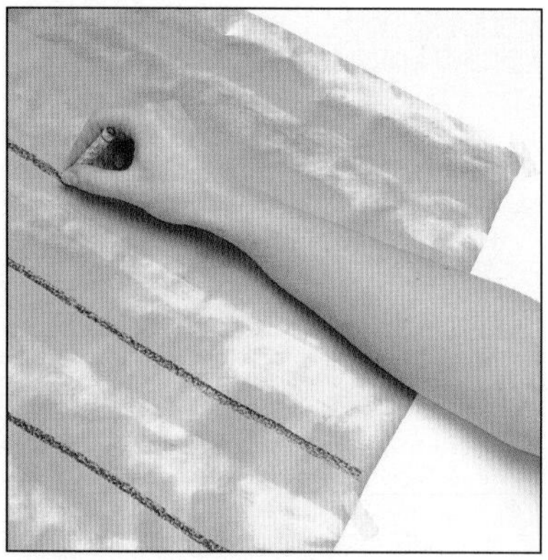

2 Add coloured or just black and white stripes to the gold. Leave the paper to dry thoroughly before using.

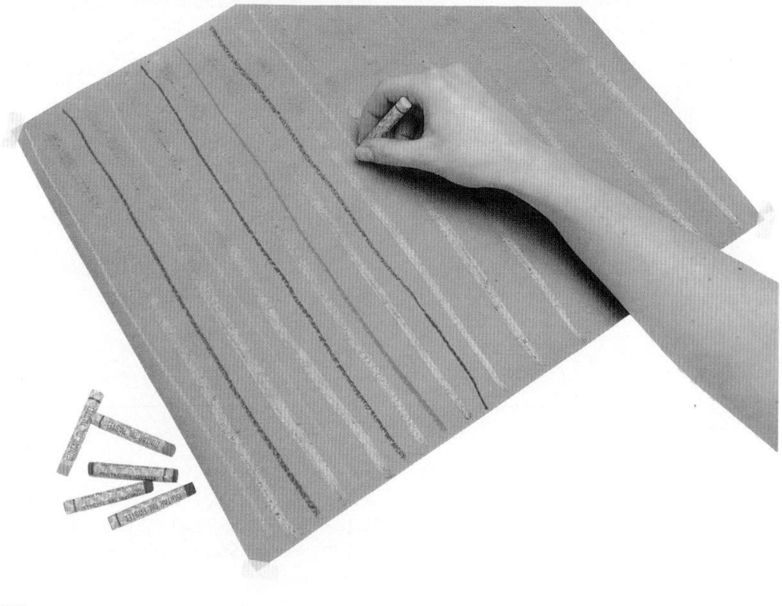

3 For an alternative look, draw vertical stripes down a piece of brown parcel wrap (packaging paper) with a chunky gold oil crayon. Experiment with different groupings and spacings for the stripes. Make several sheets to work on further.

Tin Gift Box

Embossed aluminium foil combines festive glitter with the gentle naïve appeal of tinware, and it's a perfect match for the simplicity of this Shaker box. The embossing is easy to do – simple designs really are the most successful.

YOU WILL NEED
tracing paper
heavy-gauge aluminium foil
masking tape
dried-out ballpoint pen
scissors
gift box
glue-stick

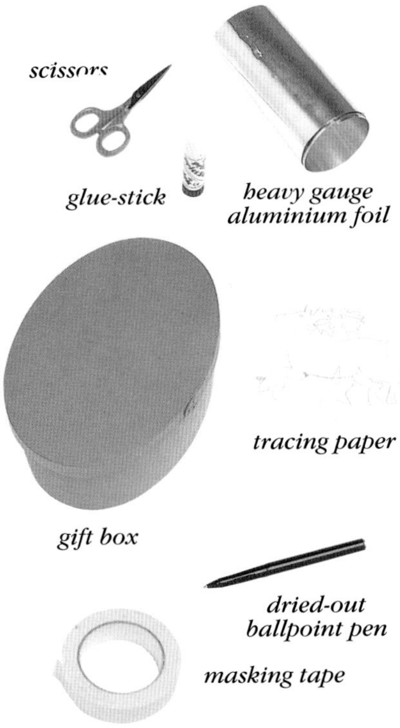

1 Trace the reindeer and stars motifs from the back of the book. Attach the tracings to the foil with masking tape and draw over the outlines with a dried-out ballpoint pen.

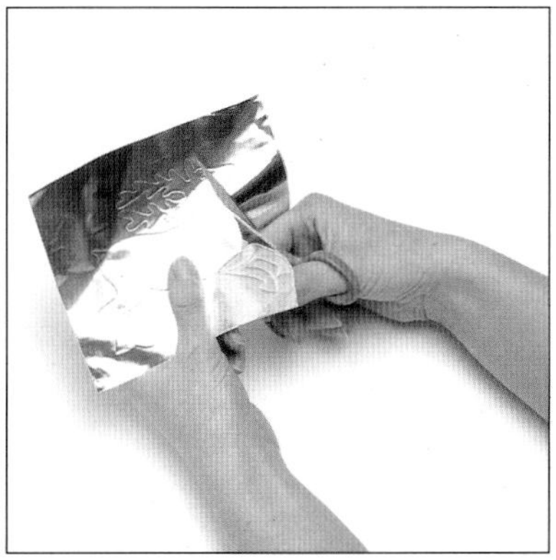

2 Remove the tracing paper and go over the embossing again if necessary. Cut out the motifs with scissors, leaving a narrow border of about 2 mm (1/16 in) around the edge – don't cut into the embossing.

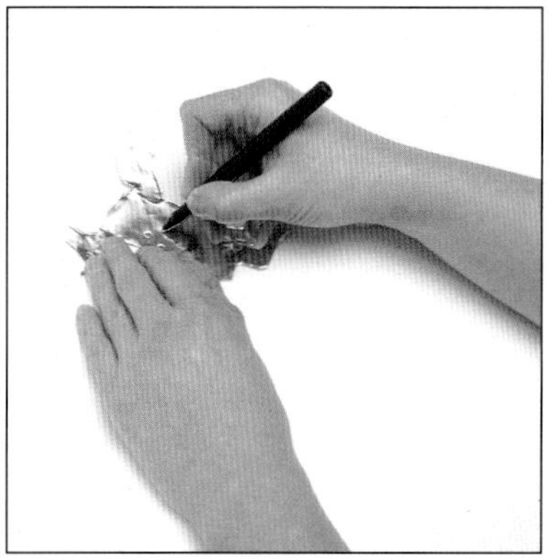

3 Add more embossed details to the motifs if you wish.

4 Turn the motifs over and arrange them on the box lid and sides. Attach them using a glue-stick applied liberally.

Place Marker Gift Bags

With these pretty copper foil tags you can plan your seating arrangement by numbers. Fill the little bags with appropriate small gifts for your dinner-party guests.

CRAFT TIP

When you're embossing metallic foil, remember that you'll be working from the back of the finished design, so always draw the motif on to the foil in reverse.

YOU WILL NEED
metallic crepe paper in bronze
craft knife
metal ruler
double-sided adhesive (cellophane) tape
tracing paper
heavy-gauge copper foil
dried-out ballpoint pen
scissors
hole punch
fine gold cord
gifts to go in the bags
ribbon

1 Cut a rectangle of the crepe paper 45 x 42 cm (18 x $16\frac{1}{2}$ in).

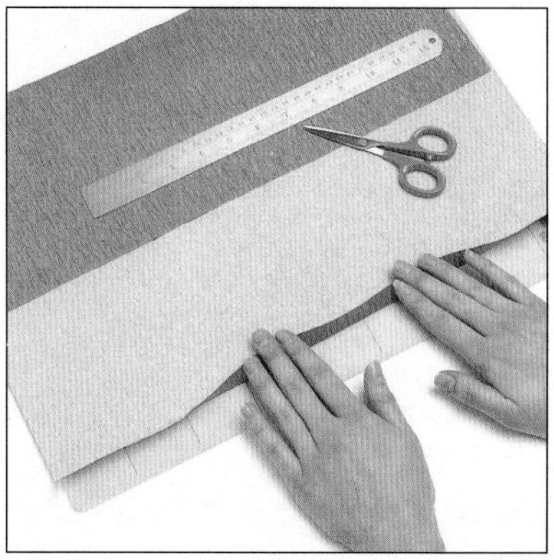

2 Fold over 15 cm (6 in) along one of the long sides, for the top, and 1.5 cm ($\frac{5}{8}$ in) along the other for the bottom of the bag.

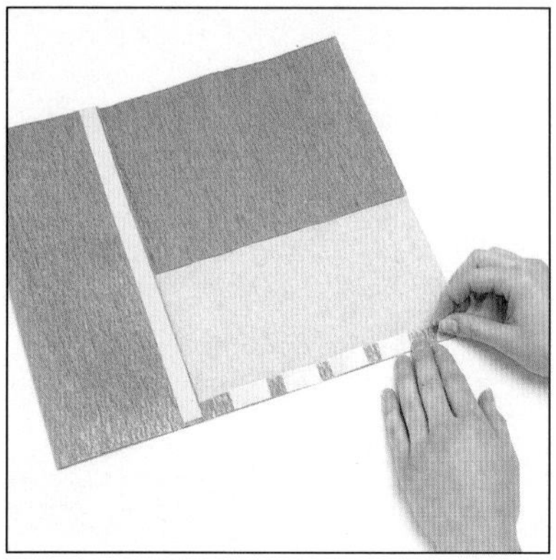

3 Use double-sided adhesive (cellophane) tape to stick together the sides of the bag and then the bottom edge of the bag.

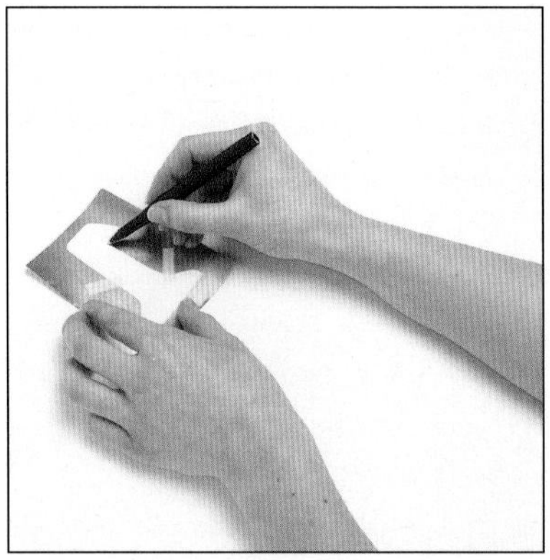

4 Trace the numeral needed for each place setting, then transfer the design in reverse to the copper foil, embossing it with a dried-out ballpoint pen.

5 Cut out the numeral with scissors. Punch a hole in the top and thread with fine gold cord.

6 Fill the bag with a suitable gift, then close. Tie the ribbon in a bow around the neck of the bag and finally attach the metal tag.

Crepe Paper Carrier Bags

When you have to wrap an awkwardly shaped gift, or a number of small things that go together, a carrier bag is a good solution. With this easy method of bag-making, you just wrap the paper around a book as if you were wrapping a package. Pull out the book and there's your bag. Match the book to the size of your gift.

YOU WILL NEED
crepe paper
book
craft knife
metal ruler
cutting mat
scissors
double-sided adhesive (cellophane) tape
hole punch
ribbon
chocolate coin

1 Place the book on top of the crepe paper and measure and mark the rectangle you will need to wrap the book with an overlap of 1.5 cm (5/8 in). Trim using a craft knife and metal ruler.

2 Using scissors, score a fold about 4 cm (1 1/2 in) from one long edge and fold it down to form the top of the bag.

3 Fold the paper over the book neatly and secure the sides with double-sided adhesive (cellophane) tape.

4 Fold in the bottom edge as if you were wrapping a package and secure to ensure the bag will take the weight of the gift. Remove the book.

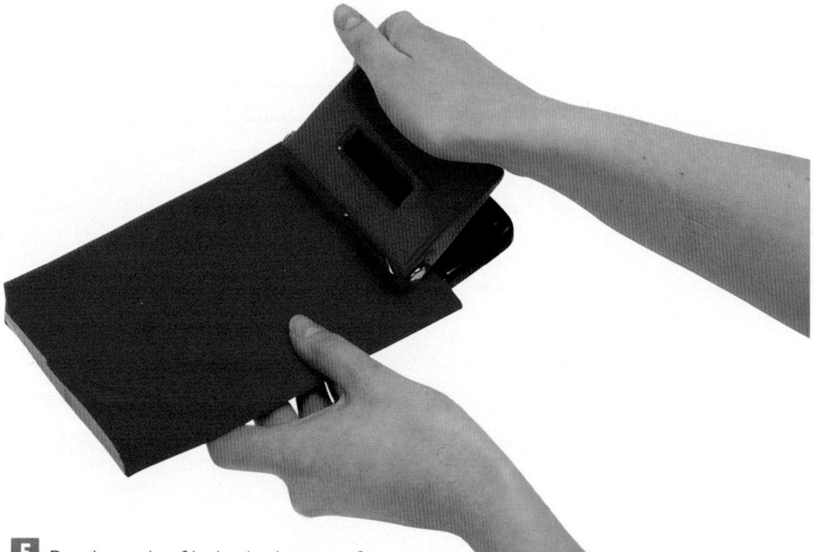

5 Punch a pair of holes in the top of the bag through the folded edge.

6 Thread a length of ribbon through the holes and knot the ends on the inside of the bag.

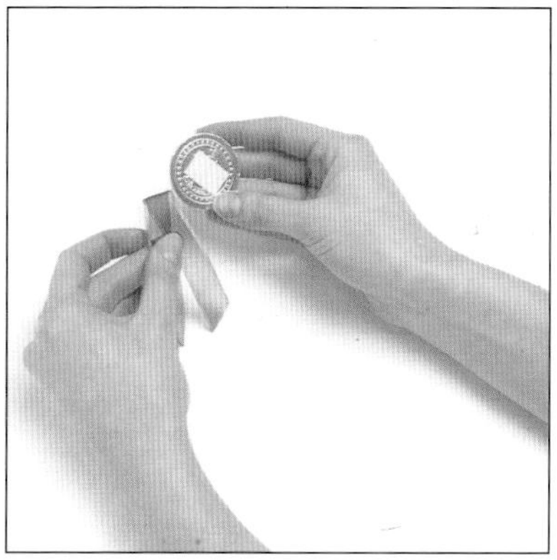

7 Decorate the bag with a chocolate coin arranged on two short lengths of ribbon to look like a medal.

Season's Greetings - the Natural Look

This project will appeal to those who feel that less is most certainly more - even at Christmas. A sheet of plain brown parcel wrap (packaging paper) is folded around the gift, then a light airy collage of festive tissue paper shapes is applied. The gift is tied up with coarse brown string and decorated with cones and pods.

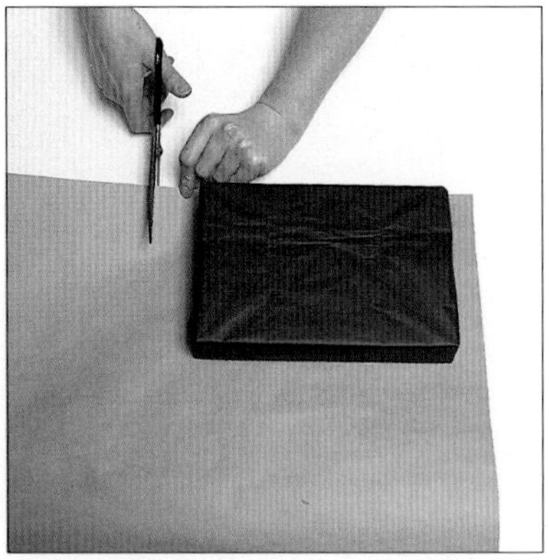

1 Use the box as a measuring guide and cut the parcel wrap to size.

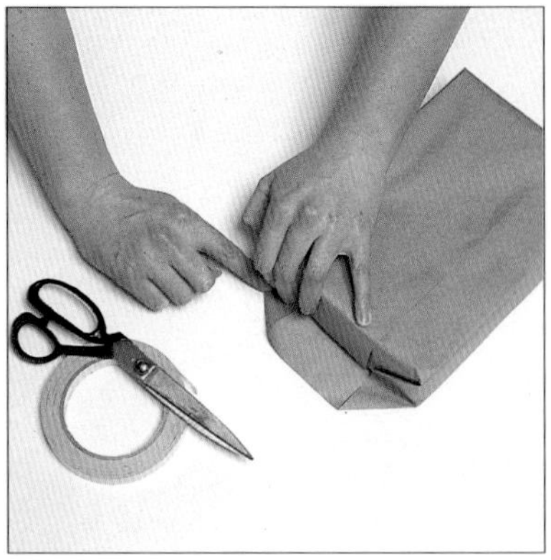

2 Wrap the box using double-sided adhesive (cellophane) tape.

YOU WILL NEED
parcel wrap (packaging paper)
scissors
double-sided adhesive (cellophane) tape
pencil
tracing paper
white chalk
dark blue and orange tissue paper
PVA (white) glue
thick coarse string
selection of dried cones and pods
hot glue gun

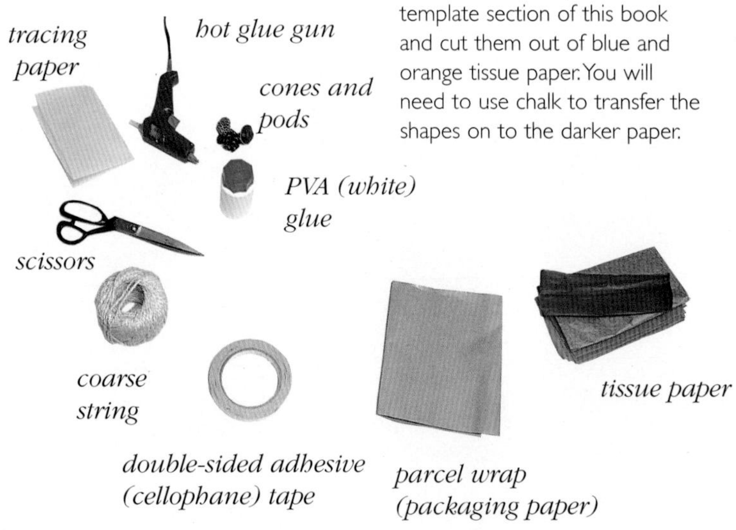

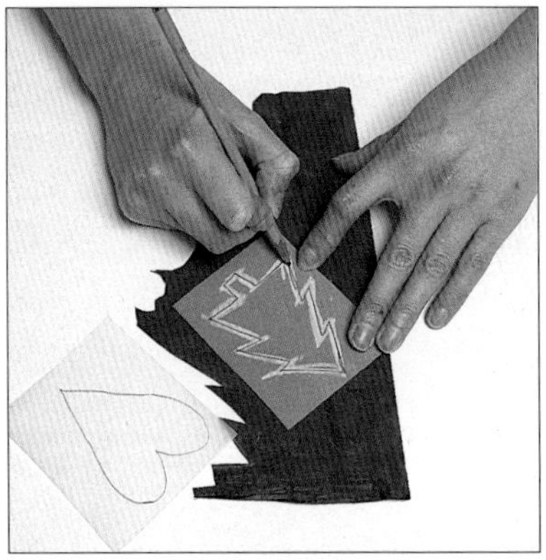

3 Trace the shapes from the template section of this book and cut them out of blue and orange tissue paper. You will need to use chalk to transfer the shapes on to the darker paper.

4 Experiment with the positioning of the shapes until you are happy with the arrangement, then apply a thin layer of glue, spread with your finger, directly on to the paper. Quickly smooth the tissue shapes on to the glue.

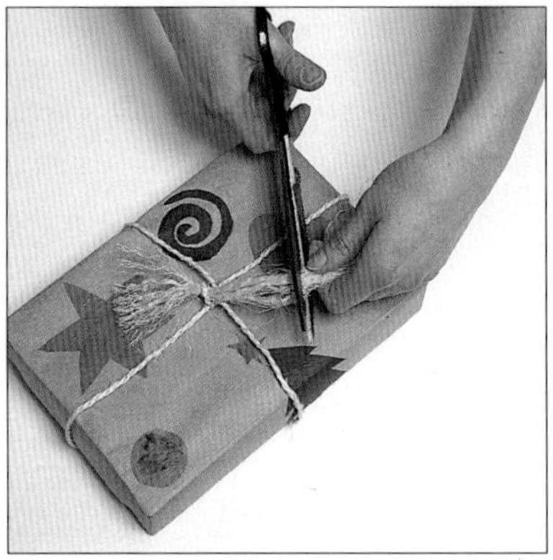

5 Tie coarse string around the gift, crossing it over underneath and knotting it on top. Untwist the string ends and fluff them out, then trim neatly.

6 Use the glue gun to stick a small arrangement of miniature cones and pods to the knotted string.

Christmas Stripes

Gift-wrap manufacturers produce thousands of variations on the Christmas theme, yet sometimes the most stylishly wrapped presents are relatively plain. This project is an example of how strong colour can be used on ordinary parcel wrap (packaging paper) for a really dramatic effect.

CRAFT TIP

You can use a small decorating roller, and the sponge versions can be cut in half to make a narrower stripe, if your gift is not large enough to show off the broad stripes. This project uses the roller full-size.

YOU WILL NEED

parcel wrap (packaging paper)
ruler
7.5 cm (3 in) decorator's rollers and tray (or small sponge brush, for smaller stripes)
dark green and white emulsion (latex) paint
saucers
scissors
double-sided adhesive (cellophane) tape
broad red moiré satin ribbon
florist's wire

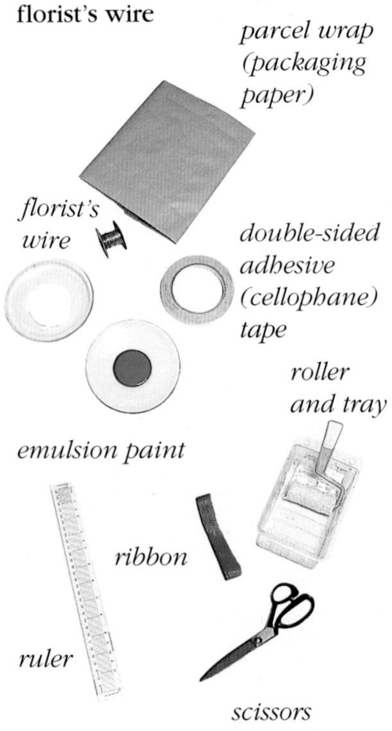

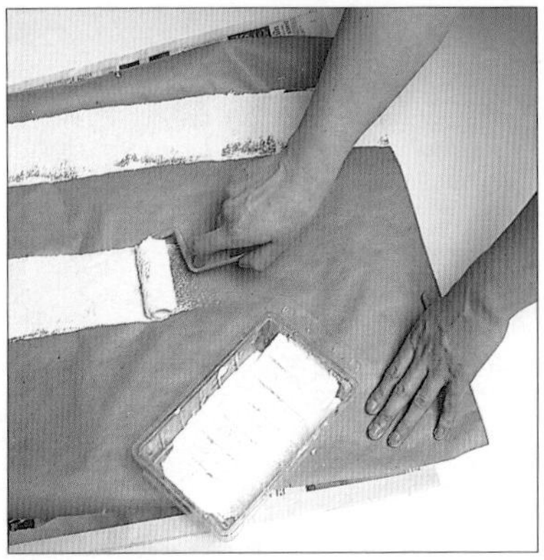

1 Lay a sheet of parcel wrap (packaging paper) on scrap paper. Use the roller to paint a white stripe, just in from the edge. Allow a roller's width plus 2 cm (¾ in), then paint the next white stripe. Repeat and leave to dry.

2 Use a fresh roller and the dark green paint. Begin painting the dark green stripe about 1.5 cm (½ in) away from the first white stripe, so that a small stripe of brown shows through. Repeat three times to complete the striped paper, and leave to dry.

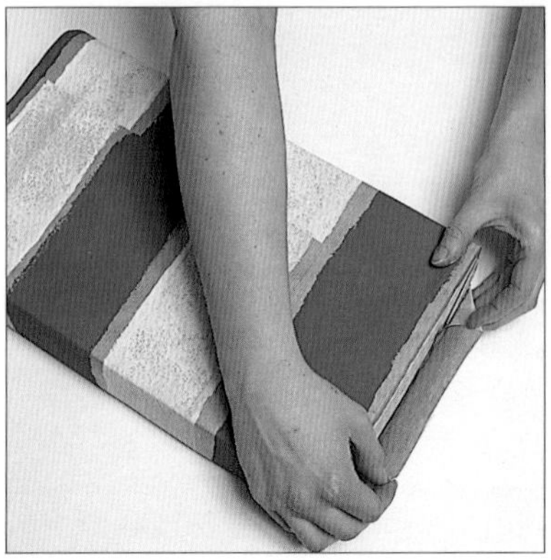

3 Using the gift as a measuring guide, trim off any excess paper. Wrap the gift, securing the edges invisibly with double-sided tape.

4 Cut a long length of ribbon, taking it around the gift, crossing it underneath and tying it at the centre point on the top of the gift.

5 Make the bow by looping the ribbon over three times on each side and securing it with florist's wire.

6 Attach the bow to the parcel with an extra piece of ribbon.

The Ice Box

A great big box under the tree always attracts attention, but this stunning present is in danger of upstaging the Christmas tree itself! The blue paper is stencilled with snowflakes, then the whole gift is bunched up in clear icy cellophane (plastic wrap). Foil ribbons and Christmas tree ornaments complete the effect.

YOU WILL NEED
tracing paper
pencil
cardboard or mylar
craft knife
bright blue paper
small sponge
bowl of water
white watercolour paint
saucer
adhesive (cellophane) tape
scissors
roll of clear, wide cellophane (plastic wrap)
silver foil ribbon
selection of Christmas tree ornaments

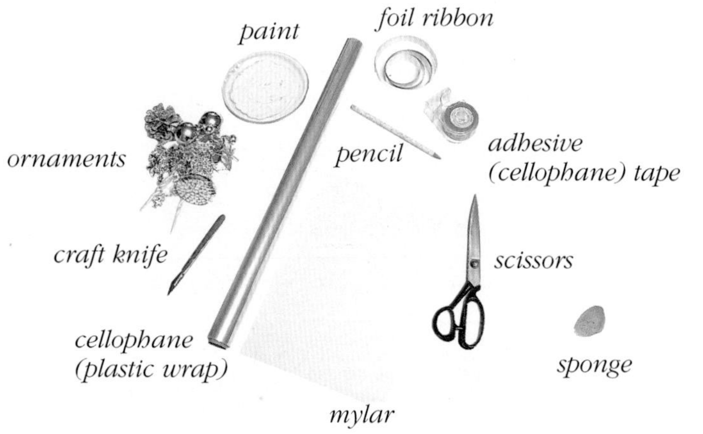

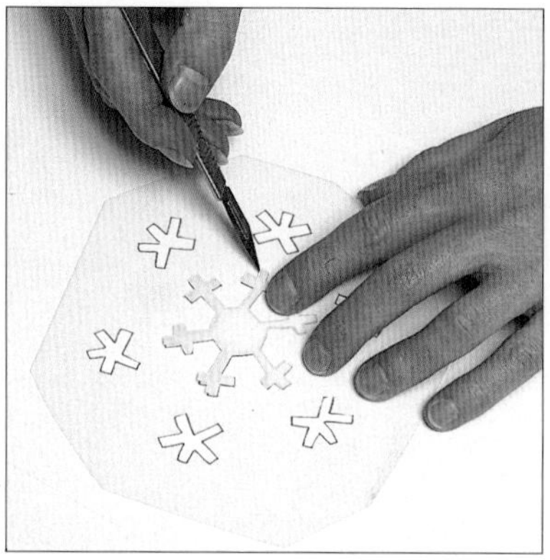

1 Trace and cut out the stencil from the template section of this book. You can use cereal box cardboard or special stencil plastic called mylar.

2 Place scrap paper on your work surface and use a small sponge to apply the white paint. Dip the sponge in the bowl of water then squeeze it out thoroughly. Stencil paints should always be on the dry side to prevent any from seeping under the stencil. Apply the snowflakes randomly all over the blue paper and right over the edges. Allow to dry thoroughly.

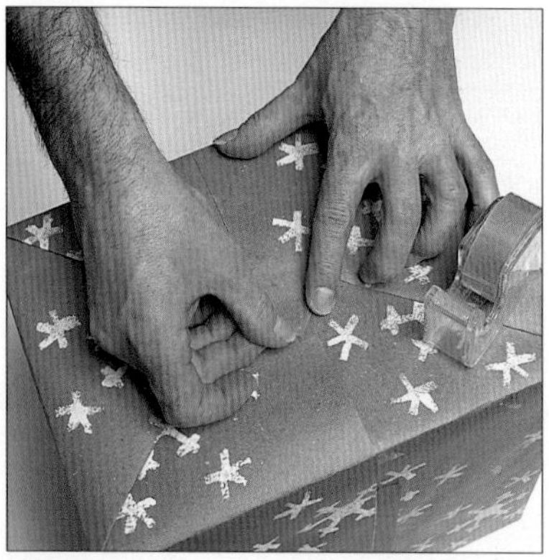

3 If one sheet of paper is not big enough to cover the box, lay two sheets side by side and run a length of adhesive (cellophane) tape along the join. Repeat with other sheets until you have a single sheet large enough for the box. Wrap up the box, using adhesive (cellophane) tape to hold the wrapping securely in place.

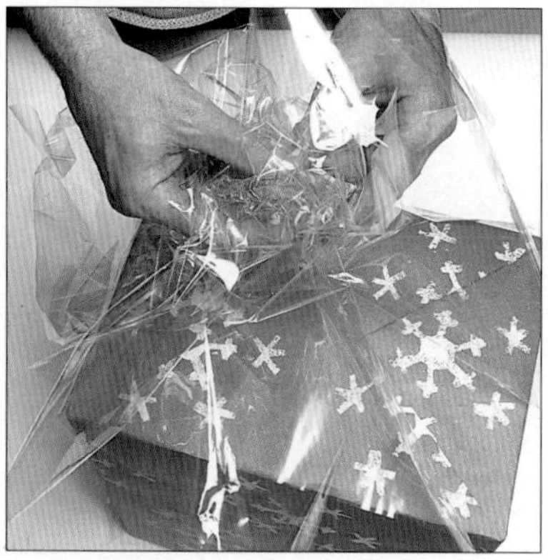

4 Unroll a length of cellophane (plastic wrap) on your work surface long enough to pass under the box, up the sides and allowing at least 30 cm (12 in) extra on both ends. Do the same in the other direction, to cross over the first sheet under the box.

CRAFT TIP

This gift-wrap works best on a large scale, so if you have a boxed toy, stereo or television to wrap, look no further.

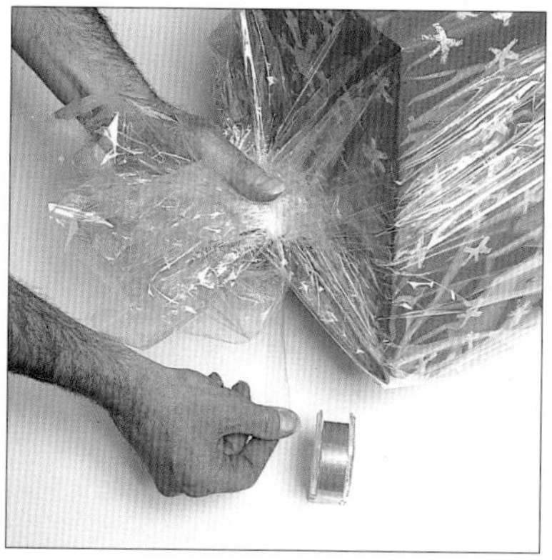

5 Gather up the cellophane (plastic wrap) on top of the box, making sure that the sides of the box are completely covered, then tape around the bunch, close to the box top.

6 Cover the adhesive (cellophane) tape with silver foil ribbon and attach the Christmas tree decorations.

Festive Fabric Card

This charming little cat is all dressed up for Christmas! If you like the design so much that you do not want to give it as a festive card, put it into a frame, sign it and give it to someone as a present.

YOU WILL NEED
coloured cardboard
felt-tip pen
paper scissors
felt squares in various colours
fabric scissors
single hole punch
PVA (white) glue
squeezy paints in various colours
artificial gemstone

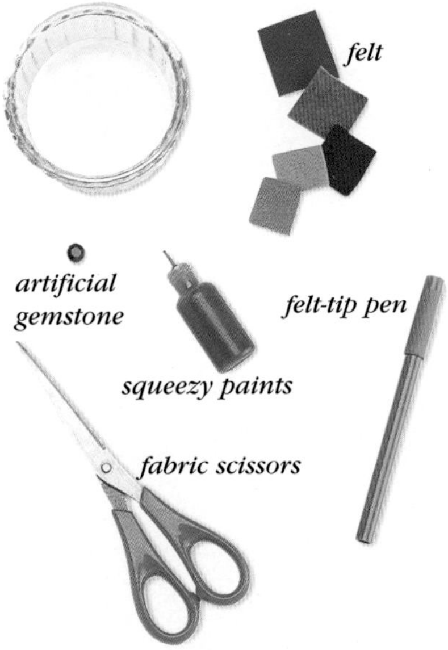

1 Fold the sheet of cardboard in half. Use a felt-tip pen to trace the templates from this book, then cut them out using paper scissors. Use the felt-tip pen to draw around the templates on the reverse side of the pieces of felt.

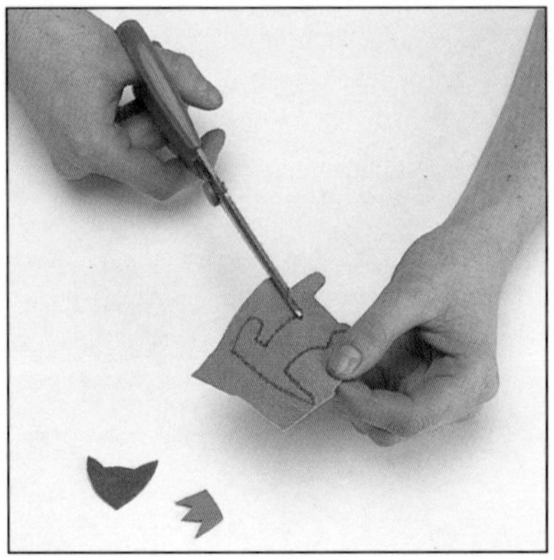

2 Use the fabric scissors to cut all of the cat shapes and the pieces for the snowy background out of the felt. Always remember to save any leftover scraps of fabric for other projects.

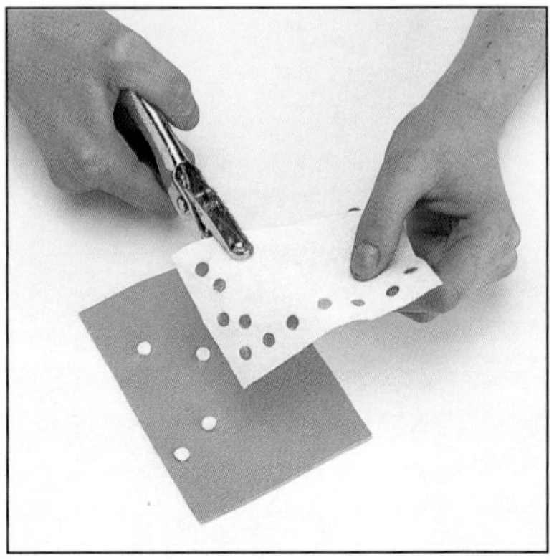

3 Punch lots of dots from a piece of white felt, using the single hole punch. These white dots will be used to make the snow that is falling around the cat.

4 Position all of the felt shapes on the background felt and, when you are happy with how they look, glue them in place with PVA (white) glue.

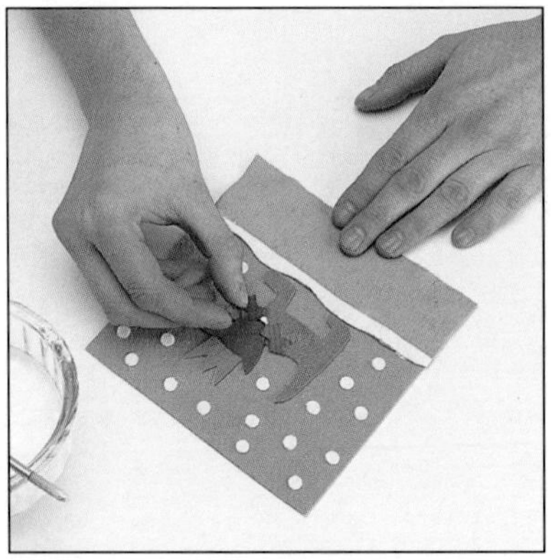

5 Using squeezy paints, decorate the cat's face to give it eyes, whiskers and a smile. If you find this too difficult, use felt-tip pens instead. Glue an artificial gemstone on the cat's collar.

6 Paint a few dabs of glue on the reverse side of the fabric design and glue it firmly in place on to the folded sheet of cardboard. Alternatively, use it as a picture and place it in a frame.

Polka-dot Wrapping Paper

You will have great fun stamping and printing to make this gift-wrap. This project uses a sponge roller and a cork to print with. Be adventurous and see what else you can use to make a printed shape.

YOU WILL NEED
coloured paper
small roller sponge
poster paints in various colours
cork
scourer pad (sponge)
scissors
single hole punch
string

small roller sponge

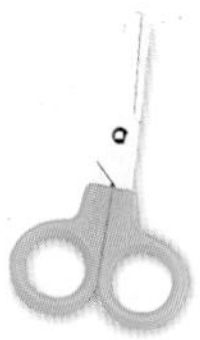

scissors

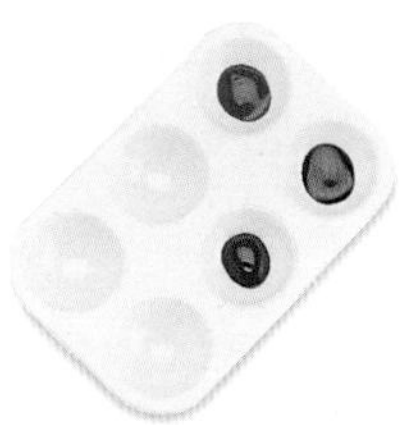

poster paints

single hole punch

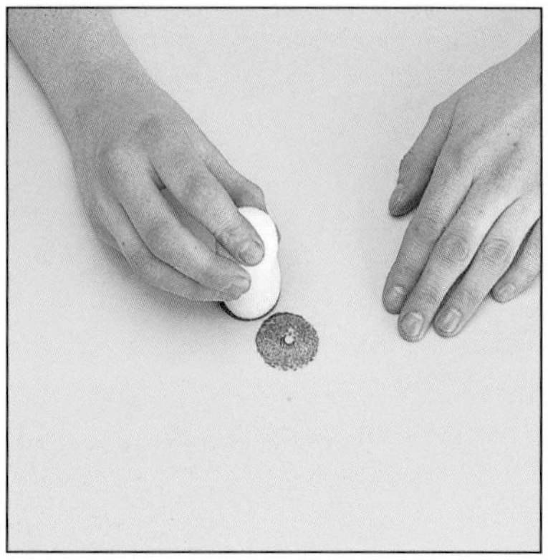

1 Lay the coloured paper on a flat, well-covered surface. Dab the end of the roller sponge in one of the paint colours. Carefully stamp dots on the paper to make a triangle shape for the Christmas tree. You may need to add more paint to the roller between prints.

2 Dab a cork in a different colour of paint and print a line of dots under the tree to make the tree trunk.

3 Cut a scourer pad (sponge) to look like a tree stand. Dab the scourer pad in a new paint colour and print it under the tree trunk.

4 To make a tag, dab a scrap piece of scourer pad in paint and print a star shape on cardboard. When dry, cut around the shape. Punch a hole in the top of the tag and thread with string.

Rope-printed Paper

This design is simple but looks very stylish. If you don't have any wood to make the printing block, you can use a piece of thick cardboard instead.

YOU WILL NEED
- wooden block
- pencil
- PVA (white) glue
- paintbrush
- thin rope
- poster paint
- scissors
- coloured paper
- single hole punch
- ribbon

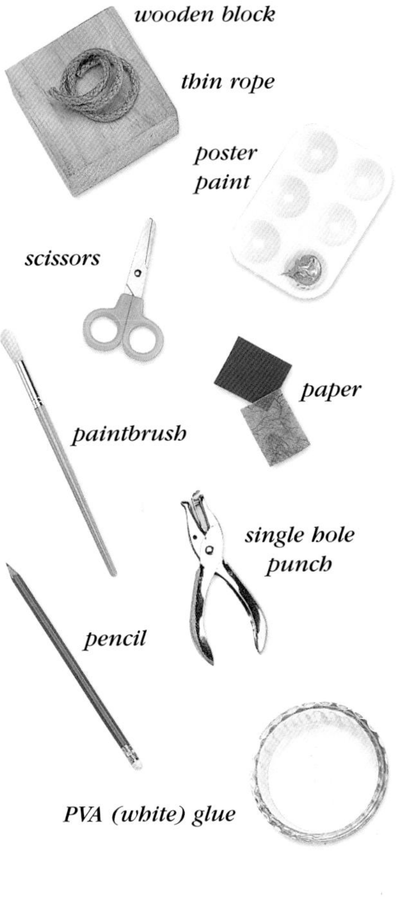

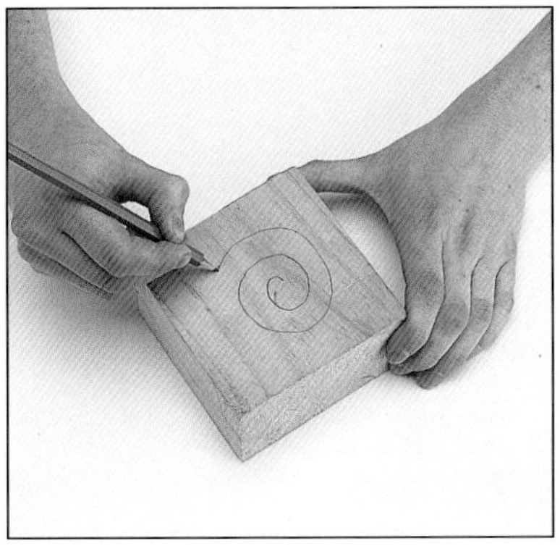

1 Draw a spiral shape on a block of wood, using a pencil so that you can rub out any mistakes. Paint a coat of PVA (white) glue over the spiral shape.

2 Begin laying the rope in place before the glue dries. Starting in the centre of the spiral, carefully wind the rope around, following the spiral design. Hold the rope in place as you work, so that it does not spring off.

3 Make sure you are working on a well-covered surface before you start to paint. Cover the rope generously with paint and then stamp the design on the paper. You will need to repaint the rope for each print you make.

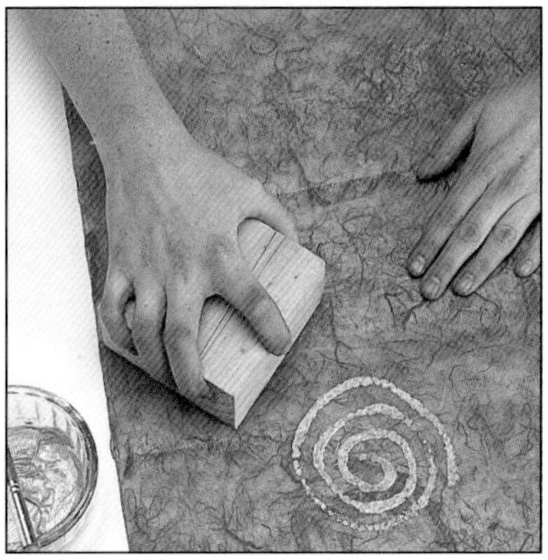

4 Make a gift tag to go with the paper. Print the design on coloured paper. When the paint is dry, cut around the design and punch a hole in the edge. Pull a length of ribbon through the hole for attaching the tag to a present.

Christmas Tree Card

Scourer pads (sponges) are usually used for cleaning pots and pans in the kitchen, but they can also be cut into shapes and used to decorate Christmas cards.

YOU WILL NEED
coloured cardboard
pencil
scissors
scourer pads (sponges) in various colours
pins
single hole punch
sequins
glitter glue
PVA (white) glue
ribbon

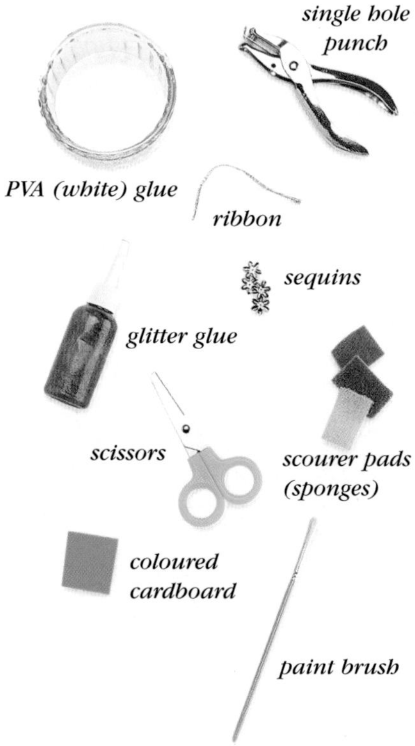

1 Fold the piece of coloured cardboard in half. Trace the templates from this book and cut them out with a pair of scissors. Lay the templates on the different coloured scourer pads (sponges) and pin them in place to make them easier to cut out.

2 Carefully cut around the templates, using a pair of scissors, then remove the pins. You should now have a Christmas tree and a Christmas tree stand.

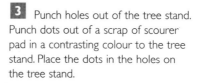

3 Punch holes out of the tree stand. Punch dots out of a scrap of scourer pad in a contrasting colour to the tree stand. Place the dots in the holes on the tree stand.

4 Decorate the tree with sequins and glitter glue, and when the glue has dried, glue the tree on to the folded piece of card. Using the same method, make a gift tag to match.

Paper Mosaic Gift Box

This glitzy box looks like a miniature treasure chest and is terrific for any presents you find too difficult to wrap in paper. If you can't find a small box, decorate an old shoe box instead.

YOU WILL NEED
shiny papers in various colours
scissors
cardboard box, sprayed silver if liked
paintbrush
PVA (white) glue
glitter glue

1 Cut up lots of strips of paper from the shiny coloured papers and then cut some of the strips into small squares. The bigger your box, the more strips and squares you will need.

2 Glue the squares on to the lid of the box, leaving a small gap in between each of the squares. Continue until you have covered the whole of the box lid.

3 Glue the strips of paper all around the sides of the box, leaving small gaps between each strip. Leave the lid and box until the glue is completely dry.

4 Carefully apply the glitter glue on the lid of the box where the gaps are. Leave it to dry: it takes quite a long time to set. If you don't have any glitter glue, use ordinary glitter and glue instead.

Three Kings Gift-wrap

Using a humble potato to print with is an easy way to create your own gift-wrap. This jewelled crown design will add a regal touch to your presents.

YOU WILL NEED
- pencil
- scissors
- coloured cardboard
- potato
- knife
- felt-tip pen
- paper towels
- squeezy paints in various colours
- glitter glue

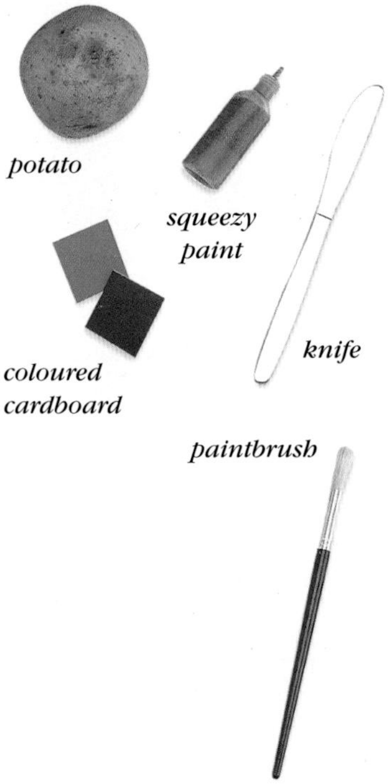

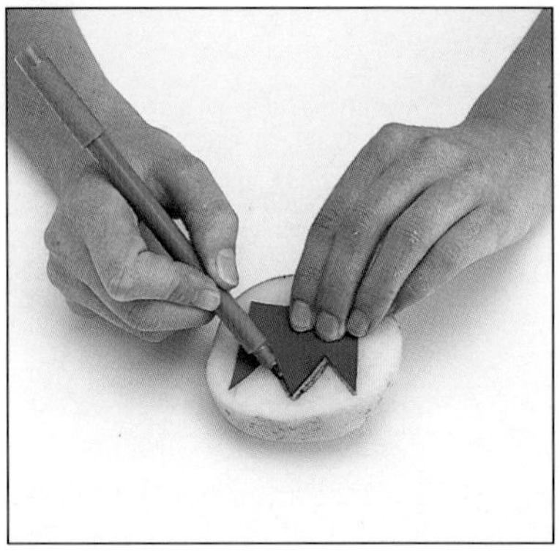

1 Trace the crown template from this book and cut it out with a pair of scissors. With the help of an adult, use a knife to cut a potato in half. Draw around the crown template on one half of the potato with a felt-tip pen.

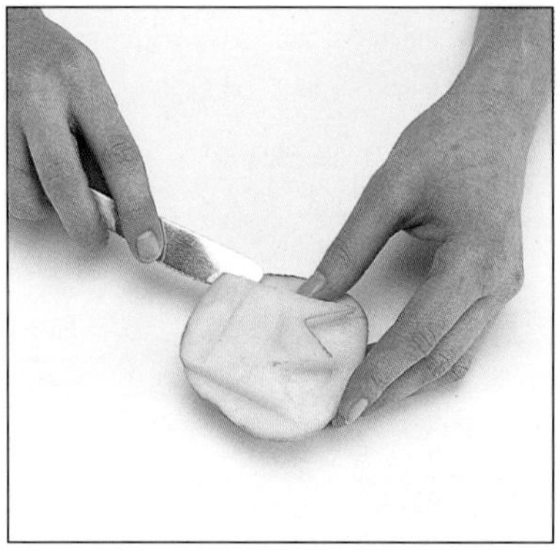

2 With the help of an adult, cut out the area around the crown shape. It is important that the shape is cut out as neatly as possible, so that the potato gives a nicely shaped print.

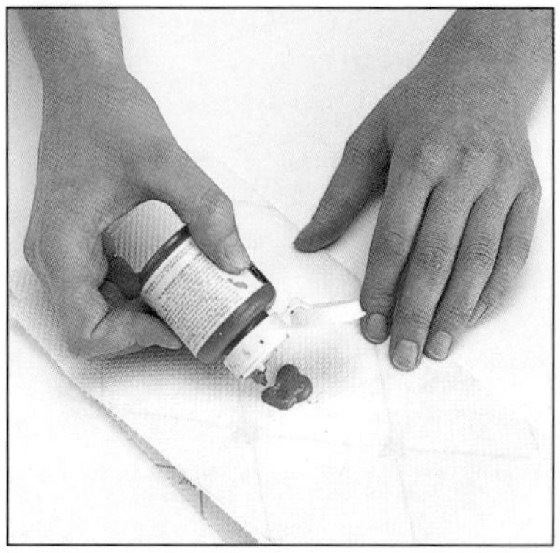

3 Squeeze a large dab of paint on a thick pad of paper towels for dipping the potato into.

4 Gently dip the potato in the paint. You can add paint directly on to the potato shape if you prefer. Carefully stamp the potato on the paper to make a print. Slowly remove the potato to reveal the print you have made.

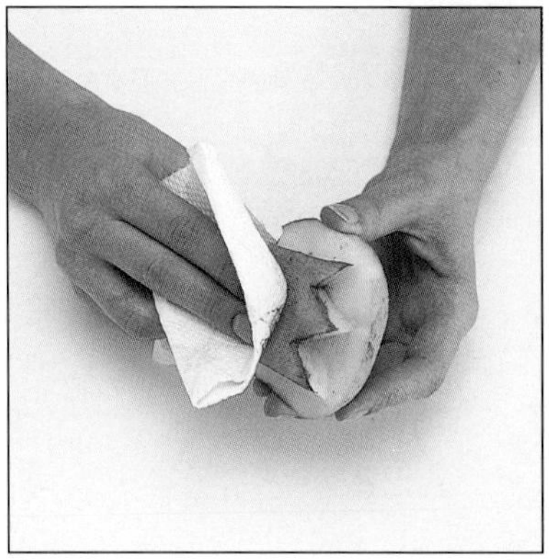

5 Use a paper towel to tidy up the printing area of the potato before you apply more paint on the paper towels or directly on to the potato. Continue printing crown shapes until you have covered the paper. Let the paint dry.

6 Add your own decoration to the printed crowns with squeezy paints and let dry. For a finishing touch, add a few dabs of glitter glue.

Disco Star Card and Tag

Use up your scraps of coloured paper and cardboard to make this groovy spinning star card and matching gift tag.

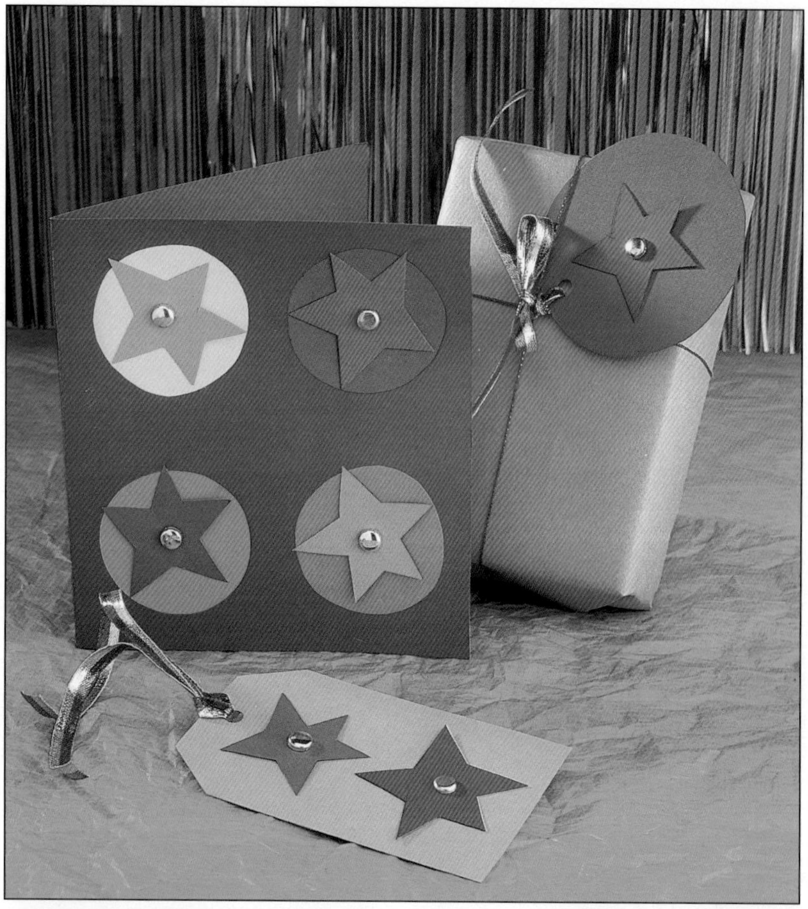

YOU WILL NEED
pencil
coloured cardboard
scissors
coloured paper
PVA (white) glue
paintbrush
paper fasteners
single hole punch
ribbon

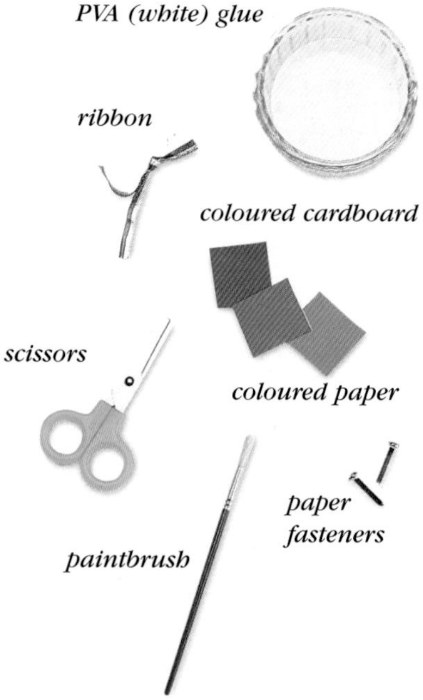

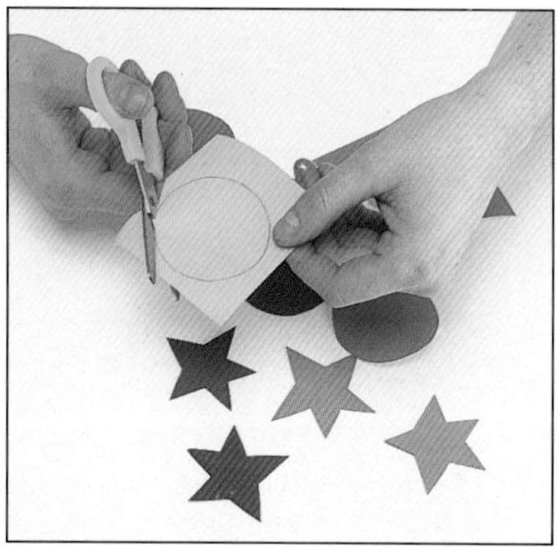

1 Trace the star and circle templates from this book and cut them out with a pair of scissors. Draw round the star template on four different coloured pieces of cardboard and cut out the star shapes. Draw round the circle template on each of the four pieces of card and cut out the circles.

2 Cut a piece of cardboard to the size you want your card to be and fold it in half. Glue the paper circles on to the front side of the card.

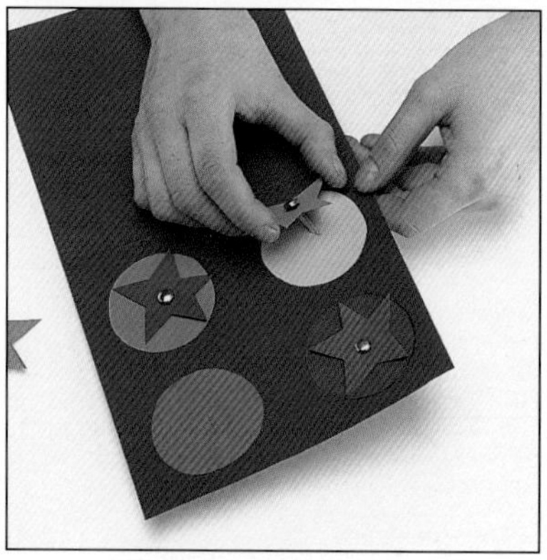

3 Ask an adult to make a slit in the centre of each star and circle with the scissors. Push a paper fastener through the centre of each star and then push it through one of the circles. Open out the fastener so that it sits flat on the card.

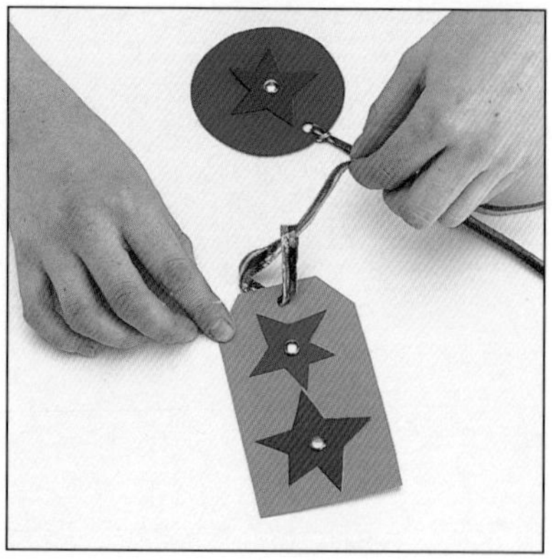

4 Make a gift tag to match the card. Punch a hole at one end of the tag to thread a piece of ribbon through.

Stained Glass Card

To enjoy the full beauty of this card you need to open it up and position it by a window. When the sun shines the light will stream through the tissue paper and light up the Christmas tree.

YOU WILL NEED
scissors
black cardboard
crayon or pencil
tissue paper in various colours
paintbrush
PVA (white) glue and
 paper glue stick
glitter glue

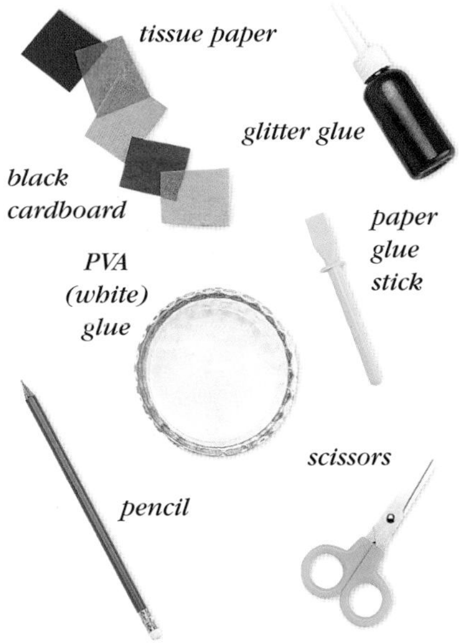

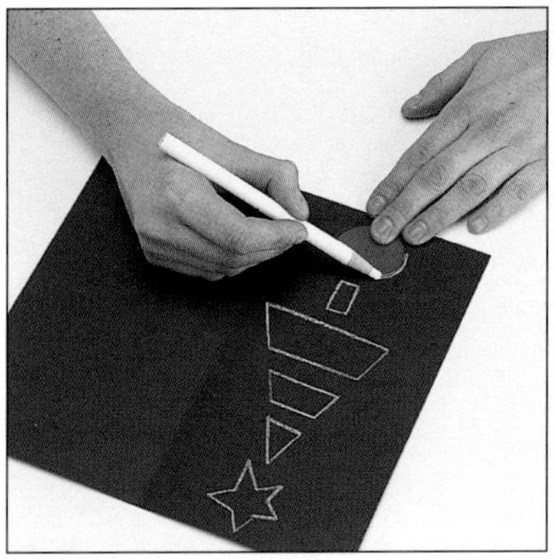

1 Cut a square shape from a piece of black cardboard, fold it in half and press down firmly on the fold. Open out the card. Trace the template from this book and cut it out. Using a crayon or pencil, draw around the template on the left side of the card.

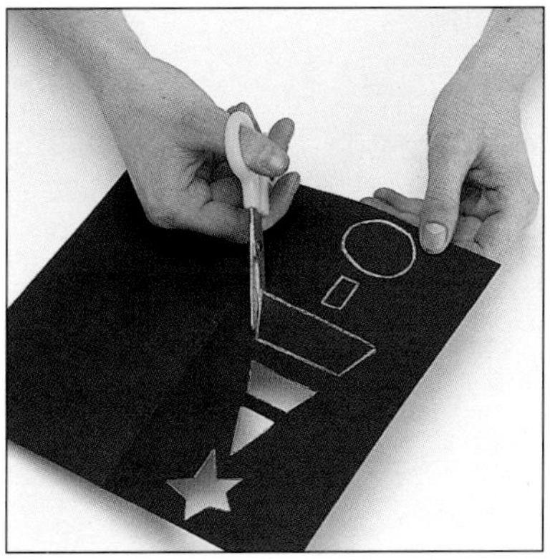

2 With the help of an adult, use a pair of scissors to cut out the Christmas tree from inside the design.

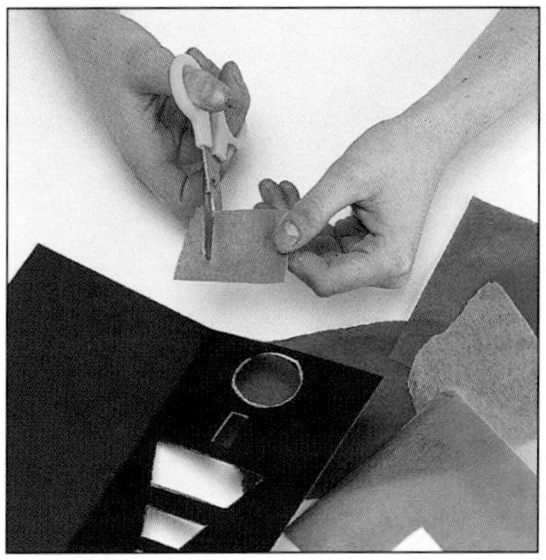

3 Cut out differently coloured pieces of tissue paper, slightly bigger than the openings in the card, and begin gluing them in place on the inside of the card.

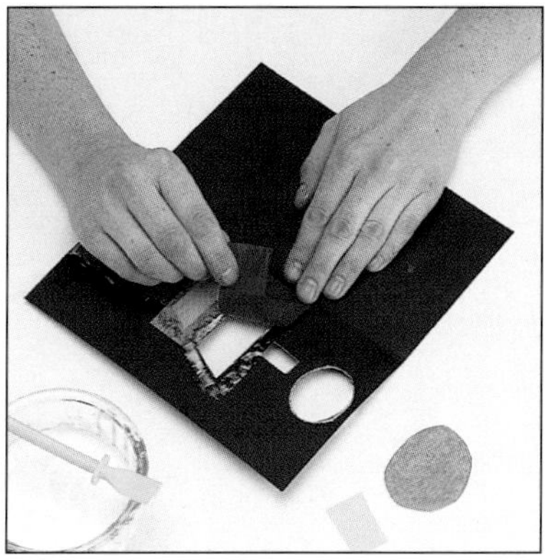

4 Continue gluing the pieces of tissue paper, alternating the colours. Allow the glue to dry before closing the card. Decorate with small dabs of glitter glue, if you wish.

Starry Gift-wrap and Tag

To make this paper project you will need to make a star stencil from a piece of stiff cardboard. You can make stencils in other shapes, too. Try out your design first on a piece of scrap paper, to make sure you are happy with it.

YOU WILL NEED
pen or pencil
stiff cardboard
scissors
single hole punch
ribbon or string
sponge
gold paint
shiny papers in various colours
PVA (white) glue

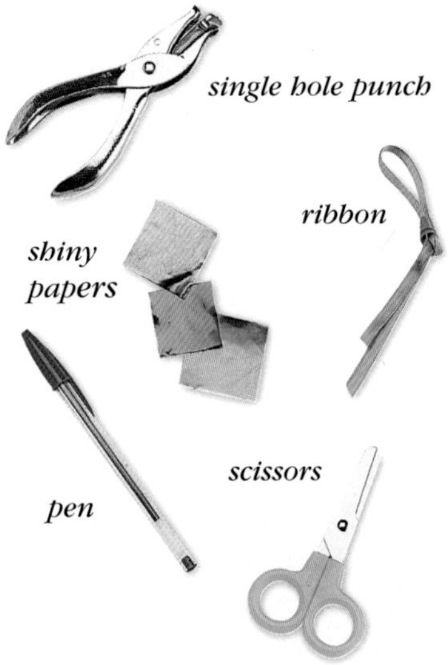

1 Trace the template for the star from this book and draw round it on a piece of stiff cardboard. With the help of an adult, cut out the inside of the star shape, so that you are left with the border as a stencil.

2 Draw round the template to make a star for the gift tag. Cut out the star. Using a single hole punch, punch a hole in the tip of one of the points and thread it with ribbon or string.

3 Dip the sponge in a small amount of paint. Position the stencil on the paper and dab through it with the sponge. Remove the stencil to reveal the print. Re-position the stencil and repeat.

4 When you have covered all of the paper with the stencilled star, cut or punch lots of dots from the shiny papers. Glue a dot on to the points of the stars on the paper, and the tag.

Snowman Card

The lovable seasonal character on this card is made from pieces of fluffy cotton wool.

You will need
- white cotton wool
- coloured cardboard
- white paper
- paintbrush
- PVA (white) glue
- scissors
- coloured papers
- single hole punch

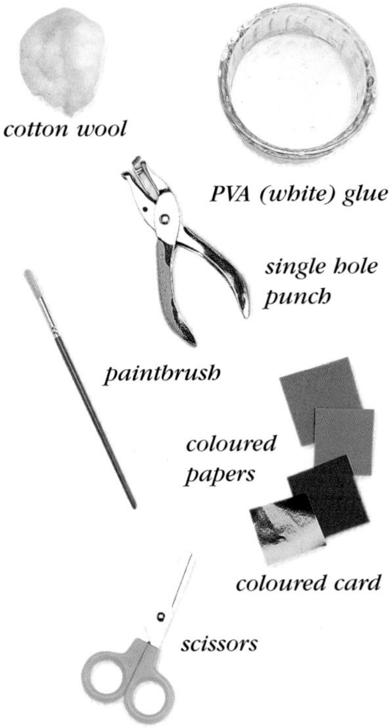

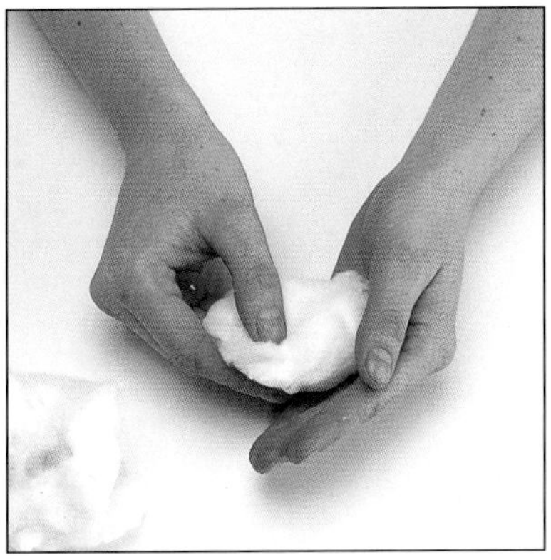

1 Gently mould two pieces of cotton wool into shapes to make the head and body of the snowman. Make sure you make your snowman nice and fat!

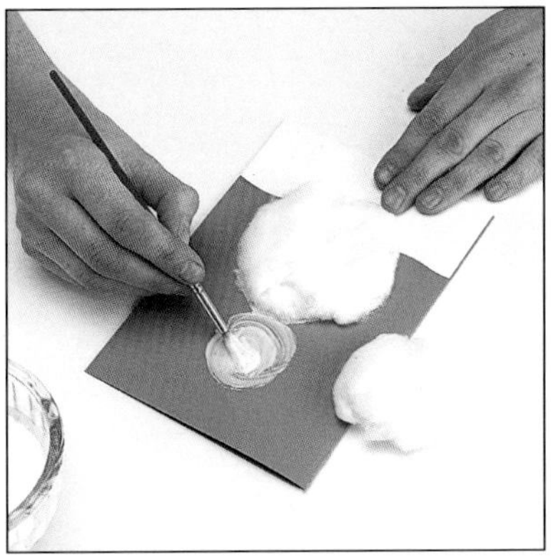

2 Fold a piece of cardboard in half, and glue a piece of white paper on the base at the front of the card, to look like a snowdrift. Glue the snowman's head and body on the cardboard.

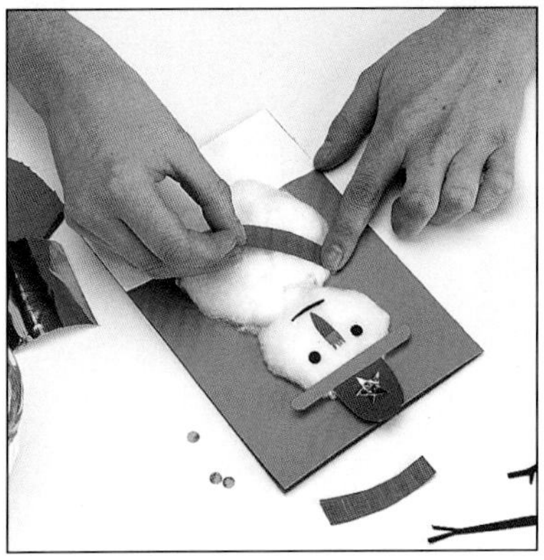

3 Trace the templates for the hat and scarf on to coloured paper and draw freehand shapes for the eyes, nose, mouth and buttons. Cut all the shapes and glue them into position.

4 Punch some dots from white paper, using the single hole punch, and glue them on the cardboard around the snowman, to look like gently falling flakes of snow. Leave the glue to dry.

Corrugated Gift Tags

These unusual gift tags, although made from humble cardboard and string, look very stylish. They are especially suitable for gift wrapping items made from natural materials such as wood.

YOU WILL NEED
corrugated cardboard
ruler
pencil
scissors
coloured corrugated card (posterboard)
non-toxic paper glue
hole punch
thick coloured twine

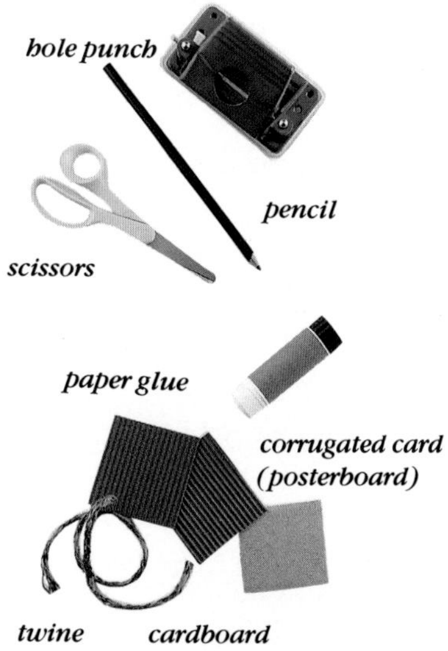

1 Draw label shapes measuring 9 × 6 cm (3½ × 2¼ in) on the corrugated cardboard.

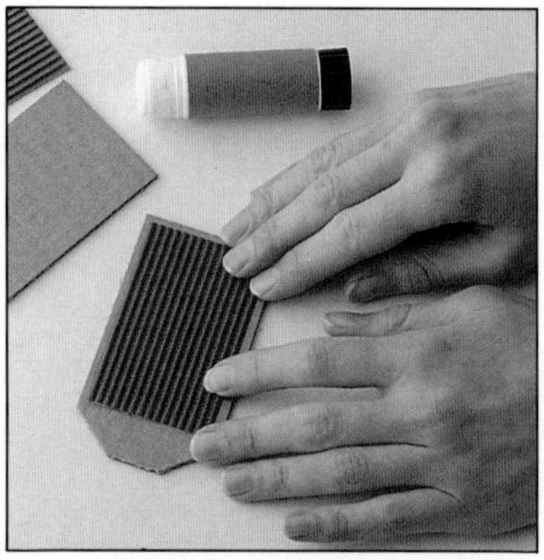

2 Cut rectangles of coloured corrugated card (posterboard) slightly smaller than the gift tags. Stick them on the front of each tag.

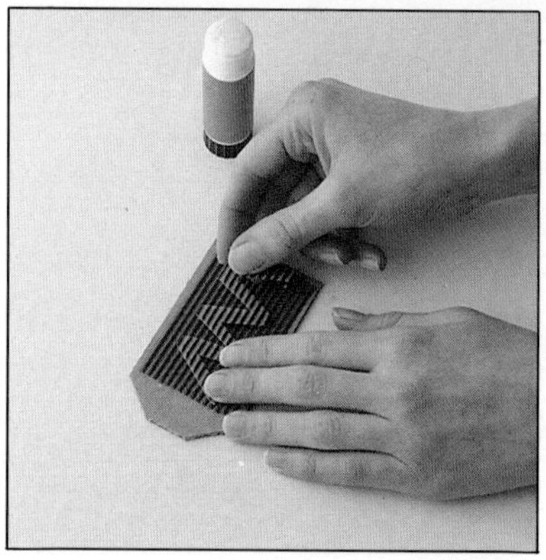

3 Cut a zig-zag shape from contrasting coloured corrugated card and stick in place on top of the card rectangles.

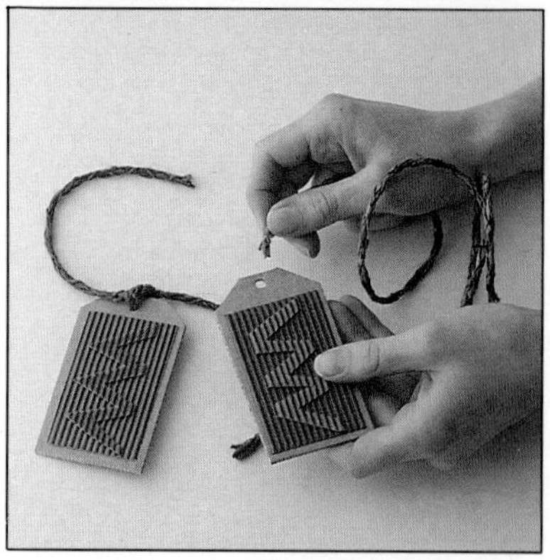

4 With adult help, make a hole at the end of each label with a hole punch. Tie a length of twine through each hole.

Felt-scrap Christmas Cards

There are always lots of leftover scraps when you make something out of felt. It's a pity to waste them, even if they're quite small, because you can use them to make bright greetings cards. Save scraps of coloured paper and card, as well, to make backings for the cards.

YOU WILL NEED
pencil
ruler
thin coloured card (posterboard)
scissors
fine felt-tipped pen
scraps of coloured felt
PVA (white) glue

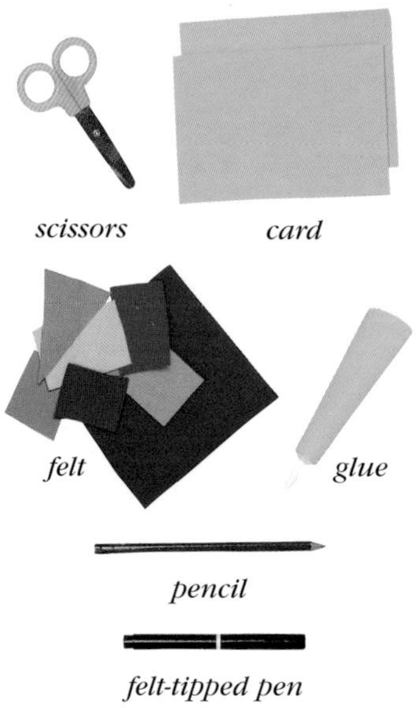

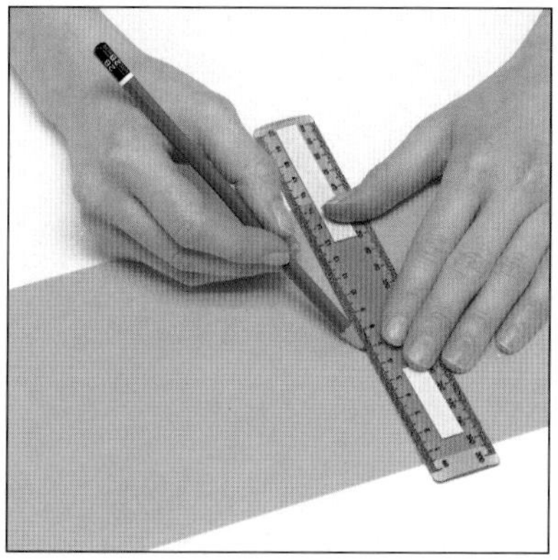

1 Draw a rectangle measuring 22 cm (9 in) x 15 cm (6 in) on the card. Cut out the rectangle and fold it in half.

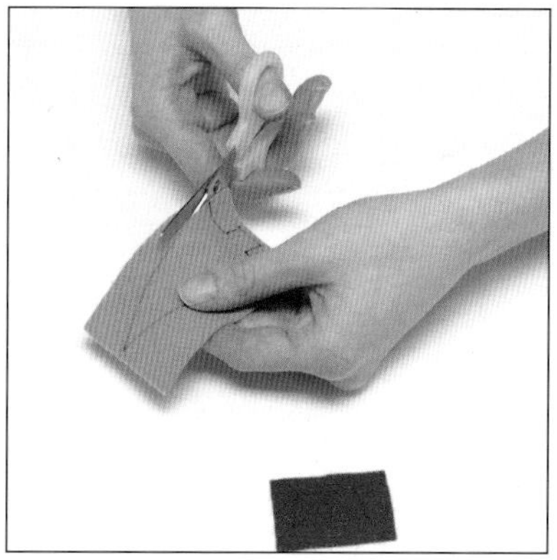

2 Draw a tree shape on a scrap of green felt and a tub on a piece of pink felt, using the fine felt-tipped pen. Cut out the shapes.

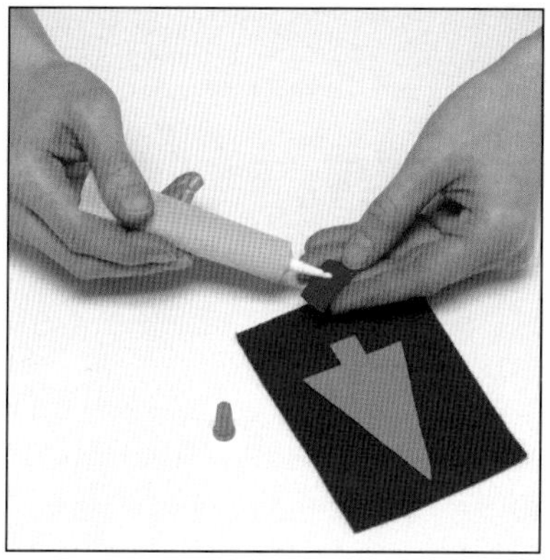

3 Cut a rectangle of blue felt slightly smaller than the card backing. Glue the tree and the tub to the blue felt.

4 Glue the picture to the front of the card. Cut small circles of coloured felt to make baubles and glue them to the tree.

Advent Table Decoration

Glue twenty-four sweets (candies) on to this terrific decoration and eat one a day in the countdown to Christmas Day.

YOU WILL NEED
green cardboard
PVA (white) glue
paintbrush
green crêpe paper
foil-wrapped sweets (candies)
pencil
scissors
gold cardboard
corrugated cardboard
terracotta flower pot
red poster paint

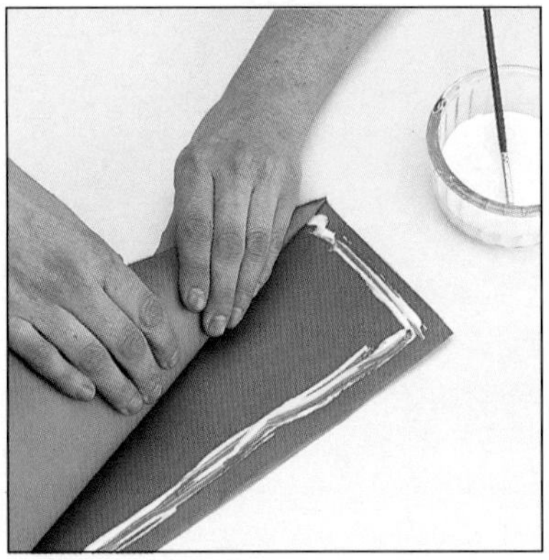

1 Roll a piece of green cardboard into a cone shape, using your hands. Glue along one edge of the cardboard, and hold the cone shape in place with your hands until the glue has dried.

2 Tear up lots of pieces of crêpe paper and scrunch them up. Paint glue on one side, and glue them all over the cone. Leave until the glue has dried.

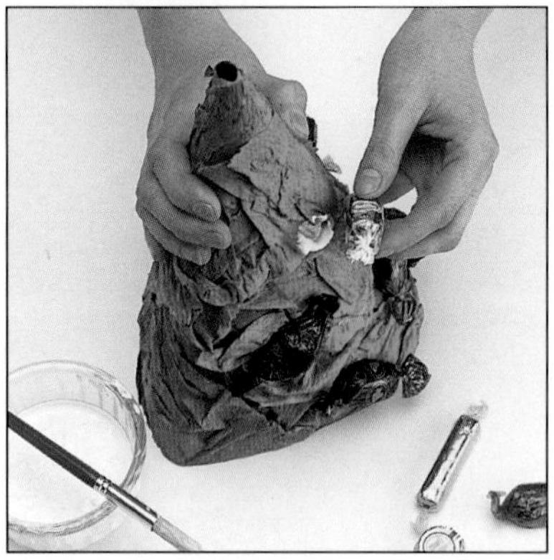

3 Glue the sweets (candies) on to the tree. Hold each sweet in place until the glue has dried.

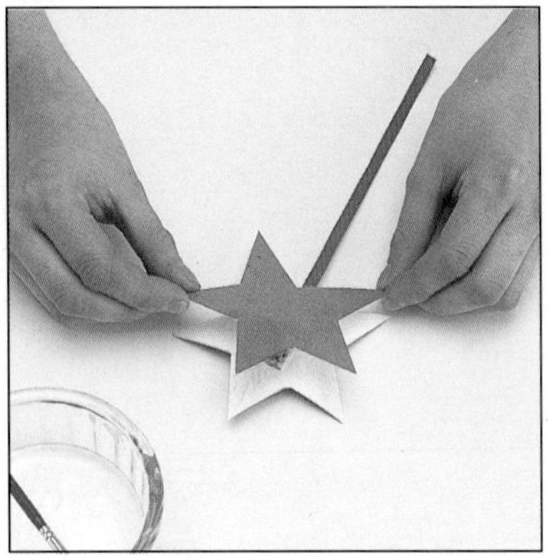

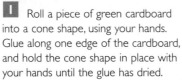

4 Trace the star template from this book and cut it out. Draw around the template on gold cardboard and cut it out. Make a second star in this way. Cut out a strip of cardboard and place it between the stars. Glue them together.

5 Cut a rectangle of corrugated cardboard and roll it up to make a tube. This makes the tree's trunk. Glue along one edge of the tube and hold in place until the glue has dried.

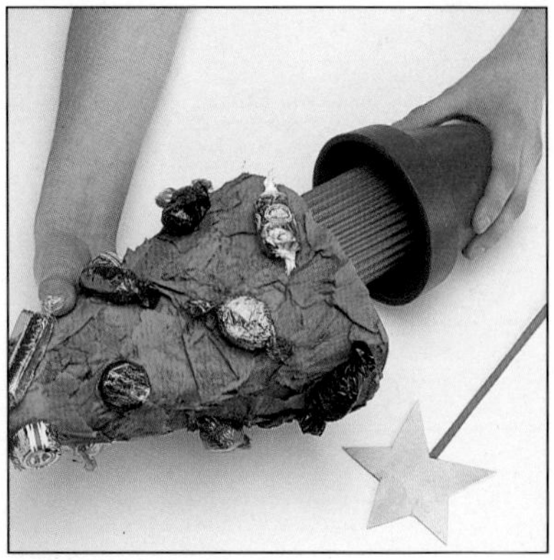

6 Paint a terracotta flower pot with red paint and, when the paint is dry, place the trunk in the pot and balance the tree on top of it. Glue the star on top of the tree.

Christmas Door Hanging

This cheerful door-decoration is easy to make from foil pie dishes (pans) and clothes pegs (clothespins). Silver foil always looks Christmassy and the smiling snowman will brighten up any door or window.

VARIATION

Any picture could go in the middle – try a gold star or a jolly Father Christmas.

YOU WILL NEED
pencil
thin coloured and white paper
scissors
paper glue
7 small foil pie dishes (pans)
strong, non-toxic glue
7 plastic clothes pegs (clothespins)
large foil pie dish (pan)
coloured ribbon

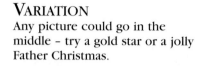

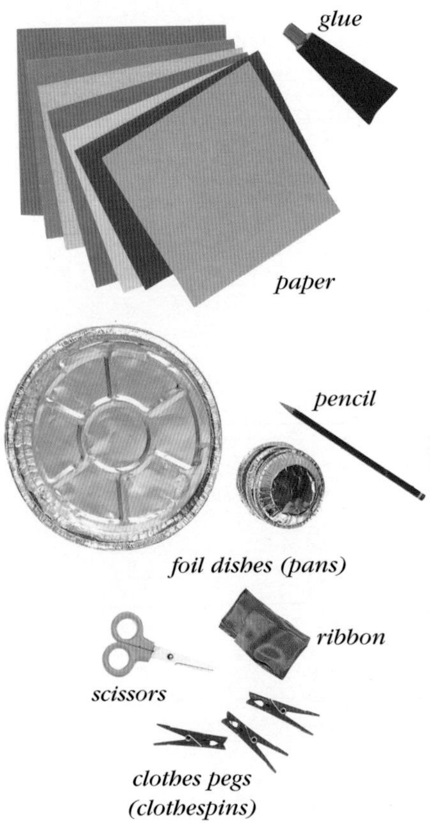

1 Draw circles the same size as the bottoms of the small pie dishes (pans) on the paper and cut them out.

2 With paper glue, glue the paper circles to the centres of the small pie dishes. Cut stars from scraps of the paper and glue one to the centre of each circle.

3 Using the strong glue, stick each of the small pie dishes to the top of a plastic clothes peg (clothespin).

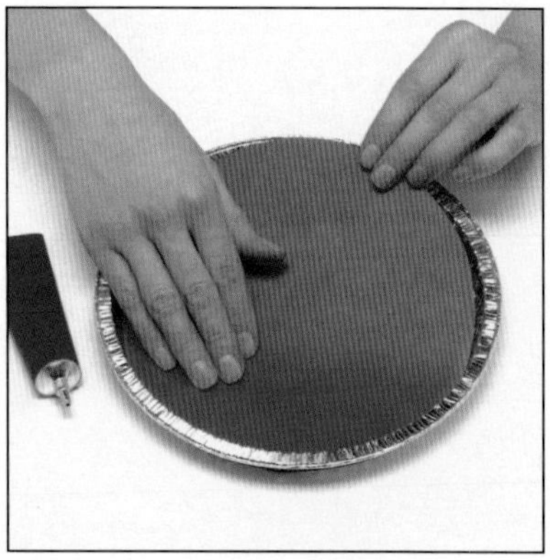

4 Draw and cut out a large circle of coloured paper to cover the bottom of the large dish. Glue it in place.

5 Cut a snowman from white paper and glue him to the middle of the large pie dish. Cut his hat, face, arms and buttons from scraps of coloured paper and glue them in place.

6 Clip the small pie dishes around the larger one, using the pegs. Tape a piece of coloured ribbon to the back of the large pie dish to make a hanger.

Christmas Wreath

Celebrate the festive season with this Christmas wreath. The leaves are lightly scored so that they have a three-dimensional effect. Use gold paper to impart an extra sparkle to the musical angel.

YOU WILL NEED
heavy red paper
ruler
pencil
scissors
tracing paper
green, white, gold and pink paper
small stapler
non-toxic paper glue
paper ribbon
thin cord

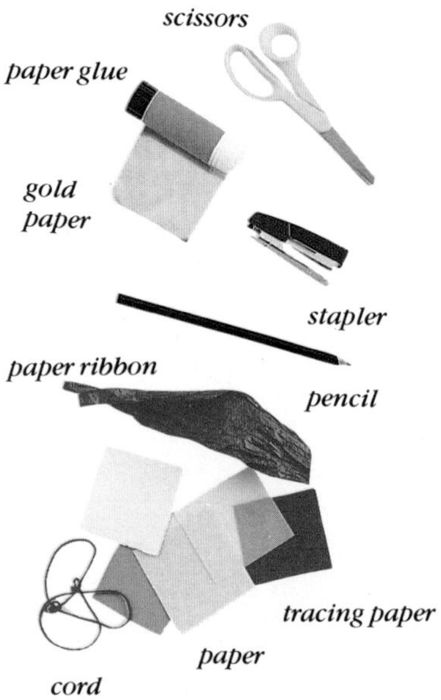

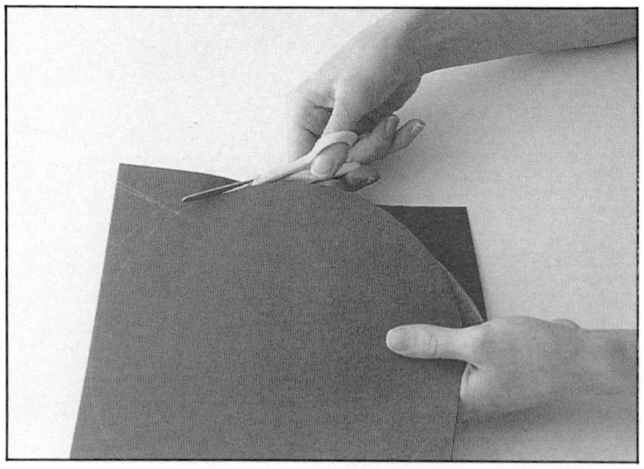

1 Draw a circle measuring 24 cm (9½ in) in diameter on a square of heavy red paper. Cut it out.

2 Trace the leaf shape from the template and transfer it to the green paper. Cut out approximately 30 leaves.

3 To make the leaves appear three-dimensional, ask an adult to help you score the centre of each one with a pair of scissors and curve the paper. Score half the leaves on the front and half on the back, so that they curve around the right- and left-hand sides of the wreath.

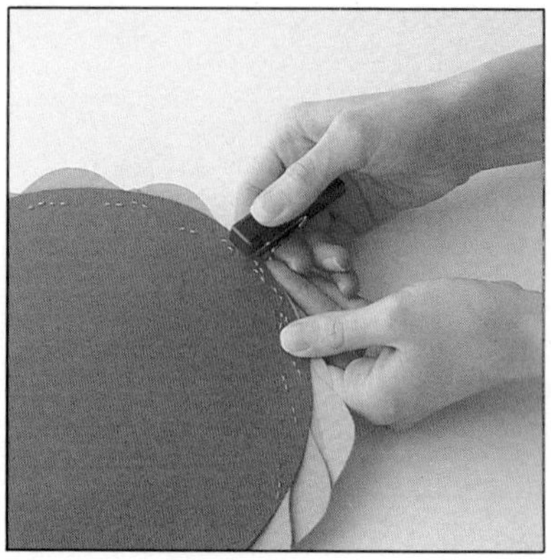

4 With adult help, staple the leaves around both sides of the wreath, overlapping them slightly.

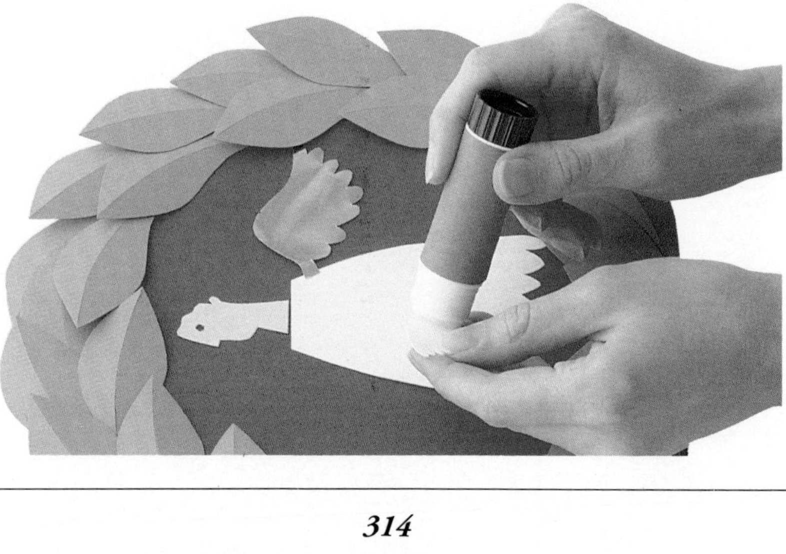

5 Trace the angel pieces from the template and transfer them to white, gold and pink paper. Cut out each of the pieces, and stick them in place on the front of the wreath.

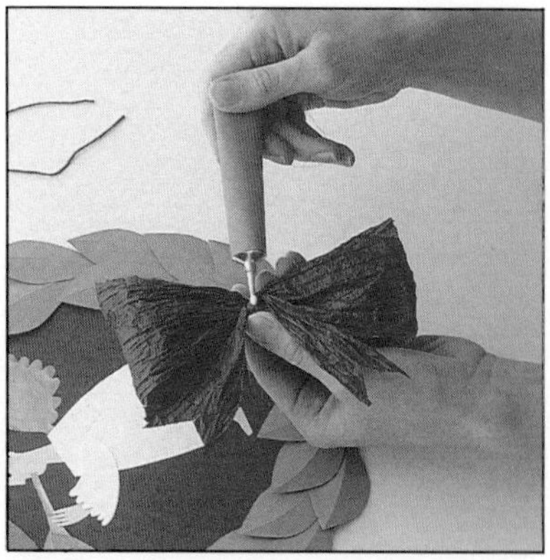

6 Open out a length of paper ribbon and tie it to form a bow. Stick it in position at the bottom of the wreath. Stick a loop of cord to the back to form a hanger.

Sparkly Sequin Baubles

Try decorating these Christmas baubles in as many different ways as you can. You could use foil sweet (candy) wrappers and small artificial gemstones to create other sparkly effects.

YOU WILL NEED
- sparkly embroidery thread (floss) or wool (yarn)
- paper baubles (styrofoam balls)
- scissors
- PVA (white) glue
- paintbrush
- poster paints
- sequins
- glitter glue

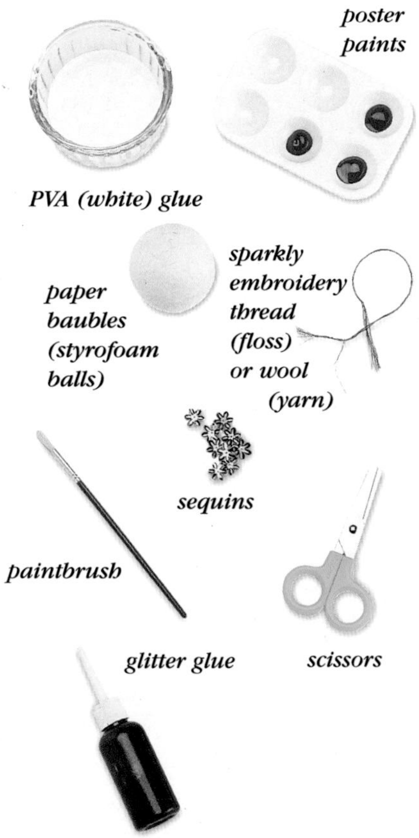

1 Cut a length of sparkly thread and fold it in half to make a loop. Glue the ends of the loop to the top of one of the paper baubles (styrofoam balls). Hold the thread in place with your hands until the glue has dried. Repeat for each of the paper baubles.

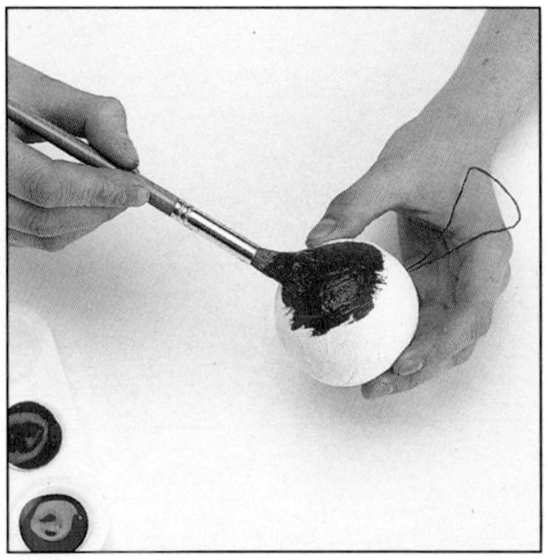

2 Paint the baubles with the poster paints. Red, purple and gold paints have been used here but you could use any colours you like. Hang the baubles up by the loops while the paint dries.

3 When the paint has dried, glue a few of the sequins on to each of the baubles. Allow the glue to dry.

4 Using the glitter glue, paint glitter dots in between the sequins and in the middle of the sequins. Leave to dry.

Pine Cone Mobile

Pine cones are lovely objects and they look great suspended from a mobile. The bars of this mobile are made from lengths of twig and the pine cones are tied at different heights. Pine cones are very much a part of winter, and you could paint your twigs and cones with gold or silver poster paint to make a Christmas mobile.

YOU WILL NEED
scissors
thin coloured cord
pine cones
2 thin twigs and 1 forked twig

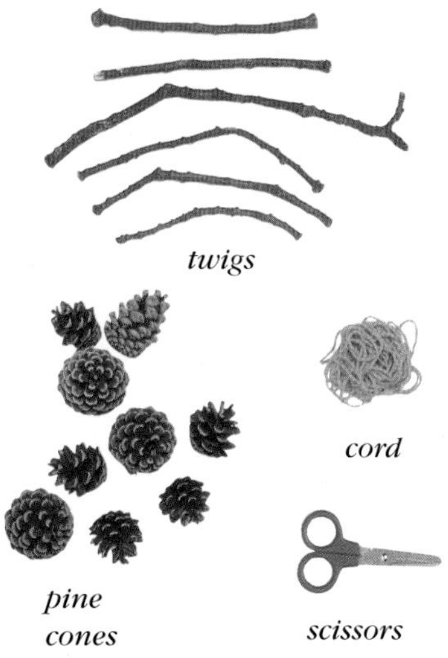

1 Cut lengths of cord and attach each one to the top of a cone. Tie a cone to both ends of two short twigs.

2 Tie the two twigs together with the cord, one above the other, to make the mobile shape.

3 Tie more small pine cones to the llower section of the mobile. Hang them at different heights.

4 Tie a large forked twig to the upper twig. Wrap the two together tightly by winding cord around them. Tie a length of cord to the top of the mobile to make a hanger.

Dove Decoration

These doves look very elegant. You could enlarge the template on a photocopier to make lots of different sized doves to hang on your tree.

YOU WILL NEED
pencil
coloured cardboard
scissors
coloured paper
gold pen
single hole punch
ribbon

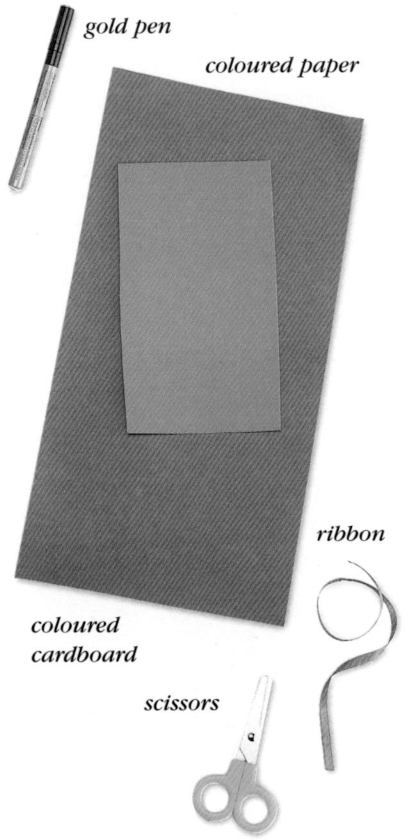

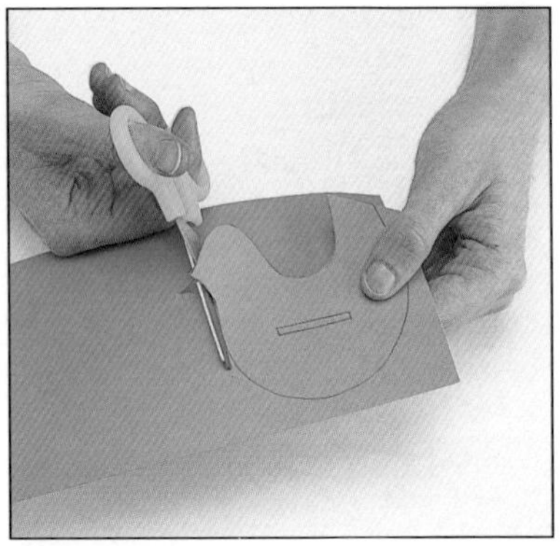

1 Trace the template for the dove's body from this book and cut it out. Draw around the template on to a piece of coloured cardboard. Ask an adult to help you make a slit in the dove's body where the wings will go. Cut out the dove shape.

2 Cut out a rectangle of coloured paper and fold it into a paper fan by turning it over each time you make a fold. This will make the dove's wings.

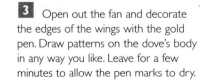

3 Open out the fan and decorate the edges of the wings with the gold pen. Draw patterns on the dove's body in any way you like. Leave for a few minutes to allow the pen marks to dry.

4 Fold up the fan and pass it through the slit in the dove. Open out the two ends so that they meet above the dove. Hold the two sides of the fan together and punch a hole through the paper. Thread a piece of ribbon through the hole and tie in a knot.

Christmas Pom-poms

These fluffy pom-poms look great hung all over a Christmas tree. They make good use of all your odds and ends of wool (yarn). Use some strands of metallic wool for a gleaming touch.

You will need
pencil
cardboard
scissors
wool (yarn) in various colours

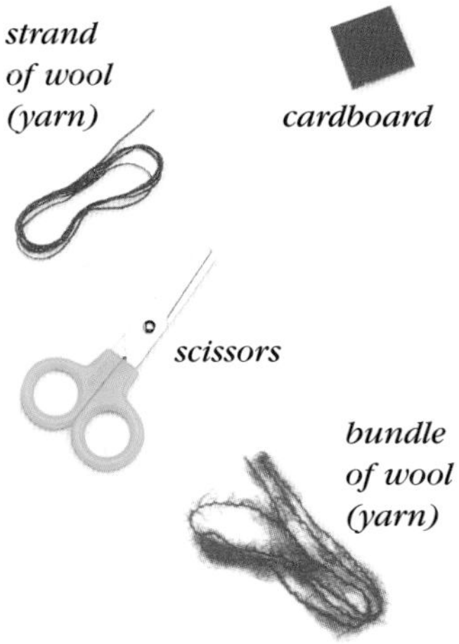

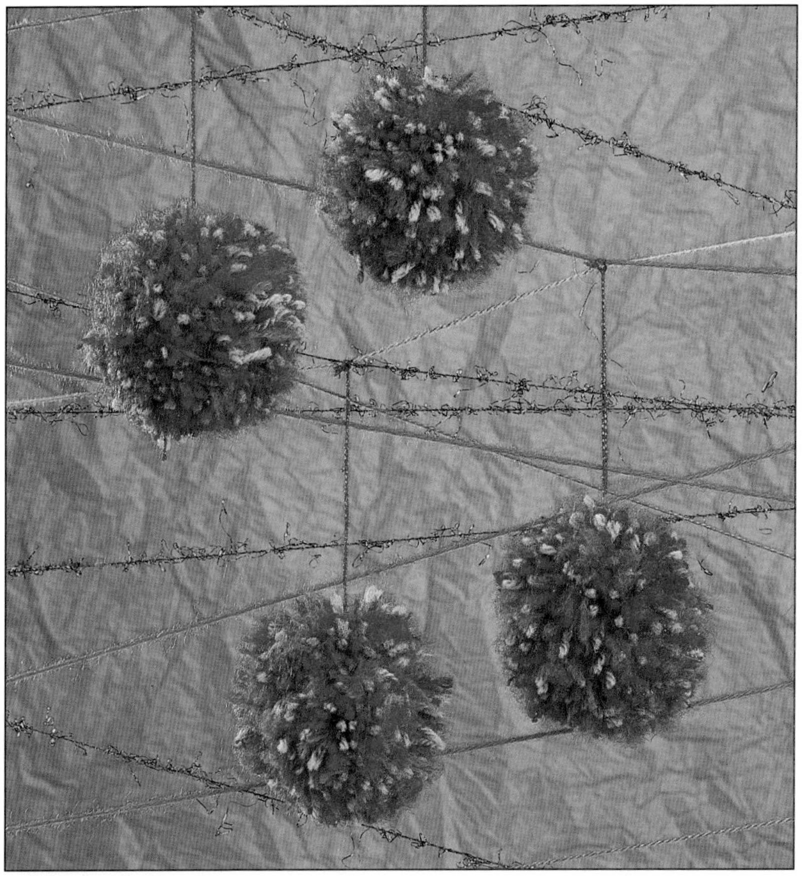

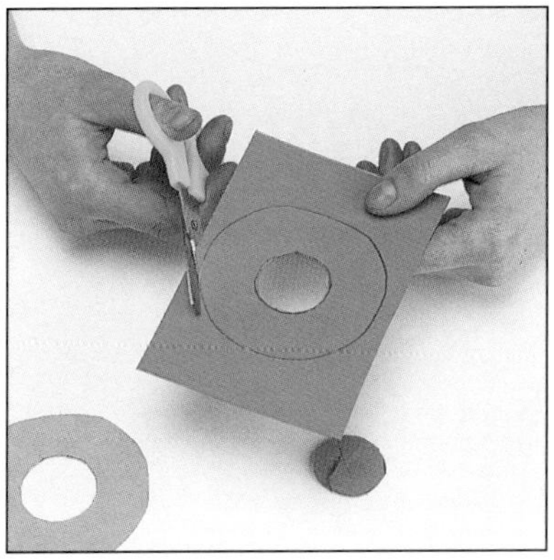

1 Trace the templates from this book and cut them out. Using the templates, draw two circles on cardboard exactly the same size, with one smaller circle in the centre of each. Cut out the circles.

2 Place the two pieces of cardboard together. Tie the end of the wool (yarn) bundle in a knot around the cardboard and thread the wool through the hole. Wrap around the whole circle until the centre hole is almost full. Tuck the ends of the wool in to stop them unravelling.

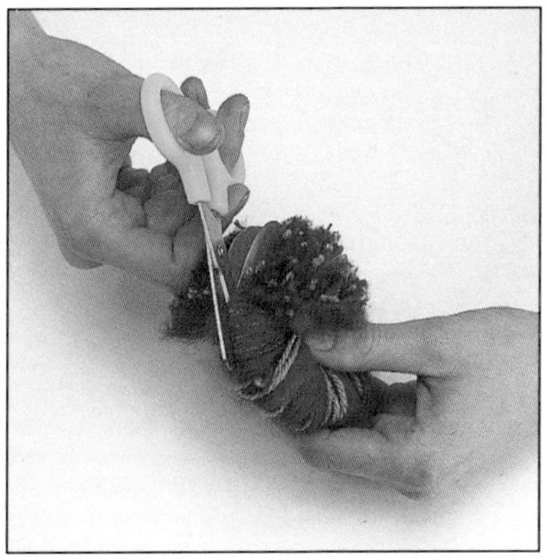

3 Place one blade of the scissors in between the two pieces of cardboard and carefully cut around the circle, snipping the wool as you go.

4 Wrap a long strand of wool in between the two pieces of cardboard and tie in a knot. Tear off the pieces of cardboard and throw them away. Fluff up the pom-pom and trim any loose ends with a pair of scissors.

Angel Tree Decoration

This decoration will add a beautiful finishing touch to your Christmas tree. If you don't have a tree, place the angel somewhere special, where everyone can see her.

YOU WILL NEED
thin white cardboard
double-sided sticky tape
scissors
silver paper doily
PVA (white) glue
pencil
gold cardboard
small cake candle
paper bauble (styrofoam ball)
paintbrush
poster paints in various colours
yellow wool (yarn)

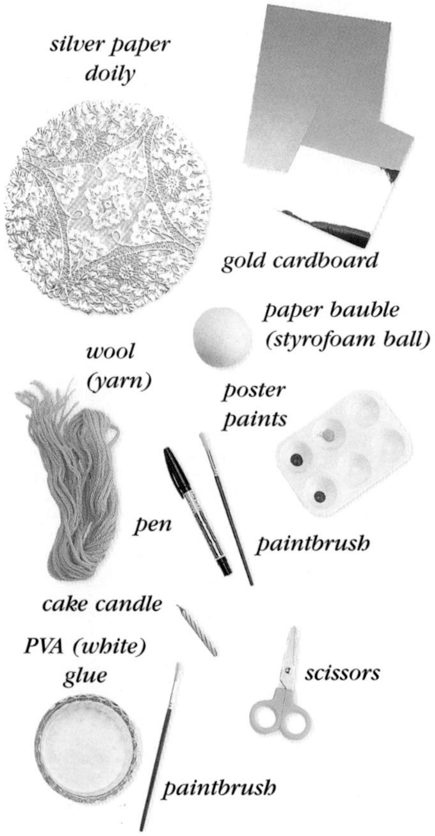

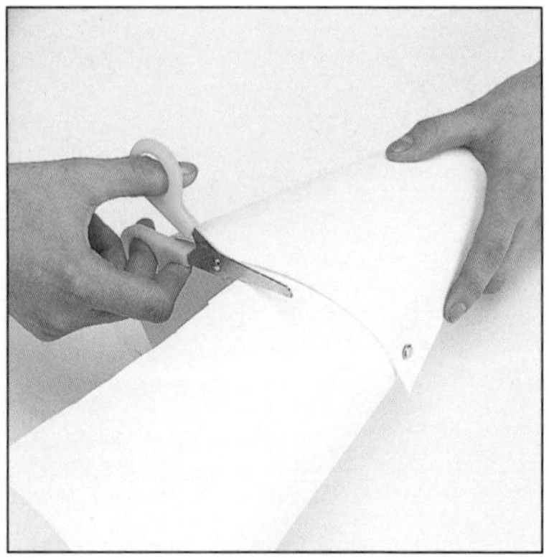

1 Make a cone shape from the thin white cardboard. Stick a strip of double-sided sticky tape under one of the edges, peel off the backing tape and stick it in place. The cone shape will make the body of the angel.

2 Cut a doily to fit around the cone shape and glue it in place. Leave to dry. Trace the templates for the arms, wings and halo and cut them out.

3 For the wings and halo, draw around the templates on gold cardboard. For the arms and hands, draw around the templates on white cardboard. Draw in the fingers yourself with a pencil.

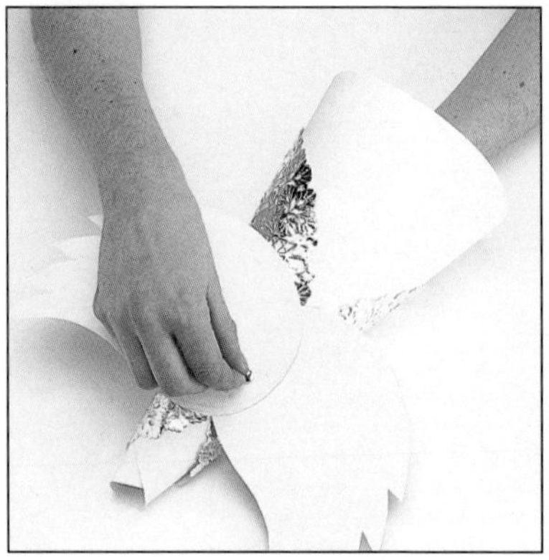

4 When you have cut out the shapes, glue the arms and wings on to the angel's body. Allow the glue to dry. Slot a small cake candle between the angel's hands.

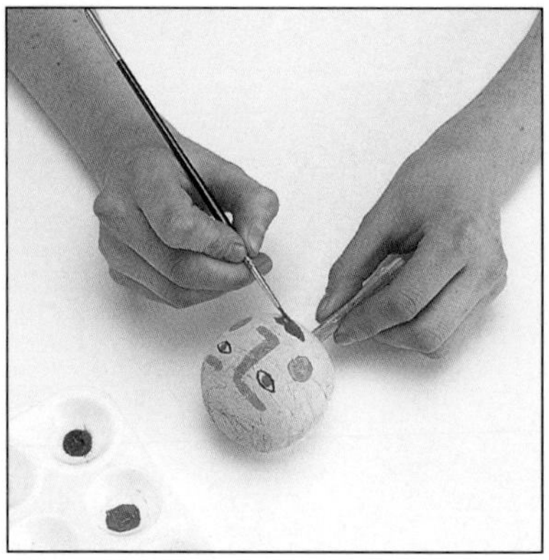

5 Ask an adult to help you stick a pencil into the paper bauble (styrofoam ball). Paint the angel's eyes, nose and mouth on the paper bauble. Leave aside for a few minutes to let the paint dry.

6 Cut about twelve strands of yellow wool (yarn) the same length and glue them to the top of the angel's head as hair. Glue the gold halo to the back of the angel's head. Attach the angel's head to her body.

Gift-wrap Advent Calendar

Instead of buying an Advent calendar this year, why not make your own, using last year's Christmas cards and a sheet of gift-wrap?

YOU WILL NEED
- sheet of gift-wrap
- ruler
- pencil
- scissors
- assorted Christmas cards
- PVA (white) glue
- number transfers
- ribbon
- backing cardboard, cut to the same size as the gift-wrap

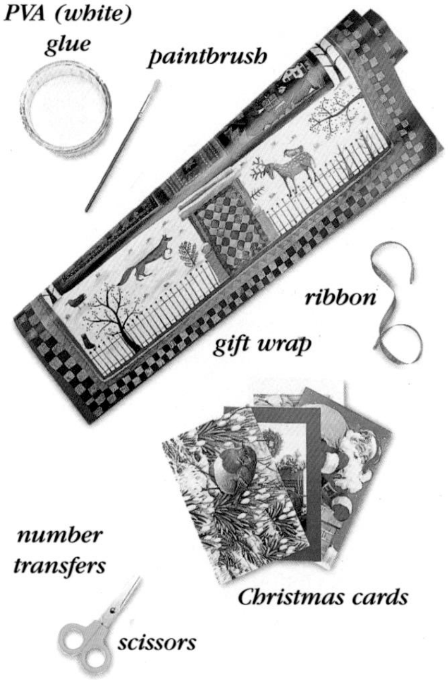

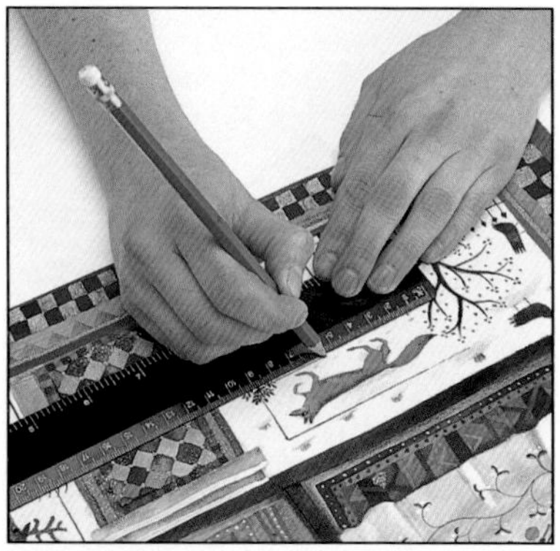

1 Carefully mark each of the twenty-four doors on the gift-wrap, using a ruler and pencil. Try to choose pretty areas of the gift-wrap for the positions of the doors. You can make the doors different sizes if you like.

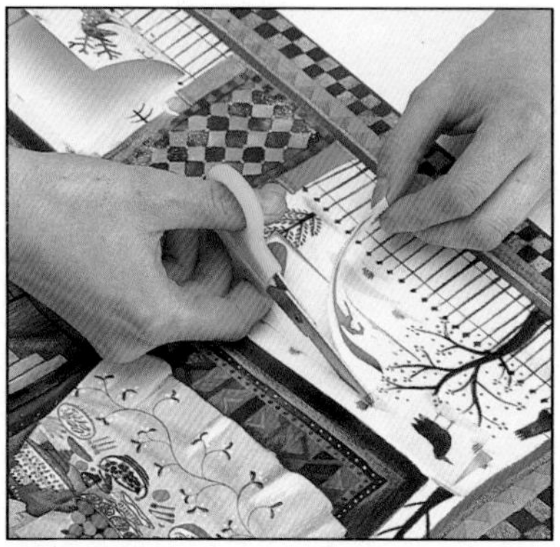

2 Cut out three sides of each door, leaving one side as a hinge so that you can open and shut the door easily.

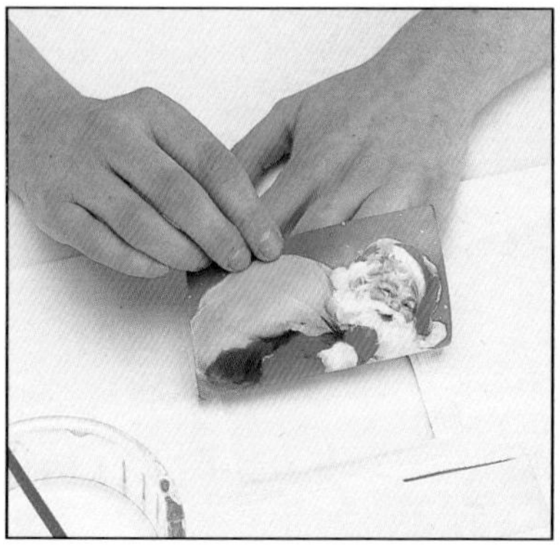

3 Cut out the pictures from some old Christmas cards and glue one picture behind each door. Leave for a few minutes to let the glue dry.

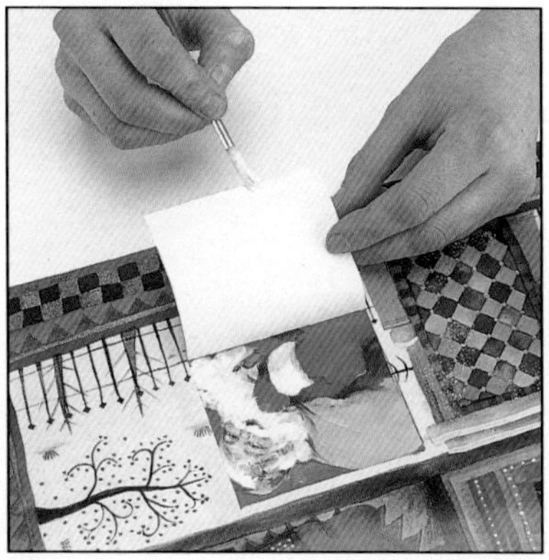

4 Dab a small amount of glue along one edge of each door and close them.

5 Using the number transfers and a pencil, rub a number between one and twenty-four on each door.

6 Cut a piece of ribbon and fold it in half to make a hanging loop. Glue the ends of the loop behind the top edge of the paper. Glue the backing cardboard to the reverse side of the calendar.

15
20
12
13
23
14
7
2
6
4
18
19
17
16
8
3
9
1
5
10
21

Christmas Cottage

You could fill this yuletide cottage with a small gift of tasty homemade fudge or Christmas cookies.

YOU WILL NEED
pencil
scissors
coloured paper
ruler
double-sided sticky tape
paintbrush
poster paints in various colours
PVA (white) glue
silver glitter

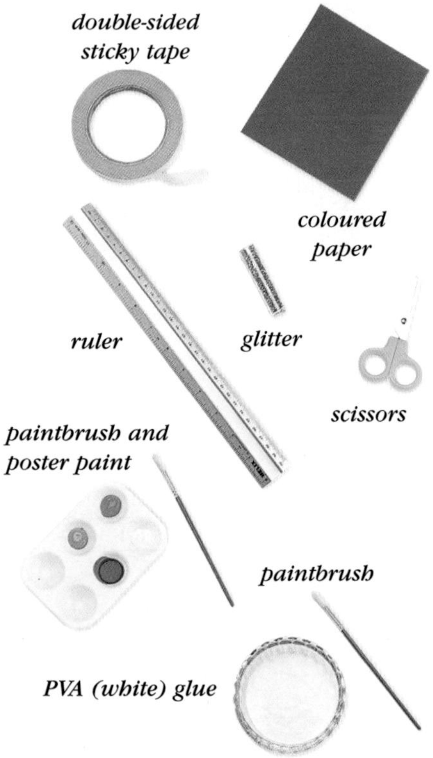

1 Trace the templates for the cottage and chimney and cut them out. Draw around the templates on coloured paper, and lightly mark out the lines of the cottage with a pencil. Use the blunt edge of a pair of scissors to score along the lines. Using a ruler to guide the scissors helps to keep the lines straight.

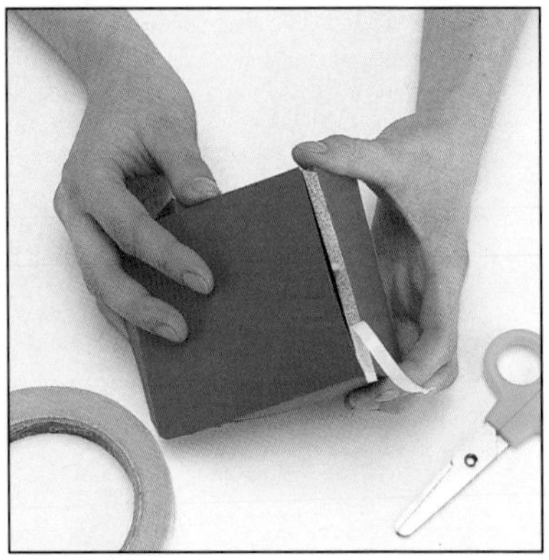

2 Make folds along the scored lines of the cottage and fold into a box. Place a small piece of double-sided sticky tape along the edges of the four tabs, peel away the backing and stick down firmly. Fold down the roof. Cut the chimney shape out of the paper.

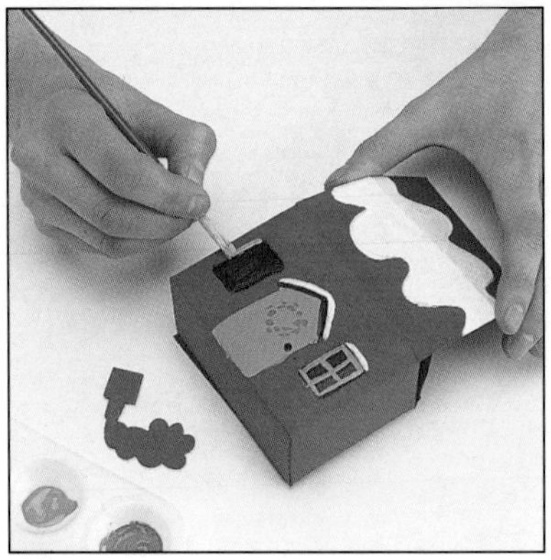

3 Paint on the door and windows and allow the paint to dry. Paint a festive holly wreath on to the front door. Allow the paint to dry. Glue the chimney pot on the roof and allow the glue to dry.

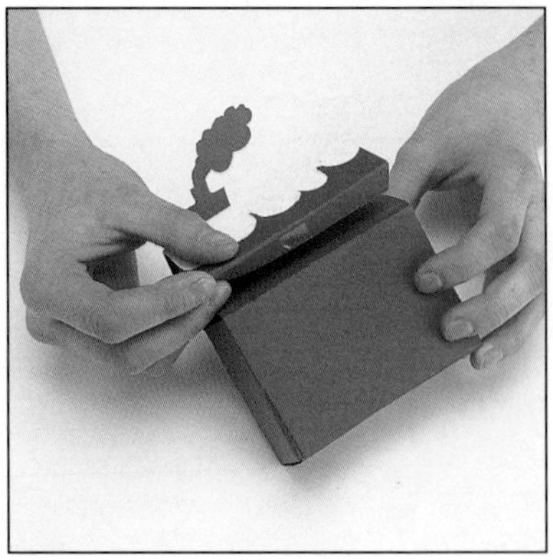

4 Stick the roof down with double-sided tape, so that you can open and close the roof. To finish the cottage, glue a line of glitter on the roof to look like a sprinkling of sparkling snow.

Rudolph the Red-Nosed Reindeer Paper Chains

These festive-looking reindeer will look great hung on a wall or around a window. Why not paint each one differently and give them funny faces?

YOU WILL NEED
pencil
coloured paper
scissors
paintbrush
poster paints in various colours
hole punch
paper fasteners

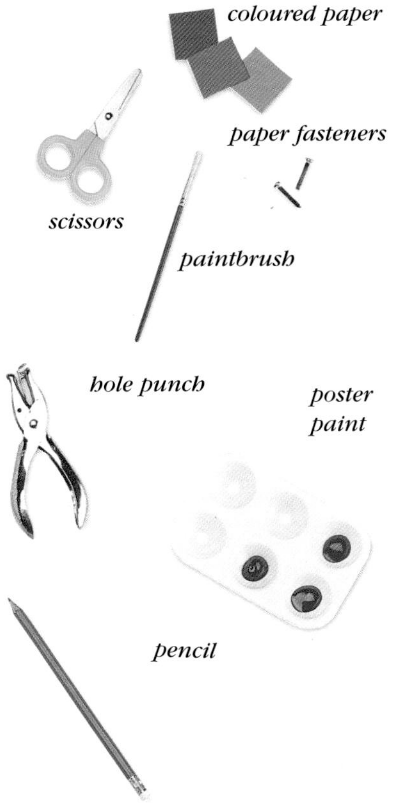

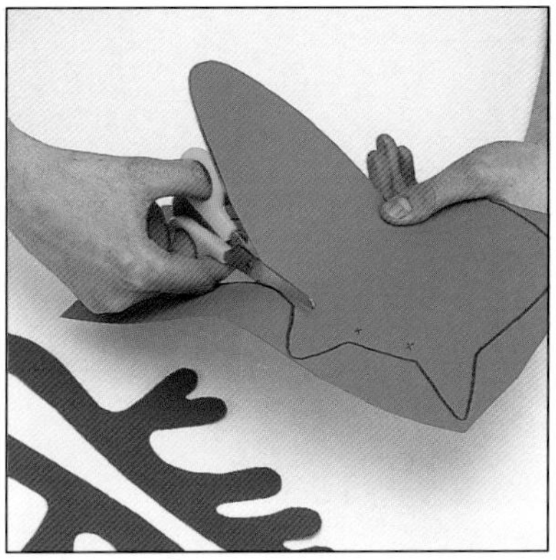

1 Draw three reindeer head shapes on the coloured paper and cut them out. Draw shapes for the reindeers' antlers and noses and cut them out. For each of the reindeer you will need two antlers, a head and a nose.

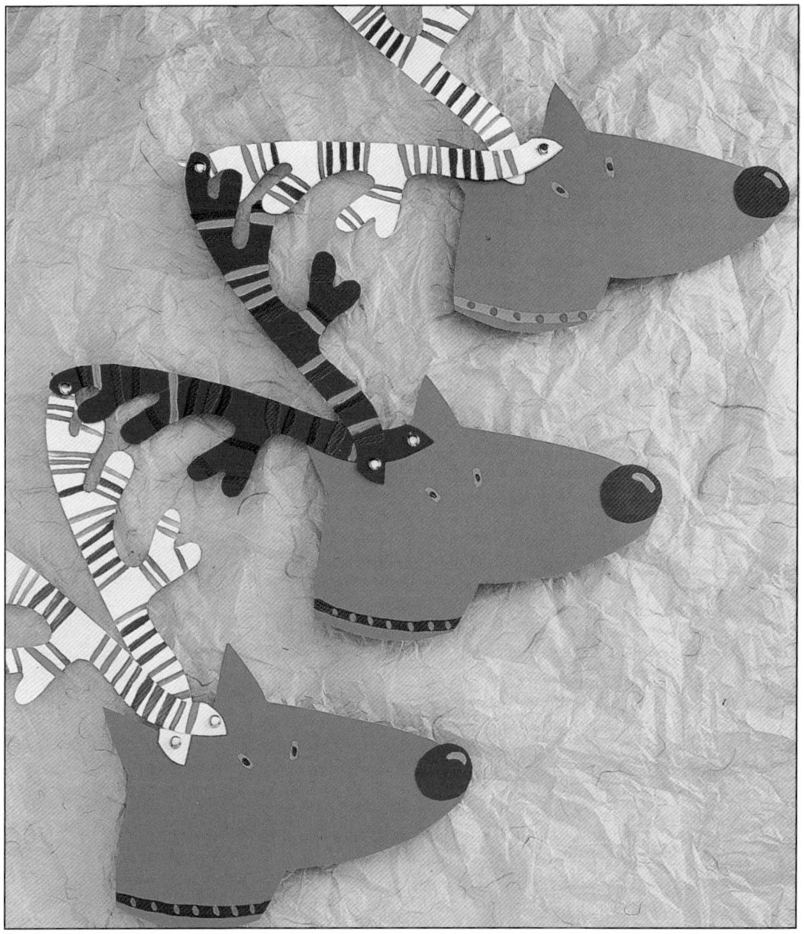

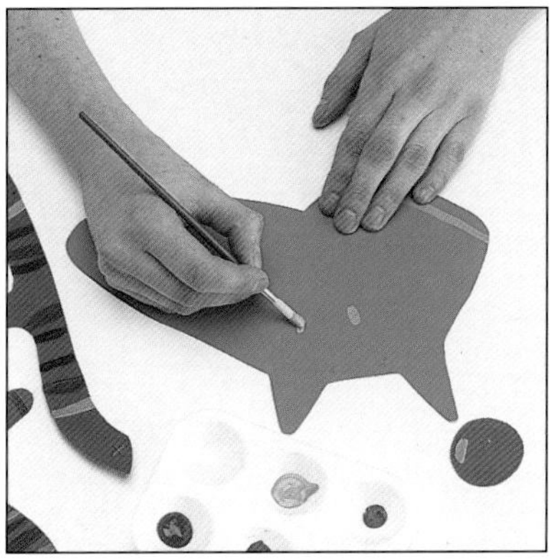

2 Paint in the details for the reindeers' faces and add patterns on the shapes if you like. Let the paint dry.

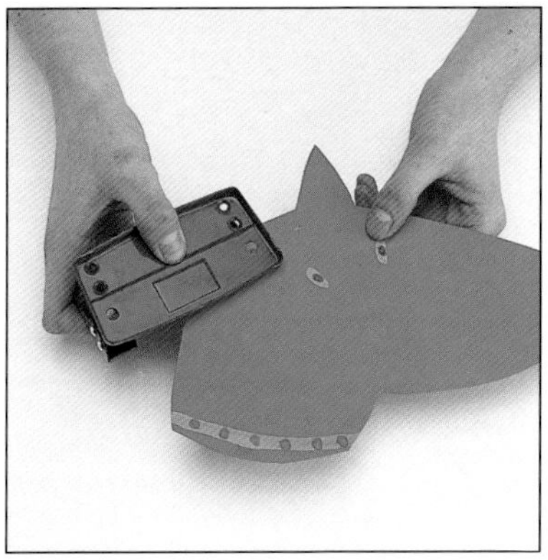

3 Mark two points between the reindeers' ears with a pencil. Punch through the marks with a hole punch.

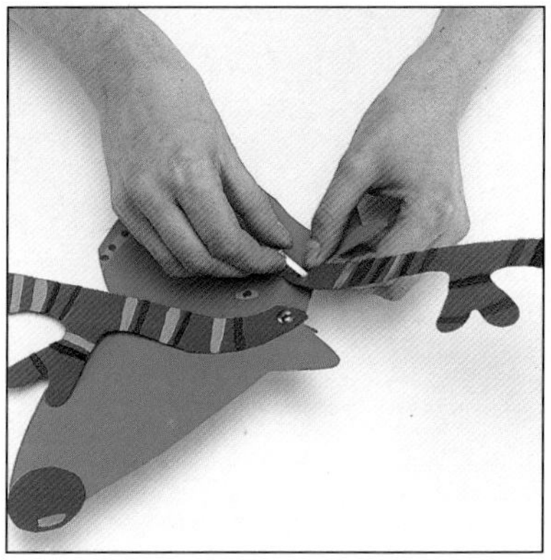

4 Thread a paper fastener through the holes and join the antlers together to make the reindeer chain. Open out the paper fasteners so that they lie flat.

Tin Heart and Star Tree Decorations

Watch these decorations dazzle on your Christmas tree or hang them up by a window to catch the light. You can buy sheets of metallic foil from specialist craft shops.

YOU WILL NEED
pencil
scissors
ballpoint pen
sheets of metallic foil in various colours
ruler
single hole punch
ribbon

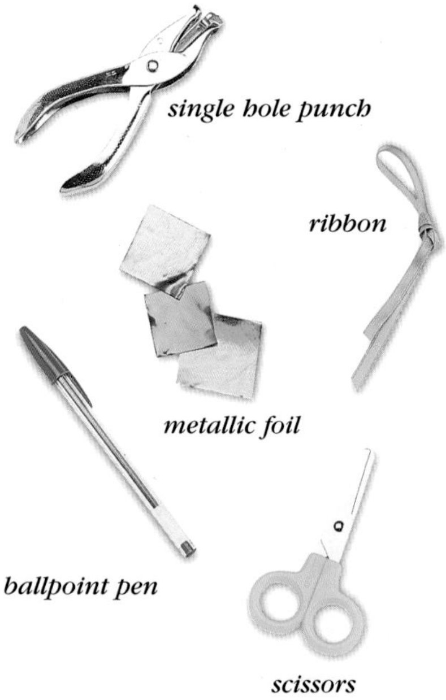

1 Trace the templates from this book and cut them out with a pair of scissors. Using a ballpoint pen, draw around the templates on the reverse of the pieces of metallic foil.

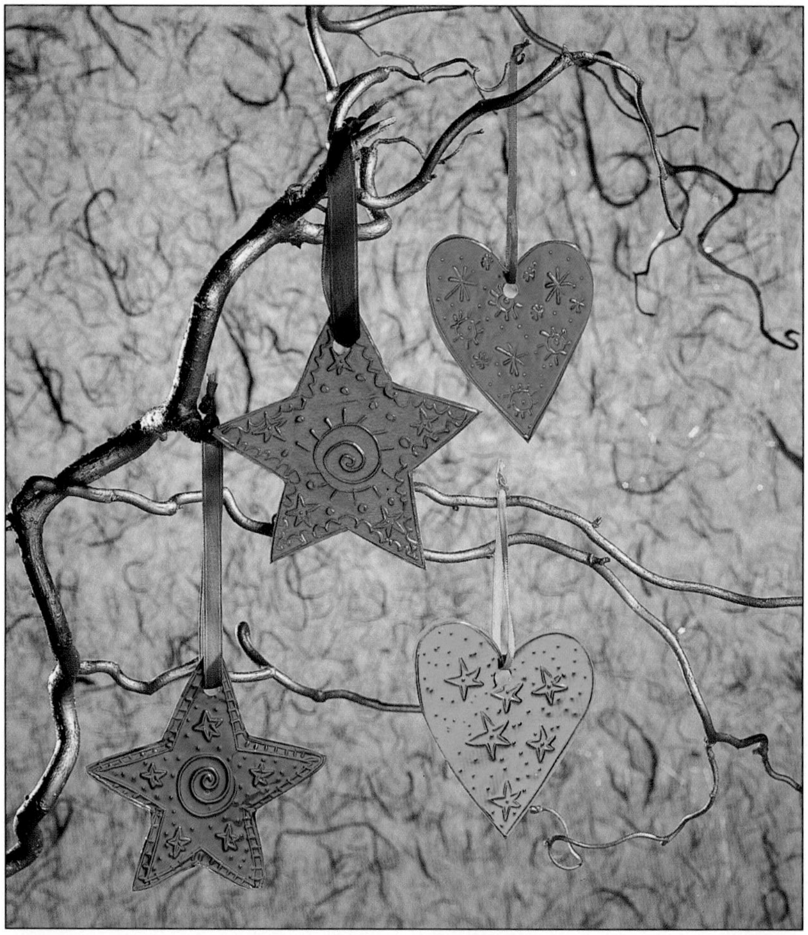

2 Using the ballpoint pen, draw lots of swirly and polka-dot patterns on the reverse side of the metallic foil.

3 Cut out the shapes approximately 3 mm (⅛ in) from the edge of the drawn line. Save any leftover foil for using in other craft projects.

4 Using a single hole punch, punch a hole in each of the decorated shapes and thread a piece of ribbon through. Tie the ends of the ribbon in a knot to make a hanging loop.

Mini Tree Stockings

These cute Christmas stockings add a festive touch to a Christmas tree. Pop a few small gifts or a couple of red and white striped candy canes inside, to make them even more appealing.

YOU WILL NEED
felt-tip pen
scissors
sheets of felt in various colours
PVA (white) glue
paintbrush
needle
sewing thread
ribbon
small bell

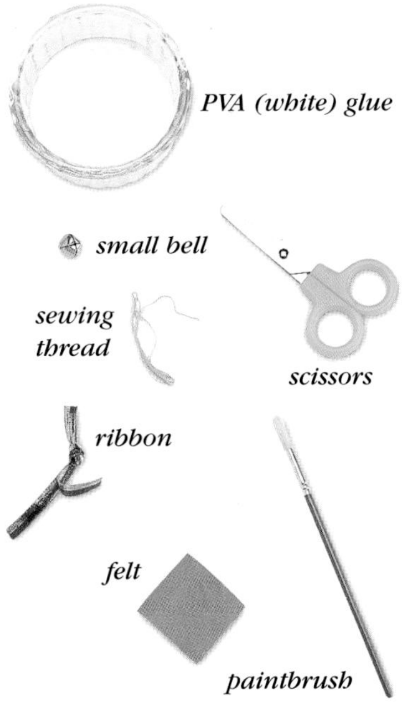

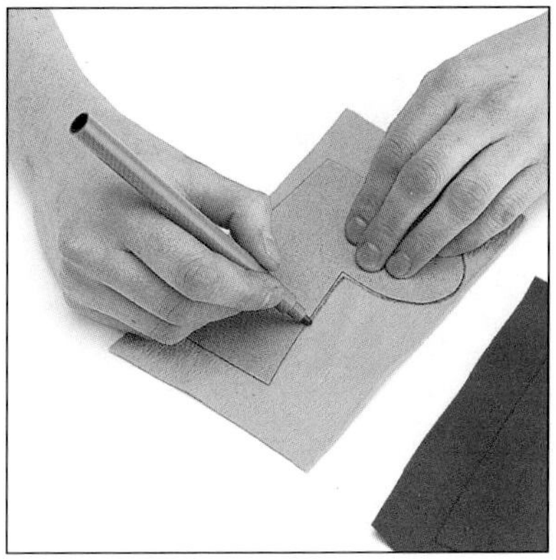

1 Trace the mini stocking template from this book and cut it out with a pair of scissors. Draw around the template on two different coloured pieces of felt. Draw some stars and dots on different coloured pieces of felt to be added to the stocking as decoration.

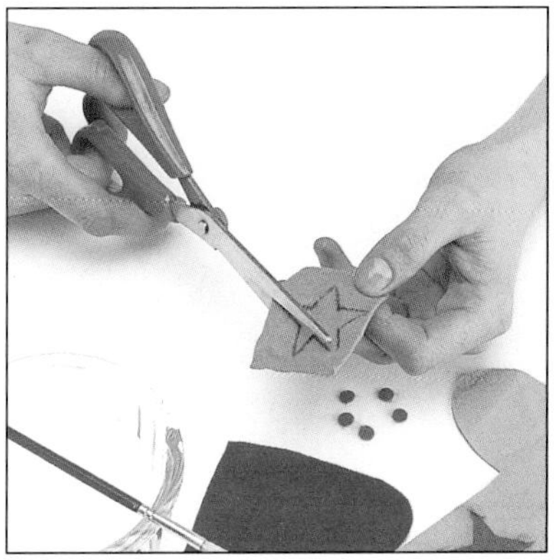

2 Cut out the stars and dots and position them on one side of the stocking. When you are happy with the positions, glue them on to the stocking and leave the glue to dry.

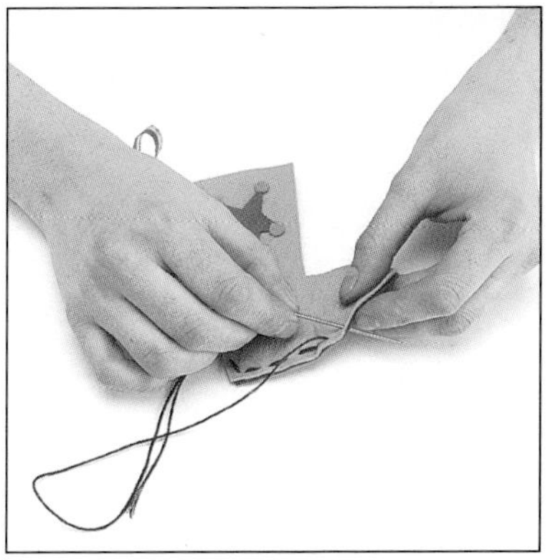

3 Sew the two shapes together, around the edge, to make the stocking. Fold a piece of ribbon in half to make a hanging loop and sew it into the side of the stocking.

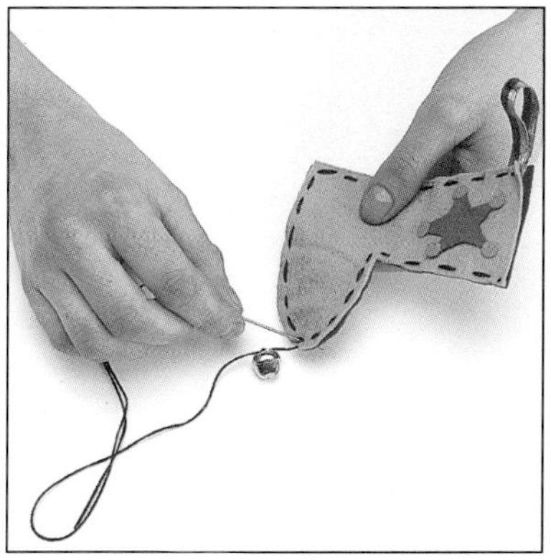

4 Sew the bell on to the toe of the stocking. Gently shake the stocking to hear the bell make a jingling sound.

Snowstorm Shaker

Carefully shake the jam jar and watch the glitter snow twinkle! If you enjoy making this project you could make other snow jars, such as a Santa Claus or a Christmas tree.

YOU WILL NEED
modelling clay in various colours, including white
jam jar with a tight-fitting lid
cold water
silver glitter

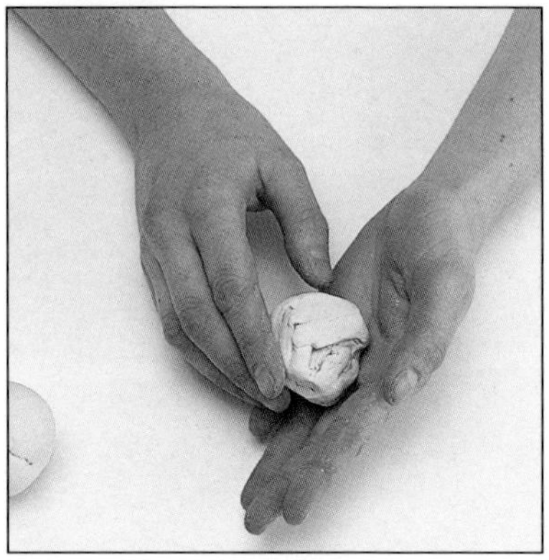

1 To make the snowman's head and body, roll two balls of white modelling clay in your hands. Make the ball for the snowman's body slightly bigger than the one for his head. Stick the smaller ball on top of the larger ball.

2 Make the snowman a hat and a scarf out of small pieces of different coloured modelling clay. Make him a carrot nose and a happy face.

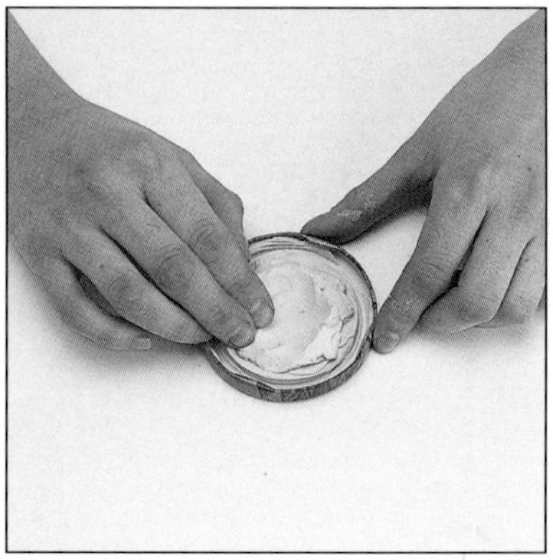

3 Make sure your jam jar is clean, with no greasy fingerprints on it! Fill the inside of the lid with another piece of white modelling clay.

4 Use your fingers to make a shallow hole in the modelling clay on the lid. Firmly position the snowman into the hole, making sure he feels secure.

5 Pour cold water into the jam jar so that it is three-quarters full. Sprinkle in at least one tablespoon of the glitter.

6 Carefully screw on the lid and slowly turn the jar upside down, so that your snowman is the right way up. Add a little more water if needed.

Christmas Crackers

Fill these fun crackers with a small gift. Write your own jokes on small pieces of paper and tuck them inside, too.

YOU WILL NEED
small gift and joke
tissue paper in various colours
cardboard toilet paper tube
PVA (white) glue
pinking shears
paper gift ribbon
pencil
scissors
coloured paper

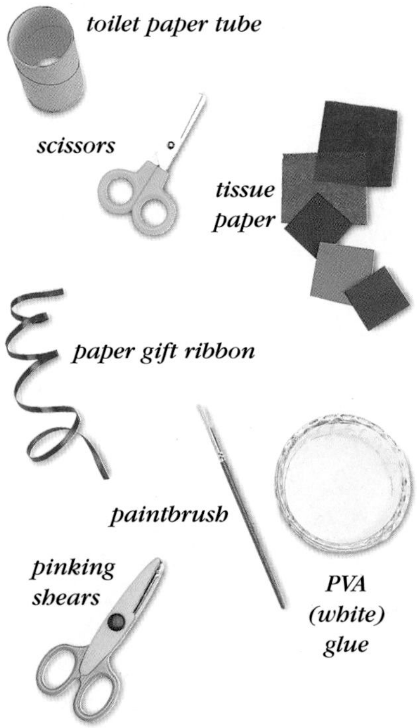

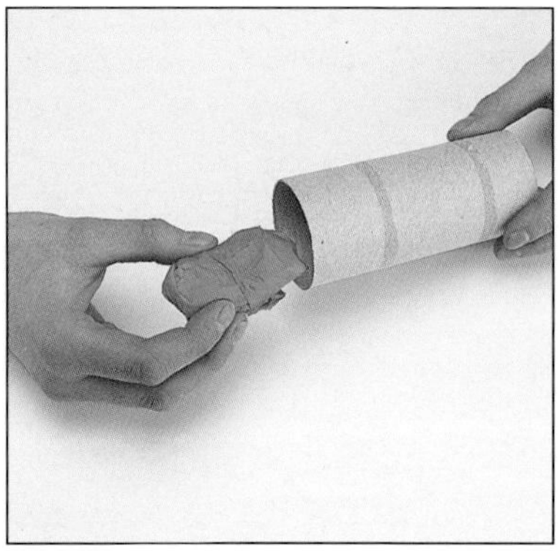

1 Neatly wrap the small gift in a piece of tissue paper and place it with your joke inside the toilet paper tube.

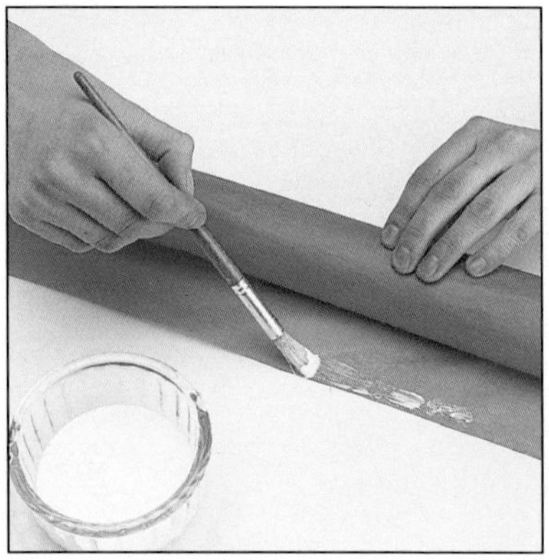

2 Cover the toilet paper tube with a large piece of tissue paper and glue the edges of the paper to hold it in place. Trim the ends with a pair of pinking shears for a decorative effect.

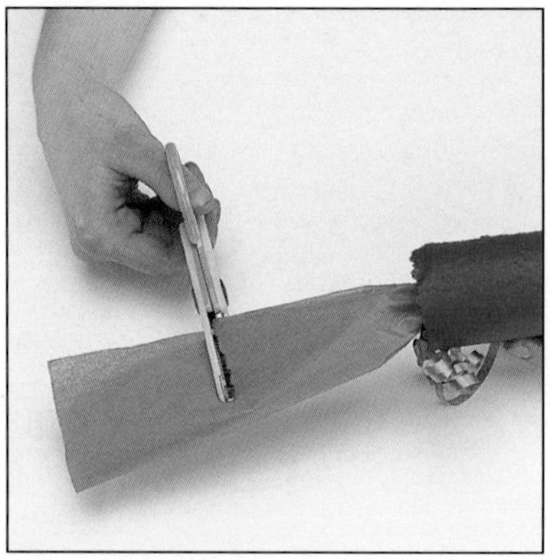

3 Glue a contrasting colour of tissue paper around the toilet paper tube. Tie a piece of ribbon around each end of the cracker. Pull along the length of the ribbon with a pencil to make it curl.

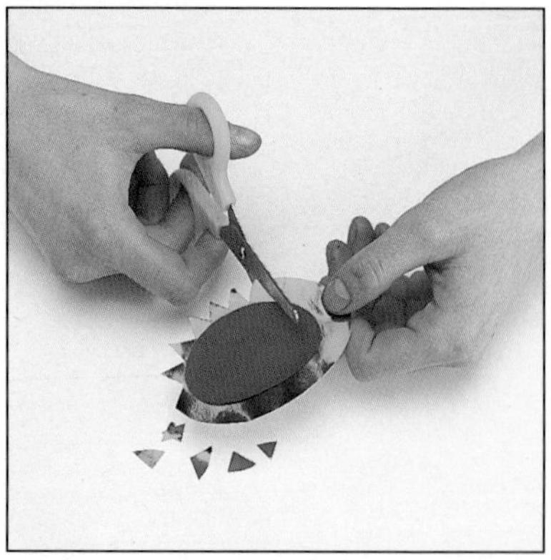

4 Using scissors or pinking shears, cut out a piece of paper in a fun shape. If you like, you can write the name of the person who will get the cracker on the paper. Glue the paper on to the cracker.

Party Paper Chains

Why not have a competition with your friends to see who can make the longest paper chain? Decorate your bedroom and use up leftover scraps of paper at the same time!

YOU WILL NEED
pencil
coloured paper
paintbrush
poster paints in various colours
glitter glue
scissors
PVA (white) glue

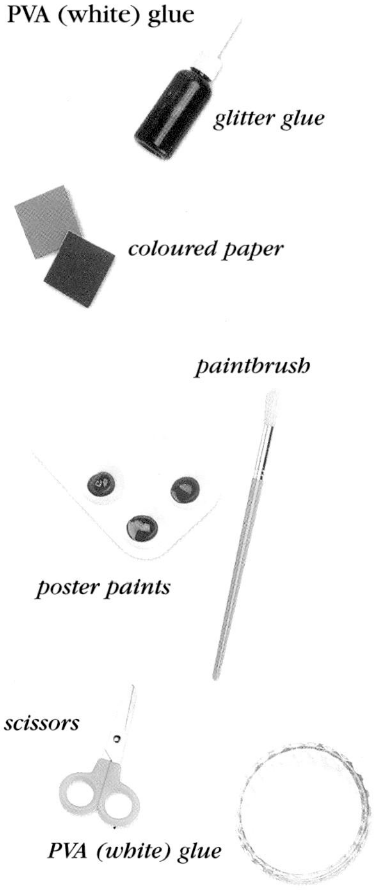

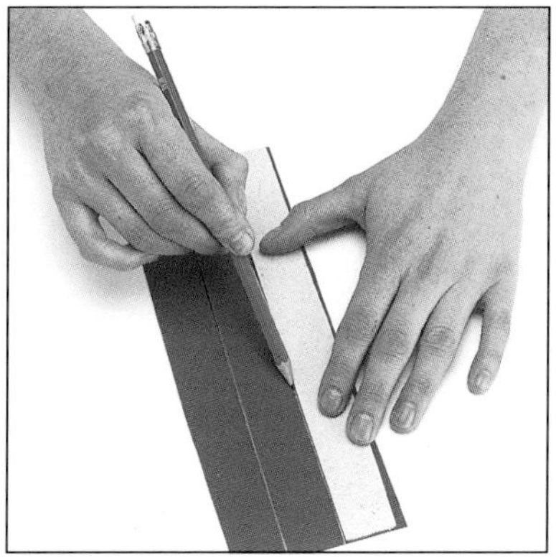

1 Make your own template for the paper chain, as long or as wide as you want. Draw around the template on a piece of coloured paper so that the strips are next to each other. Don't cut the strips out yet.

2 Paint your paper chain strips with lots of bright colours and fun swirls, stripes and dots. Allow the paint to dry.

3 If you like you can add a few dabs of glitter glue to the strips for extra sparkle. Allow the glitter to dry. Cut out all of the decorated strips of paper.

4 Curl the first strip of paper around so you can glue one end of the strip to the other. Hold it while the glue dries. Thread a second strip of paper through the first loop and glue the ends together. Continue until the chain is really long!

Felt Tree Calendar

This calendar is quick and easy to make and looks lovely hung on the wall. It will also make a very useful present, if you don't mind giving it away!

YOU WILL NEED
- felt-tip pen
- scissors
- felt squares in various colours
- fabric scissors
- PVA (white) glue
- paintbrush
- mirror tile sequins
- thin cardboard
- mini calendar
- ribbon

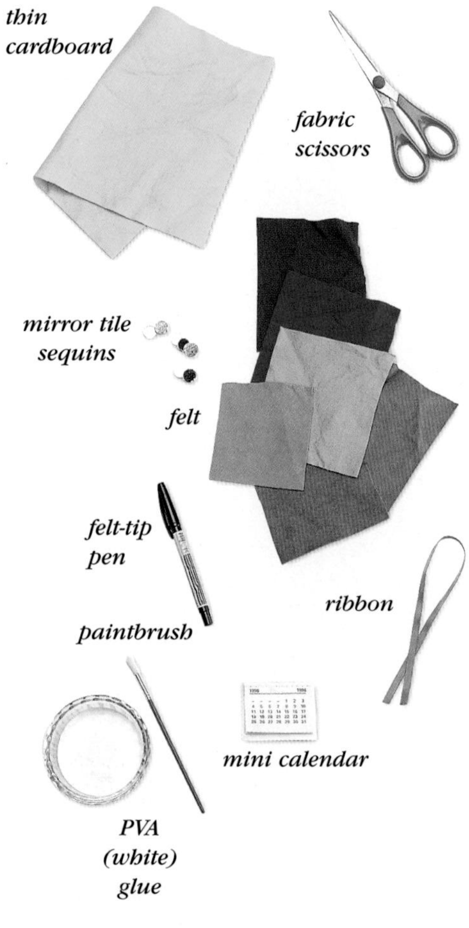

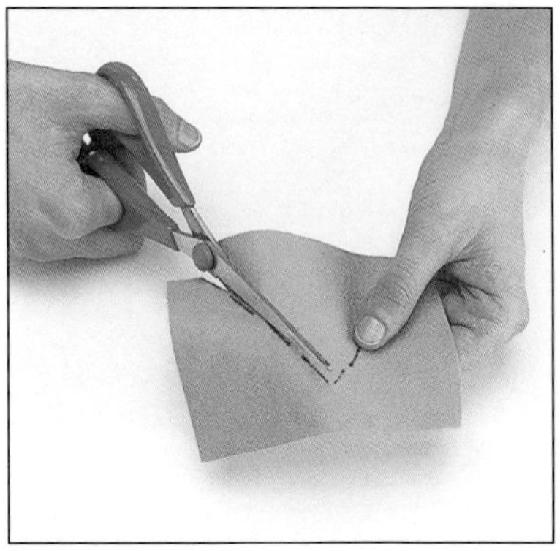

1 Trace the templates for the Christmas tree from this book and cut them out. Place the templates on the felt, draw around them and cut them out using fabric scissors. Save the leftover pieces of felt for other projects.

2 Using a pair of fabric scissors, snip a decorative fringe along the bottom edge of each section of the tree.

3 To make the background for your tree, cut out a large piece of felt. Glue on the fringed sections of felt to make the Christmas tree.

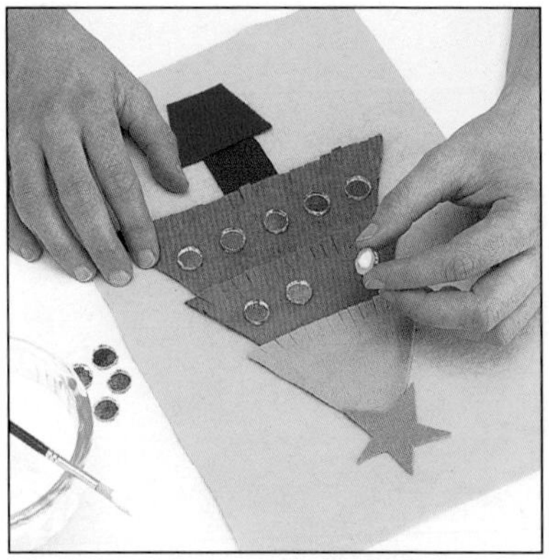

4 Glue a few mirror tile sequins on to each section of the Christmas tree to give it a bit of sparkle.

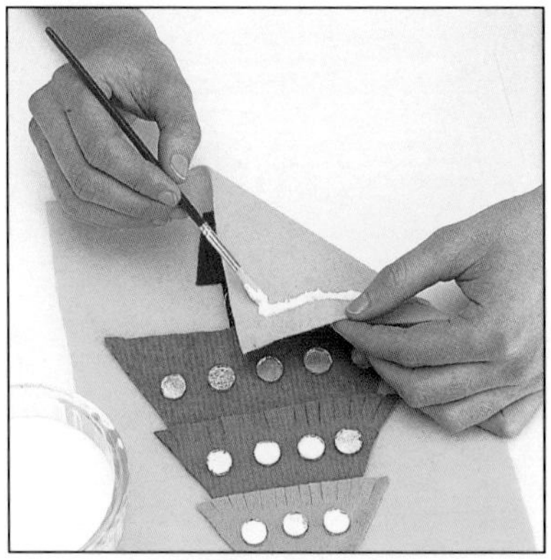

5 To make the background for your felt picture, cut out a piece of thin cardboard to the size you want. Glue the cardboard on the picture. Leave to dry.

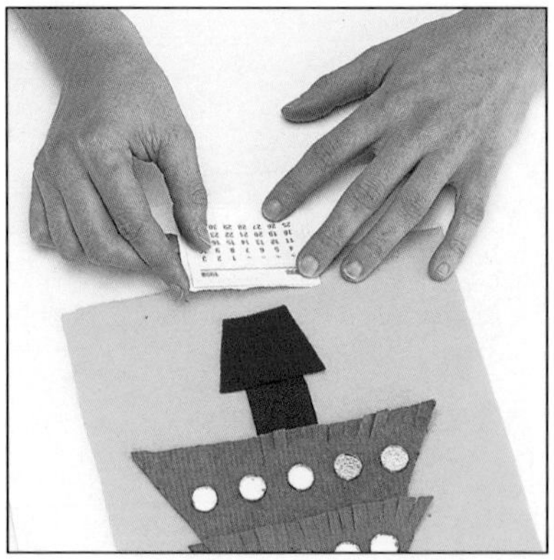

6 Glue the calendar underneath your picture. Fold a piece of ribbon in half to make a hanging loop and stick it on to the back of the cardboard at the top. Leave the glue to dry.

1998 1998
– – – – 1 2 3
4 5 6 7 8 9 10
11 12 13 14 15 16 17
18 19 20 21 22 23 24
25 26 27 28 29 30 31

Groovy Party Hats

Wearing one of these wacky hats at a Christmas party will definitely make you the envy of all of your friends.

YOU WILL NEED
- pencil
- scissors
- coloured cardboard
- paper fasteners
- coloured paper
- crêpe paper
- ribbon
- double-sided sticky tape
- PVA (white) glue
- paintbrush
- mini pom-poms or tinsel

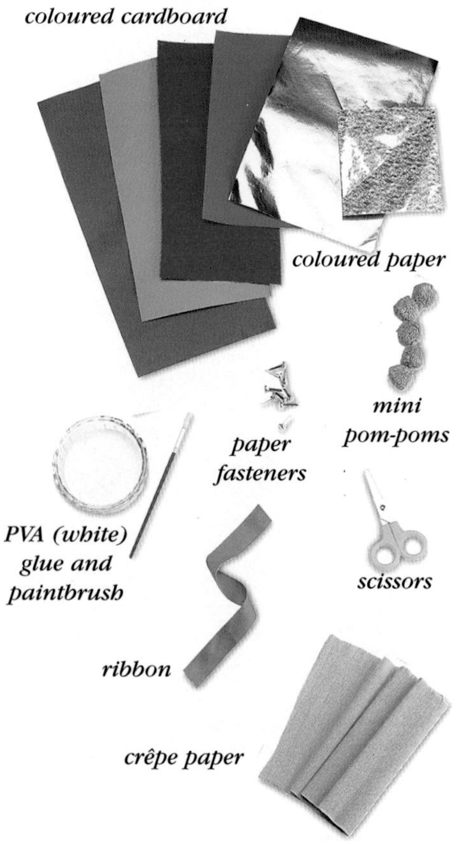

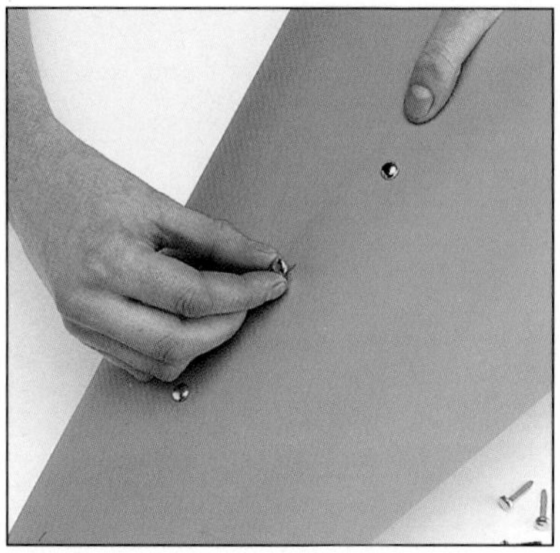

1 Trace the template for the party hat from this book, scale it up and cut it out. Draw around the template on a large piece of coloured cardboard. Cut out the hat shape and roll it into a cone. Hold the cone shape in place with the paper fasteners.

2 Cut out some circles from the coloured paper. You will need circles in two different sizes and a heart shape. Make other fun shapes, such as stars, if you like.

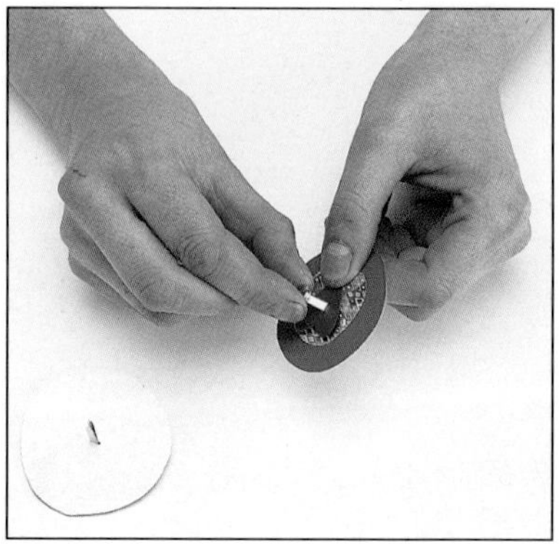

3 Starting with the large circle, place the smaller circle on top and then the heart. Pierce a paper fastener through the shapes. Make a small hole in the hat and place the paper fastener through it.

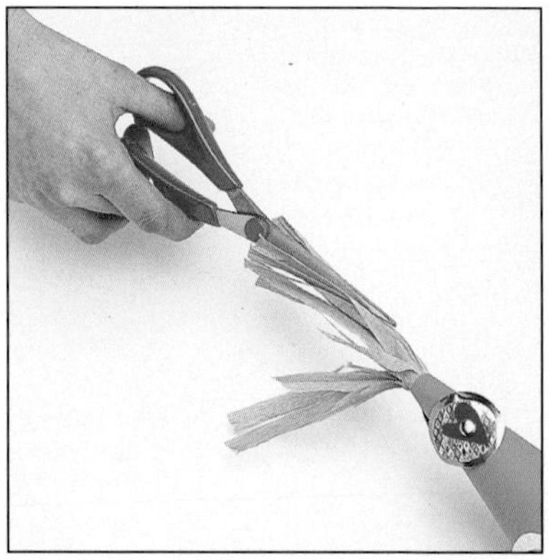

4 Open out the paper fastener so that it lies flat on the inside of the hat. Roll a piece of crêpe paper into a tight roll and place it in the top of the hat. Using a pair of scissors, snip into the top of the crêpe paper to turn it into a tassel.

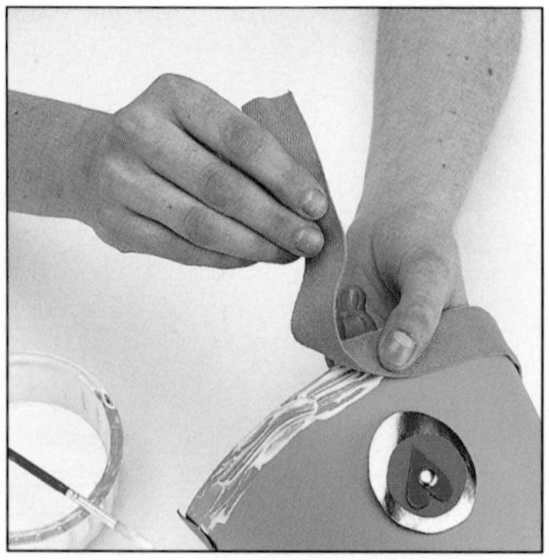

5 Measure around the base of the hat and cut a length of ribbon long enough to go around it. Using a strip of double-sided sticky tape or glue, stick the ribbon around the base of the hat.

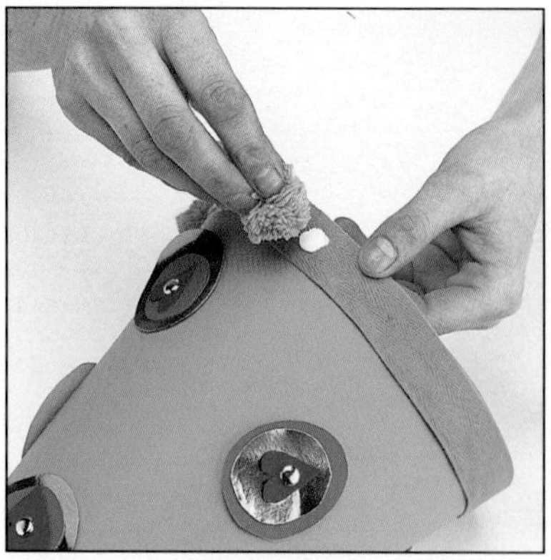

6 Glue mini pom-poms or tinsel on to the ribbon around the base of the hat. Allow the glue to dry completely before trying on your new hat.

Glittery Gift Boxes

These spectacular little gift boxes look very impressive, but are very simple to make.

YOU WILL NEED
- pencil
- small paper bauble (styrofoam ball)
- paintbrush
- poster paints in various colours
- fabric scissors
- squares of felt in red and green
- PVA (white) glue
- small cardboard boxes
- glitter in various colours
- mini pom-poms
- small glass beads in various colours

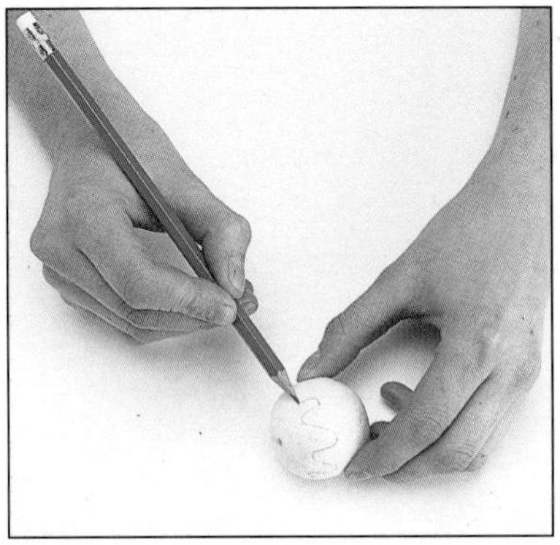

1 Using a pencil, lightly draw the outline of whipped cream on a Christmas pudding (cake) on to the paper bauble (styrofoam ball).

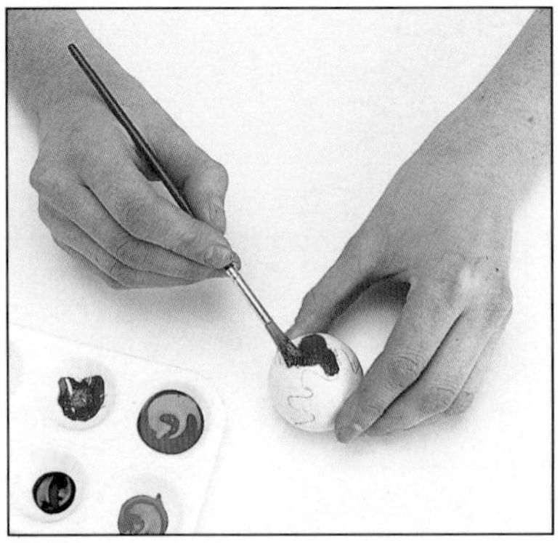

2 Paint the base of the pudding brown and allow the paint to dry. Paint small black raisins on the brown paint to make your pudding look tasty! Leave the paint to dry.

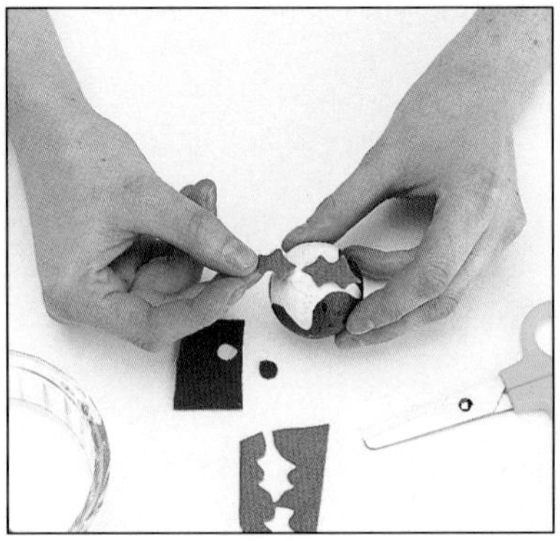

3 Use fabric scissors to cut out two mini holly leaves from a piece of green felt, then cut two small circles of red felt for the berries. Using just a tiny dot of glue, glue the holly leaves and berries on to the top of the painted pudding.

4 Glue the Christmas pudding on to the lid of the gift box. Allow the glue to dry completely.

5 Using a glue brush, paint glue all around the pudding and sprinkle on the glitter. Lightly tap the lid on a work surface to remove any excess glitter.

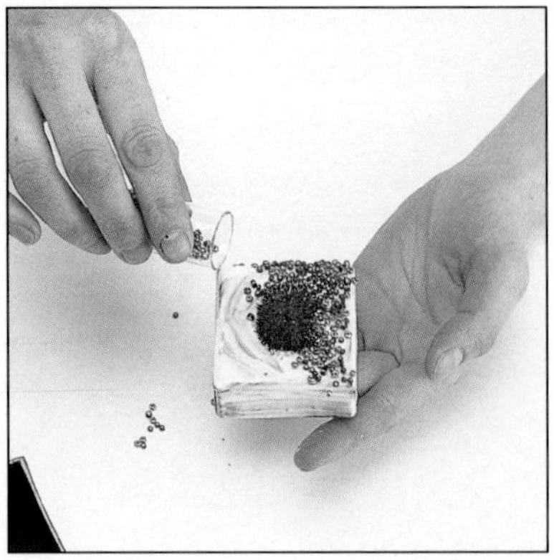

6 Another fun way to decorate a gift box is to glue a mini pom-pom on to the lid, then paint on glue around the pom-pom and sprinkle small glass beads all over it for a sparkly effect.

Winter Wonderland

This little tree scene is really magical and makes a beautiful table decoration. You can enjoy watching the trees twinkle in the light.

YOU WILL NEED
pine cone
cork
strong glue
acrylic paint in various colours
paintbrush
PVA (white) glue
glitter in various colours
coloured cardboard
scissors
small cardboard box

1 Make sure your pine cone is clean and dry. Glue the base of the pine cone on to the top of a cork using strong glue. Firmly hold the cone and the cork together for a few minutes until the glue has dried completely.

2 When the glue is dry, hold the cork in your hand and gently paint the pine cone. Stand the cork upright to allow the paint on the cone to dry.

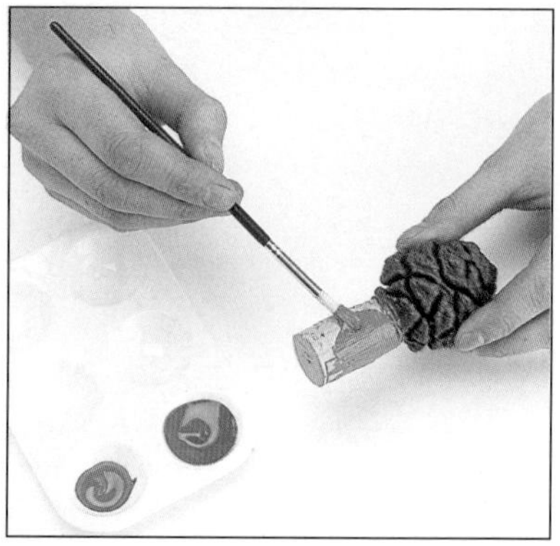

3 Paint the cork in a different colour, holding the pine cone. Allow the paint to dry.

4 Using a glue brush, paint PVA (white) glue all over the pine cone.

5 Sprinkle glitter over the cone and then tap the cork to remove the excess glitter. Cut a small star out of cardboard and glue it to the top of the cone.

6 Decorate a small gift box by gluing the glittery pine cone tree on to the lid.

Paper-clip Christmas Decorations

These shiny Christmas decorations will add a sparkle to your Christmas tree. Decorate them with scraps of bright foil from sweet wrappers, and sandwich paper clips between them to make the decorations look like icicles.

YOU WILL NEED
pencil
pair of compasses
thin card (posterboard)
scissors
silver foil
coloured foil
strong, non-toxic glue
silver paper clips
thin silver elastic

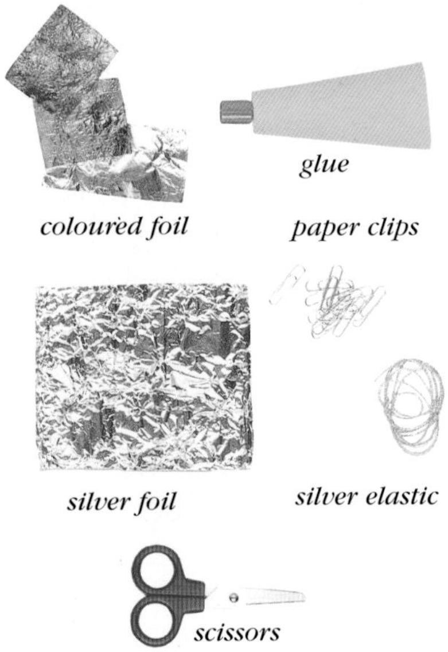

1 Using a pencil and a pair of compasses, draw two circles exactly the same size on the card (posterboard), and then cut them out.

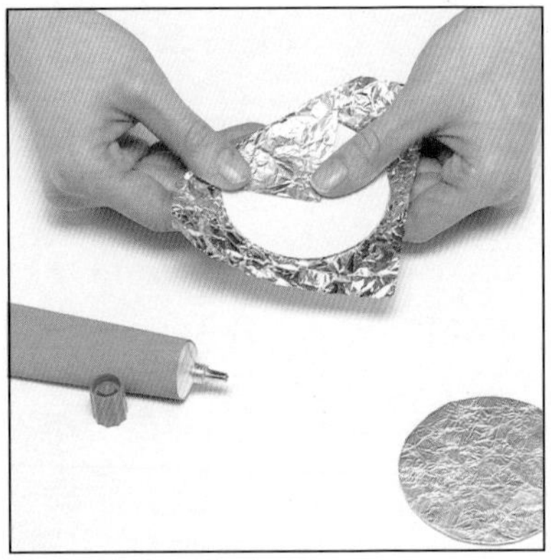

2 Cut two squares of silver foil about 4 cm (1½ in) bigger all the way around than the circles of card. Place a circle in the middle of each piece of foil. Wrap the edges of the silver foil over the card (posterboard).

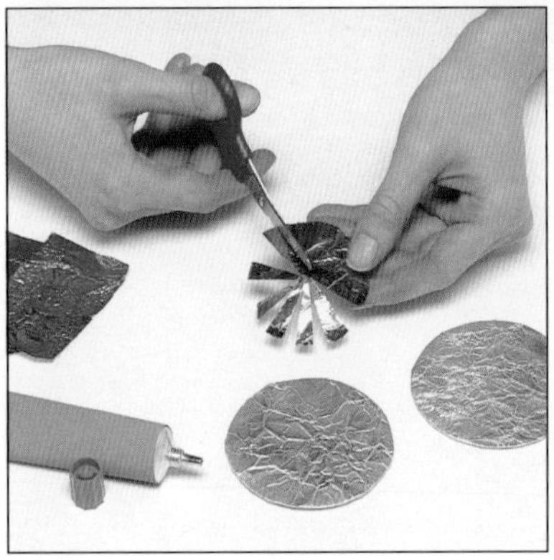

3 Cut a circle of coloured foil and snip small triangles from its edges to make a "star" shape. Glue the star to the front of one of the card circles. Cut two circles from coloured foil and glue them to the middle of the star.

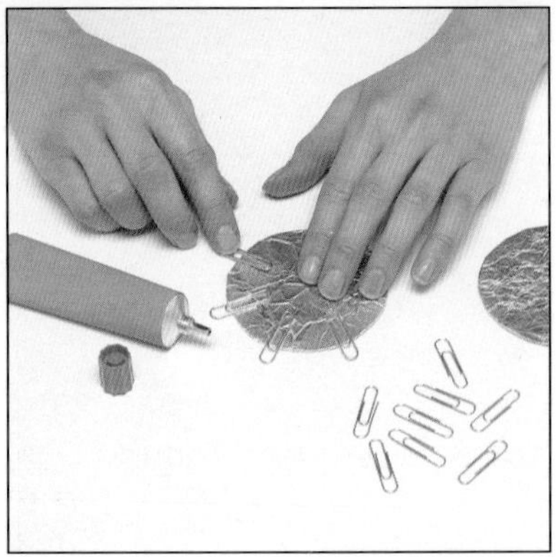

4 Glue a row of paper clips to the back of the other circle. Glue the two circles together. Tie a length of thin silver elastic to the top of the decoration to make a hanger.

Pasta-shape Christmas Tree Decorations

These Christmas-tree decorations are made from plastic pudding cartons. They are painted in bright colours and then decorated with pieces of dried pasta, which comes in lots of lovely shapes and sizes. Mix the paint with PVA (white) glue first, so that it sticks to the plastic.

YOU WILL NEED
2 plastic pudding cartons
PVA (white) glue
green, gold and pink poster paints
paintbrush
dried pasta shapes
2 gold pipe cleaners
strong, non-toxic glue

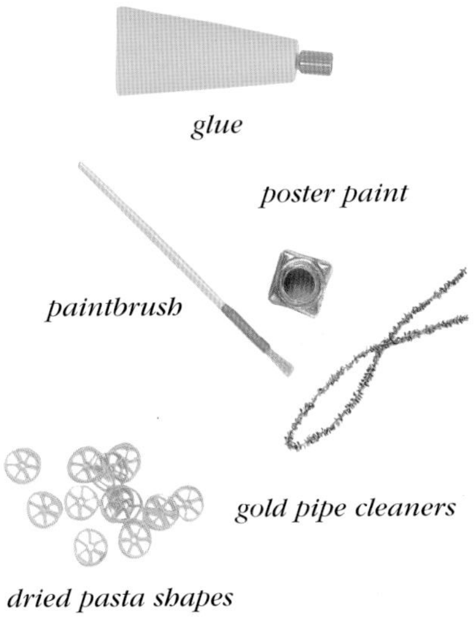

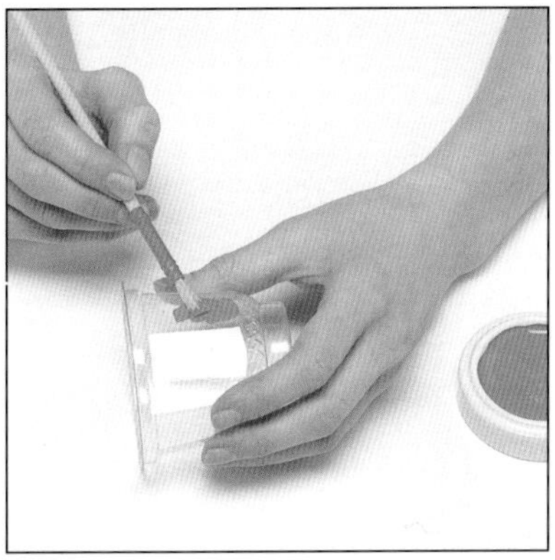

1 Wash and dry the cartons. Mix a little glue with green poster paint and paint one carton. Repeat with pink paint and the second carton. When dry, paint the top and bottom edges gold.

2 Paint the pasta shapes you have chosen with gold poster paint. Leave them to dry thoroughly.

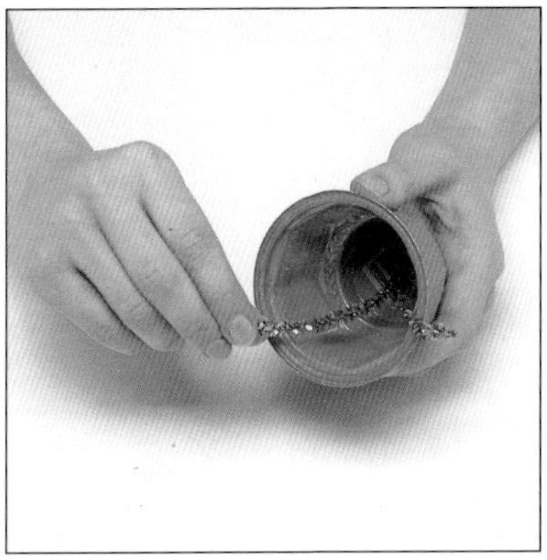

3 Ask an adult to help you to make a hole in the top of the cartons. Push both ends of the pipe cleaners through the holes. On the inside of the dishes, bend the ends of the pipe cleaners outwards to keep them in place.

4 Spread a little glue around the edge of each pasta shape. Glue the shapes around the sides of the cartons. Thread a pasta shape over the top of each pipe cleaner and glue them to the top of the decoration.

Wintry Scarf and Gloves

This designer set of accessories is sure to keep chilly winds at bay, and you can be sure that no-one else will own such an eye-catching set.

YOU WILL NEED
felt-tip pen
scissors
felt squares in various colours
fabric scissors
scarf
pins
needle
embroidery thread (floss) in various colours
small glass beads
mini pom-poms
gloves
pinking shears

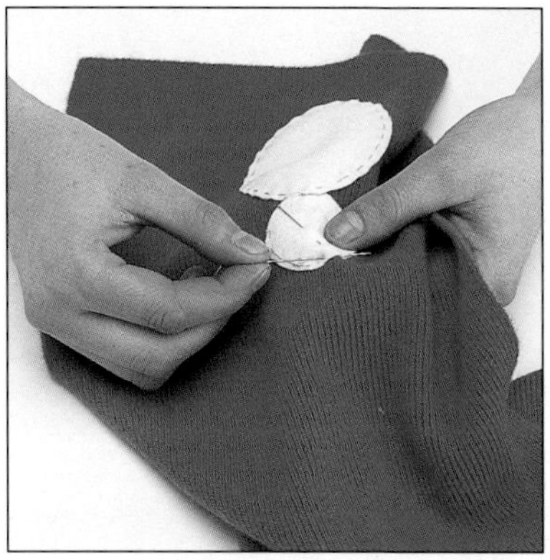

1 Trace the templates from this book and cut them out. Draw around the snowman's head and body on a piece of white felt and cut them out. Pin the snowman to one of the ends of the scarf and sew him on.

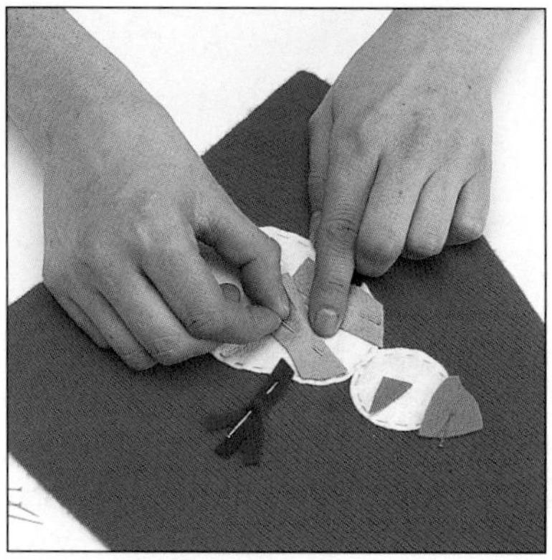

2 Using the templates, cut the snowman's carrot nose, hat, scarf and arms out of different coloured pieces of felt.

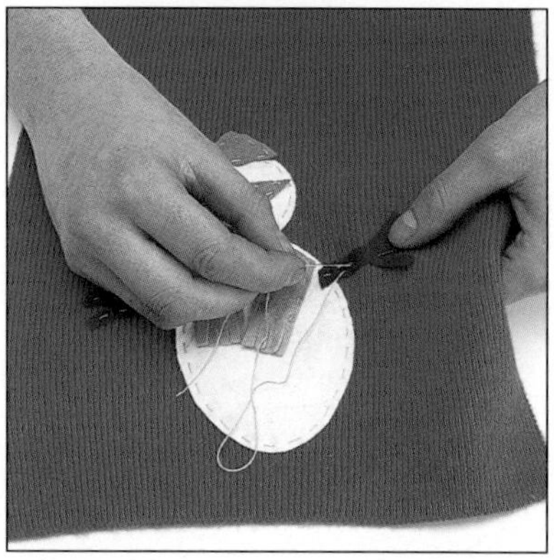

3 Position the shapes on the snowman. When you are happy with the shapes, pin them down and sew them in place.

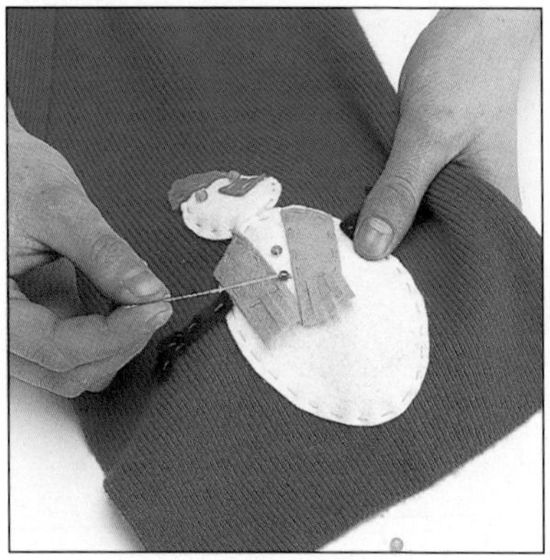

4 Sew a few beads down the front of the snowman's body for buttons and two on the face for eyes.

5 Position a mini pom-pom on the tip of the snowman's hat and sew it in place. Sew more pom-poms around the snowman and over the scarf to look like little snowballs.

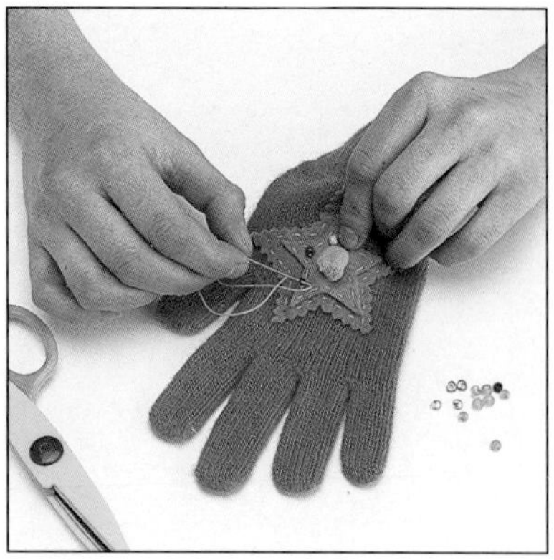

6 For the gloves, cut two large and two small stars out of felt, using pinking shears if you like. Sew one large star onto each glove. Sew the small star on to the large star. Sew on a few beads and add a pom-pom.

Christmas Message Board

This is the perfect present to give to a grown-up, especially if they are the type of person who is always losing important pieces of paper! You might find it useful to have an extra pair of hands to help you fix the ribbons in place.

YOU WILL NEED
fabric scissors
large piece of green felt
ruler
cork message board
PVA (white) glue
paintbrush
ribbons
coloured drawing pins
felt-tip pen
dark green felt

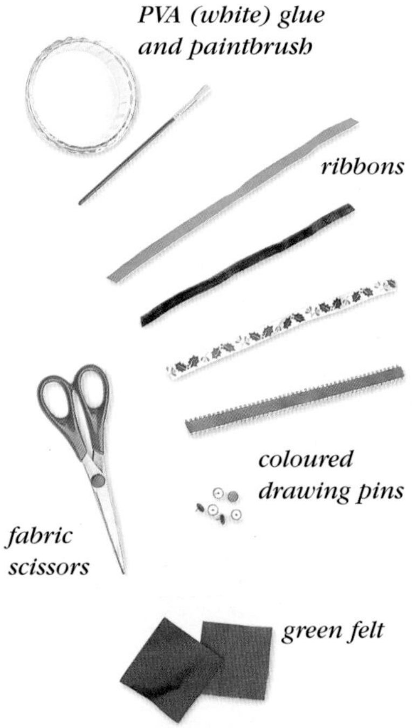

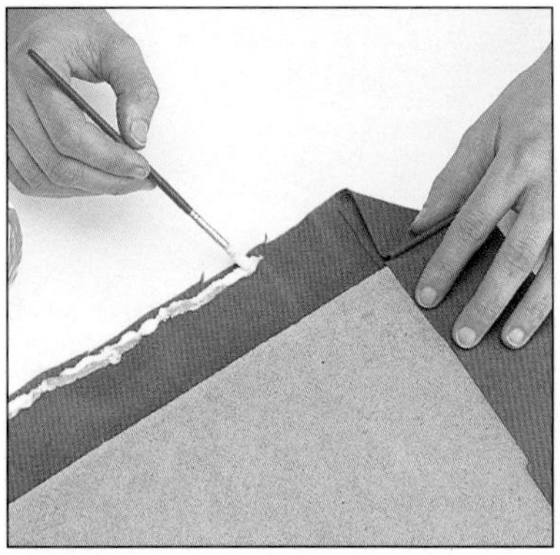

1 Cut a piece of green felt to be 5 cm (2 in) larger around each edge than the cork message board. Lay the board on top of the felt, fold the felt over the back of the board and then glue the felt firmly in place.

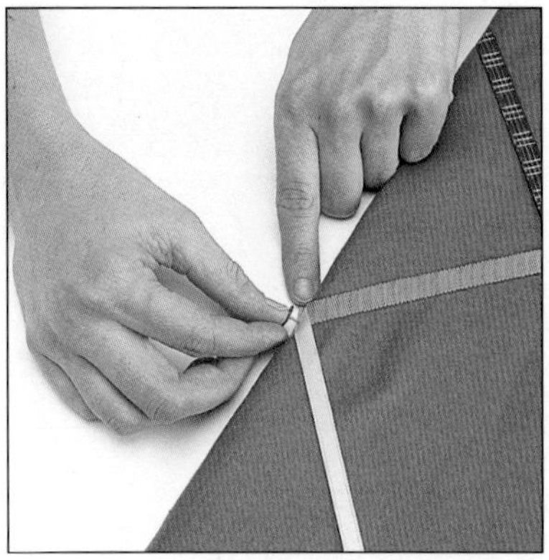

2 Cut lengths of ribbon and lay them diagonally across the board, spacing them at even intervals. Pin the ribbons on to the back of the message board.

3 Trace the holly leaf template from this book and cut it out. Draw around the template on a piece of dark green felt and cut out the shape. Repeat so that you have about sixteen holly leaves.

4 Using red drawing pins, pin the ends of the holly leaves to the board where the ribbons cross over, so that they look like holly berries.

Hair Accessories

These make brilliant presents for anyone with long hair. They are made using neoprene which is a very light, foam-like fabric that is easy to cut. It can be bought from most specialist craft shops.

YOU WILL NEED
pencil
scrap paper
neoprene sheets in various colours
fabric scissors
hair slide (barrette)
strong glue
artificial gemstones

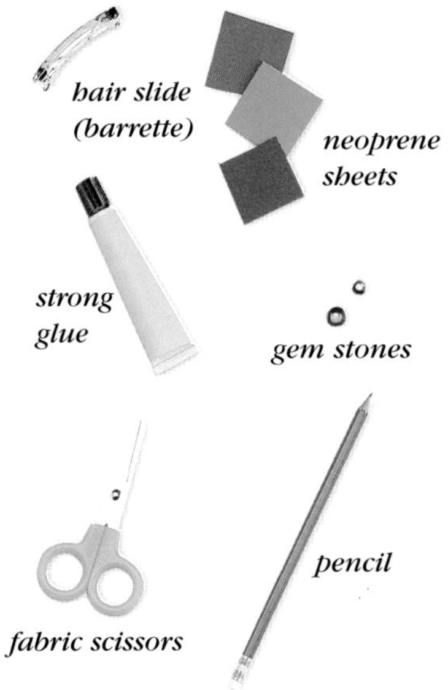

1 Draw a simple Chrtismas tree shape on a piece of scrap paper and cut it out to make a template. Draw around the template on the neoprene and cut out. Repeat to make six tree shapes.

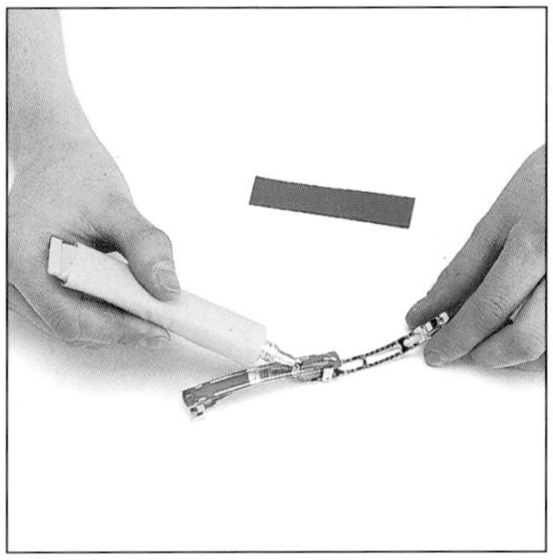

2 Cut out a strip of neoprene to fit over the hair slide (barrette) and fix it in place with strong glue. You might need to hold the neoprene in place with your hands while the glue dries.

3 Glue the shapes on the hair slide with strong glue. Allow the glue to dry before trying on the hair slide.

4 You can also jazz up a plain headband with cut-out neoprene shapes such as stars. Pile on the glamour by gluing an artificial gemstone on to the centre of each star.

Santa Puppet

Put on your own Christmas puppet show by making your own puppets. This project shows you how to make Santa Claus, but why not try making a snowman or a fairy puppet, too?

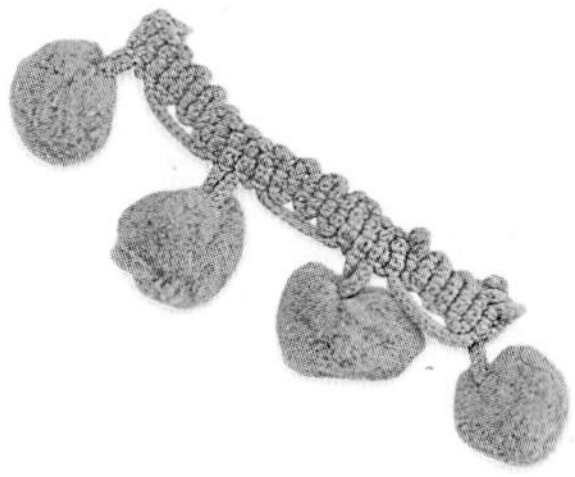

YOU WILL NEED
pencil
scrap paper
felt squares in red, pink and pale pink
fabric scissors
wadding (batting) fabric
pins
needle
sewing thread
small glass beads
pom-pom trim
small bell

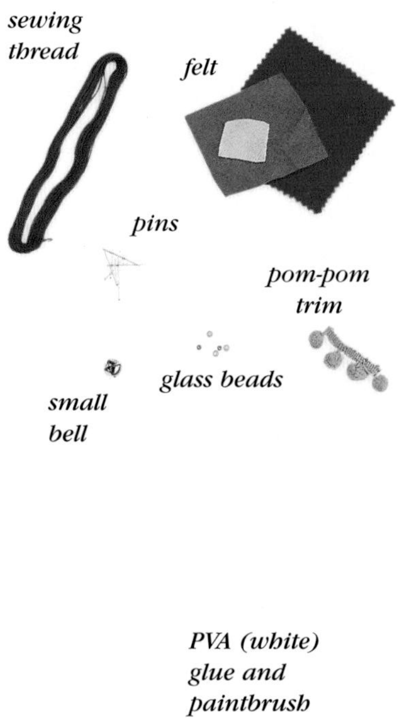

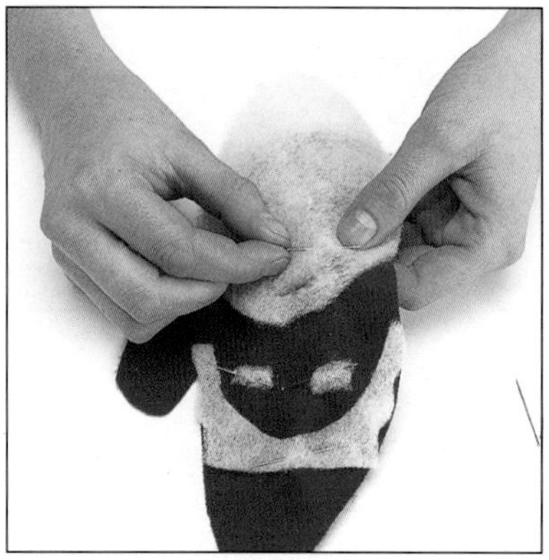

1 Draw a glove puppet shape on scrap paper and cut it out to make a template. Position the template on red felt and cut out two puppet shapes. Cut a beard, moustache and eyebrows from the wadding (batting) fabric and pin them on to one of the puppet shapes.

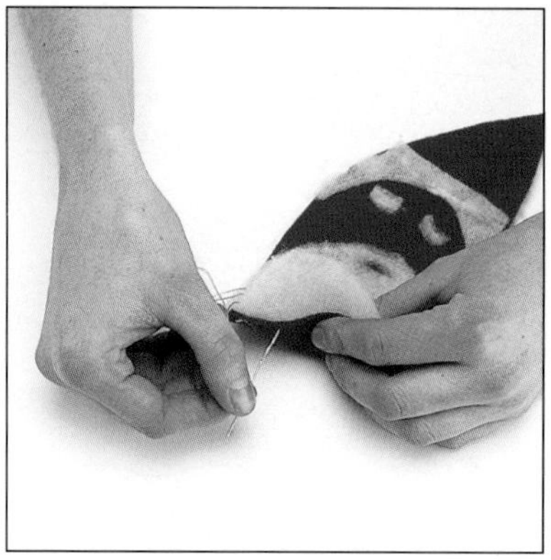

2 Thread the needle with sewing thread and start to sew the wadding in place on the puppet. Remove the pins when you have finished sewing.

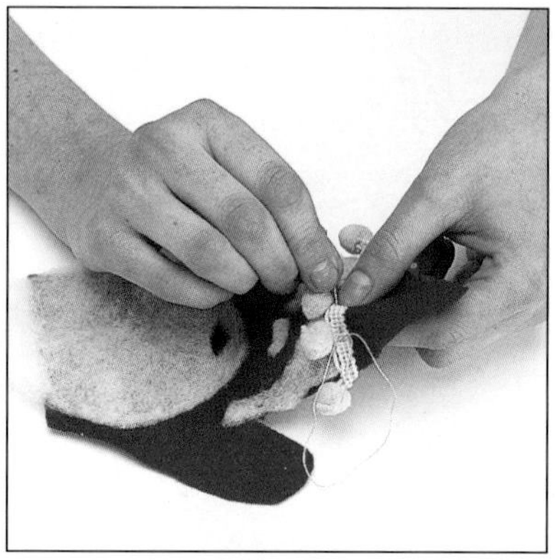

3 Sew a length of pom-pom trim just above the eyebrows.

4 Sew a blue bead under each eyebrow. Draw a hand shape on pale pink felt and cut it out. Draw two small circles for the cheeks on pink felt and cut them out.

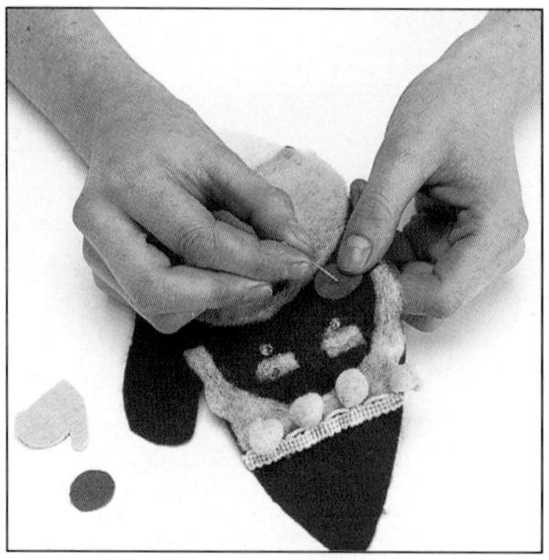

5 Sew the hand in place on the thumb of the glove and sew the cheeks on either side of the face. Place the two puppet shapes together and pin in place.

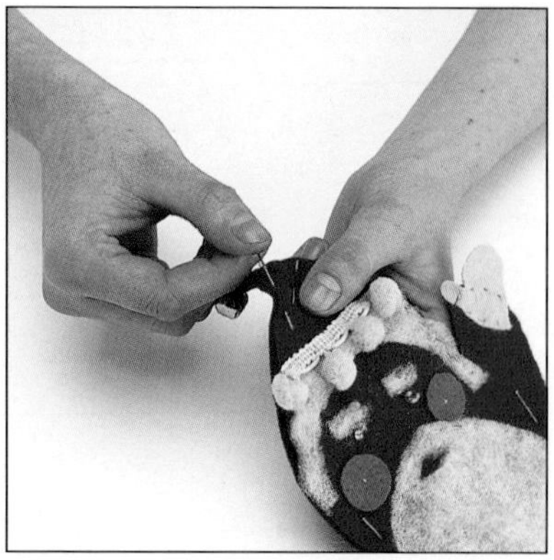

6 Sew the bell on to the top of the puppet. Sew around the edge of the glove, leaving the bottom edge open to fit your hand in. Try on the glove and hear the bell jingle as Santa moves about!

Storage Chest

This small storage chest is great for keeping little treasures safe. It is made from large, empty matchboxes and is covered with scraps of sticky-backed plastic. You can make the chest as large as you want – just keep adding more matchboxes. You can also use large and small matchboxes, so you have different-size compartments.

RECYCLING TIP

This is an ideal storage place for those buttons, beads, pins and paper clips that all good recyclers collect and keep.

YOU WILL NEED

green and red sticky-backed plastic
scissors
6 large matchboxes
strong, non-toxic glue
tracing paper
pencil
thin card (posterboard)
6 coloured plastic beads

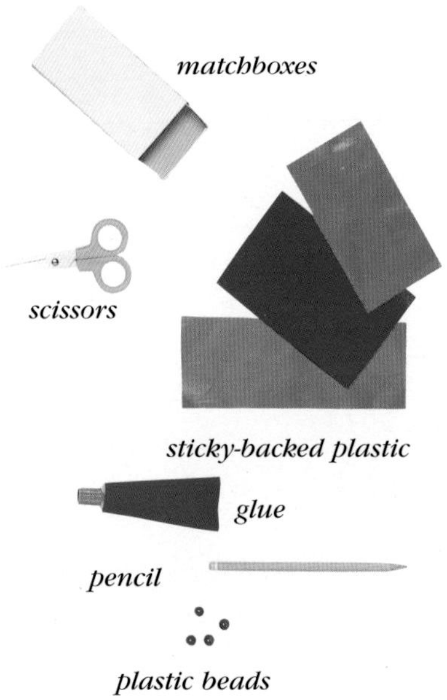

1 Cut three green and three red pieces of sticky-backed plastic the same width and long enough to fit around a matchbox, and stick them on.

2 Cut six thin strips of red and six of green sticky-backed plastic. Stick them to the front and back of the box trays; red in green boxes and green in red boxes.

3 Spread glue along the long side of one green box and glue it to a red box, and repeat so that you have three rows of two boxes.

4 When the glue has dried, glue the three rows of boxes on top of each other to make the storage chest. Make sure that the edges of the boxes line up.

5 Trace the pattern for the decoration; lay it face-down on a piece of card (posterboard); draw over the lines to transfer and cut it out. Cover the card with sticky-backed plastic and trim.

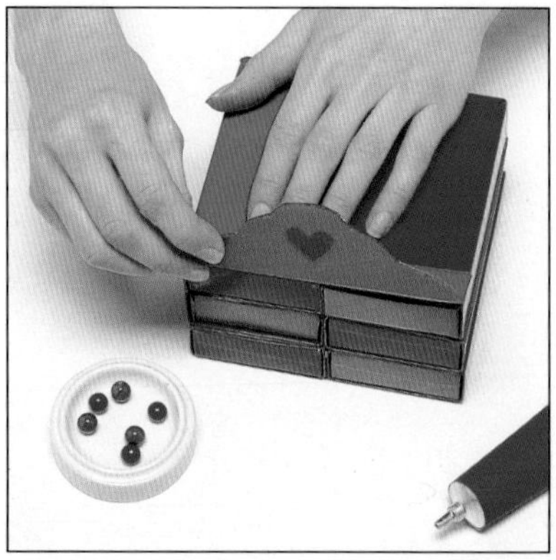

6 Cut out a small red heart and stick it to the front of the decoration. Bend back the decoration's base and glue it to the top of the chest. Glue a plastic bead to the front of each tray for handles.

Papier-mâché Bowl

Papier-mâché is like magic because you can make all sorts of things from it, using only old newspapers and glue. This bowl is decorated by gluing bright strips of wrapping paper and paper shapes to its surface, and is good for holding fruit or odds and ends.

YOU WILL NEED
petroleum jelly
plastic bowl
newspaper
PVA (white) glue, diluted
scissors
gift wrap
thin coloured paper
PVA (white) glue

glue

newspaper

plastic bowl

coloured paper

scissors

1 Grease your chosen bowl with a thin coating of petroleum jelly, so that the papier-mâché bowl will come out. Tear newspaper into 2.5-cm (1-in) wide strips. Dip the strips in the diluted PVA (white) glue and press into the mould, overlapping the edges slightly. Press in six layers and leave to dry overnight.

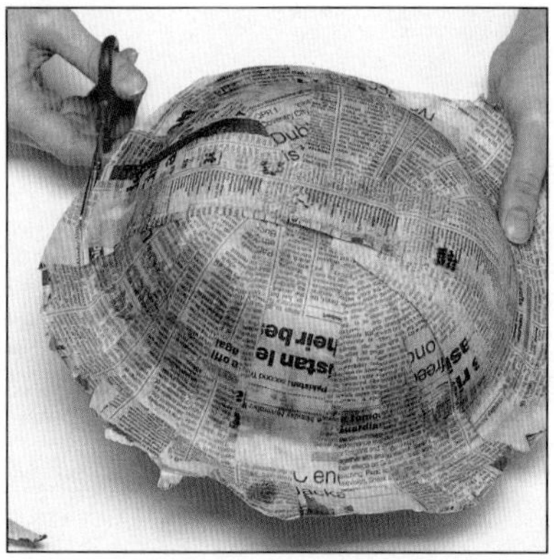

2 Gently pull the paper shape out of the mould. Leave the bowl upside-down to dry. When it has dried, cut away the rough edges from the rim of the bowl.

3 Tear the gift wrap into strips and glue them to the outside and inside of the bowl to decorate it.

4 Cut circles from the coloured paper. Snip segments out of the paper to make "stars".

5 Glue the stars to the centre and sides of the bowl.

6 Cut lots of small squares from two colours of thin paper. Glue the squares around the outside edge of the bowl.

Decoupage Santa Tray

Have some fun designing your own breakfast tray: it makes a great present and you could design it to suit whoever you are giving it to. The tray here would be great for a brother or sister.

YOU WILL NEED
fine sandpaper
small wooden tray
damp cloth
acrylic paint in various colours
paintbrushes
scissors
wrapping paper
PVA (white) glue
glitter glue
sequins
water-based clear varnish

1 To prepare the tray for painting, rub it all over with fine sandpaper to make sure the surface is completely smooth and there are no rough areas. Wipe away any dust with a damp cloth. Leave the tray to dry.

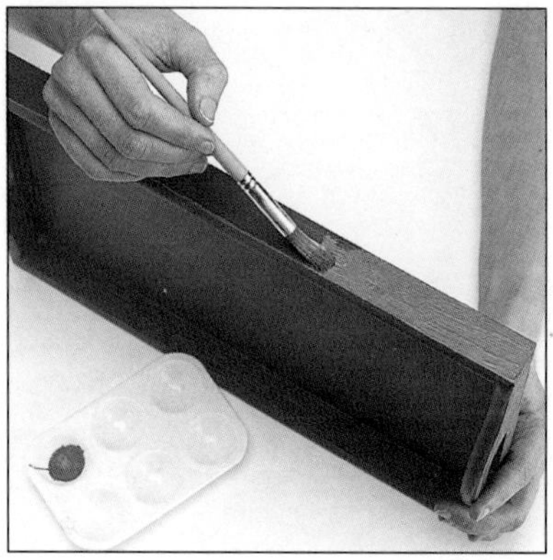

2 On a well-covered surface, paint the tray all over. Allow the paint to dry. For best results you may need to cover the tray with two coats of paint.

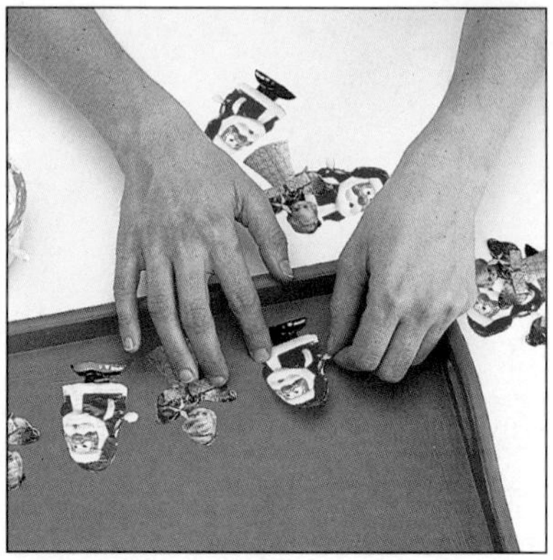

3 Cut out your favourite pictures from the wrapping paper and position the pictures on the tray. When you are happy with them, stick them on with glue. Allow the glue to dry completely.

4 Add a few dabs of paint or glitter glue around the pictures to give the tray an extra sparkle. Leave to dry.

5 Using a fine paintbrush, and a contrasting colour of paint, paint the edge of the tray with narrow stripes. Leave the paint to dry.

6 Glue some sequins on the tray and leave for several minutes to allow the glue to dry. Using a varnishing brush, paint on a few coats of clear varnish. Allow the varnish to dry.

Mini Gift Bags

These little bags are ideal for putting a small gift inside. You could also hang them up on the Christmas tree, filled with tempting chocolates.

YOU WILL NEED
ruler
fabric
fabric scissors
felt square
ribbon
needle
sewing thread
embroidery thread (floss)
braid
cord
safety pin

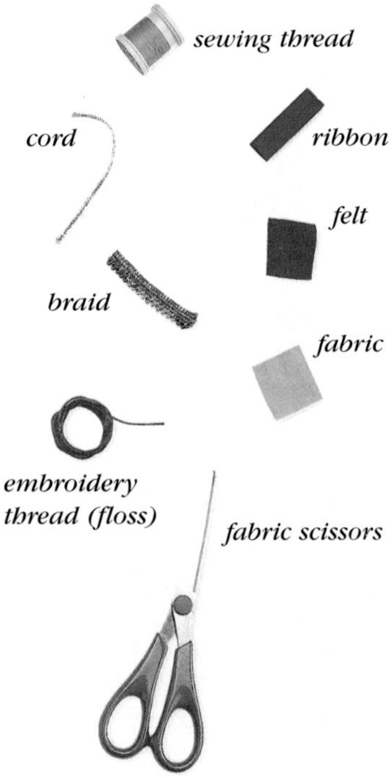

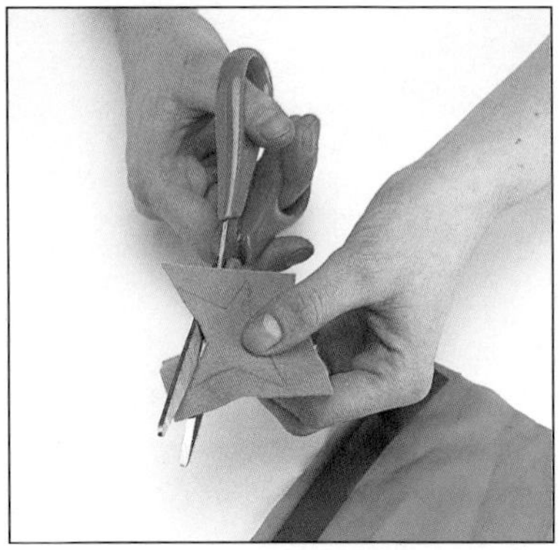

1 Cut a piece of fabric measuring 20 cm (8 in) x 15 cm (6 in) and a length of ribbon 18 cm (7 in). Trace the template from this book and cut it out. Cut around the template using paper scisors, to make a star from the felt.

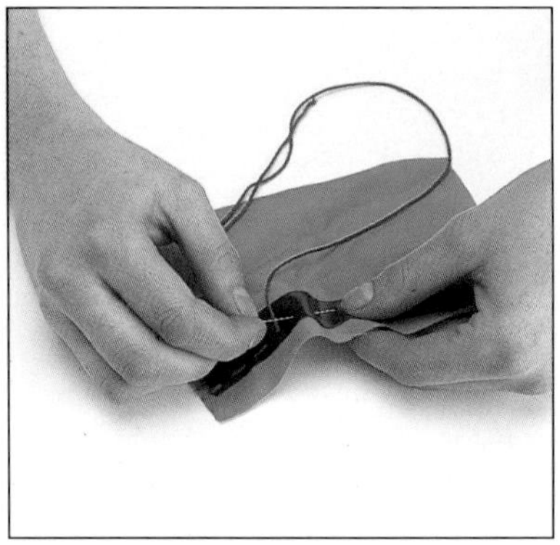

2 Sew the ribbon along one edge of the fabric 1 cm (½ in) from the top. Sew along each side of the ribbon but leave the ends open.

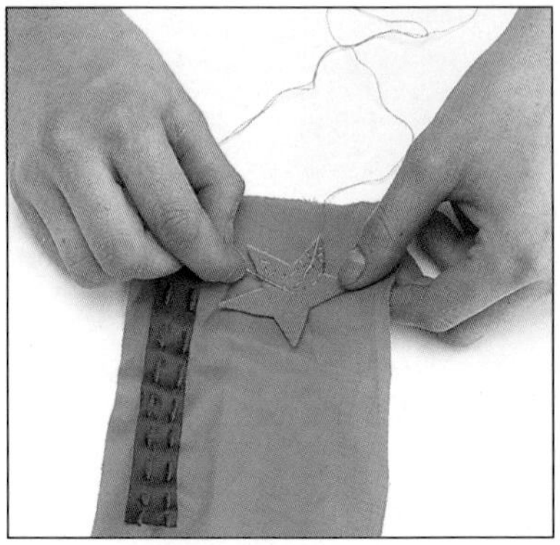

3 Sew the felt star on to one side of the fabric. If you don't want to do too much sewing, you could glue the star on with a small dab of glue.

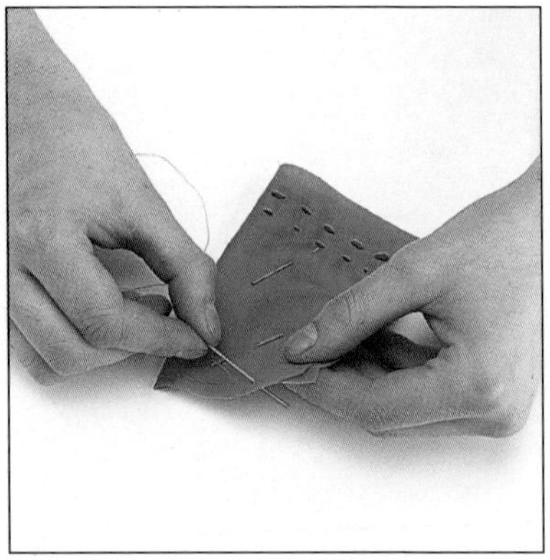

4 Fold the fabric in half with the right sides facing, making sure that all four corners meet. Carefully sew a running stitch along the bottom and side of the bag, using embroidery thread (floss). When you have finished sewing the bag, turn it the right way out.

5 Cut a piece of braid to go around the top of the bag and sew it in place with a running stitch.

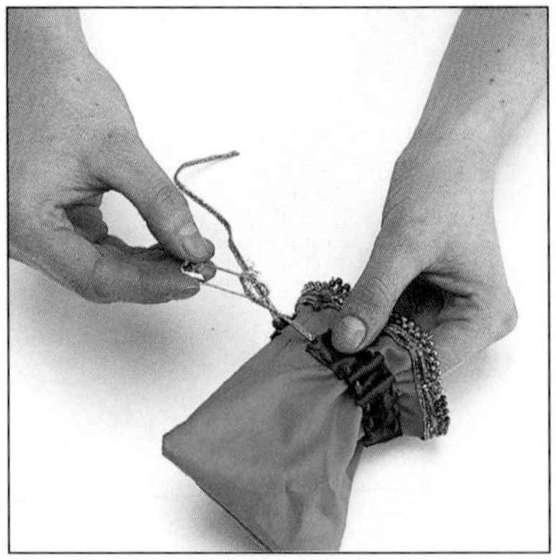

6 Cut a length of cord and secure a safety pin through one end. Thread the cord through the ribbon at the top of the bag, until it comes out at the other end. Tie the two ends in a knot. Pull the cord tight to close the bag.

Groovy Egg Cups

These jazzy egg cups will add lots of fun and colour to the breakfast table all year round. Make a special friend their own, personalized egg cup by painting on their name.

YOU WILL NEED
enamel paints in various colours
paintbrushes
china egg cups
coloured paper or wrapping paper
scissors
PVA (white) glue
paintbrush

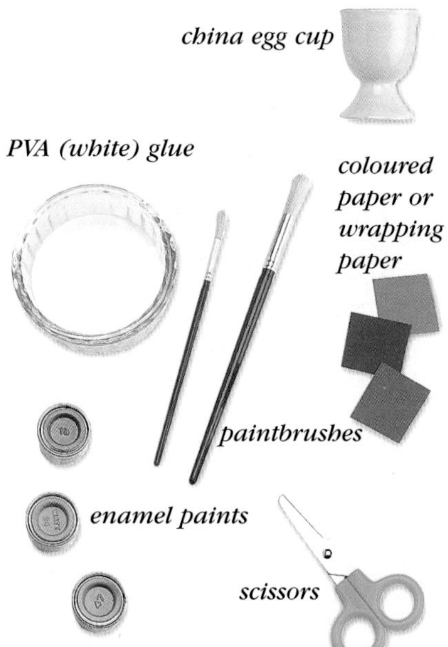

1 If you have more than one egg cup, you can give each one a different design. Paint stripes on one egg cup in a single colour. Paint slowly and carefully, and try to leave even spaces between the stripes. Allow the paint to dry.

2 Paint on some more stripes in different colours. Allow the paint to dry completely, then paint the inside of the egg cup in a single colour. Leave to dry.

3 For the tartan (plaid) egg cup, paint stripes in one colour and allow the paint to dry. In another colour, paint more stripes in the other direction and leave to dry. Paint the inside of the egg cup.

4 For the third egg cup, paint the inside and outside in contrasting colours. Let dry. Cut small squares from coloured paper or wrapping paper and glue them on. To finish, dab white paint over the egg cup to look like snow. Leave to dry.

Pomander

This is a beautiful Christmas decoration that has a subtle, spicy perfume. It would make an ideal gift for a grown-up.

You will need
ribbon
orange
scissors
cloves
PVA (white) glue
paintbrush
gold glitter

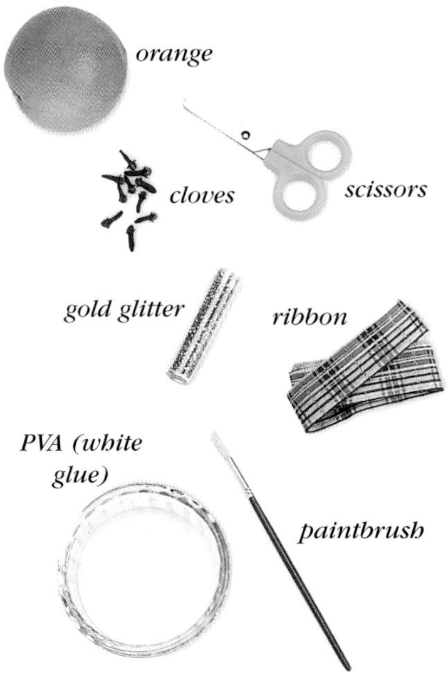

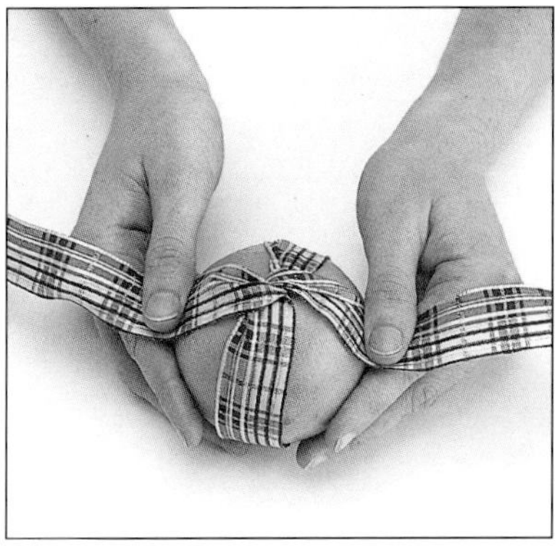

1 Holding the orange in your fingers, wrap the length of ribbon tightly around the orange. Keep hold of the ribbon.

2 Without letting go of the ribbon, twist it and wrap it around the orange in the other direction. Tie the ribbon in a large bow at the top and trim the ends.

3 Cover the whole orange with cloves by carefully piercing the pointed ends of the cloves into the orange.

4 Brush a thin layer of glue over the cloves and sprinkle glitter over the orange, shaking off any of the excess. Let the glue dry.

Christmas Pudding Apron

This apron looks delicious! As well as painting Christmas puddings, you could paint your favourite Christmas foods.

YOU WILL NEED
cardboard
scourer pad (sponge)
felt-tip pen
scissors
fabric paint in assorted colours
cotton apron
paintbrush

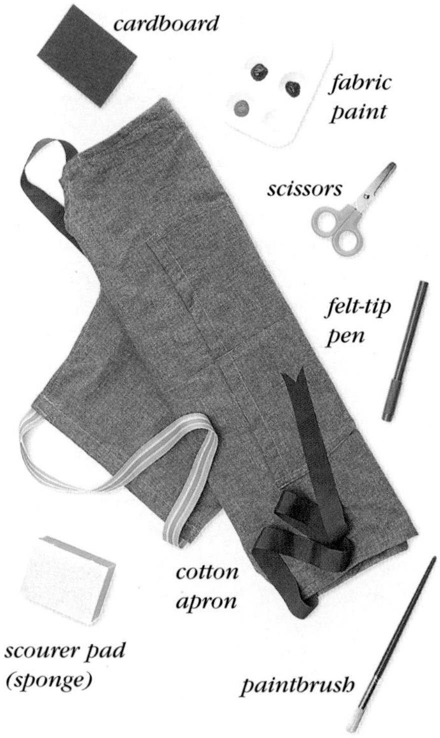

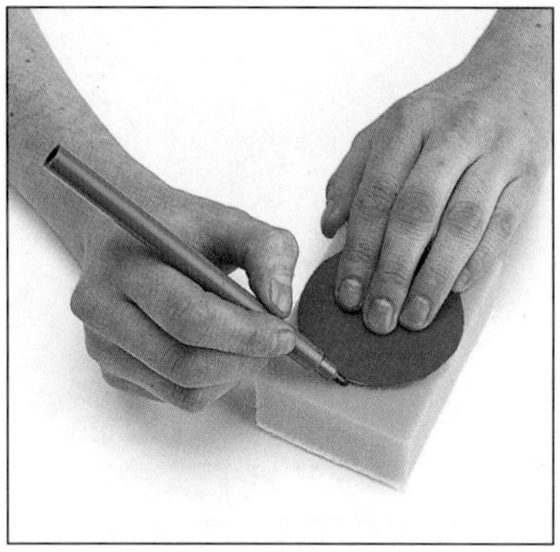

1 Trace the Christmas pudding (cake) template from this book, cut it out and draw around it on to cardboard. Cut out the pudding shape and draw around it on a scourer pad (sponge), using a felt-tip pen. With the help of an adult, cut the pudding out of the scourer pad.

2 Dab the sponge side of the scourer pad with purple fabric paint and make a practice stamp on a scrap of fabric. Then dab the sponge in the paint and stamp puddings all over the apron, dabbing the sponge in the paint after each print.

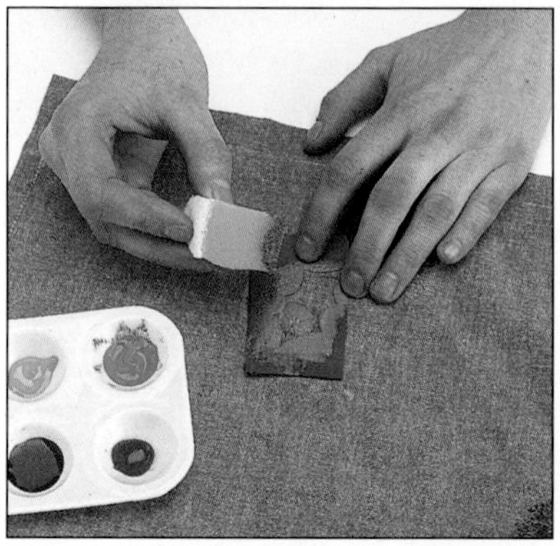

3 Trace the holly leaf template from this book, cut it out and draw around it on to cardboardand. Carefully cut out the cardboard inside the leaf to make a stencil. Position the stencil on the top of each pudding and dab the sponge, dipped in green paint, through it. Let dry.

4 Paint some white paint on to the top of the puddings to look like whipped cream. Allow to dry.

5 Using red paint, paint some red dots on to each pudding to look like glacé (candied) cherries. Allow to dry.

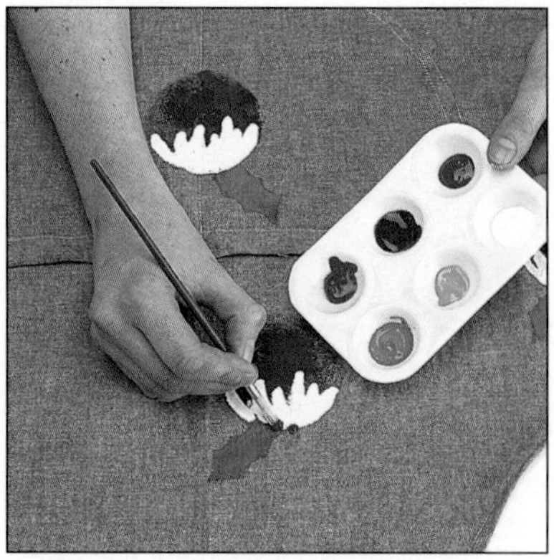

6 Finish the puddings by painting two red dots next to the holly leaves to look like festive berries.

Christmas Pudding Teapot

An ordinary cup of tea will never be the same again when served from this quirky teapot! You might need to paint on two coats of white paint, but remember to allow the first coat to dry before painting on the second layer.

YOU WILL NEED
small brown teapot
tissues
paintbrushes
ceramic paints in various colours

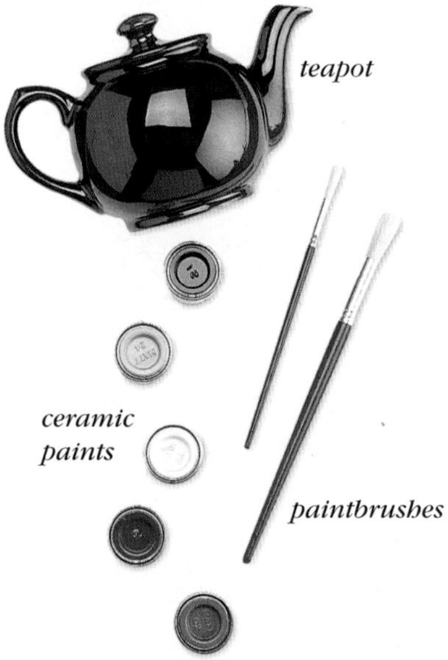

1 Before you start painting, wipe the teapot with tissues to remove all traces of grease and dirt. Leave the teapot to dry before you start to paint.

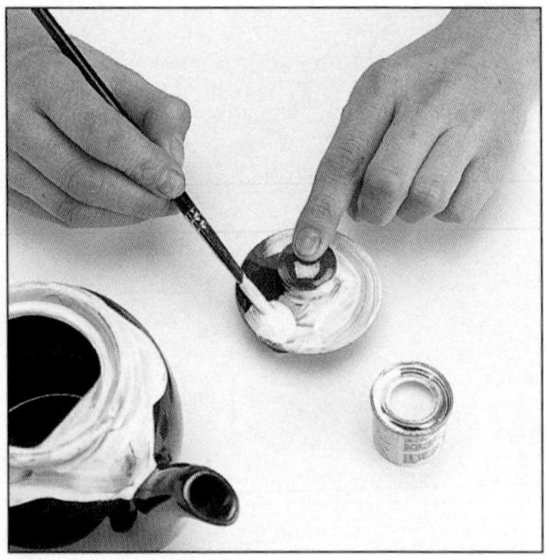

2 Remove the lid from the teapot. Paint the white "cream" on the teapot lid and around the top of the pot. Allow the paint to dry.

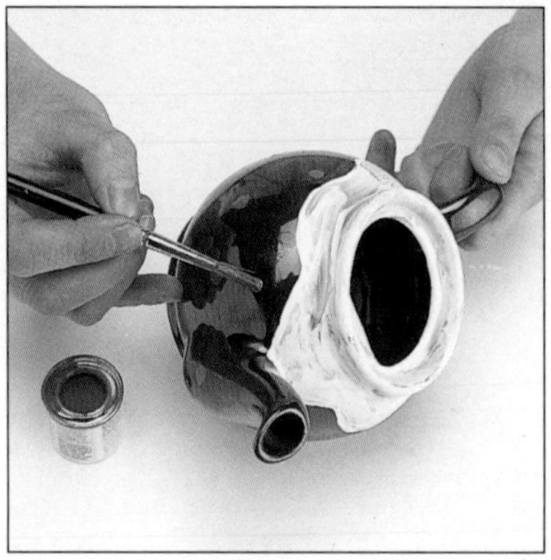

3 Paint black and brown dots on the unpainted area of the teapot to look like currants and raisins.

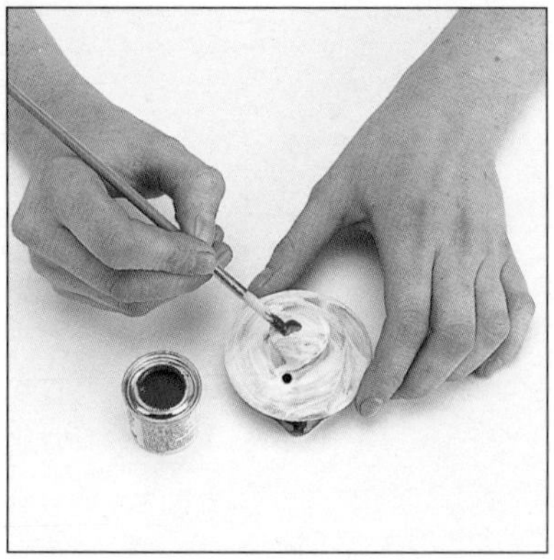

4 Paint the knob on the teapot lid red to look like a glacé (candied) cherry. Allow the paint to dry.

Snowman Mug

Warm up this chilly snowman with a nice cup of piping hot chocolate or tea!

YOU WILL NEED
mug
tissues
paintbrushes
ceramic paints in assorted colours

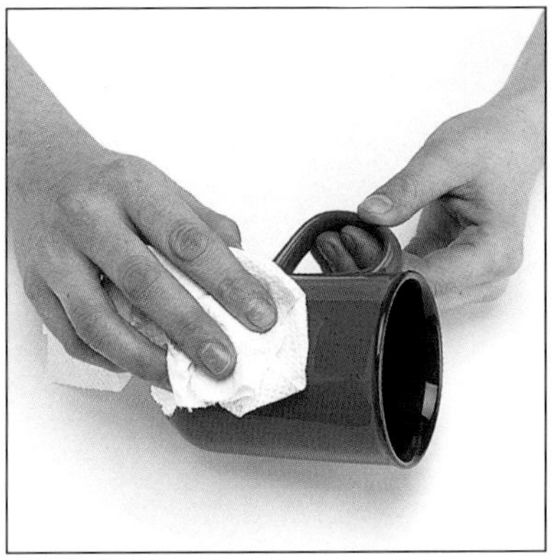

1 Before you start painting, wipe the mug with tissues to remove all traces of grease and dirt. Leave the mug to dry before you start to paint.

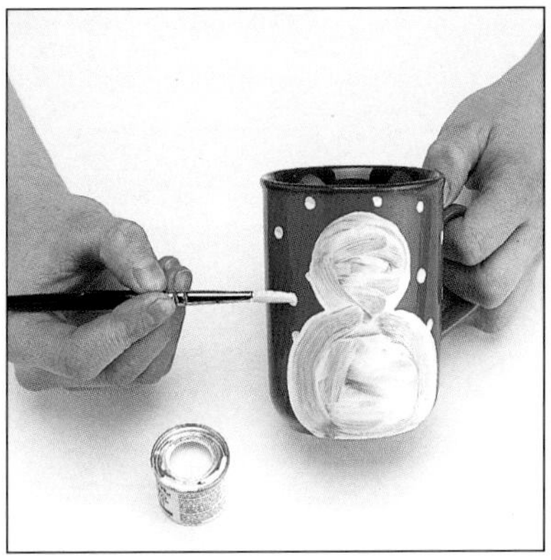

2 Using white paint, paint the snowman's head and body on the mug. Add white dots all around the snowman, to look like falling flakes of snow. Allow the paint to dry.

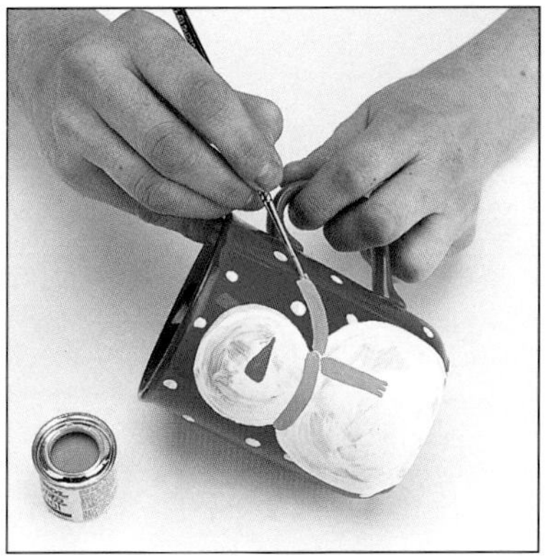

3 Using orange and blue paints, paint a carrot for the snowman's nose and give him a thick woolly scarf. Allow the paint to dry.

4 Using black paint, paint on the snowman's hat, his arms and charcoal eyes. Allow the paint to dry.

Jazzy Jewel Storage Jar

This is a great idea for making an ordinary glass container look really special. All you need are some glass paints and a handful of artificial gemstones.

YOU WILL NEED
pencil
scrap paper or cardboard
scissors
sticky-backed plastic (contact paper)
glass container with a lid
paintbrush
glass paints in various colours
strong glue
artificial gemstones in various colours
gold outline paint

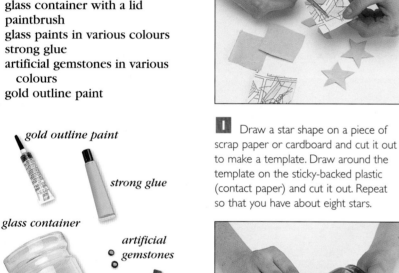

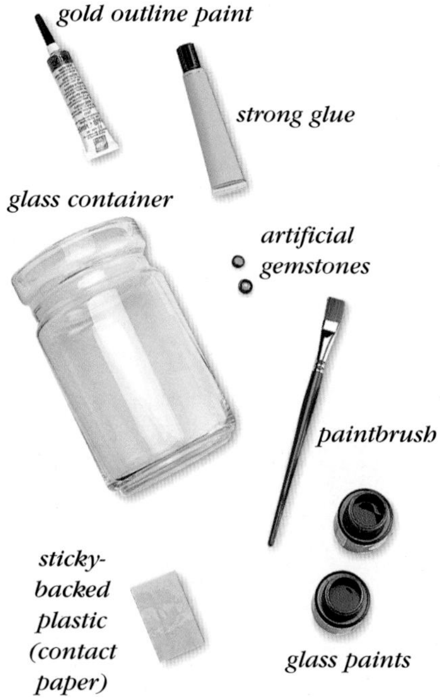

1 Draw a star shape on a piece of scrap paper or cardboard and cut it out to make a template. Draw around the template on the sticky-backed plastic (contact paper) and cut it out. Repeat so that you have about eight stars.

2 Decide where you want to position the stars on the glass container. When you are happy with them, peel off the backing and stick them in place.

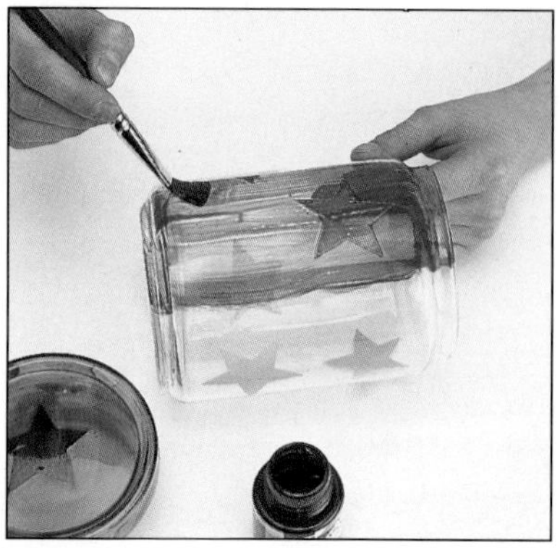

3 Paint the jar and its lid all over with glass paint. It doesn't matter if you paint over the stars, too. Allow the paint to dry completely.

4 When you are sure the paint has dried, peel the stars off the jar to reveal the unpainted stars underneath.

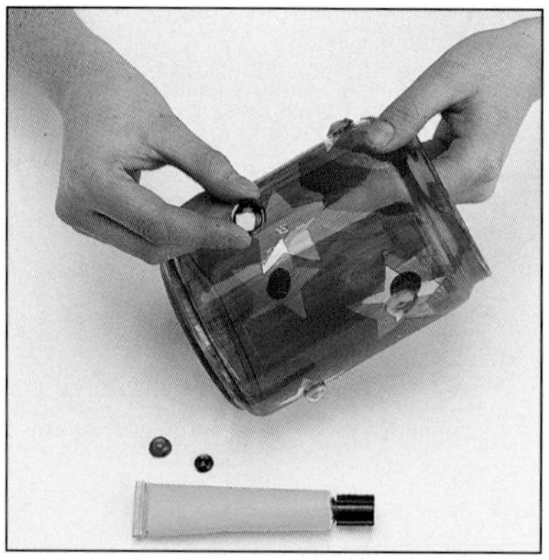

5 Using strong glue, stick an artificial gemstone in the centre of each star. Hold it in position for a few minutes until the glue dries.

6 Using the gold outline paint, decorate the edge of each star. The paint comes in a tube, so it is easy to control. Allow the paint to dry.

Appliquéd Photo Album

As well as decorating an album, you could also decorate the cover of a diary or an address book in a matching design.

YOU WILL NEED
pencil
scissors
felt squares in lilac and red
pinking shears
pins
needle
sewing thread
rick-rack braid
gold gauzy fabric
red velvet
poster paints in various colours
paintbrushes
yellow embroidery thread (floss)
tinsel ribbon
gold braid
star sequins
PVA (white) glue
fabric-covered album

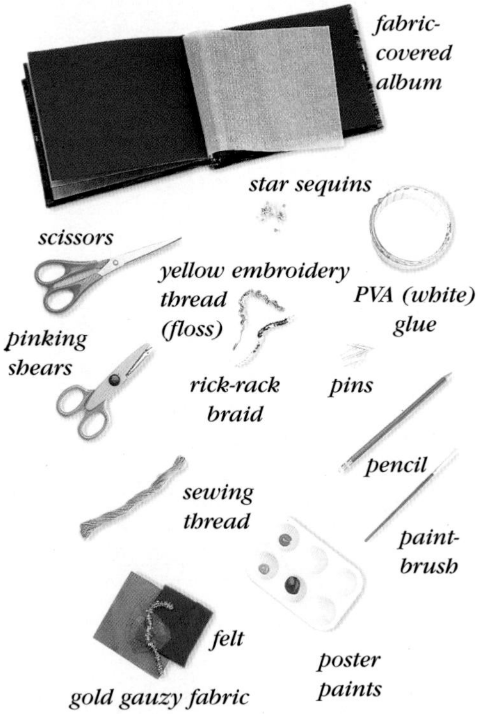

1 Trace the templates and cut them out. Draw around the background template on lilac felt and cut it out. Using pinking shears, cut out a larger square from the red felt. Sew the lilac felt on to the red felt. Pin rick-rack braid all around the edge of the lilac felt.

2 Using a small, neat running stitch, sew the rick-rack braid in place around the edge of the lilac felt.

3 Using the wing template, cut out two pieces of gold fabric. Cut a piece of red velvet to the size of the dress template. Arrange the wings behind the dress shape on the lilac felt. Sew all around the edge of the wings.

4 Cut a small circle using the template for the face and paint on the eyes, rosy cheeks and a mouth. When the paint is dry, arrange the face at the top of the triangle and sew it in place.

5 For the angel's hair, sew strands of embroidery thread (floss) to the top of her head. Sew a piece of tinsel ribbon on to her hair to look like a halo. Sew a piece of gold braid along the bottom of her dress. Sew star sequins over her dress and circular sequins on her wings. Using a small amount of glue, secure the appliqué on to the front of the album. Allow the glue to dry.

Sparkly Pencil Holder

These glitzy containers are great for storing pens and pencils. Remember to ask your friends and family to keep all their foil sweet (candy) wrappers, so that you can make a whole range of containers.

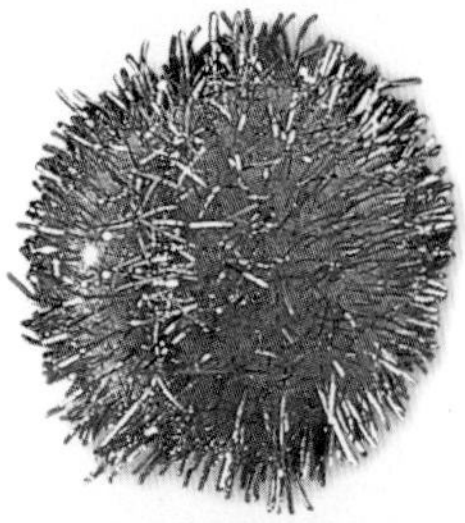

YOU WILL NEED
plastic bottle
felt-tip pen
scissors
ruler
cardboard
foil sweet (candy) wrappers
PVA (white) glue
paintbrush
double-sided sticky tape
mini pom-poms

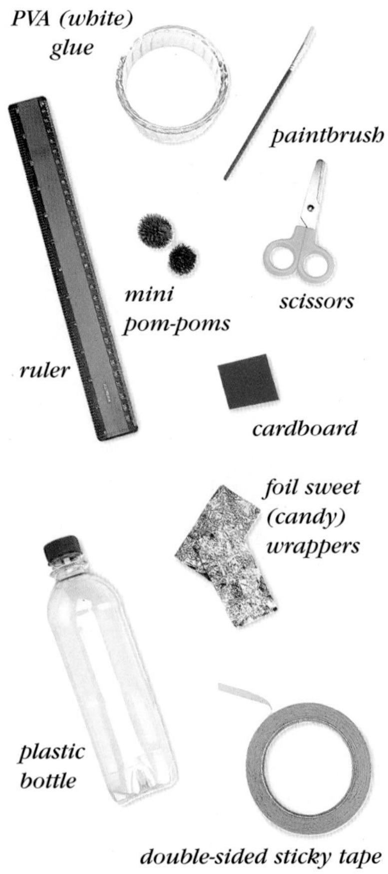

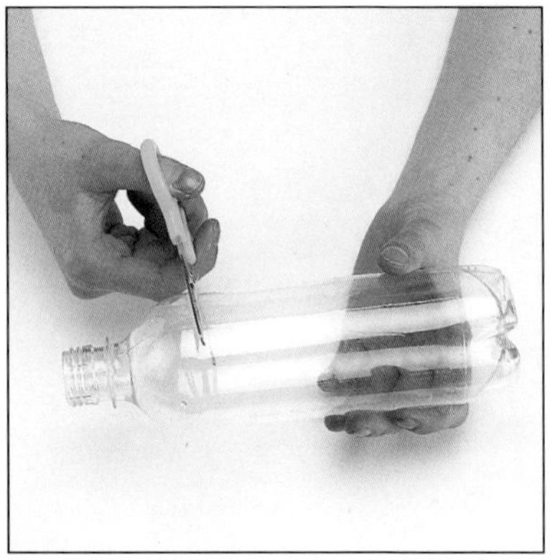

1 Decide on the height you want your container to be and draw a line around the bottle with a felt-tip pen to mark this. Ask an adult to help you cut the top off the bottle.

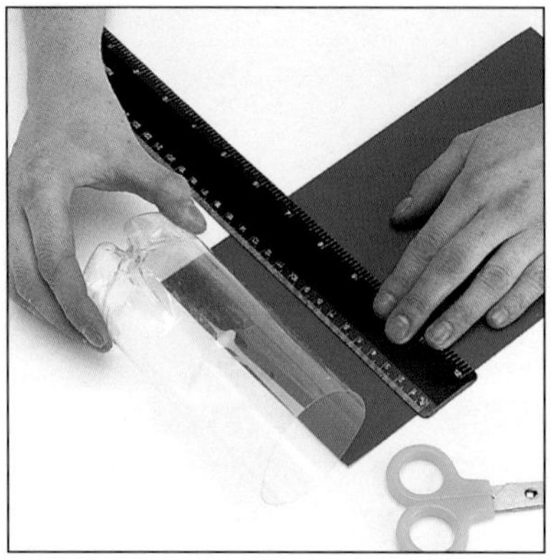

2 Measure the height of the bottle with a ruler. Allowing for a 2 cm (¾ in) overlap, cut out a piece of cardboard to fit around it.

3 Select a colourful assortment of foil sweet (candy) wrappers and smooth them out with your fingers until they are flat. Prepare enough wrappers to cover your container.

4 Glue the foil sweet wrappers on to one side of the cardboard until you have completely covered the surface. For the best pattern effect, let the wrappers overlap each other. Allow the glue to dry.

5 Stick strips of double-sided sticky tape on to the reverse side of the cardboard. Peel off the backing tape and fix the cardboard around the bottle.

6 For the finishing touch, decorate the top of the container by gluing on a selection of mini pom-poms.

Holly Leaf Picture Frame

Jazz up an old picture frame with this simple technique, using tiling grout. Put a photograph of your favourite friend in the frame, then display it, so that everyone can appreciate your handiwork.

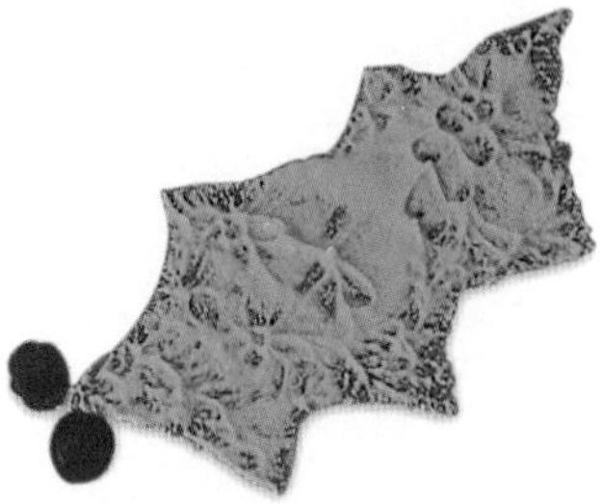

YOU WILL NEED
fine sandpaper
wooden picture frame
damp cloth
ruler
white pencil
paintbrush
acrylic paints in various colours
pencil
cardboard
scissors
tiling grout
old spoon

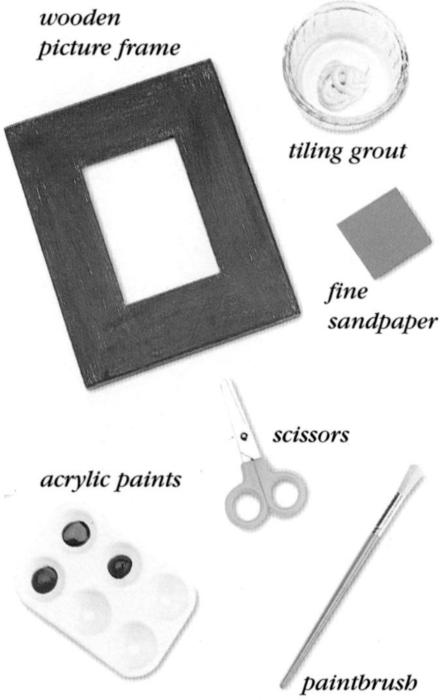

1 Using the sandpaper, lightly rub down the picture frame to remove any old paint or varnish, and to smooth the surface. Using a damp cloth, wipe over the frame to remove any dirt or dust.

2 Using a ruler and a white pencil, divide the picture frame into squares.

3 Paint on the squares as neatly as possible. Allow the paint to dry. You may find it easier to paint one colour and allow it to dry before painting on a new colour.

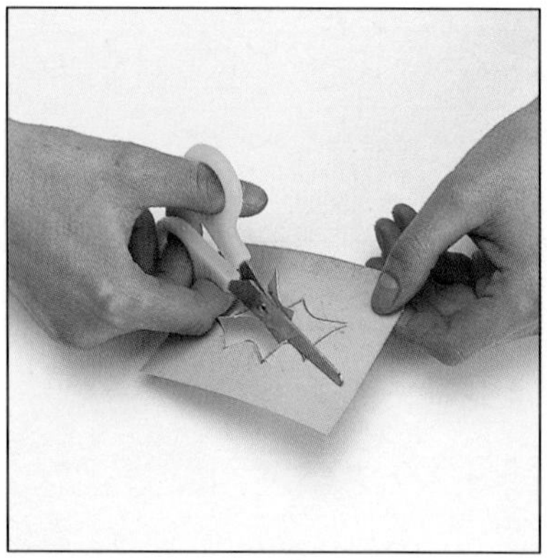

4 Trace the holly leaf template from this book and cut it out. Draw around the template on a piece of cardboard. With the help of an adult, cut out the inside leaf to make a stencil.

5 Squeeze a small amount of grout into an old container and add a small amount of paint. Using an old spoon, mix the paint into the grout until the colour is evenly mixed.

6 When the paint is dry, position the stencil on a painted square and thickly dab the coloured grout through it: it will give a lovely ridged effect to the frame. Remove the stencil and repeat on the other squares. Allow the grout to dry.

Snowflake Candlestick

Decide on who you want to give this candlestick to and then you can paint it in their favourite colours. If you like, you could also give them a Christmas candle to go with it.

YOU WILL NEED
fine sandpaper
plain ceramic candlestick
scissors
sticky-backed plastic (contact paper)
enamel paints in various colours
paintbrush
gold ceramic paint

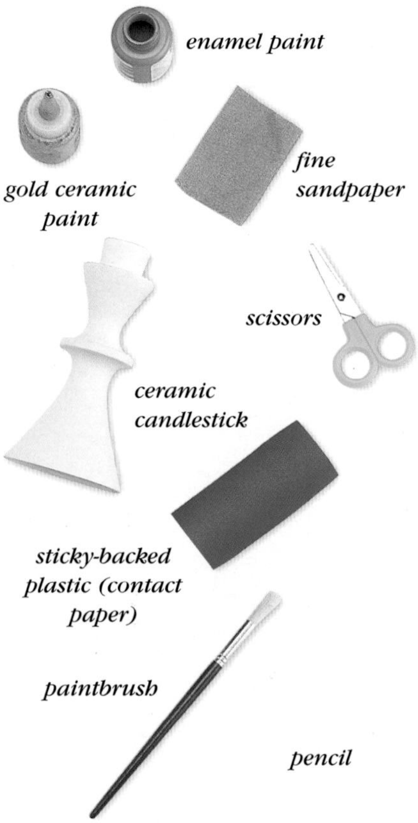

1 Using fine sandpaper, lightly rub down the candlestick to remove the glaze. This will make it easier to paint on to the candlestick.

2 Cut out small circles and strips from the sticky-backed plastic (contact paper). Stick the strips across the upper part of the candlestick and the circles around the base of the candlestick.

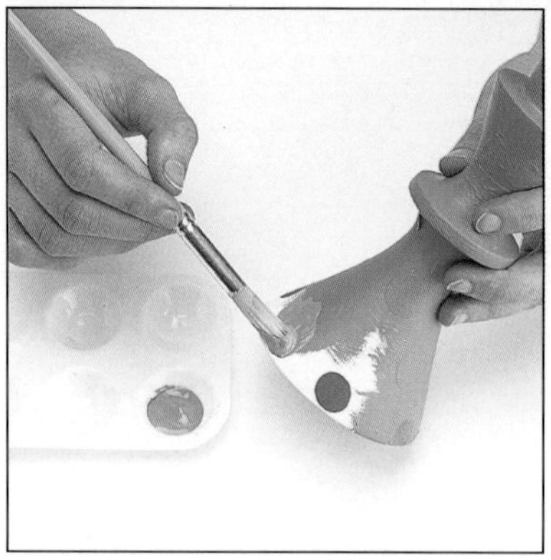

3 Paint the candlestick. Allow the paint to dry completely, then remove the sticky-backed plastic shapes.

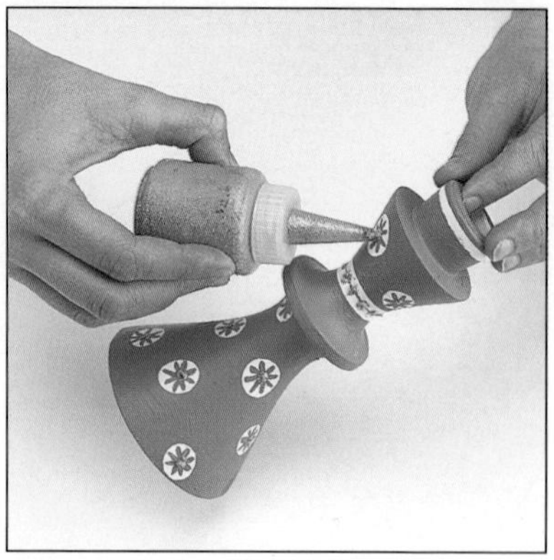

4 Paint a snowflake inside each circle and allow to dry. Then, using the gold paint, dot the centre of each snowflake to make your candlestick twinkle.

Hair Scrunchies

This is the perfect present for someone who likes to wear their hair tied back. Use fabrics that you know will match their hair colour. You could also make two smaller scrunchies for someone who likes to wear their hair in pigtails.

YOU WILL NEED
fabric 65 cm (26 in) x 14 cm (5½ in)
ruler
fabric scissors
pins
needle
sewing thread
thin elastic
safety pin

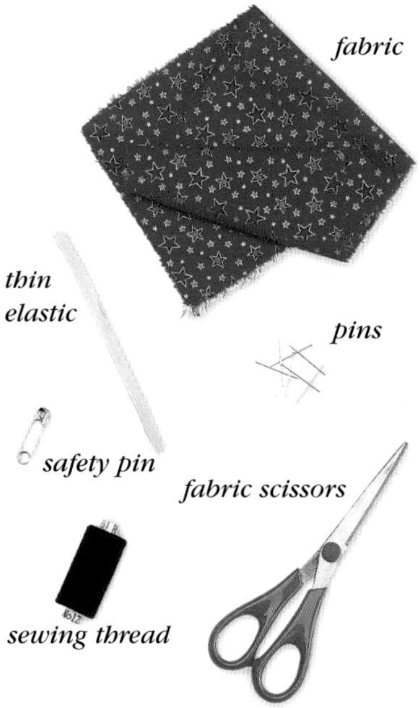

1 Fold the fabric in half lengthways, making sure that the right sides of the fabric are facing. Carefully pin the two edges together, then sew a neat running stitch along the long edge.

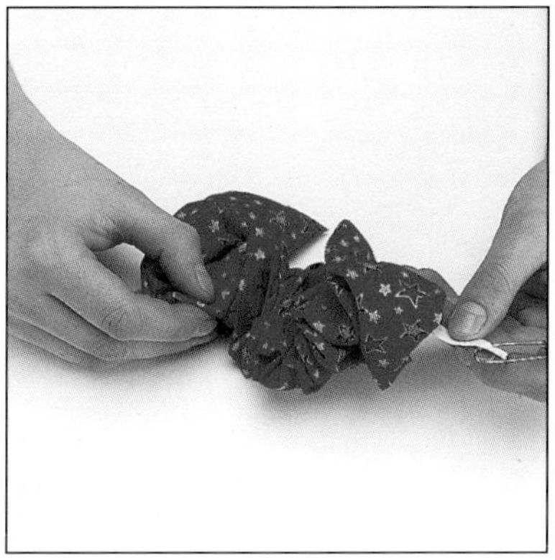

2 Turn the fabric tube right side out. Cut a piece of thin elastic 18 cm (7 in) long. Secure a safety pin through one end of the elastic. Using the safety pin to help, thread the elastic all the way through the fabric tube.

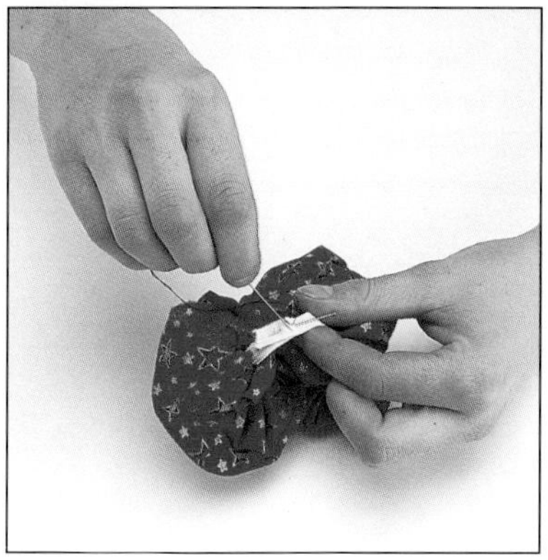

3 When the elastic comes out of the other end of the tube, remove the safety pin and pin the two ends of elastic together. Sew the ends together.

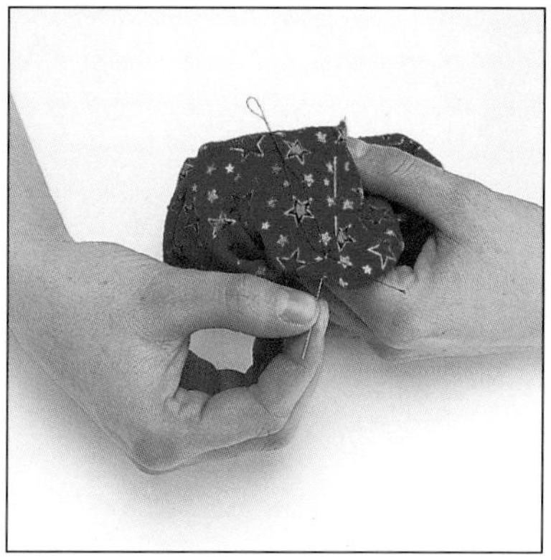

4 Turn under the raw edges of one end of the tube and pin over the other end. Sew the two together, taking care not to sew right through the scrunchie.

Friendship Bracelets

Give one of your friends or someone in your family one of these special bracelets, to show them just how much you care about them.

YOU WILL NEED
stranded cotton embroidery thread (floss) in various colours
ruler
scissors
strong sticky tape
beads in various colours

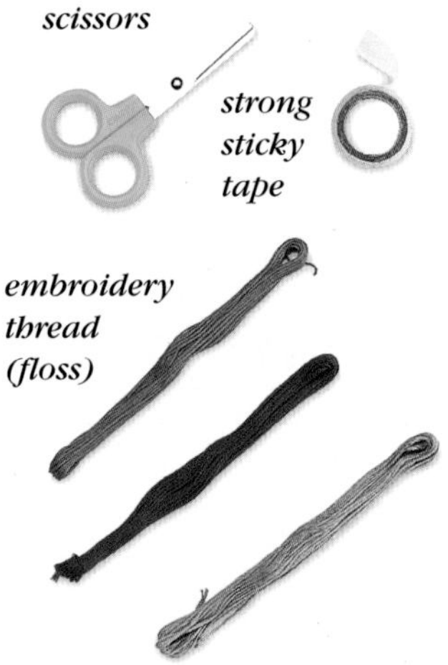

1 Decide on four colours of embroidery thread (floss) and cut two strands of each colour approximately 40 cm (16 in) long. Tie all of the strands together in a knot at one of the ends.

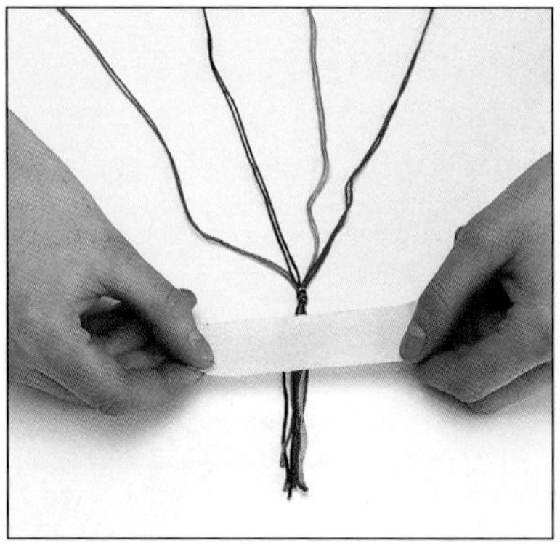

2 Using a strong piece of sticky tape, stick the strands on a flat surface just above the knot. Lay out the threads as shown.

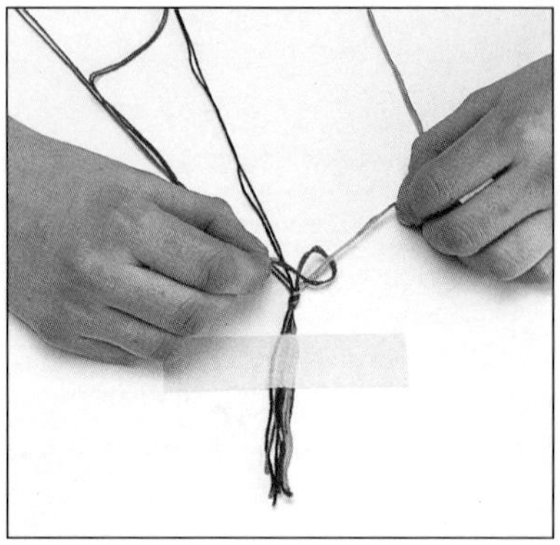

3 Take the first pair of coloured threads on the right and knot them over the pair of threads on the left.

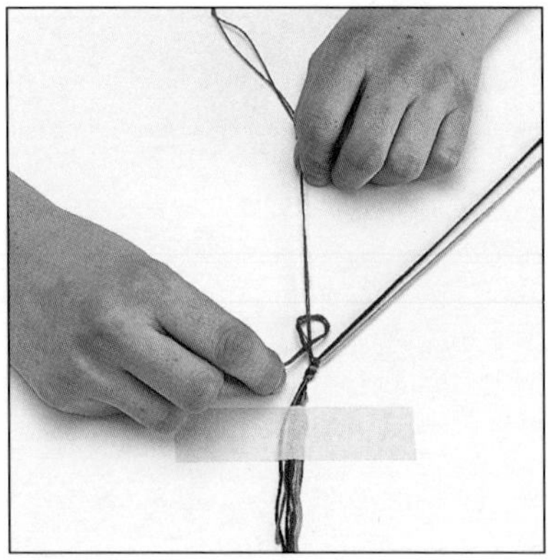

4 Tie another knot and then go on to the next pair of threads and tie two knots. Continue until you get to the end of the row.

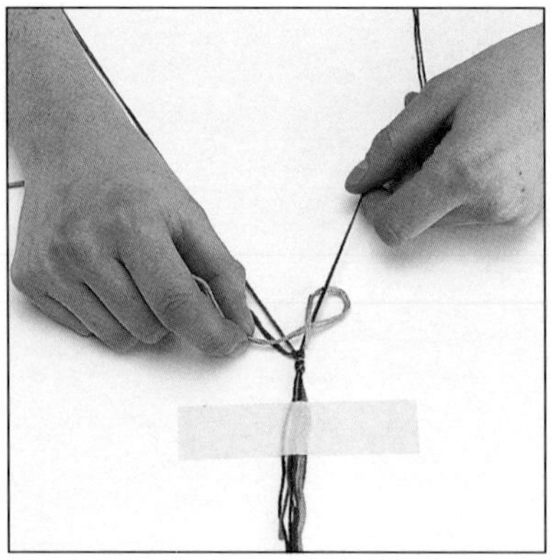

5 Go back to the new thread on the left and continue the same technique, as in step 3. Keep knotting until the bracelet is long enough to fit around the wrist of the person it will be given to.

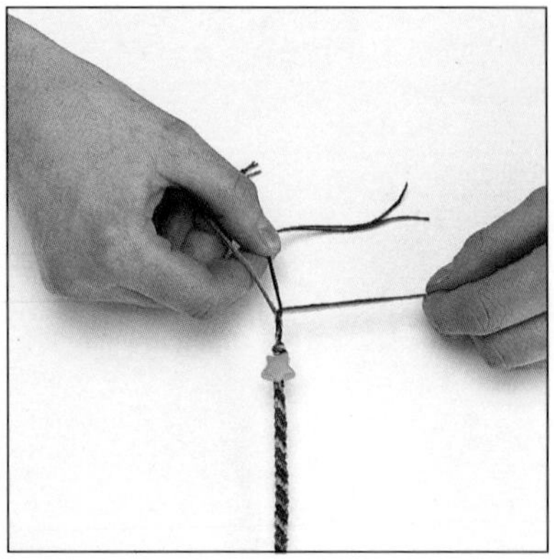

6 Divide the threads into three sections and plait (braid) them together. Thread on a bead and then tie a knot at the end, to hold the bead in place. Trim off any trailing strands.

Festive Dog Bowl

Don't forget to make your pets a present at Christmas time. If you have a cat, why not make a cat bowl instead? You'll find a fish bone template next to the dog bone one to decorate it with.

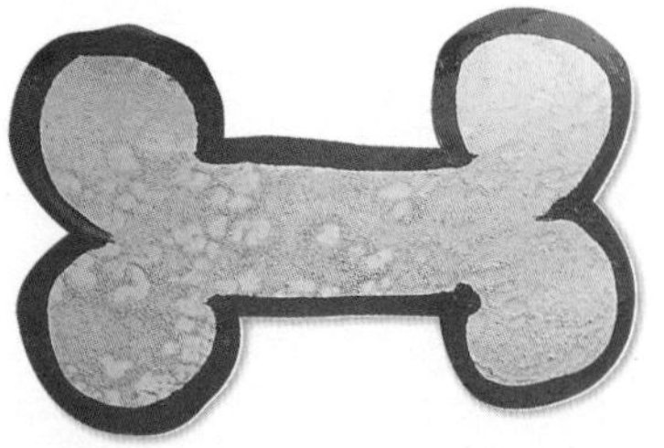

YOU WILL NEED
felt-tip pen
scissors
cardboard
masking tape
metal dog bowl
sponge
enamel paints in various colours
tissue
paintbrush
strong glue
artificial gemstones

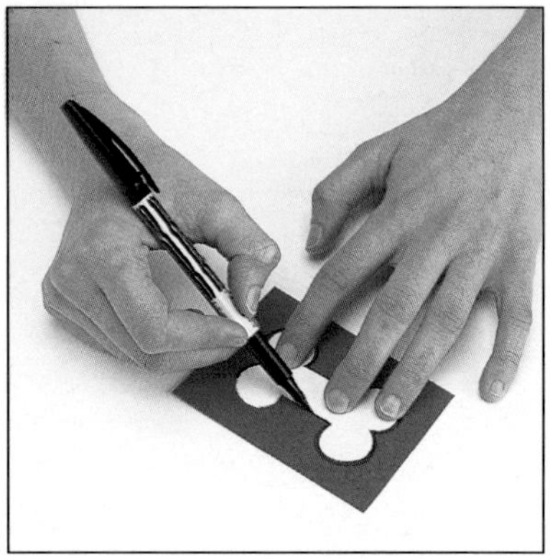

1 Trace the template for the dog bone from this book and cut it out. Draw around the template on a piece of cardboard.

2 Carefully cut out the inside of the bone shape to make a stencil. You may need the help of an adult to do this.

3 Hold the stencil firmly against the bowl or, if you find it easier, fix it to the side of the bowl with a piece of masking tape. Using a sponge, dab paint through the stencil on to the bowl. Repeat all the way around the bowl.

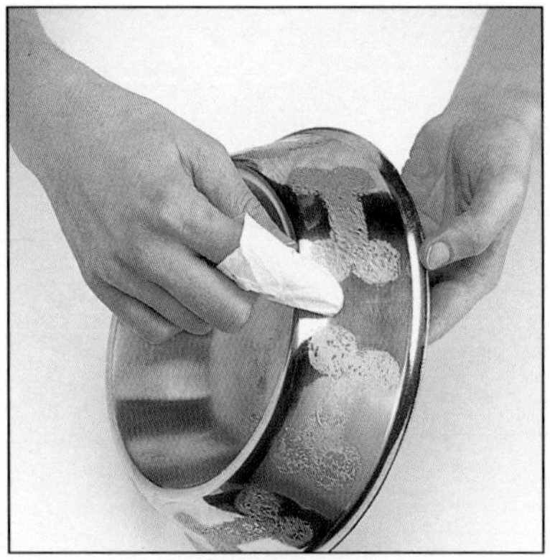

4 Neaten up the edges of the bones with a tissue. Leave the paint to dry.

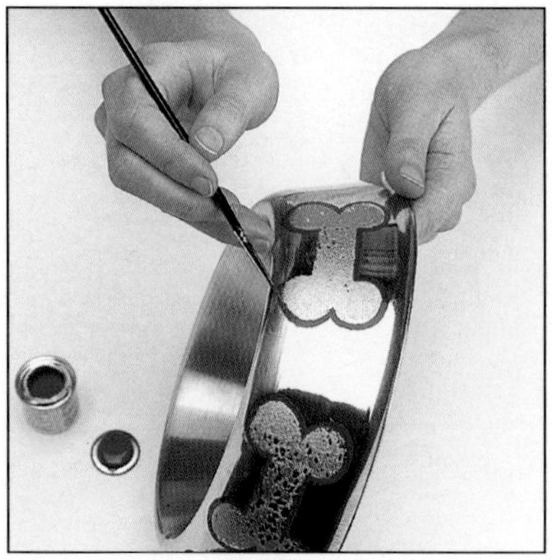

5 Paint an outline around each bone in a contrasting colour of paint.

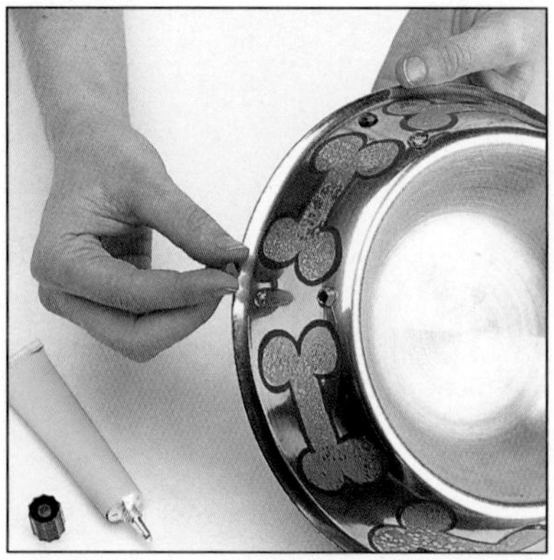

6 Using strong glue, stick the artificial gemstones on the bowl, between each of the bones.

Party Crown

You and your friends can be kings and queens for the day with this fabulous golden crown. Your Christmas party will become a royal celebration!

YOU WILL NEED
pencil
scrap paper
scissors
gold cardboard
PVA (white) glue
artificial gemstones
glitter glue
paper fasteners
double-sided sticky tape
tinsel

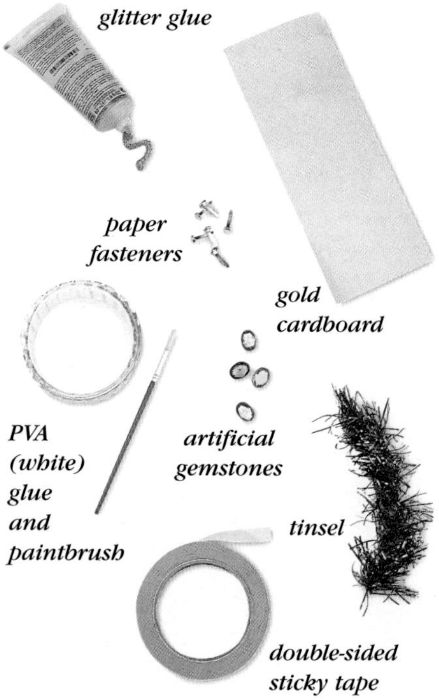

1 Draw a crown shape on a piece of scrap paper and cut it out to make a template. Make sure the crown will be the right size for your head when the ends are joined together. Draw round the template on gold cardboard.

2 Using PVA (white) glue, stick the artificial gemstones on to the crown. Leave until the glue is dry.

3 Using glitter glue, carefully highlight the edge of the crown. Leave to dry.

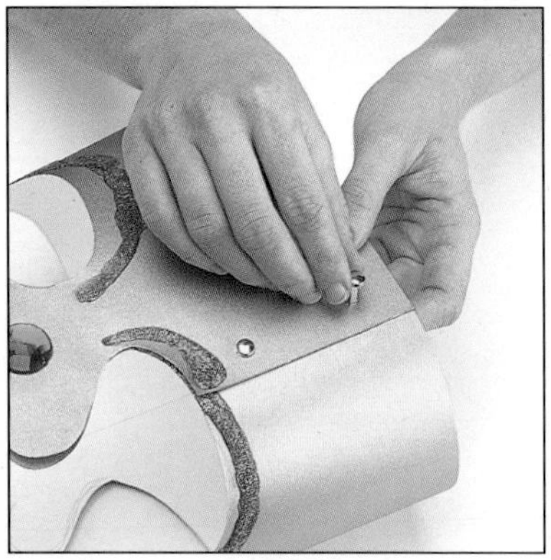

4 Join the ends of the crown together, adjusting the size to fit your head, and secure in place with the paper fasteners.

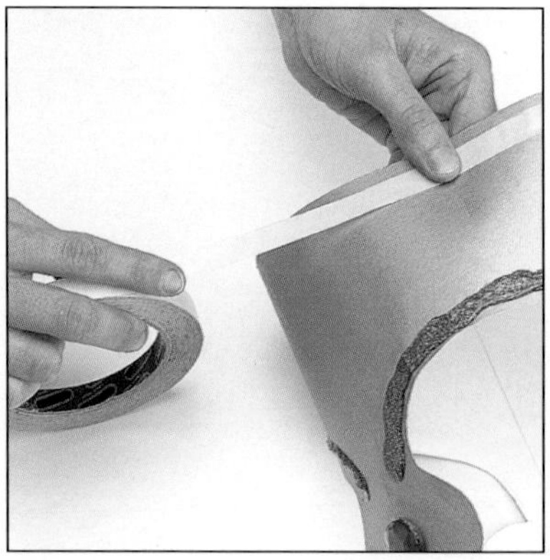

5 Stick a strip of double-sided sticky tape around the base of the crown.

6 Peel the paper backing off the sticky tape and press on the tinsel, all the way around the crown.

Christmas Tree Earrings

These festive earrings will certainly make you stand out at a party. They clip on, so you don't even have to have pierced ears to wear them.

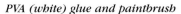

YOU WILL NEED
felt-tip pen
scissors
cardboard
gummed tape
paintbrush
gold paint
foil paper in various colours
PVA (white) glue
sequins
sewing thread
strong glue
clip-on earring findings

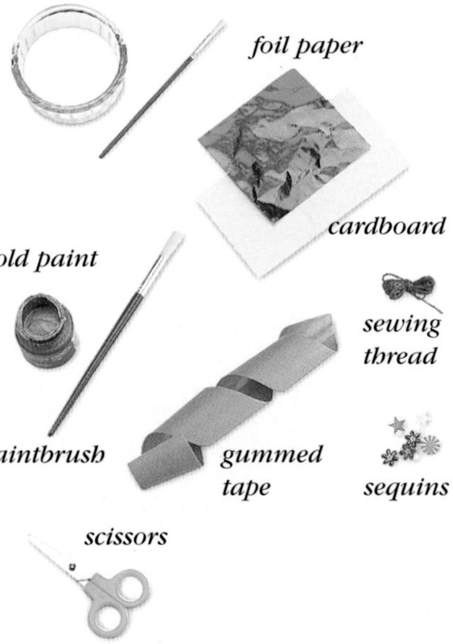

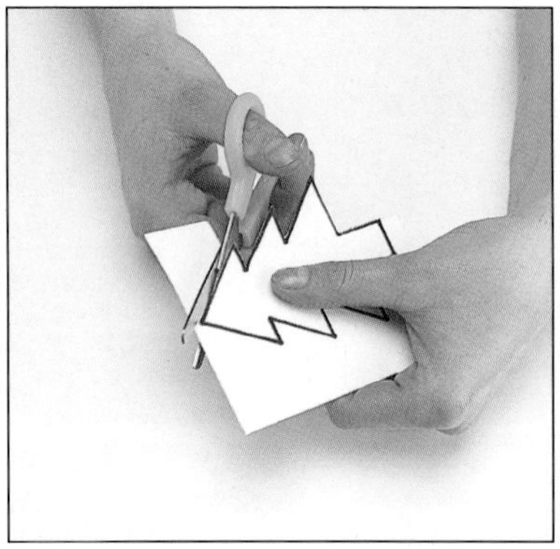

1 Trace the earring templates from this book and cut them out. Draw around the templates on a piece of cardboard. You will need to cut out two Christmas trees and two circles for each pair of earrings.

2 Tear up small pieces of gummed tape and dampen the back of them to make them sticky. Stick them on to both of the circle and Christmas tree shapes.

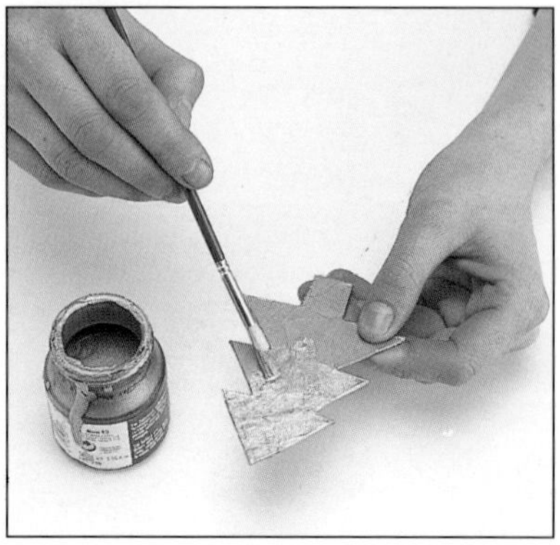

3 When the paper has dried, paint the shapes gold. Allow the paint to dry.

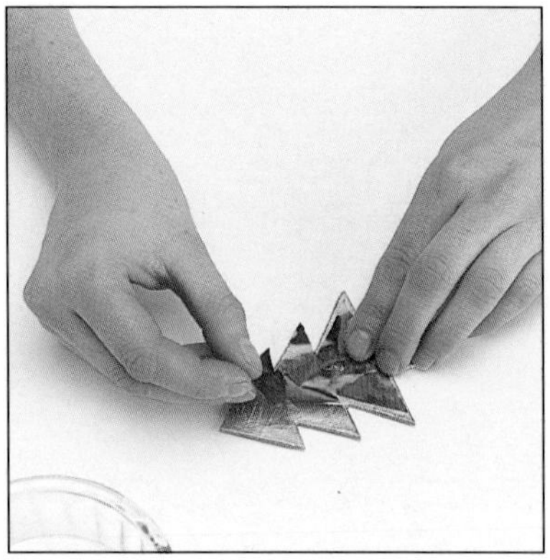

4 Cut out a tree shape slightly smaller than the cardboard tree from the coloured foil. Glue the shape on to the cardboard tree.

5 Add the decorations to the tree by gluing on a few sequins. Ask an adult to help you make a small hole at the top of the tree and at the edge of the circle, using the tip of a pair of scissors.

6 Thread a piece of thread through the hole in the circle and the hole in the tree. Tie the threads together with a small knot. Using PVA (white) glue, stick an earring finding onto the back circle part of each earring. Let the glue dry before trying on the earrings.

Party Badges

Make a party badge for your friends and family to wear on Christmas Day. Try to give each badge a different character to suit the person you are giving it to.

YOU WILL NEED
- felt-tip pen
- scissors
- cardboard
- gold paint
- poster paints in various colours
- paintbrush
- wool (yarn)
- ribbon
- PVA (white) glue
- mini pom-pom
- star sequins
- artificial gemstones
- strong glue
- brooch finding

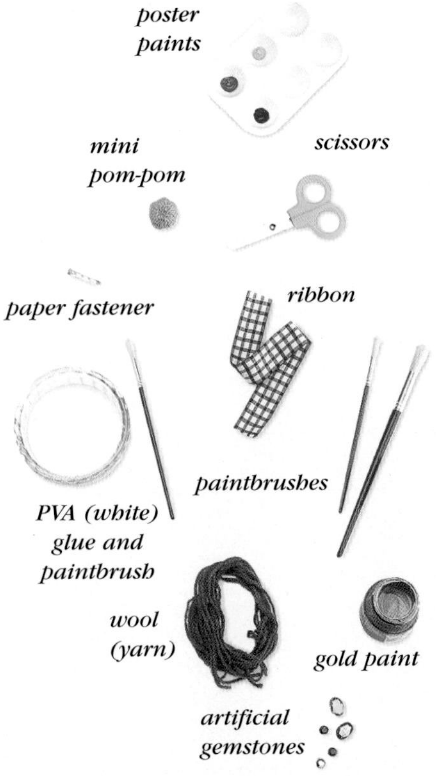

1 Trace all the badge templates from this book and cut them out. Draw around the templates on a piece of cardboard and cut them out.

2 Paint the face-shaped pieces of cardboard in a flesh colour and paint the crown shape gold. Allow the paint to dry completely.

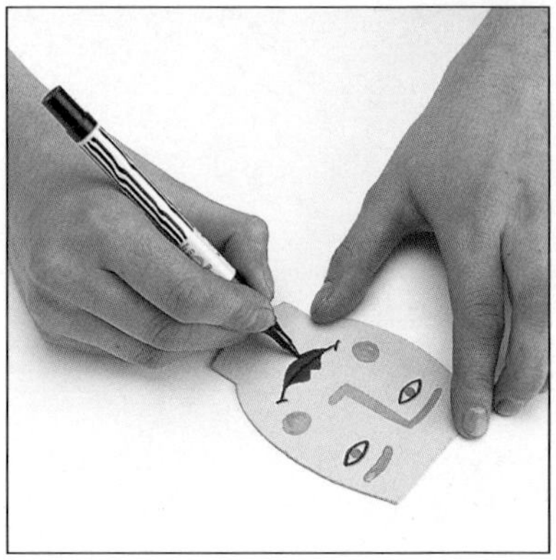

3 Using a fine paintbrush, paint the eyes, nose and mouth on the faces. Allow the paint to dry. If you find painting the details of the face too fiddly, you could use a felt-tip pen instead.

4 For the girl's hair, cut approximately nine strands of wool (yarn) to the same length. Tie them in a knot at the top and then plait (braid) them. Tie a ribbon at the end to secure the plait. You will need two plaits.

5 Glue the end of each plait to the back of the crown on either side. Allow the glue to dry. Meanwhile, paint big stripes on the boy's hat and dots on his bow tie. When the paint is dry, glue a mini pom-pom to the tip of his hat.

6 Glue the crown on to the top of the girl's head. Glue sparkly star sequins on to the crown and add artificial gemstones as a necklace. Allow the glue to dry. Using strong glue, stick a brooch finding on to the back of each badge. Leave the glue to dry.

Noughts and Crosses (Tic-Tac-Toe)

This old favourite has been brought up to date with bright jazzy colours. You could make this a portable game for journeys and holidays – use some scraps of card to form a small carrying case for board and cards.

YOU WILL NEED
medium-weight card (posterboard)
ruler
pencil
scissors
thick pink, yellow, green and blue paper
non-toxic paper glue

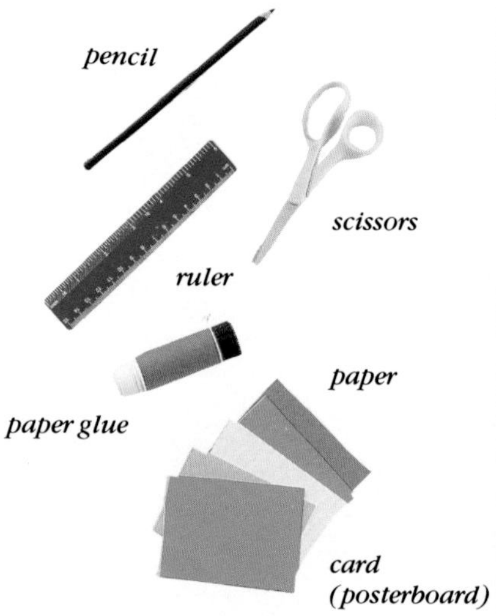

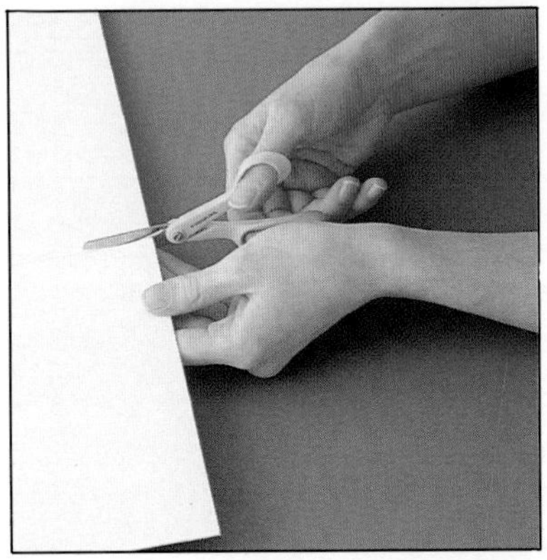

1 Mark out a square measuring 20 × 20 cm (8 × 8 in) on medium-weight card (posterboard). Cut out the square.

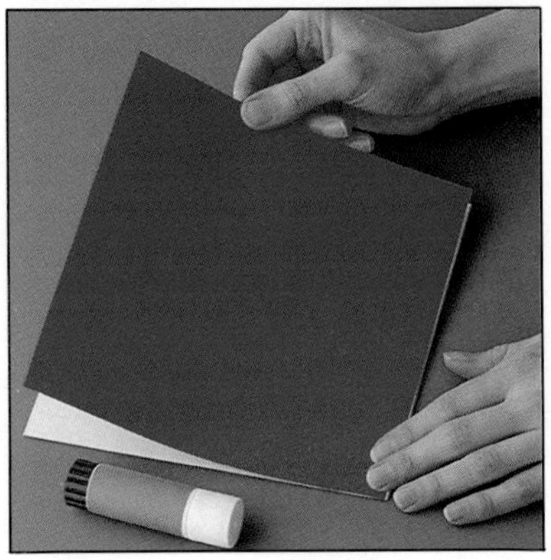

2 Place the cardboard square on the pink paper and draw around it. Cut out the paper square and stick it to the card.

3 Cut a smaller square of card measuring 15 × 15 cm (6 × 6 in). Cut a piece of yellow paper the same size.

4 Stick the yellow paper to the card and cut the card into nine squares each measuring 5 × 5 cm (2 × 2 in).

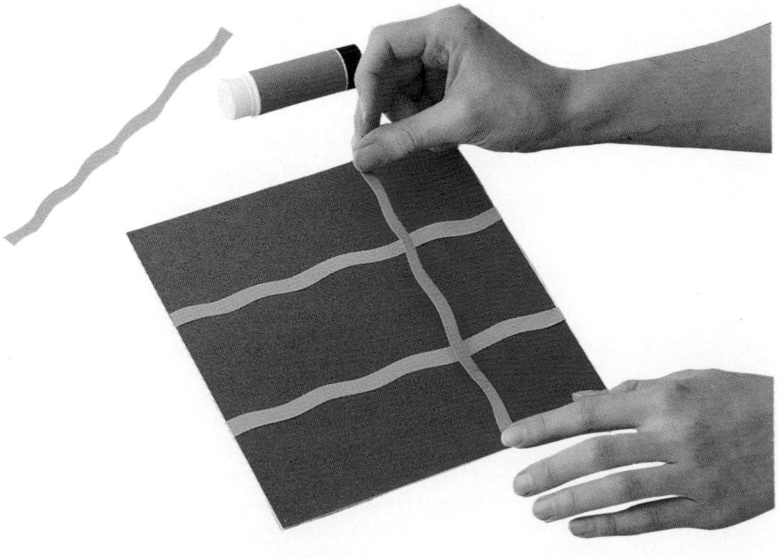

5 Cut four strips of green paper 15 × 1 cm (6 × ⅜ in). Stick them to the pink board to form nine equal squares.

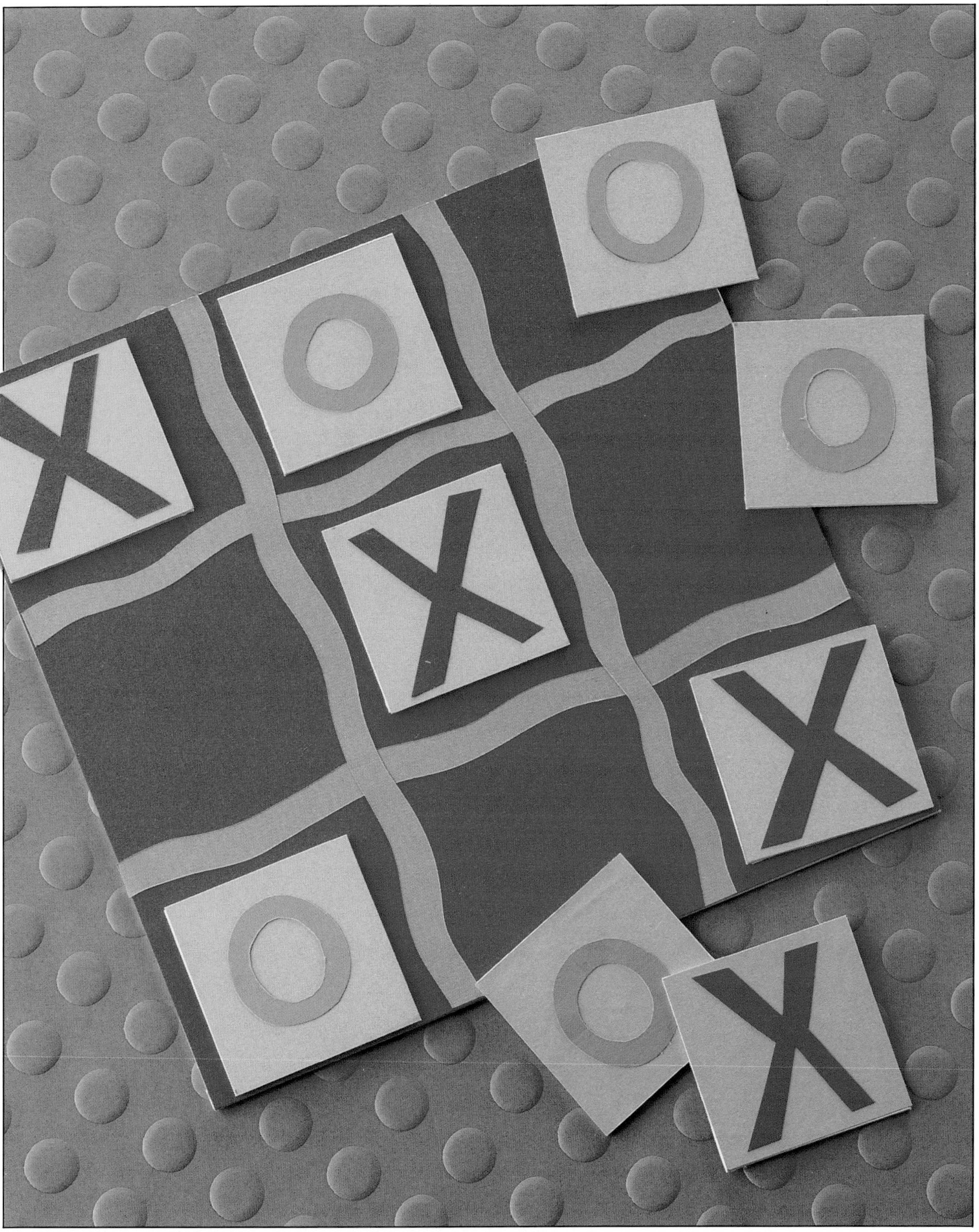

6 Draw noughts and crosses (X's and O's) on the pink and blue paper. Cut them out and stick them to the yellow squares to complete the cards.

Jigsaw

Jigsaws are a great source of enjoyment for many people. This one is cut into simple wavy pieces that slot neatly together. You could make small puzzles and give them as combined greetings cards and presents.

YOU WILL NEED
heavy card (posterboard)
ruler
pencil
scissors
stiff paper in a variety of colours
non-toxic paper glue
hole punch
craft knife (optional)

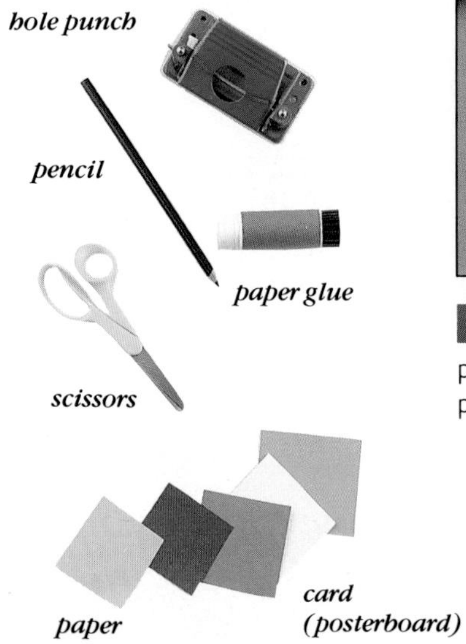

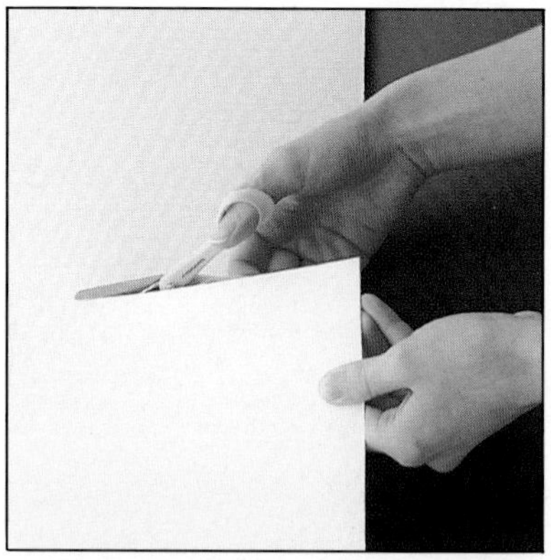

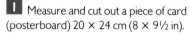

1 Measure and cut out a piece of card (posterboard) 20 × 24 cm (8 × 9½ in).

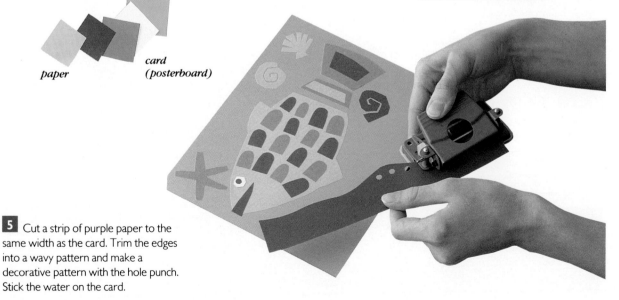

2 Place the card on a sheet of stiff blue paper and draw around it. Cut out the paper and stick it to the card.

3 Cut a fish shape from yellow paper and tail pieces from orange. Cut scale shapes from red and orange paper. Cut shells from different colours.

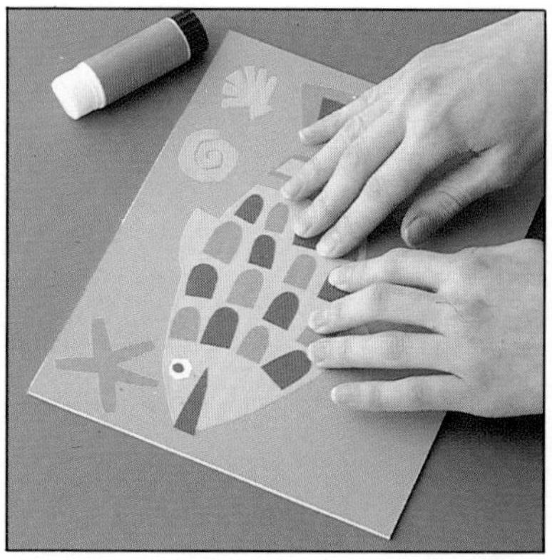

4 Stick the scales and other additions to the fish, then stick the fish to the card. Stick the shells to the background.

5 Cut a strip of purple paper to the same width as the card. Trim the edges into a wavy pattern and make a decorative pattern with the hole punch. Stick the water on the card.

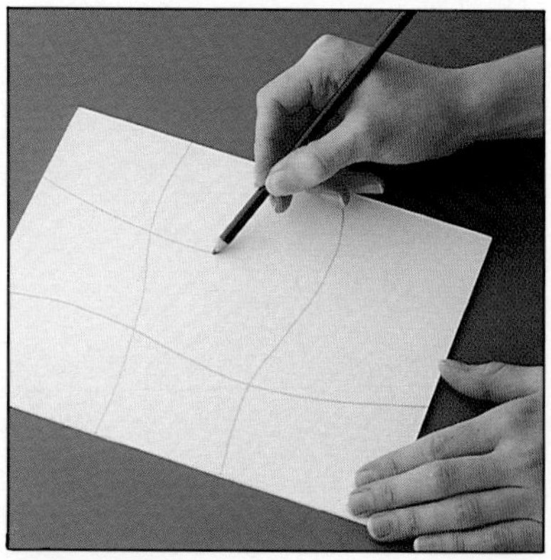

6 Draw nine uneven sections on the back of the board. Carefully cut along the lines with a pair of scissors, or ask an adult to cut using a craft knife.

Papier-mâché Earrings

These earrings would make a good gift, and the beauty of papier-mâché is that however large the earrings, they won't weigh your ears down!

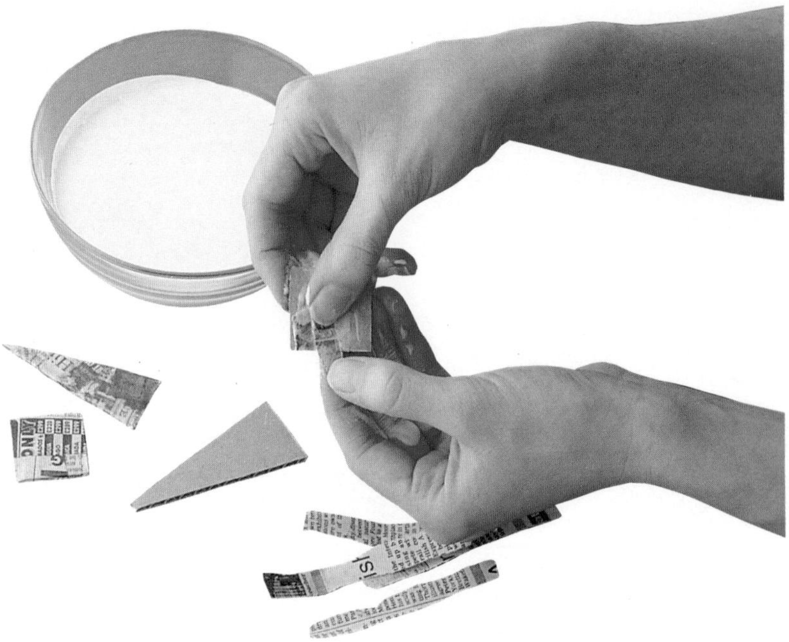

You will need
tracing paper
pencil
corrugated cardboard
scissors
newspaper
diluted non-toxic PVA (white) glue
fine sandpaper
non-toxic white paint
paintbrush
non-toxic paint in a variety of colours
non-toxic clear gloss varnish
darning needle
non-toxic strong glue
pair of eye pins
pliers
earring clips

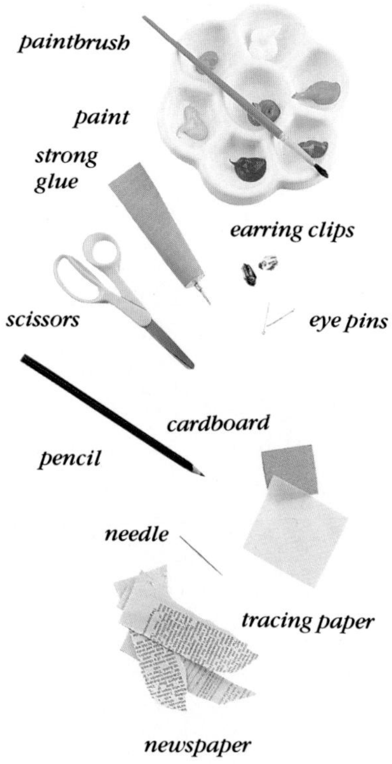

1 Trace the earring pieces from the template and transfer them to the cardboard twice. Cut them out.

2 Cover all the earring pieces in three layers of thin papier-mâché strips. Allow them to dry overnight.

3 Smooth the earring pieces with sandpaper, then prime with two coats of white paint and leave to dry.

4 Decorate the earring pieces with bright paints and leave to dry.

5 Seal the dry earring pieces with two coats of gloss varnish.

6 With adult help, make a small hole in each piece with the darning needle. Dab a little strong glue over each hole and push an eye pin into each. Leave the glue to dry. With adult help, use pliers to open the loops of the eye pins in the lower half of each earring. Hook the lower to the upper half, and close the loops. Use strong glue to attach the earring clips and allow to dry thoroughly.

Eye Masks

Even if you're not going to a masked ball, you'll have fun making and wearing these disguises! They're especially good if you're in a play or pantomime – you'll be surprised how difficult your friends find it to recognize you!

YOU WILL NEED
- tracing paper or graph paper
- pencil
- thin card (posterboard) in a variety of colours
- scissors
- paper in a variety of colours
- non-toxic paper glue
- thin wooden sticks
- paintbrush
- non-toxic paint
- non-toxic strong glue
- wax crayons
- gold paper

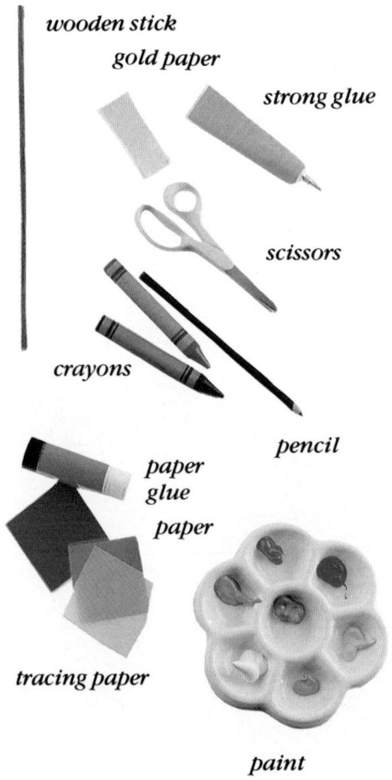

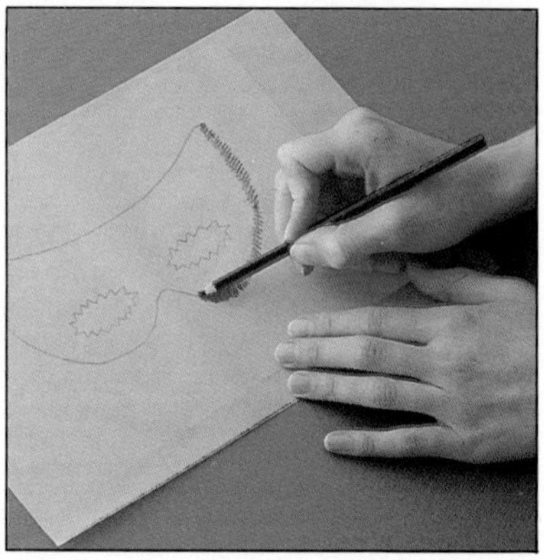

1 Trace or scale up the fiery mask shape from the template section of this book and transfer to orange card (posterboard). Cut it out.

2 Place the card on purple paper. Extend the sides and top of the eye mask with small spikes. Cut out this shape.

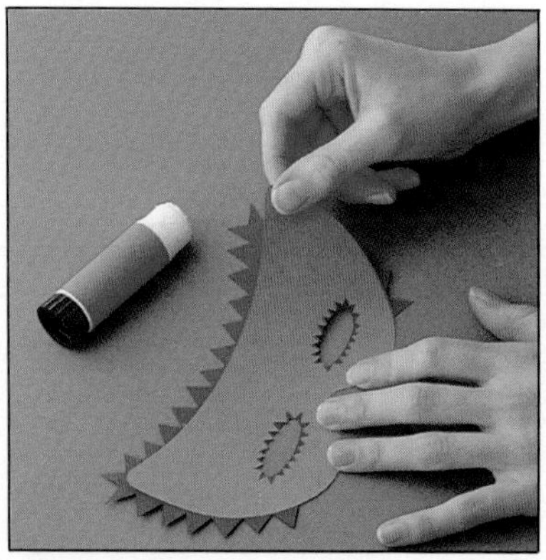

3 Using paper glue stick the orange shape in place on top of the purple one. Carefully trim the lower edge of the mask if necessary.

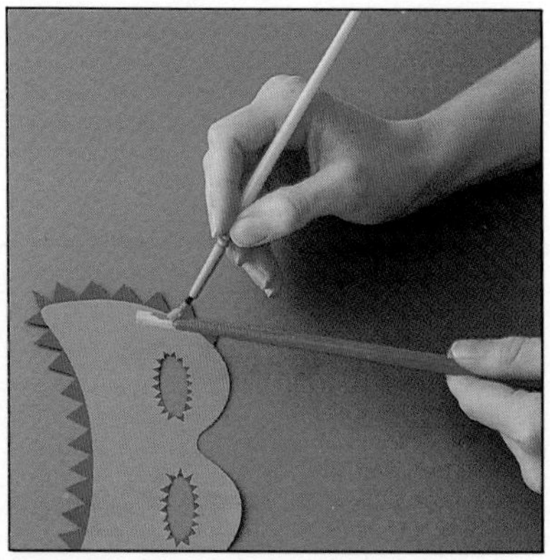

4 Paint the wooden stick a bright colour. You may have to use two coats of paint.

5 Attach the wooden stick to the side of the mask with strong glue. Stick it the right of the mask if you are right-handed and vice-versa if you are left-handed.

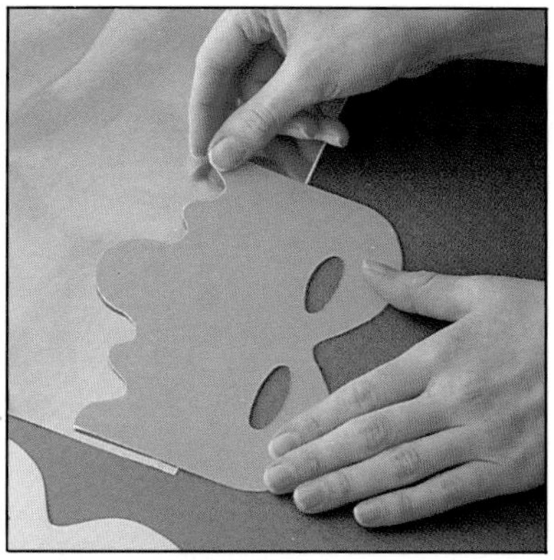

6 To make the leopard mask, use yellow card and apply the spots with wax crayon. The king has a crown made of gold paper, and his eyebrows are applied with wax crayon.

Foil-covered Frame

Do you have a favourite photograph or picture that deserves a special frame? Why not make one in papier-mâché? This one looks very impressive with its colourful foil surface and will take standard-sized photographs.

YOU WILL NEED
graph paper
thick and thin corrugated cardboard
pencil
ruler
scissors
non-toxic strong glue
newspaper
diluted non-toxic PVA (white) glue
paintbrush
non-toxic white paint
silver foil
coloured foil
2 picture hangers
thin cord

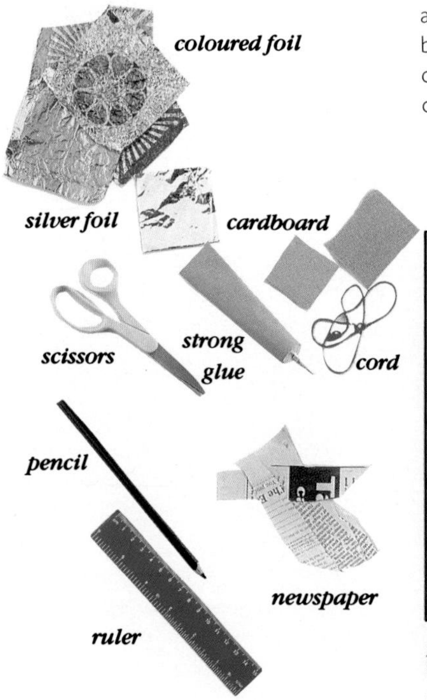

1 Scale up each piece of frame from the template in this book onto appropriate cardboard. The front and back frame should be drawn onto thick cardboard, and the spacer on thin. Cut out each piece.

2 Stick the spacer to the frame front with strong glue.

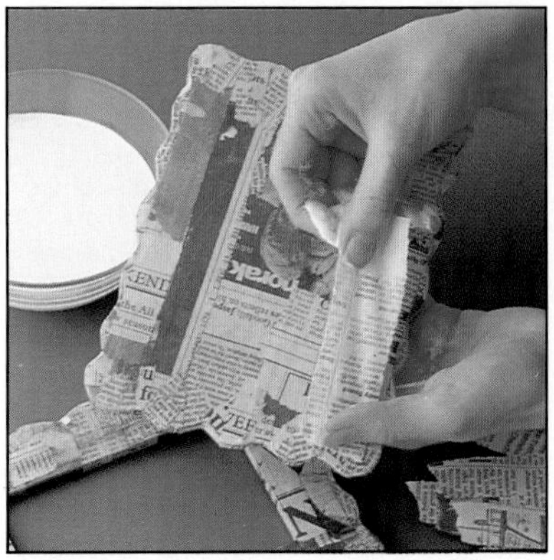

3 Cover both sections with three layers of papier-mâché strips. Allow the frame to dry overnight in a warm place.

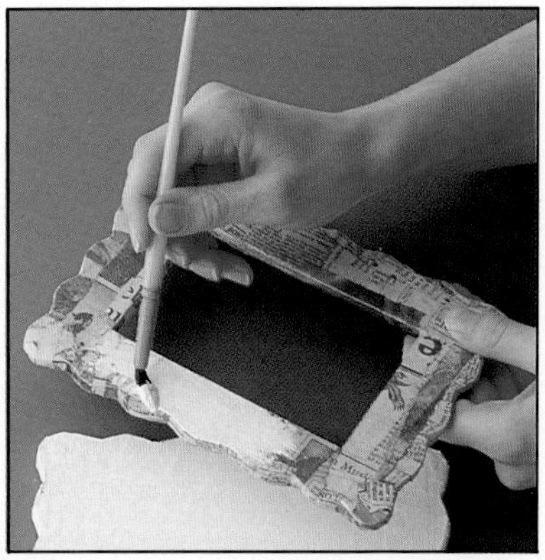

4 Prime the dry frame pieces with white paint. Although the paint won't be seen it will be easier to see where to stick the foil if the surface of the frame is white.

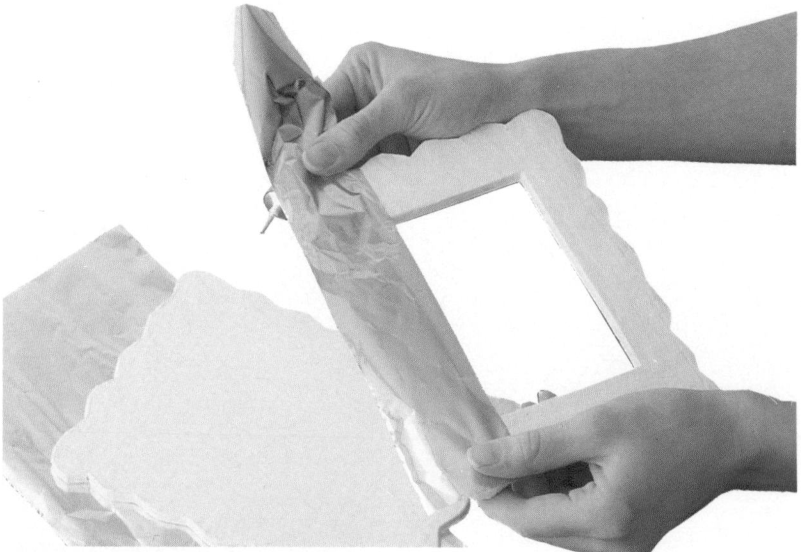

5 Cover the frame pieces with silver foil. Stick the frame front to the back. Cover the joins with strips of foil.

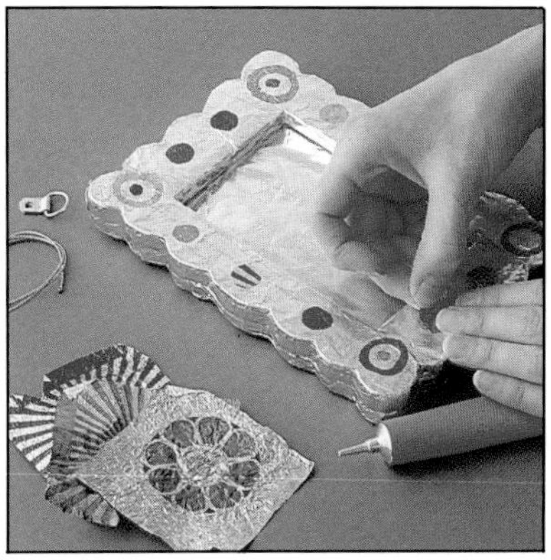

6 Cut small circles of coloured foil and stick them around the frame. Stick the hangers to the back of the frame with strong glue, and add the cord to hang the frame.

Fancy Wrapped Parcels

Turn the humblest present into an exciting parcel by making the wrappings interesting and fun. All sorts of characters are appropriate for decorating parcels. Think of the person who will receive the parcel, and of their favourite characters when choosing a design.

YOU WILL NEED
- items to wrap
- crêpe paper
- sticky tape
- paper ribbon
- pencil
- thin paper in a variety of colours
- scissors
- non-toxic paper glue
- non-toxic strong glue

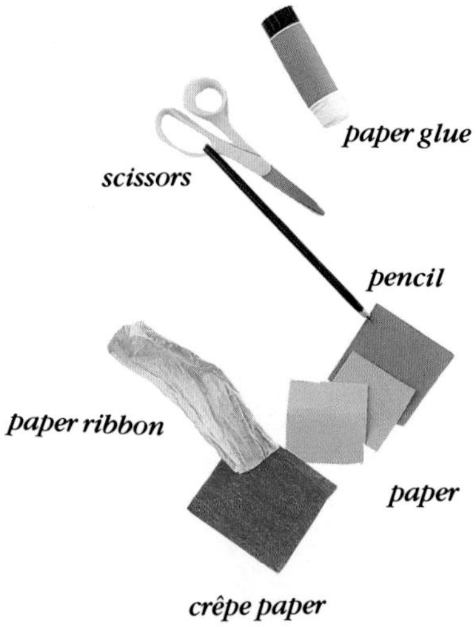

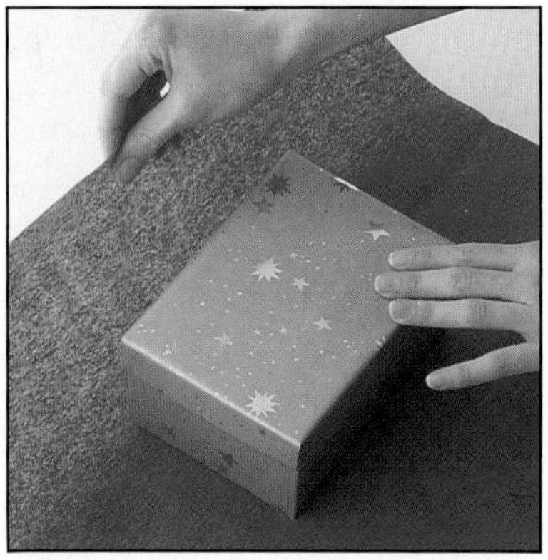

1 Wrap the parcels in crêpe paper.

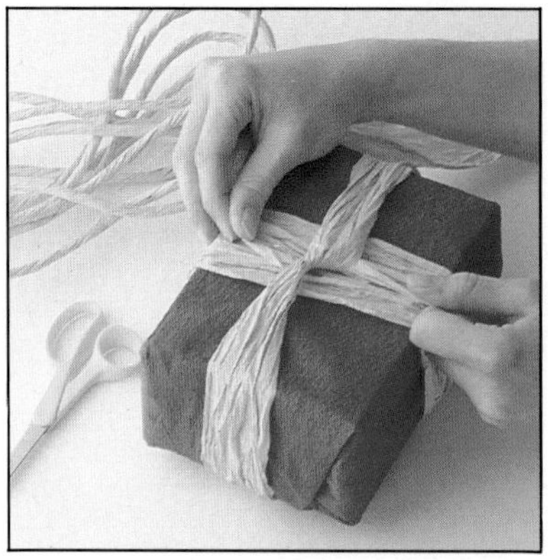

2 Open out lengths of paper ribbon and secure each parcel.

3 Draw designs onto pieces of thin coloured paper to make the head, arms and legs for each parcel (or head, legs and tail if an animal). Cut out the shapes.

4 Stick the decorative details onto each main body piece with paper glue.

5 Stick the decorations around the corners of each parcel with strong glue.

Templates

Gilded Christmas Plate

Enlarging Templates

If the templates need to be enlarged, and you do not have access to a photocopier, you can use the grid system. Trace the template and draw a grid of evenly-spaced squares over your tracing. To scale up, draw a larger grid on to another piece of paper. Copy the outline on to the second grid by taking each square individually and drawing the relevant part of the outline in the larger square. Finally, draw over the lines to make sure they are continuous.

GILDED CHRISTMAS PLATE

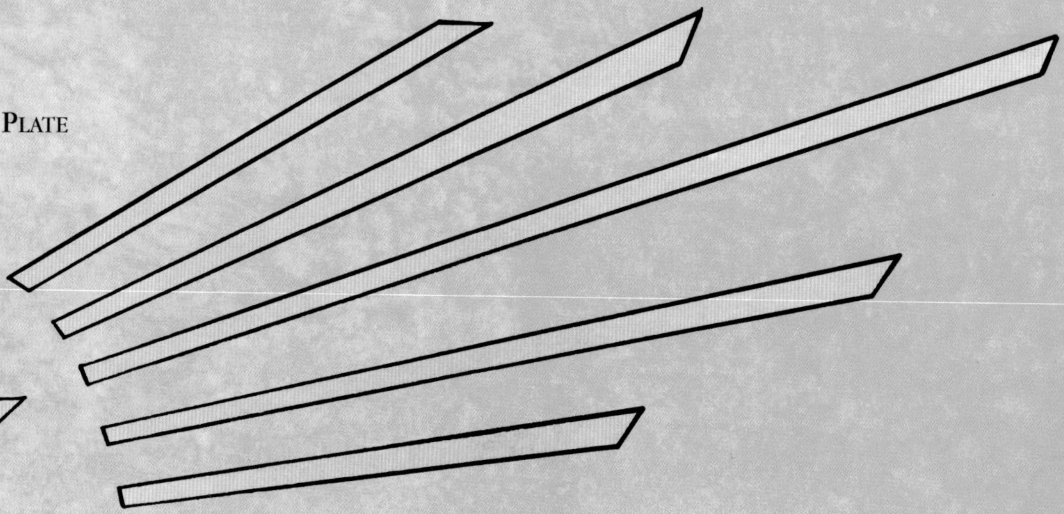

HOLLY LEAF NAPKIN

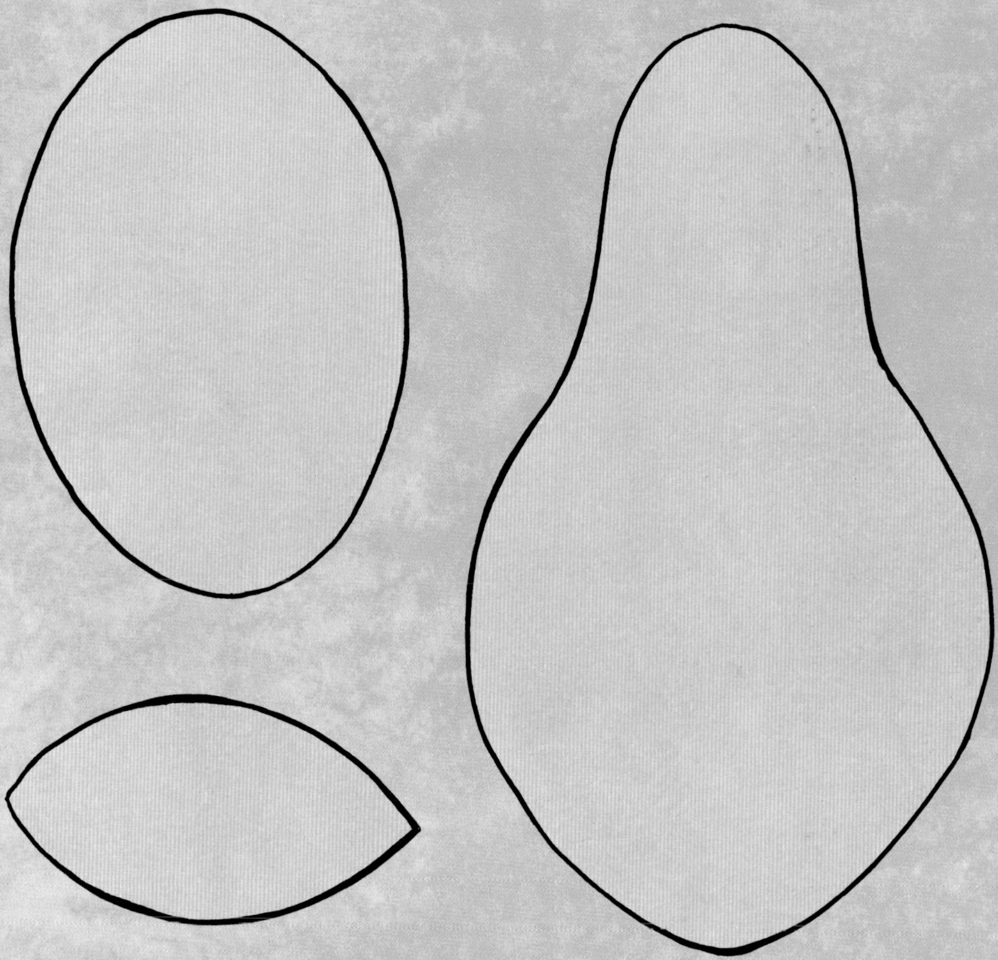

VELVET FRUITS

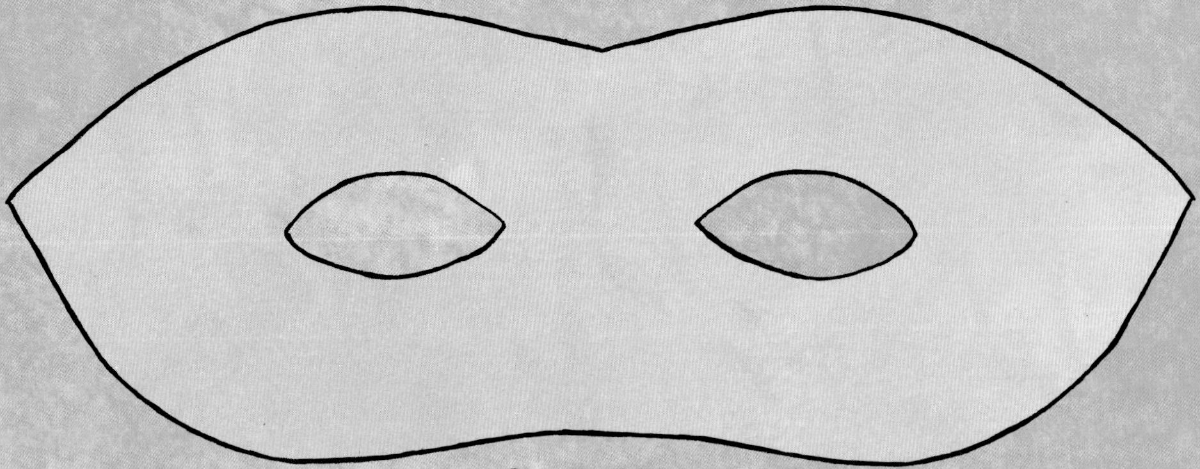

CARNIVAL MASK

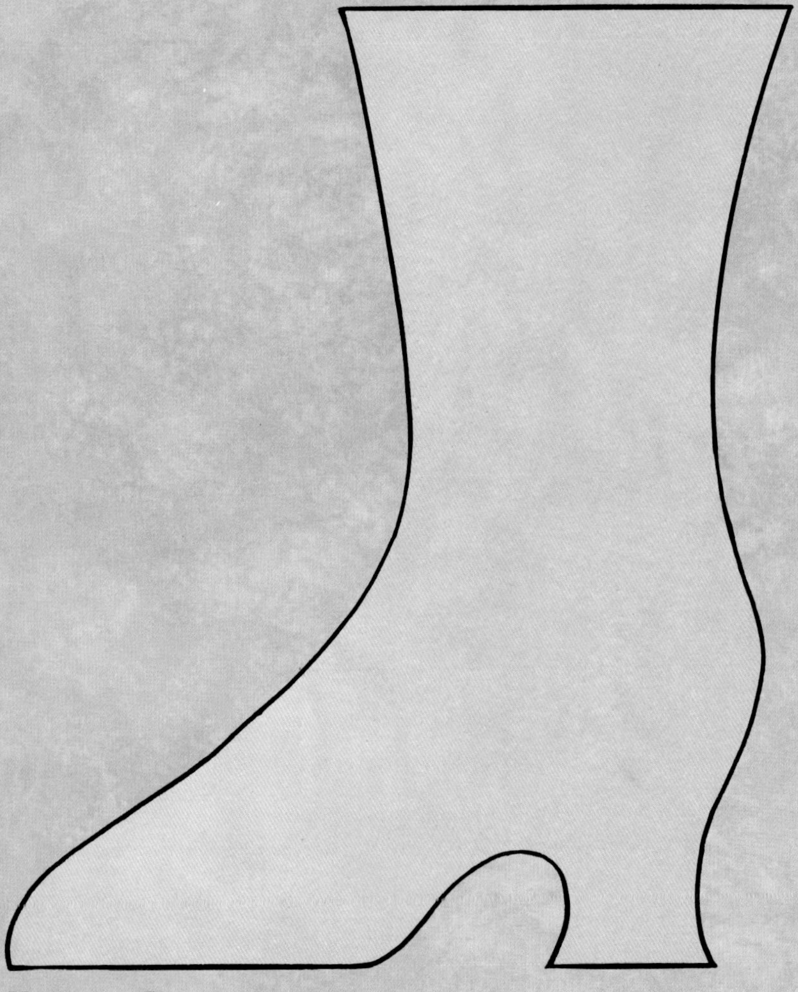

VICTORIAN BOOTS

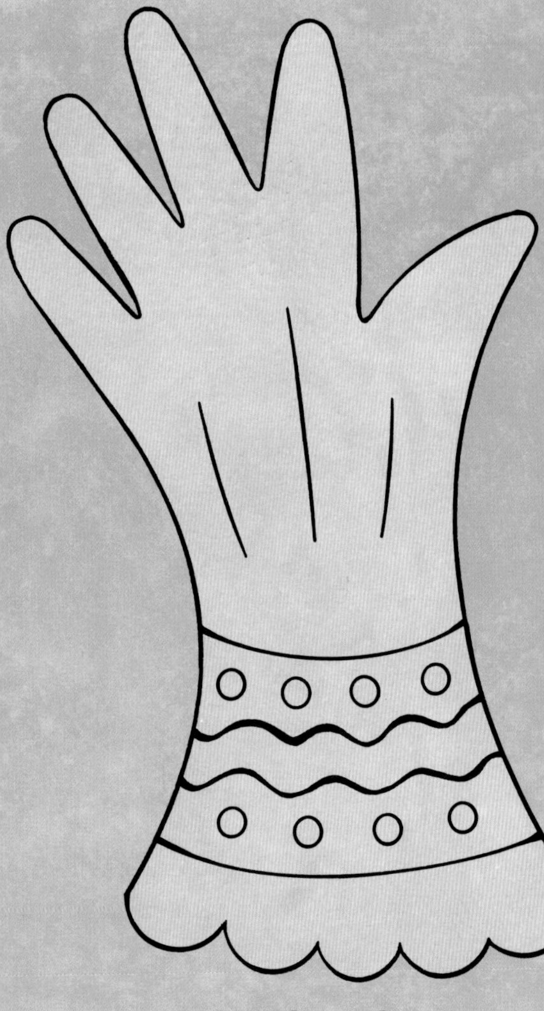

LACY SILVER GLOVES

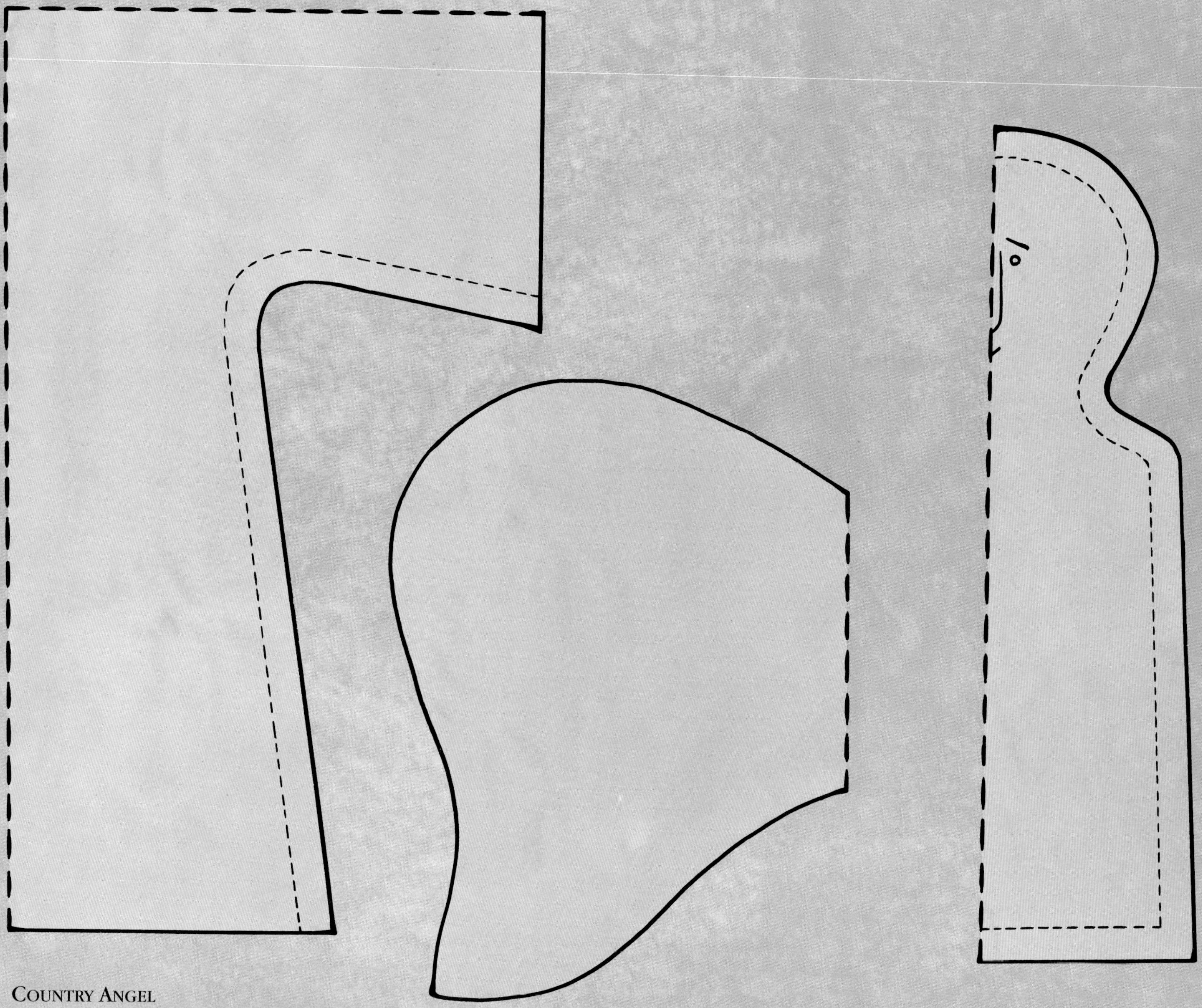

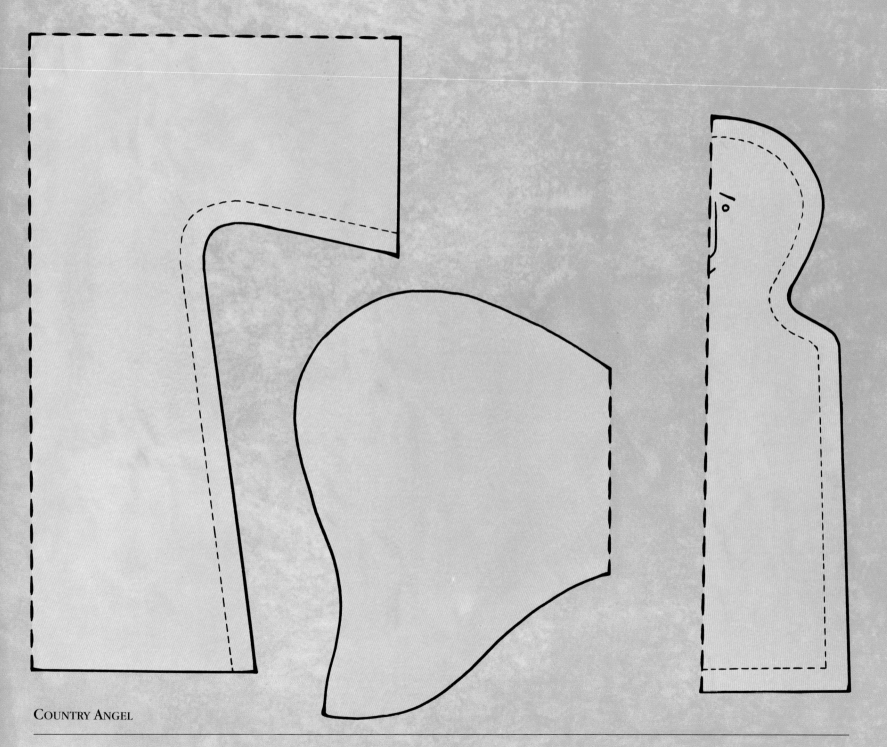

COUNTRY ANGEL

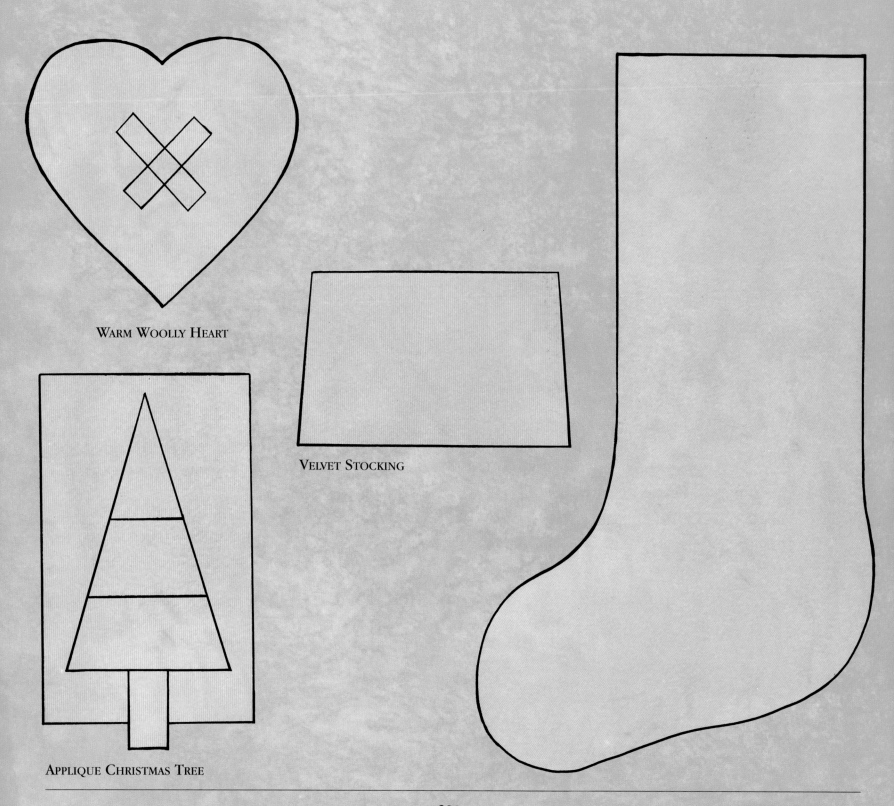

WARM WOOLLY HEART

VELVET STOCKING

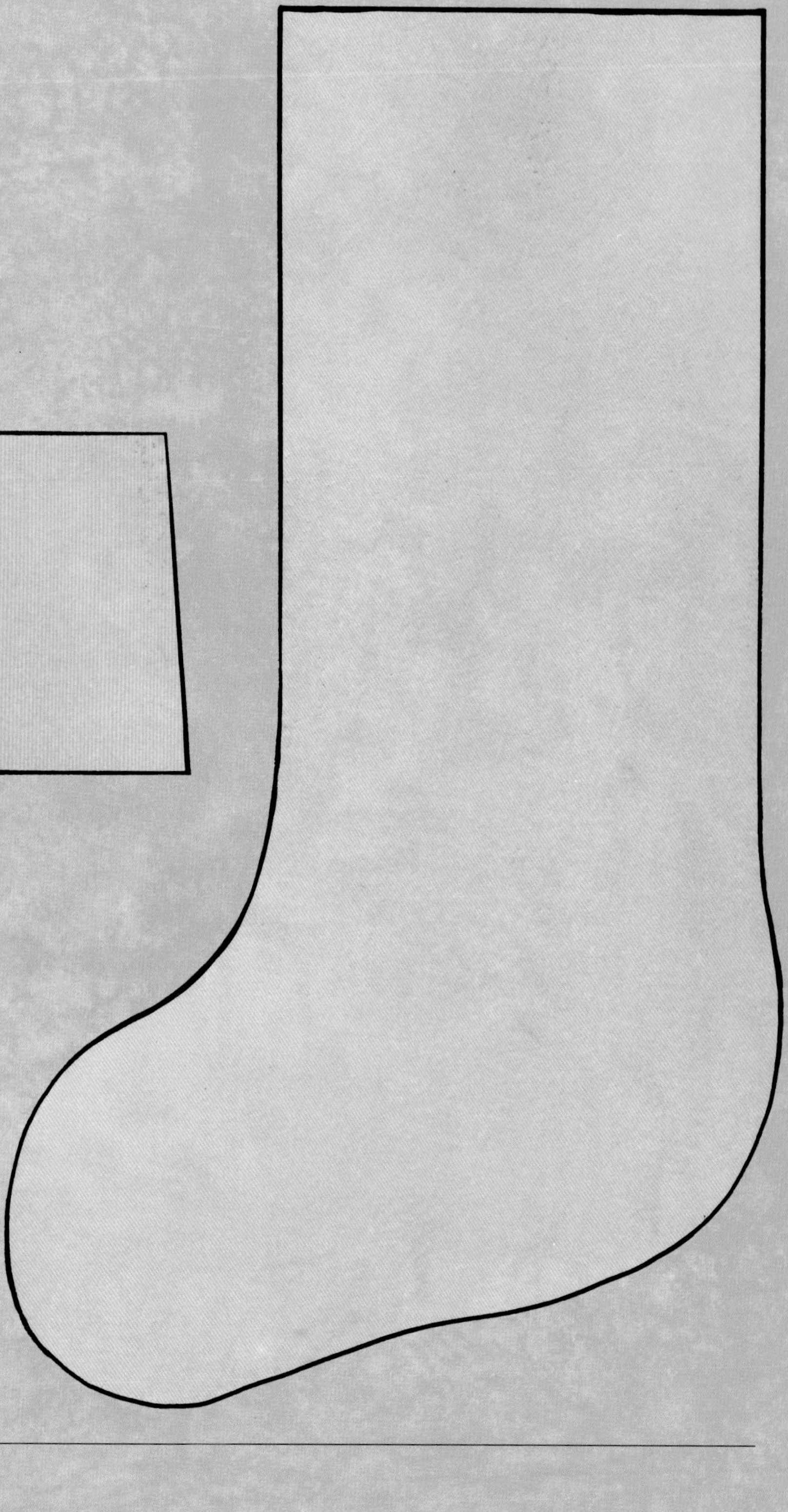

APPLIQUE CHRISTMAS TREE

CHRISTMAS COUNTDOWN

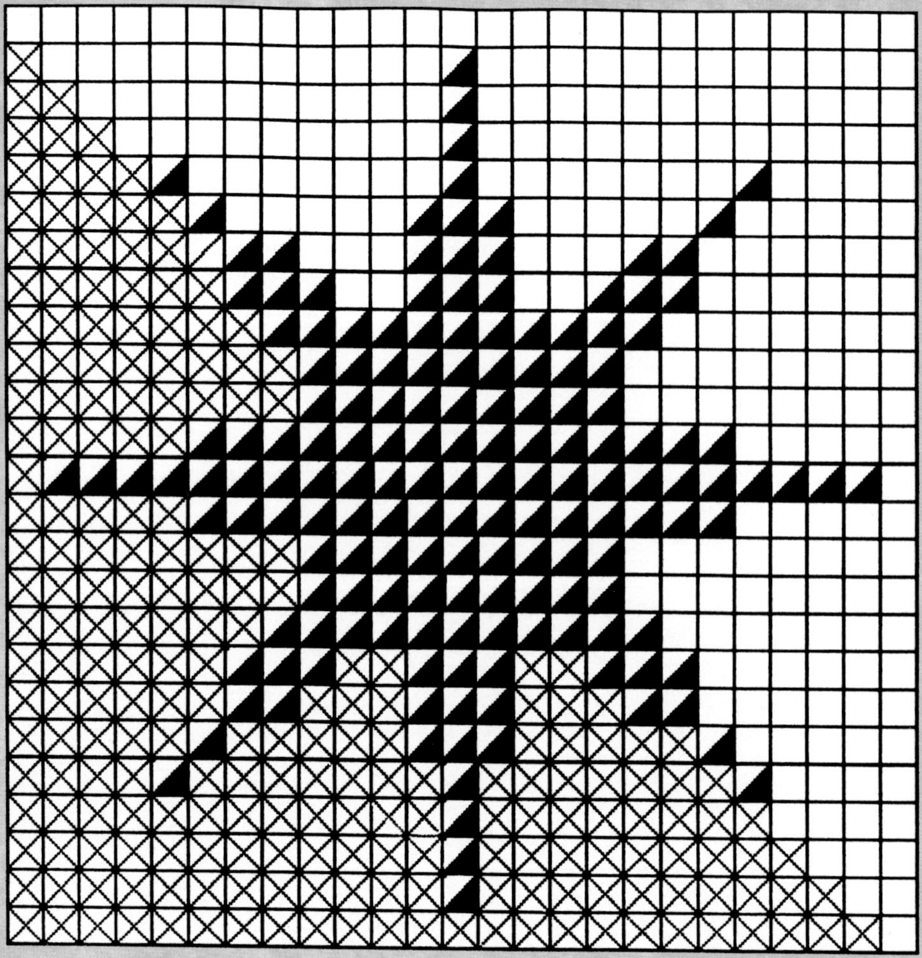

Star colour

First background colour

Second background colour

NEEDLEPOINT CUSHION

COLLAGE GIFT-WRAP AND
CHRISTMAS TREE GIFT TAGS

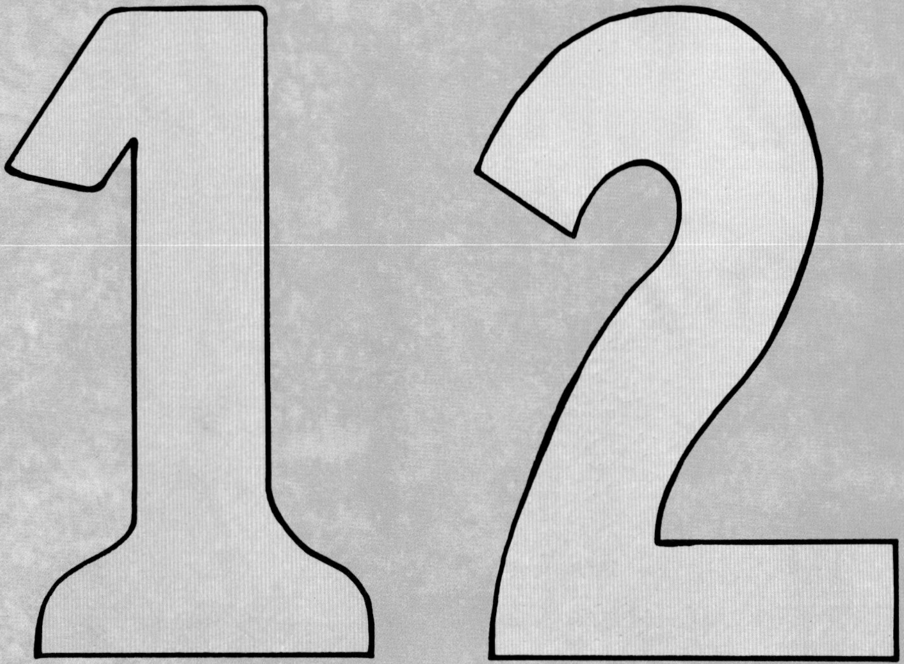

PLACE MARKER GIFT BAGS

TIN GIFT BOX

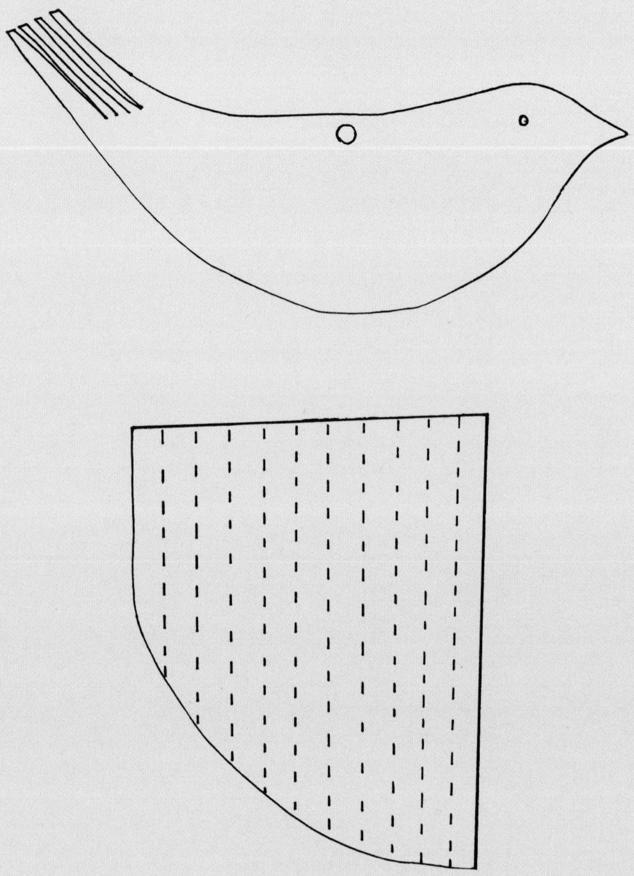

PAPER SCULPTURE BIRD

THE NATURAL LOOK

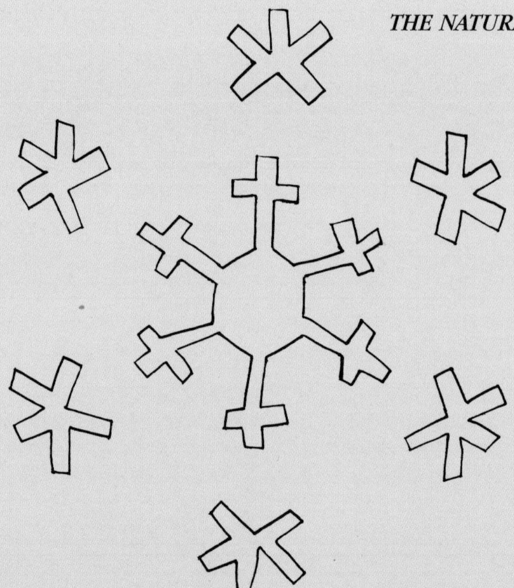

THE ICE BOX

FESTIVE FABRIC CARD

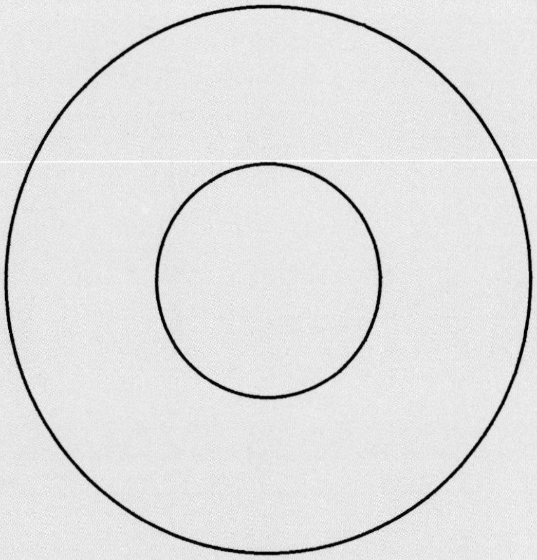

CHRISTMAS POM-POMS

CHRISTMAS TREE CARD AND TAG

STARRY GIFT-WRAP AND TAG

DOVE DECORATION

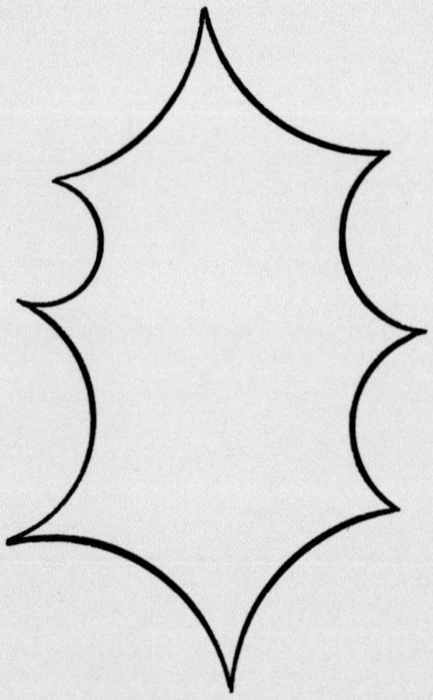

CHRISTMAS MESSAGE BOARD

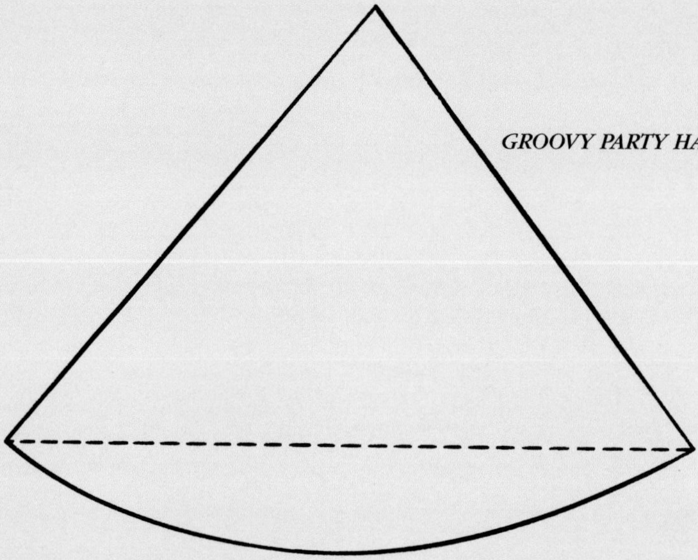

GROOVY PARTY HATS

ANGEL TREE DECORATION

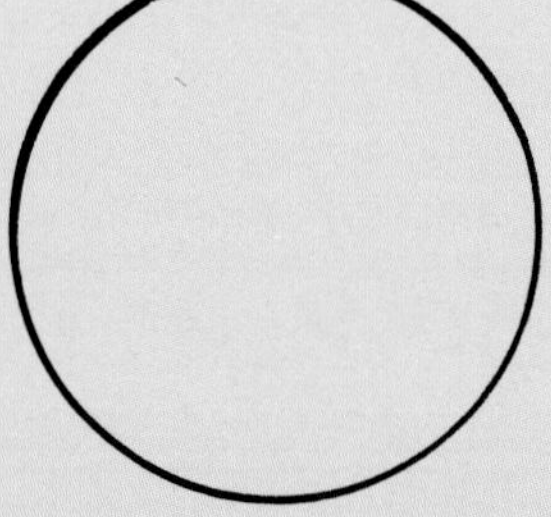

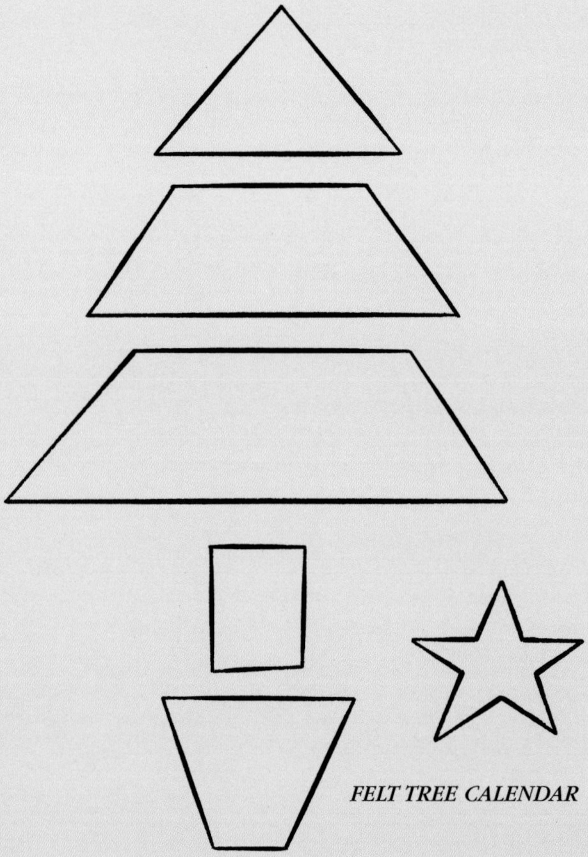

FELT TREE CALENDAR

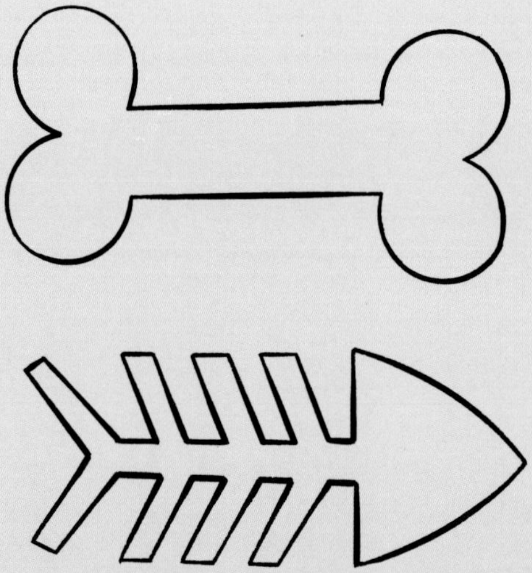

FESTIVE DOG BOWL

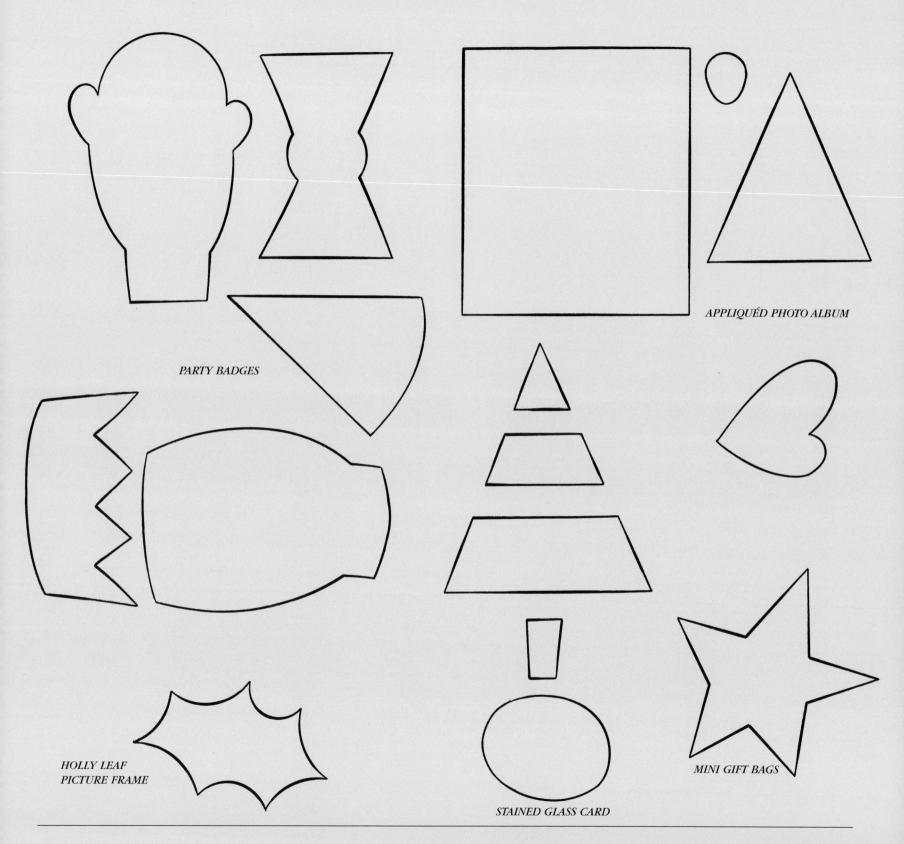

APPLIQUÉD PHOTO ALBUM

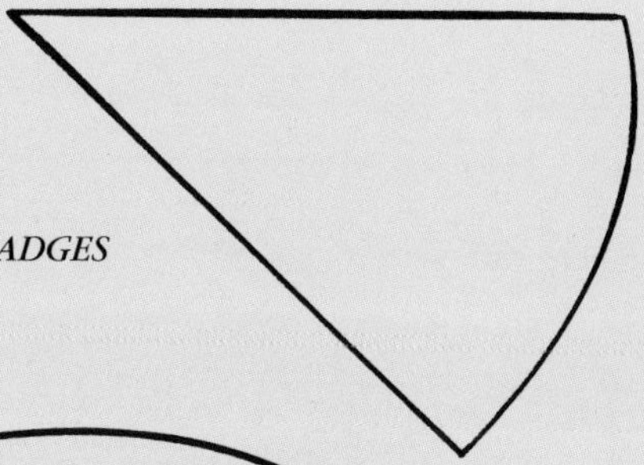

PARTY BADGES

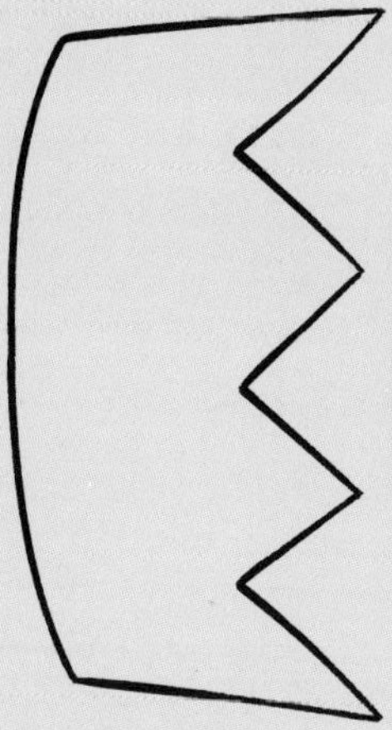
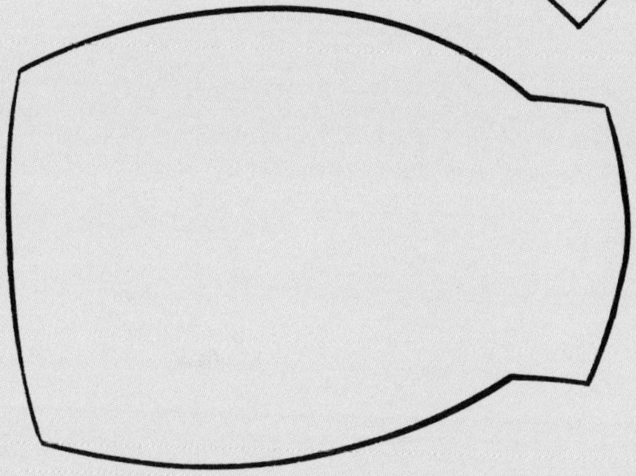

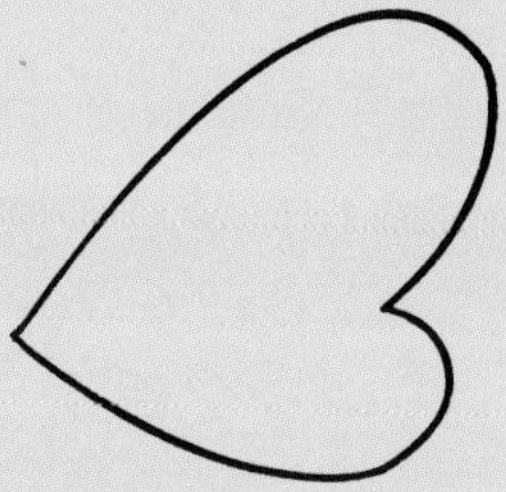

HOLLY LEAF PICTURE FRAME

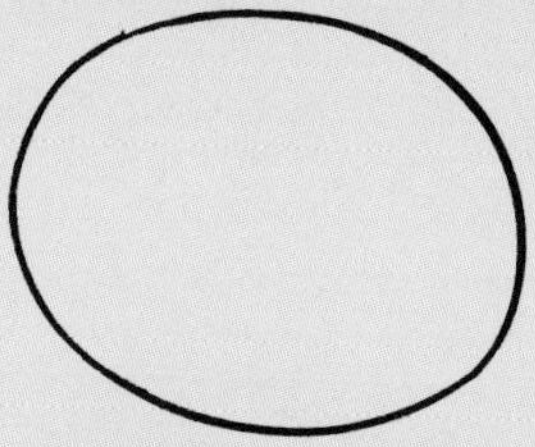

MINI GIFT BAGS

STAINED GLASS CARD

CHRISTMAS COTTAGE

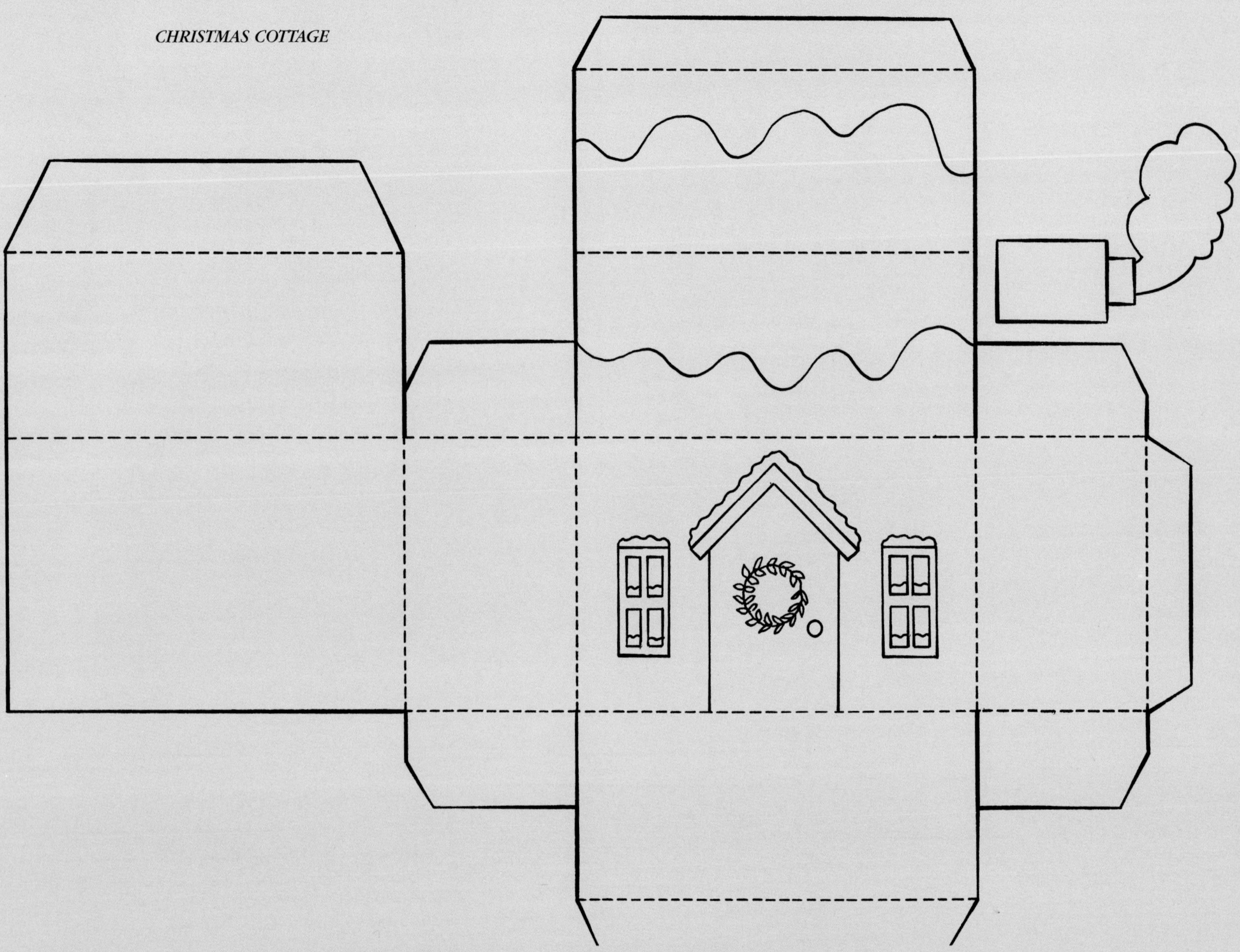

POLKA-DOT WRAPPING PAPER

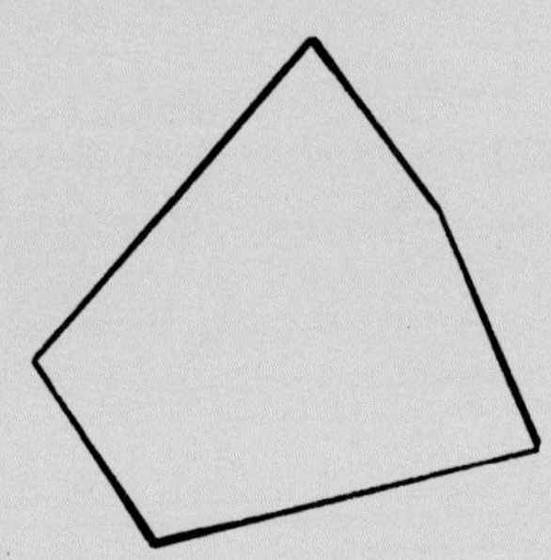

DISCO STAR CARD AND TAG

TIN HEART AND STAR TREE DECORATIONS

ADVENT TABLE DECORATION

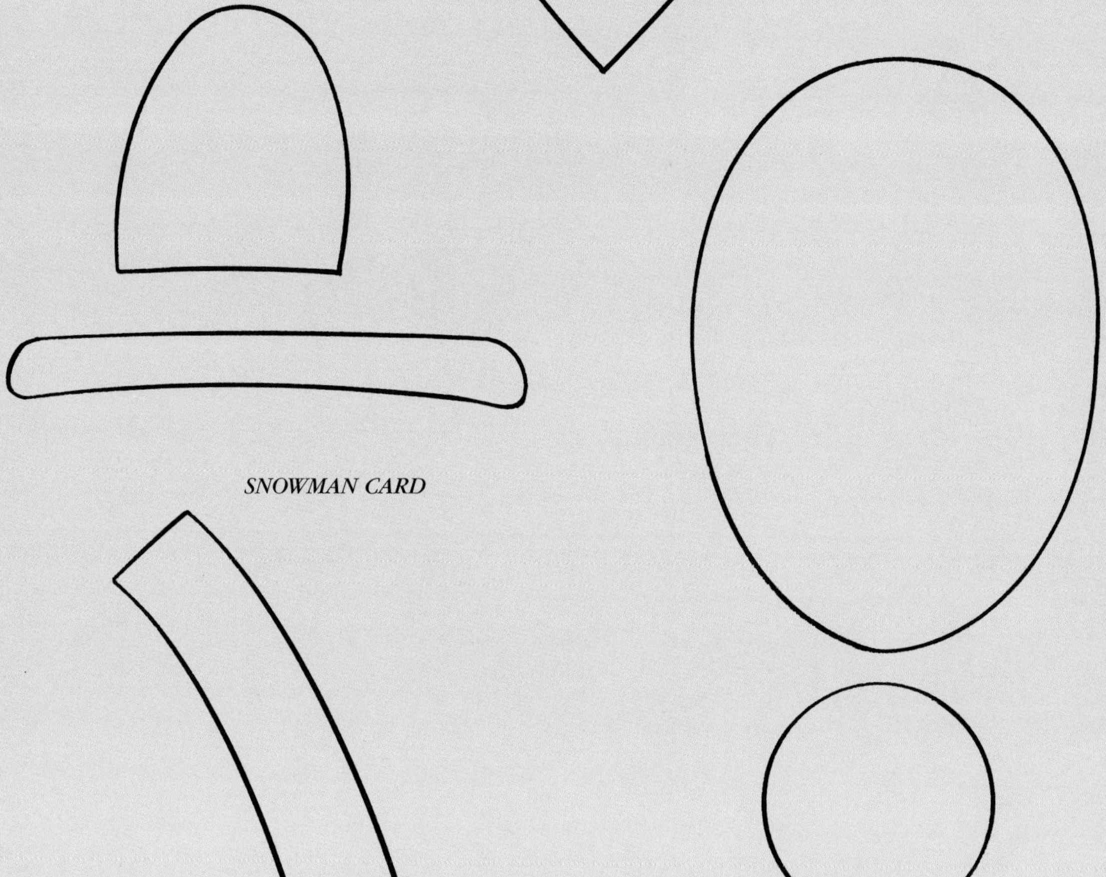

SNOWMAN CARD

WINTRY SCARF AND GLOVES

CHRISTMAS TREE EARRINGS

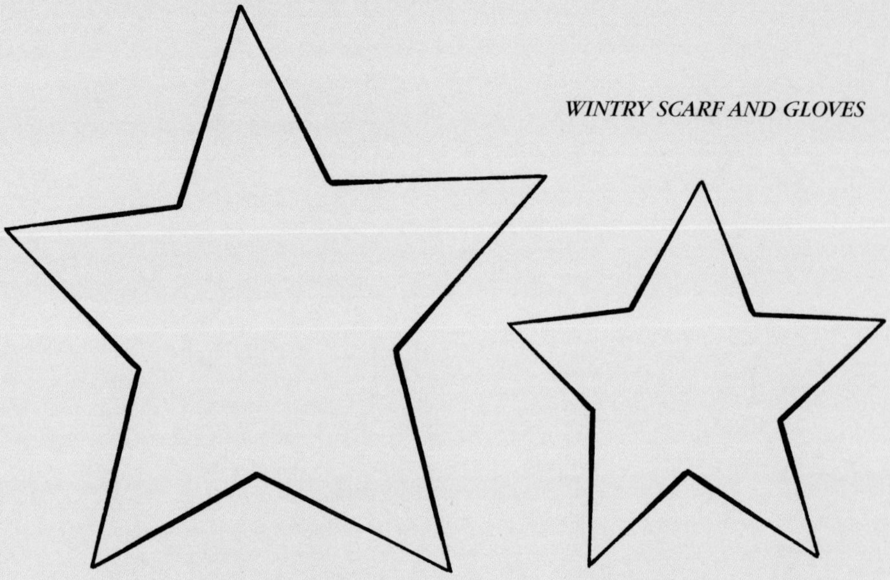

WINTRY SCARF AND GLOVES

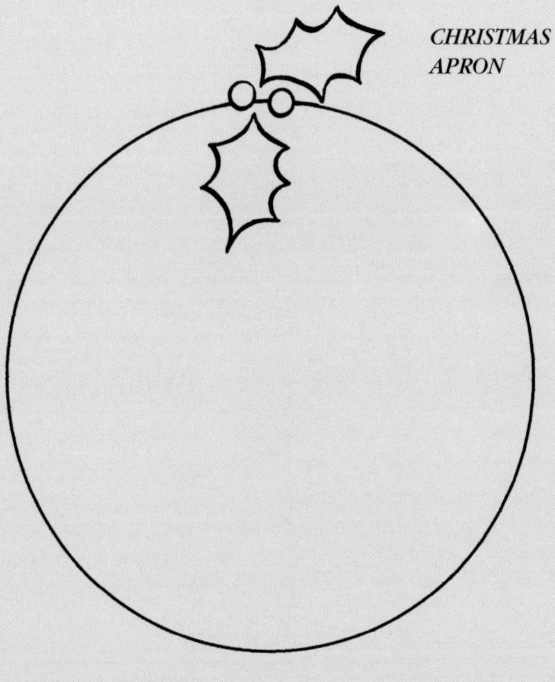

CHRISTMAS PUDDING APRON

MINI TREE STOCKINGS

CHRISTMAS WREATH

PAPIER-MACHÉ CHRISTMAS DECORATIONS

CHRISTMAS WREATH

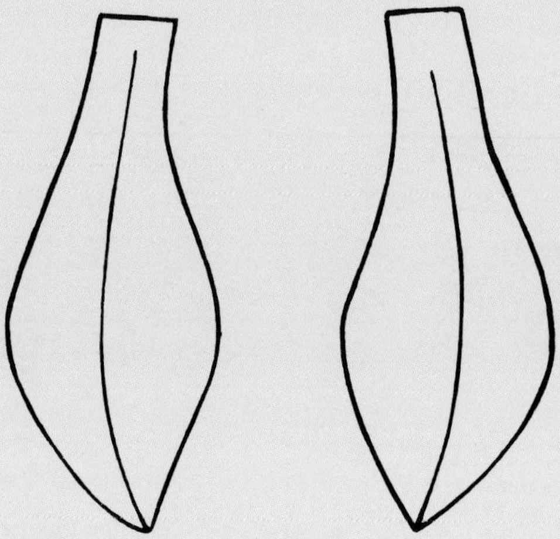

EYE MASKS

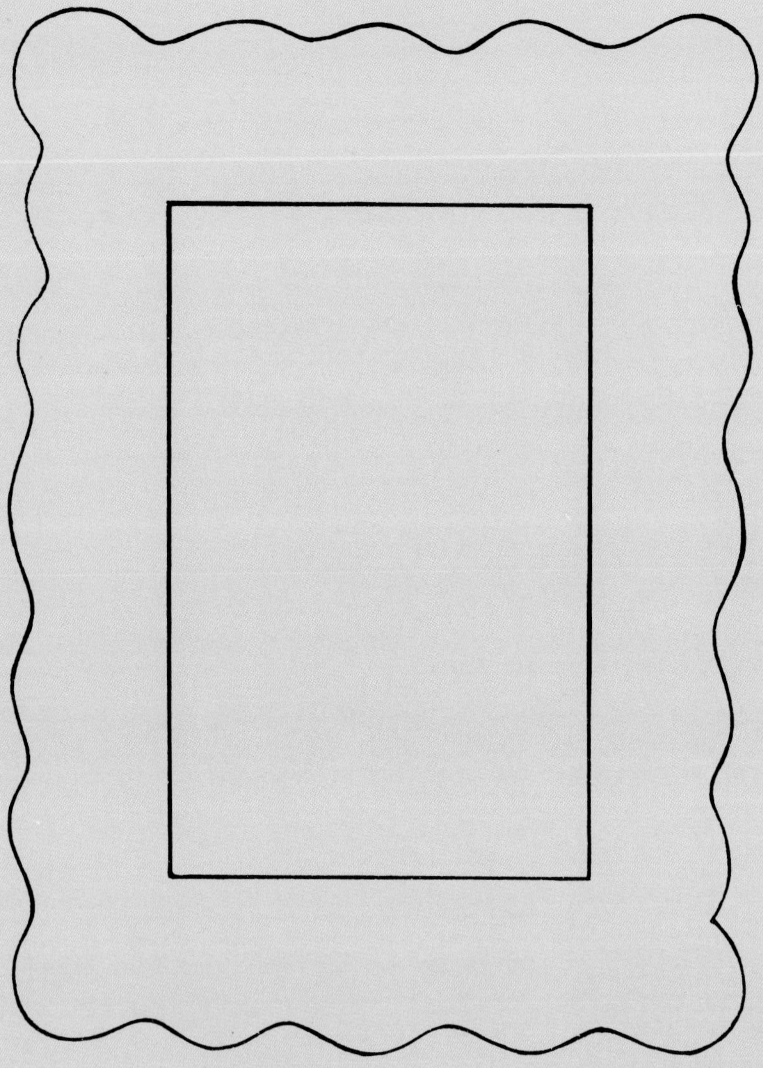

FOIL-COVERED
FRAME

PAPIER-MACHÉ
EARRINGS

STORAGE
CHEST

INDEX

ACKNOWLEDGMENTS

The publishers would like to thank the following authors for their contributions to this book:
Janet Brinkwood for the recipe for Poached Figs with Mascarpone Quenelles; Oona Van Den Berg for the Brandy Alexander, Brandy Blazer, Apricot Bellini, Virgin Prairie Oyster and Volunteer cocktails; Bridget Honour for the Stenciled Tablecloth and Painted Plate and Judy Dann for the Velvet Fruits.
The publishers would like to thank the following photographers:
Amanda Heywood for the picture of Mini Cheese Puffs and Steve Baxter for the pictures of the Brandy Alexander, Brandy Blazer, Apricot Bellini, Virgin Prairie Oyster and Volunteer cocktails.
Thanks also to Panduro Hobby, Transport Avenue, Brentford, Middlesex, TW8 8BR, Tel: 01392 4227788, for supplying craft equipment.